Ports of Call

Artist: **Anthony Flemming Thame Estuary** *Courtesy of:* **The Artist**

Editor Chris Perring

KENSINGTON WEST PRODUCTIONS

HEXHAM ENGLAND

Acknowledgements

Kensington West Productions Ltd
5 Cattle Market, Hexham,
Northumberland, NE46 1NJ
Tel (01434) 609933, Fax (01434) 600066/600422
e mail: kwp@kensingtonwest.demon.co.uk
web site: www.kensingtonwest.demon.co.uk

Editor
Chris Perring

Assistant Editors
Helen Parker, Peter Killick

Additional Research
Nicola Clements, Sarah Walton

Production & Design
Diane Ridley

Cartography
Phil Anderton, NR Design

Origination
Pre-Press Limited Hong Kong

Printing
Liang Yu Printing Factory Limited,
Hong Kong

Front Cover:
Anthony Flemming,
AT SEA,
Courtesy of: The Artist

Artist: **Anthony Flemming SCOTTISH ANCHORAGE** *Courtesy of:* **The Artist**

There have been all manner of hands that have guided the production of our first edition of Ports of Call.

The company acknowledges the kind and generous advice of many enthusiasts, harbour-masters, marina owners, RNLI administrators and staff and many others who we have listed at the back of the book. It is nigh on impossible to find such detailed information for a book such as this without this kind of help - and we are extremely grateful for it.

In our endeavour to illustrate the book, we have been kindly assisted by Rosenstiel's and other publishers of fine art as well as the artists themselves. The sea attracts to its myriad colours and moods numerous artists and we are grateful to those members of the Society of Marine Artists who kindly permitted us to use their work in Ports of Call. We are particularly grateful to Anthony Flemming a prolific artist, keen mariner and thoroughly likeable chap to boot. As you will see, his work graces many of the pages of this book and gives it a real lift.

I am also extremely grateful to Chris Perring our editor, not only for putting the book together but also helping in the compilation of the reference material and contributions provided by so many different people - a filing nightmare! I am also grateful to him for helping with the final stages of production - this somewhat harrowing time was made far more pleasant by excellent banter and bonhomie rather than the unmitigated moaning that could have ensued. Congratulations also to the team at Kensington West Productions for working so tirelessly on the project.

My thanks also go to the companies who have supported this first edition with advertising and sponsorship - this is a great help in ensuring the book is produced to a high quality and we are most grateful. I am also indebted to two great friends for endeavouring to assist with the work on their area: Robert Bickett and Russell Peters - two distinguished mariners and excellent people - thank you for your efforts.

My final thanks are reserved for the RNLI - surely one of the most noble charities of all. We genuinely hope we can make a real contribution through the sale of these books. Thanks to Peter Chennell and Frances Aldridge.
Julian West

Artist: **Anthony Flemming**
AN IDYLLIC MOORING *Courtesy of:* **The Artist**

Of changing times and unchanging values

Many things must change in the course of 175 years, but throughout massive changes in society and the march of technology the underlying principles of the lifeboat service have remained intact.

In a world which could hardly have been envisaged by Sir William Hillary, the RNLI's lifeboats are still manned by volunteers and its 222 lifeboat stations are still funded by voluntary contributions raised by an army of volunteer fundraisers. Not a penny of its income comes directly from the governments of the coasts it covers and, although there are those who might see this as strange, it is a situation which the lifeboat service, those who work on its behalf and those who find themselves in need of its services, finds entirely satisfactory.

The RNLI has but one aim in life, saving life at sea, and its independence enables it to concentrate on that aim, free from political considerations, safe from fears of cuts in its funding and able to use its experience to provide the rescue cover needed.

Independent it may be, but the RNLI forms part of a close-knit maritime rescue service, working closely with the Government, its Agencies, commercial concerns and other voluntary bodies both to save lives and to help avoid potentially dangerous situations arising.

In the 19th Century, lifeboat crews needed strength to row their open boats into the teeth of a gale and the stamina to endure conditions almost inconceivable to those who spend their lives ashore. Their seamanship, boat handling and knowledge of their own waters was second to none.

Today, up to 2,000hp of turbocharged diesel has replaced muscle power and enclosed wheel houses keep the crews of the larger lifeboats warm and dry until they reach the scene. But the dangers they face are just as real and endurance just as necessary. Skill at the oars has been replaced by skills of an entirely different kind. Now, lifeboat crews must understand their radar, their radios, and their satellite navigation systems and at the wheel they must be able to handle their 25-knot boats in seas which have driven others to shelter, and to use their powerful engines to manoeuvre with precision. One thin, however, has not changed - their seamanship, boat handling and knowledge of their own waters is still second to none.

I feel sure that Ports of Call will indeed prove to be a distinguished companion to the harbours and marinas of the UK and Ireland while, at the same time, benefiting the cause of RNLI fundraising through a generous donation from every copy sold.

I wish the publication every success. Its publication makes a fitting end to our 175th anniversary year.

Andrew Freemantle MBE
Director RNLI

175 years
of saving lives at sea

TOBERMORY LIFEBOAT, THE ANN LEWIS FRASER *Courtesy of:* **The RNLI**

Contents

Foreword 3

Contents 4

Key to Maps 5

Introduction 6

England and Wales 14

North East England 16

Northumberland 17

Tyne & Wear and Hartlepool 20

North Yorkshire 22

East Riding of Yorkshire 24

Lincolnshire 26

North East Directory 27

South East England 30

Norfolk 32

Suffolk 34

Essex 40

London and the River Thames . . 44

Kent 46

South East Directory 50

The South Coast 56

East & West Sussex 58

Hampshire 63

Isle of Wight 68

Dorset 71

South Coast Directory 76

The Channel Islands 82

Alderney 83

Guernsey 83

Jersey 85

Channel Islands Directory 88

South West England 90

South Devon 92

Cornwall 100

Isles of Scilly 107

Cornwall, North Coast 108

North Devon, Somerset & Avon . . 110

South West Directory 114

Wales, North West England
& The Isle of Man 119

Vale of Glamorgan 120

Pembrokeshire 121

Ceredigion 124

Gwynedd & Anglesey 125

Conwy 129

Merseyside 130

Lancashire 131

Cumbria 132

Isle of Man 134

Wales, North West England & . . 137

Isle of Man Directory

Scotland 144

The West Coast of Scotland &
Islands 146

Dumfries & Galloway 147

Ayrshire, Argyll & Bute 148

Highland 157

Western Isles 161

West Scotland Directory 163

East Scotland, The Shetlands
& Orkneys 167

Shetland Islands 168

Orkney Islands 170

Highland 172

Moray & Aberdeenshire 174

Angus, Fife & Edinburgh 177

East Lothian & the
Scottish Borders 180

East Scotland, Shetlands &
Orkneys Directory 182

Ireland 186

East Coast of Ireland 188

Londonderry 189

Antrim 189

Down 193

Dublin 196

Wicklow 198

Wexford 198

East Ireland Directory 201

West Coast of Ireland 204

Cork 205

Kerry & Clare 210

Galway & Mayo 213

Sligo & Donegal 216

West Ireland Directory 219

Acknowledgements 221

Index & Abbreviations 222

Artist: **Anthony Flemming** **AT SEA** *Courtesy of:* **The Artist**

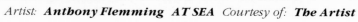

Map Key

1. **North East England**
2. **South East England**
3. **The South Coast**
4. **The Channel Islands**
5. **South West England**
6. **Wales, North West England & The Isle of Man**
7. **The West Coast of Scotland & Islands**
8. **East Scotland, The Shetland and Orkneys**
9. **The East Coast of Ireland**
10. **The West Coast of Ireland**

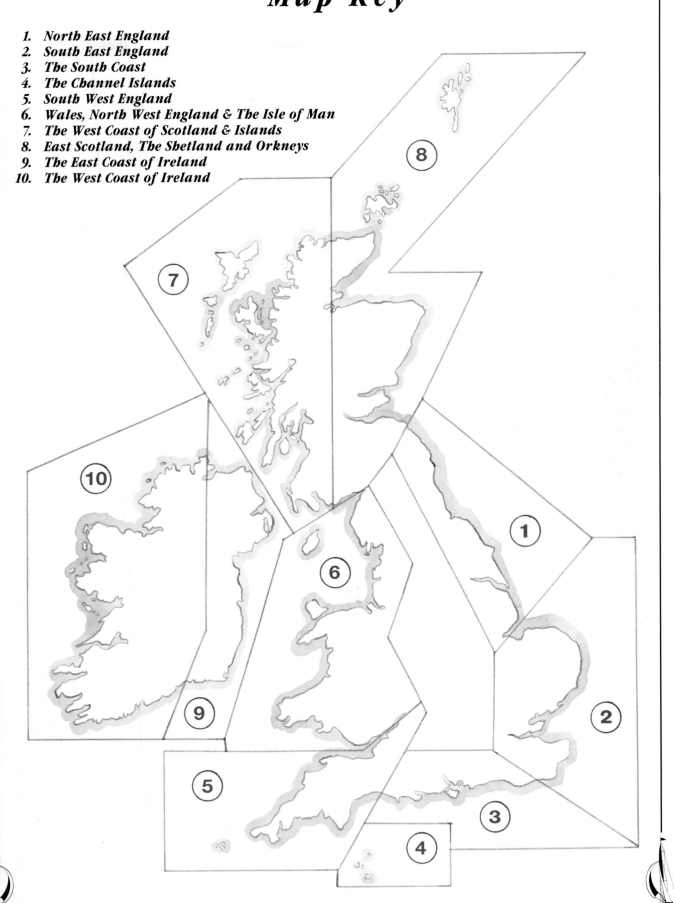

During the time we have been putting this book together, I have had a lot of fun musing and remembering favourite haunts the length and breadth of the British Isles. Our helpful contributors have also suggested numerous places which are equally uplifting. I hope that you will find that *Ports of Call* refreshes your memory of voyages and landfalls of the past, and sets you dreaming about possibilities for the future. The British Isles is very much influenced by its maritime history - it's astonishing how many figures of speech in the English language have their roots in seafaring. We are fortunate enough to have an enormously varied coastline with wonderfully contrasting scenery and a rich diversity of ports, harbours and anchorages. Sitting in front of the fire on those winter evenings, long after the rigours of laying up at the end of the season have been forgotten, we hope this is a book which will inspire the imagination and provoke dreams about destinations which may, like many of the very best dreams, never actually happen. We also hope that you will be sufficiently stirred up to set to and plan your cruises to waters new and that you will head off in search of places which will become new favourite haunts and that *Ports of Call* will be of practical use to you as a guide.

Artist: **Anthony Flemming BRIGHTLINGSEA**
Courtesy of: **The Artist**

To evoke the right atmosphere, we have included plenty of illustrations, and rather than using photographs as a great many other publications do, we have opted to use fine art. For views of coastline and seascapes, we hope you will agree that fine art really does capture the right flavour - including a suitably salty tang! Work by a number of artists is represented in the book, and we are especially pleased to have such a wide and varied selection from Anthony Flemming (see page 143 for more details about this artist and his work). The character of the book is further enhanced by the maps which Phil Anderton has created for us. These should help you to identify where the places which are described in the book are. The maps will also show you where all the RNLI stations are as well - do bear in mind that quite a lot of

these, by the very nature of their being needed where they are, are *not* places to visit by boat!

We have covered the British Isles and Ireland in ten separate geographical sections, each of which has its own character, a variety of places to visit and a selection of attractions to explore once you have gone ashore. Our intention is to tell you a little about what to expect when the sailing is done and you have arrived in port. We have usually included some historical background and suggestions about local museums and historic buildings where you can find out more. Britain's coastline boasts such a tremendously rich heritage that, regrettably, we could not possibly have examined it all in any detail but we hope we have given you some useful pointers. We have also offered suggestions of other places to visit and things to do for crew members of all ages in case you don't plan to catch the first tide out in the morning. Also included are details of a great many sailing and yacht clubs which offer the visiting yacht and her crew a warm welcome. Talking of warm welcomes, we have tried to point you in the right direction to find pubs where the beer and atmosphere is good. In many places, we have also been able to suggest a range of places which will allow you to escape the galley and head ashore for either an inexpensive meal, or perhaps something more extravagant as a reward for the hard work put in on the high seas. We hope that all the establishments which have been recommended in *Ports of Call* have a long and prosperous life and that you will find that they live up to expectations according to the details we have given. However, we all know that ownership or management can change, standards can slip and places can go out of business completely - if you find that any of these things have happened to any of the pubs, restaurants or hotels mentioned in *Ports of Call*, we would be delighted to hear from you so that we can make sure that future editions of the book are updated accordingly.

Artist: **Anthony Flemming BURNHAM-ON-CROUCH** *Courtesy of:* **The Artist**

Each geographical section has a directory which we hope you will find useful. As well as telling you where the RNLI has its stations all around the coasts of the British Isles and Ireland, and who to contact if you would like to visit them, the directory sections give a visual summary of what the place is like using a system of flags at various points on their way to the top of the mast. The scores given will not necessarily compare from one end of the country to the other, but should give you a reasonable comparison with other ports of call in the same area. Clearly, comparing shopping facilities, or indeed the selection of pubs available, in places on the Solent and parts of the West Coast of Scotland or even the Shetland Islands on exactly the same criteria wouldn't really work! So, a flag at the top of the mast means that this is about as good as it gets *in this area*. Most of the categories are self-explanatory, but some of them merit a little clarification. "Facilities for skipper" is about looking after the boat and so includes things like availability of fuel, chandlery, repair facilities and security. "Facilities for first mate" is more geared towards the needs of the crew and therefore includes factors such as how far it is to the shops and what sort of selection you will find when you get there and whether there are showers handy.

Other information given in the directory tells you who to contact for moorings or berths. Chandlers and boat-yards are listed as well. A key point to make is that *Ports of Call* is not a pilot book - there are a great many excellent publications already available, so we have also listed a selection of these in the directory sections. We are particularly grateful to all those who contributed material for inclusion in these sections and hope you will agree that this is a very practical and useful part of the book.

Those of you with an interest in racing, golf or fishing may have spotted that *Ports of Call* bears some similarity to several other books in the Kensington West Productions family. It all began with *Travelling the Turf*, now in its fifteenth edition and a widely respected "distinguished companion" for those who follow the sport of kings. *Following the Fairways* and *Fishing Forays* followed in those distinguished footsteps, and a book about sailing to complement the series has been planned for some time now. We hope that the existing titles will welcome their new stable mate!

And a final word from your editor, I have to say that I am very pleased with the way *Ports of Call* has turned out. That is not to say that I am deluding myself into thinking that it is perfect – yet! In future editions, we will update all the material contained in this book, and we'd love to hear from you if you think there is anything we have missed out, got wrong or could just have done better. We hope to add sections to cover at least those European coastlines which are within a short passage from British waters such as France, Belgium and Holland and maybe places further afield as well - if you have favourites which you would like to share with us, do get in touch.

I hope you enjoy the sailing, both imaginary and real, which *Ports of Call* inspires.

Artist: **Anthony Flemming** **TINTAGEL CASTLE**
Courtesy of: **The Artist**

Chris Perring
Editor

Important note

We hope that no one will ever think that they could use the maps in this book for anything other than giving a rough indication of where places are. Perhaps I am overly optimistic as I know of one yachtsman who used a road atlas to bridge a gap between charts while cruising off the west coast of Scotland. So while perhaps there is no accounting for what use people will put published material to, this is categorically not the purpose of the maps in this volume. Likewise, in the directory sections, where we have given approximate positions for places mentioned, these are to help you find roughly the right place on the chart, and should certainly not be used for navigation. For navigation and entering positions into electronic navigation systems, be sure to read appropriate positions off an up-to-date navigational chart, or use a Waypoint Directory or almanac to provide you with accurate information. Furthermore, the fact that any place has been included in this book does not necessarily mean that it will be suitable for all types of craft to visit in any particular conditions. The person in charge of a boat of any kind must evaluate the suitability of any destination or route using up-to-date navigational charts and taking into account the capabilities of their craft and crew, and the conditions prevailing at the time. The consequences of any decisions taken are the responsibility of the person in charge of the boat, and neither the publishers nor the editor of *Ports of Call* can accept responsibility for any accidents or mishaps which may arise as a result of acting on any information included in this volume.

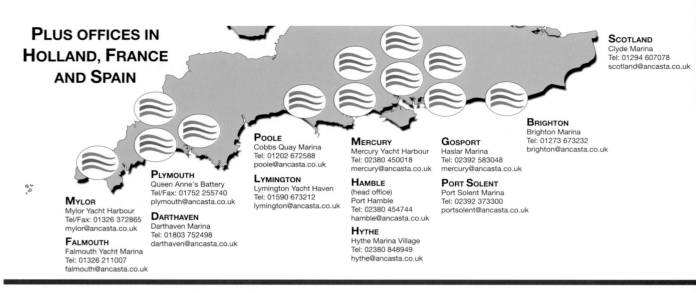

The **Ancasta** difference

INTERNATIONAL BOAT SALES

◆ **Ancasta's** database matches 9,000 potential purchasers and over 1,300 boats for sale

◆ **Ancasta's** website contains listings of all boats for sale which currently attracts over 11,000 viewers per month

◆ **Ancasta** are Europe's largest yacht brokers have 17 years experience with 22 offices throughout the UK and Europe

◆ **Ancasta** place monthly adverts in all the major boating magazines

◆ **Ancasta** have dedicated brokerage stands at International Boat Shows

◆ **Ancasta** hold six Used Boat Shows every year from Brighton to Plymouth

◆ **Ancasta** offices are open 7 days a week and linked to Ancasta's database

◆ **Ancasta's** After Sales support offers help with Finance, Insurance, registration, berthing, tuition, spare parts, valeting, engine servicing and maintenance

◆ **Ancasta** are the number one dealer of Beneteau cruising and cruiser/racer yachts, the largest independant dealer of Fairline luxury motor boats in the U.K. as well as agents for the fantastic range of Sydney racing yachts from Australia and the new range of Italian Tecnomarinc motor boats.

www.ancasta.co.uk

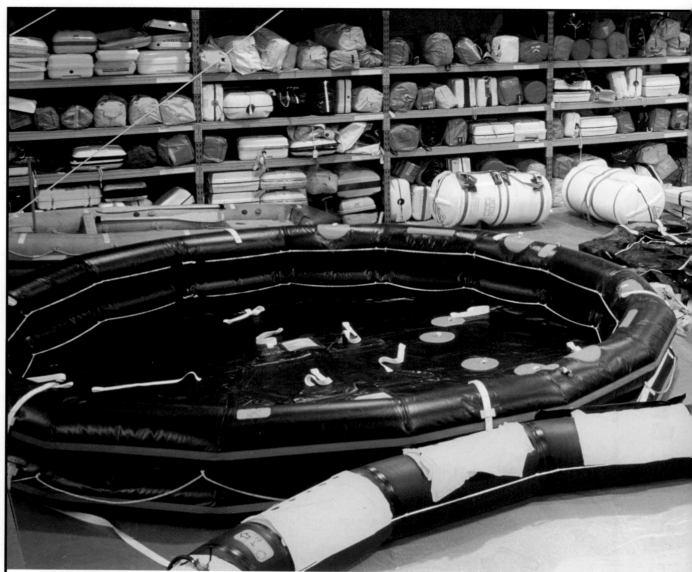

UK LIFERAFT SERVICE STATION

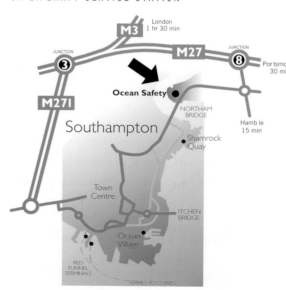

Ocean Safety Ltd
Centurion Industrial Park
Bitterne Road West
Southampton
SO18 1UB
UK

Tel +44 (0) 1703 333334
Fax +44 (0) 1703 333360
Email southampton@oceansafety.com

Ocean Safety SL
Camí Fondo
Palma de Mallorca
07007
Baleares
ESPAÑA

Tel +34 971 247 211
Fax +34 971 241 046
Email palma@oceansafety.com

a member of the
British Marine
INDUSTRIES
FEDERATION

Ocean Safety is proud to sponsor PORTS OF CALL, celebrating the RNLI's 175th anniversary. As one of the country's leading marine safety specialists we are delighted to be able to support the world's finest lifeboat organisation.

Ocean Safety, established in 1989 can supply a comprehensive range of safety products including liferafts, lifejackets, pyrotechnics, medical kits and firefighting equipment.

In addition to our extensive product range we also boast two of the largest liferaft service stations in Europe with the introduction of our new 12,000 sq foot facility in Palma de Mallorca, Spain.

Our service stations both have the capability to handle new generation large capacity liferafts as well as evacuation chutes and slides. Accredited with ISO 9002 and MCA approval in the UK and Marina Mercante approval in Spain quality workmanship is assured at all times.

Please call us for sales, service and advice on all marine safety related matters.

OCEAN SAFETY

INDEFATIGABLE

CAPITAL BANK plc is delighted to lend its support to the Royal National Lifeboat Institution. After all, we have a great deal in common. First and foremost, we are never content and will not rest until we have achieved our objectives.

Our objectives being to fulfil the wishes of our customers looking for marine funding to put their dreams and aspirations  afloat, whether they are looking for an unsecured loan of up to £25,000 to buy a sports boat, a tailored-to-suit mortgage for a substantial motor yacht or a £multi-million finance package to put a 120ft, 22 gun, wooden frigate to sea...

Because as well as supplying the necessary funding to recreate C.S. Forester's mythical 'HMS Indefatigable', skippered by the heroic Horatio Hornblower, for the hit television drama series, CAPITAL BANK Marine is also able to put more conventional vessels in the water too.

Often providing solutions above and beyond the mainstream.

In fact it is this kind of fluid financial expertise that has led to the UK's leading boatbuilders and brokers nominating CAPITAL BANK as their recommended choice for finance.

The kind of expertise that helps more people out in the water. Something CAPITAL BANK has been doing for some 50 years.

Let's hope one day we too can celebrate 175 years of unrelenting dedication and service to the job in hand, like the indefatigable Royal National Lifeboat Institution and especially the Volunteer Lifeboat Crews.

CAPITAL BANK
A BANK OF SCOTLAND GROUP COMPANY
MARINE

INTUITIVE

Adopting a tireless approach to achieving our objectives is only one facet of the service that CAPITAL BANK Marine shares with the RNLI. We also possess a special intuition which enables us to be able to react to and improvise on specific customer requirements, quickly and efficiently.

Because we have more resources at our disposal than some - we are after all a Bank of Scotland Group company - and can afford to adopt a more pliant approach, in tune with customer ideals, not vice versa.

Says Julian Gowing, National Marine Manager:
"It really makes no difference to us what type or size of vessel the customer wishes to fund. From a round the world racing yacht to a canal boat, we will almost certainly be able to find the funding solution to suit. Marine mortgages are only part of the product portfolio. We can offer unsecured loans too, of up to £25,000. It really is up to the customer which route they take. We will, of course, employ our expertise and experience to create our best all-round package to meet given customer requirements.

Our offices are open six days a week. And with northern staff coverage we can offer a truly national service. In essence, whilst we can never pretend to offer as crucial a service as the highly commendable Royal National Lifeboat Institution, we like to feel all the same that we share their commitment and dedication to the task." CAPITAL BANK Marine would like to wish the Institution its heartfelt congratulations for the stalwart work it undertakes all year round, in all weathers, with the utmost courage.

Telephone
02380 333 467

(previously 01703 333 467) **Quoting ref PC99**

and ask for Trudi or Joanne.
Fax 02380 631 514
E-mail rachel.smith@capitalbank.co.uk
Opening hours: 8.30am to 6.00pm Monday to Friday,
10am to 4pm on Saturdays

Marine loan facilities are provided, subject to status, by CAPITAL BANK plc. Written quotations available on request. You must be at least 18 and a UK resident (excluding the Channel Islands and the Isle of Man) to apply. Security over the vessel may be required. Any information provided by you may be used by CAPITAL BANK and others for marketing (by post, telephone, e-mail or fax), credit assessment and other purposes.

CAPITAL BANK
A BANK OF SCOTLAND GROUP COMPANY

MARINE

England & Wales

Artist: **Steven Dews** *SUMMER RACING OFF COWES* *Courtesy of:* **Rosenstiel's**

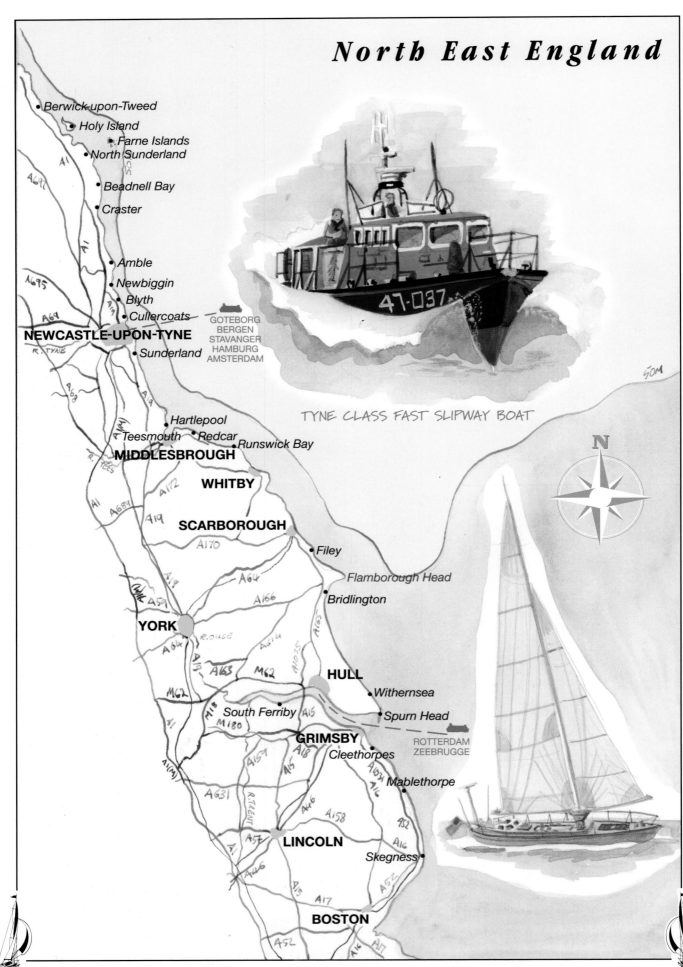

North East England

- Berwick-upon-Tweed
- Holy Island
- Farne Islands
- North Sunderland
- Beadnell Bay
- Craster
- Amble
- Newbiggin
- Blyth
- Cullercoats
- **NEWCASTLE-UPON-TYNE**
- Sunderland

GOTEBORG
BERGEN
STAVANGER
HAMBURG
AMSTERDAM

TYNE CLASS FAST SLIPWAY BOAT

47-037

- Hartlepool
- Teesmouth
- Redcar
- Runswick Bay
- **MIDDLESBROUGH**
- **WHITBY**
- **SCARBOROUGH**
- Filey
- Flamborough Head
- Bridlington
- **YORK**
- **HULL**
- Withernsea
- South Ferriby
- Spurn Head
- **GRIMSBY**
- Cleethorpes

ROTTERDAM
ZEEBRUGGE

- Mablethorpe
- **LINCOLN**
- Skegness
- **BOSTON**

N

Northumberland

England's most north-easterly stretch of coast includes great wide expanses of sandflats punctuated by looming promontories with rambling ruined castles and tiny fishing harbours clinging to the coastline. Marinas are few and far between, but for the intrepid harbour explorer there are gems to be found, especially if you are prepared to take the ground. A helpful companion for this area is The Royal Northumberland Yacht Club Sailing Directions, The Humber to Rattray Head (see directory for more details). In the main, it is a sparsely populated stretch of coast and the bird population has made the most of this. Particularly spectacular gatherings of feathered friends can be found at Lindisfarne, the Farne Islands and Coquet Island. In those places where a landfall is feasible there is much of interest to explore and find out about, and we have included a selection of places where elbows can be leaned on bars or knees placed under tables for the refreshment which is often so welcome on coming ashore.

Berwick-upon-Tweed

It's now either the first port in England, or the last port before Scotland, depending on which way you are sailing, but which ever way you look at it, Berwick-upon-Tweed has had a stormy history. Before finally ending up an English town in 1482, it changed hands over a dozen times and Berwick Castle was where Edward I decided against Robert the Bruce's claim to the Scottish throne in 1291. As you follow the river in from the sea, it curls around Berwick which is perched on a peninsula to your right on the North bank. The simple architecture of the sandstone houses topped with red tiled roofs gives a fitting sense of character and dependability. Before tucking into the Tweed Dock on the South bank, you will see the three bridges which span the river. Close to the dock, (and giving the mariner easy pedestrian access to Berwick) is the solidly stone-built Jacobean Bridge which dates from the early part of the 17th century. Beyond this is the Royal Tweed Bridge whose four spans were built in the 1920s to carry the road over the river. Curving around behind both of these are the elegant high arches of Robert Stephenson's Royal Border Bridge over which the railway has run since 1847. Look out for the flock of mute swans which can often be seen on the lower reaches of the River Tweed especially between late July and September.

The town's turbulent past can be explored in a number of museums. Berwick-upon-Tweed Barracks, the first purpose-built barracks in the country (1717), houses the Museum of the King's Own Scottish Borderers and the Borough Museum and two art galleries. Further military flavour can be found at Berwick's Castle and the 16th century Ramparts which are considered by many to be the best preserved example of their kind in Britain. The Georgian Guard House near the quay houses a permanent display, "The Story of a Border Garrison". (Details about all of these from English Heritage, ☎ 01289 304493) Looking a little further afield, a short bus ride across the border from Berwick takes you to Paxton House (☎ 01289 386291), a Palladian country mansion furnished by Chippendale whose picture gallery displays selections from the National Galleries of Scotland.

If you are finding all these historical insights rather dry and thirst-provoking, can we suggest a visit to the Wine and Spirit Museum, Palace Green (☎ 01289 305153) or if you are in search of the real thing, try the Elizabethan on North Road (☎ 01289 303244) for some liquid refreshment. Twempies Café (☎ 01289 303227) just opposite the Dock entrance offers inexpensive snacks. Popinjays in the town centre is a good choice for something a bit more substantial and if you really want to push the boat out, then try Rob Roy which is about 200 yards east of the Dock (☎ 01289 306428). Fish & chips, Chinese and Indian takeaways are all within walking distances of the dock. If you fancy a night ashore, The Kings Arms Hotel, Hide Hill (☎ 01289 307454) has a good reputation.

Berwick-upon-Tweed Harbour is quite tricky to get into, and only accessible to yachts drawing less than 1.2 metres for 4 hours each side of high water. There is room for only 8 visiting boats alongside the quay so a call to "Berwick Harbour" on Channel 12 is recommended. Facilities for yachts are limited, though water, payphone and rubbish disposal are available and engine repairs can be organised by consulting Captain Jenkinson, the Harbour-master (☎ 01289 307404). A general store, butcher and chemist are within ¼ mile and there's a supermarket within ½ mile. Captain Jenkinson is also the Honorary Secretary of Berwick's Lifeboat Station which since 1995 has boasted both a Mersea all-weather lifeboat and an inshore lifeboat. He'll be pleased to show you around the station if you give him a ring.

Taxi:	Fifes' Taxis (☎ 01289 307188)
Car hire:	Blackburn & Price (☎ 01289 330707)
	Semples (☎ 01289 307436)
	Hertz (☎ 0191 286 6748)
Bus:	local services leave from the town centre, about half a mile from the dock
Rail:	Berwick Station on the East Coast main line, about 1½ miles from the dock

for more details, see Directory Section

Berwick-upon-Tweed to Amble

Turning south, the cliffs that stretch from the border to Berwick start to give way to more open beaches and sand dunes. Turnstones, oystercatchers and purple sandpipers are regular visitors to Cocklawburn Dunes Nature Reserve. The spoil heaps of the old 18th century limekilns attract plants like the purple milk-vetch which adds strong colour to the coastline. Looking down the coast, the first of a series of imposing castles rears up from the sea – Holy Island is in sight.

Holy Island, or Lindisfarne to give it its ancient name, is still a place of pilgrimage. The religious associations date back to AD 635 when Aiden chose the island, cut off from the mainland by the tide for about 12 hours in 24, for the foundation of his monastery. The monastery was sacked by the Danes in the 9th century, and the priory which succeeded it was a victim of the dissolution of the monasteries in 1537. It appears to have fallen into total disuse by the early 18th century. The surviving ruins (Lindisfarne Priory Museum - EH ☎ 01289 389200) are impressive and provide a contrast to Lindisfarne

Castle (NT ☎ 01289 389244) which towers over the island from a surprising rocky crag in the sand dunes. The Castle was restored by Sir Edwin Lutyens in 1902 and is now managed by the National Trust which opens it to the public when tides and staff availability allow.

You can find reasonable shelter to the south west of the island where you can drop anchor next to the Priory ruins. Facilities ashore are very limited - the price you are bound to pay for visiting such a peaceful spot. There is the odd watering hole on the island which can provide a welcoming refuge from dull weather. The tranquillity of the area makes it an ideal feeding area for large numbers of birds and the island lies at the centre of the Lindisfarne National Nature Reserve which is particularly important as a wintering haven for ducks, whooper swans, pale-bellied Brent geese and numerous waders. You may also be able to see common and grey seals which sometimes bask on the sands and rocks around the island.

The sand dunes stretch on down towards **Bamburgh** where another castle perches by the coast on a rocky outcrop 150 feet high. In 1704, Bamburgh Castle was bought by Nathaniel Crew, Bishop of Durham and third Baron Crewe. When he died in 1721 without a direct heir, the Crewe Trust was founded. Among its charitable works was the establishment in the 1770s of a system of watches and courses of action to assist those in danger from shipwreck on the local stretch of coastline and outlying islands. It is believed that this is the first example of its kind and that Bamburgh can therefore justifiably claim to be the home of the first ever lifeboat sta-

tion. The tradition of lifesaving was later kept up by Grace Darling who was born in the town and also lies buried here. The story of how she and her father rescued survivors after the steamer *Forfarshire* was wrecked on the Harker Rocks in the Farne Islands in 1838 is well known - but few know of Bamburgh's early ground-breaking association with lifesaving. There is no sheltered landfall here, so visits to the Grace Darling Museum or the Castle present difficulties - regrettably, an approach by road, or at least overland is needed. The same cannot be said for the **Farne Islands** which lie a couple of miles off the coast! St Cuthbert, whose tomb became a shrine on Lindisfarne, lived as a hermit here for eight years in the seventh century. More recently, the only inhabitants of this isolated outcrop of rocky islets have been the lighthouse keepers of whom Grace Darling's father was one. The islands are owned by the National Trust and landing is restricted to only two islands to prevent unnecessary disturbance of the wide variety of seabirds which breed here during the summer. You can enjoy the antics of puffin and eider-duck, and see guillemot, shag and kittiwake here. Hats are advised if going ashore on Inner Farne as some of the terns can become quite aggressive, dive-bombing intruders to protect their nests. You can also visit the 14th century chapel dedicated to St Cuthbert. Anchor in The Kettle to the north-east of Inner Farne and enjoy the isolation of this remote spot, especially after any day-trippers have left. (Information Centre ☎ 01665 721099, Warden ☎ 01665 720651).

Back on the mainland, the dunes stretch on to

Artist: **Anthony Flemming** **LINDISFARNE CASTLE** *Courtesy of:* **The Artist**

Seahouses. Here we find the harbour for the small town of North Sunderland – not to be confused with its big brother further down the coast - and it is the home of the Marine Life Centre and Fishing Museum (☎ 01665 721257). This is an atmospheric little harbour with rows of grey stone houses looking down at the cluster of fishing cobles (local small boats) and piles of crab pots which clutter the quay. Swallow Fish is a traditional 19th century smokehouse which smokes kippers, salmon and other fish which can be bought from The Fisherman's Kitchen, South Street (☎ 01665 721052). Other shops, including a supermarket, offer general provisions and the Viking Restaurant (☎ 01665 720747) is a reasonably priced option for a meal. The pub which usually receives the highest praise is the Olde Ship (☎ 01665 720200) which is conveniently situated. There are, however, few specific facilities for the yachtsman and in summer the town gets crowded with tourists and is best avoided.

Artist: **Brian Lancaster**
DUNSTANBURGH CASTLE Courtesy of: **The Artist**

Rounding the point at **Beadnell**, the bay opens up revealing a stretch of sand dunes which reach a height of 50 feet in places. The Craster Arms Hotel, Beadnell (☎ 01665 720272) makes a run ashore inviting, though you won't find many other facilities here. The harbour is privately owned, so you need to drop anchor to the south of the Beadnell Sailing Club. This is a very pretty anchorage, but not a good place to be in strong southeasterlies or northerlies. As you continue your passage down the coast the ruins of 14th century Dunstanburgh Castle, famously immortalised in oils by Turner, stand out on the next headland. If the weather allows you to take advantage of the anchorage off Newton, you will find a glorious expanse of beach which is a characteristic trait of this stretch of coastline. Stepping ashore, you will find the thoroughly unspoiled Ship (☎ 01665 576262) which offers good but simple fodder and a pleasant situation amidst cottages owned by the National Trust. On sunny summer evenings, the light can give an almost Mediterranean hue to what we really know is the chilly North Sea. Just beyond is another small fishing village, famed for its kippers. **Craster** harbour dries and is very small, but in settled weather, you can drop anchor outside and paddle ashore to sample

the fare in The Jolly Fisherman (☎ 01665 576218). The Smokery which does first class salmon and crab as well as kippers is opposite the pub.

The last section of the Northumberland Heritage Coast to Amble includes Boulmer, home of the RAF air-sea rescue helicopters and the now silted up harbour at Alnmouth. While this is a great location for dinghy sailing, it is not suitable for larger vessels any longer. South of Alnmouth, the rocky cliffs give way to a long stretch of sand, with the Cheviot Hills rising up behind the dunes.

Artist: **Brian Lancaster**
LINDISFARNE Courtesy of: **The Artist**

Amble and the River Coquet

Amble can trace its origins back to the bronze age, though until the early nineteenth century it was merely a small agricultural hamlet. The harbour and Amble's growth date from the arrival of the coalmines and the construction of railway links to the sea. The harbour and boatyard remain, but the coal shipping stopped in the 1960s and Amble is now an attractive holiday town which appeals to visitors and residents alike. Amble's lifeboat station has an all-weather and an inshore lifeboat and, in 1969, the latter was involved in a rescue for which medals were awarded for the first time to the crew of an inshore lifeboat.

The marina is exclusively for yachts and is situated in a tidal basin just upstream from the main harbour where the fishing fleet is moored. Alternatively, visitors' moorings are available from the Coquet Yacht Club. The marina is very convenient for the quaint town centre which is compact and has all the shops, pubs, restaurants and facilities you would expect in a seaside resort town. The River Coquet marks the southern limit of the Northumberland Heritage Coast, and the outlook to the north and north-west from the marina is striking. Immediately opposite the marina is the Old Water and Saltmarsh which is a Site of Special Scientific Interest. It is a noted haven for wildlife, and eider ducklings and roosting birds can be seen here. The Amble Dunes to the south of the town constitute another designated nature reserve. Boat trips to Coquet Island, an RSPB reserve just off the coast, leave from the harbour if you fancy a closer look but would prefer to forget about navigation for a few hours! Looking beyond the saltings, Warkworth Castle (EH ☎ 01665 711423), dating back to the 12th century, provides a spectacular backdrop. Residence of the Percys, a powerful family in medieval times, Warkworth is yet another local reminder that Northumberland has had a turbulent history. You may recall that Warkworth was the setting for several scenes in Shakespeare's "Henry IV" where the Earl of Northumberland and his son Harry Hotspur conspired to overthrow the king.

The River Coquet is not navigable as far as Warkworth, but you may find a visit is worth the couple of miles' walk. As well as the castle, there are 5 pubs! The Black Bull, Dial Place (☎ 01665 711367) is renowned for good beer and pub food. The Sun Hotel, 6 Castle Terrace (☎ 01665 711259), has more of a restaurant menu and The Jackdaw, Castle Street (☎ 01665 711488) is top of the range locally. You don't need to leave Amble to find sustenance though; The Marina Arms on The Braid is a handy spot for a drink and The Blue Bell in Albert Street (☎ 01665 710431) won't burn a hole in your pocket. Charlie's (☎ 01665 710206) is rated highly for fish & chips either to eat in or take away and there are also Chinese and Indian takeaways within walking distance. The Coquet Yacht Club bar is open at weekends and visitors are welcome – there's racing every weekend in the summer and the annual regatta takes place over the late May Bank Holiday weekend.

The approaches to Amble Marina and Warkworth Harbour are straightforward and present no problems in normal weather conditions, but the marina is only accessible for between 3 and 4 hours either side of high water. Visitors should secure to the fuel pontoon just inside the marina or preferably call "Amble Marina" on Channel 80 to receive berthing instructions. All the usual facilities, including laundry and 24 hour fuel, are available and The Amble Boat Co Ltd (☎ 01665 710267) is nearby for chandlery and repairs.

Taxi:	Amble Taxis (☎ 01665 710988)
Car hire:	Aln Motors (☎ 01665 712494)
Cycle hire:	Breeze Garage (☎ 01665 710323)
Rail:	Alnmouth Station, on the East Coast mainline, about 5 miles away
Air:	Newcastle Airport 25 miles away

for more details, see Directory Section

Amble to the River Tyne

Between Amble and the next major headland at **Newbiggin** there is another fine stretch of sand – the six mile swathe of Druridge Bay. The large church of St Bartholomew is a significant landmark on the promontory which protects Newbiggin's small harbour. Local attractions include the Woodhorn Colliery Museum and the restored Saxon Church both of which are free, and a narrow gauge railway which runs through the QE II Country Park. This again is primarily dinghy territory, though you can anchor in the bay to the south of the harbour – liaise with the Coastguard on Ch 16/67 for further details. A good range of shopping facilities is available, and we recommend The Cresswell Arms in the High Street (☎ 01670 818331) and The New Ship in Gibson Street (☎ 01670 817267) if you are in search of more than just provisions.

A few miles beyond Newbiggin, **Blyth** offers a welcome secure refuge after the tricky harbour entrances and inhospitable rocky coastline of the northern part of Northumberland. However, you will quickly notice that you have left the rural beauty behind and the line of nine wind generators along the mile long breakwater bear testament to the town's motto *We grow by industry.* The port is still busy, though where once it was the point of export for Northumberland coal, coal is now imported for Blyth Power Station. Aluminium ore and wood are also major imports and the port is a supply base for North Sea oil and gas fields.

There are no tidal constraints to the entrance, and once inside, you can berth alongside pontoons or pick up a visitors' mooring at the Royal Northumberland Yacht Club in the South Harbour. From ashore, access to the pontoons is via a locked gate – you can get a key-card from the Club or the harbour-master's office. Water, electricity, payphone, rubbish disposal and showers are available at the Club, and petrol and gas can be found about a mile away.

On a brighter note, there is a broad sandy beach right next to the harbour which stretches for two miles down to Seaton Sluice, where you might like to try either The Waterford Arms (☎ 0191 237 0450) or The Astley Arms (☎ 0191 237 0057) for something to eat and drink. Back at the Harbour, the Club's bar – located in a 120 year old lightship - is open in the evenings and at weekends when meals are also available. Further exploration of Blyth and shopping for provisions means a trip to the centre of town which is over a mile away and frankly may not be top of our list of priorities. Market days are Tuesday, Friday and Saturday.

Taxi:	Phoenix Taxis (☎ 0500 50450)
Bus:	From dock gate to town centre and Newcastle (approx. 20 miles)
Rail/Air links:	from Newcastle

for more details, see Directory Section

South of Seaton Sluice and the backdrop soon begins to change as Whitley Bay, Newcastle's seaside face approaches. The line of hotels and guesthouses which stands along the shore is punctuated by Cullercoats, a small fishing harbour surrounded by a few old cottages which was swallowed up by Whitley Bay. The ruins of Tynemouth Priory (EH ☎ 0191 257 1090) stand out on the headland which protects the mouth of the River Tyne and, as the corner is rounded, the imposing statue of Admiral Collingwood, second in command to Nelson at Trafalgar, and the ruined castle come into view.

Tyne & Wear and Hartlepool

After the unspoiled coastline of Northumberland which has allowed the glories of nature to shine through, our next section offers some more cosmopolitan opportunities as a contrast. While for many, the name of Newcastle will conjure up images of fog on the Tyne and industry of old - this was where the longest grain tanker in the world was built - the modern city has seen a great deal of sympathetic redevelopment and is well worth sailing up to. The quayside area is lively and on a good night offers what many consider the best nightlife in the UK. Just down the coast from the Tyne, Sunderland has a well-equipped marina which offers easy access at any state of the tide and a good selection of things to do and places to visit once ashore. Further south, Hartlepool is another city where the decline in shipbuilding has left a quayside area ripe for redevelopment; this is an opportunity that has been enthusiastically seized to create the city's impressive "Historic Quay".

Newcastle and the River Tyne

Newcastle has a rich tradition as a maritime city both as a manufacturer of ships in the yards that greet you or more recently as a city that welcomed the Tall Ships. The Discovery Museum (☎ 0191 232 6789) in Blandford Square is a short distance from the quayside and its exhibits include the Turbinia, once the world's fastest vessel (and built on the Tyne), which is particularly well worth a look. There is also a superb maritime gallery which has one of the finest collections of ship models in the country. The Castle (☎ 0191 232 7938), which is close to the High Level Bridge, is a good example of a Norman keep, and it offers good views over the city. The Trinity Maritime Centre (☎ 0191 261 4691) on Broad Chare by the Crown Court on the Quayside has a good selection of exhibits which illustrate the maritime pedigree of Newcastle and the surrounding area and there's a very good café at the Live Theatre just thirty yards up Broad Chare. In addition to this, there are all the anticipated cultural choices of a cosmopolitan city - the Laing Art Gallery & Museum (☎0191 232 7734) just off Market Street and the Theatre Royal (☎0191 232 2061) are two for your short list.

To find a berth in what is generally regarded as the capital of the North East of England, there are a number of options open to you. There has been a lot of redevelopment around the central Quayside area, and if you want to be right in the thick of the pubs and restaurants here, you can tie up to a secure visitors' pontoon for free during the day. (Overnight - pay at the carpark opposite, about £10.00 for a 30' boat). If you are looking for marina facilities, you will have to stop short of the centre of the city at St Peter's Marina. This is quite a new development and has all the facilities you would expect plus shopping, pubs and restaurants on site, and you are only a mile away from the city centre for a much wider selection.

Newcastle is allegedly the seventh most happening city in the world - and at weekends it is easy to see why. A little way down from the marina, The Quayside, which nestles between the glorious Tyne bridges, is the place to club and party. The Pitcher and Piano is a good example of the many lively places for a drink. For more refined cuisine, visit 21 Queen Street (☎ 0191 222 0755) just back from the Quayside while lovers of Indian cuisine might try Vujon (☎ 0191 221 0601) and those peckish for Peking Duck should try the King Neptune (☎ 0191 261 6657). There are a number of pubs in the area which are quieter than the clubs, the Crown Posada is well worth a look. On the Quayside below the High Level Bridge is the Cooperage which until the early seventies was a working cooperage and is now a splendid place for a drink. Slightly further afield in the city centre, there are many more pubs worth visiting. The Bridge (opposite the Castle Keep) has a beer garden with one of the best views of the River Tyne and in a magnificent building opposite the railway station, The

Union Rooms is a good choice if you want to find somewhere to drink with no music or no smoking. For a lively city centre bar, head for Grey Street, which is noted for its fine Georgian terraces, and here you will find Fitzgeralds. If you have had enough of the solitude and the open sea - Newcastle certainly is the place to get the heart racing again.

Taxi:	(☎ 0191 276 1192)
Car hire:	Budget Rent A Car (☎ 0191 261 8282)
Rail:	Newcastle Station (☎ 0191 232 6262) - on the East Coast Intercity mainline
Airport:	Newcastle Airport (☎ 0191 232 5131)

for more details, see Directory Section

Sunderland

Just a short hop from the mouth of the Tyne, Sunderland is a straightforward harbour to get into with 24 hour access. This makes it an ideal location for a lifeboat station and Sunderland's all-weather lifeboat has been based in the marina in the North Dock since 1995 soon after the marina was completed. The marina, which is staffed round the clock, is close to the beach resort suburbs of Roker and Seaburn and about a mile and a half from the city centre. There is a reasonable general store on site, but for comprehensive restocking of the larder lockers, you will need to head for the supermarket about a mile away. Sunderland's industrial activities have included shipbuilding and glass-making and these are well represented at the town's Museum and Art Gallery on Borough Road (☎ 0191 514 1235). If you prefer, you can visit the National Glass Centre to see the processes for real - contact the Tourist Information Centre in Crowtree Road (☎ 0191 565 0960/0990) for details. A short taxi ride inland from the town takes you to the North East Aircraft Museum (☎ 0191 519 0662) which has the largest museum collection of aircraft in the North of England. On display are a Vulcan Bomber, an F100 Super Sabre, an F84F Thunderstreak and more.

There is no shortage of pubs and places to eat in Sunderland, particularly around the marina. Saltgrass (☎ 0191 565 7229) on Ayres Quay offers free transport at weekends to other local pubs, while Smugglers (☎ 0191 514 3844) on the lower promenade by the beach, is a popular family pub. Harbour View (☎ 0191 567 1402) is aptly named as it commands excellent views over the marina and harbour while being close to Roker Park and the beach. Brasserie 21 (☎ 0191 567 6594) on Wylam Wharf is an attractive converted 17th century warehouse, where booking is essential. The Swallow Hotel (☎ 0191 529 2041) makes dining enjoyable, with the restaurant overlooking Whitby Sands. The Shipwrights Hotel (☎ 0191 549 5139), despite its rather grand name, is a small riverside pub only 2 minutes from the city centre. Of course, we cannot leave the area without suggesting the Stadium of Light Sports Bar (☎ 0191 551 5100) for those of you who have more than a floating interest in football!

Taxi:	A B Taxis (☎ 0191 565 9999) or Dart Taxis (☎ 0191 565 8585)
Car hire:	Arriva Vehicle Rental (☎ 0191 514 0311) or Budget Rent A Car (☎ 0191 565 5123)

Bus:	Stagecoach enquiries (☎ 0191 567 5251), Go-Ahead Northern (☎ 0845 6060260)
Rail:	Sunderland Station, National Rail enquiries (☎ 0345 484950)
Ferry:	From Newcastle, Scandinavian Seaways (☎ 0990 333000)
Airport:	Newcastle (☎ 0191 286 0966)

for more details, see Directory Section

Hartlepool

In the early 1960s, Hartlepool's shipbuilding industry died leaving the dock area ripe for redevelopment. This opportunity has been seized enthusiastically and there is now a large and well-appointed marina. The town's current marketing motto is "A marina and much more" and you could easily spend a couple days exploring all the visitor attractions in the area. Right next to the marina is Hartlepool's "Historic Quay" (☎ 01429 860888) which is a faithful reproduction of an 18th century seaport. You can visit a range of seaport buildings and shops, relive an 18th century sea battle and learn about the history of the Royal Navy – watch out for the press-gang! A central feature is the oldest British warship still afloat, HMS Trincomalee, which was launched in 1817. What more could Patrick O'Brian readers wish for to bring to life the tales of Captain Aubrey and Dr Maturin? Just along the quay is the PSS Wingfield Castle, a restored paddle-steamer with on-board coffee shop, and the Museum of Hartlepool (☎ 01429 222255) which, unlike the Historic Quay, is free. If you fancy some serious shopping, Jacksons Landing (☎ 01429 866989) on the next quay contains outlets selling designer labels and household goods with discounts of up to 70% off normal retail prices. The Middleton Grange Shopping Centre (☎ 01429 861220) which is a bit further away has the main high street names all under one roof and an Indoor Market for the bargain hunter.

Taxi:	ABC Cabs (☎ 01429 862777) or BMW Taxis (☎ 01429 290290)
Car hire:	BR Car & Van Rental (☎ 01429 266992) or Hall & Hall Vehicle Hire (☎ 01429 234141)
Bus:	Arriva North East (☎ 01429 272904) or Stagecoach (☎ 01429 267082)
Rail:	Hartlepool Station, National Rail enquiries (☎ 0345 484950)
Airport:	Teesside International (01325 332811)

for more details, see Directory Section

North Yorkshire

The North York Moors provide a backdrop for crumbling cliffs, picturesque bays and small fishing communities clinging to the coastline along the northern stretch of coast. Further south, the picture changes and we encounter sandy beaches and the bustle of coastal holiday resorts like Scarborough and Filey. Landmarks along the shoreline stand as reminders of the industrial heritage of this area and the importance of mining and metalworking over several centuries. Though not always hospitable to the yachtsman, this is a striking stretch of coastline. The scenery is varied and there's plenty to do ashore with variety to appeal to many different tastes.

Approach to Whitby

The impressive cliffs which stretch away on both sides of the county border occasionally break down enough to offer small communities tiny harbours which are only useful to the very smallest of craft, such as the traditional local fishing cobles. Hardy fishermen still ply their trade from harbours like Staithes which is an attractive place to take a look at, but not really an option for the yachtsman. A few miles down the coast, you can drop anchor off the sandy beach at Runswick Bay where there is a sailing club which is open on Sundays. Runswick is primarily a holiday village where people come to sail, windsurf and walk. The Royal Hotel (☎ 01947 840215) is handy for a drink, and the Cliff Mount Hotel (☎ 01947 840103) offers reasonably priced meals.

Artist: **Anthony Flemming STAITHES**
Courtesy of: **The Artist**

Whitby

Whitby has many claims to fame, and landmarks stand out as reminders of many of them. Whitby Abbey (EH ☎ 01947 603568) stands at the top of a flight of 199 steps from the town. Now reduced to striking ruins on the East cliff, it was the location for the Synod of Whitby in 663 when King Oswy invited representatives of the Celtic and Roman branches of the Christian Church to settle their differences. This successful resolution resulted in improved links with the rest of Europe. Over a thousand years later came another man who is famed for establishing links overseas. The explorer Captain James Cook was not originally a Whitby man, having been born in 1728 in Marton, a village near Middlesbrough. However, he was apprenticed in Whitby to shipowner John Walker, and the ships *Endeavour, Resolution* and *Adventure* which carried him on his epic voyages around the world were built here. Cook's statue looks over the harbour from the West Bank. Near the statue, the jawbone of a whale is set up as an arch – this is a reminder that whaling was once a major source of wealth to the town. One notable local whaling captain was William Scoresby, who is credited with having invented the "crow's nest", and who brought in over 500 whales during his career in the late eighteenth and early nineteenth century.

As you sail in through the pincer of breakwaters which enclose the outer harbour, and approach the opening which forms the harbour and is the outlet for the River Esk, you will be under no illusions that Whitby is still a significant maritime town. Look out for the fishing fleet which continues to bring in herring for smoking. Harbour moorings are controlled by the Harbour Master; the marina is beyond the swing bridge which is opened on the hour and half hour for two hours each side of high water.

Artist: **Anthony Flemming WHITBY**
Courtesy of: **The Artist**

Whitby is a thriving and busy seaside tourist town with museums, a cinema, theatre, swimming pool, football club and an attractive beach – a stroll along Whitby Sands to Sandsend a couple of miles north is a good way to take control of one's land-legs. Children can play miniature golf, or have a go at fishing off the pier, and there's a funfair during the Whitby (Town) Regatta & Carnival which usually takes place on the second weekend in August. The Whitby Lifeboat Museum (☎ 01947 602001) on Pier Road includes the last pulling and sailing lifeboat to see service. Whitby's current lifeboats can be seen at the harbour and are both a great deal more sophisticated, having come on station in 1996 and 1997. The Dracula Experience on Marine Parade pays tribute to Bram Stoker's novel some of which is set in Whitby. If you have a bit more time to play with, a short train journey to Grosmont (about 5 miles away) connects you to the North Yorkshire Moors Railway (☎ 01751 472508) where full-size steam trains offer daily trips through spectacular scenery. The town centre is quite compact with all the shops, pubs and restaurants you could need within walking distance. On the east bank, the old town has characterful narrow winding streets; this is in contrast to the Victorian resort atmosphere of the West Cliff on the other bank where you will find the marina and Whitby Yacht Club. The bar at the yacht club is open on Friday and Saturday nights and Sundays on Bank Holidays. The Tap and Spile on New Quay Road (☎ 01947 381679) is within a short walk which will build up your thirst and the White Horse & Griffin (☎ 01947 604857) and the Duke of York (☎ 01947 600324), both in Church Street, serve good pub food. An inexpensive restaurant meal can be had at the Granby, Skinner Street (☎ 01947 602883) and near the Tap and Spile in New Quay Road is Trenchers Restaurant (☎ 01947 603212) if you are in the market for something a little more elaborate.

Taxi:	Station Taxis (☎ 01947 602069)
	E.T.A. Private Hire (☎ 01947 821010)
Cycle hire:	Trailways (☎ 01947 820207)
Bus:	services to Middlesbrough, N. Yorkshire, Leeds & York
Rail:	services to Middlesbrough then link to East Coast Inter City
Air:	Teeside Airport – domestic and European services

for more details, see Directory Section

Whitby to Scarborough

As you carry on south, there is some fine coastline to admire with striking headlands, cliffs and bays. As you pass, do try to have a look at Robin Hood's Bay with its unusual beach in contrasting contours of different coloured sand and shingle. This is a delightfully desolate stretch with few human habitations, lots of birdlife but no real shelter for the yachtsman until Scarborough.

Scarborough

Scarborough has been a holiday resort for over three centuries. Sandy beaches and fish & chip shops are bordered by extensive public gardens. There is a wide variety of entertainments and attractions including theatres, cinemas, a tenpin bowling alley, boat trips (the *Regal Lady* was one of the fleet of little ships at Dunkirk) and museums. In mid-May, there is a street funfair. There's a Sea Life Centre which you can get to via a miniature steam railway along the North Bay. At nearby Peasholm Park, you can hire rowing boats and canoes, listen to Organ and Brass Band Concerts, watch a water-ski circus show or the naval warfare display, which is Scarborough's unique sea battle, in 20 foot miniature warships and submarines. The naval warfare display is a clue that there is more to Scarborough's history than just the beach culture. Scarborough Castle (EH ☎ 01723 372451), perched on the headland which separates the North Bay and the South Bay, was built by Henry II in the 12th century. It was besieged twice in the Civil War by the Parliamentarians, and after it fell for the second time, Cromwell ordered it to be destroyed. Much, including most of the north west front, was demolished, but the remains of the great rectangular stone keep still stand over three stories high. In more recent military action, Scarborough was shelled by a force from the German Imperial High Seas Fleet in December 1914 and the waters off Scarborough were the scene of Scottish born American naval hero John Paul Jones's most famous battle. Throughout the American War of Independence he harassed shipping around Britain's coasts. In September 1779, he met with a Baltic merchant convoy escorted by two British warships. His squadron captured both British warships and he was given a gold-hilted sword by Louis XVI for his achievements. Happily we can report that more peaceful waters are to be found today.

Scarborough's harbour, tucked under the ruins of the castle, offers drying berths alongside the quay or on pontoons, and is just far enough away from the crowd to be reasonably peaceful. All the usual facilities are available and the area is patrolled by a 24 hour watchkeeper. A comprehensive selection of shops for provisions can be found within fifteen minutes walk (early closing on Wednesday). The Scarborough Yacht Club is based in the lighthouse on Vincent Pier which was rebuilt in 1931 after being damaged and dismantled after the German bombardment in 1914. There is 24 hour access to showers etc. and the bar is open on Wednesday, Friday and Saturday evenings and offers meals on Saturday and Sunday lunchtimes. There is a wide variety of pubs and restaurants to choose from.

Taxi:	Zcars (☎ 01723 377177)
Bus:	services to York and Leeds
Rail:	Scarborough Station offers services which link to the east Coast Inter City line
Air:	Leeds/Bradford or Humberside Airports

for more details, see Directory Section

East Riding of Yorkshire

The stretch of coast down to the River Humber has a variety of prospects. After the spectacular headland at Flamborough, a stretch of tide-swept coastline runs down to the bleak isolation of Spurn Head. The key towns along here are Bridlington and Hull which are both lively places to visit.

Bempton Cliffs to Bridlington

Pressing on south, with Filey Bay's long sweep of sand to starboard, we approach the chalky Bempton Cliffs leading to Flamborough Head which starts to loom up ahead. The cliffs, rising in places to an impressive height of 400 feet, consist of chalk and boulder clay. This mixture is highly prone to erosion, and the result is a broken line of projecting fingers and bays carved out of the coastline. Once again we are in ideal territory for bird life, and the RSPB reserve along these cliffs is home to around 200,000 of our feathered friends. You can expect to see fulmars, kittiwakes, cormorants and gannets and many others as you sail past England's largest seabird colony, though you are advised not to get too close otherwise you may be drawn in among the rocks by the tide. Once round Flamborough Head, another seaside resort comes into view. This is Bridlington, or Brid as it is affectionately known locally.

Bridlington

Bridlington Bay was the scene of tragedy in 1871 when an appalling storm wrought havoc amongst the boats which were sheltering there. Over 70 men were drowned and 30 ships lost. This provoked Samuel Plimsoll MP to argue that overloading was causing needless danger and a law was passed in 1876 which introduced the requirement for the now familiar marking to be painted on ships' hulls. The splendid lifeboathouse was built at the turn of the century and is well worth a visit. The station mechanic will be delighted to show you around and, while you are in the area, the Bridlington Harbour Museum and Aquarium (☎ 01262 670148), close by on Harbour road, includes exhibits relating to the RNLI.

Bridlington's harbour is another which dries at low water, but you can tie up to the quay in the south harbour by arrangement with the harbour-master. The fishing fleet is kept separate in the northern section. Though there is no marina as such, most facilities are available from the harbour authorities or the Royal Yorkshire Yacht Club which is based here. The clubhouse is open

seven days a week in the summer and welcomes the crews of visiting yachts. As well as the usual attractions of a seaside resort (you can discover how rock is made and even personalise your own stick at the John Bull World of Rock, ☎ 01262 678525), Bridlington has its quieter charms. The older part of the town has an impressive Priory Church and an interesting museum in a fourteenth century building. This is also where you will find Ellie Mae's Bistro, 55 High Street (☎ 01262 677605) for first class feeding and there are several pubs in the area which serve food if you are feeling a little more frugal. Nearer the harbour, The Windsor Hotel, Windsor Crescent (☎ 01262 673623) is a good option for a drink, and Beamont's Café (☎ 01262 400357) just opposite the RYYC offers inexpensive meals. If you have the time and are willing to travel (details of cycle hire below – or you might prefer a taxi!), The North Star at Flamborough (about 5 miles away, ☎ 01262 850379) does a good pub lunch.

Taxi:	Coastline Cabs (☎ 01262 400150)
Cycle hire:	Kirbys (☎ 01262 674946)
Bus:	National coach services/local bus services
Rail:	Links to Scarborough and Hull, thence to East Coast main line
Airports:	Humberside and Leeds Bradford

Bridlington to Spurn Head

From Bridlington, a long sandy beach stretches all the way to Spurn Head with bordering cliffs undulating from 100 feet to just above sea level. This is a tide-swept length of coastline where no fewer than 30 towns and villages have been lost to the encroaching sea since Roman times. Some unfortunate development between the wars has not done the area any favours, but many sections offer attractive vistas over rolling agricultural land interspersed with woodland. The projecting finger of Spurn Head itself is a nature reserve, designated as Heritage Coast. The three mile stretch shelters the northern approach to the Humber and leads to one of the most isolated Lifeboat stations in the British Isles. Such is its remoteness that Humber Lifeboat Station is unique for having the only full-time crew the RNLI operates.

The Humber

You have to go a long way north or south before finding another inlet which offers sheltered and deep access so, unsurprisingly, there is considerable commercial traffic - and some of it is pretty big. The tides run quickly as well, and channels are prone to considerable movement, especially in the upper reaches. This makes for some challenging navigation which may not be everyone's cup of tea. Before we put you off too much though, this is a popular sailing area, claiming as much space as the Solent with considerably less overcrowding. One attraction is the wildlife; Spurn Head itself is a haven for many migrant birds including pink footed geese, and there are several more nature reserves on both sides of the river on the way up to Hull. There are also a number of ports with plenty to see and do if you are not in any particular hurry to press on. There are several options if you are looking for a pontoon to tie up to and Grimsby is quite near the mouth of the estuary if you don't fancy the half day's sail up to Hull itself or beyond.

Kingston-upon-Hull

Ferries, fishing boats, oil tankers and container ships are all regular visitors to Hull's docks in the late 20th century. The port on the River Hull received a charter from King Edward I in 1299, and from then on, its formal name has been Kingston upon Hull. A number of museums illustrate Hull's history since then, and particularly its significant role in North Sea fishing and in Arctic whaling in the 19th Century. The old offices of the Hull Dock Company house the Maritime Museum (☎ 01482 613902) which is just the other side of the Princes Quay Shopping Centre from the Marina. A little further from the centre, in High Street, you can find the Hull and East Riding Museum (☎ 01482 613902), Hull's Museum of Transport (☎ 01482 613902), and interestingly the birthplace of William Wilberforce (1759-1833). His battle to abolish slavery and the slave trade is commemorated with depictions of the slave trade and a collection of relics in the dignified and attractive building called Wilberforce House (☎ 01482 613902). While much of Hull was seriously damaged during World War II, there are parts of the Old Town which survive from the 18th century and earlier. Look for the narrow cobbled lanes and old quays on the West Bank of the River Hull, where you will also find Holy Trinity Church which was founded in 1285 and is reckoned to be the largest parish church in England. It has some of the earliest known medieval English brickwork. While you are in the area, The King William (☎ 01482 227013) in Market Street is inviting. You may like to get hold of *The Hull Ale Trail*, a comprehensive guide to Hull's Heritage Pubs; contact Hull Tourism (☎ 01482 615726). If you are looking for food, head south for Nelson Street on the point looking over the Humber between the River Hull and the marina, where you will find pub meals at the Minerva Hotel (☎ 01482 326900) or something smarter at Ceruttis (☎ 01482 328501). There are also several bars and restaurants around the waterside Quay at the marina if you prefer not to stray too far. The Olde White Harte (☎ 01482 326363) off Silver Street , is worth a visit to experience its six bars and its varied menu with everything from sandwiches to three course meals. Regular events which may be of interest are the Hull Marina Regatta which takes place in early July, the Jazz Festival in early August and the International Sea Shanty Festival in early September.

The Marina is conveniently placed near the centre of the town, but not right in it for reasonable peace at pub closing time! All the usual facilities are available on site - the Marina boasts a four anchor award and there's 24 hour security with CCTV. Access to the marina is through a lock which is open 3 hours each side of high water, and while the strong currents in the Humber should be treated with respect, the channels are well marked and navigation is reasonably easy if you follow the buoys.

Taxi, car hire & cycle hire:
details on notice board at Marina reception
Bus: 5 mins walk, local and national services
Rail: 5 mins walk, Intercity and local
Air: Humberside Airport half an hour away by road.
for more details, see Directory Section

Upriver

The intrepid estuary explorer might like to venture further up the Humber and there are several havens to head for. A major landmark is the imposing Humber Bridge with its 500 foot towers and span of over 450 feet, and soon after passing this, you can nip into **South Ferriby** Marina on the south bank. Again, this marina is entered via a lock whose gates are open three hours each side of high water. Be sure you have an up to date chart as the buoyed channel above Hull changes frequently. Even further up river, **Winteringham Haven** and **Brough Haven** offer moorings (which dry) and limited facilities. Both are run by the Humber Yawl Club (☎ 01482 667224) and you should contact them before starting up river in order to check on mooring availability and for up to date details of the approach channels.

Grimsby

Grimsby's large deep-sea fishing fleet is now a thing of the past, but the tradition has not been forgotten and North Sea fishing is still a key part of this port, as is commercial shipping. Like Hull, having deep water access and good shelter made it almost inevitable that this would be a great maritime centre. The National Fishing Heritage Centre (☎ 01472 323345) offers much in the way of both educational and fun insights into this great British industry. You can also have a look around Ross Tiger, a fully restored traditional deep sea trawler which is moored next to the centre. Just along the coast, almost merged together with Grimsby, is Cleethorpes which is a classic English seaside resort. Here you can stroll along the promenade, visit the pier, get out the buckets and spades and indulge in all the other traditional seaside pursuits. There's a narrow gauge railway which runs along the coast and an unusual attraction is the Discovery Centre which introduces the natural life of the sea and foreshore with exhibits, computers and an observatory overlooking the Humber Estuary. The sands and mudflats off Cleethorpes are recognised as a site of Special Scientific Interest and offer the chance to see rare migrating birds and the opportunity for some fine (and very un-hilly) walking. Another wildlife attraction is the Deep Sea Experience. Here you can see fish from all around the world including sharks, rays and lion fish - and at close quarters too!

Grimsby is on the south bank of the Humber, and considerably closer to the mouth than Hull. This makes it an easier option to get to if time is not on your side. Grimsby Marina is accessible from three and a half hours before high water to two and a half hours after via Royal Dock and Union Dock. Alternatively, you can try the Meridian Quay Marina which is managed by the Humber Cruising Association and is inside No. 2 Fish Dock. Grimsby and Cleethorpes Yacht Club organises racing on Sundays throughout the season. It's based at Alexandra Dock near the National Fishing Heritage Centre and visiting yachtsmen are always welcome.

Willy's Pub & Brewery (☎ 01472 602145) in Cleethorpes, is a popular seafront bar serving home-cooked food and it holds an annual beer festival in November. A stone's throw away is the recently refurbished Smugglers (☎ 01472 200862) which is popular with both locals and tourists. Kingsway Hotel (☎ 01472 601122)

overlooking the Humber Estuary, is noted for the local fish it features on its menus. Close neighbour, Grimsby, offers a choice of pubs including the Tap & Spile (☎ 01472 357493) on Garth Lane, which is basic but good for real ales and unusual dishes. The Hope & Anchor (☎ 01472 342565) on Victoria Street is relaxing with reasonably priced bar food and the Travel Inn (☎ 01472 242630) in Europa Park serves meals in its grill restaurant.

Taxi:	AA Radio Cars (☎ 01472 696969) or Bob's Taxis (☎ 01472 692846)
Car hire:	Avis Rent A Car (☎ 01472 343600)
Bus:	Stagecoach (☎ 01472 358646)
Rail:	Grimsby Station, National Rail Enquiries (☎ 0345 484950)
Airport:	Humberside (15 minutes), enquiries (☎ 01652 688456)

for more details, see Directory Section

Lincolnshire

The Humber to the Wash

This low lying stretch of coastline is great for marshes and sandy beaches, but there are few anchorages, let alone inlets until you get to the very tricky tidal waters and muddy bleakness of the Wash. Just beyond Skegness and at the edge of the Wash, there is a viable option for those with a hankering for peace and quiet and no worries about resting on the bottom.

Skegness

The Skegness Yacht Club, based at Gibraltar Point about three miles south of Skeggy (as it is familiarly known) sails out of a drying creek. Twin or lifting keels are most definitely an advantage here and the creek is only accessible for a couple of hours each side of high water. Gibraltar Point is a National Nature Reserve and its Visitor Centre is right next to the club. Visiting birds include Brent Geese, fieldfares, twites and redwings and the reserve provides one of the few regular nesting places on the Lincolnshire coast for little terns. This is definitely a port of call for those in search of a peaceful spot which is off the beaten track. Facilities for yachtsmen are very limited, but all the usual shopping and holidaymaking facilities can be found in Skegness itself. There's no public transport link, so you might find it handy to have John Lee's phone number (☎ 01754 761441) as he runs a local taxi service. (*for more details, see Directory Section*)

Artist: **Anthony Flemming** **ENTRANCE TO THE CREEK** *Courtesy of:* **The Artist**

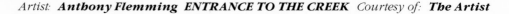

BERWICK-UPON-TWEED 55.46.0N 01.59.0W

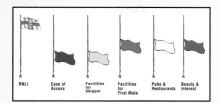

Capt. J.H. Jenkinson: Harbourmaster
Harbourmaster's Office, Tweed Dock,
Berwick-upon-Tweed, TD15 2AA
Tel: 01289 307404
VHF Ch: 12 VHF Name: Berwick Harbour

Repairs: contact Harbourmaster

Berwick-upon-Tweed Lifeboat
Dock Road, Tweedmouth
Open to visitors: Contact Hon. Sec. Capt J
Jenkinson Tel: 01289 307404

HOLY ISLAND 55.40.0N 01.48.0W

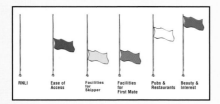

Ralph Wilson: Harbourmaster
Tel: 01289 389217

NORTH SUNDERLAND

North Sunderland Lifeboat
Seahouses, Northumberland
Open to visitors: contact boathouse
Tel: 01665 720370

BEADNELL BAY 55.33.0N 01.37.0W

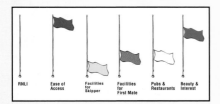

Beadnell Sailing Club
G.S. Howlett: Secretary
Harbour Road, Beadnell, NE67 5BJ
Tel: 0191 285 6398

Craster 55.28.5N 01.35.0W

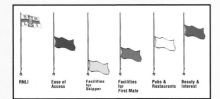

Anchor outside the harbour, in fair weather
only

Craster Lifeboat
Craster Harbour, Craster, Alnwick
Open to visitors: weekends in summer
For details contact: David Clarke, Coxswain
Boathouse Tel: 01665 576050

AMBLE 55.20.5N 01.34.0W

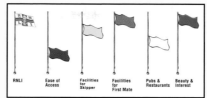

Amble Marina
Mrs Linda Sweaney: Manager
Amble, Northumberland, NE65 0YP
Tel: 01665 712168 Fax: 01665 713363
VHF Ch: 80 VHF Name: Amble Marina

Coquet Yacht Club
Neal Hill: Secretary
The Braid, Amble, Northumberland
Tel: 01665 711179
VHF: Ch: 37 VHF Name: Coquet Base

Chandlers:
Amble Boat Company Ltd, The Boatyard,
Amble, Northumberland NE65 0DJ
Tel: 01665 710267 Fax: 01665 711354

Repairs: contact chandler

Amble Lifeboat
Amble, Northumberland
Open to visitors: Contact Hon. Sec. M.
Pritchard Tel: 01670 760447

NEWBIGGIN 55.10.5N 01.30.0W

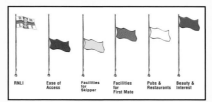

Limited facilities for yachts

Newbiggin Lifeboat
Bay View East, Newbiggin-by-the-Sea
This is the oldest operational lifeboat
boathouse in the UK
Open to visitors: on weekdays generally –
contact Hon Sec for details.
Boathouse Tel: 01670 817320
Hon. Sec. Tel: 01670 817320

BLYTH 55.07.0N 01.29.5W

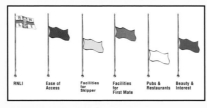

Captain Steven Tong: Harbourmaster
Tel: 01670 352678
VHF Channel: 12/11/16
VHF Name: Blyth Harbour Radio

Royal Northumberland Yacht Club
P.S. Guellard: Secretary
South Harbour, Blyth NE24 3PB
Tel: 01670 353636

Blyth Lifeboat
South Harbour, Blyth
Open to visitors: Contact Hon Sec J Scott
Tel: 0670 368466

CULLERCOATS

Fair weather anchorage only.

Cullercoats Lifeboat
Front Street, Cullercoats
Contact J.W.K. Smith (Hon. Sec.) to arrange to
visit.
Boathouse Tel: 0191 2521820
Hon. Sec. Tel: 0191 2520394

NORTH SHIELDS 55.01.0N 01.24.0W

Tynemouth Lifeboat
Fish Quay, Eastern Jetty, North Shields, NE30
1YX
Open to visitors: Mon-Fri 0900-1700
Boathouse Tel: 0191 2570913

NEWCASTLE-UPON-TYNE 54.58.0N 01.35.0W

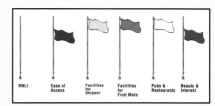

River Tyne/ North Shields Harbourmaster
Tel: 0191 257 2080
VHF: Channel 12/16/11/14
VHF Name: Tyne Harbour Radio

St Peter's Marina
Contact: Manager
St Peter's Basin, Newcastle-upon-Tyne, NE6 1HX
Tel: 0191 265 4472 Fax: 0191 276 2618
VHF: Ch: 80/37 VHF Name: St Peter's Marina

Royal Quays Marina
Contact: Manager
Albert Edward Dock, Coble Dene Road,
North Shields, NE29 6DU Tel: 0191 272 8282
VHF: Ch: 80 VHF Name: Royal Quays Marina

Hebburn Marina Tel: 0191 4832876

Friars Goose Marina Tel: 0191 4692545

Chandlers:
Storrar Marine Store, 181-183 Coast Road,
Newcastle-upon-Tyne
Tel: 0191 266 1037 Fax: 0191 270 1950

Fox & Hounds Marine Ltd, 166 Brinkburn St
South, Newcastle-upon-Tyne NE6 2AR
Tel: 0191 276 1161 Fax: 0191 276 5846

Repairs:
J. Southern & Sons, 10 Cliffords Fort, Fish
Quay, N. Shields, Tyne & Wear NE30 1JE
Tel: 0191 257 4981 Fax: 0191 257 6958

SUNDERLAND 54.55.0N 01.21.0W

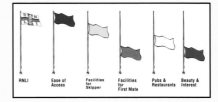

Harbourmaster
Tel: 0191 553 2148
VHF: Channel 14/16
VHF Name: Sunderland Harbour Radio

Sunderland Marina
Mr P. Murray: Manager
Sunderland, SR6 0PW
Tel: 0191 514 4721 Fax: 0191 514 1847
VHF: Ch: 37 VHF Name: Sunderland Marina

No chandler or repairs on site

Sunderland Lifeboat
Sunderland, Tyne and Wear
Open to visitors: contact Boathouse
Tel: 0191 567 3536

HARTLEPOOL   54.41'.3N 01.11'.5W

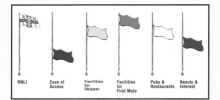

Captain J Drewitt: Harbourmaster
Tel: 01642 277205

Hartlepool Marina
Paul Lane: Manager
Lock Office, Slake Terrace, Hartlepool, TS24 0RU
Tel: 01429 865744 Fax: 01429 865947
VHF: Ch: 37/80 VHF Name: Hartlepool Marina

Chandler:
Hart Marine, Marina Boatyard, Hartlepool
Tel: 01429 862932

Repairs:
Hartlepool Marine Engineering, Marina
Boatyard, Hartlepool Tel: 01429 867883

Hartlepool Lifeboat
Irvines Quay, Ferry Road, Hartlepool
Open to visitors: 0900-1500 all week - you'll
get a friendly welcome and a nice cup of tea
Boathouse Tel: 01429 266103

TEESMOUTH

Teesmouth Lifeboat
Teesdmouth, Redcar & Cleveland
Open to visitors: Week days 0900 - 1400,
weekends 1400 - 1700 Easter to Nov Contact
Hon Sec N Marson Tel: 01642 481203 or
Graham Petite Tel: 01642 486636

REDCAR

Redcar Lifeboat
Redcar, Redcar & Cleveland
Open to visitors: Contact Hon Sec I Readman
Tel: 01642 486877
Boathouse Tel: 01642 484491

RUNSWICK BAY   54.32'.0N 00.44'.0W

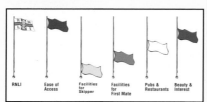

Anchorage only - unsuitable in north-easter-
lies

Runswick Bay Sailing Club
Richard Willis: Secretary
c/o The Moorings, Guisborough Road,
Moorsham, Nr Saltburn, Cleveland
Tel: 01287 660119 Fax: 01287 660119

Staithes & Runswick Lifeboat
The Lifeboat House, Northside, Cowbar,
Saltburn by Sea.
Open to visitors: daily in summer -
contact Hon Sec at other times
Boathouse Tel: 01947 840001
Hon Sec Tel: 01947 840141

WHITBY   54.29'.5N 037'.0W

Captain W Estill: Harbourmaster:
Harbour Office, Pier Road, Whitby YO21 3PU
Tel: 01947 602354 Fax: 01947 600380
VHF: Ch: 16/11 VHF Name: Whitby Port
Radio or Whitby Marina

Whitby Yacht Club
Samantha Fielding: Secretary

WHITBY cont.

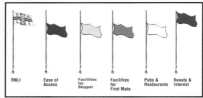

The Pier, Whitby, North Yorkshire YO21 3PU
Tel: 01947 603623

Chandlers:
M.R. Coates Marine, The Marina Boatyard,
Longbourne Rd, Whitby YO21 1GU
Tel: 01947 604486

Repairs: contact Coates Marine

Whitby Lifeboat
Whitby, North Yorkshire
Open to visitors: All year Contact Mech G
Goodberry Tel: 01947 602216/601293

SCARBOROUGH   54.17'.0N 00.23.5W

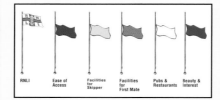

Captain W Estill: Harbourmaster
18 West Pier, Scarborough, North Yorkshire
YO11 1PD
Tel: 01723 373530 Fax: 01723 373530
VHF: Channel: 16/12
VHF Name: Scarborough Lighthouse

Scarborough Yacht Club
Mrs S. Scholes: Secretary
The Lighthouse, Vincent Pier, Scarborough
Tel: 01723 373821 Fax: 01723 373821

Chandlers:
Scarborough Marine, 36 Sandside,
Scarborough YO11 1PQ
Tel: 01723 375199

Repairs: contact Scarborough Marine (no sail
repairs)

Scarborough Lifeboat
Foreshore Road, Scarborough YO11 1PB
Open to visitors: times vary.
Contact Coxswain/mechanic for further
details. Cox'n/Mech. Tel: 01723 360520

FILEY   54.13'.0N 00.16'.0W

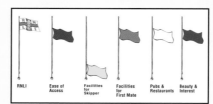

Anchorage only

Filey Lifeboat
Filey, North Yorkshire
Open to visitors: All year Contact Hon Sec G
Cammish Tel: 01723 891992

FLAMBOROUGH

No facilities for yachts

Flamborough Lifeboat
Flamborough, East Riding of Yorkshire

Open to visitors: All year Contact Hon Sec
Capt C Hoskison Tel: 01262 851108 or DLA J
Hughes Tel: 01262 850916

BRIDLINGTON   54.05'.0N 00.11'.0W

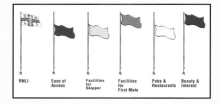

Mr Wright: Harbourmaster:
West End, Bridlington Harbour
Tel: 01262 670148
VHF: Ch: 16 VHF Name: Bridlington Harbour

Royal Yorkshire Yacht Club
J.H. Evans: Secretary
c/o 1 Windsor Crescent, Bridlington, East
Yorkshire YO15 3HX
Tel: 01262 672041 Fax: 01262 678319

Chandlers:
C & M Marine, West End, Bridlington Harbour
Tel: 01262 672212

Engine repairs:
Auto Electrical Fuel Injection Services,
Havelocks Crescent, Bridlington
Tel: 01262 400622

Bridlington Lifeboat
Bridlington, East Riding of Yorkshire
Open to visitors: All year Contact Mech S
McKie Tel: 01262 672450

WITHERNSEA

No facilities for yachts

Withernsea Lifeboat
Withernsea, East Riding of Yorkshire
Open to visitors: East to September Contact
Hon Sec B Brigham
Tel: 01964 613723

SPURN HEAD

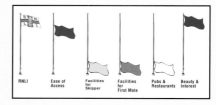

Anchorage behind Spurn Head in settled
conditions.

Humber Lifeboat
Spurn Point, HU12 0UG
NOT SUITABLE FOR VISITORS
Tel: 01964 650228

HULL

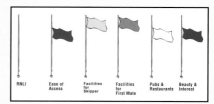

Paul Hames: Humber harbourmaster (Hull)
Tel: 01482 327171

Hull Marina
Howard Anguish: Manager
Warehouse 13, Kingston Street,
Kingston-upon-Hull HU1 2DQ

Tel: 01482 613450
VHF: Channel 80
VHF Name: Hull Marina

Chandlers:
Kildale Marine, Hull Marina
Tel: 01482 227464

Repairs: consult marina office – all repairs available locally

Upriver - River Humber

South Ferriby Marina
Contact: Manager
Barton-on-Humber DN18 6JH
Tel: 01652 635620
Fax: 01652 660517
VHF: Channel 80
VHF Name: South Ferriby Base

Humber Yawl Club – offers some visitors moorings at: Brough Haven
(Tel: 01482 667224) and
Winteringham Haven (Tel: 01724 734452)

GRIMSBY   53.35'.0 N 00.04'.0W

M Gough: Dockmaster
Tel: 01472 359181
VHF: Channel 74/18/79
VHF Name: Grimsby Docks Radio

GRIMSBY cont.

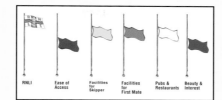

Grimsby Marina
Contact: Harbourmaster
Corporation Road, Grimsby DN31 1UE
Tel: 01472 360404 Fax: 01673 828596

Humber Cruising Association
Meridian Quay, Aukland Road DN31 3RP
Tel: 01472 268424 Fax: 01472 268424

CLEETHORPES

No facilities for yachts

Cleethorpes Lifeboat
Cleethorpes, North East Lincolnshire
Open to visitors: All year, Sunday by arrangement Contact Hon Sec W Barlow
Tel 01472 698244 or 01469 571000 ext 3510

MABLETHORPE

No facilities for yachts

Mablethorpe Lifeboat
Central Promenade, Mablethorpe, Lincs
Open to visitors any reasonable time, contact R Stones, Tel: 01507 477585
Boathouse Tel: 01507 477848

SKEGNESS

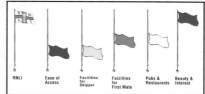

Skegness Yacht Club   53.05'.0N 00.20'.0E
Marilyn Walsham: Secretary
Gibraltar Point, Skegness Tel: 01507 607761

Skegness Lifeboat
Tower Esplanade, Skegness
Open daily during summer and at weekends during winter. Boathouse Tel: 01754 763011

North East England - Chart Agents

Lilley & Gillie, Newcastle Tel: 0191 2572217
Yacht Brokerage, Hartlepool Tel: 01429 865433
Scar Marine Eng, Scarboro Tel: 01723 375199
Coates Marine, Whitby Tel: 01947 604486
B Cooke & Son, Hull Tel: 01482 223454

North East England - Pilot Books

Tidal Havens of the Wash & Humber, Henry Irving. 4th Edition 1991
published by Imray, Laurie, Norie & Wilson Tel: 01480 462114, ISBN 0852 881 592

Sailing Directions: Humber to Rattray Head, Royal Northumberland Yacht Club 1990
published by Royal Northumberland Yacht Club Tel: 01670 353636

North Sea Waypoint Directory, Peter Cumberlidge
published by Adlard Coles Nautical Tel: 0171 2420946 ISBN: 0713 647 99X

North Sea (West) Pilot. 4th Ed. 1997
published by United Kingdom Hydrographic Office, ISBN: 0707 710 545

St Peters Marina, Newcastle-upon-Tyne

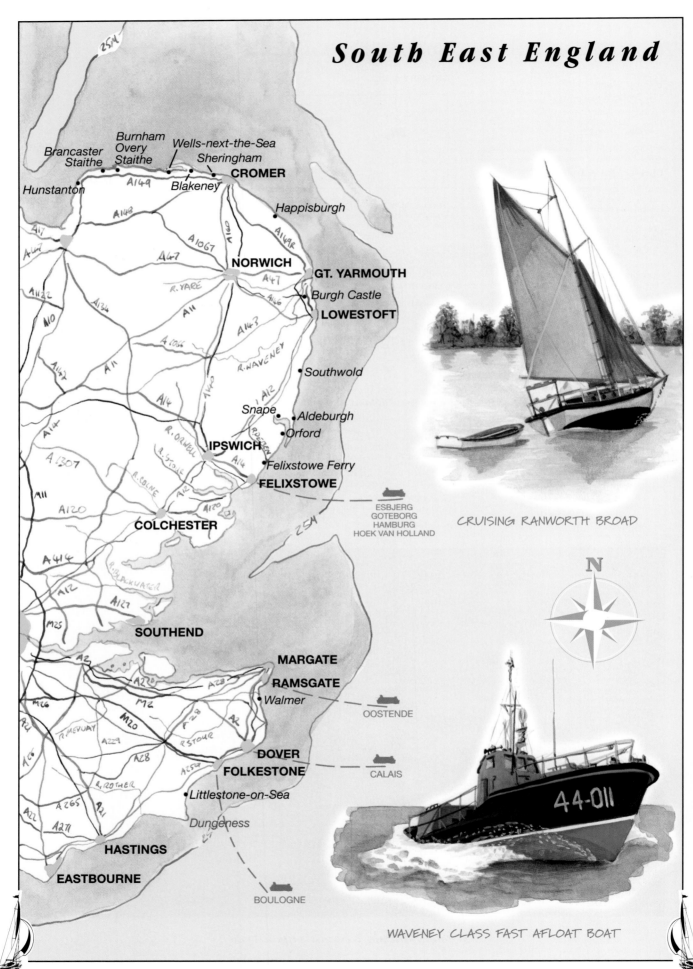

South East England

Brancaster
Staithe

Burnham
Overy
Staithe

Wells-next-the-Sea

Sheringham

CROMER

Hunstanton

Blakeney

A149

A148

Happisburgh

A1067

A1065

A140

A149R

A47

NORWICH

R. YARE

A47

GT. YARMOUTH

A11

A146

Burgh Castle

A1066

LOWESTOFT

A143

R. WAVENEY

A140

Southwold

A12

A14

Snape

Aldeburgh

R. DEBEN

Orford

R. ORWELL

IPSWICH

R. STOUR

A14

Felixstowe Ferry

A1307

R. COLNE

A120

FELIXSTOWE

A12

A120

COLCHESTER

254

ESBJERG
GOTEBORG
HAMBURG
HOEK VAN HOLLAND

CRUISING RANWORTH BROAD

A414

R. BLACKWATER

A12

A127

M25

A2

SOUTHEND

A20

A28

MARGATE

N

M26

M2

RAMSGATE

Walmer

OOSTENDE

M20

R. MEDWAY

A229

A2

R. STOUR

DOVER

CALAIS

A20

A28

FOLKESTONE

R. ROTHER

Littlestone-on-Sea

A265

A21

Dungeness

A22

A271

HASTINGS

EASTBOURNE

BOULOGNE

44-011

WAVENEY CLASS FAST AFLOAT BOAT

Felixstowe to Margate - Close up

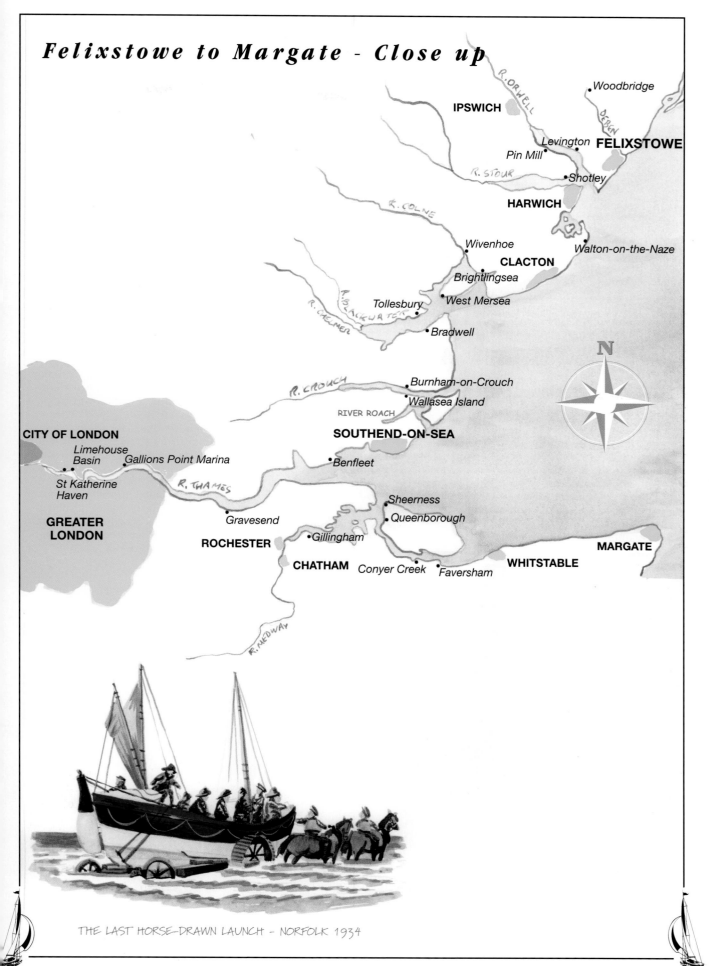

R. ORWELL

Woodbridge

IPSWICH

DEBEN

Levington **FELIXSTOWE**

Pin Mill

R. STOUR

Shotley

HARWICH

R. COLNE

Wivenhoe

Walton-on-the-Naze

CLACTON

Brightlingsea

R. CHELMER

R. BLACKWATER

Tollesbury

West Mersea

Bradwell

R. CROUCH

Burnham-on-Crouch

Wallasea Island

RIVER ROACH

SOUTHEND-ON-SEA

N

CITY OF LONDON

Limehouse
Basin

Gallions Point Marina

Benfleet

St Katherine
Haven

R. THAMES

Sheerness

**GREATER
LONDON**

Queenborough

Gravesend

ROCHESTER

Gillingham

MARGATE

CHATHAM

Conyer Creek

Faversham

WHITSTABLE

R. MEDWAY

THE LAST HORSE-DRAWN LAUNCH - NORFOLK 1934

Norfolk

The coast here tends to be low lying, as is much of inland Norfolk as well. Backed by sand dunes and marshland, this sparsely populated coastline is a popular destination for birdwatchers as there are numerous species to see. Haven for wildlife it may be, but it is not quite so accommodating for the yachtsman. There isn't a marina until Great Yarmouth, and that is well upstream in the Broads, and other than that, most of the harbours dry. These deterrents have their advantages – there are rich rewards for the intrepid and you get to enjoy the area without having to fight through hordes of other boats. The Norfolk coastline can be hazardous if the wind comes from the wrong direction and there are very limited opportunities to find shelter of any sort in strong northerlies. It is well worth keeping in touch with Yarmouth Coastguard who can refer you to local harbour authorities for advice and local knowledge, and who will be happy to keep track of what you are up to.

The Wash to Wells-next-the-Sea

Yachts are not really encouraged to visit the commercial port of Kings Lynn, so sailing east from the Wash, following a coastline which consists of sand dunes backed by salt marshes, the first feasible port of call is Brancaster Staithe. This small drying harbour is surrounded by nature reserves with Titchwell Marsh RSPB Reserve to the West and Scolt Head Island National Nature Reserve to the East. Avocets, marsh harriers and migrating waders can be seen here, and between April and mid August, the western end of Scolt Head is closed to the public to allow common and sandwich terns to breed in peace (EN warden ☎ 01485 518559). Known as Branodunum in Roman times, Brancaster was the site of one of the first of ten forts built to deter the Saxon pirates from the South East coast. An ulterior motive for this choice of location may be hinted at by the fact that ever since then Brancaster has been famous for shellfish, and locally grown oysters and mussels are a delicacy to look out for.

The entrance to the harbour is accessible for about two hours each side of high water; it can be tricky and should not be attempted in onshore winds which are anything more than a gentle breeze. Consult the harbour-master or sailing club for local knowledge as the sandbanks shift frequently.

Within walking distance, The Jolly Sailor (☎ 01485 210314) is a good basic pub for food and drink and the sailing club, offering a bar and food, is open at weekends, Bank Holidays and school summer holidays. Provisions shopping is rather limited, though there is a reasonable general store and a good fishmonger. Cycles can be hired at Dial House, (NT ☎ 01485 210719).

At the other end of Scolt Head, a winding creek leads up to **Burnham Overy Staithe**. This is one of a group of attractive villages known as the 'Seven Burnhams', which includes Burnham Thorpe a mile and a half away, birthplace of Lord Nelson in 1758. Sadly, the rectory he grew up in was demolished at the beginning of the nineteenth century. However, it is said that he was born in the flint barn next to the Inn as his mother didn't reach home in time, and that still stands. The Lord Nelson (☎ 01328 738241) is a traditional pub with stone flagged floor, old wooden settles, bar food and real ale served straight from the barrel. Adjacent Burnham Market has Georgian houses and bow windowed shops around its green, and Fishers' (☎ 01328 738588) restaurant is worth a visit if you are looking for an excellent meal. A call to the local taxi firm (☎ 01328 730440) will save you the walk. Back in Overy Staithe, good food and beer can be found in The Hero.

The entrance to the creek between Scolt Head and Gun Hill is not easy and to be avoided in onshore winds (NW to E). The tide runs quickly in the creek resulting in constant variations in the channel, so you are advised to consult those with local knowledge before attempting to get in. *(for more details, see Directory Section)*

Wells-next-the-Sea

After the quiet little villages further west, the small town of Wells seems quite metropolitan. Visiting yachts can moor up alongside at the west end of the quay before you get to the Fish Quays, or a visitors' mooring

Artist: **Clive Madgwick HOME WITH THE CATCH** *Courtesy of:* **Rosenstiel's**

may be available. You should contact the harbour-master to get permission to enter the harbour – if you are worried about the channel, or the conditions are difficult, the Harbour launch may be prepared to guide you in. Once moored up, you are right in the heart of the town where atmospheric old streets run all the way down to the quay. Pop into the Harbour Office and pick up a copy of the Wells Harbour Commissioners excellent Welcome Brochure which is packed with useful local information. This is a beach resort town, so there are amusement arcades on the front, but the beach, campsite and caravan park are all to the north of the town. A miniature railway saves the mile long walk up to the beach, and for those who can't get enough of this sort of thing, there is also a narrow gauge steam railway which takes you four miles inland to Walsingham. On the Quay itself just by the Harbour Office, the Old Lifeboat House is now a maritime museum (☎01328 711646) with displays of the history of Wells' lifeboats, floods, harbour history, coastguards and smuggling, fishing, natural history and wildfowling. There are good shopping facilities and everything you could need is within a couple of hundred yards of the quay. There is also quite a choice of pubs and restaurants. The Ark Royal is not far from the Harbour Office on Freeman Street which makes it handy for a pint. Up the hill a bit, on Station Road, the Edinburgh Hotel (☎ 01328 710120) or, round the corner in the Georgian elegance of The Buttlands, the Crown Hotel both offer good pub-type meals. Probably the best restaurant in town is The Moorings (☎ 01328 710949) which is near the Harbour Office.

Artist: **Anthony Flemming NORFOLK CREEK**
Courtesy of: **The Artist**

Taxi:	Betjemens (☎ 01328 738309)
	mobile (☎ 0385 378786)
Car hire:	Bussey's, Fakenham (10 miles away)
Cycle hire:	Walsinghams, Polka Road, (☎ 01328 710522)
Bus:	Local services from town centre
Rail:	Sheringham, 14 miles
Airport:	Norwich 30 miles

for more details, see Directory Section

Wells to Great Yarmouth

Less than five miles along the coast, a more tranquil haven is in store. The four mile spit of Blakeney Point curls around a marshy tidal estuary and sheltered anchorage. At high water, the channel up to **Blakeney** is not difficult and you can lie alongside the quay in a drying berth for no charge. An easier option is the channel up to Morston Quay, or you can lie at anchor in 'The Pit'. Morston does not offer much in the way of facilities though there is an information centre at the Quay. Blakeney has a reasonable range of shops and The Kings Arms fifty yards from the quay is a good pub for a drink or a snack. Even closer is the Blakeney Hotel for more refined hospitality. Blakeney is an attractive spot with traditional local flint and brick buildings running down to the Quay. Blakeney Point is part of a National Trust Nature Reserve where terns, ringed plover and shelduck nest. You may well also get the chance to see common and grey seals in the estuary.

East of Blakeney are Sheringham and **Cromer**, both providing useful bases for the RNLI, though not hugely hospitable to the passing yachtsman. Neither offers any shelter, though you can drop your anchor off Cromer and take a dinghy ashore in settled conditions. Cromer has long been a popular seaside resort and has a pier, a Carnival and all the trimmings. There's a good selection of pubs, hotels and restaurants ashore, though given the exposed nature of the anchorage, any run ashore is likely to be brief. For a quick meal or a drink, The White Horse in West Street (☎ 01263 512275) is a good option. Cromer was the home of Henry Blogg, the RNLI's most decorated lifeboatman, who was Coxswain here from 1909 to 1947. During those thirty-eight years, he didn't lose a single man under his command, and is believed to have been responsible for saving more than 870 people. He received three gold and four silver medals from the RNLI, each representing a separate feat of outstanding bravery. The lifeboat museum here is named in his memory and his exploits are suitably recorded. The museum is open from 10.00 to 15.30 seven days a week between Easter and the end of September.

Bus:	local services from town centre
Rail:	local station connects to Intercity at Norwich.

The coastline continues to be fraught with sandbanks, tricky tides and scant shelter and the next place which offers sanctuary is not until Great Yarmouth, the northern gateway to the Norfolk Broads.

Great Yarmouth & the South Broads

Yarmouth is East Anglia's biggest seaside resort with two piers. The Pleasure Beach has a good range of white knuckle fairground rides and four miles of sandy beach. The Elizabethan House Museum on the South Quay (NT ☎ 01493 855746) is a 16th century building and 19th century frontage where the theme is the domestic life of families who have lived there in the past. A combined ticket also gives you access to the Maritime Museum for East Anglia and the Tollhouse Museum and Brass Rubbing Centre. English Heritage also have a variety of properties in the same area which portray life in times gone by (☎ 01493 857900). For seafaring history, head for the Maritime Museum (☎ 01493 842267) on marine parade which includes a collection of lifeboat models, or for the real thing, give the RNLI's Great Yarmouth Gorleston Station Honorary Secretary a ring to arrange a visit to the extensive double lifeboathouse near the river mouth at Gorleston.

When you think of the considerable extent of the waterways that make up the Norfolk Broads, it will come as little surprise to discover that the tide fairly sluices in and out through the mouth of the River Yare at Great Yarmouth. Strong south easterlies cause dangerous sea conditions in the mouth, especially on the ebb. It's also a busy commercial port, and you should contact Yarmouth Harbour radio (VHF Ch 12) for entry and departure and observe the International Port Traffic Signals.

You can moor up at the Town Hall Quay in the centre of the town, two miles up from the mouth, if you want to be in the thick of the action. However, there are no helpful facilities for yachts here. Comprehensive Marina facilities are available at Burgh Castle Marina which is another four miles inland at the far end of Breydon Water. There are two bridges which you will probably need to have opened before passing through. These are manned and open regularly during the week – contact Breydon Bridge on Channel 12 to arrange opening. At weekends, it is worth booking in advance – or checking to see what times others have booked for – by phoning the Harbour Office before 1500 on Friday (☎ 01493 335500).

Burgh Castle is set in spectacular scenery. Breydon Water, to the north east, is a Site of Special Scientific Interest and the marina is surrounded by Broadlands landscape and views. To the west, the Berney Arms Windmill (EH ☎ 01493 700605) is one of the last and best remaining examples of a marsh mill in Norfolk. Its seven floor height makes it a landmark for miles around. Latterly, it was used to pump water to drain the surrounding marshes, though it was originally built to grind an ingredient for cement. The castle here is Gariannonum, a Roman fort built in the late 3rd century as part of a chain to protect the coast from Saxon raiders. It has impressive walls and projecting bastions and is locally claimed to be the largest Roman ruin in Britain other than Hadrian's Wall. It's managed by the Norfolk Archeological Trust, and entry is free at any reasonable time.

The marina and adjacent boatyard offer a full range of facilities, and your mooring charge includes the use of the heated swimming pool when it's open in the summer. The Fisherman's (☎ 01493 780729) is a good pub which also serves meals and is 300 yards from the marina. For our recommendations for more elaborate meals, you either need to take your boat or a taxi 4 miles upstream to St Olaves to Spinnakers (☎ 01493 488332) or head back to Yarmouth to try the Rambouillet Restaurant (☎ 01493 842000). Fish & chips and other takeaway food is available at Liffen's Holiday Park which is half a mile from the marina.

Taxi:	Anglia Taxis (☎ 01493 855855)
Car hire:	Economy Drive (☎ 01493 658336)
Bus:	stops at Park Entrance, to Great Yarmouth
Rail:	Great Yarmouth links to Norwich
Airport:	Norwich Airport - Domestic/International

for more details, see Directory Section

Upriver from Burgh Castle

Those who remember Arthur Ransome's books will hardly need reminding about the wealth of wildlife and the rural scenery which can be enjoyed in the Broads. Incidentally, thinking about Coot Club, there are those who suggest that the availability of cheap beach and sun holidays in Southern Europe has improved the Broads by significantly reducing your chances of running into the Hullabaloos. Between the sea and the heads of navigation on the Waveney, Yare and Chet Rivers, the South Broads offer 55 miles of navigable water and over 35 miles of this can be cruised from Burgh Castle without passing under any fixed bridges. You can get to within 3 miles of Norwich before Postwick Viaduct restricts access to allow only those requiring less than 10.6 metres clearance. Breydon Water and the lower reaches of the Yare and Waveney Rivers are uncrowded and wide, providing ideal inland sailing and motor cruising conditions unlike the North Broads where some channels are narrow and can be busy with hire cruisers, and navigation is restricted by numerous fixed bridges. For those who can easily lower their masts, the North Broads can also be approached via Yarmouth under a tricky fixed bridge at the mouth of the River Bure. This opens up access to another 150 miles of navigable waterways and Broads. The narrower river channels, more numerous interlinked Broads and riverside homes with their own boathouses make for a quite different character to the more open vistas and huge skies of the South Broadland area. You do need a licence to cruise on the Broads - you can get one in advance from The Broads Authority in Norwich (☎ 01603 610734) or from a River Inspector when you come across one.

The Ferry Inn at Reedham Ferry on the Yare and The Bell in at St Olave's further up the Waveney provide suitable watering holes for lunch and back cruises. For those with plenty of time on their hands, varied cruising in marshland, river valley and Broads settings is provided by exploring to the heads of navigation of the Yare (Norwich), the Chet (Loddon) and the Waveney (Gedleston Lock below Bungay). Norwich has only recently ceased to be a commercial inland port and since river transport was the lifeline of this region until early this century, there are numerous safe moorings, rustic inns and footpaths with which to explore neighbouring villages. Very few hire cruisers ply these waterways, which are the haunt of private owners whose craft range from classic Broads sailing cruisers to sleek gin palaces more often seen in warmer climes. From the Waveney, it is also possible to reach Oulton Broad which leads to the sea at Lowestoft. Another option is a circular cruise linking the Waveney and the Yare via the Haddiscoe Cut, a route used by local sailors in their annual round the island race.

Suffolk

The Suffolk coast is low lying and getting lower as the coastline subsides and the shingle beaches, sand cliffs and dunes are eroded by the sea. A number of the towns and villages are now considerably smaller than they were several centuries ago, most notably Dunwich which used to boast several churches and now consists of only a handful of houses. This stretch of coastline might, at first glance, seem rather uninteresting to the

The marina enjoys a beautiful riverside location which is central for Broadland cruising. It is surrounded by stunning views and overlooked by its own holiday park. The whole complex is reserved exclusively for private owners of boats and holiday homes (many are owners of both). The marina is open all year and offers serviced pontoons accessible at all tides up to a minimum depth of one metre with a soft mud bottom. Visitor berths are usually available. Vessels requiring up to two metres minimum draft presently use river quay moorings. A slipway, winch and dry berths also serve trailer launched craft (minimum weekly tickets), with the adjoining boatyard providing lift-outs (maximum 32 tons), pump-outs, diesel, full repairs and servicing. Ample car parking alongside the marina is restricted to keyholders, who also enjoy use of the park's showers, toilets, launderette and heated outdoor pool. Besides cruising inland, day sailing at sea is an option (one hour with the tide to Haven Bridge, Great Yarmouth: bridge openings by appointment). There is also a designated water skiing area close by.

The park is on a gentle hill slope and has a low density layout with many mature trees, flowering shrubs and grass surrounds. Each holiday home is connected to full mains services with parking alongside. There is a separate touring section with hook-ups and screened pitches. Wash-up facilities and a disabled suite will open later in 1999. Cooking is by bottled gas (sold at park reception). The Fisherman's free public house, riverside terrace and garden is open all year (restricted hours in winter), serves meals and snacks and also operates a small shop from which fresh supplies can be ordered in advance by phone (01493-780729). A regular, year round bus service to Gorleston and Great Yarmouth stops at the park entrance (approximately 1 km from the marina berths).

The complex is independently owned and managed and aims to provide high standards of comfort and convenience for those who prefer quiet relaxation and leisure pursuits in attractive surroundings. It is a popular base for walkers, anglers, bird watchers, landscape painters and photographers as well as for boating enthusiasts. A short stroll along Angles' Way (a long distance footpath) provides easy, direct access to the Roman shore fort built to defend against Saxon raiders and to Breydon Water. The park publishes its own range of local explorer leaflets and is developing an extensive information and exhibition centre on the neighbouring marshlands and the magnificent Roman ruins.

Burgh Castle Marina & Caravan Park
Butt Lane, Burgh Castle
Norfolk NR31 9PZ
Tel. 01493 780331
Fax. 01493 780163
E-mail: rdw_chesham@compuserve.com

Member, BMIF and BHHPA.

yachtsman. Despite the lack of anchorages on the coast however, there are several rivers that are readily navigable, offering a wide variety of different scenery and access to many delightful towns and villages. The area also benefits from spectacular birdlife thanks to a number of bird sanctuaries and the relatively low density of human population.

Lowestoft

Lowestoft Harbour is the most easterly town in Britain (as The Sunrise Coast, the Tourist Board point out it's the place to be to see the earliest dawn of the new millennium in the UK - just a few months off at the time of writing) and it's also another busy commercial port. The fishing fleet is not as large as it once was, but still consists of a couple of dozen trawlers. There's a Maritime Museum (☎ 01502 561963) which charts the history of the fishing fleet, and also the Royal Naval Patrol Service Museum. Lowestoft is a popular seaside resort town and there are sandy beaches to the north and south of the mouth of the river. Other attractions include historic vessels on display at the yacht basin such as a steam fishing boat and a wooden drifter. A more modern resident in the Yacht Basin is the RNLI's Tyne class all-weather lifeboat which Mr Chapman, the station's Honorary Secretary, will be pleased to arrange for you to see. The Excelsior Trust (☎ 01502 585302) run the annual Lowestoft Smack Race for old fishing vessels and wooden yachts – it's good to see elderly craft still being pushed to sail fast. Lowestoft Carnival is in mid-August and there's an Air Show towards the end of July.

As you make your approach to the harbour, you should make every effort to contact Lowestoft Harbour Control on VHF Channel 14 to let them know what your intentions are (contact them when you are departing as well). Yachts have the exclusive use of the south west harbour which is where the Royal Norfolk and Suffolk Yacht Club is based. Visiting yachts are welcome and the Club has a bar and restaurant, T.V. room and snooker room. There is also 24 hour access to the showers and laundry room. There is a good supermarket which is close to hand and chandlery is round by the entrance to the fish dock. To get a better flavour of the town, you might like to try the Triangle Tavern (☎ 01502 582711) in St Peter Street for a drink or The Jolly Sailor (☎ 01502 561398) for a pub meal. Both of these are a couple of miles from the yacht basin, as is Sgt. Pepper's (☎ 01502 566754) in the High Street which serves inexpensive meals.

Taxi:	Atlas (☎ 01502 500000)
	Bluebird (☎ 01502 589999)
	Ace (☎ 01502 566690)
Car hire:	Europ Car (☎ 01502 516982) or
	Economy Drive (☎ 01502 537777)
Cycle hire:	Broadland Bikes (☎ 01502 519999)
Bus:	1/2 mile – national network
Rail:	100 yds, links to Norwich, Ipswich & Intercity
Airport:	35 miles to Norwich Airport

for more details, see Directory Section

Upriver

For more peaceful and picturesque surroundings, it's well worth heading a couple of miles inland. Beyond the Lowestoft Harbour Bridge (contact Lowestoft Harbour Control on Channel 14 or telephone ☎ 01502 572286), moorings are sometimes available from Lowestoft Cruising Club or Oulton Broad Yacht Station. Access to the Broads is via a lock at Mutford for which there is a charge (around £5.00). You also need a temporary licence for the Broads which you can get at the lock office. At Oulton Broad, the Flying Dutchman is a good pub for a drink, and the Waveney (☎ 01502 573940) and The Commodore (☎ 01502 565955) offer good pub meals. The Wherry Hotel (☎ 01502 573521) has a reasonably priced menu, and The Parkhill Hotel (☎ 01502 730322) is highly rated. Ivy House Farm (☎ 01502 501353) is also a good choice for a more extravagant eating experience. While you are in the area, you might be interested by the collection of some 300 vessels kept by the International Sailing Craft Association at their museum on Caldecott Road (☎ 01502 585606).

Southwold

About ten miles south of Lowestoft, Southwold is a charming little town which the twentieth century largely seems to have passed by. Beer from the famous local brewers, Adnams, is still delivered by horse-drawn dray – you can sample their wares at the Sole Bay Inn, and The Crown Hotel is recommended for pub meals. A line of brightly coloured beach huts is backed by brick and flint and colour washed houses which stand around a series of open greens. The lighthouse and church stand out as the tallest buildings on the town's skyline. To the south of the harbour, and rather closer than Southwold itself to the north, is Walberswick which stands at the top of a stretch of marshy coastline which forms the Walberswick National Nature Reserve. Two pubs here are worth a mention, namely the Bell and the Anchor. The substantial Church of the Holy Trinity at Blythborough, which is at the head of the estuary, is a notable local landmark and a reminder of the fluctuating fortunes of coastal towns, now serving a small village where once there was a bustling port.

Southwold Harbour is another one which can be tricky to get into thanks to its strong currents and the shifting shoals around the entrance. Once again, the harbour-master should be consulted before attempting the entrance - the office is usually manned for 4 hours each side of high water, and Ken Howells, the harbour-master, is very helpful, and will guide you in by VHF from the harbour wall if required.

Southwold to Shingle Street

Twenty five miles of rather desolate shingle and sand beach offer no sheltered spots for anchoring between Walberswick and the mouth of the River Alde or Ore at Shingle Street. Looming up in the distance, modern engineering is responsible for the striking dome (or blot on the landscape, depending on your point of view) of Sizewell Nuclear Power Station. No amount of engineering of any sort seems to be able to stall the power of wind and tide at poor disappearing Dunwich which you pass a few miles south of Walberswick. Not far south of Sizewell, you may be struck by the bizarre architectural absurdities of the Victorian holiday village of Thorpeness - look out for The House in the Clouds.

From here, it's only a couple of miles to Aldeburgh – the sea side of Aldeburgh that is. However, if you are hoping to find shelter here, you have another twenty odd miles to go to get down to the mouth and back thanks to the substantial longshore drift of Orford Ness. Admire the prospect of the town and the RNLI's impressive 'Penza' lifeboathouse, which was built in 1993, and press on to Shingle Street to enter the river.

The River Ore and Alde

The entrance to the River Ore at Shingle Street is over a shingle bar which can alter considerably during the winter storms, and sometimes after heavy weather in the summer. A regularly updated local survey is available from the Alde & Ore Association or the Secretary of the Aldeburgh Yacht Club *(see directory)*. Orford Ness is a spit about twelve miles long which stretches from Aldeburgh, where the River Alde went out to sea in Roman times, to the present mouth at Shingle Street. Now owned by the National Trust, this isolated peninsula was used by the Ministry of Defence for secret testing and is reputed to be one of the places where radar was developed in the Second World War. The river changes its name from the Ore to the Alde between Orford and Aldeburgh.

Once you have successfully negotiated the entrance, the river takes you along the coast, with the sea still in earshot for a couple of miles. You soon reach Havergate Island, an RSPB bird sanctuary where landing is prohibited unless you have a permit from the warden: J.

Partridge (aptly named), 30 Mundys Lane, Orford, Woodbridge, Suffolk IP12 2LX. Tucked up behind the island is the Butley River which is a favoured spot for a peaceful evening at anchor.

The impressive castle and traditional East Anglian flint-clad church stand out above **Orford**, which is a little further up river, sheltering behind the widest part of the shingle spit. A stroll ashore along the street of rustic cottages will give you the chance to investigate a couple of good pubs, though watch out for the slightly unhelpful custom of closing at 2.00 p.m. sharp at lunch time. Don't miss the Butley Oysterage (☎ 01394 450277) whose widespread reputation for excellent seafood is complemented by a lack of pretension that is summed up by the Formica topped tables. It is also well worth visiting the smokery next door to stock up on vacuum packed delicacies that are ideal for stowing aboard.

The view as you approach **Aldeburgh**, another five miles up river, has changed remarkably little since Turner painted it. Guarded to the south by the most northerly of the Napoleonic Martello Towers, the town is steeped in local history and still operates a fleet of 16 foot open fishing boats which are hardly launched off the beach through the breakers. Looking west across fields of reclaimed marshland, a glimpse of The Snape Maltings Concert Hall draws attention to Aldeburgh's world-wide reputation for the annual music festival which was founded in 1948 by the composer Benjamin Britten who lived in Aldeburgh. Careful navigation on a rising tide can take you right up past Iken, with its

Artist: **Anthony Flemming ORFORD NESS** *Courtesy of:* **The Artist**

thatched church, to **Snape** and the opportunity for very much better than just pub grub at the Crown Inn (☎ 01728 688324). Aldeburgh itself is well provided for with a variety of restaurants, take-aways and pubs. The beer is well kept in the White Hart, which is handily placed next to an excellent Fish & Chip shop. At the other end of the High Street, The Cross Keys serves good pub food, including locally caught fish dishes. The Lighthouse (☎ 01728 453377) offers a more upmarket evening, and Cafe 142 (☎ 01728 454152) is a good choice for a late breakfast or lunch. You may also enjoy the opportunity to browse in the town's interesting antique shops, art galleries and the Moot Hall, where the Mayor and town council have met for the last 400 years and which is now also an informative museum.

Moorings are sometimes available from Bryan Upson (☎ 01728 453047), or you may anchor in good holding to the south of the Yacht Club near the Martello Tower. Aldeburgh Yacht Club has good facilities which visiting yachts are welcome to use. The club is open at weekends, bank-holidays and throughout the summer holidays, offering a bar and a good selection of food. There's a reasonable range of shops for provisions, though it's a walk of about a mile from the Yacht Club and anchorage to the centre of the town. You can buy fresh fish direct from the fishermen's huts on the beach. Chandlery and fuel are available from the Aldeburgh Boatyard which isn't far from the Yacht Club.

Taxi:	Amber Taxis
Car hire:	Wards Garage (☎ 01728 452721)
Cycle hire:	Wards Garage (☎ 01728 452721)
Bus:	Services from town centre or boatyard.
Rail:	5 miles from Saxmundham which links to Ipswich for Intercity

for more details, see Directory Section

The River Deben

The mouth of the River Deben is another tricky one with a shifting shingle bar, but there are great rewards for the intrepid as this is a very pretty river with a number of towns and villages which are well worth visiting. A current sketch map of approaches can be sent to you if you send Tidemill Yacht Harbour an SAE and 2 first class stamps (for the RNLI). There is also a pilot at Felixstowe Ferry who you can contact if needed. The mouth is flanked to the north by **Bawdsey Quay** and the south, **Felixstowe Ferry**. Contact the Felixstowe Ferry Boatyard or the harbour-master to arrange moorings or for advice on suitable anchorage. During the day, there's a water taxi which might encourage a run ashore to sample the wares of the Felixstowe Ferryboat Inn. A couple of miles further upriver, the Ramsholt Arms, close to the quay, does good food. Ask the harbour-master, George Collins, about moorings by hailing the small staging near the Ramsholt Arms – don't go too close as it's shallow except at high water springs. Alternatively, you may prefer to anchor at The Rocks a mile further up, a popular anchorage with holding in sand, clay and rocks, and stroll down the bank to the pub. Another option on the south bank a little further up is the Maybush at Waldringfield. Try to make sure you have the time to get to **Woodbridge** a few miles further inland. This is a lovely town, dating from Saxon times, with plenty of things to see and do. Local museums include the Suffolk Horse Museum and the Woodbridge Museum, both on Market Hill, and there's a cinema and swimming pool both within a few minutes walk of the Quay. As well as plenty of shops for provisions, there are numerous antique shops and boutiques for gentle browsing in a setting of narrow medieval streets.

The Tide Mill Yacht Harbour is a tempting alternative to drying out on a mooring or at anchor; access is via a

Artist: **Melvyn Brinkley THE DEBEN AT RAMSHOLT** *Courtesy of:* **The Artist**

Artist: **Melvyn Brinkley LOW TIDE ON THE DEBEN AT WOODBRIDGE** *Courtesy of:* **The Artist**

Artist: **Melvyn Brinkley WOODBRIDGE FROM THE NORTH BANK** *Courtesy of:* **The Artist**

Artist: **Melvyn Brinkley WOODBRIDGE SOUTH BANK** *Courtesy of:* **The Artist**

tidal sill and just outside there are moorings to wait on until there is enough water to get over - there's a tide gauge which makes this easy to judge. It's worth booking a space in advance - see directory for contact details. The Tide Mill is a striking landmark and is built on a site where there is believed to have been a mill of one sort or another since the 12th century. Those in favour of environmentally friendly sources of energy will be pleased by the existing 18th century mill, now carefully restored, which harnesses power from the tidal rise and fall in the river.

There's a wide selection of pubs, restaurants and hotels to choose from. The Anchor is a good choice for a drink and bar food is available at most of the pubs in town. The restaurant at The Bull Hotel on Market Hill (☎ 01394 382089) offers more elaborate meals and Seckford Hall Hotel (☎ 01394 385678) is the one to go for if you're in the mood for a blowout. This is a couple of miles from the Quay, so a taxi is probably needed. Visiting yachtsmen are welcome at the Woodbridge Cruising Club which is based on the Promenade and offers a bar and food at weekends. Slightly less accommodating is the Deben Yacht Club where you need to join as a temporary member before they offer the use of their facilities.

Taxi:	M.R. Cars (☎ 01394 386191)
Bus:	Local services, links to Ipswich and national coach network.
Rail:	Woodbridge Station, close to Quay - links to Ipswich for Intercity

for more details, see Directory Section

The River Orwell

With the major container shipping port of Felixstowe at its mouth, and access to Harwich (see ESSEX) as well, be prepared for some heavy traffic - in particular, watch out for the high speed catamaran ferry which travels at speeds in excess of 40 knots. You should keep well clear of Felixstowe, but you would probably wish to anyway when you realise that its docks handle about half the container traffic in and out of Britain each year! The container vessels and passenger ferries do not go far up the river though, and separation arrangements at the mouth are well buoyed and charted. Once past the hectic commercial ports at the entrance, the river heads up through fine countryside and offers the chance to see and visit a number of attractive and interesting places. As you head up the Orwell, the Shotley Peninsula to port offers a variety of prospects. What used to be the Royal Navy training base of HMS Ganges is now the National Police Training Centre. However, the buildings soon give way to more rural scenery and the opportunity to see a wide variety of birdlife. This is a popular wintering ground and, late in the sailing season, you can see redshanks, black-tailed godwit and dunins. Black and white oystercatchers, curlews, knot and turnstones are also often around as are large flocks of shelduck, mallard and wigeon. You may also see cormorants feeding on fish at the water's edge, and heron fishing in slightly deeper water.

A convenient stop-off is **Suffolk Yacht Harbour** at Levington which is about five miles up river and has pontoon berths and a converted lightship offering bar,

dining and washing facilities. Chandlery and basic provisions are also available on the site, but there is no town or village of any size in the immediate area. Pinmill, a couple of miles further up on the South Bank, is a beautiful little village where at high water on spring tides, you can tie up so close to the Butt and Oyster that you don't need to go ashore to order drinks. There's good, inexpensive food here as well. Pinmill is famous for its connections with sailing barges, many of which still sail out here, or are used as houseboats. An annual event well worth watching if you are in the area is the Pin Mill Barge Match which takes place in late June or early July (it's organised by Pin Mill Sailing Club, so contact them for details). Not much further up the south bank, you come to Woolverstone Marina which is set amid beautiful parkland, and is the home of the Royal Harwich Yacht Club. There's good food available on site, and all the facilities you would expect from a Marina Developments Marina.

Artist: **Clive Madgwick** **LOW TIDE AT PIN MILL**
Courtesy of: **Rosenstiel's**

Ipswich

Passing on up river under the majestic Orwell Bridge, which carries the A14 and its container traffic to Felixstowe, you approach Ipswich, Suffolk's county town. Before the centre of Ipswich, with its harbour which is only accessible for a couple of hours around high water, you pass another comprehensive marina, Fox's at Wherstead, which again has a yacht club and a good range of facilities. The centre of Ipswich is only three miles away if you feel like some town exploring. Another option is to head through the lock (contact Ipswich Port Radio on VHF Channel 14 before you approach), into Ipswich Docks and moor up at Neptune Marina. The clubhouse here has washing facilities and security is very good. Ipswich is a lively town with a wide variety of pubs and restaurants, a theatre, cinemas, art galleries and plenty of history and the docks are about ten minutes walk from the centre of the town.

In the Middle Ages it became a prosperous port exporting wool and the docks still export agricultural produce. The town is also noted for its local beer, and you will have passed the splendid Victorian Tolly Cobbold Brewery, rebuilt in 1896, on the east bank of the river on your way into the town. Aspirations to become a great centre of academia to rival Oxford and Cambridge were thwarted in Tudor times when Cardinal Wolsey's (born in the town in about 1475) plan to found a college was stopped by Henry VIII as Wolsey fell from favour. Nothing more than the gateway, which still stands in College Street, was ever built. The town has over 650 listed buildings and twelve medieval churches and all periods of English architecture are represented. The Isaac Lord Buildings on Fore Street by the Wet Dock are an interesting complex of medieval timber framed buildings including the original merchant's house and warehouses. The Old Customs House is an example of Victorian classical architecture, and Sir Norman Foster's Willis Corroon Building in Friars Street had the unusual distinction of achieving listed building status as an historic building within 25 years of being built. The Ipswich Museum, housed in another fine Victorian building has a wide range of displays relating to local history, wildlife, geology and many other subjects.

You will not go thirsty or hungry in Ipswich. The town centre is awash with fine establishments and the aroma from the brewery will hopefully lead you in the right direction, but not before you have passed the Brewery Tap (☎ 01473 281508) which is a waterfront pub at the foot of Tollys old brewery, now a museum and visitor centre. The Fat Cat (☎ 01473 726524) on Spring Road, is good for bar food and the Greyhound (☎ 01473 252862) on Henley Road / Anglesea Road, has lots of home cooking and varied ales. For restaurant dining, try the Marlborough Hotel (☎ 01473 257677) on Henley Road, with its country house atmosphere, seasonally changing menu and contemporary bar. Conveniently placed, are Scott's Brasserie (☎ 01473 230254) which has a definite cosmopolitan feel to it, and Dhaka (☎ 01473 251397) which serves Indian food, both of which are on Orwell Place. Finally, Mortimer's Seafood (☎ 01473 230225) on Wherry Quay, is great for an à la carte meal.

Taxi:	Avenue Taxis (☎ 01473 407070)
Car hire:	National Car Rental (☎ 01473 219851)
Cycle hire:	(☎ 01473 259853)
Bus:	Ipswich Bus Company (☎ 0800 919390)
Rail:	Ipswich Station enquiries (☎ 0345 484950)
Airport:	Stanstead (☎ 01279 680500)

for more details, see Directory Section

Essex

There are those who might think that Essex is only worth making poor jokes about at the expense of the fairer sex. They would of course be wrong as there is some wonderful countryside - Constable painted lots of it - and some interesting towns. Rather like Suffolk, Essex has a number of rivers which offer interesting cruising away from the open sea in sheltered waters, though these are not without their navigational challenges as the tides can be fierce. There's a mixture of opportunities for peace and solitude and getting right in amongst it all at the resort towns with their crowds of holidaymakers.

Harwich & the River Stour

In spite of the considerable amount of ferry traffic which might at first glance make Harwich seem to be a place worth avoiding, the centre of the town has its charm and there's lots of history to explore as well. The harbour proved useful as a naval base early in The Hundred Years War when, prior to defeating the French at Sluys, the English fleet was gathered here in 1340. Over the intervening centuries, Harwich has played a major part in the maritime activities of the British Isles as a naval dockyard and a base for commercial activities both in freight and passenger transportation. The old town of Harwich has seen a great deal of restoration and preservation and much of its historic flavour is still in evidence. There are several museums, including a Maritime Museum (☎ 01255 503429), a Lifeboat Museum (☎ 01255 503429), The Harwich Redoubt Fort (☎ 01255 503429) - a striking example of the military fortifications built in the Napoleonic era - and the National Wireless and Television Museum (☎ 01206 322606). Harwich is also the home of the oldest working cinema in England (☎ 01255 503429). To the south east of the town, there are sandy beaches which look out to sea for less energetic and mind taxing relaxation. There's a good selection of hostelries serving local beers and locally caught seafood. On the Quay in the Old Town, The Angel (☎ 01255 507241) is recommended for a drink and The Alma (☎ 01255 503474) in Kings Head Street serves good pub food. For a restaurant meal, we suggest you try the Sign of the Bear (☎ 01255 242628) in Kings Quay Street, or if you are feeling extravagant, the Pier Hotel (☎ 01255 241212) which is also on The Quay and is believed by many to be the best around.

The Harwich and Dovercourt Sailing Club in Gas House Creek has a bar which is open on Tuesday and Friday evenings and Saturday and Sunday lunchtimes. They have moorings and you might be able to pick up a vacant one, or you can lie alongside the quay around high water - contact the secretary for details. Facilities are a little limited; showers are available at the Harwich Town Sailing Club which is about 400 yards away and also has a bar boasting incomparable views across the harbour. General shopping facilities for provisions can all be found within a few hundred yards, or there's a supermarket about a mile away if you prefer to do it all under one roof. Full marina facilities are available on the other side of the river at Shotley Point Marina which is accessible at all states of the tide, and there are regular ferries throughout the day between Harwich, Shotley and Felixstowe, and a water taxi is also sometimes available.

While under way in the Harwich Harbour area, you are advised to listen out on Channel 71 for traffic movement announcements (transmit on this channel only in emergency). Fear not however, there is plenty of room for yachts without using the main shipping channel. The Stour Valley is attractive and inspired at least one of its sons to become a painter. John Constable (1776-1837) remarked: "I associate my careless boyhood with all that lies on the banks of the Stour; those scenes made me a painter and I am grateful". Thomas Gainsborough (1727-1788) was also born in the same area. The river is navigable all the way to Manningtree which takes you well into what is often referred to as Constable Country.

Taxi:	(☎ 0800 123444)
Bus:	links to Clacton, Colchester and thence national network
Rail:	Intercity from Harwich to London
Airport:	Stanstead is the nearest

Ferries: locally to Shotley and Felixstowe, or Holland, Denmark, Sweden & Germany if you so wish.
for more details, see Directory Section

Walton-on-the-Naze

A short hop down the coast from Harwich brings you to the entrance to the Walton Backwaters, snugly tucked in behind the Naze. The Walton Channel is quite busy and full of moorings, but there's much more to explore if you are looking for a quiet anchorage alongside one of the reedy islands. Much of the Backwaters is rather shallow for large yachts, but a trip in the dinghy may evoke the mood of the Swallows and Amazons exploring their 'secret water'. Arthur Ransome's book of that name was actually inspired by this collection of islands and creeks. The Walton Channel leads up to Walton's landward side, and you can either find a mooring in the yacht basin by the Walton & Frinton Yacht Club (contact Bedwell & Co), or up the Twizzle Creek at Titchmarsh Marina.

The seaside of Walton is just that, boasting a 3/4 mile pier which is second only to that at Southend in length, and a fine sandy beach. Walton is at the north end of a strip of holiday resorts which takes in Frinton-on-Sea and Clacton-on-Sea. This is a family resort and is restrained by comparison to many – neighbouring Frinton is similar and doesn't have a single pub! Walton's Pier has many amusements, stalls, rides, refreshments and tenpin bowling and is a berthing point for excursion steamers. More firmly ashore, there's a Maritime Museum (☎ 01255 678259) in the Old Lifeboat House on East Terrace with displays of lifeboats, piers, mills and coastguards. Local history and the geology of the Naze are also examined. The current Lifeboat Station is about a mile along the coast. To the north of the town, the Naze is a popular area for a stroll, for birdwatching and for observing the seaborne traffic moving in and out of Felixstowe and Harwich.

There's a good selection of shops for provisions and these are mostly only a few hundred yards from the yacht basin – it's more like a mile and a half from the marina. You can also buy freshly caught fish on the Sea Front. The Marine (☎ 01255 674000) and the Walton Tavern (☎ 01255 676000) are good choices for a drink and The Victory (☎ 01255 577857) also does good bar meals. There's also a wide selection of takeaways including Fish & Chips and Chinese. The best restaurant in town is the Harbour Lights (☎01255 851887)which is at the Titchmarsh Marina. There's a bar which does food at the marina, and the Yacht Club Bar also offers food and their facilities are open from 8am to 10.30pm.

Taxi: Town Taxi (☎01255 675910) or (☎ 01255 850888)
Bus: services to Clacton and Colchester, thence national network
Rail: services from Walton to London
Airport: Stanstead
for more details, see Directory Section

The Rivers Colne & Blackwater

There's a wonderful collection of tidal creeks and islands to explore in this area. Bustling centres of yacht-ing and maritime history are interspersed with tranquil nature reserves offering variety and plentiful facilities to the visiting yachtsman. Once one of the Cinque Ports, **Brightlingsea** is the first possible port of call up the River Colne, tucked off to one side up a creek which becomes very narrow at low water and the Railway Tavern (☎ 01206 302581) is a welcome pub stop near the promenade, which even hosts a cider festival every May.

The Rose & Crown (☎ 01206 826371) with its quayside position overlooking the River Colne, is handy for a drink, or the Black Buoy (☎ 01206 822425) is famous for its convivial atmosphere and choice of good food. A little way out of the village, the Horse & Groom (☎ 01206 824928) serves good value, home-cooked food.

Artist: **Anthony Flemming BRIGHTLINGSEA**
Courtesy of: **The Artist**

There are three yacht clubs in this backwater alone, and all the facilities you might need. This is also the home of the Smack Preservation Society where the historical importance of fishing is practically demonstrated by a collection of old Essex fishing smacks. The isolated creeks off the River Colne are home to a wide variety of birds and butterflies and the intrepid navigator can work his way past the tide barrier to **Wivenhoe**. The backdrop of the concrete buildings of Essex University belie the appeal of the largely residential jumble of 18th and 19th century houses and old boatyards.

Artist: **Anthony Flemming WIVENHOE**
Courtesy of: **The Artist**

West of the Colne, **Mersea Island** is the home of the local lifeboat and the West Mersea Yacht Club - contact the boatman (VHF Channel 37, callsign YC1) for free moorings. It's narrow and shallow at low water, but if you follow the line of moorings, you should keep out of too much trouble. Mersea Island has a long history of welcoming visitors dating back to the Romans who used it as a holiday island. There's lots of Roman history in the area, and much has happened since and the small museum specialises in local history. There's a good selection of shops for provisions and plenty of places to enjoy a drink or meal ashore. The club has a bar which serves meals and The Victory (☎ 01206 382907), The Waterfront Café (01206 386061) and Willow Lodge (01206 383568) all offer reasonably priced food and are conveniently placed on the waterfront. For a more elaborate meal, try the Blackwater Hotel (☎ 01206 383338) in the centre of the village.

Venturing further west into the Blackwater, there's a wide selection of places to stop and several marinas offering full facilities. The Tollesbury Fleet leads between Tollesbury Wick Nature reserve and the Old Hall Marshes RSPB Reserve. **Tollesbury** Yacht Harbour is at the top of Woodrolfe Creek amongst a delightful maze of tiny winding creeks which are used by many as berths which are linked by an elaborate network of boardwalks. It's a spectacular sight at any state of the tide. The marina is accessible for a couple of hours each side of high water and is only a short walk from the village where there is a general store, butcher, baker and post office as well as two pubs. There's chandlery and a comfortable clubhouse at the marina itself. Facilities include a bar with snacks, a restaurant and a covered heated swimming pool.

you want to remain afloat at low water, you need to be back just above Osea Island as there's only a couple of feet of water at Maldon at low water. Alternatively, the lock at Heybridge Basin operates during the hour before high water in daylight hours, and it's then about a mile and a half walk up the canal towpath to Maldon. The river is still used for transporting grain and you will come across the traditional craft for this job, Thames barges, a number of which are berthed at the Hythe, Maldon's waterfront. The town is relatively unspoilt by modern development, and there are two unusual churches, a Moot Hall, one of the oldest lending libraries in England, and houses and pubs from almost every recent century. There are a couple of good pubs at the Hythe, namely the Jolly Sailor (☎ 01621 853463) and the Queens Head (☎ 01621 854112), and many more in the town - The White Horse in the High Street has a good selection of beers. De Vere's Restaurant at The Blue Boar (☎ 01621 852681) in Silver Street is worth a visit for a meal in the centre of the town.

Taxi:	Arrow (☎ 01621 855111)
	Banyards (☎ 01621 853569)
Car hire:	Euro Car & Van Rental in Tillingham (☎ 01621 779259)
Cycle hire:	From Little Baddon, Retreat Farm Campsite (☎ 01245 225440)
Bus:	Essex Bus Line (☎ 08457 000333)
Rail:	Nearest station Burnham-on-Crouch
Airport:	Stanstead airport enquiries (☎ 01279 680500)

for more details, see Directory Section

Artist: **Anthony Flemming MALDON**
Courtesy of: **The Artist**

Artist: **Anthony Flemming HEYBRIDGE BASIN**
Courtesy of: **The Artist**

More easily reached on the south bank of the river, **Bradwell** Marina is only inaccessible for three hours around low water. This is a rather isolated spot; Bradwell-on-Sea is built on reclaimed marshland, and the looming presence of Bradwell Nuclear Power Station would not be everyone's preferred choice of view. The visitor centre and tour of the power station are free if you'd like to find out how a nuclear power station works (☎ 01621 873395). There's a restaurant in the Bradwell Cruising Club's premises and the Green Man is just along the road. If time or inclination allow, you can follow the river all the way up to Maldon, though if

The River Crouch

The Crouch is a popular sailing centre which is often referred to as the Cowes of the East Coast. The river is readily accessible and offers a good selection of facilities - it has been a focal point for yachtsmen for over a century and there are no less than six marinas or yacht harbours and numerous yacht clubs. While the entrance is straightforward, the numerous sandbanks around the mouth make an approach in daylight prudent for the visitor. Once you have passed Foulness Island and the entrance to the River Roach, you soon reach **Burnham-on-Crouch** and its ranks of moored boats. Originally,

Burnham was centred around the Parish Church of St Mary's to the north of the present town. However, the growth in sea-borne trade during the Middle Ages drew the nucleus of the town to the quayside. This is an area full of olde-worlde charm and many of the substantial houses which front the river and quayside are listed buildings including, you might be surprised to learn, the rather out of keeping 1930s clubhouse of the Royal Corinthian Yacht Club towards the east end of the waterfront. The elegant High Street is principally Georgian, and the Clock Tower is an ornate landmark which has dominated the old part of the town since 1877. There is a variety of shops which cater both for stocking up on provisions and for browsing, and there are plenty of restaurants and watering holes to choose from as well. The Olde White Harte (☎ 01621 782106) has good views from the jetty and a good selection of local beers, and The Star, also on The Quay, is also recommended and has the advantage of being a bit nearer the Yacht Harbour. There's a bar, food and a warm welcome to visiting yachtsmen at the Crouch Yacht Club's Clubhouse on Corinthian Road which is on the way from the marina to the centre of town. All on the High Street, and in ascending order of sophistication (and expense!), try one of the following for a restaurant meal: Sgt. Pepper's Restaurant (☎ 01621 786500), Clouds (☎ 01621 782965), The Contented Sole - it is widely respected, so reservation is generally needed (☎ 01621 782139).

Pontoons along the waterfront belonging to yacht clubs and boatyards provide convenient places to nip ashore. However, for anything longer than the briefest stop, you will need to find a mooring or head for Burnham Yacht Harbour which is a short way upstream of the town and has 24 hour open access. The marina is situated between agricultural land and Burnham Country Park which offers a pleasant open outlook. With around 500 berths, this is a pretty big marina and has levels of facilities to match. There's a bar which also offers snacks on site as well as chandlery and boatyard facilities. the unusual floating boathouse in the marina is the home of the Burnham-on-Crouch inshore lifeboat and it's open to visitors on some weekends and bank-holidays (*see directory for contact details*).

Taxi:	B&H Taxis (☎ 01621 784878) Mobile: 0860 714852
Car hire:	Euro Car & Van Rental in Tillingham (☎ 01621 779259)
Bus:	connections to Chelmsford
Rail:	Burnham Station, connections to London
Airport:	Southend, 20 miles, or Stanstead (☎ 01279 680146), 40 miles

for more details, see Directory Section

Upriver

Almost opposite Burnham Yacht Harbour on **Wallasea Island** is Essex Marina and its associated yacht club which serves food at weekends in the summer. Also at weekends during the summer, there's a ferry to take you across to Burnham - you'll need this if you want anything more than the most basic provisions. The river is navigable for ten miles above Burnham, and it does become more peaceful. There's a very old inn

and a fifty yard boardwalk out into the river at **North Fambridge** where there is also a boatyard and marina offering moorings and facilities and another yacht club to welcome visitors. A few miles further upriver at Hullbridge, the delightfully named Brandy Hole Yacht Station and its associated club has moorings and facilities. You should check that there is space and as this spot is close to the navigable limit of the river, it is perhaps surprising that the tidal restrictions on access are as good as being accessible for four hours each side of high water.

The River Roach

For a different atmosphere, you might like to nip into the River Roach rather than following the Crouch up to Burnham. The shelter here is often better than in the Crouch, and you have access to a network of out-of-the-way creeks which wind through the quiet desolation of Foulness Point. Foulness is owned by the Ministry of Defence, and public access is forbidden. It's a haven for migrating Brent geese who pass through in their 1000s in the autumn - Foulness means promontory of birds. In settled weather, this route is often used by yachts wanting a shortcut to the Thames Estuary as the Havengore Creek links through here. The remote nature of this area means there are few facilities. "We love it because it has no facilities and is remote" says John Langrick, Secretary of the Roach Sailing Association. Lacking a clubhouse, they meet in the Plough and Sail (☎ 01702 258242) at Paglesham Eastend - it's the only pub for miles. Be sure to show an anchor light when you drop your hook as there is the possibility of commercial traffic in these narrow waterways around the clock. Before passing Shoeburyness Range you should give 24 hours notice to the Range Officer (☎ 01621 292271).

Artist: **Anthony Flemming SOUTHEND-ON-SEA**
Courtesy of: **The Artist**

Southend-on-Sea

Southend-on-Sea has the longest pleasure pier in the world - it's nearly a mile and a half long. The usual seaside resort attractions are all on offer here, though the beach gets a bit muddy at low tide. You can lie alongside the pier, though it dries for most of its length.

Facilities for yachts are rather scattered and there are several thousand small boat moorings around the pier which makes it difficult to find a spot to anchor. You might manage to arrange a visitors' mooring from one of the numerous yacht clubs, but be warned that strong southerly winds make moorings lively - that is until they dry out. There's lots to do ashore, and a wide range of places to eat and drink. Finding provisions may be a bit of a walk - it depends where you come ashore, and Southend is a big place.

Taxi:	ABC Radio Cars (☎ 01702 334455)
	(☎ 01702 345678)
Car hire:	Steve's (☎ 01702 612047
Bus:	Local links and links to London
Rail:	Southend to London Fenchurch Street
Airport:	Southend

for more details, see Directory Section

Benfleet

As a quieter option than Southend, if you can take the ground, you will be made welcome at the Benfleet Yacht Club which is tucked up the Benfleet Creek behind Canvey Island. Access is only possible for about two hours each side of high water, but like at many clubs in inaccessible places, the intrepid visitor gets credit for perseverance. There's a good range of provisioning options, and the club has a bar and does food. Check with the Honorary Secretary to find out when it's open.

London and the River Thames

Artist: **Anthony Flemming THAMES ESTUARY**
Courtesy of: **The Artist**

The Thames offers a multitude of places to moor up. There's a selection of marinas throughout the tidal section of the river, and by arrangement with the appropriate authorities, you can land at a number of different piers between Greenwich and Richmond. At the risk of stating the blindingly obvious, there is an enormous amount to see and do in London, and with the Thames winding its way right through the centre, arriving by boat and then having your own mobile base to explore different parts of the city will give you new insights into the capital. The Thames is managed by the Port of London Authority (PLA) and is a major thoroughfare for commercial and leisure traffic. Detailed pilotage notes and instructions for navigation can be found in almanacs such as Macmillan-Reeds. The PLA also publish several informative and helpful guides for users of the Thames which they will be happy to supply free of charge and are well worth getting hold of *(see directory section for further details).*

The importance of the Thames as a transport link and port for overseas trade cannot fail to make itself obvious as you head up the river. Sailing ships might have found the long, winding estuary awkward at times, but the strong tides would have made it practicable to get in and out. Steam powered vessels made access much easier, and the multitude of docks and wharves throughout the east end of London are testament to the importance of London as a centre for global trade.

Gravesend, as location of the headquarters of the Port of London Authority, has an important part to play in the ongoing role of the river. As such, it might not seem to be a place for the yachtsman, but this is not the case. The Gravesend Sailing Club offers a refuge from the commercial traffic in the river, and you can either pick up a mooring or lock into the Gravesend Basin immediately behind the club (accessible for the hour before high water). This is one of the oldest sailing clubs in the country, founded in 1894, and their comfortable clubhouse offers good facilities and a warm welcome to visitors. Within easy walking distance, there are plenty of pubs and restaurants to choose from in the town itself. The town is interspersed with parks and gardens, and points of interest include the Gordon Promenade, named after Gordon of Khartoum fame who, in the late 1860s, supervised the construction of a series of forts to protect the Thames against the marauding French, and the statue of Pocahontas, the Native American Princess who was the first American Christian to be received at the court of James I in 1616 and who is buried in the churchyard at St George's which is close to the waterfront (this might interest a few younger mariners with an appetite for Disney characters).

Artist: **Anthony Flemming GREENWICH**
Courtesy of: **The Artist**

Pressing on up the river, the magnificent span of the Queen Elizabeth II bridge starts to dominate the skyline. Having passed under (and over the other carriageway

Artist: **Anthony Flemming LONDON FROM THE RIVER** *Courtesy of:* **The Artist**

which goes through the tunnel) the M25, London is not far off now, and the huge tower at Canary Wharf may mislead you into thinking it is even closer than it really is. There's a recently built marina at Gallions Point at the east end of the Royal Albert Dock which is accessible for 5 hours each side of high water. Transport links are good from here as the Docklands Light railway provides transport into town until 0030 and for crew changes from all over the British Isles, London City Airport is just at the other end of the dock.

It seems a shame to stop here in many ways as, having come so far, the centre of London is not much further, and passing through Tower Bridge and past Westminster by boat are memorable experiences. The Thames Tidal Barrier is also a spectacular feature to navigate past and this is in the next stretch of the river (the landscape is also now altered by a certain dome). Greenwich is just around the corner, reminding us of Britain's influence as a seafaring nation as we cross from Eastings to Westings. Greenwich Park is well worth a visit for anyone with an interest in matters maritime as it contains the Royal Naval College, The National Maritime Museum, The Queen's House and the Old Royal Observatory. Gypsy Moth IV and the Cutty Sark are also kept here and there's much more besides. Contact the PLA if you wish to land at Greenwich Pier, but bear in mind that berthing against the Thames' piers can be uncomfortable given the wash created by the traffic on the river.

More comfortable accommodation can be found at the Limehouse Basin a few miles further up. This locked marina is accessible at all times other than about 3 hours around low water. This is where the Cruising Association

has its headquarters, and their well appointed and comfortable clubhouse is made available to visiting yachtsmen. Or, alternatively, you may prefer to head for the heart of the City of London, and moor up at St Katherine's Haven which is about another mile up right next to the Tower of London.

Navigation above Tower Bridge becomes a little trickier and you need to check the clearance on the various bridges which you will now need to pass under. There's a well equipped marina at Chelsea Harbour which has a selection of outstanding places to eat and drink on site to suit various depths of pocket, and the rest of the West End of London is within easy reach either on foot or just a short taxi ride away.

Artist: **Anthony Flemming TALL SHIPS AT GREENWICH** *Courtesy of:* **The Artist**

Kent

From the marshy and muddy low lying creeks, rivers and islands on the north to the dramatic harbours crouching by high cliffs in the south with a dash of beach holiday resorts thrown in on the Isle of Thanet – there's plenty of variety to Kent's coastline. The isolation around the Isle of Sheppey contrasts with the bustle and traffic of the English Channel and the major ports of Dover and Ramsgate.

The Medway and the Swale

While the entrance between the Isle of Grain with its gas and oil storage tanks and the commercial harbour of Sheerness may not look all that enticing, there are good secluded anchorages and interesting towns and villages to visit up the Medway. In 1667, this was the scene of the destruction of half the ships in the English Navy by the Dutch fleet. Things are a bit more tranquil these days; it is now a popular yachting area offering some peaceful anchorages and there are marinas with all the facilities you might need as well. Just beyond Sheerness, **Queenborough** is a welcome harbour for those awaiting the tide to carry them up the Thames to London or indeed for those about to delve further into what the Medway has to offer. You can pick up a mooring here, or for landing or a short stay, you can lie alongside the all-tide pontoon which belongs to the Queenborough Yacht Club. There's a water taxi at weekends. You will stop here for the convenience of the facilities – there's water, fuel, power and showers all on hand – though this end of the Isle of Sheppey is a rather industrial area,

and not one which you will probably want to hang about in.

The wide expanses of water at high tide – and mud at low water, interspersed with islands and creeks lead up to the conurbation of Gillingham, Chatham and Rochester. **Gillingham** Marina, offering a full range of marina facilities, is at the western end of what is mainly a residential town, and not far from Chatham. The tree-lined locked basin is accessible for $4^{1}/_{2}$ hours each side of high water, and visitors can make use of the club facilities as temporary members. It's a popular marina so you are advised to book a space at least 24 hours in advance. This is an area steeped in maritime and military history. In Gillingham, you can find out about the history of military engineering since 1066 at the Royal Engineers Museum (☎ 01634 406397) and in neighbouring **Chatham**, the naval dockyards were an important element of Britain's naval strength for several centuries. Henry VIII established this base which built several hundred ships, including Nelson's *Victory* during its lifetime. The dockyard was closed in 1984 and is now managed by Chatham Historic Dockyard Trust and is open to the public from April to October. Of interest to those who go to the sea in ships of any size, The Historic Dockyard is the home of Lifeboat!, the Royal National Lifeboat Collection, where there is a collection of 15 historic lifeboats, archive film and artefacts. Other displays at the dockyard include a dramatic reconstruction of the building of a wooden warship, the $^{1}/_{4}$ mile long Ropery and you can visit the submarine Ocelot which was the last warship built for the Royal Navy at Chatham. On the opposite bank and close to the

Artist: **Anthony Flemming EARLY MORNING ON THE MEDWAY** _Courtesy of:_ **The Artist**

Medway Yacht Club, 16th century Upnor Castle (☎ 01634 718742) is a well-preserved example of a gun fort built to protect naval shipping in the Medway. All in all this is a place to give lovers of maritime history something of a pilgrimage.

A little further up the Medway, now a narrow winding river by contrast to the great wide expanses further downstream, you arrive at **Rochester** with its fine cathedral (☎ 01634 401301) which dates back to Norman times. Rochester Castle (EH ☎01634 402276) on the waterfront also has Norman roots and was built on the old Roman city wall. Charles II stayed at Restoration House just before the monarchy got back on the throne in 1660, and Charles Dickens used this house as a model for Miss Havisham's House in Great Expectations. Dickens lived just outside Rochester from 1858 until his death 12 years later, and based several of his books in the area. He is widely fêted by the town which holds an annual Dickens Festival, during which the townspeople dress appropriately to stage scenes from his books, and also has a Charles Dickens Centre (☎ 01634 844176) which pays tribute to his life and work. There's limited clearance at Rochester Bridge, but for those with the capacity to easily lower their mast or who don't need to, the river is navigable for a considerable distance through the Kent countryside. There are plentiful facilities as there are four marinas in the stretch between Rochester and Allington Lock, which is over 21 miles from the river mouth.

Artist: **Anthony Flemming ROCHESTER**
Courtesy of: **The Artist**

The Isle of Sheppey, east of the mouth of the Medway, is cut off from the mainland by **The Swale**. This tidal passage can be reached from the open sea at Whitstable or from the Medway at Queenborough, though this latter route is narrow and shallow, and there's a lifting bridge to negotiate. This is a desolate and sparsely populated area and the marshlands which make up much of the south of the Isle of Sheppey are a haven for wildlife. Intrepid visitors to the RSPB Elmley Marshes Reserve have quite a trek to get to it. Passing by on the water may give you sight of lapwings, redshanks and shovelers which breed here and sometimes also avocets and mallard. Marsh and Montagu's harriers have also been seen here, and if you are cruising at hardy times of the year, you may see teal, wigeon and white

fronted geese which winter here. There are several creeks which offer drying moorings, and several boatyards which offer moorings in the stretch of the river between **Faversham Creek** and Conyer Creek. At the head of its now silted creek, Faversham is an attractive town. Its prosperity since the port silted up rested on the manufacture of gunpowder, though you may be relieved to hear that production in the 18th century mills stopped in about 1930. The town has a number of other interesting historic buildings to visit. The Swale Marina at **Conyer Creek** has pontoon berths for a few visitors and has a reasonable range of facilities. There are also a couple of pubs in Conyer which is about a quarter of a mile away.

Artist: **Anthony Flemming FAVERSHAM CREEK**
Courtesy of: **The Artist**

The Swale to Ramsgate

Whitstable Harbour is small and dries, but offers good shelter if needed. Yacht berths are limited to genuine refuge seekers as priority is given to commercial shipping. Passing Herne Bay, the coastline's character changes as the yellow-brown clay of Bishopstone Cliffs leads along to the ruins of St Mary's Church at Reculver. Several miles of sandy beach then give way to a series of bays and coves as we near the end of the Isle of Thanet. **Margate** has a small drying harbour and some facilities for yachts. This is a traditional seaside resort and can claim a place in the history of seaside resorts as the home town of Benjamin Beale who invented the covered bathing machine. There are shops and boutiques, amusements and fun parks for children and young at heart grown-ups and a number of museums and other local features such as the Margate Caves, dug out of the chalk and reputedly the haunt of smugglers, and not forgetting the famous Shell Grotto where millions of shells have been used to decorate 2000 square feet of passages in what is believed to be a 2000 year old temple.

Ramsgate

Work started on the building of Ramsgate Harbour in 1750 in response to public perception of a need for a safe refuge on this coast following a violent storm in December 1748. Numerous ships were wrecked and on this occasion, as on many others before and since, the treacherous Goodwin Sands, which lie about 5 miles from Ramsgate, claimed many lives. The Harbour became "Royal" in 1820, to show George IV's appreciation for the hospitality which the town offered him when he used the harbour to depart for and return from Hanover. Ramsgate boasts both a Maritime Museum (☎ 01843 587765) which is in Pier Yard and a more general town museum (☎ 01843 593532) where you can explore the role Ramsgate has played in history both ashore and at sea. The Motor Museum (☎ 01843 581948) at West Cliff Hall has a range of exhibits dating from Edwardian times to the 1950s and the Model Village (☎ 01843 592543) at the top of the cliffs on West Cliff Promenade is popular with children.

Taxi:	Mini Cabs (☎ 01843 581581)
Car hire:	Compass Car Hire (☎01843 582324)
	Station Approach Road
	Spains Self Drive (☎ 01843 592149)
	9 Prices Avenue
Cycle hire:	Spains Car Hire (☎ 01843 592145)
	9 Prices Avenue
Bus:	East Kent Buses (☎ 01843 581333)
	National Express Coaches
	(☎ 01843 240101)
Rail:	Rail links to London from town centre -
	timetable enquiries (℅ 01732 770111)
Airport:	RAF Manston-Kent International Airport
	(℅ 01843 823333)

for more details, see Directory Section

Artist: **Anthony Flemming WHITSTABLE**
Courtesy of: **The Artist**

Artist: **Anthony Flemming OFF NORTH FORELAND**
Courtesy of: **The Artist**

The original harbour is now a locked inner harbour, known as the Inner Royal Marina which is accessible for roughly 2¹/₂ hours each side of high water. The Outer Royal Marina offers 24 hour access to the sea, regardless of the state of the tide, and is protected by a wavebreak though can sometimes be uncomfortable. All the facilities you would expect to find at a large marina are here and, in addition, the Royal Temple Yacht Club offers a warm welcome to all visiting yachtsmen. Be warned that this is also a busy commercial harbour with considerable amounts of ferry and fast catamaran traffic. It's worth getting details of the most suitable approaches from the harbour office in advance if you can, and anyway, keep a watch on Channel 14. Call Ramsgate Port Control on the same channel to get permission to enter the harbour or cross the shipping channel. Channel 14 can also be used to call the Dock Office to reserve a berth. Pet owners are advised that strict anti-rabies byelaws forbid animals ashore or afloat within the harbour limits regardless of whether you have come from overseas or not.

Jarvis Marina (☎ 01843 588276) on Harbour Parade, is definitely worth a visit and it serves bar lunches from Monday to Saturday, and now an a la carte dinner menu. There are several characterful pubs dotted throughout the town, such as the Artillery Arms (☎ 01843 853282) which is alleged to have been a brothel in Victorian times and Honeysuckle (☎ 01843 597532) on Honeysuckle Road, which has been standing since 1789.

Dover

The approach to Dover is a spectacular one with the famous white cliffs which guard it on both sides. Shakespeare Cliff, to the west reaches 300 feet above sea level, dwarfing even the biggest ships which are approaching the harbour.

Dover Harbour itself is on a massive scale and not the place to go if you are in search of peace and quiet. As well as the considerable ferry and commercial traffic, the marina is a busy one which is clearly popular as it logs around 5000 visiting yachts and motor boats a year. Entry and exit is strictly monitored and permission must be granted before making passage in or out. There are plenty of spaces for visitors in both the locked Wellington Dock and the Inner Harbour which has 24 hour access. Alternatively, you can anchor for free in the outer harbour between the deep draught vessel anchorage and the Prince of Wales Pier, but note that anchored vessels should not be left unattended.

There is evidence to suggest that there has been a harbour at Dover since Roman times - there are the remains of a Roman lighthouse just beside the castle. With France not much more than 20 miles away, it's an obvious place to choose to make the shortest possible channel crossing from. Little wonder that this spot was key in two historic channel crossings. In 1875 Matthew Webb started the first cross-channel swim here and, 35 years later, Louis Bleriot touched down here after the first successful cross-channel flight. The Marina is well removed from the ferry terminal being more favourably located near to the town centre where there is plenty to see and do. The Dover Museum and The White Cliffs Experience are nearby and it's not far to the Town Hall and Old Town Gaol. Dominating the harbour is Dover Castle (EH ☎ 01304 211067) some of which dates back to the 1180s. There is a wide range of interesting displays which illustrate the castle's role over the centuries and you have the opportunity to explore the warren of secret underground tunnels which was most recently used and much developed in World War II. Also well worth a look are both the Dover Transport Museum (☎ 01304 204612) at Old Park in Whitfield and the St Margaret's Museum (☎ 01304 852764) in St Margaret's Bay. There are RNLI related exhibits and much more at both of these informative museums.

Artist: **Anthony Flemming DOVER**
Courtesy of: **The Artist**

The Royal Cinque Ports Yacht Club, which is close to the marina, welcomes visiting yachtsmen, and you are likely to meet up with the crews of boats making pas-

sages from all over Europe. They have a bar and restaurant, both of which are open at lunchtime and in the evening. There are plenty of pubs to choose from – we suggest the Mogul (☎ 01304 205072) in Chapel Place, or the Flagship (☎ 01304 204653) in Snargate Street, because both are within 5 minutes walk, although there are many more which are worth visiting. Likewise there are any number of restaurants to choose from, but for a top class meal, try the Churchill Hotel (☎ 01304 203633). The Curry Garden Indian Restaurant (☎ 01304 206357) in the High Street will deliver direct to your boat if you so wish.

Taxi:	Clubs Taxis (☎ 01304 211777/201915)
	Victory Cars (☎ 01304 228888)
Car hire:	All major companies represented locally
Cycle hire:	
Bus:	100 yards to bus stop, local & national services from Dover
Rail:	Dover Station connects direct to London.
Airport:	Gatwick, 1 hour away. Heathrow 1½ hours away.

for more details, see Directory Section

Dover to Rye

Pressing on from Dover, the coastline makes a dramatic change from the high cliffs to the low lying ground of the Romney Marshes as you approach the bleak shingle promontory of **Dungeness**. The RSPB manages the pits and pools on this headland to encourage migrating and wintering visitors and it's an important breeding ground for gulls and terns which you will be able to see as you sail by. With the somewhat uninspiring prospect of Dungeness A and B Nuclear Power Stations, this windswept spot offers little shelter, so you will probably wish to speed your passage towards the Sussex coast and fresh opportunities to explore ashore.

Artist: **Anthony Flemming ROUNDING THE GOODWIN LIGHT** *Courtesy of:* **The Artist**

HUNSTANTON

No facilities for yachts

Hunstanton Lifeboat
Sea Lane, Old Hunstanton, Norfolk
Open to visitors 0900-1200 every Sunday -
contact Hon. Sec. David Harrison
Hon. Sec. Tel: 01485 534110

BRANCASTER STAITHE   52.59'.0N 00.38'.5E

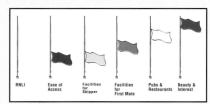

Mervyn Nudds: Harbourmaster
Tel: 01485 210638
VHF: Channel 16/37   VHF Name: The Ferry

Brancaster Staithe Sailing Club
Anne Webb: Secretary
Tel: 01485 210249 Fax: 01485 210399

Chandlers:
Snelling Marine, North Shore, Brancaster
Staithe Tel: 01488 210381

BURNHAM OVERY STAITHE
52.59'.0N 00.46'.5E

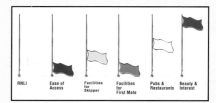

Burnham Overy Staithe Sailing Club
Peter Beck: Secretary
The Boathouse, Burnham Overy Staithe,
Norfolk PE31 8JF
Tel: 01328 738348 Fax: 01328 730550

Chandlers:
Burnham Overy Boathouse Ltd, Burnham
Overy Staithe Tel: 01328 738348

WELLS-NEXT-THE-SEA   52.59'.5N 00.49'.5E

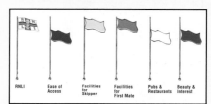

Graham Walker: Harbourmaster
Harbour Office, Old Lifeboat House, West
Quay, Wells-next-the-Sea, NR23 1AT
Tel: 01328 711646
VHF: Ch: 12/16 VHF Name: Wells Harbour

Chandlers and Repairs: contact
Harbourmaster who will advise

Wells Lifeboat
Beach Road, Wells-next-the-Sea, NR23 1AT
Open to visitors most days, or by appoint-
ment - contact Coxswain-mechanic Allen
Frarey Boathouse Tel: 01328 710230
Cox'n/mech: 01328 710950

BLAKENEY   52.59'.0N 00.58'.5E

Harbourmaster
Tel: 01263 740362

BLAKENEY cont.

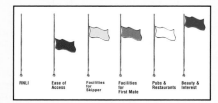

Chandler:
Stratton Long, Blakeney Harbour, Norfolk
Tel: 01263 740362

Repairs: contact Stratton long

SHERINGHAM

Not suitable for yachts.

Sheringham Lifeboat
West Promenade, Sheringham
Open to visitors every day 1000-1600
between Easter and October or contact
senior helmsman Boathouse Tel: 01263 823212
Senior helmsman (P.M. Jackson) 01263 822728

CROMER

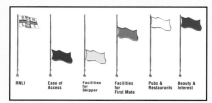

May anchor off in settled weather only

Cromer Lifeboat
No 2 Boathouse, The Promenade, Cromer
Open to visitors every day 1000-1530
between Easter and end of September or
contact museum curator
Boathouse Tel: 01263 511294 Curator
(Frank Muirhead) Tel: 01263 513018

HAPPISBURGH

Unsuitable for yachts

Happisburgh Lifeboat
Beach Road, Happisburgh, Norfolk
Open daily 1000-1200 and 1400-1700 between
May and September or contact Hon. Sec.
Boathouse Tel: 01692 651308 Hon. Sec.
(Mr C. Cox) Tel: 01692 650727

GREAT YARMOUTH   52.34'.5N 01.44'.5E

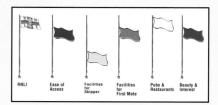

Captain Alec Goodlad: Harbourmaster
Tel: 01493 335511
VHF Channel: 12
VHF Name: Yarmouth Harbour Radio

Breydon Bridge
VHF Ch: 12   VHF Name: Breydon Bridge

Great Yarmouth & Gorleston Lifeboat
Open to visitors: daily during summer or by
appointment with N. Duffield (Hon. Sec.)
Hon. Sec. Tel: 01493 661776

THE SOUTH BROADS
The Broads Navigation Authority,

18 Colegate, Norwich Norfolk NR3 1BQ
Tel: 01603 610734

Burgh Castle Marina

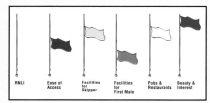

B. Humphrey: Manager
Butt lane, Burgh Castle, Norfolk NR31 9PZ
Tel: 01493 780331

Chandlery and repairs:
Goodchild Marine, Butt Lane, Burgh Castle,
Norfolk NR31 9PZ
Tel: 01493 782301 Fax: 01493 782306

LOWESTOFT & OULTON BROAD
52.28'.5N 01.45'.5E

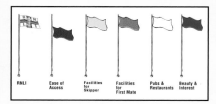

Harbourmaster and Bridge Control
Associated British Ports, The Bridge,
Lowestoft Tel: 01502 572286
VHF: Channel 14/16/11
VHF Name: Lowestoft Harbour Control

Royal Norfolk & Suffolk Yacht Club
Andrew Donovan: Secretary
Royal Plain, Lowestoft, Suffolk NR33 0AQ
Tel: 01502 566726 Fax: 01502 517981
VHF Ch: M/14   VHF Name: Yacht Club

Lowestoft Cruising Club
Mrs Coles: Secretary
Harbour Road, Oulton Broad, Lowestoft,
Suffolk Tel: 01502 574376

Oulton Broad Yacht Station
Contact: Manager
Oulton Broad, Suffolk Tel: 01502 574946

Chandlers:
Frithvales, Battery Green Road (opposite Fish
Dock entrance), Lowestoft Tel: 01502 517992
Lowestoft Yacht Services, Halls Boatyard,
Harbour Road, Oulton Broad, Lowestoft,
Suffolk, NR32 3LX Tel/Fax: 01502 585535

Repairs: contact Lowestoft Yacht Services for
all repairs

Lowestoft Lifeboat
Open to visitors: daily - check with Hon. Sec.
for times. Hon. Sec. Tel: 01986 892218 (home)
01502 572974 (office)

SOUTHWOLD   52.18'.5N 01.40'.5E

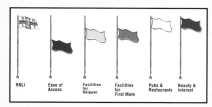

Ken Howells: Harbourmaster
Harbour Office, Southwold, Suffolk
Tel: 01502 724712
VHF Channel: 12

VHF Name: Southwold Harbour Radio

Chandlery & repairs:
Harbour Marine Services, Blackshore,
Southwold Harbour, Southwold IP18 6TA
Tel: 01502 724721

Southwold Lifeboat
The Lifeboathouse, Southwold Dock, Ferry
Road, Southwold
Open to visitors: daily Easter to September.
Contact G Doy (Mechanic) or J. Huggins
(Hon Sec) for times.
Mech. Tel: 01502 723380
Hon. Sec. Tel: 01502 722672/724253

THE RIVER ALDE   52.02'.0N 01.27'.5E

Orford

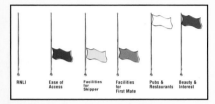

The Alde and Ore Association,
Send £1.50 and large s.a.e. for chart of mouth
of River Alde Contact: The Secretary
Hill House, Snape Bridge, Suffolk IP17 1ST

Orford Quay Administration
Clerk to the Town Trust, The Hollies, Market
Hill, Orford, Suffolk Tel: 01394 450481

Aldeburgh

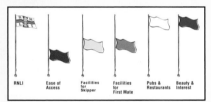

Aldeburgh Yacht Club
Mr Neville Bromage
Slaughden, Aldeburgh, Suffolk
Tel: 01728 452562 or 452504

Chandlery and repairs:
Aldeburgh Boatyard, Fort Green, Aldeburgh,
Suffolk, Proprietor: Peter Wilson
Tel: 01728 452019

Moorings, Chandlery & Repairs:
R.F. Upson & Co, Slaughden Quay,
Aldeburgh, Suffolk IP15 5NA
Tel: 01728 452896

Aldeburgh Lifeboat
Crag Path, Aldeburgh, Suffolk IP 15 5BP
Open to visitors every day between 1000
and 1600. Recent "Penza" lifeboathouse.
Boathouse Tel: 01728 452552

RIVER DEBEN

Bawdsey   51.59'.0N 01.22'.5E

Bawdsey Haven Yacht Club
Nicholas Rose: Secretary
Bawdsey, Suffolk IP12 3AY
Tel: 01394 410258

Felixstowe Ferry

Pilot: Robert Brinkley
Tel: 01394 270853 or 0411 002825 (mobile)
VHF Channel: 8 VHF Name: Late Times

Felixstowe Ferry Boatyard
Felixstowe Ferry, Felixstowe IP11 9RZ
Tel: 01394 282173
VHF Ch: 16/8 VHF Name: Deben Worker

Felixstowe Ferry cont.

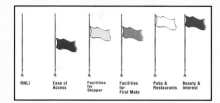

Felixstowe Ferry Sailing Club
Tel: 01394 283785

Ramsholt

George Collins: Harbourmaster – hail at quay

Waldringfield

Waldringfield Sailing Club Tel: 01394 736633

Moorings, Chandlery & Repairs:
Waldringfield Boatyard, The Quay,
Waldringfield, Suffolk IP12 4QL
Tel: 01473 736260

Woodbridge

Tidemill Yacht Harbour
Contact: Manager
Tidemill Way, Woodbridge, Suffolk IP12 1BP
Tel: 01394 385745 Fax: 01394 380735
VHF Channel: 80/M
VHF Name: Tidemill Yacht Harbour

Woodbridge Cruising Club   52.05'N 01.19'S

Richard Sampson: Secretary
River Wall, Woodbridge, Suffolk IP12 4BB
Clubhouse Tel: 01394 386737
Secretary Tel (Home): 01394 382028

Chandlers & Repairs:
contact Tidemill Yacht Harbour or:
Robertsons Boatyard, Lime Kiln Quay,
Woodbridge, Suffolk IP12 1BD
Tel: 01394 382305 Fax: 01394 388788
Melton Boatyard Ltd, Dock Lane, Melton,
Woodbridge Suffolk IP12 1PE
Tel: 01394 386327
Frank Knights (Shipwrights) Ltd, Ferry Quay,
Woodbridge, Suffolk
Tel: 01394 382318 Fax: 01394 388958
Woodbridge Boat Store, Lime Kiln Quay,
Woodbridge, Suffolk Tel: 01394 380390

Sailmakers & repairs:
Suffolk Sailcare, Quayside Buildings,
Woodbridge IP12 1BY Tel: 01394 386323

RIVER ORWELL

Captain John Swift: Harbourmaster (Ipswich)
& Orwell Navigation Service
. Tel: 01473 231010
VHF Channel: 14/16/12
VHF Name: Ipswich Port radio

Levington

Suffolk Yacht Harbour
Contact: Manager, Levington, Ipswich, Suffolk
Tel: 01473 659465 or 659240
Fax: 01473 659632
VHF Channel: 80/M
VHF Name: Suffolk Yacht Harbour

Haven Ports Yacht Club
Contact: Secretary
Suffolk Yacht Harbour, Levington, Suffolk
Tel: 01473 659658

Chandlery & Repairs:
Seamark Nunn & Co, 400 High Road, Trimley
St. Martin, Ipswich IP10 0SG
Tel: 01394 275327 Fax: 01394 670329

Sail makers & repairs:
Parker & Kay Sailmakers (East), Suffolk
Yacht Harbour, Levington, Ipswich Suffolk
Tel: 01473 659878 Fax: 01473 659197

Pin Mill

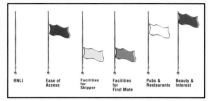

Tony Ward: Harbourmaster Tel: 01473 780276
Pin Mill Sailing Club
Contact: Secretray Tel: 01473 780271

Chandlery:
Wards Tel: 01473 780276

Woolverstone

Woolverstone Marina
Contact: Manager
Woolverstone, Ipswich, IP9 1As
Tel: 01473 780206 or 780354
VHF Channel: 80/37(M)
VHF Name: Woolverstone Marina

Engine repairs:
Volspec, Woolverstone Marina, Ipswich,
Tel: 01473 780144 Fax: 01473 780174

Ipswich

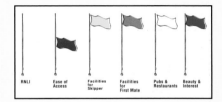

Fox's Marina
Contact: Manager
The Strand, Wherstead, Ipswich, IP2 8SA
Tel: 01473 689111 Fax: 01473 601737

Neptune Marina
Contact: Manager
Neptune Quay, Ipswich, Suffolk IP4 1AX
Tel: 01473 215204 Fax: 01473 215206
Office: 01473 780366

Debbage Yachting Services
Contact: Manager
The Quay, New Cut West, Ipswich IP2 8HN

Chandlery & Repairs: available at Fox's
Marina

RIVER STOUR

Captain Ian Whale: Harbourmaster (Harwich)
Tel: 01255 243030
VHF Channel: 71/11/14/16
VHF Name: Harwich Harbour Radio

Harwich

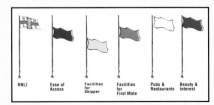

Harwich & Dovercourt Sailing Club
                    51.56'.5N 01.17'.0E
Peter Phillips: Secretary
Sailing Club, Gas House Creek, Harwich
Tel: 01255 551153

Harwich Town Sailing Club
T.C. Rogers: Hon. Sec. Tel: 01255 508054

Harwich Lifeboat
Open to visitors: by appointment, contact
Capt. R Shaw (Hon. Sec.)
Hon. Sec. Tel: 01255 552441 (home)
01255 508881 (office)

Shotley Point

Shotley Point Marina
Contact: Manager
Shotley Gate, Ipswich, Suffolk IP9 1QJ
Tel: 01473 788982 Fax: 01473 788868
VHF Channel: 80/37
VHF Name: Shotley Point Marina

WALTON-ON-THE-NAZE   51.54'.5N 01.17.0E

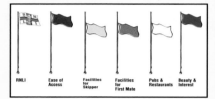

Titchmarsh Marina
Contact: Manager
Coles Lane, Walton on the Naze CO14 8SL
Tel: 01255 851899 Marina Office: 01255 672185
VHF Ch: 37/80 VHF Name: Titchmarsh Marina

Moorings:
Bedwell & Co, Mill Lane, Walton-on-the-Naze
Tel: 01255 675873
VHF Ch: M1 VHF Name: Bedwell & Co

Walton & Frinton Yacht Club
Diana Pickard: Secretary
Tel: 01255 675526 Fax: 01255 678161

Chandlers & Repairs:
Bedwell & Co or:
Frank Halls & Son, Mill Lane, Walton-on-the-
Naze Tel: 01255 675596

Walton & Frinton Lifeboat
47 High Street, Walton-on-the-Naze, Essex
Open to visitors: most afternoons or by
appointment, Contact: Hon Sec
Boathouse Tel: 01255 675650
Hon. Sec. Tel: 01255 675549

CLACTON-ON-SEA

No facilities for yachts

Clacton-on-Sea Lifeboat
Open to visitors: June-September – contact
R Smith (Hon.Sec.) Tel: 01255 861844 (home)
01255 421090 (office)

RIVER COLNE

Brightlingsea

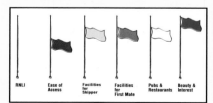

Captain T Coupland: Harbourmaster
Harbour Office, 4 Copprass Rd, Brightlingsea,
Essex CO7 0AP Tel: 01206 032200
VHF Channel: 68
VHF Name: Brightlingsea Harbourmaster

Moorings:
Town Hard, Brightlingsea, Tel: 01206 303535

Colne Yacht Club, Brightlingsea
Tel: 01206 302594

Wivenhoe

Harbourmaster Tel: 01206 827316

VHF Channel: 68
VHF Name: Colchester Harbour Office

Colne Marine & Yacht Co, Wivenhoe, Essex
Tel: 01206 222417

RIVER BLACKWATER

West Mersea

Moorings:
West Mersea Marine
Contact: Manager
110 Coast Road, West mersea, Nr Colchester,
C05 8NA Tel: 01206 382244 Fax: 01206 384455
VHF Channel: M VHF Name: CC 1

West Mersea Yacht Club, West Mersea,
Colchester, Essex
VHF Channel: 37 VHF Name: YC1

West Mersea Lifeboat
Coast Road, West Mersea, Colchester CO5
Open to visitors: by appointment - contact
Anthea Wade Tel: 01206 382874
Hon. Sec. Tel: 01206 385558

Tollesbury

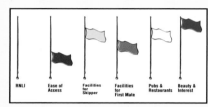

Tollesbury Marina
Contact: Manager
Woodrolfe Boatyard, The Yacht Harbour,
Tollesbury, Tel: 01621 869202 Fax: 01621 868489
VHF Ch: 37/80 VHF Name: Tollesbury Marina

Moorings:
Tollesbury Saltings Ltd,
Contact: Manager
The Sail Lofts, Woodrolfe Road, Tollesbury,
Maldon CM9 8SE
Tel: 01621 868624 Fax: 01621 868227

Tollesbury Cruising Club Tel: 01621 869561

Engine repairs:
Volspec, Woodrolfe Road, Tollesbury, Essex
Tel: 01621 869756 Fax: 01621 868859

Bradwell-on-Sea

Bradwell Marina
Roy Smith: Harbourmaster
Waterside, Bradwell-on-Sea, Essex CM0 7RB
Tel: 01621 776235 Fax: 01621 776393
VHF Ch: 37/80 VHF Name: Bradwell Marina

Bradwell Quay Yacht Club
Roger Price: Commodore
Quay House, Waterside, Bradwell-on-Sea,
CM0 7QX Tel: 01621 776539 or 01621 783437
(Moorings officer)

Marylandsea

Blackwater Marina
Contact: Manager
The Marina Office, Marine Parade,
Marylandsea, Essex CM3 6AM
Tel: 01621 740264 Fax:01621 742122
VHF Ch: M VHF Name: Blackwater Marina

Marylandsea Bay Yacht Club
Mr J. Weedon: Sailing Secretary
Tel: 01621 858532

Harlow (Blackwater) Sailing Club
Mrs M. Mayo: Secretary
Tel: 0181 367832

Maldon

Moorings:
Chris Reynolds-Hole: River Warden
River Bailiff's Office, Hythe Quay, Maldon

Maldon cont.

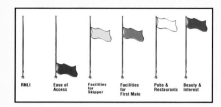

Tel: 01621 856487 Fax: 01621 852575
VHF Channel: 16 VHF Name: Highspirits

Fairways Marine Engineers
Contact: Manger
Bath Place Wharf, Downs Road, Maldon,
CM9 7HU Tel: 01621 852866 Fax: 01621 850902

Heybridge Basin

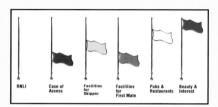

Colin Edmond: Lockmaster
Lock House, Lock Hill, Heybridge Bsin,
Maldon Tel: 01621 853506

Moorings:
Holt & James Wooden Boats Ltd
The Boatyard, Heybridge Basin, Maldon
CM9 7RS Tel: 01621 854022 Fax: 01621 854022

Chandlery, Sail makers & repairs:
Valiant marine, Stock Chase, Heybridge,
Maldon Tel/Fax: 01621 853558

RIVER CROUCH

Burnham-on-Crouch

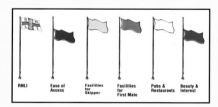

Captain Ian Bell: Harbourmaster
Tel: 01621 783602
VHF Ch: 80 VHF Name: Couch Harbour

Moorings:
Burnham Yacht Harbour
Contact: Manager
Foundry Lane, Burnham-on-Crouch, CM0 8BL
Tel: 01702 258531 Fax: 01702 258227
VHF Channel: 80/37
VHF Name: Burnham Yacht Harbour

R.J. Prior & Sons Ltd,
Contact: Manager
Quayside, Burnham-on-Crouch CM0 8AS
Tel: 01621 782160 Fax: 01621 784220

Rice & Cole Ltd
Contact: Manager
Sea End Boathouse, Burnham-on-Crouch
CM0 8AN Tel: 01621 782063 Fax: 01621 782063
VHF Channel: M VHF Name: Rice & Cole

Royal Corinthian Yacht Club
Mrs M. Pollard: Club Controller
Tel: 01621 782105

Burnham Sailing Club
Victor De Sarandy: Hon. Secretary
Tel: 01621 782812

Crouch Yacht Club
Miss Mary purves: Hon. Secretary
Coronation Road, Burnham-on-Crouch, Essex
Tel/Fax: 01621 782252

Royal Burnham Yacht Club
Mrs L. Bayliss: Office Secretary
Tel: 01621 782044

Chandlery:
Cruisermart, Burnham Yacht Harbour,
Burnham-on-Crouch CM0 8BG
Tel: 01621 782890 Fax: 01621 782730

Fairways Chandlery Ltd. The Quay,
Burnham-on-Crouch CM0 8AT
Tel/Fax: 01621 782659

Repairs: contact Burnham Yacht Harbour

Sailmakers & repairs:
Hyde Sails
Contact: Richard Franks
The Sail Loft, Burnham Business Park,
Burnham-on-Crouch, Essex CM0 8TB
Tel: 01621 782108 Fax: 01621 782669

Lonton & Gray, 61C High Street, Burnham-
on-Crouch, Essex CM0 8AH
Tel: 01621 786200   Fax: 01621 786201

Wilkinson Sails, The Sail Loft, Quayside,
Burnham-on-Crouch, Essex CM0 8AS
Tel: 01621 786770 Fax: 01621 786817

Burnham-on-Crouch Lifeboat
Burnham Yacht Harbour, Burnham-on-Crouch
Open to visitors: weekends and Bank
Holidays – check with D Glaze (Hon. Sec.) or
Mrs M Milton (Admin Officer)
Boathouse Tel: 01621 786670 Hon. Sec.
Tel: 01621 776397
Admin Officer Tel: 01621 784345

Wallasea Island

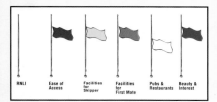

Essex Marina Ltd
Contact: Manager
Wallasea Island, Nr Rochford, Essex SS4 2HG
Tel: 01702 258531 Fax: 01702 258227
VHF Ch: 80/37 VHF Name: Essex Marina

Essex Marina Yacht Club   51 37'.3N 00.47'.9E
R.J.L. Stace: Secretary
Essex Marina, Wallasea Island, Essex
Tel: 01702 258352

Repairs: contact Trevor Taylor at Essex
Marina

North Fambridge

North Fambridge Yacht Centre Ltd
Contact: Manger
Ferry Road, North Fambridge,
Nr. Chelmsford, CM3 6LR Tel: 01621 740370

West Wick Marina
Contact: Manager
Church Road, North Fambridge, Nr
Chelmsford CM3 6LR Tel: 01621 741268
VHF Ch: 80/M VHF Name: West Wick Marina

Hullbridge

Brandy Hole Yacht Station
Contact: Manager
Pooles Lane, Hullbridge, Essex SS5 6QB
Tel: 01702 230248

Althorne

Bridgemarsh Marine

Contact: Manager
Bridge Marsh lane, Althorne, Essex CM3 6DQ
Tel: 01621 740414 Fax: 01621 742216

RIVER ROACH   51 35'.5N 00.48'.5E

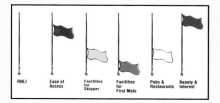

Roach Sailing Association
John Langrick: Secretary
c/o 10, St James Av. Thorpe Bay, Essex
Tel: 017025 88199 Fax: 017025 89021

Moorings:
Paglesham Boatyard,
Contact: Manager
Waterside Road, East End Paglesham, Rochford,
Southend SS4 2ER Tel: 01702 258885

Repairs:
Miracle Boat Repairs, Paglesham Boatyard.
Tel: 01702 258292

SOUTHEND-ON-SEA   51 31'.0N 00.47'.0E

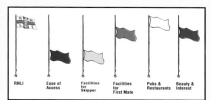

Southend-on-Sea Pier
Mr Ged Bowes: Pier Manager
Tel: 01702 215620
Mr Jim Mackie: Foreshore Manager
Tel: 01702 611889

Alexandra Yacht Club Tel: 01702 340363
Leigh-on-Sea Yacht Club Tel: 01702 76788
Thorpe Bay Yacht Club Tel: 01702 587563

Thames Estuary Yacht Club   51 32'.0N 00.42'.0E
David G. Brown: Secretary
3 The Leas, Westcliff-on-Sea SS0 7ST
Tel: 01702 345967

Halfway Yacht Club
Contact: Hon. Secretary
217 Eastern Esplanade, Thorpe Bay, Essex
Tel: 01702 582025

Chandlers:
Shoreline (Cruisermart), 36 Eastern
Esplanade, Southend-on-Sea Tel: 01702 460055

Repairs:
Lower Thames Marine, High Street, Leigh-on-Sea
Tel: 01702 79009
Seacraft, High Street, Old Town, Leigh-on-Sea
Tel: 01702 713151

Southend-on-Sea Lifeboat
Open to visitors: weekends April-October –
or by arrangement with C Sedgewick (Hon.
Sec.) Tel: 01702 338997 or 01702 713151 or
01702 480092 (office)

CANVEY ISLAND

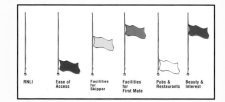

Moorings:
Halcon Marine Ltd
Contact: Manager
The Point, Canvey Island, Essex SS8 7TL
Tel: 01268 511611
VHF Channel: M VHF Name: Mississippi

Dauntless Yacht Co,
Contact: Manager
Canvey Bridge, Canvey Island, Essex SS8 0QT
Tel: 01268 793782

Pitsea Hall Marina
Contact: Manager
Pitsea Hall Country Park, Pitsea Hall Lane,
Pitsea, Basildon, Essex SS16 4UW
Tel: 01268 550088 Fax: 01268 581093

Benfleet Yacht Club
Contact: Hon. Secretary
Canvey Road, Canvey Island, Essex SS8 0QT
Tel: 01268 792278

Repairs: contact Dauntless Yacht Company

RIVER THAMES

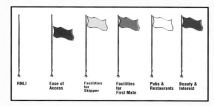

Port of London Authority, Devon House, 58-
60 St Katherine's Way, London E1 9LB
Tel: 0171 265 2656 Fax: 0171 265 2699

Gravesend

Moorings:
Port of London Authority, London River
House, Pier Road, Gravesend DA12 2BG
Tel: 01474 562212

Gravesham Marina   51.22'.5N 00.23'.0E
Contact: Manager
The Canal Basin, Gravesend, Kent
Tel: 01474 353392

Gravesend Sailing Club
Valerie Green: Secretary
Promenade East, Gravesend, Kent DA12 2RN
Tel: 01474 533974 Fax: 01474 333414

Upriver

Thurrock Yacht Club
Contact: Secretary
Kilverts Wharf, Argent Street, Grays, Essex
Tel: 01375 373720

Chandlers:
Sharbucks, 73 West Street, Gravesend
Tel: 01474 350671

Repairs: contact chandler or ask at club

Gallions Point Marina 51 30'.3N 00.04'.8E
Contact: Manager
Gate 14, Royal Albert Basin, Woolwich
Manor Way, North Woolwich E16 2PU
Tel: 0171 476 7054
VHF Ch: 13 VHF Name: Gallions Point Marina

Greenwich Yacht Club
Contact: Secretary
Riverway, London SW10 0BE Tel: 0181 858 7339
VHF Ch: M VHF Name: Greenwich Yacht Club

South Dock Marina
Contact: Manager
Lock Office, Rope Street, Plough Way,
London SE16 1TX
Tel: 0171 252 2244 Fax: 0171 237 3806
VHF Ch: M/80 VHF Name: South Dock Marina

Limehouse Basin
British Waterways Lock Office
Tel: 0171 308 9930

Moorings:
Limehouse Marina (The Cruising Association)
Contact: Manager
1 Northney Street, Limehouse Basin, E14 8BT
Tel: 0171 537 2828 Fax: 0171 537 2266
VHF Ch: 80 VHF Name: Limehouse Basin

St Katherine Haven
Contact: Manager
50 St Katherine's Way, London E1 9LB
Tel: 0171 481 8350 Fax: 0171 702 2252
VHF Ch: M (37) VHF Name: St Katherine's

Fuel:
Westminster Petroleum Ltd – fuel barge is
400 yards below St Katherine's Lock
Tel: 0831 110681
VHF Channel: 14 VHF Name: Thames Refueller

Chelsea Harbour   37.28'.5N 00.10'.7W
Chelsea Harbour Marina
Contact: Manager
Lotts Road, Chelsea Harbour, SW10 0XF
Tel: 0171 351 4433 Fax: 0171 352 7868
VHF Ch: 80 VHF Name: Chelsea Harbour

Chandlers and repairs:
Chas Newmans Marine, The Boathouse,
Putney Embankment, London
Tel: 0181 788 4587

QUEENBOROUGH

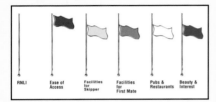

John Chapman: Harbourmaster
Queenborough Harbour Office, Town Quay,
South St, Queenborough, Kent ME11 5AF
Tel: 01795 662051 Fax: 01795 662051

Queenborough Yacht Club
Contact: Secretary
Tel: 01795 663955
VHF Ch: M/80/M2 VHF Name: Queen Base

THE MEDWAY

Peter White: Harbourmaster
Tel: 01795 561234
VHF Ch: 74/16 VHF Name: Medway Radio

Gillingham   51.24'.0N 0034'.5E

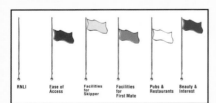

Gillingham Marina
Contact: Manager
F. Parham Ltd, 173 Pier Road, Gillingham,
ME7 1UB Tel: 01634 280022 Fax: 01634 280164
VHF Channel: 80
VHF Name: Gillingham Marina Lock

Medway Pier Marine
Contact: Manager
Pier Head Buildings, Gillingham Pier,
Gillingham, ME7 1RX Tel: 01634 851113
VHF Channel: 16 VHF Name: Medway Pier

Hoo

Hoo Marina (Medway) Ltd
Contact: Manager
Vicarage Lane, Hoo, Rochester, ME3 9TW
Tel: 01634 255880 Fax: 01634 253606

VHF Channel: 80/M VHF Name: Hoo Marina

Moorings:
Whitton Marine
Contact: Manager
Vicarage Lane, Hoo, Rochester ME3 9LB
Tel: 01634 250593 Fax: 01634 280593

Hundred of Hoo Sailing Club
Mrs J Thorne: Secretary
Vicarage Lane, Hoo, Rochester
Tel: 01634 250102
Repairs: contact Whitton Marine

Rochester and above

Medway Bridge Marina
Contact: Manager
Manor Lane, Rochester, Kent ME1 3HS
Tel: 01634 43576 Fax: 01634 843820
VHF Ch: 80/M VHF Name: Medway Bridge

Port Medway Marina
Contact: Manager
Station Road, Cuxton, Rochester ME2 1AB
Tel: 01634 726604 Fax: 01634 720315
VHF Ch: 80/M VHF Name: Port Medway

Cuxton Marina
Contact: Manager
Station Road, Cuxton, Rochester ME2 1AB
Tel: 01634 721941 Fax: 01634 250853

SHEERNESS

No facilities for yachts

Sheerness Lifeboat
Open to visitors: by arrangement, usually
Sundays. Contact Capt. W Patterson (Hon.
Sec)
Hon. Sec. Tel: 01795 664624

FAVERSHAM

Faversham Creek

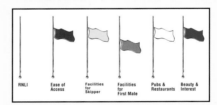

Moorings:
Hollowshore Services
Contact: Manager
Hollowshore, Faversham, Kent ME13 7TU
Tel: 01795 532317

Brents Boatyard
Contact: Manager
The Old Shipyard, Upper Brents, Faversham,
ME13 7DR Tel: 01795 591159 Fax: 01795 538656

Iron Wharf Boatyard
Contact: Manager
Iron Wharf, Abbeyfields, Faversham ME13 7BT

Oare Creek

Moorings:
Youngboats
Contact: Manager
Oare Creek, Faversham, Kent ME13 7TX
Tel: 01795 536176

Conyer Creek

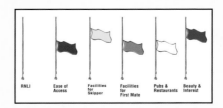

Conyer Marine
Contact: Manager
Conyer Quay, Teynham, Sittingbourne Kent
ME9 9HW Tel: 01795 521285
VHF Ch: 16/37/80 VHF Name: Alberdina

Swale Marina   51.21'.0N 00.49'.0E
Contact: Manager
Conyer Wharf, Teynham, Sittingbourne, Kent
ME9 9HP

Conyer Cruising Club
Mrs L Weekes: Secretary
c/o Swale Marina, Conyer, Sittingbourne,
Kent ME9 9HP

Repairs: contact Swale Marina Office for all
repairs
Wilkinson Sails, The Sila Loft, Conyer,
Teynham, Kent Tel: 01795 521503

Kingsferry Bridge
VHF Ch: 10 VHF Name: Kingsferry Bridge

WHITSTABLE

John Clayton: Harbourmaster
Tel: 01227 274086 Fax: 01227 265441
VHF Channel: 9/12/16
VHF Name: Whitstable Harbour Radio

Whitstable Yacht Club
Tel: 01227 274086

Chandlers:
Goldfinch Sails, Sea Wall, Whitstable
Tel: 01227 272295

Whitstable Lifeboat
Open to visitors: Easter to September – check
with D Lamberton (Hon. Sec.)
Hon. Sec. Tel: 01227 262305

MARGATE

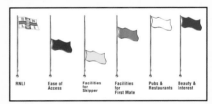

Margate Yacht Club 01843 292602

Margate Lifeboat
The Rendezvous, Margate, CT9 3XJ
Open to visitors: usually daily 1000-1430
between Whitsun and end of September but
please phone to check
Boathouse Tel: 01843 221613

RAMSGATE   51.19'.5N 01.25'.5E

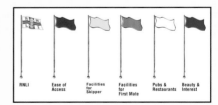

Ramsgate Royal Harbour and Marina
Capt. Ken Gray: Harbourmaster
Harbour Office, Military Road, Ramsgate
CT11 9LQ Tel: 01843 592277 Fax: 01843 590941
VHF Ch: 80 VHF Name: Ramsgate Marina

Before entering or leaving Royal Harbour,
call Ramsgate Port Control on Channel 14

Chandlers:
Bosun's Locker
Military Road, Ramsgate, Kent
Tel: 01843 582158 Fax: 01843 597158

General repairs:
Nicholls & Bailey Tel: 01843 582389
Engine repairs:
Davis Marine Tel: 01843 586172
Sail repairs:
Northrop Sails, 29 Military Road, Ramsgate
Tel: 01843 851665

Ramsgate Lifeboat
Open to visitors: All year by arrangement
with Capt. G Tully (Hon. Sec.) or Ron
Cannon (Cox'n)
Hon. Sec. Tel: 01843 227324
Cox'n Tel: 01843 602905

DOVER

Kevin Richardson: Harbourmaster
Tel: 01304 240400 Fax: 01304 241274
VHF Channel: 74/12/16
VHF Name: Dover Port Control

Dover Marina
Tony Greening & Dave Austen: Marina
Supervisors

DOVER cont.

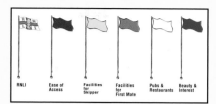

RNLI / Ease of Access / Facilities for Skipper / Facilities for First Mate / Pubs & Restaurants / Beauty & Interest

Dover, Kent CT17 9TF
Tel: 01304 241663 Fax: 01304 242549
VHF - use only when within the harbour:
Channel 80 VHF Name: Dover Marina

Chandlers:
Dover marine Supplies, The Clock Tower
Building, Western Dock, Dover
Tel: 01304 201677 Fax: 01304 201542
Sharp & Enright, Snargate Street, Dover
CT16 9DA Tel: 01304 206295

Repairs:
Dover Yacht Company, Cambridge Road,
Dover, Kent CT17 9BY
Tel: 01304 201073 Fax: 01304 207458

Engine repairs:
Ensign Marine Services Ltd, Wellington Dock,
Union Street, Dover Kent CT13 9BY
Tel: 01304 240004
Parts: 01304 241200
Fax: 01304 242520

Royal Cinque Ports Yacht Club
Carol Partridge: Secretary
Waterloo Crescent, Dover, Kent CT16 1LA
Tel: 01304 206262

Dover Lifeboat
Tug Haven, Clarence Quay, Western Docks,
Dover Kent CT17 9TF
Open to visitors: by appointment to view
lifeboat only – contact Capt. P. White (Hon.
Sec.) Boathouse Tel: 01304 204280
Hon. Sec. Tel (Home): 01304 812534

South East England - Chart Agents

Stratton Long, Sheringham Tel: 01263 740362
Charity & Taylor, Lowestoft Tel: 01502 581529
Aldeburgh Boatyard, Aldeburgh Tel: 01778 452019
Small Craft Deliveries, Woodbridge Tel: 01394 386664
Fox's Marina, Ipswich Tel: 01473 689111
Wyatt's Chandlery, Colchester Tel: 01206 384745
Cruiser Mart, Southend-on-Sea Tel: 01702 444423
Bosun's Locker, Ramsgate Tel: 01843 597158
Sharp & Enwright, Dover Tel: 01304 206295

South East England - Pilot Books

North Sea Waypoint Directory
published by Adlard Coles Nautical Tel: 0171 2420946 ISBN: 0713 647 99X

North Sea Passage Pilot 3rd Ed. 1998, Brian Navin
published by Imray, Laurie, Norie & Wilson Tel: 01480 462114, ISBN 0852 883 935

The East Coast. New 4th Ed. 1998, Derek Bowskill
published by Imray, Laurie, Norie & WilsonTel: 01480 462114, ISBN 0852 881 584

East Coast Rivers. New 16th Ed. 1998, Jack Coote
published by Airlife Publishing Tel: 01743 232944 ISBN: 1852 771 461

North Sea (West) Pilot. 4th Ed. 1997
published by United Kingdom Hydrographic Office, ISBN: 0707 710 545

Dover Strait Pilot, 1997
published by United Kingdom Hydrographic Office, ISBN: 0707 710 286

Yachting Guide to Harwich Harbour and its Rivers.
free from Harwich Haven Authority Tel: 01255 243030

Yachtsman's Guide, Pleasure Users Guide, Leisure Guide
all free from Port of London Authority, Devon House, 58 - 60 St Katherine's Way, London E1 9LB Tel: 0171 265 2656

The South Coast

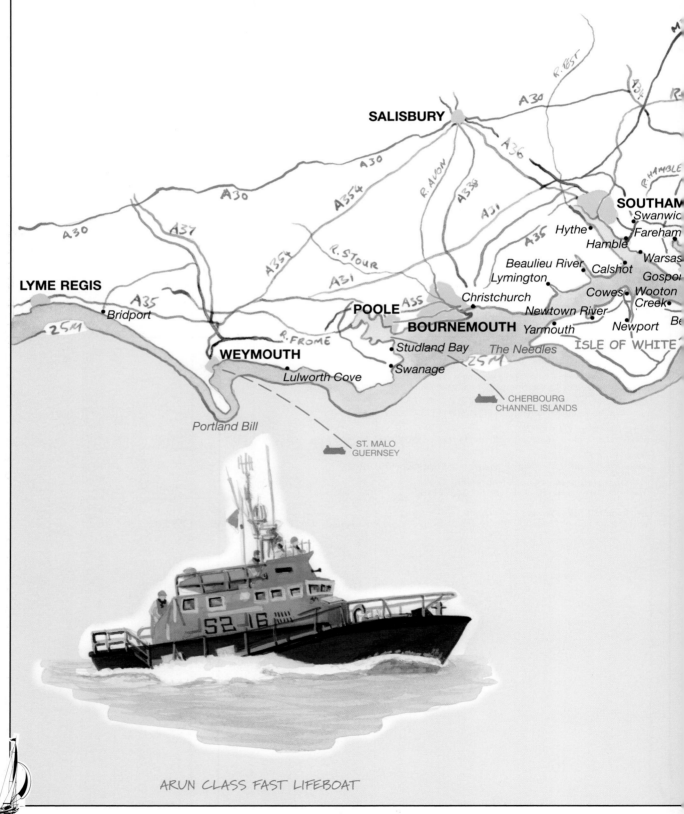

SALISBURY

SOUTHAM

Swanwic

Hythe

Fareham

Hamble

Warsas

Beaulieu River   Calshot   Gospo

Lymington   Cowes   Wooton

Christchurch   Newtown River   Creek

POOLE   Newport   Be

BOURNEMOUTH   Yarmouth

LYME REGIS   ISLE OF WHITE

Bridport

Studland Bay   The Needles

WEYMOUTH   Swanage

Lulworth Cove

CHERBOURG
CHANNEL ISLANDS

Portland Bill

ST. MALO
GUERNSEY

A30, A354, A37, A35, A31, R. STOUR, R. AVON, A338, A36, R. FROME, R. HAMBLE, R. TEST, 25M

ARUN CLASS FAST LIFEBOAT

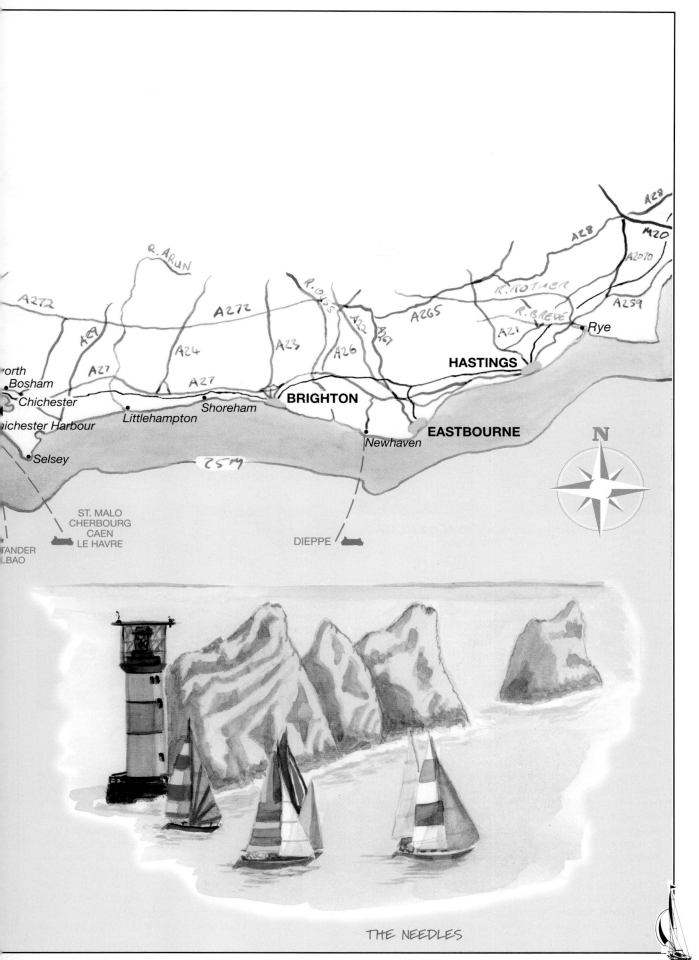

THE NEEDLES

East & West Sussex

After the rather grim bleakness of Dungeness with its dour view of power station and deserted foreshore, the atmosphere changes completely soon after you pass the border between Kent and East Sussex. The East and West Sussex coast is extensively built up with a series of seaside holiday resorts which boast sandy beaches, piers and Punch and Judy. There are marinas at Eastbourne, Brighton and Bognor Regis for you to get ashore with your bucket and spade easily. There's variety as well, with the rivers at Rye, Newhaven and Shoreham offering opportunities to visit places with more of a maritime than seaside emphasis. The impressive bulk of recently modified Beachy Head and its new extended foreshore is the central landmark on this stretch.

Artist: **Anthony Flemming BEACHY HEAD**
Courtesy of: **The Artist**

Rye

One of the ancient Cinque Ports, Rye no longer has large amounts of commercial traffic, though there is some - listen on Channel 14 to find out if anything is about to arrive or depart. This is a river which offers challenging pilotage with strong tides and limited time to work with as it dries out completely (soft mud) and the entrance is only readily navigable for a couple of hours each side of high water. Beware of the training wall which runs up the middle of the river and is submerged (but clearly marked) at high water. Rye Harbour Nature Reserve is on the west bank, and is a breeding ground for black-headed and herring gulls, grey herons, little and common terns, oystercatchers and ringed plovers. **Rye Harbour** is about 3/4 mile upriver, and is a small village separate from Rye itself. Here you will find the harbour-master's Office (Be sure to contact the harbour-master to get a river licence) and a reasonable selection of yachtsmen's facilities and the William the Conqueror which has a good menu of pub food. You probably don't want to stop here for long as Rye itself is another 2 miles up river - and that is where you want to be.

The Strand Quay is close to the heart of old Rye. Narrow cobbled streets climb up to St Mary's Church which dates back to Norman times. Mermaid Street, with its famous half-timbered inn The Mermaid, is a classic example, and was traditionally the haunt of smugglers. The attics of several of the houses interconnect for easy escape from the excise men! From 1898 to 1916, Rye was the home of the American novelist Henry James, and you can visit Lamb House (NT ☎ 01892 890651) where he lived - another author, E.F. Benson, also lived in the same house later. There are a number of museums including the Rye Heritage Centre on Strand Quay and the Ypres Tower, all that remains of Rye Castle, where one of the world's oldest fire engines is among the exhibits.

As well as the Mermaid (☎ 01797 223065), there are many good places for a drink or a meal. The Ypres Castle (☎ 01797 223248) behind the Ypres Tower has good views across the harbour from its garden and benefits from being slightly off the beaten track. The Old Forge Restaurant (☎ 01797 223227) on Wish Street and Casa Conti (☎ 01927 222574) are good options for a restaurant meal. Budgens supermarket is about 400 yards from the quay, and you can also buy fresh fish from the fishing boats which moor in the Rother.

Taxi:	Sean's Taxis (☎ 01797 225774)
	mobile (☎ 0468 854980)
Car hire:	Rye Service (☎ 01797 225535)
Cycle hire:	Rye Hire, Cyprus Place (☎ 01797 223033)
Bus:	South Coast Buses (☎ 01424 433711)
Rail:	direct services to Brighton and London, Charing Cross
Airport:	Gatwick Airport is about 35 miles away.

for more details, see Directory Section

Artist: **Anthony Flemming RYE**
Courtesy of: **The Artist**

Rye to Eastbourne

A strip of muddy, shingly beach runs west from the mouth of the River Rother. By the time you reach **Hastings**, this is backed by imposing sandstone cliffs. Hastings, another of the ancient Cinque Ports, is now still a fishing town and also a beach resort with a pier. In settled weather, you can anchor and there are landing places on the pier. The old town is built on steep hillsides and is interesting to explore, though the lack of facilities for yachts will probably result in a short stay. The Stag in All Saints Street does bar meals at weekends, and good beer and lunch can be found at The First In, Last Out on the High Street, or for a simple meal, try

Roser's Restaurant (☎ 01424 712218) in Eversfield Place on the seafront.

Pressing on from Hastings, you pass the dignified resort town of Bexhill whose shingle beach was, racily, the first place in Britain to allow mixed bathing at the turn of the century. The long sweeping curve of Pevensey Bay has a coastline rather cluttered with chalets and small houses; this is real summer holiday country, and Eastbourne is heaving into view.

Artist: **Anthony Flemming HASTINGS**
Courtesy of: **The Artist**

Eastbourne

The Sovereign Harbour Marina offers comprehensive facilities and is right next to a retail park which includes an Asda Superstore and a multi-screen cinema. There are shops, pubs and restaurants along the The Waterfront which borders the marina. This is not a quaint or historic harbour as it was only recently created in the early 1990s, but being a purpose built leisure marina, all facilities and services are conveniently located and considerable trouble has been taken to offer everything you could hope for in a new development. You can get into the marina at any state of the tide via a two metre dredged channel and twin locks to the inner basin. The Sovereign Harbour Yacht Club welcomes visitors and the bar is open seven days a week during the season. Meals are available at weekends or by prior arrangement. This well appointed marina attracts visitors from all over Europe, and even further afield, so you will have the opportunity to meet the crews of yachts with a wide variety of home ports.

The centre of Eastbourne itself is a couple of miles away, but there is a regular bus service from the marina. Eastbourne is a large beach resort town with three miles of seafront which includes a pier, bandstand and well maintained public gardens. The architecture is largely Victorian - giving a clue to the period in which the town achieved major popularity as a holiday destination. The old lifeboat station on King Edward Parade is now a Lifeboat Museum (☎ 01323 730717) with models of lifeboats, photographic history of Eastbourne lifeboats and other memorabilia. The Lifeboat is now based at Sovereign Harbour. Next door to the Lifeboat Museum in a restored Martello Tower is The Wish Tower Puppet Museum (☎ 01323 417776) which has puppets from all over the world and of course the

local staple, Punch and Judy. More military contents can be found in the Redoubt Fortress (☎ 01323 410300) which claims to be the South East's largest military museum with 14 large galleries of exhibits. Also towards the east end of the seafront and not far from the marina, you can play crazy golf, try being land-locked for a change on the Boating Lake (☎ 01323 415465) or get behind the wheel at Formula Fun Go-Karts (☎ 01323 642833).

Taxi:	Pier Cars (☎ 0500 515250) or freephone by pressing *1 on the public phone in the shower block
Car hire:	Practical Car & Van Hire (☎ 01323 412219)
Cycle hire:	Marina Office, May-September
Bus:	services to town centre
Rail:	from town centre to other coastal destinations and London Victoria
Airport:	Gatwick Airport is about 35 miles away

for more details, see Directory Section

Artist: **Anthony Flemming THE SEVEN SISTERS**
Courtesy of: **The Artist**

Eastbourne to Newhaven

Leaving Eastbourne and looking west, the massive shoulder of Beachy Head stands out over 500 feet high. As you approach and the lighthouse emerges from behind the cliff, you may be able to see the recent extension to the foreshore where collapsing cliffs have all but linked the lighthouse to the beach. The undulating clifftops of the Seven Sisters stretch away into the distance as you clear the headland - while they are nothing like as high as Beachy Head, the flowing lines of chalky cliffs are an impressive sight.

Newhaven

Here is a more traditional harbour between the new and artificial havens which have been created at Brighton and Eastbourne - or so you might think. In fact, in the overall scheme of things, this is quite a new harbour as well as it was created in 1579 when a great storm caused the River Ouse to find a new mouth - it previously having joined the sea at Seaford a few miles down the coast. Hence 'New' haven - as distinct from the old one! Visit the Newhaven Local and Maritime Museum (☎ 01273 514760) to find out more about the history and background of the town. You might be interested to learn that the RNLI station here was, in

1904, the first to use a motor lifeboat which was sent here for trials (see directory for details of the station if you would like to visit it). The river runs through the town down to the marina on the outskirts. There's a maritime tradition here as well, so watch out for ferries and other commercial vessels as you come in - remember to pay attention to traffic signals. The marina has pontoon berths available for visitors and most facilities (but no petrol, gas or laundry), and chandlery and repairs are close to hand. There is also a Yacht Club on site with bars, restaurant and showers as well as an excellent Italian Restaurant, Villa Adriana (☎ 01273 513976). The Coral Cabin Café (☎ 01273 516143), also on site, offers more modest meals and if you are in search of a pub meal, we would suggest either the Hope Inn (☎ 01273 515389) or the Sheffield Arms which are both in Fort Road and only a short walk from the marina. There's a reasonable general store close by, but for comprehensive shopping facilities, you need to get to the centre of town which is just under a mile away.

Taxi:	Newhaven Taxis (☎ 01273 611111)
Bus:	local services from town centre
Rail:	Newhaven Town Railway Station – services to London Victoria via Lewes
Airport:	London-Gatwick 45 minutes away by road or accessible by rail

for more details, see Directory Section

Brighton

Brighton's roots as the small fishing village of Brightelmstone have long since been submerged in the South Coast's most famous seaside resort. A Dissertation Concerning the Uses of Sea Water in Diseases of the Glands by Dr Richard Russell of Lewes recommended bathing in and drinking seawater for the prevention of a wide range of ailments. Attendants were on hand to ensure that the fashionable visitors to Brighton took their medicine and were totally immersed in it. Brighton's centrepiece, the Royal Pavilion, owes its existence to the Prince Regent, later George IV. Indeed, the growth of the town, and its Georgian elegance, are largely a result of George's extravagant patronage. The Pavilion was completed in about 1820 and was the work of the architect John Nash, perhaps better known and respected for his elegant terraces in the West End of London. The Pavilion is a whimsical combination of styles representing George's interests in Chinese and Indian influences and was not popular with the population at large. It provided a focus for dissatisfaction with the lavish Royal lifestyle at a time when many were suffering deprivation. Members of the public are now welcome to enjoy the Pavilion for themselves, though our enjoyment of its finery may well be tempered by astonishment at the indulgence with which those who were entertained there were treated! There is a vast range of other interesting buildings, museums, galleries and other attractions to explore, including the pedestrianised narrow streets of the old village where you can indulge yourself in a little boutique browsing.

The marina is well placed at the end of the Volks Electric Railway, the first of its kind, which runs between the marina and the Palace Pier. The Prince Regent's tendency to do things on a large scale is clearly still part of Brighton's culture, and Brighton Marina is no exception being, as it is, the largest marina in Britain. You can get in at all states of the tide, though sometimes low water springs might cause slight difficulties, and the entrance is not easy in south easterly gales. There's an Asda Superstore right next to the marina and a wide range of shops and eating and drinking establishments not to mention the multi-screen cinema and 10 pin bowling centre just west of the marina. There's also quite a lot of waterside residential development which does mean that you don't need to feel that you have come to rest in a retail park. The beach to the west is reserved for naturists, though rest assured, this is a refined area - Roedean School is just across the road!

Taxi:	Streamline (☎ 01273 747474)
Car hire:	Avis (☎ 01273 673738)
Bus:	services from marina to town centre, thence national network
Rail:	Brighton Station, links to other coastal destinations and London
Airport:	Gatwick Airport (☎ 01293 535353) 25 miles, Shoreham Airport (☎ 01273 452304), 5 miles

for more details, see Directory Section

Artist: **Anthony Flemming BRIGHTON**
Courtesy of: **The Artist**

Shoreham

Old Shoreham and its Saxon Church of St Nicholas lie well up the River Adur and found themselves superseded as the river silted up. The Normans began a newer town further south on the peninsula to give easier access to the sea. Southwick on the north bank merges with Hove and Brighton, but still has its own focus - the village green survives and is a good spot for a stroll. Shoreham has continued to value transport links into the twentieth century and boasts the oldest airport in Britain which has an interesting art deco terminal building. Also at the airport, you will find the Museum of D-Day Aviation (☎ 0374 971971). The Marlipins Museum (☎ 01273 462994) in Shoreham High Street is also worth a visit - you'll find displays relating to local history, especially the town's maritime history. After 43 days on the run following his defeat by Oliver Cromwell at Worcester in September 1651, it was in Shoreham that Charles II found a ship to enable him to escape to France. Whether this is a claim to fame or infamy it is difficult to say!

The current harbour and marina (managed by the harbour authority) are in the East Arm and canal which lie to the South of Southwick. The Sussex Yacht Club has clubhouses both at Shoreham - up the West Arm which dries and has limited moorings for visitors - and at Southwick by the Lady Bee Marina which is through the lock in the East Arm. There is a good range of possibilities for provisioning within reach of the marina, and the intimacy of this small refuge with just over a hundred berths may well appeal to those who feel that neighbouring Brighton is just too big! The Crown and Anchor in Shoreham High Street is a good pub for a drink and the Schooner (☎ 01273 592252) in Southwick does good pub meals. There is a wide variety of restaurants within easy reach of either of the Sussex Yacht Club's locations including Indian, Italian and Vietnamese cuisine. One of the best in the area is the Indian Cottage Tandoori (☎ 01273 453379) in Shoreham High Street.

Littlehampton

It's about ten miles from the mouth of the Adur at Shoreham to the mouth of the Arun at Littlehampton. This resort town enjoys good sandy beaches though the sand might not be quite so popular with the yachtsman - there's a sandbar at the entrance to the river which makes access to the river difficult or impossible for a couple of hours each side of low water. This narrow river has strong tides, so you will need to plan your arrival accordingly. There's a choice of moorings available. The first you come to as you head up the river is the Littlehampton Sailing and Motor Club which is accessible for three hours each side of high water for shallow draft vessels. Adjacent is the Arun Yacht Club which also has some moorings for visitors. On the town side of the river, the east bank, you can berth at the Town Quay, or you might prefer to head on up to the Littlehampton Marina which is about 3/4 mile from the mouth of the river. Contact the Harbour Office in advance to arrange for the footbridge below the marina to be opened. This is a well equipped little marina with no tidal access constraints other than those generally applying to navigation on the river. There's a floating pub and restaurant and a café on site and the marina is set on the edge of the town about half a mile from the centre. There are good shopping facilities in the town, but it is about a mile to the supermarket.

Small vessels can navigate further up river, and those without masts can get well beyond Arundel which is a characterful town and has a spectacular castle which towers over the flood plain. The Wildfowl & Wetlands Trust (☎ 01903 883355) manages a Site of Special Scientific Interest here and you can see ducks, geese and swans from all over the world. At Ford, which is about halfway to Arundel, there's another small marina for shallow draft boats.

Chichester Harbour

Chichester Harbour, set in an area of outstanding natural beauty, is a vast natural harbour with over 11 square miles of water and 17 miles of navigable channels. This is a haven for wildlife as well as yachtsmen, and the vast areas of mudflats are a popular wintering ground for a variety of wildfowl and waders. During the breeding season, you can see common and sand-wich terns, redshanks, shelduck and ringed plover. For wildlife and yachtsman alike, there's good shelter to be had throughout, and a mixture of open countryside and attractive villages for a variety of outlooks. Just inside the entrance, there's a good sandy beach on the east shore which is a popular place for bucket and spade work – drop the anchor and paddle ashore. This is a popular cruising ground, so there are plenty of facilities for yachts. While it can be quite busy as something of the order of 10,000 boats are kept here, you can find tranquil spots for peace and quiet.

Artist: **Anthony Flemming BIRDHAM, CHICHESTER HARBOUR** *Courtesy of:* **The Artist**

At the east end of the harbour's series of channels is Chichester itself. As the channel narrows to round Chaldock Point, Bosham Channels winds off to the north and you pass **Itchenor** on the south bank. This is where the Chichester Harbour Conservancy is based, and the harbour-master will direct you to a mooring or pontoon berth if you wish to stop here. This is a popular base for dinghy sailing, though you will find most facilities are available for yachts as well (early closing day is Thursday). As you head on up the channel, you come to two marinas not far from **Chichester**. The Birdham Shipyard at Birdham Pool is a small marina with a good range of facilities and it's situated not far from the small village of Birdham. There are not many berths for visitors, and access is limited to three hours each side of high water. Access to neighbouring Chichester Marina is less constrained by the tide as it is only inaccessible for about three hours around low water. This is a large marina run by Premier Marinas set in open agricultural countryside. There's a bar and restaurant on site and it's also the home of the Chichester Yacht Club which has bar and restaurant facilities and welcomes visiting yachtsmen.

The town of Chichester is only a short bus or taxi ride away and is well worth a visit. The main street plan was laid out by the Romans who founded the town in AD70 and built the original city walls. Rebuilt in flint in Medieval times, you can walk round the walls and enjoy splendid views both into and out of the city. The centre of the town around the Tudor Market Cross is pedestrianised making it attractive for visitors to stroll around. Close to the centre is Chichester Cathedral (☎ 01243 782595) which was dedicated in 1108 and boasts a window by Chagall, a painting by Sutherland, a tapestry by Piper, Lambert Barnard's beautiful Lady Chapel ceiling

Artist: **Anthony Flemming BOSHAM QUAY, CHICHESTER HARBOUR** *Courtesy of:* **The Artist**

and it's the final resting place of composer Gustav Holst (1874-1934). Also close to the centre is Pallant House (☎ 01243 774557), a fine Queen Anne town house which houses a major collection of recent (c.1890-1965) paintings and fine antique furniture, porcelain, glass and textiles. Also worth a look while in the town are the Chichester District Museum (☎ 01243 784683) at 29 Little London and The Guildhall (open on Saturdays or by appointment – contact the museum) in the Priory Park. Just outside the town, the Mechanical Music and Doll Collection (☎ 01243 785421) offers an unusual and interesting historical perspective, and not far away, the Tangmere Military

Aviation Museum (☎ 01243 775223) provides a contrast. At the top of the Chichester Channel, and just to the west of the city, you may be interested by the excavations of the Roman Palace at Fishbourne (☎ 01243 785859). Here you can see fine mosaic floors, under-floor heating systems and the bath suite (all under cover) and a replanted formal Roman garden.

Off the Chichester Channel and before you reach Birdham, the **Bosham** Channel winds up to the pretty waterside village of Bosham. If you are happy to take the ground, you can tie up to the Quay, or you can contact the Quaymaster who might be able to find you a mooring (anchoring is forbidden in this channel). Alternatively, you may prefer to visit with someone else at the helm by taking the ferry up from Itchenor. On the Quay, you will find Bosham Sailing Club which welcomes visiting yachtsmen, and close to the waterfront, the Anchor Bleu (☎ 01243 573956) which is handy for a drink or a pub meal. A good alternative is the Barclay Arms (☎ 01243 573167) which is a short walk away up the High Street. It's worth the trip to East Ashling for good beer and grub at the Horse & Groom (☎ 01243 575339) and if you want a good restaurant meal, The Millstream Hotel & Restaurant (☎ 01243 573234) is the best place to head for.

Roughly parallel to Bosham Channel and to the west, running up the east side of Thorney Island is Thorney Channel. You can anchor off Pilsey Island which is an RSPB bird sanctuary (no landing) at the mouth, or further up you might be able to use the visitors' mooring at

Emsworth Yacht Harbour

Emsworth Yacht Harbour is found at the northern extreme of Chichester Harbour and offers a comprehensive range of facilities for the visiting yachtsman.

The sheltered site which has been recently dredged has 200 berths on four pontoons and is only 10 minutes walk away from the village which boasts several shops, pubs and restaurants.

To make your stay a comfortable one, the marina can offer showers and toilets, water and electricity, and diesel, calor and camping gas.

If your craft requires any repairs or maintenance you will find that you are well catered for at Emsworth, with workshops, chandlery and an outboard specialist as well as a 25 tonne mobile crane, a launching slipway, a drying out grid and a mast crane. Longer stays can be arranged in the serviced hardstanding and storage areas.

This friendly marina is set in a sheltered area of outstanding natural beauty and is an excellent port of call for any yachtsman.

Emsworth Yacht Harbour
Thorney Road
Emsworth
Hants PO10 8PB
Tel: (01243) 377727
Fax: (01243) 373432

Thorney Island Sailing Club. There are drying berths at Thornham Marina which is accessible for about an hour each side of high water. Between Hayling Island and the west of Thorney Island, the Emsworth Channel marks the west edge of Chichester Harbour. This is popular yachting territory and there are numerous sailing clubs and two more marinas. At the head of the channel, you will find **Emsworth** which is an attractive waterside village with a long maritime pedigree. The oyster fishing and boat building which were the main local trades continue, though now on a reduced scale. Striking features at the harbour front are the mill ponds which served the two tide mills which have been restored for use by a gallery, sailing club, several small businesses and for residential accommodation. Brick and rendered Georgian houses make up many of the charming narrow streets and there are plenty of pubs, restaurants and boutiques for gentle browsing.

For a meal ashore, 36 On the Quay (☎ 01243 375592) on South Street, overlooking Chichester Harbour, comes highly recommended for intimate dining, as does Spencers (☎ 01243 375592) on North Street, with à la carte dinners and a brasserie downstairs. Julie's (☎ 01234 377914) also on South Street, is good for a relaxed meal. The Crown (☎ 01243 372806) on High Street is handy for a drink as is the Kings Arms (☎ 01243 374941) on Havant Road where you will find good, reasonably priced food.

The Tarquin Yacht Harbour is accessible for about two hours each side of the high water, offering pontoon berths close to the centre of Emsworth. On the other side of the channel and right at the north end of Hayling Island, Northney Marina has unrestricted access and all the facilities you would expect from a Marina Developments marina. About half a mile away, you'll find a good general store, but it's three or four miles to more comprehensive shopping facilities, so this is not an ideal spot for major re-provisioning. There's a bar and restaurant on site, or you might like to nip across the bridge to Langstone where The Ship Inn (☎ 023 9247 1719) is a good spot for a drink or a pub meal (taxi: 023 9245 1440). At the south end of the island, the Sparkes Yacht harbour is usefully accessible at all states of the tide. It offers a good refuge for those just popping into Chichester Harbour as it's just inside the entrance, or might provide a good launch pad for further exploration or indeed a jumping off point for those leaving the harbour with the next favourable tide. Chandlery and repair facilities are available as are full marina facilities and it's a short walk to Hayling Island Sailing Club where there is a bar and restaurant and a welcome for visitors from outside Chichester Harbour as long as you contact them in advance. The Mariners Tavern at the marina is comfortably furnished and offers a range of food from sandwiches to three course meals. It's a bit of a hike to shopping or other pubs and restaurants in South Hayling, so a taxi might be called for (☎ Somerfield Cars 023 9246 7381 or AJS Taxis 023 9246 9333) to get you to the supermarket or the shops in Mengham Village. The Lifeboat Inn (☎ 023 9246 3624) a couple of miles away on the Sea Front is a good place for a drink, and it's about a mile to the Kittiwake (☎ 023 9246 3489) on Sandy Point Road which does pub food. On the west side of the island, Ma Baker's (☎ 023 9246 3226) is worth the taxi ride, as is the Newtown House

Hotel (☎ 023 9246 6131) in Manor Road. Also in Manor Road, the Barley Mow does good pub food.

Hampshire

Hampshire can justly claim to be the central focus for yachting in the British Isles in terms of the number of places you can sail to and, perhaps less thrillingly, in terms of the colossal number of boats which are kept along the coast here. Stretching from Chichester Harbour to Lymington, it includes Portsmouth, the Hamble, Southampton and the Solent. This is a popular and populated place to go sailing and with good reason. Easy access to the Isle of Wight is also an attraction. The sheltered waters of the Solent may become rather busy at times, especially during sunny summer weekends, but there are spectacular views to be enjoyed, attractive and interesting towns and villages to visit and even occasional opportunities for peace and quiet.

Langstone Harbour

Though Langstone Harbour is accessible from Chichester Harbour via a narrow and shallow channel around the north end of Hayling Island, the bridge and electricity cables which link the island to the mainland mean that only small craft can pass through. Most will have to enter from the sea between Portsmouth and Hayling Island. Langstone offers a welcome haven to those who would rather not fight with all the commercial shipping in the entrance to Portsmouth Harbour, and also to those who may prefer to avoid the tricky entrance to Chichester Harbour and all its leisure traffic. The entrance is narrow, but not difficult unless the wind is strong from the south when it can be dangerous. Once inside, visitors should report to the harbourmaster. You can pick up a mooring or go alongside briefly to pick up stores on the Hayling (east) side which is where the harbour office is based. If you wish to anchor further up in the harbour, it's worth consulting the harbour-master to check on how to avoid the gravel dredgers which operate in the harbour day and night. Don't let this put you off, there's plenty of tranquillity here and many of the mudflats and low islands are owned by the RSPB. This is a Site of Special Scientific Interest, and an important breeding ground for little terns, ringed plovers and redshanks.

If you are in search of a pontoon berth, Southsea Marina, just inside the entrance on the west side, is not far from Portsmouth and gives you the opportunity to visit the town without sailing into the harbour (see next entry for details). There's a bar and a restaurant and it's not too far to go to get provisions - marina staff will gladly give you a lift. Chandlery, diesel and gas are available 24 hours a day, and the marina is accessible for about 3 hours each side of high water.

Portsmouth Harbour

The large natural harbour at Portsmouth has played a significant role in Britain's maritime history for well over half a millennium. As well as being a centre for fishing and a major terminal for ferry traffic, Portsmouth is perhaps most famous for its role in military history. The Naval Dockyard, which was established in Tudor times, formalised its role as a key element in the defence of the realm, and the considerable fortifications around the town and the entrance to the harbour bear testament to how highly its strategic importance has been valued. Much of Portsmouth's shoreline within the harbour is still run by the Navy. Much of what is of historic interest can be visited under the banner "Flagship Portsmouth" (☎ 023 9286 1512). The centrepiece for most people is Nelson's flagship HMS Victory, and there are older and newer warships to see as well. The Mary Rose, which capsized and sank in 1545, is preserved here and there's a museum of artefacts which have been recovered from the wreck site. Also on display is HMS Warrior which was the world's first iron-clad warship, serving usefully as a deterrent to foreign naval powers after her launch in 1860. For those who would like a look at more modern warships, tours by motorboat offer a view of some of the Royal Navy's current state-of-the-art vessels. The Royal Navy Museum is also well worth a look and gives a good overview - it includes fine paintings and displays which illustrate the history of the "Senior Service". Never quite leaving the dockyards behind, you can explore the atmospheric narrow streets of the Old Town - in places little has changed since Jack Aubrey and Stephen Maturin might have known them (as readers of Patrick O'Brian's Napoleonic War stories will appreciate). Literary connections do not end there as, in 1812, Charles Dickens was born here (visit the Charles Dickens Birthplace Museum ☎ 023 9287 2261 at 393 Old Commercial Road) and Arthur Conan Doyle was resident in Portsmouth when, in 1886, he first wrote of the great detective Sherlock Holmes. Portsmouth's seaside face at Southsea has more of a resort feel and there's a large funfair at Clarence Pier, though the military connections are still obvious with Southsea Castle (☎ 023 9282 7261) and the D-Day Museum (☎ 023 9282 7261) on Clarence Esplanade. Don't overlook the Royal Marines Museum (☎ 023 9281 9385) which is just along the coast at Eastney.

Artist: **Anthony Flemming** **PORTSMOUTH HARBOUR** *Courtesy of:* **The Artist**

Traffic in the narrow entrance to the harbour is strictly controlled, and most yachts will need to stick to the Small Boat Channel. The tide can be quite strong, so unless you have a very powerful engine, you will need to pick your moment to enter accordingly. The options for finding a berth along the Portsmouth harbourfront are limited. If you are lucky, you might be able to get a visitors' mooring from the Royal Naval Club and Royal Albert Yacht Club which has splendid premises in Old Portsmouth, or there's very limited space at the Town Quay in the Camber (contact "Portsmouth Harbour Radio" on Channel 11 or 14) close to Portsmouth Sailing Club. Most will content themselves with one of the big marinas on the **Gosport** (west) side where pontoon berths and comprehensive yachting facilities are available. Gosport Marina (formerly Camper & Nicholson's) has some visitors' berths or you could try Gosport Boatyard, but you will probably find it easiest to get into Haslar Marina which is the first one you come to anyway. Most facilities are on hand here, though if you require diesel or petrol you need to go to the fuel barge just inside the entrance to Gosport Marina. There's a full range of shops for provisions including a supermarket on Gosport High Street which is within walking distance and there's a street market here every Tuesday and Saturday. You needn't feel cut off as there's a ferry close at hand to take you across to Portsmouth. You might also be interested to visit the Royal Navy Submarine Museum (☎ 023 9252 9217) which is on this side of the harbour just over the Haslar Bridge. Here you can explore the WWII submarine HMS Alliance and learn about the history of submarines through a number of hands-on displays.

Artist: **Anthony Flemming** **PORTSMOUTH** *Courtesy of:* **The Artist**

A converted lightship in the marina, "The Mary Mouse" (☎ 023 9260 1819) has washing and laundry facilities and a good bar and restaurant. If you fancy a stroll ashore to find a meal, The Castle (☎ 023 9258 3991) which is on Mumby Road just by the Gosport-Portsmouth Ferry does a reasonable pub meal. Here you will also find the De Café for an inexpensive restaurant meal, or if you want something a bit more elaborate, try The Pebble Beach (☎ 023 9251 0789) which is a short taxi ride away by the Stokes Bay Sailing Club. Local knowledge suggests that one of the best in the area is The Great Wall of China (☎ 023 9250 3388) which is also just by the ferry in the High Street.

Taxi: Streamline (☎ 023 9252 2222)
Car hire: Avis (☎ 0990 900500)

Bus:	from Gosport High Street, services to Southampton, Portsmouth, Fareham and links to national network
Rail:	via ferry to Portsmouth Harbour Station, direct services to London
Ferry:	local ferry to Portsmouth. from Portsmouth to Isle of Wight and France
Airport:	Southampton or London Heathrow or Gatwick

for more details, see Directory Section

Artist: **Moira Huntly THE DONALD SEARLE OFF GOSPORT** *Courtesy of:* **The Artist**

Inland

At the north end of Portsmouth Harbour, there's a large marina at Portchester with a full range of first class facilities including shops, restaurants, cafés and a pub all on site or close to hand. From **Port Solent Marina**, the centre of Portsmouth is a bus or taxi ride away. You may, however, be content to explore Portchester Castle (EH ☎ 023 9237 8291) which frowns down at the marina, or a little further away, the Royal Armouries – Museum of Artillery (☎ 01329 233734) at the sprawling mass of Fort Nelson on Down End Road. For more modern entertainment, there's a six screen cinema by the marina. Alternatively, you might consider the smaller scale of things up towards Fareham. Moorings are often available from Wicor Marine or, if you can get under the electricity cables and don't mind a channel which dries, there are drying pontoons at Fareham Yacht Harbour and, at the lower quay by the town, Fareham Marina has a few visitors' berths and some moorings. Basic facilities are available on site. The Fareham Sailing and Motor Boat Club just next door welcomes visitors from other clubs and there's a pub adjacent as well. The Bird in Hand (☎ 01329 280841) on Gosport Road boasts good beer and live music, and about ten minutes walk away in the High Street, Edwins Brasserie (☎ 01329 221338) serves restaurant meals. A good range of reasonable shops for provisions, including a supermarket, can be found in the High Street.

River Hamble

There are moorings and berths for several thousand boats in the River Hamble, but this is hardly surprising given the convenience of the long stand at high water and regular double high tides.The attractive countryside and waterside villages add to the appeal. The mouth is bordered on the east bank by Hook Nature Reserve and Hamble Common to the west. There will be oystercatchers, turnstones and ringed plovers hunting for shellfish and worms when the mud is exposed, and you may

also see herons and redshanks. The navigation would be straightforward were it not for both the heavy traffic which can be mind-boggling during sunny summer weekends (there's good reason for banning the use of spinnakers throughout most of the navigable length of the river) and the apparently never-ending lines of moorings. As anchoring is not permitted, it's just as well that some spaces are reserved for visitors! The Harbour Authority has pile moorings for visiting yachts at both Warsash and Hamble, and there is a bewildering choice of marinas as well - Marina Developments have all of three for starters! Port Hamble Marina has a good range of facilities and is not far from the centre of Hamble, or you might like to try Mercury Yacht Harbour a little further up if there's no room, though be warned that there's no petrol or diesel here. However, Hamble is very definitely a "yachtie" centre, so generally facilities are comprehensive. Once ashore, The White Hart in the High Street is a popular pub for a drink and, also in the High Street, both the Victory and the King & Queen offer reasonably priced restaurant meals. There's also a good range of takeaway food including fish & chips, Indian and Chinese. Phipps Taxis (☎ 023 8045 2241) might ease the strain if you are at Mercury. If you land on the other side of the river at Warsash, good pub meals are available at the Jolly Farmer (☎ 01489 572500) and Pacinos (☎ 01489 573720) in Brook Lane offers a reasonably priced restaurant meal.

Good transport links for exploring the surrounding area or the need to make crew changes might well draw you further upriver to Swanwick Marina which is as far as boats with masts can go anyway. The Moody family, who still run the marina, have been building boats here since the beginning of the 19th century, and the boatyard here has launched many well-known yachts. It's only five minutes walk from the marina to Burlesdon railway station which has services to Southampton and Portsmouth, and buses to Southampton and Gosport stop just outside the marina's gate. A comprehensive range of facilities is available including a bar and restaurant called The Doghouse (☎ 01489 571602). Venturing outside the marina, you might like to go for a drink at the Jolly Sailor (☎ 023 8040 5557) which is just over the river in Burlesdon - the quickest way is to take your dinghy over. Those who remember BBC TV's "Howard's Way" might find the surroundings familiar. In easy walking distance in Swanwick, The Ship (☎ 01489 575646) does good pub food, and also in Bridge Road, you might like to try The Spinnaker (☎ 01489 572123) for cheap and cheerful meals. Still in Bridge Road, the Riverside Chinese (☎ 023 8040 4100) is excellent and it also does takeaways. You might be asking if all the pubs and restaurants in the area choose their names according to the same theme. Here's one that doesn't - for a good but maybe pricey meal it's well worth taking a short taxi ride to Ennio's (☎ 01489 782068) in The Square in Botley (Taxi: ☎ 01489 573573).

Southampton

The busy channel of Southampton Water offers a variety of prospects as you approach what has been a major seaport since Roman times. The marshy coast on the west bank includes Calshot Marshes Nature Reserve just next to the castle, though the backdrop of Fawley

Power Station and the oil refinery isn't all that pleasing. Perhaps you will prefer the other bank which includes stretches of parkland and mature mixed woodland before you reach the outskirts of Southampton. Most of the yachting facilities are located at or near Ocean Village on the peninsula between the Itchen and the lower reaches of the River Test which means you don't have to get involved in the commercial traffic manoeuvring at the Western Docks. This is a major terminal for freight and passenger traffic, so there are considerable numbers of large vessels coming and going – among others, the QEII is a regular visitor. Be sure to consult a good almanac or pilot book to find out where you should and shouldn't go. Most of us will know Southampton as the home of the annual Boat Show and as the base for both the Whitbread and BT Global Challenge round-the-world yacht races. Many other famous voyages have begun or ended here. Richard I sailed from Southampton to join the Crusade in 1189 and in 1415 Henry V embarked here on his way to defeat the French at Agincourt. About a hundred years later in 1620, the early pilgrim colonists left for America in the tiny Mayflower, and on 10th April 1912, a much larger ship left for America though this voyage was not destined to be completed. Five days later, the "unsinkable" Titanic sank with the disastrous loss of life which shook the world. The Maritime Museum (☎ 023 8063 5904) on the Town Quay examines the recent history of Southampton's maritime role since 1838 – hardly surprisingly, the Titanic gets thorough coverage as well as many other "great liners" –

there's a fine 22 foot long model of the Queen Mary. The museum is located in "The Wool House" which is an ancient medieval warehouse of interest in its own right. Also on the Town Quay, the Museum of Archaeology (☎ 023 8063 5904) explores the earlier history of Southampton through Roman, Saxon and Medieval times. This museum is housed in "God's House Tower" which is a striking stone building dating from the 1400s. Though Southampton suffered severe bombing in the last war, many historic buildings escaped. In French Street, you can visit both The Medieval Merchant's House (EH 023 8022 1503) which was built in about 1300 and the more recent Tudor House (☎ 023 8063 5904) which was built 200 years later in about 1500. About half of the medieval town walls survive including 13 of the original towers and 6 of the 8 gates. There's a guide to the walls which you can pick up from the City museums or at theVisitor Information Centre (☎ 023 8022 1106). You will get good views and there's lots of historical interest. Close to Ocean Village on Albert Road South, more recent history is brought to life at the Hall of Aviation (☎ 023 8063 5830). The Solent area played an important role in the development of both civil and military aircraft and there are a number of aircraft on display as well as models, photographs and paintings.

There are several large marinas to choose from. Ocean Village Marina is part of a purpose built development which includes shops, bars and restaurants as well as residential housing and is reasonably close to the centre of the town. It's where the round-the-world races start

Artist: **Geoff Hunt ASHLETT MILL** *Courtesy of:* **The Artist**

from and is also the base for the Royal Southampton Yacht Club. Alternatively, the Town Quay Marina is right alongside the walls of the Old Town and a good base for exploring ashore. If they have space, this is probably the least expensive option for a berth in the area. It's right next to the Boat Show site, so worth avoiding in September. If you need fuel, repairs or chandlery, the best equipped marina is probably Hythe Marina Village which is on the south bank of Southampton Water just opposite the town. Bar and restaurant facilities are available on site, but you will probably want to get across to Southampton to explore. If so, there's a ferry service across to the Town Quay. There's a good yachtie atmosphere at Los Marinos in Ocean Village if you're thirsty, and for an informal meal, we suggest you try Simon's Wine Bar (☎ 023 8063 6372) in Vernon Walk off London Road or Buffalo Bills in Commercial Road. La Lupa (☎ 023 8033 1849) in the High Street offers good Italian food, and a taxi ride up the road to Romsey (a little over 5 miles away) takes you to La Parisienne (☎ 01794 512067) which is highly rated if you are feeling extravagant.

Taxi:	Streamline (☎ 023 8022 3355)
Car hire:	Avis (☎ 023 8022 6767)
	or Budget (023 8063 8833)
Bus:	First Bus enquiries (☎ 023 8022 4854)
Rail:	Southampton Station
Airport:	Southampton Airport (☎ 023 8062 0021)

for more details, see Directory Section

Beaulieu River

Those with basic school French should have no difficulty in decoding the name of the river and village at its head (it's locally pronounced Bew-ley), and it's no lie either. The river winds its way into the south eastern part of the New Forest through mature woodland and is a sheltered and delightful place to explore. You can drop your anchor in the lower reaches of the river, but do at least potter up the river a bit before doing so. The landing stages and slipways are mostly private until you get to **Buckler's Hard** which has pile moorings or pontoons available for visitors. This small yacht harbour is popular, so you may end up with other yachts rafted up with you, but this is a small price to pay for a stay here. Even though you won't be able to moor further up river, it's well worth following it up around high water as the river is navigable for another mile or so, though keep an eye on the depth. With good access to plentiful timber from the New Forest, Buckler's Hard was an important shipyard building wooden warships between 1745 and 1822. The village has been owned by the Montagu family since it was founded in 1724, and the wide grass mainstreet flanked by rows of original houses has remained largely unchanged. There's an interesting maritime museum (☎ 01590 616203) and some of the cottages have reconstructions of 18th century village life. If you are feeling energetic, you might like to stroll the 2 ¹/₂ miles up the river bank to Beaulieu itself (taxis ☎ 0800 521520 or ☎ 023 8084 1100). Here there is a variety of attractions including the National Motor Museum with over 250 vehicles on display, the ruins of a 13th century abbey - the Palace House - home of the Montagu family since 1538 - all set

in elegant gardens in the middle of the New Forest (☎ 01590 612123). At the end of the day, we suggest you return to the Master Builder's House Hotel (☎ 01590 616253) in Buckler's Hard which has a couple of good bars, a restaurant and a garden where you can eat al fresco when it's fine. There's also a well stocked general store in the village which is open seven days a week in the summer.

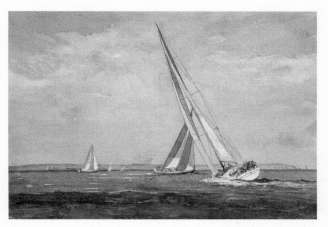

Artist: **Anthony Flemming SAILING IN THE SOLENT** _Courtesy of:_ **The Artist**

Lymington

A stretch of saltmarsh, mudflats and open shore with low sandy cliffs stretches between the mouth of the Beaulieu and Lymington and much of it has been set aside for wildlife and walkers as the North Solent National Nature Reserve. The backdrop of the New Forest offers continuing unspoilt outlooks. Lymington itself is surrounded with pleasing wooded countryside and the marinas are set in the spacious and leafy outskirts of the town. This west Solent yachting centre is a good jumping off place to prepare to break out of the Solent with Poole an easy day's sailing away. Lymington Yacht Haven is on the west bank right at the mouth of the river, and Berthon Lymington Marina is a few hundred yards further upriver and closer to the centre of the town. Both have a full range of facilities and the Yacht Haven has a bar and restaurant on site which is handy as it's a bit of a walk to the town centre. Anchoring is not permitted, but an alternative is to lie alongside the Town Quay or get a visitors' mooring close to it - contact the harbour-master for details. These are both inexpensive options, but be warned that while you are well placed for the centre of the town, you'll have to manage without showers. In the town centre, there are lots of attractive and interesting shops, and there's a street market on Saturdays. A full range of shops for provisions can also be found in the town centre. Lymington Town Sailing Club just next to the Yacht Haven welcomes those from visiting yachts and The Royal Lymington Yacht Club is pleased to admit visitors from other clubs with reciprocal facilities. Their clubhouse is between the Yacht Haven and Berthon Marina. The Kings Head (☎ 01590 672709) on Quay Hill is a good choice for a drink, and the Chequers (☎ 01590 673415) in Lower Woodside is a popular choice for pub meals and worth a short taxi ride. Both Preachers (01590 675370) in

Ashley Lane and The Old Bank House (☎ 01590 671118) on the High Street are good choices for reasonably priced meals, and Limpets (☎ 01590 675595) in Gosport Street is the place to go for something more extravagant.

While you may decide that Lymington is a good place to stop – and many do as it's well connected by road and rail, so a popular place to keep a boat – you should be itching to press on as there are excellent options in every direction from here. Turn right and head for Dorset to open up your way to the West Country, turn left to explore further into the Solent, or head straight across to the Isle of Wight for a variety of destinations which we will be looking at in the following pages. Or what about a quick hop across the Channel? Cherbourg and the Channel Islands are both less than 100 miles away and that shouldn't be more than a 24 hour passage given a decent breeze.

Isle of Wight

A ridge of chalk which runs through the middle of the Isle of Wight is carved through on the coastline in several places to give spectacular cliffs and, most famously, the line of chalky teeth which stretch out from the west end of the island to form The Needles. Low lying ground on the north side of the island has allowed the development of several rivers and natural harbours, and this is where the majority of the yachting destinations on the island are located. The island is a popular holiday centre, and so there are plenty of things to do and places to visit all over the island, and whilst parts are rather built up, there are attractive vistas and tranquil spots to be found as well.

Yarmouth

Opposite Lymington at the west end of the island, Yarmouth offers an attractive harbour presided over by a castle which proved to be the last of Henry VIII's coastal defences and was completed in 1547. From last to first, Yarmouth's lifeboat has pioneered several technical improvements including the introduction of diesel rather than petrol engines in 1936 and the use of radar on the Earl and Countess Howe which went on station in 1963. Yarmouth Castle (EH ☎ 01983 760678) has exhibitions of photographs of the village and paintings of the Isle of Wight. There are moorings or alongside berths in the harbour, though the harbour can get very busy in the summer so you may have to anchor or pick up a visitors' mooring just outside. If the harbour-master has no moorings left, you might be lucky enough to get one from the Royal Solent Yacht Club (just east of the castle) who have a couple for visitors. Once ashore, the Yacht Club will make you welcome and has a bar, restaurant and showers (there are also showers at the harbour). As you wander around the narrow streets, look out for the Wheatsheaf Hotel (☎ 01983 760456) on Bridge Road which is a good choice for a drink, or the Kings Head (☎ 01983 760351) on Quay Street which does good pub food. The Lobster Pot (in Wheatsheaf Lane) is a cheap and cheerful restaurant which also does take-away food and the Harbour View (☎ 01983 760054) on Quay Street is worth a try for a moderately priced meal. Also on Quay Street, The George Hotel (☎ 01983 760331) is as good as it gets for a meal out here. Provisioning shops are a bit limited, but there is a reasonable general store and a chemist, or you can take a bus or taxi to neighbouring Freshwater which is a bit bigger.

Artist: **Steven Dews** **BRITANNIA 1933 RACING IN THE SOLENT** *Courtesy of:* **Rosenstiel's**

Artist: **Steven Dews BRITANNIA RACING WESTWARD** *Courtesy of:* **Rosenstiel's**

Taxi: I Drive Car Service (☎ 01983 755490)
Car hire: ☎ 01983 760395
Bus: local services connect to Freshwater and Newport
for more details, see Directory Section

Newtown River

If you are looking for somewhere which is a bit off the beaten track, the estuary of the Newtown River with its network of creeks and saltings is a good choice, though regrettably it too can be busy at weekends in the summer. You would hardly know that this natural harbour was once a busy port, and much of the estuary is now a nature reserve. You should consult the warden to see where landing is permitted before going ashore to the north east of the harbour - find him at the School's Reception Centre in Newtown. There are a few visitors' moorings or you can drop anchor but be careful to avoid the oyster beds which occupy several of the creeks (check in your almanac or pilot book). Tidal channels lead up to the small villages of Shalfleet and Newtown which are pretty villages for a run ashore. Facilities are limited - though there is a pub which serves good food at Shalfleet (The New Inn) and a village store. In Newtown, the Old Town Hall (NT ☎ 01983 741052) is an interesting old building which is open to the public in the afternoon on Mondays, Wednesdays and Sundays from March to October and also on Tuesdays and Thursdays in July and August.

Cowes and the River Medina

Cowes is probably the most famous yachting centre in the British Isles, and Cowes Castle has been the home of the prestigious Royal Yacht Squadron since 1856. A number of other yacht clubs line the waterfront at West Cowes and there are several marinas offering pontoon berthing and easy access to the town. Given its popularity as a racing and cruising centre, it is hardly surprising that it can be very busy, especially around the beginning of August when the world famous regatta week takes place. Don't let this deter you - there is a buzz which is exciting when the town is busy, or if you can't face that, try to visit on a weekday outside Cowes Week - you will find it much less hectic. The Cowes Maritime Museum (☎ 01983 293341) will give you a feel for Cowes' traditional role as a shipbuilding centre and its current role as a major yacht building centre. For more background, the Sir Max Aitken Museum (☎ 01983 295144) in the High Street in West Cowes (on the other side of the river) has a collection of paintings and other bits and pieces connected with yachting. The architectural character of the town is mostly Victorian reflecting the period when it became a popular leisure resort, and it is an attractive place to browse in. Cowes is centrally positioned on the island for exploration further afield. It's not far to Osborne House (EH ☎ 01983 200022) which was built for Queen Victoria and Prince Albert to be "a place of one's own, quiet and retired" which rather understates its elegance and spaciousness. Further Victoriana can be found at the Isle of Wight Steam Railway (☎ 01983 882204) which has Edwardian and Victorian engines and carriages and a 5 mile stretch of track running through attractive countryside. In Cowes itself, there are plenty of pubs and restaurants to choose from. Both the Pier View (☎ 01983 294929) in the High Street and The Woodvale (☎ 01983 292037) at Gurnard, which is a further half mile stroll along the Esplanade, offer good pub meals and are worth popping into for a drink as well. The Baar Thai (☎ 01983 291917) in Bath Road is a good choice for something oriental and, for a reasonably priced restaurant meal, why don't you try either Bijoux or The Red Duster (☎ 01983 290311) in the High Street.

Artist: **Geoff Hunt NIRVANA, FASTNET RACE**
Courtesy of: **The Artist**

There is quite a range of moorings to choose from. By the centre of the town, there are visitors' moorings off the waterfront by The Parade. Close by, The Island Sailing Club has a short stay pontoon for access to the club where there is a bar and restaurant and showers which the crews of visiting yachts may be invited to use. Cowes Yacht Haven is slightly further up river and has a comprehensive range of facilities, and further up still, there are more visitors' berths managed by the Harbour Authority as well as a couple more marinas. For a comprehensive directory of all yachting facilities it is well worth getting hold of the Port Handbook and Directory which is free and is available from the harbour-master, harbour launches and marinas etc.

Taxi: Alpha Cars (☎ 01983 280280),
             Jill's Taxis (☎ 01983 292678)
Car hire: Solent Self Drive (☎ 01983 282050)
Cycle hire: Isle of Wight Cycle Tours
             (☎ 01983 292723)
Bus: Local network by Southern-Vectis
             (☎ 01983 827005)
Ferry: Red Funnel to Southampton
             (☎ 023 8033 4010)
Airport: Southampton International Airport
             (ferry & rail link takes 50 mins)
for more details, see Directory Section

Upriver

The river is navigable all the way to Newport in the centre of the island where you can lie alongside the quay if you don't mind taking the ground. There's a good choice of pubs and restaurants and all the shops you could need for provisions and more. Well worth a look just outside the town is Carisbroke Castle (EH ☎ 01983 525450) which was the power base on the island for many centuries. About halfway between Cowes and Newport, there are visitors' moorings at Folly Point which is a popular place to stop, not least because of the well-known yachting oasis there, the Folly Inn.

Artist: **Anthony Flemming COWES**
Courtesy of: **The Artist**

Cowes to Bembridge

As you head out of Cowes and follow the coast round to starboard in the direction of Bembridge, you soon reach the elegant parkland which surrounds Osborne House. Osborne Bay is a popular place to drop anchor for lunch or longer as it has a good backdrop and you get good views over the Solent back to the mainland. Just along from Osborne Bay, a dredged channel gives access to **Wooton Creek** where there are a limited number of visitors' moorings and a distinct contrast from the hurly-burly of Cowes. It's not difficult to get in here, and there's good shelter but, while it is an attractive harbour, facilities are rather limited. Contact the Royal Victoria Yacht Club (☎ 01983 882325) who manage the moorings and have a clubhouse with bar and restaurant. You get another option a couple of miles further east at **Ryde**. Here, a small drying harbour offers a refuge for smaller yachts which don't mind taking the ground – it's accessible for a couple of hours each side of high water. This seaside holiday resort town has a splendid stretch of sand and all the traditional seaside holiday trappings – there's also an ice rink and tenpin bowling close to the harbour. The Island Line Railway has a station next to the harbour which opens up much of the west of the island for exploration and links to the Isle of Wight Steam Railway (see Cowes for details). Facilities for yachts are a bit limited, but there's enough to get by. Most of the shops you might need are within easy walking distance and there's a launderette just opposite the harbour in Monkton Street. Pubs within handy reach are the Solent Inn (☎ 01983 563546) in Monkton Street and the Simeon Arms (☎ 01983 614954) in Simeon Street. Budget meals can be had from the Harbour Café (☎ 01983 567035), and a good spot for a reasonably priced meal is The Manor Inn (☎ 01983 564777) which is about a mile away in Appley Road (Taxi: ☎ 01983 811111). The best in the area is probably Biskra Beach House Restaurant (☎ 01983 567913) in St Thomas's Street.

Bembridge

The large natural harbour at Bembridge is close to the Isle of Wight's eastern-most tip. Woodland and the attractive villages of Bembridge and St Helens surround this appealing haven. There's an interesting Maritime

Museum (☎ 01983 872223) in Bembridge which includes a collection of models and half-models and numerous interesting finds from wrecks, many discovered by the museum's owner Martin Woodward. Bembridge also boasts the only remaining windmill on the island (NT ☎ 01983 873945). It was built around 1700 and still has its original wooden machinery. Bembridge and St Helens also have a good range of pubs and restaurants. In Bembridge itself, the Row Barge and the Pilot Boat, both in Station Road, are good choices for a drink, and the Crab and Lobster (☎ 01983 872244) in Forelands Field Road does good food. You might like to try the Square Rigger (☎ 01983 872734) on Sherborne Street for tea or an inexpensive restaurant meal, and Bembridge Sailing Club has a bar which is open daily between July and September and most days for the rest of the year – food is generally available when the bar is open. In St Helens, and therefore nearer the marina, the Vine Inn (☎ 01983 872337) on Upper Green Road will see to it that your thirst is quenched, and Baywatch (01983 873259) on The Duver will serve you a good meal which shouldn't burn a hole in your pocket. Slightly more upmarket is Ganders (☎ 01983 872014) on Upper Green Road, and the St Helens Restaurant (☎ 01983 872303) in Lower Green Road is currently top of the local league.

Once inside the harbour, you can find deep water or drying berths, but around neaps the depth on the bar can make access difficult or impossible depending on your draft. Have a good look at the tide gauge which is not far from St Helens Fort if you are in any doubt. The marina and floating visitors' pontoon in the harbour are exclusively for yachts, or you can join the fishing boats at the Fisherman's Wharf. Catamarans and bilge keelers can anchor fore and aft in the bay close to the Bembridge Sailing Club, but only if prepared to dry out. Facilities are a bit limited though most basics can be found if you are prepared to go some distance – there's a chandlery near the Bembridge Sailing Club, and petrol and gas are a bit of a hike from the marina. Likewise, provision shopping is not extensive immediately by the marina, but there is a full range in Bembridge itself – maybe a taxi for that mile and a half journey to save stretching the arms as well as the legs!

Taxi:	Flint Taxis(☎ 01983 874787)
	Bembridge Harbour Taxis
	(☎ 01983 874132)
Car hire:	GP Rentals (☎ 01983 872904)
Cycle hire:	GP Rentals (☎ 01983 872904)
Bus:	Local services to Ryde, Sandown &
	Newport (☎ 01983 522456)
Rail:	Island Line from Brading (3 miles) links
	to Ryde
Ferries:	Cowes, or hovercraft/passenger ferries
	from Ryde

for more details, see Directory Section

Dorset

Making our escape from the confined and sometimes rather frantic waters of the Solent, we head towards the West Country along some spectacular coastline which gives access to several splendid Ports of Call. The natural harbours at Christchurch and Poole offer contrasting inland cruising opportunities and Weymouth is a handy refuge to pause and think about tackling Lyme Bay.

Artist: **Geoff Hunt JUNO, ADMIRAL'S CUP** *Courtesy of:* **The Artist**

Artist: **Steven Dews SIGMA 38S RACING OFF RYDE** *Courtesy of:* **Rosenstiel's**

Bridport and Lyme Regis are havens for smaller boats, saving you from the need to make a passage all the way to Devon before your next stop. The clifftops are largely unspoiled by any regrettable outbreaks of housing, and the coastline has several striking features - including Lulworth Cove where you might like to drop anchor, Portland Bill which you will treat with considerable respect, Chesil Beach which is amazing but not really exciting to look at from the sea, and Golden Cap near Lyme Regis which really is.

Christchurch

The sprawling seaside resort town of Bournemouth is flanked on each side by a pair of splendid natural harbours. To the west are the extensive open lagoons of Poole Harbour and to the east, the more compact and fiercely tidal creeks and channels of Christchurch Harbour. You will need to pick your moment to attempt the entrance as it is narrow and only deep enough around the double high waters (or stand at neaps) to say nothing of avoiding swift currents which pick up quickly as the tide starts to run. Draft is a major constraint here, and not more than three foot is ideal, although boats drawing up to four will probably manage around springs. It's quite a challenge for those who are unfamiliar with this harbour to find their way across to the Rivers Stour and Avon which empty into it - be prepared to encounter the bottom! It may be worth consulting the Honorary Secretary or Cruiser Class Captain of the Christchurch Sailing Club for some local knowledge. Members of other recognised Yacht Clubs will be made welcome by the club, which is open seven days a week (though the bar is closed on

Mondays at lunchtime, so there's no food available then either). There are various options for anchoring as you make your way upstream, but now you are in you really ought to head up to Christchurch which is an attractive spot with historic interest and good pubs, restaurants and shops as well. Between the sailing club and the High Street, Christchurch Priory is a striking landmark and boasts the longest nave of any parish church in England. There's also a castle (EH ☎ 01202 673555) and younger crew members may well enjoy the Alice in Wonderland Family Park (☎ 01202 483444) which is a short taxi ride away in neighbouring Hurn and includes the largest hedge maze in the South of England. Stanpit Marsh between Christchurch and Mudeford is a Site of Special Scientific Interest and offers scope for tranquil communion with nature. Once you have built up a thirst, the Castle Tavern (☎ 01202 485199) on Church Street, or the Ship Inn (☎ 01202 484308) may well be what you are looking for, or for a pub-type meal, try Thomas Tripp in Wick Lane. Another inexpensive option for a meal is La Mama (☎ 01202 471608) in Bridge Street, or a more elaborate choice would be Pommerys (☎ 01202 484494) in Church Street. Splinters (☎ 01202 483454) is also in Church Street, and is where to take the crew for a treat.

Taxi:	(☎ 01202 478786), (☎ 01202 484848)
Car hire:	Kenning Car Hire (☎ 0870 1555900)
Bus:	local services to Bournemouth
Rail:	Christchurch Station direct services to London, Bournemouth, Poole and Weymouth

Airport: Bournemouth Airport for UK domestic
services

for more details, see Directory Section

Poole Harbour

This large natural harbour, second only to Sydney Harbour in Australia in size, is a popular base for boating of all sorts – yes, sadly, those accursed jet-skiers do rather spoil the tranquillity of parts of the harbour. However, the harbour authorities seem determined to address this sort of problem by designating different sections for different uses, and there should be plenty of room for everyone in a harbour whose banks stretch for something like a hundred miles. The approach and entrance can be tricky as there are brisk tides to contend with as well as the traffic, so plan accordingly and, once inside, it is advisable to stick to the marked channels as much of the harbour is shallow. This is particularly the case in the southern half which is designated a "Quiet area" where speed should be kept down to minimise wash. Though much of this area dries, there are good places to anchor peacefully, but take care to avoid the oyster beds. The harbour and its surrounding area are good places to see wildlife and there are something like a dozen different nature reserves in the immediate area. To the south, you have views over the lowland heath of Studland Heath which is home to reed, sedge and Dartford warblers as well as a breeding ground for woodpeckers, nightjars and sparrowhawks. In the middle of the harbour, the different landscape of Brownsea Island which is largely covered in woodland is home to a large colony of herons, and common and sandwich terns also breed here. This is also one of very few places in the south where you might be lucky enough to see red squirrels which still have a healthy colony here. The northern half of the harbour is more populated with the resort areas of Parkstone and Sandbanks bridging the gap between Bournemouth and Poole itself. There are several marinas offering pontoon berthing and good facilities – Salterns which is the first you reach has the Yacht Harbour Association's 5 Gold Anchor award for excellence and enjoys fine views over much of the harbour. While it is not cheap, you get a full range of first class facilities including the use of the yacht club bar and restaurant. Neighbouring Parkstone Yacht Haven and Parkstone Yacht Club is only marginally less expensive. The Beehive (☎ 01202 708641) at 234 Sandbanks Road has good beer and does pub food if you want to get out of the marina. If you want to be right in the thick of it, and close to shops and a wide range of pubs and restaurants as well, you'd better lie alongside at Poole Quay, though the council-run shower block is not all it might be. The Quay can get very busy in the high season, but it's the best place to explore the town centre from. Contact the berthing master to be directed to a space – the office is open between 8.00 am and 10.00 pm. While you are in the area, perhaps you would like to pay your respects to the RNLI whose headquarters in West Quay Road receive a cheque from all of us at least one a year! It's not far from the Quay, and visitors are welcome on weekdays. You can see a collection of paintings, photographs, models and equipment. Just in case you don't have the number with you, you can contact the office on ☎ 01202 663000. You don't need to go far from your boat to find a drink or a meal. The Lord Nelson (☎ 01202 673774) and the Portsmouth Hoy (☎ 01202 673517) on the waterfront are good spots to quench your thirst or have a light meal. For an Italian restaurant meal, why not try La Lupa (☎ 01202 670660) which is also on the Quay, or a little further afield in the High Street, The Warehouse Brasserie (☎ 01202 677238) has a good selection of fish dishes. The Guildhall Tavern (☎ 01202 671717) in Market Street is also highly rated locally. Try Mansion House (☎ 01202 685666) on Thames Street, just off the busy quay for stylish dining and bar snacks; it is very popular with the sailing fraternity. Banks Road by the harbour has a wide choice of pubs and restaurants such as the Haven Hotel (☎ 01202 707333) and the Sandbanks Hotel (☎ 01202 707377) which both have excellent menus. The popular Saltern's Hotel (☎ 01202 707321) overlooking Poole Marina, is definitely worth a visit with spectacular views over to Brownsea Island making for very pleasurable dining. To quench your thirst try Custom House (☎ 01202 676767) on The Quay which has a French style bar menu and a terraced restaurant upstairs, or Sandacres Free House (☎ 01202 707244), handy for the beach with stunning views over Poole Harbour.

Upriver

Not far beyond the lifting bridge (which opens every couple of hours) near the end of the Quay, Cobbs Quay Marina has some spaces for visitors, and offers a full range of facilities less lavishly and less expensively than Salterns out at Lilliput. Another alternative is available to those who don't draw too much. At the far end of Poole Harbour, a narrow channel winds its way up the River Frome through tranquil marshland to the ancient village of Wareham. Moorings are available from the Ridge Wharf Yacht Centre half way up to the town, or you might be able to go alongside at Wareham Quay or at the Yacht Club's pontoons. The Quay (☎ 01929 552735) on South Street, is handy for its namesake with seating out on the quay, and it serves varied bar food, while the Priory (☎ 01929 551666) on Church Green is a good choice for something a little smarter.

Artist: **Anthony Flemming WAREHAM**
Courtesy of: **The Artist**

Poole to Lyme Regis

A cruise along this stretch of coast offers good views of some spectacular coastline with a variety of cliffs, rocky coves and bays before you reach Portland Bill. This striking lump of rock remains imposing despite intensive quarrying which has hardly made much impact. It's connected to the mainland by the impressive and impenetrable Chesil Bank which runs for over ten miles along the coast, enclosing the Fleet and providing a superb bird sanctuary which is closed to human interference for the breeding season. In fair weather, **Studland Bay** and **Swanage Bay** to the south of the entrance to Poole Harbour are good places to lie at anchor, and a run ashore in the dinghy at either gives access to sandy beaches and seaside holiday resort facilities. Once you have rounded Durlston Head, a spectacular stretch of cliffy coastline offers a fine prospect but little shelter and few anchorages until you get to Weymouth tucked in behind Portland Bill. Erosion by the waves has created a series of geological features which include Lulworth Cove and Stair Hole just next to it, and Durdle Door which is about a mile further west. **Lulworth Cove** is a tempting little natural harbour, though not a good place to be if there is a big swell from the south. Backed by high cliffs, this is a very picturesque haven, though not a very comfortable sanctuary in poor weather. Thanks to the considerable expanse of Lulworth Range, the coast here has seen little development. When approaching from the east, it is worth checking on what activity is planned on the firing range – details are circulated to harbour-masters and yacht clubs in the area.

ers, bars, restaurants and shops here, though for chandlery you do have to walk up to Commercial Road by the marina. Apart from that, most of the usual facilities for yachts can be found nearby. This seaside resort was a favourite of King George III so, as you would expect, much of the seafront has a Georgian flavour. Local attractions include a couple of castles and forts, "The Deep Sea Adventure", Radipole Lake and Nature Reserve in the middle of the town, The Sea Life Centre, and not far away, the Portland Museum and Portland Castle (EH ☎ 01458 250664) – no prizes for guessing what it's made of! There's also a good sandy beach, and plenty of places for shore leave. The Dorset Brewery on Brewers Quay (☎ 01305 777622) is recommended for a drink, and pub food can be found at the Kings Arms (☎ 01305 770055) in Trinity Road which isn't far away. There's a complete range of restaurants and take-aways at the Custom House Quay. The Harbour Side Bistro (☎ 01305 773394) won't burn a hole in your pocket, and The Ship Inn (☎ 01305 773879) is a bit more elaborate. The best of the bunch is probably The Sea Cow (☎ 01305 783524).

Taxi:	(☎ 01305 783636)
Car hire:	(☎ 01305 777172)
Cycle hire:	(☎ 01305 776977)
Bus:	Local services from esplanade and Town Bridge
Rail:	Weymouth Station - services to London
Airport:	Bournemouth Airport for UK domestic services

for more details, see Directory Section

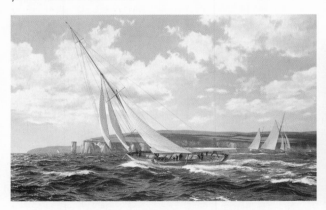

Artist: **_Steven Dews_ LULWORTH, OFF OLD HARRY ROCKS** _Courtesy of:_ **_Rosenstiel's_**

Artist: **_Anthony Flemming_ WEYMOUTH** _Courtesy of:_ **_The Artist_**

While **Portland Harbour** may look tempting, apparently offering good shelter and there is certainly plenty of room, facilities are relatively limited at the time of writing. You might like to lie at anchor in Castle Cove in the north part of the harbour and go ashore to explore Portland Bill while you steel yourself to contend with the Portland Race. Plans for major re-development of this harbour do include provision of a marina as well as extending the facilities for commercial shipping. This is one for a future edition so for the time being, we recommend that you put into neighbouring **Weymouth** which has 24 hour access and where you can moor up in the centre of the town in the 17th century harbour. There's a new marina beyond the lifting bridge which should ease the congestion on the pontoons managed by the harbour authority at "The Cove". There are show-

Tucked in behind an almost surprising outcrop of spectacular golden cliffs after the bleak line of Chesil Beach, West Bay, which is the old and relatively quiet harbour for nearby **Bridport,** might seem familiar. This is where the recent TV series "Harbour Lights" was filmed - try not to be surprised when the harbour master turns out not to be Nick Berry. There is not much room for visitors here and most of the harbour dries. The entrance can be tricky if an onshore wind is much more than a breeze as swell builds up in the narrow entrance. Facilities ashore are limited, but the hotel is very close to the harbour for drinks and basic meals.

Just before the Dorset-Devon border, the harbour at **Lyme Regis** is spectacularly set between cliffs and enjoys views across Lyme Bay to Golden Cap which is the highest cliff on the South Coast. This harbour has also been immortalised on film as those who saw "The French Lieutenant's Woman" may notice, the historic buildings and old fashioned quay giving just the right atmosphere. The cliffs here are widely famed for the fossils which can be found, and examples of many of these can be seen at the Lyme Regis Philpot Museum (☎ 01297 443370) which also has material relating to local history and literary connections with writers such as Jane Austen and John Fowles. There's more fossil related material at "Dinosaurland" and the marine aquarium is also worth a look. Though the harbour dries, it is home to an active fleet of small cruisers and there is space for a handful of visiting yachts to dry out alongside the quay. In settled weather, you can anchor just outside, or you may be able to pick up a visitors' mooring. Contact the harbour-master who controls all the moorings as you arrive to see what's available. Once ashore, there are first-class facilities at the new clubhouse of the Lyme Regis Sailing Club – contact the harbour-master if the club is closed but you would like a shower. The club is a good spot for a drink and sometimes does food, or you might like to try The Nags Head (☎ 01297 442132) on Silver Street or The Cobb Arms (☎ 01297 443242) which is adjacent to the harbour. There is also a selection of bistros and restaurants close to the harbour to choose from. The supermarket is a bit of a hike (if you want a taxi, try Blueline Taxis (☎ 01297 444747), but there is a full range of shops close to the harbour catering for most needs. There is a good choice of watering holes in this part of the world. A good option is the nautically themed seaside bar, the Pilot Boat (☎ 01297 443242) which offers popular, reasonably priced pub grub. The Royal Standard (☎ 01297 442637) and the Harbour Inn (☎ 01297 442299) both on the seafront are good spots for a drink and some well priced, tasty food. Try the Alexandra Hotel (☎ 01297 442010), within walking distance from the beach, for traditional English cooking, while in the centre of town the thatched Kersbrook Hotel (☎ 01297 442596) is good value for traditional country cooking.

Artist: **Anthony Flemming** **YACHTS OFF THE NEEDLES** _Courtesy of:_ **The Artist**

RYE   50.55'.5N 00.46'.5E

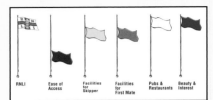

Rye and Rye Harbour
Mr C Bagwell: Harbourmaster
Harbour Office: Camber, Rye, TN31 7QS
Tel: 01797 225225 Fax: 01797 227429
VHF Ch: 14/16 VHF Name: Rye Harbour

Rye Harbour Sailing Club Tel: 01797 344645

Chandlers (Rock Channel, Rye)
Sandrock Marine Tel: 01797 222679
Sea Cruisers Tel: 01797 222070

Moorings (Rock Channel, Rye)
H J Phillips Ltd Tel: 01797 223234
Rye Yacht Centre Tel: 01797 225399

Rye Harbour Lifeboat
Open summer weekends, Contact: R Tollet
(Hon Sec) Tel: 01797 223631/222622

HASTINGS   50.51'.0N 0035'.5E

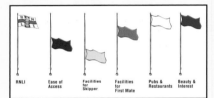

Hastings & St Leonard's Sailing Club
Tel: 01424 420656

Hastings Lifeboat Station & Visitor Centre
The Stade, Old Town, Hastings
Open to visitors all year, except at Christmas;
guided tours by appointment
Tel: 01424 425502

EASTBOURNE   50.47'.5N 00.20'.0E

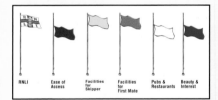

Mr D Hughes: Harbour Manager
Tel: 01323 470099
VHF Ch: 17/15 VHF Name: Sovereign Harbour

Sovereign Harbour Marina
Tel: 01323 470099 Fax: 01323 470077
Pevensey Bay Road, Eastbourne BN23 6JH

Sovereign Harbour Yacht Club
Tel: 01323 470888

Chandlers:
Russell Simpson Marine Tel: 01323 470213
Smith & Gibbs Boatyard Tel: 01323 723824

Eastbourne Lifeboat Station
Open to visitors daily, Contact Coxn/Mech D
Corke or Hon Sec Captain J Hart Tel: (Coxn)
Tel: 01323 730836 or (Hon Sec) Tel: 01323 735883

NEWHAVEN   50.47',0N 00.05'.0E

Peter Doran: Harbourmaster
Tel: 01273 514 131
VHF Ch: 12/16 VHF Name: Newhaven Harbour

NEWHAVEN cont

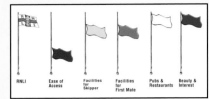

Newhaven Marina
Contact: Manager
The Yacht Harbour, Newhaven BN9 9BY
Tel: 01273 513881 Fax: 01273 517990
VHF Ch: 80 VHF Name: Newhaven Marina

Newhaven & Seaford Sailing Club
Tel: 01323 890077
Newhaven Marina Yacht Club
Tel: 01273 513976
Newhaven Yacht Club
Tel: 01273 513770

Chandlers:
Cantell & Son Tel: 01273 514 118
Russell Simpson Marine Tel: 01273 612612

Repairs:
Peter Leonard Marine, The Moorings, Denton
Island, Newhaven BN9 9BA
Tel: 01273 515987 Fax: 01273 513032

Moorings:
Cantell & Son Tel: 01273 514118
Meeching Boats Tel: 01273 514907

Newhaven Lifeboat
Open to visitors Sundays 1400-1700 (May-
Sept - other times by arrangement)
Contact: M Tubb
Tel: 01323 897576 or 01273 513608

BRIGHTON   50.48'.5N 00.06.5'W

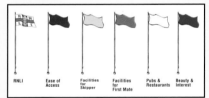

Brighton Marina
Contact: Andrew Lay, Manager,
Brighton Marina Co Ltd, Brighton, BN2 5UF
Tel: 01273 819919 Fax: 01273 675082
VHF Ch: 80/16 VHF Name: Brighton Control

Brighton Marina Yacht Club Tel: 01273 818711

Chandlers:
Russell Simpson Marine Tel: 01273 681543

Repairs:
Brighton Marina Moorings (all repairs)
Tel: 01273 609235
Felton Marine (engine spares, stainless steel
fabrication) Tel: 01273 601779
Garth GRP (glass fibre boat repairs)
Tel: 01273 600004
Southern Masts & Rigging (yacht rigging)
Tel: 01273 818189
Terry Pachol & Son (shipwrights)
Tel: 01273 682724
The Sail Loft (on-site sail repairs - contact:
Ursula Wilkinson) Tel: 01273 677758

Brighton Lifeboat
Open to visitors all year round
Contact: Hon Sec C Maltby Tel: 01273 462670

SHOREHAM   50.49'.5N 00.15'.0W

Captain Brian Fountain: Harbourmaster
& Lock
Tel Habourmaster: 01273 598100
Tel Lock: 01273 592366

SHOREHAM cont.

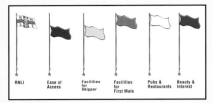

Lady Bee Marina
Contact: Manager
Shoreham Harbour, Albion St, Southwick,
Brighton, E Sussex BN42 4EG
Tel: 01273 59801 Fax: 01273 870349
VHF Channel: 14/16
VHF Name: Shoreham Harbour Radio

Sussex Yacht Club
Secretary: Alan Rudkin
85/89 Brighton Road, Shoreham-by-Sea,
W Sussex BN43 6RE Tel/Fax: 01273 464868

Shoreham Sailing Club Tel: 01273 494064

Chandlers:
G P Barnes Tel: 01273 596680
Sussex Marine Centre Tel: 01273 454737

Moorings:
Riverside Marine
The Boathouse, 41/43 Riverside Road,
Shoreham Beach, W Sussex BN43 5RB
Tel: 01273 453793 Fax: 01273 453514

Shoreham Harbour Lifeboat Station
Open to visitors all year round
Contact J Silverson Tel: 01273 592339 or
J Langridge Tel: 01273 736428

Marlipins Museum
Open to visitors May-Sept, Tuesday to
Saturday & Sunday afternoons
Tel: 01273 462994

LITTLEHAMPTON   50.48'.0N 0032.5'W

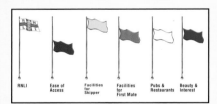

John Sherwood: Harbourmaster
The Harbour Office, Town Quay, Pier Road,
Littlehampton BN17 5LR
Tel: 01903 721215
VHF Ch: 71 VHF Name: Littlehampton Harbour

Littlehampton Marina
John Mitchell: Manager

Ferry Road, Littlehampton, BN17 5DS
Tel: 01903 713553 Fax: 01903 732264
VHF Ch: 37 VHF Name: Littlehampton Marina

Ship and Anchor Marina
Ford, Arundel, W Sussex BN18 0BJ
Tel: 01243 551262 Fax: 01243 555256

Arun Yacht Club
Riverside West, Littlehampton, BN17 5DL
Tel: 01903 714533/716016

Littlehampton Sailing & Motor Club
90-91 South Terrace, Littlehampton, BN17 5LJ
Tel: 01903 715859

Chandlers:
Aruncraft Chandlers Tel: 01903 723 667
Canvas Rope & Rigging Ltd Tel: 01903 732561
Davis Yacht Chandlers Tel: 01903 722778

Littlehampton Lifeboat
Open to visitors all year round
Contact: J M Jones (Hon Sec) Tel: 01903 722216

SELSEY
(No facilities for visiting yachts)

Selsey Lifeboat Station and Museum Boathouse with slipway open to visitors 365 days 10.00-12.00 and 14.00-16.00
Museum open daily March-October and weekends during winter months
For more details contact Martin Rudwick:
Coxswain Tel: 01243 602833 (boathouse and museum)

CHICHESTER HARBOUR 50.47'.0N 00.56'.0W

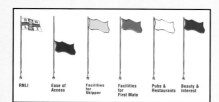

Chichester Harbour Conservancy
Lieutenant Colonel J Q Davis RM:
Harbourmaster
Harbour Office, West Itchenor, Chichester
PO20 7AW
Tel: 01243 512301 Fax: 01983 513026
VHF Channel: 14
VHF Name: Chichester Harbour Radio

Chichester Channel

Birdham Pool Marina
Tel: 01243 512310

Chichester Marina
Contact: Manager
Chichester Yacht Basin, Birdham, Chichester, W Sussex P020 7EJ
Tel: 01243 512731 Fax: 01243 513472
VHF Ch: 37/80 VHF Name: Chichester Marina

Chichester Yacht Club
Ian Clarke: Secretary
Chichester Marina, Birdham, Chichester, West Sussex PO20 7EJ
Tel: 01243 512918 Fax: 01243 512627

Chichester Cruising and Racing Club
Tel: 01243 371731
Itchenor Sailing Club Tel: 01243 512400

Bosham Channel

Bosham Sailing Club Tel: 01243 572341

Thorney Channel

Thornham Marina Tel: 01243 375335

Emsworth Channel

Northney Marina
Northney Road, Hayling Island, PO11 0NH
Tel: 023 92 466321/2 Fax: 023 92 461467

Sparkes Marina Tel 023 92 463572
VHF Channel: 80
VHF Name: Sparkes Marina

Tarquin Yacht Harbour Tel: 01243 377727

Emsworth Sailing Club
Secretaries: Susan Stewart-Fitzroy/
Alan Hounsham
55 Bath Road, Emsworth, Hants PO10 7ES
Tel: 01243 372850

Emsworth Slipper Sailing Club
Eileen Higham: Secretary
The Quay Mill, The Quay, South Street, Emsworth, Hants PO10 7EG
Tel: 01243 372523

Hayling Island Sailing Club
David Morley: Secretary
Sandy Point, Hayling Island, Hants PO11 9SL
Tel: 02392 463768 Fax: 02392 469381

Mengeham Rythe Sailing Club
Tel: 023 92 463 337

Hayling Island Lifeboat:
Open to visitors Wednesday evenings 19.30-21.00 and weekends all year
Contact: N Roper (Hon Sec)
Tel: 02392 465733

Fishbourne Channel

Dell Quay Sailing Club Tel: 01243 785080

Chandlers:
Dinghy Den Tel: 02392 464333
Emsworth Chandlery Tel: 01243 375500
Express Marine Service Tel: 01243 771000
Fast Tack Tel: 02392 461895
Ostar Marine Tel: 01243 376414
Peters Chandlery Tel: 01243 511033
Sportline Chandlery Tel: 02392 461669
Yacht & Sports Gear Tel: 01243 784572

Repairs:
AJS Marine Service Tel: 01243 572692
Combes Boatyard Tel: 01243 573194
Emsworth Shipyard Tel: 01243 375211
Tim Gilmore Tel: 01243 373234
Haines Boatyard Tel: 01243 512228
Hayling Yacht Co Tel: 023 92 463592
Holman Rigging Tel: 01243 514000
Peters Shipyard Tel: 01243 512831
Porter Brothers Tel: 01243 377522
Sparkes Boatyard Tel: 023 92 463 572
Wyche Marine Tel: 01243 782 768

LANGSTONE HARBOUR 50.47'.0N 01.01'.5W

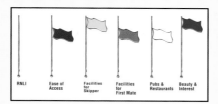

Captain Nigel Jardine: Harbourmaster
Langstone Harbour Board, Ferry Point, Hayling Island, Hants PO11 0DG
Tel: 02392 463419 Fax: 02392 467144
VHF Ch: 12 VHF Name: Langstone Harbour

Southsea Marina
Fort Cumberland Road, Southsea, PO4 9RJ
Tel: 02392 822719 Fax: 02392 822220

Langstone Sailing Club Tel: 02392 484577

Eastney Cruising Assoc Tel: 02392 734103

Chandlers:
Auto Marine Chandlery Tel: 02392 825602
Chris Hornsey Tel: 02392 734728
Southsea Marina Tel: 02392 822719

Repairs:
Goodacre International Tel/Fax: 02392 872662
Tip Top Sail Loft Tel: 02392 873997
Silverwood Yacht Services Tel: 02392 838335

PORTSMOUTH HARBOUR 50.47'.5N 01.06'.5W

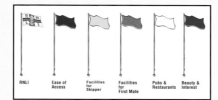

Commander P Chapman-Andrews:
Queen's Harbourmaster
Tel: 02392 723124
VHF Channel: 11
VHF Name: Portsmouth Harbour Radio

Portsmouth Sailing Club
Kathy Cropper: Secretary
21 Bath Square, Old Portsmouth, PO1 2JL
Tel: 02392 820596

Portsmouth Harbour Yacht Club
Tel: 02392 222228 or 222334
Fax: 02392 219827

Royal Naval Sailing Assoc
Tel: 02392 823524 Fax: 02392 870654

Royal Naval Club & Royal Albert Yacht Club
Lt Cdr J McDermott: Secretary
17 Pembroke Road, Old Portsmouth, PO1 2NT
Tel: 02392 825924 Fax 02392 875009

Chandler:
W G Lucas & Son Tel: 02392 826629

Repairs:
Ken Brown Tel: 02392 814246

Portsmouth Lifeboat
Open to visitors Sundays after 10.00
Contact: B R Taylor (Hon Sec) Tel: 02392 664781

Gosport

Gosport Marina
Peter J Wright: Manager
Mumby Road, Gosport, Hants PO12 1AH
Tel: 02392 524811 Fax: 02392 589541
VHF Ch: 80/37 VHF Name: Gosport Marina

Hardway Marine
Stephen Duncan-Brown: Manager
97-99 Priory Road, Gosport, Hants PO12 4LF
Tel: 02392 580420

Haslar Marina
Steven Godden: Manager
Haslar Road, Gosport, Hants PO12 1 NU
Tel: 02392 601201 Fax: 02392 602201
VHF Ch: 80(M) VHF Name: Hasalar Marina

Hardway Sailing Club
Bryan Gurling: Secretary
103 Priory Road, Gosport, Hants PO12 4LF
Tel: 02392 581875

Chandlers:
Aladdin's Cave Tel: 02392 504434
R Arthur Tel: 02392 526522
Frederikson UK Tel: 02392 525377
Ron Hale Marine Tel: 02392 732985
Hardway Marine Tel: 02392 580420
Solent Marine Chandlery Tel: 02392 584622

Repairs:
Camper & Nicholsons Tel: 02392 580221
Gosport Boatyard Tel: 02392 586216
The Maritime Workshop Tel: 02392 527805

Fareham and Portchester

Fareham Marine
Caroline Millar: Manager
Fareham Marine, Lower Quay, Fareham, PO16 0RA
Tel: 01329 822445

Fareham Yacht Harbour (Wicormarine)
Contact: Manager
Wicormarine, Cranleigh Road, Portchester, Fareham, Hants PO16 9DR
Tel: 01329 237112 Fax: 01329 825660

Port Solent Marina
Contact: Manager
South Lockside, Port Solent, Portsmouth, Hants PO6 4TJ
Tel: 02392 210765 Fax: 02392 324241
VHF Ch: 80 VHF Name : Port Solent

Fareham Sailing & Motor Boat Club
Contact: Secretary
Tel: 01329 280738

Portchester Sailing Club
Mick Worsfold: Secretary
The Old Vicarage, Waterside Lane, Portchester, Hants PO16 9QN
Tel: 02392 376375

Chandlers:
Fairweather Marine Tel: 02392 283500
Hill Head Chandlery Tel: 02392 664621
Marine Superstore Tel: 02392 219843
Trafalgar Yacht Services Tel: 02392 822445

Repairs:
Clarence Marine Tel: 02392 511555
Fax: 02392 581013
Goodacre International Tel/Fax: 02392 210220
Madge Marine Services Tel: 02392 214881
Fax: 02392 214882
Wicormarine Tel: 02392 237112

RIVER HAMBLE 50.51'.0N 01.18'.5W

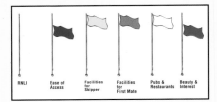

Hamble Harbour
Captain R B Exley: Harbourmaster
Harbour Master's Office, Shore Road,
Warsash SO31 9FR
Tel/Fax: 01489 576387
VHF Channel: 68
VHF Name: Hamble Harbour Radio

Warsash

Stone Pier Yard
Contact: Harbourmaster
Stone Pier Yard, Warsash, Southampton,
Hants SO3 9FR
Tel: 01489 885400 Fax: 01489 885340

Warsash Sailing Club
Contact: Secretary Tel: 01489 583575

Hamble

Hamble Point Marina
Contact: Manager
Satchell Lane, Hamble, Southampton SO31 4NB
Tel: 02380 452464 Fax: 02380 456164
VHF Ch: 80 VHF Name: Hamble Point Marina

Mercury Yacht Harbour
Debbie Burns: Manager
Satchell Lane, Hamble, Southampton SO31 4HQ
Tel: 02380 455994 Fax: 02380 457369
VHF Channel: 80
VHF Name: Mercury Yacht Harbour

Port Hamble Marina
Contact: Manager
Satchell Lane, Hamble, Southampton SO31 4QD
Tel: 02380 452741 Fax: 02380 455206
VHF Ch: 80 VHF Name: Port Hamble Marina

Hamble River Sailing Club
Contact: Secretary Tel: 02380 452070

Royal Air Force Yacht Club
Wing Commander Stanley Pratt:
Commodore; Bill Oakley: Secretary
RAFYC, Riverside House, Hamble,
Southampton, SO3 5HD Tel: 02380 452208

Royal Southern Yacht Club
Contact: Secretary Tel: 02380 453271

Burlesdon & Swanwick

Swanwick Marina
Jane Moody: Manager
Swanwick, Southampton, Hants SO31 1ZL
Tel: 01489 88 000 (after hours 885262)
Fax: 01489 885509
VHF Ch: 80 VHF Name: Swanwick Marina

Chandlers:
Aladdin's Cave (Swanwick Marina)
Tel: 01489 575828
(Deacon's Boatyard, Bursledon)
Tel: 02380 402182

(Mercury Marina) Tel: 02380 454849
Compass Point Chandlery Tel: 02380 452388
Sea Fever Yacht Chandlery Tel: 01489 582804

Repairs:
Moody Service & Construction
Tel: 01489 885000
Richardson Sails Tel: 02380 403914
Shore Sailmakers Tel: 01489 589450

Moorings:
Cabin Boatyard Tel: 02380 402516
Eastlands Boatyard Tel: 02380 403556
Elephant Boatyard Tel: 02380 403268
Foulkes & Son Tel: 02380 406349
Hamble River Boatyard Tel: 02380 583572
Universal Shipyards Tel: 02380 574272

SOUTHAMPTON 50.53'.0N 01.23'.5W

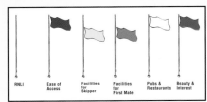

Southampton Port
Contact: Duty VTS Harbour Control Officer
ABP Southampton, Ocean Gate, Atlantic
Way, Southampton SO14 3QN
Tel: 02380 339733 (all hours)
Fax: 02380 232991
VHF Ch: 12/14 VHF Name: Southampton
VTS (for vessel traffic services)

Hythe Marina Village
Peter Bedwell: Manager
Shamrock Way, Hythe, Southampton, Hants
SO45 6DY
Tel: 02380 207073 Fax: 02380 842424
VHF Ch: 80 VHF Name: Hythe Marina

Kemps Quay Marina
Bob Kemp: Manager
Quayside Road, Bittorne Manor,
Southampton SO18 1BZ
Tel: 02380 632323 Fax: 02380 226002

Ocean Village Marina
Alan Tribbeck: Manager
2 Channel Way, Southampton SO14 3TG
Tel: 02380 229385 Fax: 02380 233515
VHF Ch: 80 VHF Name: Ocean Village Marina

Shamrock Quay Marina
Cuan Marsh: Manager
William Street, Northam, Southampton
SO14 5QL
Tel: 02380 229461 Fax: 02380 333384
VHF Ch: 80 VHF Name: Shamrock Quay

Town Quay Marina Tel: 02380 234397

Hythe Sailing Club Tel: 02380 846563

Marchwood Yacht Club Tel: 02380 666141

Royal Southampton Yacht Club
Tel: 02380 223352

Chandlers: at Kemps Quay and Shamrock
marinas, also:
Kelvin Hughes Tel: 02380 634911
Marine Connections Tel: 02380 336200
Resin Store Tel: 02380 449338
Wessex Marine Equipmt Tel: 02380 510570

Repairs:
Bruce Bank Sails Tel: 01489 582444
Richardson Sails Tel: 02380 403914

CALSHOT

No facilities for yachts

Calshot Lifeboat
Open to visitors Sundays 10.00-1.00 and
Wednesdays 17.00-19.00
Contact: J Horton (Hon Sec) Tel: 02380 893509

BEAULIEU RIVER 50.47'.0N 01.22'.0W

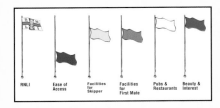

Buckler's Hard Yacht Harbour
John Edward: Harbourmaster
Harbourmaster's Office, Buckler's Hard,
Beaulieu, Hants SO42 7XB
Tel: 01590 616200/616234 Fax: 01590 616211

Beaulieu River Sailing Club Tel: 01590 672383

Chandler/Repairs:
Buckler's Hard Boatbuilders Tel: 01590 616 214

LYMINGTON 50.45'.0N 0131'.5W

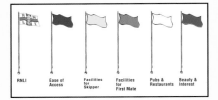

Lymington Harbour
Alan Coster: Harbourmaster
Harbour Office, Bath Road, Lymington, SO41 3SE
Tel: 01590 672014 Fax: 01590 671823

Berthon Lymington Marina
Brian May: Manager
The Shipyard, Bath Road, Lymington, SO41 3YL
Tel: 01590 673312 Fax: 01590 676353
VHF Ch: 80 VHF Name: Lymington Marina

Lymington Yacht Haven
Contact: Manager
Kings Saltern Road, Lymington, SO41 3QD
Tel: 01590 677071 Fax: 01590 678186
VHF Channel: 80/37
VHF Name: Lymington Yacht Haven

Royal Lymington Yacht Club
Tel: 01590 672677

Lymington Town Sailing Club
Tel: 01590 672096

Chandlers:
Nick Cox Tel: 01590 673489
Yachtmail Tel: 01590 672784

Repairs:
Berthon Boat Co Tel: 01590 673312

Lymington Lifeboat Station
Open to visitors on Sunday afternoons,
Easter through September
Contact: M J Webb (Hon Sec) Tel: 01590 676404

YARMOUTH 50.42'.5N 0130'.0W

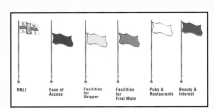

Yarmouth Harbour
Nick Ward: Harbourmaster
Harbour Office, The Quay, Yarmouth,
IOW PO41 0NT
Tel: 01983 760321 Fax: 01983 761192
VHF Ch: 68 VHF Name: Yarmouth Harbour

Royal Solent Yacht Club
Secretary: Mrs Sue Tribe
The Square, Yarmouth, IOW PO41 0NS
Tel: 01983 760256 Fax: 01983 761172

Yarmouth Sailing Club Tel: 01983 76020

Chandlers:
Harwoods Tel: 01983 760258
IOW Outboards Tel: 01983 760436

Repairs:
Harold Hayles Tel: 01983 760373

Yarmouth Lifeboat Station
Open to visitors Sats 09.00 - 16.00 during July
and August
Contact: B Turner (Hon Sec) Tel: 01983 753625

NEWTOWN RIVER   50.43'.5N 01.24'.5.W

D Flannagan: Harbourmaster
Tel: 01983 531424 Fax: 01983 531914

Chandler:
Eddies Farm Shop Tel: 01983 531547

COWES   50.46'.0N 01.17'.5W

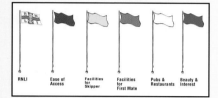

Cowes Harbour
Captain Stuart McIntosh: Harbourmaster
Harbour Office, Town Quay, Cowes, IOW
PO31 7AS
Tel: 01983 293952 Fax: 01983 290018
VHF Channel: 69
VHF Name: Cowes Harbour Radio

Cowes Yacht Haven
Contact: Manager
Vectis Yard, High Street, Cowes, IOW PO31 7BD
Tel: 01983 299975 Fax: 01983 200332
VHF Ch: 80 VHF Name: Cowes Yacht Haven

Island Harbour Marina
Contact: Manager
Mill Lane, Binfield, Newport, IOW PO30 2LA
Tel: 01983 822999 Fax: 01983 526020
VHF Ch: 80/37 VHF Name: Island Harbour

East Cowes Marina
Contact: Manager
Clarence Road, East Cowes
Tel: 01983 293983 Fax: 01983 299276
VHF Ch: 80 VHF Name: Cowes Marina

Cowes Combined Clubs Tel: 01983 295744

East Cowes Sailing Club Tel: 01983 294394

Island Sailing Club
Alan Young: Cruising Secretary
High Street, Cowes, IOW
Tel: 01983 296621 Fax: 01983 293214

Royal Corinthian Yacht Club Tel: 01983 293581

Royal London Yacht Club Tel: 01983 299727

Royal Yacht Squadron Tel: 01983 292191

Chandlers:
Aqua-Togs Tel: 01983 295071
Hunter & Coombes Tel: 01983 299599
Pascall Atkey Tel: 01983 292381

Repairs:
Adrian Stone Yacht Services Tel: 01983 297898
Groves & Guttridge Tel: 01983 294862
McWilliam Sailmakers Tel: 01983 281100
Powerplus Marine Tel: 01983 200036
Regis Electronics Tel: 01983 293996
Souter Shipyard Tel: 01983 294711
Spencer Rigging Tel: 01983 292022
Victory Yard Tel: 01983 200226

D G Wroath Marine Tel: 01983 281467

Water Taxi:
David Jones Tel: 01983 325928

Moorings/Repairs:
Shepards Wharf Boatyard, Medina Road, Cowes
Contact: Manager Tel: 01983 297821

UK Sailing Academy
Contact: Manager
Arctic Road, West Cowes, IOW PO31 7PQ
Tel: 01983 294941 Fax: 01983 295938

NEWPORT AND THE RIVER MEDINA
        50.42'.0N 01.17'.5W

Newport Yacht Harbour
W G Pritchett: Harbourmaster
Harbour Office, Town Quay, Newport, IOW
PO30 2ED
Tel: 01983 525994
VHF Channel: 69
VHF Name: Newport Yacht Harbour

Folly Reach
Contact: Harbourmaster
Tel: 01983 295 722
VHF Ch: 69 VHF Name: Folly Launch

Island Harbour Marina
Contact: Manager
Tel: 01983 8222999 Fax: 01983 526020

Mooring:
Medina River Services (Folly Inn)
Contact: Manager Tel: 01983 295772

Repairs:
Richardsons Boatbuilder Tel: 01983 821095

RYDE   50.44'.0N 01.09'.0W

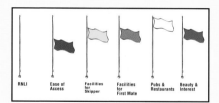

Ryde Leisure Harbour
David Brown & Don Hickman: Harbourmaster
The Esplanade, Ryde, IOW PO33 1JA
Tel: 01983 613879 Fax: 01983 823841
VHF Ch: 80 VHF Name: Ryde Harbour

Royal Victoria Yacht Club
Contact: Secretary Tel: 01983 882325

Moorings:
Wootton Creek Contact: Harbourmaster
Fishbourne Quay, IOW PO33 4EE
Tel: 01983 882200 Fax: 01983 883132

BEMBRIDGE   50.41'.5N 01.06'.5W

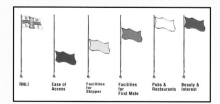

Bembridge Harbour
Captain G R Hall: Harbourmaster
Harbour Office, Bembridge Marina, St Helen's
Quay, IOW PO33 1YS
VHF Ch: 80 VHF Name: Bembridge Harbour

Bembridge Marina
Tel: 01983 872828 Fax: 01983 872922

Bembridge Sailing Club
Lt Col M J Samuelson RM: Secretary
Embankment Road, Bembridge, IOW

Tel: 01983 872237 Fax: 01983 874950

Brading Haven Yacht Club
Contact: Secretary Tel: 01983 872289

Chandler:
Spinnaker Yacht Chandelry Tel: 01983 874324

Bembridge Lifeboat Station
Open to visitors May-Sept, Weds, Thurs,
Suns & Bank Hols 14.00-16.00
Contact: J Francis Tel: 01983 872192

Maritime Museum & Shipwreck Centre
Providence House, Sherborne Street,
Bembridge, IOW
Open March-Oct and in closed season by
appt Tel: 01983 872223/873125

CHRISTCHURCH & MUDEFORD
        50.43'.5N 01.44'.5W

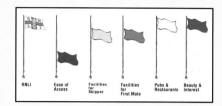

Christchurch Harbour
Contact: Harbourmaster
Harbour Dept, Christchurch Borough
Council, Civic Offices, Bridge Street,
Christchurch, Dorset BH23 1AZ
Tel: 01202 495070 Fax: 01202 482200

Christchurch Sailing Club
Paul Reakes: Secretary
The Quay, Christchurch, Dorset BH23 4QF
Tel: 01202 483150

Moorings:
Elkins Boatyard Tel: 01202 483141

RIBS Marine
Little Avon Marina, Stony Lane South,
Christchurch, Dorset BH23 1HW
Tel: 01202 477327 Fax: 01202 471456

Rossiter Yachts
Bridge Street, Christchurch, Dorset BH23 1DZ
Tel: 01202 483250 Tel: 01202 490164

River Stour Moorings
c/o Bournemouth Borough Council, Parks
Dept, Town hall,Bournemouth, Dorset
Tel: 01202 552066 Tel: 01202 297592

Strides Boatyard
The Watch House, Coastguard Way,
Mudeford, Christchurch, Dorset BH23 3NP
Tel: 01202 485949 Tel: 01425 614058

Chandlers:
Christchurch Boatshop Tel: 01202 482751
South Coast Marine Tel: 01202 482695

Repairs:
Rossiter Yacht Builders
Tel: 01202 483250

Mudeford Lifeboat Station
Open to visitors all year
Contact: V Derham (Hon Sec)
Tel: 01202 482366

POOLE HARBOUR   50.41'.0N 01.57'.0W

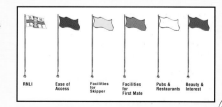

Poole Harbour (Poole Town Quay)
Peter Booth: Harbourmaster
The Harbour Office, 20 New Quay Road,
Hamworthy, Poole, Dorset BH15 4AF
Tel: 01202 440233 Fax: 01202 440231
VHF Ch: 14 VHF Name: Poole Harbour Control

Cobb's Quay Marina
Contact: Manager
Hamworthy, Poole, Dorset BH15 4EL
Tel: 01202 674299

Quay West Marina
Contact: Manager
23 West Quay Road, Poole, Dorset BH15 1HX
Tel: 01202 675071 Fax: 01202 681646

Salterns Marina
Contact: Manager
40 Salterns Way, Lilliput, Poole, BH14 8JR
Tel: 01202 707321/709971 Fax: 01202 700398

Sunseeker International Marina
Contact: Manager
Tel: 01202 685335

Ridge Wharf Yacht Centre
Contact: Manager
Ridge, Wareham, Dorset BH20 5BG
Tel: 01929 552650

North Haven Yacht Club Tel: 01202 708830

Poole Yacht Club Tel: 01202 672687

Redclyffe Yacht Club Tel: 01202 561227

Royal Motor Yacht Club
D Grierson: Secretary
Panorama Road, Sandbanks, Poole BH13 7RE
Tel: 01202 707227 Fax: 01202 708775

Moorings:
Arthur Bray's Yard Tel: 01202 676469
Davis's Boatyard Tel: 01202 674349
Dorset Yacht Co Tel: 01202 674531
Harvey's Pleasure Boats Tel: 01202 666226
Lake Yard Tel: 01202 674531
Lilliput Yacht Station Tel: 01202 707176
Mitchell's Boatyard Tel: 01202 747857
Moroconium Quay Tel: 01202 674531
Parkstone Yacht Haven and Yacht Club
Tel: 01202 738824
Poole Boat Park Tel: 01202 680843
Sandbanks Yacht Co Tel: 01202 707 00

Chandlers:
CQ Chandlers Tel: 01202 682095

Force 4 Chandlery Tel: 01202 723311
Quay West Chandlers Tel: 01202 742488
Piplers Tel: 01202 673056
Pumpkin Marine Tel: 01202 723211
Salterns Chandlery Tel: 01202 701556

Repairs:
Boatyard Marine Services Tel: 01202 660150
Mitchell's Boatyard Tel: 01202 747857
K Latham Tel: 01202 748029
Quay sails Tel: 01202 681128
Poole Rigging Service Tel: 01202 623681
Salterns Boatyard Tel: 01202 707391
Tabb sails Tel:01202 684638

Poole Old Lifeboat House
Open to visitors daily between 11.00 and 16.00
Tel: 01202 671133 Fax: 01202 670128

Poole Lifeboat Station
Open to visitors by appointment
Contact: R W Parry (Hon Sec) Tel: 01202 665607

SWANAGE

Swanage Lifeboat Station
Open to visitors all year round
Contact: boathouse Tel: 01929 423237

WEYMOUTH   50.36'.5N 02.26'.5W

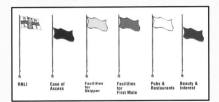

Weymouth Harbour
Captain D T Stabler: Harbourmaster
Municipal Offices, North Quay, Weymouth,
Dorset DT4 8TA
Tel/Fax: 01305 206342
VHF Channel: 12
VHF Name: Weymouth Harbour

Weymouth Marina
Contact: Manager
Tel: 01305 767576 Fax: 01305 767575

Royal Dorset Yacht Club Tel: 01305 786258

Weymouth Sailing Club Tel: 01305 785481

Chandlers:
W L Bussell Tel: 01305 785633
Kingfisher Marine Tel: 01305 766595
Weymouth Chandlers Tel: 01305 771603

Repairs:
Ferrybridge Marine Services Tel: 01305 781518

Weymouth Lifeboat Station
Open to visitors all year round
Contact: W Macey Tel: 01305 774019

PORTLAND HARBOUR   50.35'.0N 02.25'.0W

Portland Harbour
Contact: Port Controller Tel: 01305 824044
VHF Channel: 13
VHF Name: Portland Harbour Radio

Castle Cove Sailing Club Tel: 01305 783708

BRIDPORT   50.42'.5N 02.46'.0W

Bridport Harbour
Harbourmaster Tel: 01308 423222
VHF Ch: 11/16 VHF Name: Bridport Radio

LYME REGIS   50.43'.0N 02.56'.0W

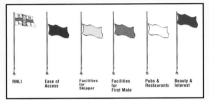

The Cobb Harbour
Mike Ponpard: Harbourmaster
Lyme Regis Harbour Office, The Cobb, Lyme
Regis, Dorset Tel/Fax: 01297 442137
VHF Channel: 16
VHF Name: Lyme Regis Harbour radio

Lyme Regis Power Boat Club
Tel: 01297 443788

Lyme Regis Sailing Club Tel: 01297 442800

Chandlers:
Axminster Power Tel: 01297 33980
Jimmy Green Marine Tel: 01297 20744

Lyme Regis Lifeboat Station
Open to visitors all year round
Contact: Clifford Travis Tel: 01297 442687

The South Coast - Chart Agents

Russell Simpson, Eastbourne Tel: 01323 470213
Auld at Sea, Hayling Island Tel: 02392 461669
Trafalgar Yacht Services, Fareham Tel: 01329 822445
Hardway Marine, Gosport Tel: 02392 580420
R Arthur & Co, Gosport Tel: 02392 602265
Aladdin's Cave, Hamble Tel: 02380 454849
Kelvin Hughes, Southampton Tel: 02380 634911

Bucklers Hard Boatyard, Beaulieu Tel: 01590 616214
Pascall & Atkey, Cowes, I.O.W. Tel: 01983 292381
Spinnaker Chandlers, Bembridge, I.O.W. Tel: 01983 874324
Rossiter Yachts, Christchurch Tel: 01202 483250
W L Bussel, Weymouth Tel: 01305 785633
Serendip Fine Books, Lyme Regis Tel: 01297 442594

The South Coast - Pilot Books

The Shell Channel Pilot, the South Coast of England, Edited by Tom Cunliffe. Rev'd. 1997 Ed.
published by Imray, Laurie, Norie &Wilson Tel: 01480 462114, ISBN 0852 883 862

Waypoint Directory, Peter Cumberlidge. 1995
published by Adlard Coles Nautical Tel: 0207 2420946 ISBN: 0713 641 177

Wight Hazards, Peter Bruce
published by Boldre Marine ISBN: 1871 680 018

Solent Hazards 4th Ed. 1994, Peter Bruce
published by Boldre Marine ISBN: 1871 680 026

Cruising Guide to the Solent, Derek Bowskill
published by Imray, Laurie, Norie &WilsonTel: 01480 462114 ISBN 0852 288 1401

South Coast Cruising, Mark Fishwick
published by Yachting Monthly ISBN: 1852 770 83X

Inshore Along the Dorset Coast, Peter Bruce
published by Boldre Marine ISBN: 1871 680 069

Channel Pilot. 3rd Ed. 1996
published by United Kingdom Hydrographic Office ISBN: 0707 710 278

Artist: **Steven Dews** **THE WIND PIPED LOUD FROM THE WEST** *Courtesy of:* **Rosenstiel's**

Artist: **Steven Dews** **GERMANIA RACING METEOR IV** *Courtesy of:* **Rosenstiel's**

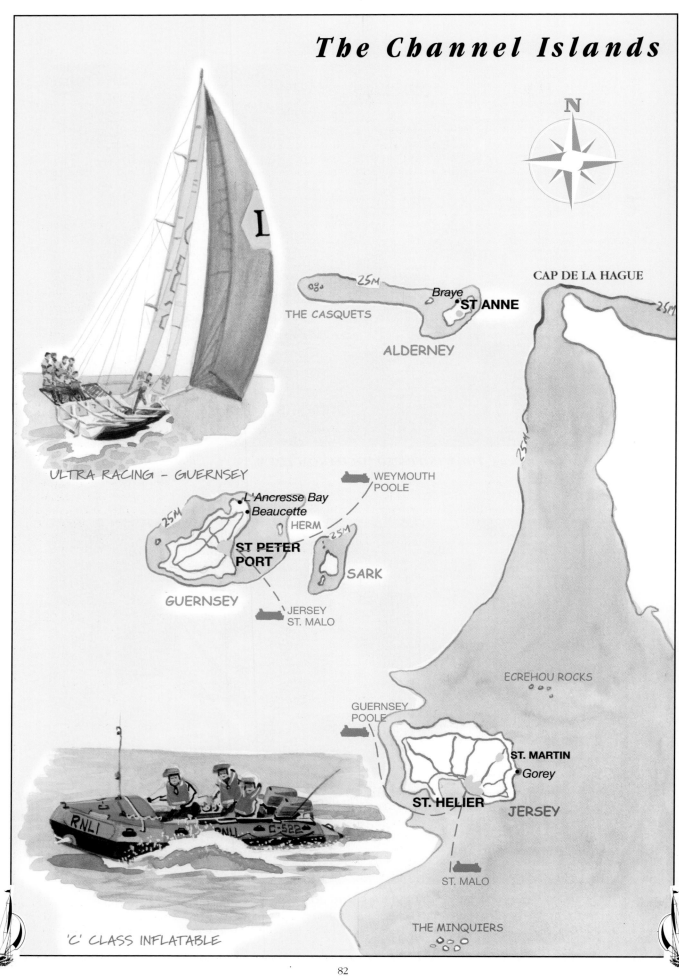

The Channel Islands

N

CAP DE LA HAGUE

THE CASQUETS

25M

Braye •**ST ANNE**

ALDERNEY

25M

ULTRA RACING - GUERNSEY

WEYMOUTH POOLE

L'Ancresse Bay
• Beaucette

25M

HERM

25M

ST PETER PORT

SARK

GUERNSEY

JERSEY
ST. MALO

ECREHOU ROCKS

GUERNSEY POOLE

ST. MARTIN
• Gorey

ST. HELIER

JERSEY

RNLI C-522

ST. MALO

THE MINQUIERS

'C' CLASS INFLATABLE

The Channel Islands are a spectacular cruising area and, as they are between 60 and 100 miles from the south coast of England, they are well within range for most cruising yachtsmen who are prepared to make a passage of up to 24 hours. The scenery is often rugged, and the rocks which are scattered over the chart can be forbidding, but in fine weather this is an outstandingly beautiful place to be, and the mixture of British and French cultures and the variety of atmospheres to be found on the different islands is intriguing and appealing. We would not wish to underplay the challenges to the navigator in these waters. Tidal streams can be very brisk and there are plenty of hazards to be avoided, so you will need large scale charts and detailed pilotage instructions in order to explore this area safely. Even experienced navigators will be kept on their toes if they are unfamiliar with these waters, and as things can happen very quickly, good preparation and careful planning are essential. For those who are not deterred, there are rich rewards to be reaped. There are some really lovely anchorages and atmospheric harbours and, on going ashore, you will find interesting places to visit, wonderful scenery and, thanks to the French influence, some tremendous places to eat and drink. Be aware that the Channel Islands are not part of the UK and you will need to observe customs formalities on arrival from both Britain and France, and indeed on movement from the Guernsey administration to that of Jersey.

Alderney

Alderney is the most northerly of the Channel Islands, and consequently the closest to mainland Britain, but much closer to France. Though the island owes allegiance to the English Crown and there are pubs to make you feel at home, French influences can be felt as well. With a spectacular rocky coastline hinting at hidden hazards, and equally spectacular tidal ranges and currents which can occasionally reach over 10 knots, the island might seem a bit forbidding to the visiting yachtsman. However, with reasonably careful planning, you will be able to avoid the worst of these, and you should manage to get the tides to work to your advantage. As you approach, and once ashore, you cannot fail to be struck by the fortifications which impose themselves on the coastline. These include Roman, Elizabethan, Victorian and Second World War structures many of which can be easily reached and explored. You can discover more about the island's turbulent history at the Alderney Museum which is beside the old clock tower in the centre of the island's small town, St Anne. The museum also examines the island's natural history which is something many visitors come to enjoy. Boat trips around the island or further afield on Lady Maris (☎ 01481 822051) or Voyager (☎ 01481 823666) offer an opportunity to view the coastline and its considerable variety of seabirds; it's also a good way to spare you the challenges that navigation around the island present if you take your own boat! For a sedate view of the north eastern part, you can make use of the island's railway, whose familiar carriages have a strangely urban feel. However, as the island is less than four miles in length, it won't take you long to walk to almost anywhere, and probably the best beach if you are looking for some bucket and spade action is in Braye Bay which is right next to the harbour.

The harbour authorities welcome visiting yachts and are very helpful. If you contact them in advance, they will send you pilotage instructions and comprehensive details of facilities ashore. In settled weather, some of the sandy bays around the island's coast offer peaceful anchorages, or for shelter and the convenience of facilities close to hand, you may opt for the harbour next to Braye Bay. There is space to anchor in the bay and over 60 visitors' moorings in the harbour which offers good shelter except in strong north to north easterlies. At the harbour, you will find showers, launderette, fuel and most other facilities you might wish for close to hand, and as most of the island's population of about two and a half thousand people live within a mile of the harbour, it's not far to the shops. All things considered, there's a good range as well, including a small supermarket a couple of hundred yards from the waterfront.

For such a small place, you will be impressed by the selection of places to have a drink or a meal. At the harbour on Braye Street, the Divers Inn (☎ 01481 822632) is handy for a drink and the Moorings (☎ 01481 822421) serves good pub food as does the Harbour Lights (☎ 01481 822168) just inland in Newtown. The First and Last (☎ 01481 823162) in Braye Street is a good choice for a moderately priced meal. Slightly further away in St Anne, The Rose and Crown (☎ 01481 823414) is a good choice for a drink and has the best off-license on the island, and you will find inexpensive meals at G&T's Bistro (☎ 01481 824232) on Victoria Street and Marais Hall (☎ 01481 822683) on Marais Square. The Bellevue Hotel (☎ 01481 822844) in The Butes offers something a bit more upmarket and the jury is out on which is the best on the island – it's either the Inchalla Hotel (☎ 01481 823220) in The Val or Chez Andre (☎ 01481 822777) in Victoria Street.

Water taxi:	Mainbrayce (☎ 01481 822772) or VHF Ch. 37 or 80 ("Mainbrayce Taxi")
Taxi:	Alderney Taxis (☎ 01481 822611 or 822922)
Car hire:	Alderney Hire Cars (☎ 01481 823352) or Central Car Hire (☎ 01481 822971)
Cycle hire:	Puffin Cycles (☎ 01481 823725) JB Cycle Hire (☎ 01481 822294) Top Gear Cycle Hire (☎ 01481 822000)
Bus:	local services around the island
Airport:	flights to Guernsey, Jersey & Southampton. Aurigny Air Services (☎ 01481 822886)

for more details, see Directory Section

Guernsey

Guernsey, like the other Channel Islands, became part of England in 1066 when William the Conqueror linked Normandy and England. When King John lost control of the Duchy of Normandy in 1204, he managed to retain possession of the Islands and they have remained possessions of the English Crown ever since. However, the islands have total administrative autonomy and are self governing, though the Queen is still loyally toasted as "Our Duke". The visitor will soon spot some of the differences, one significant advantage being the absence of

VAT which will appeal to committed shoppers, and you will be struck by the continental atmosphere, and all in a place which still has the silhouette of the Queen on its stamps! Most sailors will be familiar with the name of the island for its association with splendid thick woolly jumpers. The absence of VAT should mean you can pick one up inexpensively, though we hope you won't need it as the climate here is traditionally warm and sunny, certainly at the height of the sailing season. Guernsey's climate has been a great asset to its economy, and the cultivation of tomatoes and flowers has been an important source of employment and income. On a sunny day, anyone arriving by plane to join their boat will see the island sparkle with the sun's reflection on the acres of glass houses which boost the benefit of the island's benign climate. To get the full background on the island's history and culture, it's well worth a visit to the Guernsey Museum and Art Gallery (☎ 01481 726518) on Candie Road in the capital, St Peter Port. Here you will be able to find out about the island's archaeology and there is an interesting collection of artefacts from the island and all over the world. The section entitled "The Story of Guernsey" gives a full chronological view of the history of the island. For more historical insight and culture, Castle Cornet (☎ 01481 721657), which has guarded the mouth of the harbour since the 13th century, is close to the marina on the south arm of St Peter Port Harbour. Displays here include The Armoury, The Guernsey Militia Museum, The 201-Squadron Museum, The Hatton Art Gallery, The Maritime Museum and "The Story of Castle Cornet" Museum. Further exploration of this attractive town's narrow cobbled streets and perhaps slightly surprisingly English architecture will give you more flavour and may bring you to the house where Victor Hugo, who lived here between 1855 and 1870 while in exile, wrote Les Miserables. Heading out of St Peter Port, the island's road network can be a bit mystifying to visitors and so most stick to the coast. This is fine for getting to any of the island's tremendous selection of beaches and clifftop walks, but do make sure that you head inland to find the Little Chapel which is made entirely from shells and broken porcelain, and the Folk Museum (NTG ☎ 01481 728451) at Summarez Park (☎ 01481 55384) which is not quite so well hidden. There's another Maritime Museum which concentrates on shipwrecks along the infamous west coast. This is located in a Martello Tower at Fort Grey (☎ 01481 65036) on Rocquaine Coast Road, St Peters - we don't recommend you try to sail here. There is also the German Occupation Museum (☎ 01481 38205) near the airport which tells the story of this unhappy episode in the island's all-too-recent history.

Like much of the rest of the Channel Islands, the approaches to Guernsey are somewhat fraught with

Artist: **Geoff Hunt** *ST PETER PORT* *Courtesy of:* **The Artist**

hazards, so a large scale chart and pilot book with good local coverage are essential. Your pilot book will also guide you to the numerous sandy bays which variously give shelter from weather from all points of the compass and are good places to lie at anchor. Pontoon berthing with all services in deep water is available in two marinas, and if you are approaching from the north, the small marina at **Beaucette** may well be attractive. Located on the north east point of the island, this old quarry has been converted into a sheltered marina by Premier Marinas and offers a good range of yachting facilities and has space for a few visitors. The marina is accessible for about three and a half hours each side of high water, and the approach channel is clearly buoyed, but you must call the marina before trying to enter to make sure they have space for you. Shopping for provisions is a little limited here, but there are several places to eat within walking distance including the Marina Restaurant (☎ 01481 47066) at the marina and the Symphony House Hotel (☎ 01481 43581) in Hacse Lane, L'Ancresse. L'Ancresse Bay, probably the best bathing beach on the island, is just a few minutes walk from the marina, and for exploration further afield, the marina office will be pleased to help you with car or cycle hire. For the more cosmopolitan feel of Guernsey's capital and main port, head to **St Peter Port** less than five miles south of Beaucette. Of the three marinas here, Victoria Marina which is inside the main harbour has 240 pontoon berths exclusively for the use of visitors and there are mooring buoys available as well. Access to the marina berths is constrained by the tide to two and a half hours each side of high water. A full range of facilities for yachtsmen is available close to hand, and the marina couldn't be better placed for exploring the town. Shops for provisions and much, much more are available in profusion within a couple of hundred yards walk, and we recommend that you seek out the Market Halls just behind the town church for fresh produce and locally caught fish.

As Guernsey's capital, St Peter Port has an abundance of fine places to eat and drink. A good pub for a drink or a meal is the Ship & Crown (☎ 01481 721368) on the North Esplanade. This busy pub opposite the marina is, as you might expect, very popular with the yachting fraternity as it shares a building with the Royal Guernsey Yacht Club, and it serves good value food. The Drunken Duck (☎ 01481 725045) at Le Charroterie, is also well worth a visit. It is popular and serves a good choice of real ales and some popular bar food.

For a more formal meal, try Moore's Central (☎ 01481 724452) on Le Pollet where their two restaurants will offer you a good choice. La Fregate (☎ 01481 724624) in Les Cotils commands outstanding views of the town and the harbour, making it an idyllic place to enjoy a delicious à la carte meal. Battens (☎ 01481 729939) on Fountain Street, is another great place to have a meal, and it's very popular so booking is advised. Le Nautique (☎ 01481 721714) on Quay Steps is a pleasantly situated restaurant with harbour views, for a really sumptuous meal, we recommend Victor Hugo (☎ 01481 728282) at St Pierre Park Hotel which is at Rohais, about 1 1/2 miles west of St Peter Port, by Grange Road. The seafood here is tremendous.

Taxi:	(☎ 01481 44444)
Car hire:	Harlequin Car Hire (☎ 01481 39511)
Bus:	Quay Cycle Hire (☎ 01481 714146)
Ferry:	services to Poole, Weymouth, France, Jersey and other Channel Islands
Airport:	Guernsey Airport (☎ 01481 37766) 6 miles from St Peter Port

for more details, see Directory Section

Herm and Sark

Temptingly within sight from the harbour at St Peter Port, these two small islands are both well worth a day trip. You will find contrasting characteristics, but both offer good walking and have hostelries for refreshment once you have built up your appetite. Herm is closer, smaller and most famous for its "Shell Beach" where the Gulf Stream has deposited millions of shells and fragments from as far afield as the Gulf of Mexico. Neither island has motorised traffic, though a tractor and trailer is available to carry people up the hill from the landing stage on Sark. Governed by a hereditary feudal seigneur, Sark has a spectacular coastline of high cliffs and there's a striking narrow causeway 250 feet above sea level which links the main island with Little Sark to the south. Consult your pilot book for details about where to anchor, or if you prefer to have a rest from navigating your way around all the rocks, you can hop on a small ferry from St Peter Port to either island.

For a meal ashore on Herm, head for the White House (☎ 01481 722159). This restaurant is part of the Ship Inn which is in a great spot by the harbour. It is nautically decorated and has plenty of seating outside, and it serves decent bar food. The restaurant upstairs has a good carvery buffet and excellent local seafood.

Sark offers a wider choice. La Moinerie (☎ 01481 832089) is an attractive stone-built pub which serves good, well priced bar food and also has a restaurant with an open fire to keep diners warm on those chilly days. There is outside seating on the lawn area, too. The Dixcart (☎ 01481 832015), a 16th century farmhouse, is another good choice for a meal, as is the Petit Champ (☎ 01481 832046) which has outstanding views of the coast, Herm, Jetou and Guernsey. Founiais (☎ 01481 832626) on Harbour Hill is another upmarket dining option, as is La Sablonnerie (☎ 01481 832061) on Little Sark.

Jersey

Jersey is the furthest south of the Channel Islands and is also the largest. Because of the huge tidal ranges which can be up to 40 feet, the surface area of the island increases from 45 to 63 square miles at low tide. Like the other main islands, in the group, the coastline is a mixture of impressive rocky cliffs and sandy bays which are popular with holiday makers. Much of the scenery and many of the landmarks will be familiar to viewers of the BBC detective series 'Bergerac' which was filmed here. Places of interest to visit on the island range from prehistoric sites to contemporary visitor attractions, and the variety on offer means that there should be something to occupy everybody. If you don't mind taking the ground, one of the most spectacular places to moor is in **Gorey Harbour** over which looms

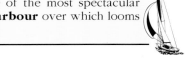

the massive stronghold of Mont Orgueil Castle (☎ 01534 853292). This impressive 13th century fortification contains interesting tableaux which illustrate its history - though frankly, what is far more memorable is just looking up at the castle when it is floodlit at night. Showers are on hand, and there are some provisions shops by the harbour. For a full range of shops, it's a ten minute walk to Gorey Village. As Gorey Harbour dries, you may prefer one of the marinas at the island's capital St Helier as a base for major re-provisioning and exploring the rest of Jersey. For a run ashore, conveniently close on Gorey Pier, you will find the Fisherman's Bar and Grill, or the main restaurant in The Dolphin Hotel (☎ 01534 855343), or the Moorings Hotel (☎ 01534 853633) serve good meals in civilised surroundings. Ming's Dynasty Chinese Restaurant (☎ 01534 856886) is a few doors along and has an excellent reputation. For a more informal atmosphere, try the Mont Orgueil Restaurant (☎ 01534 853291) where you can dine 'al fresco' on the terrace or The Drive In Bar.B.Q (☎ 01534 851266) on the Coast Road has a garden restaurant with a wide range of seafood and children's menus. Another option for a good meal is the Apple Cottage Restaurant (☎ 01534 861002) at Rozel Bay which is just round on the north coast and is an attractive anchorage in fine weather. Exploration of the north coast is rewarding as there are some idyllic anchorages. However, newcomers are advised to plan to visit this area at neap tides, and large scale charts and a thorough pilot book are, as ever in the Channel Islands, essential for safe navigation.

Artist: **Moira Huntly MOORINGS**
Courtesy of: **The Artist**

St Helier

Set at the east end of the wide sandy sweep of St Aubins Bay, St Helier is a bustling town and a major financial centre. It is, however, an agreeable place to spend some time and faces south west making it ideal for pavement cafes which give it that continental atmosphere. At the harbour, you are well placed to learn about Jersey's sea-faring past at the Maritime Museum (☎ 01534 811043) on New North Quay in 19th century warehouse buildings beside St Helier Marina. The same site is also home to the Occupation Tapestry Museum where you can see the results of a massive community project to depict the story of the German Occupation in tapestry form. Older European animosities are brought to mind by Elizabeth Castle (☎ 01534 723971) which stands guard at the entrance to the harbour and was built by Sir Walter Raleigh in the 1590s while he was governor of the island and named in honour of his monarch, the first Queen Elizabeth. At low tide, you can walk out to the castle along the causeway, or there are shuttle services when the sea gets in the way. Fort Regent (☎ 01534 500200) on the east of the harbour was built to keep Napoleon at bay in the early years of the 19th century and is now a sports and leisure centre. A wide range of sporting facilities including a swimming pool is complemented by the Gloucester and Queen's Halls where concerts, exhibitions and fairs take place and a range of cafés, bars and shops are found. A stroll along the ramparts gives good views over the town. The history, traditions and culture of the whole island are explored at the Jersey Museum (☎ 01534 633300) which is by the bus station at the top of New North Quay. Heading out of town, the road network is not too complex to find your way around, or you may find the bus services perfectly adequate for excursions to explore the rest of the island. For animal lovers, a must is Jersey Zoo (☎ 01534 864666) near Trinity, which was founded by Gerald Durrell and is the headquarters of the Jersey Wildlife Preservation Trust which works to save endangered species from all over the world. Animals on view in enclosures which seek to capture their natural environments include families of gorillas, orang-utans, gibbons and lemurs as well as a good cross-section of birds and other exotic creatures. Also in the area, you will find the Pallot Heritage Steam Museum (☎ 01534 865307) in Rue de Bechet, Trinity, where there is a collection of steam engines and machinery as well as a display which commemorates Jersey Railways and a collection of organs including a Compton cinema organ. Between Gorey and St Helier at Grouville, La Hogue Bie (☎ 01534 853823) is a significant prehistoric monument. At this site, there is a sizeable burial mound which dates from 3800 BC, a Neolithic passage grave, and more recent buildings including two Medieval chapels and a German underground command bunker. Information is on hand at the galleries and Discovery Centre. Jersey's most extensive subterranean construction is the German Underground Hospital (☎ 01534 863442) at Meadowbank, St Lawrence where you can explore the underground passages and find out about the German Occupation. There's more information and a collection of uniforms, equipment and documents and a short film about life under enemy occupation at the Island Fortress Occupation Museum (☎ 01534 734306) which is on the Esplanade in St Helier.

Facilities for visiting yachts at St Helier are comprehensive, though this is a popular destination and the marinas can be very busy at peak times. The La Collette Yacht Basin is accessible at all states of the tide and can be used as a waiting area until the tide allows access to one of the larger marinas, and there are a few spaces for short stays of up to 24 hours. To the west of the harbour area, the new Elizabeth Marina was opened in 1998 and is primarily for local boats, though there are a few spaces for visitors. There is more space for visitors at the St Helier Marina in the inner harbour, and there's a holding pontoon just outside it if you need to wait for enough water to get over the sill. You will need to keep a look out for commercial traffic as you approach and pay attention to traffic control signals. A listening watch on Channel 14 is advised as are sharp eyes as there are new high speed ferries operating in the area. Both Elizabeth and St Helier Marinas are accessible for about 3 hours each side of high water. Fuel is available at the Elizabeth Marina, or on the South Pier by the St Helier Yacht Club in the approach to St Helier Marina. There's a chandlers on the New North Quay, and most shops you will need for provisions can be found within half a mile. The Indoor Market off Beresford Street is a good source of fresh local produce.

You will certainly find no shortage of places to eat well in St Helier. We would suggest you try Victoria's (☎ 01534 872255) at De Vere Grand Hotel, on Peirson Road, which has live music and dancing on Friday and Saturday and an à la carte menu, or La Petite Pomme (☎ 01534 66608) at Pomme d'Or Hotel, which will also serve you an excellent meal. You will have striking ocean views whilst dining at the Chateau de la Mer (☎ 01534 33366) on Havre des Pas, and this will also be the case if you pay a visit to the De La Plage (☎ 01534 723474) which is a bit further down the coast; it serves a bar lunch and dinner, and if you feel like something a bit smarter, they also have an à la carte menu.

For some lighter refreshment, why not try the Admiral (☎ 01534 300095) on St James Street. This delightful pub is festooned with candles and all manner of curious memorabilia and it serves very good value bar food. Alternatively, the Tipsy Toad Town House (☎ 01534 615000) on New Street is another one that is worth a visit. It has two floors with downstairs being the more traditional, and serving excellent bar food. If you need a respite from some serious shopping, then the Dog & Sausage (☎ 01534 30982) on Hilary Street is perfect.

Or for the complete picture, The Good Eating Guide is a local publication based on nominations by both residents and visitors and is well worth getting hold of for an up to date catalogue of the full range on offer. It can be purchased (50p) from the Visitors' Services Centre in St Helier.

In St Helier:

Taxi:	Luxi Cabs (☎ 01534 887000),	
	Yellow Cabs (☎ 01534 888888)	
Car hire:	Charles Street Car Hire (☎ 01534 21242),	
	Hireride (☎ 01534 31995),	
	Holiday Autos (☎ 01534 888700),	
	Zebra Car Hire (☎ 01534 36556)	
Cycle hire:	Zebra Cycles (☎ 01534 36556) or	
	Holiday Auto (☎ 01534 888700)	
Bus:	local bus services from main bus station	
Ferry:	services to other Channel Islands, France and the UK	
Airport:	Jersey Airport offers services to other Channel Islands and France	
	Aurigny (☎ 01534 44735) and the UK	
	Jersey European (☎ 0990 676676),	
	British Airways (☎ 0345 222111),	
	British Midland (☎ 0345 554554)	

for more details, see Directory Section

Artist: **Carlo Rossi BREAKERS AT SUNSET** *Courtesy of:* **Rosenstiel's**

ALDERNEY   49.44'.0N 02.11'.5W

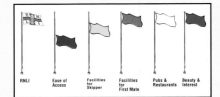

Braye Harbour
Mr Shaw: Harbour Master
Harbour Office, Alderney GY9 3XX
Tel:01481 822620 Fax: 01481 823699
VHF Channel: 74
VHF Name: Alderney Radio

Alderney Sailing Club
Open from: 1800 - 2000 (Welcomes visiting
yachtsmen) Contact: The Manager
Tel: 01481 822758

Chandlers:
Mainbrayce Marine, Braye Harbour,
Alderney, Channel Islands, GY9 3XX
Tel: 01481 822772
VHF Channel: 37,80 VHF Name: Mainbrayce

Repairs:
Mainbraye Marine, as above
Boat Repairs. Engine Repairs. Sail Repairs.

Alderney Lifeboat
Braye Harbour, Alderney GY9 3XX
Open to visitors: All Year
Contact: Harbourmaster Tel: 01481 823456
Harbourmaster Tel: 01481 822620

BEAUCETTE   49.30'.5N 02.30'.0W

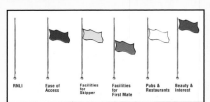

Beaucette Marina
Neil Rhys-Evans: Harbour Master
Vale, Guernsey, Channel Islands, GY3 5BG
Tel: 01481 45000 Mobile Tel: 04481 102302
VHF Ch: 80 VHF Name: Beaucette Marina

Channel Islands - Pilot Books

North Brittany & Channel Islands Cruising, Peter Cumberlidge
published by Yachting Monthly, ISBN: 1852 770 694

Normandy & Channel Islands Pilot, Mark Brackenbury
published by Adlard Coles Nautical, Tel: 0171 2420946 ISBN: 0713 641 940

The Shell Channel Pilot, Ed. Tom Cunliffe Revised 1997 Edition
published by Imray, Laurie, Norie & Wilson, Tel: 01480 462114 ISBN: 0852 882 785

The Channel Islands, Nick Heath
published by Imray, Laurie, Norie & Wilson, Tel: 01480 462114 ISBN: 0852 883 617

Waypoint Directory (English Channel), Peter Cumberlidge 1995
published by Adlard Coles Nautical, Tel: 0171 2420946 ISBN: 0713 641 177

ST PETER PORT   49.27'.5N 02.32'.0W

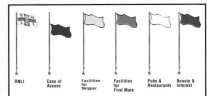

Capt. Robert Barton: Harbourmaster
Tel: 01481 720229 Fax: 01481 714177
VHF Channel: 12 VHF Name: Port Control

Victoria Marina
Graham Trebert: Manager
St Julian's Emplacement, St Peter Port, GY1 2LW
Tel: 01481 725987 Fax: 01481 714177
VHF Channel: 20
VHF Name: St Peter Port Radio

Chandlers:
Marquands Bros., Nort Quay, St Peter Port
Tel: 01481 720962
Boatworks +, Castle Emplacement, St Peter Port,
Tel: 01481 726071

Repairs:
Boatworks + as above
Boat repairs. Engine Repairs. Sail Repairs.

St Peter Port Lifeboat
Open to visitors: Contact Hon Sec Capt R
Barton, Hon Sec Tel: 01481 36434
(office)720229

St Peter Port Maritime Museum, Castle Cornet
Open to visitors: Apr - Oct; 7 days, 1000 - 1700
Contact: Mr P Sarl Tel: 01481 721657

ST HELIER   49.10'.5N 02.06'.5W

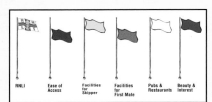

Capt. Brian Nibbs: Harbourmaster
Tel: 01534 885588 Fax: 01534 885599
VHF Channel: 14
VHF Name: St Helier Port Control

St Helier Marina
Contact: Manager Tel: 01534 885508

Elizabeth Marina
Contact: Manager Tel: 01534 885530

La Collette Yacht Basin
Contact: Manager Tel: 01534 885529

St Helier Yacht Club
M L Goulder: Hon Sec
South Pier, St Helier, JE2 3NB
Tel: 01534 721307 Fax: 01534 20842

Chandlers:
Kufra's, New North Quay, St Helier, JE2 3ND
Tel: 01534 36955

Repairs:
Kufra's as above
Boat Repairs. Engine Repairs. Sail Repairs.

St Helier Lifeboat
open to visitors: by arrangement with
Capt. Brian Nibbs (Hon. Sec.)
Boathouse Tel: 01534 24173
Hon. Sec. Tel: 01534 885500

GOREY   49.12'.0N 02.01'.5W

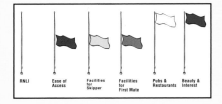

Gorey Harbour
Captain Brian Nibbs: Harbour Master
Tel: 01534 885588
VHF Channel: 74 VHF Name: Gorey Harbour

ST. CATHERINES

Limited facilities for yachts

St Catherine Lifeboat
La Route de St Catherine, St Martin, Jersey,
JE3 6DD. This is the most southerly
Inshore Lifeboat Station in the RNLI.
Open to visitors: By appointment only
Contact: Bruce Ferguson, Senior Helmsman
Tel: 01534 853457 Senior Helmsman
Tel: 01534 851186

Artist: **Steven Dews** **RANGER AND ENDEAVOUR** *Courtesy of:* **Rosenstiel's**

Artist: **Steven Dews** **COLUMBIA AND SHAMROCK** *Courtesy of:* **Rosenstiel's**

South West England

SEVERN CLASS LONG RANGE BOAT

N

Bude

Boscastle

Padstow • • Rock

NEWQUAY

Charlestown P

Fow

St Agnes • Mevagisse

Truro

R. FAL

St Ives Mylor

Hayle Penryn

FALMOUTH St Mawes

PENZANCE

Land's End Newlyn St Michael's • Helford

Mousehole Mount

Porthleven

Lizard Point

• St Mary's

ISLES OF SCILLY

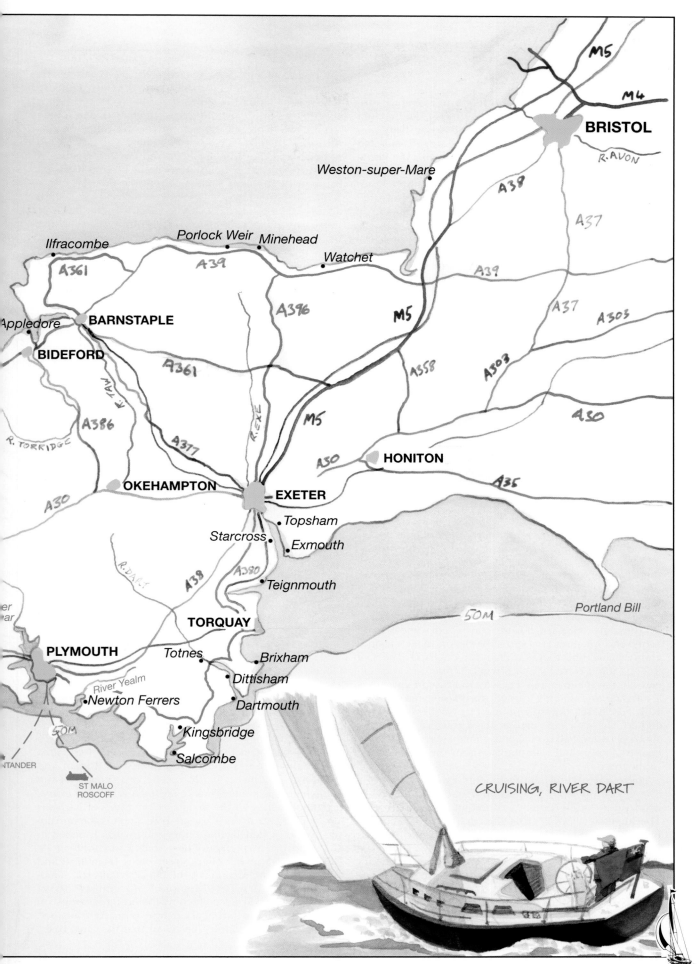

M5

M4

BRISTOL

R. AVON

Weston-super-Mare

A38

A37

Porlock Weir   Minehead

Ilfracombe

A39

Watchet

A39

A361

A396

A37

A303

Appledore

BARNSTAPLE

M5

BIDEFORD

A361

A39

M5

A558

A303

A50

R. TAW

A303

R. TORRIDGE

A386

A361

A377

R. EXE

M5

A30

A30

A30

HONITON

OKEHAMPTON

EXETER

A35

Topsham

Starcross

Exmouth

R. DART

A38

A380

Teignmouth

50M

Portland Bill

TORQUAY

PLYMOUTH

Totnes

Brixham

River Yealm

Dittisham

Newton Ferrers

Dartmouth

50M

Kingsbridge

NTANDER

Salcombe

ST MALO
ROSCOFF

CRUISING, RIVER DART

South Devon

Devon's southern coastline offers a tremendous variety of cruising waters and places to visit. The coastal scenery includes spectacular cliffs and sandy bays, and places for you to put in or explore include the sheltered sanctuaries of the Rivers Exe, Dart and Yealm, the hectic resort atmosphere of Torbay with its marinas at Torquay and Brixham, and the wealth of maritime history and extensive inland cruising opportunities offered by Plymouth Sound and the rivers which run into it. There really is something for everybody here and it is not hard to see why this is such a popular area for yachtsmen and landlubbers alike. It's also not quite as hectic and crowded as the sailing centres around the Solent, though obviously some of the places you might like to visit may well be blighted by overcrowding at the height of the season. If you are able to avoid the bigger resort areas and tourist traps during sunny weekends, so much the better.

River Exe

The wide sands which greet you as you approach the entrance to the River Exe make this a popular area with holidaymakers. After the spectacular cliffs which form the Devon Coast thus far, the narrow entrance at Exmouth is the first refuge for the yachtsman. It's quite a tricky one at that, with swift tides to chastise the unwary who might be lulled into a sense of false security by the tranquil holiday atmosphere. Once through the entrance, the estuary opens up into one of the best birdwatching areas in the South West. Birds which breed here include lapwings, redshanks, reed and sedge warblers and shelduck, and there is a colony of herons at Powderham halfway up the west bank of the estuary. If you are cruising out of season, there is a wide variety of waders which winter here as well. You have a choice of places to stop. For peace and tranquillity, you can drop your anchor in the shelter of Warren Point, or you might even find a visitors' mooring. If you prefer to go alongside, the old commercial harbour in **Exmouth** is now mainly used for leisure craft (and some fishing boats) and has pontoon berths for visitors. Basic facilities are available, and there's a chandler on hand. The Exe Sailing Club is close by and offers bar and food at weekends and in the evenings Tuesday to Friday. Exmouth is a pleasing and smartly turned out seaside resort town with an elegant atmosphere and plenty of things to see and do. There's a supermarket and a reasonable range of shops between half a mile and a mile away, and a good choice of pubs and restaurants within the same stretch of the town.

There are several establishments near the seafront. The Grove (☎ 01395 263444) on The Esplanade, serves good value, locally caught seafood and is a family pub. The Imperial (01395 274761) also on The Esplanade, and Barn (☎ 01395 224411) approximately 1 mile East on Foxholes Hill, via The Esplanade, both serve food. The Seafood (☎ 01395 269459) on Tower Street, is pleasant for dinner and concentrates its menu on seafood!

On the other side of the estuary at the village of **Starcross** you can lie alongside the quay as long as you don't mind drying out, or you might find a visitors' mooring. Anchoring anywhere near is tricky because of the numerous moorings. Isambard Kingdom Brunel left his mark when he built the Great Western Railway which runs along the shore here, and you will notice the Pump House by the jetty which was part of an experimental propulsion system for the trains on this section of the line. The Starcross Fishing & Cruising Club is situated in the Brunel Tower, and has a well stocked and "atmospheric" bar and offers home cooked meals on Saturdays – the club is not open all the time, so check with them about access before you arrive. If you stroll about a mile south to Cockwood, you'll find a brace of pubs: The Anchor (☎ 01626 890203), and The Ship Inn (☎ 01626 890373) which has an inexpensive restaurant. Back in Starcross, there's a general store, bakery and chemist, but if you want to do more comprehensive shopping, you can catch the passenger ferry which runs across to Exmouth during the summer. There are more facilities at **Topsham** which is at the head of the estuary. You can find out about the town's past as a centre for shipbuilding and trade at the Topsham Museum (☎ 01392 873244) or you may prefer to just stroll in its charming streets. There's a good range of shops for provisions close to the waterfront, though if you want a supermarket you'll have to head towards Exeter. Contact one of the boatyards or the Topsham Sailing Club for a visitors' mooring. The club has a bar and showers and is open at weekends and when the tide is right for racing. Other places for sustenance are The Bridge Inn (☎ 01392 873862) about half a mile from the club on Bridge Hill, or you might like to take your dinghy a couple of miles up the canal to the Double Locks Hotel. Close to the club on Ferry Road, The Passage House Inn (☎ 01392 873653) or a little further away on Fore Street, The Globe (☎ 01392 873471) both offer good pub food. Try The Gallery (☎ 01392 876078) on Fore Street or Nellos Ristorante Italiano (☎ 01392 877937) for reasonably priced restaurant meals, or for a special night out, take a taxi the 2 miles to the Ebford House Hotel (☎ 01392 877658) just round the head of the estuary.

Taxi:	Topsham Cabs (☎ 01392 877905)
Bus:	from the Town Quay to Exeter and Exmouth
Rail:	from Topsham Station to Exeter and Exmouth
Airport:	Exeter Airport. UK domestic routes

for more details, see Directory Section

Exeter

Exeter has been the central urban focus of the area since Roman times and there's plenty of Roman and medieval flavour to explore. The centrepiece is the cathedral which dates back to Norman times and enjoys a tranquil setting in the middle of the town. St Nicholas Priory (☎ 01392 265858) just off Fore Street is the remaining part of a Benedictine Priory which was founded in 1087 and has a splendid Guest Hall. The Guildhall (☎ 01392 265524) in the High Street dates from 1330 and nearby there are sections of the old city walls still standing. The Royal Albert Memorial Museum (☎ 01392 421252) has a varied collection including sections on Roman and more recent local history, natural history, fine art and west country silver. Around the canal basin, you will find antique shops, bistros, boutiques, pubs and restaurants all housed in historic buildings dating from the time of the construction of what is the oldest ship canal in England. This once busy wool export port might seem familiar to those who remember the BBC's Onedin Line some of which was filmed here. Contact the Exeter harbour-master for details about access to the canal and berthing arrangements in the canal basin in Exeter. If you don't fancy the trip up the canal to Exeter, or your mast is too high to get under the M5 bridge, but you would still like to explore the city, you can easily hop on the train up from Starcross or Topsham.

Torbay

The wide open bay of Tor Bay is pretty much built up on all three sides by what the local tourist board styles as "The English Riviera". This is real holiday resort land, and the almost adjoining towns of Torquay, Paignton and Brixham are full of hotels and guest-houses ready to disgorge their patrons onto the bay's sandy beaches and into the pleasure boats which tour the harbour. If this sounds a bit negative, let it just be a warning that the waterfront areas of these towns can be hectic and the main emphasis is not really on yachting, though there are plentiful facilities and lots of attractions and entertainment to keep yachtsmen and other visitors amused. Both Torquay and Brixham have marinas, and both have quite different atmospheres so each is worth visiting in its own right. At the north end of the bay, **Torquay** is the largest of the three towns. The marina is big with around 500 berths and takes up about half of the harbour. It has a good number of berths for visitors, though there is always the risk of demand exceeding supply at popular holiday times. The harbour office also administers some moorings for visitors. The waterfront is elegant and boasts carefully nurtured palm trees, and with white Italianate villas on the hillsides which climb up from the front, there is a genuinely Continental atmosphere when the sun shines. Local attractions include Aqualand (☎ 01803 294439) at the harbour which is an aquarium where local marine life and exotic fish from more tropical climes can be seen. The restored Edwardian Pavilion (☎ 01803 214624) on the Harbourside near the marina is also worth a visit and here you will find shops, cafes and restaurants. Appropriately while thinking of that era, you are not allowed to forget that Agatha Christie was born in Torquay in 1890 and is widely feted, and there are exhibitions celebrating her life at Torquay Museum (☎ 01803 293975) in Babbacombe Road and at Torre Abbey (☎ 01803 293593) in Kings Drive. The latter is an interesting mixture of the remains of an old 11th century abbey and Georgian mansion and now houses an interesting variety of exhibitions. A bit further away in Babbacombe, which is a suburb on the cliffy north side of the headland, the Bygones Museum (☎ 01803 326108) in St Marychurch features a life-size Victorian street with 20 shops and period rooms. There's also a large model railway if you prefer to see something a bit more dynamic. While on the subject of miniature things, not far from here in Hampton Avenue is the Model Village (☎ 01803 315315). Here, there are more model trains and an amazing array of other models (including Stonehenge, a castle, a car ferry, open fields and a city centre) all set in a landscape planted with suitably miniature trees and

plants. It really is very cute and there are good views out to sea as well if you take the free bus service from the Harbour to the Village.

The choice of places to eat and drink is considerable. You won't have to go far to find something which suits you - here are some suggestions to get you started.

Beach Road fields the Cary Arms (☎ 01803 327110) which enjoys sea and cliff views, while serving plentiful bar food. On Park Lane, near the harbour, the Hole in the Wall (☎ 01803 298020) is an unspoilt local which is open all day, while the London (☎ 01803 380003) on The Strand, serves good value food in its enviable position, overlooking the harbour and the marina. In the centre of town the atmospheric Pig in Black (☎ 01803 213848) is lively, especially in the evenings and at weekends. There is a wealth of seafront hotels with superb restaurants; the Imperial Hotel (☎ 01803 294301) on Park Hill Road, just north of the new harbour enjoys its stunning aspect, serving dinner and bar food at lunch time. Corbyn Head Hotel (☎ 01803 213611) on Torquay Road has two restaurants which look out over the harbour while The Osbourne Hotel (☎ 01803 213311) on Hesketh Crescent serves both lighter brasserie meals and dinner only in the Langtry restaurant. The Grand (☎ 01803 296677) on the Sea Front, provides Edwardian surrounding and a varied menu.

Taxi:	BB Taxis (☎ 01803 322500)
Car hire:	Hertz (☎ 01803 294786)
Cycle hire:	Colin Lewis Cycle Hire (☎ 01803 553095)
Bus:	Stagecoach Buses (☎ 01803 613226)
Rail:	National Rail enquiries (☎ 0345 484950)
Ferry:	services to Paignton (dependent on tide) and Brixham
Airport:	Exeter Airport

for more details, see Directory Section

Artist: **Moira Huntly BRIXHAM**
Courtesy of: **The Artist**

On the southern arm of Tor Bay, **Brixham** has a more maritime flavour and its harbour is very much the focus of the town. Attractive small houses line the waterfront and narrow streets climb up the hillsides which surround the harbour. Brixham has been an important fishing port since the Middle Ages, and was said to be the largest fishery in England by 1850. There are still plenty of fishing boats in the harbour, and also a few small fishing boats in the marina. A slightly unexpected resident in the harbour is a replica of the Golden Hind, the ship in which Francis Drake became the first Englishman to sail around the world between 1577 and 1580. You can climb aboard, and will probably be astonished at how small she is. Brixham is also notable as the landfall for the invading army of William of Orange in 1688 at the start of his happily bloodless campaign to overthrow King James II - which he successfully did, arriving triumphant in London 43 days later on December 18th. Brixham Museum (☎ 01803 856267) on Bolton Cross includes material about the history of the town and port and an interesting collection of old shipbuilding tools, and also has displays relating to lifeboats, coastguards and smuggling. The Torbay all-weather lifeboat is also moored in the harbour and the station here has an inshore lifeboat as well (see directory for details if you would like to visit). Being a smallish town, you don't have to go far to get out and see some countryside. There's a nature reserve and some splendid old fortifications on Berry Head not far from the marina, though in the tourist season this can get pretty crowded. Visiting yachts are confined to the marina which is large and boasts a comprehensive range of facilities. It is located close to the centre of the town where there is a full range of shops for provisions and browsing and a wide variety of pubs and restaurants. Spinnakers Restaurant and Bar is on site or, for a popular harbourside pub, the Blue Anchor (☎ 01803 859373) offers live music and reasonably-priced food and drink. Quayside (☎ 01803 855751) on King Street is good for a bar lunch or an à la carte dinner.

Taxi:	Brixham Taxis (☎ 01803 853000)
Car hire:	consult marina office
Bus:	local services to Paignton, Torquay & Newton Abbot
Rail:	from Paignton or Torquay - services to Dartmouth and all stations to London
Ferry:	services to Paignton (dependent on tide) and Torquay
Airport:	Exeter Airport

for more details, see Directory Section

River Dart

The River Dart is a real treat. Its spectacular narrow entrance between the twin castles is only the beginning as there is wonderful scenery up the valley, and the prospect of **Dartmouth** itself with the Royal Naval College looming large in the background is attractive as well. Fine old houses line the waterfront and narrow streets climb up the hill behind, steeped in history and full of interest. The sheltered natural harbour has meant that Dartmouth has a maritime history stretching back over a thousand years, and the Crown recognised its strategic importance for trade and defence by adopting the right to control traffic on the river in 1327. You can find out about local history at the Dartmouth Museum (☎ 01803 832923) which is based in an old merchant's house which dates from 1640 at The Butterwalk. Commercial use of the port has dwindled, but its superb location for the yachtsman has meant that it has not been abandoned! There is a good choice of places to berth, probably the most conveniently placed for exploring the town being Dart Marina just below the Naval College. This was the first pontoon-based marina to be built in Britain back in the 1960s. It has recently been refurbished and over-

hauled and offers first class up-to-date facilities. It is also not far from a full range of shops for provisions, including a supermarket. Less expensive options are available on the other side of the river. Dart Haven Marina is in **Kingswear**, and close to the Royal Dart Yacht Club which has a comfortable clubhouse and welcomes those who arrive on visiting yachts to enjoy its good facilities which include bar and restaurant, some visitors' moorings and showers. A little further up river in a more rural setting, Noss Quay Marina has a chandler and most facilities (no diesel or petrol). There are general stores at both, but for a full range of shops and to explore the town you will probably want to take advantage of ferry or water taxi services. These will carry you across to the waterfront in Dartmouth. The harbour authority also has visitors' moorings, and you can sometimes get a pontoon berth from the Dartmouth Yacht Club close to the south end of the quay on the west bank. Once ashore, a popular place to go for a drink is the Royal Castle Hotel (☎ 01803 833033) which is on The Quay. Porter's Restaurant (☎ 01803 835850) at 6 Church Close will feed you inexpensively, or you could try The Cutters Bunch Bistro (☎ 01803 832882) at 33 Lower Street for something a little more elaborate. The best in town (so make a reservation) is The Carved Angel (☎ 01803 832465) at 2 South Embankment. If you are based at Dart Haven on the east bank there's the Royal Dart Yacht Club of course, or you could head for The Ship for a drink or the Steampacket Inn for pub food if you don't want to cross over.

Artist: **Anthony Flemming**
DARTMOUTH *Courtesy of:* **The Artist**

Taxi:	Devon Taxis (☎ 01803 833778)
Cycle hire:	available at Dart Marina
Bus:	Dartmouth Embankment to Totnes, Kingsbridge and Plymouth. Kingswear to Brixham and Torquay.
Rail:	Scenic steam railway from Kingswear to Paignton (☎ 01803 555872), which links to national rail network
Ferries:	passenger and vehicle ferries between Dartmouth & Kingswear river cruisers land at Totnes
Airport:	Exeter Airport

for more details, see Directory Section

Upriver

We haven't told you about the river cruisers or the scenic steam railway along the river bank as the best way to enjoy the river is from your own boat - unless you are feeling idle! If you don't know the river, it would be a crime not to explore upstream for at least some distance. The countryside is lovely and there are several interesting and attractive towns and villages on the way. The Dart is navigable for about 10 miles all the way up to **Totnes** which has an inviting waterfront, Elizabethan houses, a castle and plenty of old world charm. Drying berths are available alongside the quay, but there's not much space so do check with the berthing master before committing yourself to a stay any further up than **Dittisham**. There are visitors' mooring buoys at Dittisham which, we hardly need to say, is another attractive little place and it's worth a run ashore to sample the fare at the Ferry Boat Inn (☎ 01803 722368). The boatyard at Dartside Quay in **Galmpton** Creek just opposite might be able to let you have a berth, but access is quite severely limited by the tide. If you go ashore here, The Manor Inn (☎ 01803 842346) is a good spot for a drink, and Squires (☎ 01803 842169) is an inexpensive eatery. Alternatively, you are really very close to Paignton and Brixham, so you might like to take a short taxi ride to the more abundant options at either of these. Further afield at Galmpton, overlooking the River Dart, the Maypool Park Hotel (☎ 01803 842442) is good for dishes which make use of local seafood.

Salcombe and the Kingsbridge Estuary

The headlands of Start Point and Prawle Point mark the most southerly point of Devon. Just round the corner to the west, there's a deep water natural harbour offering good shelter once you have crossed the bar – not something you should contemplate in strong southerlies. The Kingsbridge Estuary with Salcombe at its mouth is a marvellous cruising ground with a network of attractive creeks extending five miles inland to the picturesque town of Kingsbridge itself. A lot of the estuary is pretty shallow, so it is perhaps most suitable for smaller yachts and dinghies. However, with care, boats which draw up to two metres can get all the way to Kingsbridge as long as they are happy to take the ground which is soft mud. Check with the harbour office for availability of pontoon or drying berths before committing yourself to a stay up here. After you pass Salcombe, there are several places where you can anchor in deep water to enjoy the surroundings in peace and quiet after all the dinghies and dayboats have gone home for the night. Most of the estuary is a designated nature reserve, so you will not be alone as there are plenty of birds to watch at all times of the year. **Salcombe** itself is a popular holiday base for sailors and can be busy in the high season, especially around the Festival in June and the Regattas in August. Narrow streets with old stone houses crowding their way right to the waterfront give the quay area a delightful atmosphere, and there are attractive sandy coves on both sides of the narrow estuary for bucket and spade work. For local history, just outside the town, the Overbecks Museum and Garden (☎ 01548 842893) has an interesting collection and is set in an attractive landscape. The Salcombe Museum in the lifeboat station includes a model of every Salcombe lifeboat since 1869 and other RNLI memorabilia.

The harbour authority has about 50 pontoon berths (not connected to land) and 100 moorings for visitors that are all accessible at all states of the tide. The pontoon by the harbour office is for short stays (up to 1 hour) for visitors to load stores etc. Visiting yachts can leave their tenders on the inside of this pontoon. Facilities are provided at Salcombe Yacht Club on Cliff Road which is close to some of the visitors' moorings (tie up your tender at the steps by the Club starting box), or by the Island Cruising Club in Island Street (or by prior arrangement you may be able to moor alongside their floating sailing school - _Egremont_). Showers, bars and food are available at both clubs. There's also a full range of shops for provisions within a couple of hundred yards of the harbour office and visitors' pontoon and most don't observe the early closing day on Thursdays. Pubs and restaurants are abundant along Fore Street which runs along the waterfront. For food and drink, The Fortescue Inn, The Kings Arms (which offers Indian takeaway food as well) and the Victoria Inn are all worth a visit, or for a restaurant meal try Dusters (☎ 01548 842634), The Galley (☎ 01548 842828) or Clares (☎ 01548 842646). For a day's cruise or a break in your journey, drop your hook in Hope Cove - here the Hope and Anchor (☎ 01548 561294) run in superb style by several old sea dogs should not disappoint.

Taxi:	Select Taxis (☎ 01548 561577)
	D&C Taxi Services (☎ 01548 852906)
	H.W. Duderstadt (☎ 01548 842739)
Car hire:	not locally, see Plymouth
Bus:	services from Shadycombe Road to Kingsbridge
Rail:	nearest stations at Totnes or Plymouth
Airport:	Exeter, Plymouth or Bristol

for more details, see Directory Section

River Yealm

Tucked away on the east side of Wembury Bay, the casual passing mariner might fail to notice the entrance to the River Yealm behind the headland. That would be a mistake as this is a delightful place to explore with attractive woodland running down to the river banks. There are rocks to avoid in the bay, and a sandbar at the river mouth and inner spit as you approach The Pool, but with reasonable attention this is not a particularly difficult entrance except in strong westerlies. You can drop anchor just inside the entrance in Cellar Bay if the weather is settled, but do have a potter upriver first to enjoy the scenery. There is a visitors' pontoon (without direct access to the shore) in The Pool and another on the west bank just beyond the mouth of the Newton Arm - the creek which runs up to Newton Ferrers and Noss Mayo. Alternatively, you may be able to pick up a vacant mooring - consult the harbour-master. If you are happy on the bottom, you might be able to anchor up in the Newton Arm between the villages, but as this creek dries completely, getting ashore can be tricky or at least mucky! There are public landing places at Wide Slip at the south of the mouth to the Newton Arm or at the Parish Steps just a little further south which give access to Noss Mayo. The harbour office is near the imposing Yealm Hotel on the north bank which is accessible by steps just below the hotel. While the hotel

CREW
CLOTHING Co.®

Crew clothing started in 1993 and in just a few years has established itself as an outstanding manufacturer of the finest stylish casual clothing for men, women and children. This season sees the launch of the new Crew W for women. The new range boasts the full spectrum of stylish and elegant ladies wear; from fitted fleeces and sweatshirts to sleeveless shirts and lightweight trousers. As with all clothes under the Crew brand, Crew W is characterised by its fresh and vibrant colours and the high quality of its fabrics and workmanship.

All this, along with Crew's exceptional
attention to detail has meant that its unique
identity has been recognised by some of the
sports world's foremost sponsors who have
asked Crew to produce shirts for teams and
companies. You will find the Crew range on
sale at some of the country's major sporting
events, or in one of the seven Crew shops.
Alternatively, the unbeatable Crew range can
be accessed by mail order or over the internet.

Crew Clothing Co.
Mail Order,
62 New Kings Road,
London SW6 4LT.
tel +44 (0) 7000 900 100
fax +44 (0) 7000 27 39 26
Brochure Hotline: tel +44 (0) 7000 900 200
Internet: www.crewclothing.co.uk

looks like a convenient refuge, you would do much better by strolling for ten minutes to Newton Ferrers which has an attractive old waterfront. The Yealm Yacht Club welcomes visitors to use its facilities and has a bar and restaurant. The Dolphin Inn (☎ 01752 872007) almost next door is charming and a good spot for a drink and the Bistro Ferrers (☎ 01752 873146) is a bit smarter than the Yacht Club for a meal. There's a full range of good shops for provisions including a supermarket within half a mile of the waterfront. If you go ashore on the south side, a similar stroll takes you to Noss Mayo where there are a couple of pubs. The Ship is the one to head for if you are after a simple pub meal or fish & chips to take away.

Water Taxi:	VHF Channel 8 "Yealm Water Taxi"
Taxi:	Nearby in Wembry, Wembry Cabs (☎ 01752 862151)
Bus:	local service to Plymouth
Rail:	National network from Plymouth
Airport:	Plymouth Airport
Ferries:	from Plymouth to the continent

for more details, see Directory Section

Artist: **Brian Lancaster NEWTON FERRERS**
Courtesy of: **The Artist**

Plymouth

Plymouth Sound is a large natural harbour which has played a key role in the maritime history of Britain. We all know the story about Drake and his game of bowls which didn't prevent him from taking his place as second in command of the fleet assembled here to see off the Spanish Armada in 1588 (with a little help from the weather) but there is a lot more to Plymouth than this. The Naval Base at Devonport to the west of Plymouth is still an important part of Britain's defence forces and Plymouth's position which gives easy access to the open oceans has made it a popular point for departure on voyages of exploration and international trade. So be warned, you will need to watch out for and keep clear of ferries, warships and submarines - check in your almanac for details of advance warning on naval activities, and be prepared to obey traffic signals and instructions given by the harbour authorities. With a population of around a quarter of a million people, Plymouth is the largest town in the south west and is a bustling place to visit, especially after the peace and tranquillity you may have enjoyed in some of the neighbouring

backwaters. There are loads of things to see and do here. For historical flavour, try the Royal Citadel (☎ 01752 775841 - tickets from Plymouth Dome nearby) next to The Hoe, or The Prysten House (☎ 01752 661414) in Finewell Street which is a fine 15th century house in the heart of the city centre. The City Museum and Art Gallery (☎ 01752 264878) has interesting collections of paintings, silver and china as well as local and natural history exhibitions, and Crownhill Fort (☎ 01752 793754) in Crownhill Fort Road is a bit of a hike from the town centre, but offers a fine outlook and has much to explore and see. In the Elizabethan Barbican area close to the Royal Citadel, you can look round the 200 year old Plymouth Dry Gin Distillery (☎ 01752 665292) which still makes gin in the traditional way. You should also explore the narrow streets of this area if you are in search of antique shops and art galleries. The more spacious Georgian street plan of the centre of the town has a good selection of shops as well. Don't be too disappointed if you don't find as many historic streets as you would like, Plymouth has paid the price for being an important military stronghold. This has not, however, affected the grassy expanse of The Hoe which is always a good place to take your ease and gaze out over the sound, picturing the historic scenes which have been enacted there. If you yearn for real countryside and open spaces, Plymouth is a good base to explore Dartmoor - the closest parts of which are 15 or 20 minutes away by car or bus.

Artist: **Brian Lancaster THE HARBOUR,
PLYMOUTH** *Courtesy of:* **The Artist**

There is an almost bewildering choice of places offering berths to the visiting yacht. For the convenience of being close to the centre of the town, you will probably want to aim for Sutton Harbour Marina or Queen Anne's Battery Marina both of which lurk close to the citadel. Both marinas have over 300 moorings and are therefore comprehensively equipped. The latter is where the prestigious and ancient Royal Western Yacht Club of England has its splendid premises (where the crews of visiting yachts are welcome). The club is famous for organising or instigating a variety of ocean races including the Single-Handed Transatlantic Race first sailed by Francis Chichester and Blondie Haslar in 1960, and it organises the finishing arrangements for the Fastnet Race. Visitors are also welcome at the Royal Plymouth Corinthian Yacht Club which is on Madeira

The Mayflower International Marina
Plymouth

The Mayflower International Marina, Plymouth is ideally situated on the banks of the River Tamar overlooking Mount Edgecumbe Country Park at the heart of one of the United Kingdom's finest cruising areas.

Attractive south coast inlets such as Salcombe, Fowey, Dartmouth or the Fal Estuary are just perfect for local cruising and Plymouth is a natural departure point for the Channel Islands, France, Ireland or beyond.

Owned and run by its own berth-holders, Mayflower International Marina has established a unique and highly successful operation and holds the industry's highest accolade, The Five Gold Anchor Award, for its high standards, facilities and value for money.

A very relaxed atmosphere surrounds the Marina, which nevertheless is renowned for its strict security. Continuous manning 24 hours a day ensures that property and privacy are protected alike. Full facilities are available all year round.

The Marina enjoys a deep water access at all states of the tide - there are no cills or lock gates to negotiate.

Mayflower International Marina
Ocean Quay
Richmond Walk
Plymouth
PL1 4LS
Tel: 01752 556633
Fax: 01752 606896
E-mail: mayflower@mayflowermarina.co.uk

Road on the Hoe waterfront. A few swinging moorings for visitors are available from both these clubs. Visitors' moorings can sometimes also be had at the Millbay Marina Village opposite Drake's Island which is a small but comfortable base with limited facilities. If you plan to explore up the Tamar, you might take advantage of the excellent facilities and 24 hour access and services offered by the Mayflower International Marina in The Narrows close to Devonport. This is a bit further away from the centre of town, but there is a courtesy bus service from the marina.

For a drink or meal in town, if it is harbour views that you are after, then China House (☎ 01752 260930) on Marrowbone Slip, is the pub for you with seating on the verandah and varied bar food. For a more eccentric atmosphere, try the unspoilt Dolphin (☎ 01752 660876) on the Barbican, where the clientele includes fishermen, actors and artists and there are several Beryl Cook original art pieces displayed here. The Ship (☎ 01752 667604) on the Quay, is worth a visit for its pleasant harbour views and various offers on food. For dining with a continental flavour, Chez Nous (☎ 01752 266793) on Frankfort Gate, is a little bit of France with à la carte menu and the Duke of Cornwall (☎ 01752 266256) on Millbay Road near the town centre is a personally run hotel with wide ranging and inventive cuisine.

Taxi:	Express (☎ 01752 669999), or (☎ 01752 222222)
Bus:	local services link to Western National (☎ 01752 222666)
Rail:	Plymouth Station other side of town centre (☎ 0345 484850)
Ferry:	to Santander (summer only) & Roscoff (Brittany Ferries ☎ 0990 360360)
Airport:	Plymouth Airport 12 miles from city centre (BA reservations ☎ 0345 222111)

for more details, see Directory Section

Artist: **Brian Lancaster DRAKE'S ISLAND, PLYMOUTH** *Courtesy of:* **The Artist**

Upriver - The River Tamar

Pick up a copy of the Small Craft Guide to Plymouth's waterways which gives information about what you can see and where there are facilities. There are a number of areas of Special Scientific Interest up the Tamar and its tributaries, and there is a wealth of wildlife to enjoy. A major claim to fame is the significant number of avocet which winter here, though you're unlikely to benefit from this unless you are being quite hearty about your choice of cruising season. There's easily navigable water to the bridges at Saltash, where the banks of the river stop being built up and the countryside opens out. The rail bridge by Brunel is magnificent and was completed in 1859, the year he died. Shortly before you reach the bridges, you have the option to head off west up the St Germans or Lynher River which is readily navigable to St Germans Quay (which belongs to the Quay Sailing Club and is about five miles up) and further for those with shallow draft. However, if you don't want to dry out, you will need to anchor below the village of Antony just a bit more than a mile from the Tamar. Antony House close to the river bank is a fine 18th century house (built in about 1711) with lovely woodland gardens to visit or admire from the river (NT ☎ 01752 812191 - phone to check which days it's open). Heading on up the Tamar, you share the valley with the Tamar Valley Line (☎ 01392 476338) which is a lovely country branch line and offers an alternative way of enjoying the scenery. From Cargreen onwards it gets pretty shallow, but if you don't mind sitting on the bottom, and your mast's not too high to get under the power cables near Weir Quay, you can explore for several miles as the river winds its way up the valley. There's food and drink ashore at the small villages at Cargreen (where there is also a village shop and post office) and up by the imposing railway viaduct at Calstock. You can pick up fuel and water at the boatyards at Weir Quay and at Calstock.

Cornwall

There's a good variety of places to visit along the coasts of Cornwall. Some of the smaller coves and harbours are really only suitable for small boats and those who are happy to dry out. If you can't, or are unwilling to do this, you may well miss some of the best places to visit. However, you can find deep water moorings and anchorages in the rivers at Fowey and Falmouth, and there are locked yacht basins at Penzance and Padstow. The Rivers Tamar and St Germans are also good cruising grounds. While they are to a greater or lesser extent (the Tamar forms the boundary) in Cornwall, they are accessible via Plymouth which is not, and so were covered at the end of the last section. The Cornish coastline is spectacular with fine cliffs, rocky bays and luxuriant vegetation. The climate benefits from the Gulf Stream and you will find plants growing here which are surprising at this northern latitude. There are wonderful cultivated gardens to visit, and the countryside and clifftops are often decorated with wild flowers and shrubs in glorious profusion. Cornwall's industrial heritage has also left its mark on the coastline, though the frequent chimneys from the pumping and winching stations along the coast are hardly a blight as they blend into the scenery, often having been part of it for centuries. They stand as a reminder of the extensive mining operations for both copper and tin which in places stretched for miles under the sea in intricate networks of shafts and tunnels.

Artist: **Moira Huntly** POLPERRO
Courtesy of: **The Artist**

Penlee Point to Fowey

Looe is a popular holiday resort which is a delight to visit and it still boasts a busy fishing fleet. It's also where the Shark Angling Club of Great Britain has its headquarters and it's a popular place for anglers in search of salmon, sea trout and brown trout. Though the harbour dries, there's plenty of depth at high water. However, it's only really accessible for an hour and a half each side, and the rather fine seven arched bridge which links East Looe and West Looe will prevent those with any sort of mast from getting far upriver. When the fishing boats are in harbour, it can be crowded, though there are some designated visiting yacht berths on the west bank. The harbour office manages facilities for ablutions or you can arrange to use the premises of the Looe Sailing Club (☎ 01503 262559) which is in Buller Street in East Looe.

For refreshment, the Olde Salutation on Fore Street is an old fashioned pub with lots of atmosphere and nautical memorabilia. It serves good, simple food, is open all day, and is not far from the coast path. For dinner only, Klymiarven (☎ 01503 262333) on Barbican Hill in East Looe, is accessible from the town on foot and has great views of Looe itself and the harbour.

Just along the coast, the pretty town of **Polperro** has a tiny drying harbour with very limited space for visitors. The town can be very busy with tourists during the day, but that is only because it is a most pleasant place to visit. You will however, find it delightful out of season and a visit is recommended. Facilities are limited, but you don't come to a place like this for shopping or maintenance, so head ashore to try out some of the town's hostelries. Blue Peter (☎ 01503 272743) on The Quay is a small and friendly pub which serves no food, but allows you to bring your own sandwiches. Crumplehorn Mill Inn (☎ 01503 272348), converted from an old mill, boasts a history with a mention in the Domesday Book, and has good food and beer. The Kitchen (☎ 01503 272780) located by the harbour at The Coombes, provides a fine menu of local produce with international flavour, while the Three Pilchards (☎ 01503 272233) above the harbour, is a fisherman's local with generous, good value seafood. There are lots of other little pubs tucked away in this small village which are easily found on foot.

Fowey

Set in craggy coastline decorated with coves and castles, we find our next port of call. The small town of Fowey is tucked inside the river behind the headland village of Polruan on the opposite bank. The port has been an important trading haven for around 2000 years, and both the Romans and Phoenicians used it as a base for dealings with Ireland, and you would probably be surprised to learn that it is still one of the dozen busiest ports in Britain. This is thanks to the china clay dock upriver to the north of the town whence about three million tons of Cornwall is shipped out each year. The docks are out of sight of the entrance and moorings at Fowey so they don't spoil the view, though it can be quite disconcerting to be reminded about them by occasionally meeting a 15,000 ton freighter in a river which is barely 200 yards wide! This mustn't be allowed to put you off, and the stretch of river with most of the visitors' moorings and pontoons has plenty of room for everyone. The town's waterfront has changed very little since the turn of the nineteenth century and, with the rows of bright, neat, little houses rising up the hill, gives a cheerful and inviting prospect. Visit the Fowey Town Museum (☎ 01726 833513) in Trafalgar Square for local historic background, and St Catherines Castle (EH ☎ 01209 719988) which is a small fort built by Henry VIII at the river mouth, mostly for the view and access to the wonderful coves nearby. There are various options for mooring, all under the management of the Harbour Commissioners, so give them a call on Ch 12 ("Fowey Harbour Radio") as you come in. The pontoons by Albert Quay near the harbour office are for short stays of not more than a couple of hours. Most of the visitors' moorings and unconnected pontoons are on the Polruan side where the shelter is good. There is some limited space to anchor just outside the entrance to Pont Pill if you prefer. There are ferries and water taxis to save you having to flog across the river in your dinghy, and once ashore, you will find a good range of shops close to the waterfront downstream of the Albert Quay. Though reaching the nearest supermarket involves a five mile bus or taxi ride to Holmbush, you probably won't need it as there's a good general store and excellent butcher, fishmonger and delicatessen. Whilst it could be (and has been for your editor!) frustrating to be storm-bound here while waiting to get across to the food and drink to be had in Brittany, there's plenty to keep you well fed and watered here for several days. There are a number of good pubs, mostly offering food as well as drink, and for the best home-made bar food, The Galleon (☎ 01726 833014) on the Town Quay is the one to head for. The Lugger (☎ 01726 833435) in Fore Street and The Ship in an elegant old town house are also both worth a visit, and at the King of Prussia on the Town Quay, the juke box will probably save you having to make conversation if you like your atmosphere noisy. For restaurant meals, we suggest The Commodore (☎ 01726 833594) opposite Albert Quay for a reasonably priced menu which includes Sicilian fare. Sam's (☎ 01726 832273) is run by the owners of the splendid deli almost next door and specialises in fish dishes. Try the Globe Posting House (☎ 01726 833322) in Fore Street for something a little more elaborate or alternatively Cordon Bleu (☎ 01726 832359) in The Esplanade. If you want to

Artist: **Clive Madgwick FISHING BOATS, POLPERRO** *Courtesy of* **Rosenstiel's**

push the boat out, the top of the range is Food for Thought (☎ 01726 832221) which is on the Town Quay.

Upriver

To best enjoy the scenery upriver, it's probably worth leaving the boat at the visitors' pontoon at Mixtow Pill, opposite the docks, and continuing by dinghy. Given a favourable tide and a reasonable outboard, there are several miles more river running through attractive countryside and woodland with a number of creeks and interesting villages to explore.

Water taxi:	VHF Ch. 9 "Fowey Water Taxi"
Taxi:	Fowey Taxis (☎ 01726 832676)
Car hire:	St Austell - Enterprise (☎ 01726 75700) or Beech Motors (☎ 01726 74743)
Cycle hire:	Cranks 01726 832864 - answerphone booking system
Bus:	Western National (☎ 01208 79898)
Rail:	Par Station (5 miles away)
Airport:	Newquay or Plymouth

for more details, see Directory Section

Fowey to the River Fal

Charlestown has a small, privately owned harbour which is now the base for a fleet of tall ships which are used for making period films. This is rather nice as you can easily imagine what the harbour must have been like when it was first built for exporting clay and other such missions . . . unless they are all off on location elsewhere! You need to contact the harbour-master in advance for permission (which is not always given) to use the harbour. (Harbour-master: 01726 67526 or VHF

Ch. 14.) The inner basin is appealingly locked but not usually accessible for visiting yachts which should moor in the outer harbour which dries. There are a number of attractions for tourists around the harbour which can make it busy, but are interesting all the same. Charlestown itself is almost as far from the harbour as the much larger market town of St Austell where there is a full range of shops.

For a convenient drink or meal, try Rashleigh Arms (☎ 01726 73635) and the Harbour, both overlooking the harbour with good food and great views. Pier House Hotel (☎ 01726 67955) is right next door to Harbour, and is handy for one of their à la carte meals.

Mevagissey has a small harbour a lot of which almost dries at low water. There is very limited space for visitors, but room for some, in nearly 2 metres at low water, just inside the South Pier where shelter is not great in strong easterlies. Most facilities you could hope for in a small place are available. There is still an active fleet of small fishing boats, and a number of tourist boats, so the harbour remains very much in use for business. (Harbour-master: 01726 843305, VHF Ch. 16.) This is another pretty little place with a good range of pubs, bars and restaurants to cater for the numerous visitors who are drawn to the village. Cars are not allowed in the steep narrow streets which is a bonus, and there is a museum, and aquarium and an extensive model railway exhibition to see. For more peace and quiet, the clifftop paths to north and south are recommended for glorious views of sea, village and Cornish countryside.

For such a small village, we are able to recommend a fair sprinkling of pubs including the Fountain Inn (☎ 01726 842320) on Fore Street, whose atmosphere is enhanced by slate floors, beams and historic photographs. For a smaller, but no less welcoming pub, the Kings Arms (☎ 01726 843869) provides cheap and cheerful food while near the harbour, on Fore Street, the Ship (☎ 01726 843324) serves generous food, quick and well with nice touches inside, such as open fires and nautical decor.

Falmouth

Flanked by Pendennis Castle to the west and St Mawes Castle to the east, the entrance to Carrick Roads as the lower estuary of the Fal is known is a striking one. Falmouth owes its existence to this excellent natural harbour, and would probably have become one of the most important ports on the south coast were it not for the fact that it is just too far from the centre of things. Falmouth's history is not as long as one might expect since the port, and the town which grew with it, was only founded in the latter part of the 17th century and up until then, Truro and Penryn, both further up their respective rivers, had been the major centres of maritime business. Until the railway link was built in 1863, Falmouth was relatively inaccessible by land, though the deep water and good shelter made it popular with passing commercial traffic in the days of the great sailing ships. The arrival of powered vessels made this staging post less crucial, and while still busy to this day, the role of the port has diminished. As commercial activity waned, Falmouth quickly took advantage of the area's benign climate and stunning scenery to become a popular holiday destination, and the collection of creeks and rivers which connect to the estuary made it an inevitable choice with yachtsmen as sailing grew in popularity as a leisure pursuit. Opinion is divided over whether you need to take as much as a couple of weeks to explore the area thoroughly, or whether in fact it could keep you occupied for a whole season. Suffice it to say that with 12 miles of navigable water up to the ancient market town of Truro and numerous other creeks and rivers in attractive countryside, there is plenty to explore in these sheltered waters. The Cornish climate makes the area a horticulturalist's dream and Falmouth has three splendid municipal gardens for you to enjoy. Fox Rosehill Garden (☎ 01872 224355) in Melville Road has many exotic trees and shrubs and the Queen Mary Gardens on the seafront offer good views out to sea. The Gyllyngdune Gardens provide a fine setting for the Victorian veranda and bandstand near the town's elegant theatre Princess Pavilion (☎ 01326 211222), which, together with the Arts Centre (☎ 01326 212300) and Art Gallery (☎ 01326 313863), provides a programme of cultural events throughout the year. To find out about Falmouth's historical context within the rest of Cornwall, head for the Cornwall Maritime Museum (☎ 01326 316745) in Bell Court where the collection includes material prints, pictures, models and a gallery dedicated to the Falmouth Packet Boat Service. It would be difficult to forget about Pendennis Castle (EH ☎ 01326 316594), built by Henry VIII, proud on its headland where fine views are complemented by exhibitions which illustrate the strategic role of this fortress until as recently as the last world war.

The entrance to Carrick Roads is straightforward at all states of the tide, and clearly lit so not too taxing by night even to strangers. There is a selection of places to moor at Falmouth with visitors' moorings and berths available from the harbour-master at the North Quay where there is a full range of facilities. Just along the quay to the southeast is Port Pendennis Marina which may also have space for visiting yachts. These two are in the most convenient location for exploring the town, for provisions and more general shopping. The Royal Cornwall Yacht Club also has a few moorings for visiting yachts a little further up river and visitors are welcome to use their facilities which include bar, restaurant, showers and a launch service. Another option is Falmouth Marina which is half a mile further up the River Penryn and has most facilities including a bar which does food on site. There's also a supermarket three minutes walk away. Once you've done your shopping and exploring, you may be ready for a drink; in which case repair to the Chain Locker, the Old Ale House or the Quayside Inn (☎ 01326 312113) on Custom House Quay where you can get pub meals. Nearby, the Warehouse Bistro (☎ 01326 313001) won't break the bank for a restaurant meal, and the Seafood Bar (☎ 01326 313001) in Quay Street is also a good choice. For good food that's a bit more pricey, try Prestons (☎ 01326 312774) at 21 Church Street, or a short taxi ride away, Pennypots (☎ 01326 250251) at Maenporth Beach is worth the journey.

Taxi:	Aaron Taxis (☎ 01326 314691)
Car hire:	Europcar (☎ 01326 319357)
	Avis (☎ 01326 211511) (at Falmouth Marina)
Bus:	local services from town centre pass Falmouth Marina
Rail:	Falmouth and Penryn Stations for services to Truro on London-Penzance mainline
Airport:	Newquay Airport (☎ 01736 860551) for domestic services

for more details, see Directory Section

Upriver

Not far above Falmouth Marina the old port of Penryn, which to some extent Falmouth usurped, has an older historic feel with its interesting buildings and courtyards. There's a boatyard with basic facilities and a few visitors' moorings, though tidal constraints do come into play. In fact, it's so close to Falmouth, especially to the marina, that probably the best way to get here is by dinghy. The same is true of the quaint and elegant village of Flushing just opposite Falmouth. Alternatively, you could take the ferry which runs across from the Prince of Wales Pier.

St Mawes

On the opposite side of the entrance to Carrick Roads, St Mawes is much less of a metropolis than Falmouth and may appeal if you want somewhere a little quieter. By day though, it can be rather overrun with trippers across from Falmouth on the ferry. Like them, you can visit St Mawes Castle (EH ☎ 01326 270526), and if open, Lamorran House Gardens (☎ 01326 270800), which overlook the sea and include interesting water gardens, are well worth seeing. The harbour-master can direct you to a space alongside the quay or a visitors' mooring, or the

St Mawes Sailing Club may have a mooring available. The club is where to head to for a shower and has a bar which welcomes visitors and sometimes offers food as well. The Rising Sun (☎ 01326 270233) in the Square serves a good pint, and nearby the Idle Rocks Hotel (☎ 01326 270771) and The Victory Inn (☎ 01326 270324) on Victory Steps do good pub food. Broomers (☎ 01326 270440) on Marine Parade and the Old Watch House (☎ 01326 270279) in Kings Road both serve inexpensive meals. For more elaborate fare, try La Roche (☎ 01326 270293) on Marine Parade or The Tresanton Hotel (☎ 01326 270055) which is a couple of minutes walk away and extremely good.

Taxi:	Roseland Taxi (☎01872 580530)
Car hire:	Roseland Taxi (☎01872 580530)
Bus:	from the Square to Truro
Rail:	nearest stations St Austell or Truro
Airport:	Newquay Airport

for more details, see Directory Section

Upriver

The River Percuil is easily navigable for a mile or so above St Mawes, though moorings for visitors are hard to come by. Given the number of private moorings, anchoring isn't easy, and there are also oyster beds to contend with. This is probably another place to get the outboard going and potter up in the dinghy as this way you will be able to get much further and enjoy some splendid countryside.

River Fal

The Fal estuary and its various tributaries offer interesting cruising through spectacular scenery. If you don't mind drying out, you can get all the way to Truro, and there's deep water as far as Malpas. Following the River Fal as it winds its way up, there are numerous places of interest on the way. Several areas are designated Sites of Special Scientific Interest, so be sure to follow instructions from your almanac or pilot book on where to anchor, and there is a good range of wildlife to watch out for including dolphins and a variety of birds. If you are lucky, in the autumn you may see ospreys, and there are healthy contingents of waders and others which stay longer here than elsewhere, sometimes all winter, because of the mild climate. Heading up the Carrick Roads, there's a well equipped marina at the mouth of the **Mylor Creek**. Moorings and pontoon berths are available for visitors and there's a yacht club to welcome you as well. The Ganges Fish Restaurant (☎ 01326 374320) is on site and is one of the best in the area. This reminds us that this was once where HMS Ganges, a hulk used for training youngsters for the Navy, was moored. For provisions, you will need to stride a mile and a half up the lane which runs along the creek to Mylor Bridge, where there is also a good pub, The Lemon Arms, which serves meals. (taxi: Able taxis ☎ 01326 373007). Tucked just inside the next creek is the Pandora Inn (☎ 01326 372678) which is a good place to stop for a drink or a meal. The **Restonguet Creek** is very shallow, so you need to anchor just outside and take your dinghy up to the pontoon by the pub on the south west bank. There are good anchorages off Loe Beach

just below Feock and at Channels Creek which is close to Trelissick House (NT ☎ 01872 862090). Though the house is not open to the public, the lovely gardens and woodlands are (for a price!) and there is an art and craft gallery and a couple of places to eat lunch or tea. The river continues to wind between wooded banks giving tidal access to the small village of **Malpas** where there is a boatyard with some facilities and moorings. From here there's a bus or ferry service to Truro if you don't fancy the pilotage of the last stretch of the river, and the Heron Inn is an excellent watering hole.

At the head of navigation at **Truro**, you can moor alongside the Town and Worths Quays and the Garras Wharf - unless you draw next to nothing, you will need to arrive near high water as all the quays dry out. The city contains a marvellous mixture of Georgian buildings, cobbled streets and tiny alleyways and has a good variety of shopping, eating and drinking. At the centre of the town, Truro Cathedral is one of the country's more recently constructed cathedrals. It is only a little more than a hundred years old, having mainly been built during the 1880s. Its three spires dominate the town, and it is pleasingly constructed from a variety of local stone. Also worth a visit while in the area is the Royal Cornwall Museum (☎ 01872 272205) which is the leading museum and art gallery in the county. There are boat models and marine paintings as well as archaeological collections - which include Egyptian, Greek, Roman and oriental material. Local and natural history, ceramics, costume and Cornish minerals are also represented. These are all examined in permanent exhibitions and there are regular special exhibitions as well. The city is also famous for its Three Spires International Arts Festival which takes place in late May-early June and there's a splendid theatre and concert hall, The Hall for Cornwall (☎ box office 01872 262466) where there are cultural events throughout the year.

There are lots of places to quench a thirst in this delightful town, starting with the Old Ale House (☎ 01872 271122) on Quay Street which has sawdust on the floor, and serves very good, reasonably priced bar food and a great selection of real ales!

The Wig & Pen (☎ 01872 273028) and City Inn (☎ 01872 272623) are both friendly with a good mix of locals and tourists. For more sophisticated dining, Alverton Manor (☎ 01872 276633) on Tregolls Road is an attractive former bishop's house and convent, and Oliver's Restaurant (☎ 01872 273028) on Castle Street in the city centre, favours the use of fish on the menu and also serves good bar food.

Taxi:	City Taxis (☎ 0800 318708) or Ava Cab (☎ 01872 241214)
Car hire:	Car Rental (☎ 01872 276797) or Vospers (☎ 01872 223676)
Cycle hire:	Truro Cycles 01872 271703
Bus:	Western National (☎ 01209 719988) or Truronian (☎ 01872 273453)
Rail:	Truro Station, mainline between Penzance and London
Airport:	Newquay Airport (25 miles away)

for more details, see Directory Section

Helford River

Here's another scenic river which carries you inland through beautiful Cornish countryside. Though not as extensive as the Fal and its tributaries (or maybe because of this!) it is a charming haven offering good shelter in anything other than strong easterlies. Facilities are rather limited, and there's nowhere to berth alongside unless you dry out at the delightful Quay in Gweek, but for heaven's sake, we can manage without pontoons can't we? Falmouth is just round the corner if we do need that sort of thing! You can anchor in the bay on the north side of the entrance below the little village of Durgan where there's a beautiful garden owned by the National Trust: Glendurgan Garden (☎ 01208 74281 for opening times). Alternatively, you might be able to pick up a visitors' mooring in The Pool between the villages of Helford and Helford Passage. Consult the mooring officer if there are no obvious spaces. Above the pool, anchoring is not permitted because of the oyster beds - it's also all pretty shallow, so if you do want to explore up to **Gweek**, you might prefer to do so in your dinghy. Gweek was once a Roman port, and still has a couple of boatyards. A popular place to visit here is the Cornish Seal Sanctuary where stranded seals are nursed back to full strength before being released. Visitors are warmly welcomed at the Porth Navas Yacht Club up Navas Creek, and at the Helford River Sailing Club at Helford on the south bank. Here you will also find the Shipwrights Arms (☎ 01326 231235) which offers excellent simple food. There's also a general store with a post office counter. At Helford Passage on the north bank, the Ferry Boat Inn (☎ 01326 250625) serves food and drink and also lets visiting yachtsmen have a shower. Just outside the mouth of the Helford, there's an anchorage in **Gillan Creek** just by the village of St Anthony-in-Meneage. Contact Sailaway St Anthony to see if there are any vacant moorings - this is a pretty spot, though facilities are very limited.

Helford River to Penzance - Round the Lizard

With its cliffs and coves, this is a fierce looking stretch of coastline, and the tides that run around Lizard Point and over occasionally shallow outcrops can cause fierce sea conditions as well - even in apparently fine weather. Judicious poring over almanacs, pilot books and tide tables is advisable before starting any passage along here. There's also not really anywhere to hide if the weather gets nasty between Falmouth and Penzance. However, if the weather is settled, there are a number of lovely little anchorages where you can spend a few hours peacefully enjoying the spectacular coastline and wildlife which it harbours. Porthoustock and Coverack Coves are both east facing and close to their respective villages. Beware the Manacles, site of numerous wrecks which make the area a mecca for divers, which lie about a mile offshore between these two coves. South of Coverack the cliffs rear up to the headland at Black Head. As you start to clear Black Head (which should be given at least half a mile's clearance) on a fine day, Bass Point and just behind it, Lizard Point, the most southerly part of mainland Britain, peep out from behind. As the coastline starts to head north, you soon reach Mullion Cove tucked in behind the island where there is good shelter in easterlies.

Porthleven is less than five miles further on, and here there is an atmospheric little fishing harbour (which dries) giving access to easily the biggest centre of population we've seen since Falmouth. However, with about 3000 people living here, it's hardly a metropolis and is probably more popular with divers than with yachtsmen as it is tricky to get into and can be closed in poor weather - check with the harbour-master (☎ 01326 574270 or 563472) or Falmouth Coastguard if in doubt. Do not expect to find clear buoyage or navigational aids at any of these remote anchorages. You will need a chart with a large scale and probably a local pilot book or at least a comprehensive almanac to be sure of finding your way in and out safely.

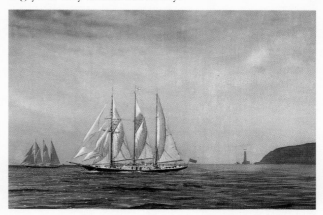

Artist: **Anthony Flemming SAILING SHIPS OFF THE LIZARD** *Courtesy of:* **The Artist**

The geography of the shore along much of this stretch of coastline makes it popular territory for surfing, so it will not come as much of a surprise to learn that it does not offer much refuge for yachts! However, there is a picturesque anchorage (but only in offshore winds) at **St Michael's Mount** close to the ancient town of Marazion. The Mount (NT 01736 710507) was originally the site of a Benedictine priory, and the castle dates back to the 12th century. Perched on the top of this rocky outcrop, and now set in beautiful gardens, it became a private house in the 17th century and consists of fine rooms steeped in history and a network of narrow passages. There's room for a few visitors inside the drying harbour on the island, or you might prefer to anchor just to the west of the harbour. Facilities on the island itself are very limited but there's more at the other end of the tidal cobbled causeway in Marazion. The Mounts Bay Sailing Club at Godolphin Steps is open in the evenings except on Mondays and Wednesdays and welcomes visitors to use its bar and showers. Other hospitable spots locally include The Godolphin Arms (☎ 01736 710202) and The Kings Arms (☎ 01736 710291) which are good choices for a drink - the latter serves good food as well. For a restaurant meal, the Clipper (☎ 01736 711060) is a good choice. The local museum is based in the Old Fire Station close to the end of the causeway and explores the history of this interesting town and the surrounding area. Just outside the town, the RSPB reserve at Marazion Marsh (☎ 01736 711682) boasts two unusual summer visitors, the spotted crake and the aquatic warbler, and this is the best place in

Artist: **Anthony Flemming** **ST MICHAEL'S MOUNT** Courtesy of: **The Artist**

Cornwall to see all sorts of birds which breed in reedbeds. The warden takes guided tours around the reserve every Wednesday morning.

Penzance and Newlyn

At last for the itinerant yachtsman, here is a secure harbour which offers reliable shelter. Even here though strong south or south easterlies can make the entrance dangerous. The growth of the town was mainly as a result of the tin industry in the 17th century, and Penzance's harbour was developed to capitalise on this. Though still something of a commercial port, and the base of the Scillonian which links the Scilly Isles to the mainland, yachts are welcome in the Wet Dock where there are 50 berths for visitors and which is accessible for a couple of hours each side of high water. There may be drying moorings available in the outer harbour, though these are usually all taken up by local boats. There is usually space to dry out alongside the harbour wall, or in fair weather you can drop anchor just outside the entrance. Penzance is the last town in England, but because of its traditional commercial role and ongoing attractiveness to visitors, it has a buzzing atmosphere. You can discover more about local history at the Penlee House Art Gallery and Museum (☎ 01736 363625) in Morrab Road, and for those of us who depend on their services, Trinity House National Lighthouse Museum (☎ 01736 60077) on Wharf Road, is somewhere which you will find interesting and ought to visit. Of slightly more tangential interest is the Cornwall Geological Museum, nearby in Alverton (☎ 01736 330183). There is a good range of shops in the town close to the harbour, and it's not far to the supermarket which is a slightly regrettable, albeit welcome, landmark on the waterfront to the east of the town. There are showers at the harbour office and a launderette near the railway station. If you fancy a run ashore for sustenance, The Turk's Head (☎ 01736 363093) is a popular, bustling pub, with good and varied food. Admiral Benbow (☎ 01736 363448) on Chapel Street is, as the name suggests, nautically themed, serving decent food and the downstairs restaurant is open all day during the summer months. The Abbey Hotel (☎ 01736 366906) is a pleasant 17th century house, close to the sea, and Beachfield Hotel (☎ 01736 362067) on The Promenade, is handily placed next to the quay to enjoy bar lunches or a more refined à la carte meal in the evening. For value for money, try Tarbert Hotel (☎ 01736 363758) on Clarence Street near the centre of town. This former sea captain's residence serves good fish dinners and bar lunches.

Taxi:	Carne's Taxis (☎ 01736 363572)
Car hire:	Europe Car Hire (☎ 01736 368340)
Cycle hire:	The Cycle Centre (☎ 01736 351671)
Bus:	Western National (☎ 01209 719988)
Rail:	Penzance Station – terminus for Intercity services to London
Airport:	Newquay Airport

for more details, see Directory Section

In adjoining **Newlyn**, the small harbour is home to a large fleet of fishing boats, but you might decide to brave this to take advantage of access with no tidal limitations. No specific visiting yacht moorings or berths are provided so you have to jolly along with the fishing boats which can be noisy and somewhat mucky neighbours. Most facilities are available, though mainly geared towards the needs of fishermen rather than yachtsmen. There are shops and hostelries on hand, and you are close to Penzance for a wider selection as well.

In Newlyn, the Tolcarne Inn (☎ 01736 363074) on Tolcarne Place is clean and well kept with a good choice of food. On Fore Street, the Fisherman's Arms (☎ 01736 63399) has superb views over Mount's Bay and the harbour and offers good simple food. If you want to get away from the pub atmosphere, Higher Faugan (☎ 01736 362076) about 3/4 of a mile south west of Newlyn serves a good dinner and bar lunches are available.

A prettier place to put in is **Mousehole** which is a couple of miles along the coast. This is a very small drying harbour with limited facilities for visiting yachts, but if that doesn't deter you, well worth putting into. The Lobster Pot Hotel (☎ 01736 731251) has an excellent restaurant and there are several other hospitable hostelries to look into as well. The Ship (☎ 01736 731234) should not be passed by. Right on the harbour, this bustling, friendly pub is popular with both locals and visitors, serving up decent bar food. Apparently it makes a good vantage point to enjoy the elaborate harbour lights at Christmas! For restaurants try Cornish Range (☎ 01736 731488) a delightful former smuggler's haunt, now a seafood restaurant on Chapel Street (booking, is advised.) Old Coastguard Inn (☎ 01736 731222) on The Parade offers both a popular bar menu and a restaurant blackboard with daily fish specials. Be warned, however – this delightful little place can be a bit of a honeypot for tourists in high season, so it's probably one to avoid at least at weekends.

Artist: **Brian Lancaster MOUSEHOLE**
Courtesy of: **The Artist**

Scillies

Lying less than 30 miles from Land's End, the Scilly Isles can be easily reached in a day's sail from Penzance given suitable conditions, or further afield if you are prepared to push it. This collection of something over 50 rocky islands of varying sizes is a wonderful cruising ground, though they present considerable navigation and pilotage challenges to those who are new to the area. It is not a place for the faint-hearted, and only experienced yachtsmen with good navigation skills should attempt to cruise here. Large scale charts and a pilot book with good coverage of this area (A Yachtsman's Guide to Scilly by Norman Gooding is helpful) are essential, and even those who are relatively familiar with the area's hazards will tend to choose to make a daylight landfall. Having said all that, don't be put off if you are up to it. This is somewhere where you will really be able to get away from the crowds, as there are numerous secluded anchorages, and even the centres of population are intimate. There are superb opportunities to enjoy wildlife in incomparable scenery, and some truly amazing cultivated gardens on Tresco.

St Mary's

St Mary's is the largest of the five inhabited islands, and is where you will find Hugh Town and the only harbour in the islands. This is where the ferry from the mainland docks daily and is also the base for fishing boats and a dozen or so launches which carry visitors on cruises to other islands in the group. While you are finding your way around, a trip on one of these might well help you to familiarise yourself with the area before setting off to explore in your own precious vessel. There are visitors' moorings at Hugh Town which is also the best place to head for if you need showers, fuel, repairs or provisions. Pick up a copy of the booklet "Duchy of Cornwall – Information for visiting craft" from the harbour-master as this gives important information about where you may and may not land throughout the group of islands and is a useful complement to your pilot book. Having come to the Scillies probably to get away from it all, you may not want to hang around in Hugh Town, but it is an attractive place and provides a good base to get the feel of the area.

Ashore, you will find a reasonable range of shops for provisions. However, bearing in mind that most of the stock has to be shipped from the mainland, you will do well to bring as much as you can with you. You can also browse in a variety of craft shops and art galleries which offer locally produced work. For historical background, the small St Mary's Museum has information about the local area including its numerous ancient monuments which range from stone-age tombs and settlements to Civil War fortifications. For those who fancy a bit of diving, this offers another way to explore. Contact Mark Groves who takes underwater safaris (☎ 01720 422732). For such a small place, Hugh Town does well to boast five pubs! The Atlantic (☎ 01720 422323) on The Strand in Hugh Town, is a popular low-beamed, nautical pub. Both locals and visitors enjoy the convivial atmosphere either sampling the bar food or surveying the harbour from the restaurant upstairs. The Bishop and Wolf (☎ 01720 422790) on Silver Street, provides much the same as the Atlantic with its food noted for fish dishes. Mermaid (☎ 01720 422701) on The Quay, is a typical stone-floored seafaring pub with an idyllic view of the harbour. As if that wasn't enough choice, Lock, Stock & Barrel both in Old Town (☎ 01720 422301) and in St Mary's (☎ 01720 423033), manages to combine the feel of a locals' bar and social club, serving food from sandwiches to pizzas and it is open all day! For an historic feel, we recommend the 16th century Star Castle Hotel (☎ 01720 422317) on The Garrison. It is about ¼ of a mile from the town centre, but as a nice touch, the hotel taxi meets guests from the quay, or the airport for that matter, and has a bar and two restaurants where you can enjoy the ambitious and successful cooking which incorporates local produce.

Taxi:	St Mary's Taxi Services (☎ 01720 422555)
	Scilly Cabs (☎ 01720 422901)
Car hire:	(☎ 01720 422431)
Cycle hire:	Buccabu (☎ 01720 422289)
Bus:	Local services and tours from Hugh Town
Rail:	Ferry & air links to Penzance for Intercity mainline to London
Ferry:	Isles of Scilly Steam Ship Co (☎ 01736 62009)
Airport:	Helicopter flights to Penzance & Tresco by British International Helicopters (☎ 01736 363871). Planes to Land's End Aerodrome near St Just by Skybus (☎ 01736 787017)

for more details, see Directory Section

Cruising the Islands

Where you choose to head for as you explore further afield will very much depend on weather conditions and forecasts, and your confidence at navigation through the often rock-strewn waters which interlock between the islands. The uninhabited island of Annet has particularly spectacular birdlife to admire (no landing in the breeding season) and throughout the islands, there are plenty of birds to look out for and identify. The spring and autumn migration seasons bring numerous species which are not often seen in much of mainland Britain, and some which are - including migrant birdwatchers who know that this is a good place to be at these times of the year. The inaccessibility of the Scillies means that this is not an invasion so large as to spoil the tranquillity, thankfully! There's a good variety of habitats on the second largest island in the Scillies which is **Tresco**, and you mustn't leave the area without visiting the Tresco Abbey Gardens (☎ 01720 22849) which include an astounding array of sub-tropical plants. There's a good anchorage in New Grimsby Sound where you might be able to pick up a mooring to enjoy the scenery with the ruins of Cromwell's Castle standing guard on the promontory. This, like a couple of other old military strongholds on the island, is managed by English Heritage who make no charge for the privilege of exploring the ruins. There's a general store and art gallery in the village and The Island Hotel with bar and restaurant gives the opportunity for a break from the galley.

Cornwall, North Coast

The coast on the north side of Cornwall is spectacular with jagged cliffs and rock-strewn bays. It is therefore hardly surprising that many yachtsmen tend to choose to make for Milford Haven to the north in Wales, or even further afield to the excellent cruising areas in

Artist: **Anthony Flemming CROMWELL'S CASTLE, SCILLIES** *Courtesy of:* **The Artist**

Southern Ireland, rather than getting involved with this rather inhospitable and, at times downright alarming, stretch of coastline. However, if you relish a challenge and the weather conditions and your level of experience are in the right balance, then there are interesting and attractive places for the intrepid to visit.

Artist: **Anthony Flemming LAND'S END** *Courtesy of:* **The Artist**

St Ives

After the rocky cliffs and headlands which line the coast from Land's End, St Ives Bay provides a change of prospect. This broad inlet is bordered with wide sandy beaches and there are anchorages along the west side close to St Ives itself, or you may prefer to pick up a visitors' mooring in the shelter of the drying harbour. A word of warning: this is not a good place to be in onshore winds or, you might be surprised to hear, during and after south westerly gales. Yachting facilities are a bit limited though water and diesel are available at the harbour.

St Ives is a popular seaside resort and busy fishing port.

For over a century, it has also been a favourite place to work for a large number of artists, so there are numerous galleries including the splendid country branch of the Tate Gallery (01736 796226), housed in a spectacular building overlooking the sea, where there is a good collection of interesting recent work. Your entry ticket here also entitles you to visit the former studio of the sculptor Barbara Hepworth which is now a museum. The St Ives lifeboat is also housed in a new building which was completed in 1993 - the architecture demonstrates dependability contrasting with the showmanship of the Tate Building. The town is an attractive place to wander around and has two contrasting waterfronts divided by St Ives Head. There's a full range of shops for provisions including a reasonable supermarket within a few minutes walk from the harbour. For entertainment, St Ives boasts a theatre and a cinema, and in September there's an extensive arts festival. Also close to the harbour on The Wharf, The Sloop Inn (☎ 01736 796584) is a good pub for a drink or a pub meal, though you will find there are many others which are worth visiting. There are also numerous restaurants to choose from: the best in town is probably Russets (☎ 01736 794700) in Fore Street. St Ives is set in superb country for walking and also worth a mention is the RSPB reserve on the **Hayle Estuary** (☎ 01736 711682) which is a couple of miles along the bay and plays host to numerous migrating and wintering wildfowl – go and have a look if you are in the area during the autumn. You can berth in the estuary (which dries) alongside one of the Quays, and there's a harbour-master should you require advice on the approach. You can get across the bar in good weather for about an hour each side of high water, and there are basic facilities on hand.

From St Ives:
Taxi: D.J. Cars (☎ 01736 796633)
Car hire: St Ives Motors (☎ 01736 795156)
Bus: services to Penzance, Truro and
            Falmouth
Rail: St Ives Station. Services to London, the
            Midlands and the North
for more details, see Directory Section

Newquay

This popular town is a calm weather option only as with any groundswell, this becomes no place for yachts. Newquay's drying harbour is also kept busy with fishing boats. Visiting yachts can lie beside the harbour wall, or anchor a quarter of a mile to the north of the harbour. Basic facilities are here as they are needed by the fishing boats, and there is a chandlers and a full range of shops for provisions. This is a popular holiday town and has a cosmopolitan feel, with a fine sandy beach that is popular for surfing. Ye Olde Dolphin Restaurant (☎ 01637 874262) is an excellent steakhouse, claimed by some to be the best in the county, and the Red Lion and the Sailors Arms are good pubs not far from the harbour.

Padstow

Padstow's maritime roots lie in fishing and latterly as a port for shipping the output from Cornish mines. Though both these activities have now declined, or died off completely, the harbour still has a business-like feel.

Artist: **Anthony Flemming TIN MINE**
Courtesy of: **The Artist**

The town is now a popular holiday resort and the Camel Estuary which it lies on is popular for sailing and boating of all sorts. Care is needed in the entrance to the estuary and you should not attempt to cross the bar too close to low water, especially when there's any swell running, or at all in strong north westerlies when seas may be breaking on the bar. The inner harbour is locked and offers good shelter with tidal access for a couple of hours each side of high water. There are no pontoons, so it's a case of lying in rafts against the quay sides, and in quiet periods there may be some fishing boats in as well. However, this really is quite bearable on the basis that there isn't a marina for miles – or any sort of sheltered all tide harbour come to that and there are all the facilities you could need at or close to the harbour. Alternatively, there is some space to anchor near The Pool, or you might be able to pick up a mooring. A further possibility is to find a visitors' space at the quay by the Rock Sailing & Waterski Club opposite Padstow which will give you a different perspective. There's a ferry service which links Padstow and Rock. As well as for all the sailing and boating, people come to Padstow and Rock for the good sandy beaches and fine countryside for walking. If the weather is poor, or you'd like some variety, there are plenty of shops to browse in (as well as for provisions – head for the fish dock for very fresh fish) and several museums to fill you in on all the local history and culture including The Padstow Museum (☎ 01841 532574) in Market Place which has displays covering shipwrecks, lifeboats and shipbuilding. If you have time, it's worth a trip to the Padstow Lifeboat Station which is about five miles from the town and is spectacularly located at Trevose Head where there are glorious views. Closer to town, Prideaux Place (☎ 01841 532411) is an interesting Elizabethan House which is still lived in by the family that first built it. Set in grounds that include woodland and formal gardens, it's open throughout the summer from Sunday to Thursday in the afternoons. In town, the Capitol Cinema is open in the evenings in the summer, and in the afternoon if the weather is wet. Talking of getting wet, there are numerous pubs to choose from, and the choice of restaurants is good as well – the famous chef Rick Stein owns several. Of these, try The Seafood Restaurant (☎ 01841 532700/532485) which is close to the inner basin and is probably the best known. For inexpensive pub food, the London Inn is only two minutes from the quay. If you are looking for places to go over on the Rock side, you will be made welcome at the bar of the Rock Sailing Club, or for pub food, try the Rock Inn (☎ 01208 863498) or The St Enedoc Hotel (☎ 01208 863394) for something a little more elaborate.

Water taxi:	VHF Ch 16, 12
Taxi:	(☎ 01841 521092) or (☎ 01841 532903)
Car hire:	In nearby Wadebridge, Tregonning Garage (☎ 01208 816066)
Cycle hire:	(☎ 01841 533533)
Bus:	local buses, including to Bodmin for station, national coach network links
Rail:	nearest is Bodmin Station
Airport:	Newquay Airport for domestic flights

for more details, see Directory Section

Artist: **Anthony Flemming CAMEL ESTUARY**
Courtesy of: **The Artist**

Bude

Bude is a popular beach resort noted for good conditions for surfing. There is a small drying harbour, and when there is not too much swell, it is possible to enter the lowest reach of the old Bude Canal which is a very sheltered haven where you could leave a boat unattended if there is space. Be warned, however - the lock fees are very high. Basic facilities are available, though not necessarily close to hand, and there is a good range of local shops within walking distance. Local inventor Sir Goldsworthy Gurney was the first man to travel from London to Bath by steam carriage and was involved in installing lighting in the Houses of Parliament. He is remembered in the local museum which also explains the role and workings of the Bude Canal which climbs over 300 feet in little more than five miles. There are plenty of places to take refreshment of one sort or another: The Brendon Arms (☎ 01288 352713) is a good choice for a drink and The Falcon Hotel (☎ 01288 352005) offers good value pub food in a bustling atmosphere. For restaurant meals, the Atlantic Hotel (☎ 01288 352451) on Summerleaze Crescent, has both restaurant and bar menus, and good views of the River Neet and the sea beyond. The Hartland (☎ 01288 355661) on Hartland Terrace offers a choice of both bar lunches and restaurant dinners, as does the Cliff (☎ 01288 353110) on Crooklets Beach.

Taxi:	Triangle Taxis (☎ 01288 356729) or Vodden (☎ 01288 354411)
Car hire:	Beech Motors (☎ 01288 355345) or Bude Car Rental (☎ 01288 353679)
Cycle hire:	North Coast Cycles (☎ 01288 352974)
Bus:	local services and national network

for more details, see Directory Section

Artist: **Anthony Flemming BOSCASTLE**
Courtesy of: **The Artist**

North Devon, Somerset & Avon

There is some spectacular scenery as the coast marks the north edge of Exmoor with the highest cliffs in England which reach a dizzying 1200 feet. Sheltered places to put into are relatively scarce, and most dry out. If you do manage to put in, you will find some attractive and interesting places to visit, and you will have the opportunity to enjoy some of the landscape of Exmoor and rural Somerset. Tidal ranges and currents become impressive as you get towards the mouth of the Severn Estuary making it a very tricky area to cruise in. There are good facilities in Bristol, and it's an interesting city with a great maritime pedigree and good transport links to the rest of the country, so it may be a good spot to change crew or leave the boat if necessary. However, with places which are easier to sail to on the south coast of Wales, most will probably choose to strike north and leave the swirling Severn and its bore to be admired from terra firma or one of the bridges rather than getting involved afloat.

Ilfracombe

The sheltered harbour here brought Ilfracombe prosperity that has subsequently been built on as it has gained popularity as a holiday resort. This is a picturesque place clinging to a steep rocky hillside and there is access to good walking and birdwatching countryside. Tucked behind the rocky peninsula, the harbour offers drying moorings and some space to lie to against the harbour walls. This is a working harbour, so you may have to contend with fishing boats and the like. There are showers and all the usual facilities, and the Ilfracombe Yacht Club also has facilities which visitors will be welcome to use. There is a good range of shops for provisions within a few minutes walk of the harbour, and there is a museum, theatre, cinema and art gallery for entertainment. Just along the coast, the theme park at Watermouth Castle (☎ 01271 867474) offers family entertainment for all ages through the summer. The Victorian Celebrations which take place in mid-June and the Carnival week at the end of August are high points in the calendar of events the town hosts for its visitors' and indeed its own amusement. The Pier Hotel (☎ 01271 866225) on Quay Road is by the harbour for a drink and from there it's not far to the Waverley (☎ 01271 862681) in St James Place. The George and Dragon (☎ 01271 863851) on Fore Street does good pub food, and for a restaurant meal, try the Capstone Restaurant (☎ 01271 863540) in St James Place, or The Bath House Hotel (☎ 01271 866859) in Runnacleave Road which is highly rated.

Taxi:	(☎ 01271 864607)
Car hire:	Foxhunters Garage (☎ 01271 863104)
Bus:	local services and nationwide links
Rail:	nearest station at Barnstaple
Airport:	Exeter Airport for domestic and international services

for more details, see Directory Section

Porlock Weir

Taking advantage of a break in the cliffs which make up the spectacular north edge of Exmoor, Porlock Weir nestles in a small inlet surrounded with wooded hillsides. There is a handful of moorings here, and a few spaces to dry out alongside the quay and, once you are in, this is a snug and sheltered harbour. Facilities at Porlock Weir itself are very limited, but you will find more in Porlock which is a couple of miles inland. There you will find a full range of local shops, but no supermarket - it just wouldn't really fit in with the thatched cottages. The scenery around here is wonderful and there is the whole of Exmoor on the doorstep. The break in the high cliffs leaves room for some marshland here which is a refuge for lots of birds, and the views are superb if you clamber up and stroll along the clifftops. Porlock Weir Sailing and Boatowners Club doesn't actually have a clubhouse, so they use the pub and hotel by the quay for food, drink and showers. The Ship Inn (01643 862753) is right by the harbour and serves pub food. Adjoining it, the Anchor Hotel (same telephone number as The Ship) has a restaurant for a slightly grander meal. There's more choice in Porlock itself where The Ship (☎ 01643 862507) is a good choice for a meal or a drink - it's known locally as The Top Ship to distinguish it from the other. The Oak also does bar food, and for a restaurant meal, try the Cottage Hotel (☎ 01643 862687).

Taxi:	Colin Strange, based on the quay
Cycle hire:	available in Minehead
Bus:	local services from harbourside
Rail:	Taunton Station (8 miles away)
Airport:	Bristol Airport or Exeter Airport

for more details, see Directory Section

Minehead

This is real seaside resort land. There are amusement arcades along the seafront and there's a vast expanse of sand and shingle beach. It is here that Butlins have a huge holiday camp called Somerwest World (☎ 01643 703331) - you don't have to stay, day tickets are available if you fancy it. The harbour is right at the other end of town from all this. It's the older end of town and does have a bit more dignity. It's not a large harbour, so you'll have to take what space is available as it is popular. It is also only accessible for about two hours each side of high water, but does offer reasonable shelter from most quarters. Facilities at the quayside are very limited, but there is a good range of shops in the town. Minehead is at the western end of the West Somerset Railway (☎01643 704996) which offers excursion rides on steam trains along a twenty mile route following the attractive coastline before heading inland towards Taunton through delightful countryside. There's also a railway museum at Blue Anchor Station just along the bay. Dunster Castle (NT ☎ 01643 821314) overlooks the delightful old village of Dunster and is set in beautiful parkland and gardens. A lot of it was rebuilt in Victorian times, but bits survive from the 13th century and the whole melange is rather fine. You can also visit a fully functioning 17th century water mill (☎ 01643 821759) which is set in breathtaking scenery on the banks of the River Avill in Mill Lane not far from the centre of the village. Back in Minehead, to slake your thirst after a hearty walk ashore, or after a hard day's sailing and navigating, The Old Ship Aground (☎ 01643 702087) on Quay Street is a good choice for a drink and the Queens Head Hotel (☎ 01643 702940) on Holloway Street serves good pub food.

Taxi:	Taxi rank in town centre
Car hire:	Mersons Garage (☎ 01643 706296)
Cycle hire:	Pompy's Cycles (☎ 01643 704077)
Bus:	local services from town centre
Rail:	nearest station is at at Taunton or Tiverton
Airport:	Bristol Airport, or Exeter Airport, or Cardiff Airport

for more details, see Directory Section

Watchet

At the west end of Blue Anchor Bay, Watchet is an alternative place to base yourself while you explore this area. The West Somerset Railway (see Minehead for details) has a stop here and there are several museums, one of which covers local history and you can see historic local boats being restored and built at the other. Currently, the harbour at Watchet is only accessible for a couple of hours each side of high water and dries. There is a certain amount of small commercial traffic including charter fishing trip boats and small coasters. Plans are in hand for a 250 berth marina with pontoon berths, and a full range of facilities which should be open by 2001. Consequently, the year 2000 sailing season may well see construction work which might make access to the harbour more difficult than it usually is. There's a reasonable range of shops for provisions within a few hundred yards of the harbour including a good supermarket. There are also a number of pubs and restaurants to try. The Star Inn (☎ 01984 631367) on Mill Lane is a good spot for a drink and serves home made pub nosh. A little further away in Swain Street, the West Somerset Hotel (☎ 01984 634434) is well respected for the beers it keeps and the food it serves. The Corner House Café (☎ 01984 631251) and Skyburns Restaurant (☎ 01984 631208), both on Market Street, serve inexpensive meals and Gennaro's (☎ 01984 631479) is the place to go for a more continental flavour.

Taxi:	(☎ 01984 631973)
Car hire:	in Minehead
Cycle hire:	in Minehead
Bus:	local services to Minehead and Taunton, summer only to Bristol, Lynton & Ilfracombe
Rail:	bus service connects West Somerset railway to national network at Taunton
Airport:	Bristol Airport (☎ 01275 474444)

for more details, see Directory Section

Weston-super-Mare

At the mouth of the Severn Estuary, Weston-super-Mare boasts sandy beaches and an impressive Grand Pier. This is a popular resort for people from the big towns and cities in the Midlands, and can get a bit over-run in the summer. Perhaps its greatest claim to fame is that it's where John Cleese comes from – does this say something about the local hotels, or was Fawlty Towers really based on Torquay? There is a good range of things to see and do here as you would expect in a holiday resort. There are donkeys on the beach, amusements on the pier and the Tropicana Pleasure Beach which has a pool and offers entertainment in the evenings. A splendid turn of the century boathouse is attached to the pier and is the launching station for the RNLI's two inshore lifeboats which are based here. (see directory for more details.)

You have two options for berthing and both dry out – the tidal range here is very impressive. Knightstone Harbour is closest to the town centre or you can head for the mouth of the River Axe at Uphill just to the south. Here there is a boatyard which has chandlery and repair facilities – Uphill Boat Services – and you should contact them for a visitors' mooring as well.

Taxi:	Apple Central (☎ 01934 613613) or Woodspring Taxis (☎ 01934 414141)
Car hire:	Eurodrive Car Rental (☎ 01934 414551) or Pearce Bros Autorentals (☎ 01934 415550)
Cycle hire:	In nearby Hutton village - Wheel (☎ 01934 888800)
Bus:	Badger Line (☎ 0117 9553231)
Rail:	National Rail enquiries (☎ 0345 484950)
Airport:	Bristol Airport (☎ 01275 474444)

for more details, see Directory Section

Bristol

Bristol has been a merchant city for over a thousand years. Its prime location on a major sea inlet which places it close to the heart of the south of England meant it was a key commercial centre until the industrial revolution when the focus of industrial activity in the north meant that this became a relative backwater. There is plenty to see here, and for mariners, a visit to the Maritime Heritage Centre (☎ 0117 9260680) close to

Artist: **Anthony Flemming** THE AVON GORGE Courtesy of: **The Artist**

Bristol Marina is a must. Close by, you will be able to see Brunel's S.S. Great Britain which is being restored. She was the first iron-built propeller-driven passenger liner, launched in 1843 to ply the Atlantic. The Industrial Museum (☎ 0117 9251470) by the Floating Harbour gives a flavour of the city's industrial heritage, and the Floating Harbour is itself noteworthy. The result of work done at the beginning of the 19th century to create a harbour with constant water levels, it was no mean feat when you consider the tidal ranges outside in the Bristol Channel. While the currents outside may be alarming, once in the locked sanctuary offered by Bristol's various waterways, you have a range of options for berthing. With the high river banks, the approach is quite splendid, including the fine spectacle of passing under Brunel's Clifton Suspension Bridge. There is space for visiting yachts at both the City Docks and at Bristol Marina which is also in the Docks. Security is better at the marina if you are thinking of leaving your boat unattended. For a drink or a meal ashore, Bristol is a typically bustling city. For those seeking a quieter corner to enjoy a drink, Bristol Marina is not badly placed for you

to sample the delights of Clifton Village near Brunel's bridge. You will find plenty of choice for good pubs, bistros and restaurants here. In the city centre, for those in search of good food and fine wines, Harveys (☎ 0117 9275034) in Denmark Street is a good option or The River Café (☎ 0117 9872270) at Redcliff Quay with its riverside setting is a handy choice within walking distance of most of the berthing options.

Taxi:	Streamline (☎ 0117 9264001) or Bristol Hackney Cabs (☎ 0117 9538638)
Car hire:	Avis Rent A Car (☎ 0117 9292123) or British Car Rental (☎ 0117 9253839)
Cycle hire:	Whistle Stop Cafe (☎ 0117 9665069) Mud Dock Cycle Works (☎ 0117 9292151)
Bus:	First Bus City Line (☎ 0117 9553231)
Rail:	Bristol Station, National Rail enquiries (☎ 0345 484950)
Airport:	Bristol (☎ 01275 474444)

for more details, see Directory Section

Artist: **Anthony Flemming** **THE PENDEEN LIGHTHOUSE** *Courtesy of:* **The Artist**

RIVER EXE
50.37'.0N 03.25'.0W

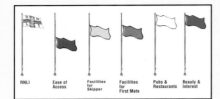

Exmouth

Exmouth Dock
Keith Graham: Dock Master Tel: 01395 269314
VHF Ch: 14 VHF Name: Exmouth Docks

Exe Sailing Club
Mike Hill: Secretary Tel: 01395 264607

Moorings:
Yacht Basin Tel: 01395 269314

Chandlers:
Peter Dixon Chandlery Tel: 01395 273248
Small Boat Chandlers Tel: 01395 516656

Exmouth Lifeboat Station
Open by appointment, contact: B Cole
Boathouse Tel: 01395 263463
B Cole Tel: 01395 274328

Starcross

Cockwood Boat Club
E S Tucker: Secretary Tel: 01626 890789

Starcross Fishing & Cruising Club
Peter Harris: Secretary Tel: 01626 891996

Starcross Yacht Club Tel: 01626 890470

Chandler:
Retreat Boatyard Tel: 01392 875934

Topsham

Topsham Sailing Club Tel: 01392 877524

Chandler:
The Fo'c'sle Tel: 01392 874105
Retreat Boatyard Tel: 01392 875 934
Fax: 01392 876182

Repairs:
Sails & Canvas Tel: 01392 877 527

Mooring/Repairs:
Retreat Boatyard or
W Trout & Sons Boatyard
Tel: 01392 873 044 Fax: 01392 875 176

Exeter

Exeter Harbour
Jack West: Harbourmaster Tel: 01392 274 306

Chandler:
John Bridger Marine Tel: 01392 250970

Maritime Museum
Open daily except Xmas Day & Boxing Day
Tel: 01392 58075

TEIGNMOUTH
50.32'.5N 03.30'.0W

Reg Matthews: Harbourmaster (East Quay)
Tel: 01626 773165
VHF Channel: 12/16 (Office hours, incl Sat
Mornings) VHF Name: East Quay

Teignmouth Corinthian Yacht Club
Tel: 01626 772 374

Chandler:
Brigantine Tel: 01626 872 400

Teignmouth Lifeboat Station
Open to visitors all year round
Contact: P Barczok
Tel: 01626 776845 (day) and 776772 (eve)

TORQUAY
50.27'.5N 03.31'.5W

Torquay Harbour
Capt. Mowatt: Harbourmaster

Torquay Harbour Office, Beacon Quay,
Torquay, Devon TQ1 2BG
Tel: 01803 292 429 Fax: 01803 299 257
VHF Channel: 16 VHF Name: Torquay Port

Torquay Marina
Contact: Manager
9 Vaughan Parade, Torquay, Devon TQ2 5EQ
Tel: 01803 214624 Fax: 01803 291634
VHF Ch: 80 VHF Name: Torquay Marina

Royal Torbay Yacht Club Tel: 01803 292006

Chandlers:
Torbay Boating Centre Tel: 01803 558760
Torquay Chandlers Tel: 01803 211854

BRIXHAM
50.24'.0N 03.31'.0W

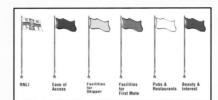

Brixham Harbour Office
Capt. Paul Labistour: Harbourmaster
Tel: 01803 853 321
VHF Ch: 14/16 VHF Name: Brixham Harbour

Brixham Marina
Neil Salter: Manager
Berry Head Road, Brixham, Devon TQ5 9BW
Tel: 01803 882929

Chandler:
Brixham Chandlers Tel: 01803 882055

Repairs: consult marina office

Brixham Yacht Club Tel: 01803 853332

Brixham Museum
Open Mon-Fri 10.00-17.00 and Sat 10.00-13.00
from Easter through October
Contact: Dr Philip Armitage Tel: 01803 856267

Torbay Lifeboat
Open to visitors by appointment
Contact: Captain H East Tel: 01803 853435

RIVER DART

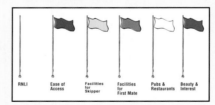

Dartmouth
50.20'.5N 03.34'.0W

Dart Harbour
Captain Colin Moore: Harbourmaster
Harbour Office, Dart House, Oxford Street,
Dartmouth TQ6 9AL
Tel: 01803 832337 Fax: 01803 833631
VHF Channel: 16
VHF Name: Dartnav

Dart Marina
Tony Tucker: Manager
Tel: 01803 833351 Fax: 01803 832307
VHF Channel: M VHF Name: Dart Marina

Darthaven Marina
Contact: Manager Tel: 01803 752 545
VHF Channel: 80
VHF Name: Darthaven Marina

Noss-on-Dart Marina
Tony Tucker: Manager
Tel: 01803 833351 Fax: 01803 832307
VHF Channel: M VHF Name: Noss Marina

Dartmouth Yacht Club
Contact: Secretary Tel: 01803 832305

Royal Dart Yacht Club
Contact: Secretary
Tel/Fax: 01803 752496

River Moorings contact Dart Marina

Chandlers:
Dart Chandlers Tel: 01803 833772
Darthavon Chandlers Tel: 01803 752733
Dartmouth Yacht Chandlers Tel: 01803 834896
Sport Nautique Tel: 01803 832532

Dartmouth Museum
Open to visitors daily
Contact: Mrs S Cawthorne Tel: 01803 832923

Dittisham, Galmpton and Totnes

Contact: Dartmouth Harbourmaster

Dartside Quay Marina
Ian Quick: Manager
Tel: 01803 845445 Fax: 01803 843558
VHF Channel: 80 VHF Name: Dartside Quay

Chandler:
Dart Chandlers Tel: 01803 845886

SALCOMBE
50.13'.5N 03.46'.5W

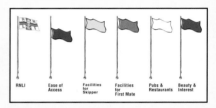

Salcombe Harbour
Steve Tooke: Harbourmaster
Harbour Office, Whitestrand, Salcombe,
Devon TQ8 8BU
Tel: 01548 843791 Fax: 01548 842033
VHF Ch: 14 VHF Name: Salcombe Harbour

Island Cruising Club
M A Gaunt: Secretary
Tel: 01548 843481 Fax: 01548 843929

Salcombe Yacht Club
Contact: Secretary Tel: 01548 842593

Moorings:
J Stone & Son Tel: 01548 51242
Winters Marine Tel: 01548 843838
Yeoward & Stone Boatyard Tel: 01548 844261

Chandlers:
Salcombe Boatstore Tel: 01548 843708
Salcombe Chandlers Tel: 01548 842620
Sport Nautique Tel: 01548 842130

Repairs: J Alsop Sailmakers Tel: 01548 843702
Richard Lewis (Elec Eng) Tel: 01548 843223
Lincombe Boatyard Tel: 01548 843655
VHF Channel: 13 (830-5.00)
VHF Name: Lincombe Boatyard

Quayside Marine Services
Tel: 01548 844300/843249
Sailing Marine Engineers Tel: 01548 842094

Salcombe Lifeboat Station & Museum
Open to visitors every day Easter through Xmas
Contact: P Hodges Tel: 01548 842975

RIVER YEALM
50.18'.5N 04.04'.0W

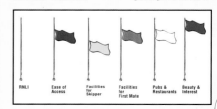

River Yealm Harbour

Julian Stapley: Harbourmaster
Harbour Office, Yealm Hotel Drive, Newton
Ferrers, Devon PL8 1BL
Tel: 01752 872533

Thorn Pool Moorings
Contact: Manager Tel: 01752 880104

Yealm Yacht Club
Don Taylor: Secretary
Riverside Road East, Newton Ferrers, Devon
PL0 1AE Tel: 01752 872291
Chandlers:
The Stock Shop Tel: 01752 872728

Repairs:
Phil Carter Tel: 01752 872189

PLYMOUTH   50.20'.0N 04.09'.0W

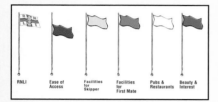

Port of Plymouth

Shaun Taylor: Queen's Harbourmaster
Long Room Port Control, Stonehouse
Barracks, Stonehouse, Plymouth PL1 3RT
Tel: 01752 836528
VHF Channels: 16/14/13
VHF Name: Queen's Harbourmaster

Long Room Port Control
VHF Channel: 14
VHF Name: Long Room Port Control

Cattewater Harbour
Tim Chalesworth: Harbourmaster
Tel: 01752 665934
VHF Ch: 16 VHF Name: Cattewater Harbour

Clovelly Bay Marina
Contact: Manager
The Quay, Turnchapel, Plymouth PL9 9TF
Tel: 01752 404231 Fax: 01752 484177
VHF Ch: 80/M VHF Name: Clovelly Bay

Mayflower International Marina
Robin Page: Manager
Ocean Quay, Richmond Walk, Plymouth,
Devon PL1 4LS
Tel: 01752 556633/567106 Fax: 01752 606896
VHF Ch: 37/80 VHF Name: Mayflower Marina

Millbay Marina Village
H G Smith: Manager
Great Western Road, Millbay Docks,
Plymouth PL1 3EQ Tel/Fax: 01752 226785
VHF Ch: 80/37A VHF Name: Millbay Marina

Plymouth Yacht Haven
A Barber: Manager
Shaw Way, Mount Batten, Plymouth PL9 9XH
Tel: 01752 404231 Fax: 01752 484177

Queen Anne's Battery
Contact: Manager
Queen Anne's Battery Marina, Plymouth,
Devon PL4 0LP
Tel: 01752 671142 Fax: 01752 266297
VHF Channel: 80
VHF Name: Queen Anne's Battery Marina

Sutton Harbour Marina
Contact: Manager
Harbour Office, Sutton Harbour, Plymouth,
Devon PL4 0ES
Tel: 01752 664186 Fax: 01752 223521
VHF Channels: 12/16/80/37/M
VHF Name: Sutton Harbour Radio

Royal Plymouth Corinthian Yacht Club
Tel: 01752 664327

Royal Western Yacht Club Tel: 01752 660077

Chandlers:
Chas R Cload Tel: 01752 663722
Mount Batten Boathouse Tel: 01752 482666
Ocean Marine International Tel: 01752 500121
Yacht Parts Plymouth Tel: 01752 252489

Repairs:
Complete Yacht Service Tel: 01752 482445
Marine Wise Tel: 01752 484288
Osen Sails Tel: 01752 255066
Plymouth Lifeboat Station
Open to visitors all year round
Contact: D Studden
Tel: 01752 662623 (mornings)

River Tamar & St Germans

Calstock Boatyard
Contact: Manager
Lower Kelly, Calstock, Cornwall PL18 9RY
Tel: 01822 832502 Fax: 01822 823118

Southdown Marina
Contact: Manager
Southdown Quay, Millbrook, Torpoint,
Cornwall PL10 1HG Tel/Fax: 01752 823084
VHF Channel: 16/M
VHF Name: Southdown Marina

Torpoint Yacht Harbour
Contact: Manager
The Ballast Pound, Marine Drive, Torpoint,
Cornwall PL11 2EH Tel/Fax: 01752 813658
VHF Channel: M
VHF Name: Torpoint Yacht Harbour

Weir Quay Boatyard
Contact: Manager
Heron's Reach, Bere Alston, Devon PL20 7BS
Tel: 01822 840474 Fax: 01822 840948

Tamar River Sailing Club Tel: 01752 362741

Moorings (St Germans river):
Quay Sailing Club Tel: 01503 250370

Chandler:
Saltash Boat Market & Mooring Services
Tel: 01752 845482

LOOE

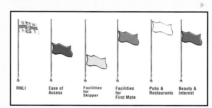

E T Webb: Harbourmaster Tel: 01503 262839

Looe Sailing Club
Contact: Secretary Tel: 01503 262559

Looe Lifeboat Station
Open to visitors by appointment
Contact: J Brice Tel: 01503 265223

FOWEY   50.19'.5N 0438'.5W

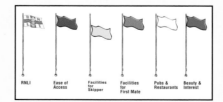

Fowey Harbour
Captain Mike Sutherland: Harbourmaster
Harbourmaster's Office, Albert Quay, Fowey,
PL23 1AJ Tel: 01726 832471/2 Fax: 01726 833738
VHF Channels: 12/16
VHF Name: Fowey Harbour Radio

Fowey Golants Sailing Club
Contact: Secretary Tel: 01726 832335

Royal Fowey Yacht Club
Contact: Secretary Tel: 01726 832245

Fowey Crusing School
Principal: John Myatt
32 Fore Street, Fowey, Cornwall PL23 1AQ
Tel: 01726 832129 Fax: 01726 832000

Chandlers:
Outriggers Tel: 01726 833233
Upperdeck Marine Tel: 01726 832287

Repairs:
Fowey Boatyard, refer Harbour Commission
Fowey Marine Electronics Tel: 01726 833101
Fowey Marine Engines Tel: 01726 832899
Hunkins Boatyard Tel: 01726 832874
Mitchell Sails Tel: 01726 833731
C Toms & Son Tel: 01726 870232

Fowey Lifeboat
Open to visitors weekday mornings
Contact: K Stuart Tel: 01726 832156/832277

RIVER FAL   50.08'.5N 05.01.5W

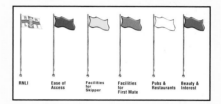

Falmouth

Falmouth Harbour
Captain David Banks: Harbourmaster
44 Arwenack Street, Falmouth, Cornwall
TR11 3JQ Tel: 01326 314379 Fax: 01326 211352
VHF Channel: 16
VHF Name: Falmouth Harbour Radio

Falmouth Marina
John Young: Manager
North Parade, Falmouth, Cornwall TR11 2TD
Tel: 01326 316620 Fax: 01326 313939
VHF Ch: 80/37 VHF Name: Falmouth Marina

Falmouth Yacht Haven
Contact: Manager
Tel: 01326 312285 Fax: 01326 211352

Port Pendennis Marina
Contact: Manager Tel: 01326 311113

Royal Cornwall Yacht Club
Michael Prescott: Secretary
Green Bank, Falmouth, Cornwall TR11 2SW
Tel: 01326 312 126
VHF Channel: 37
VHF Names: Club Base or Club Launch

Flushing Sailing Club
Contact: Secretary Tel: 01326 374043

Restronguet Sailing Club
Contact: Secretary Tel: 01326 374536

Falmouth Boat Construction
Contact: Manager
Little Falmouth Yacht Yard, Flushing,
Falmouth TR11 5TJ Tel: 01326 374309

Chandlers:
Boat Store Tel: 01326 318314
Bosuns Locker Tel: 01326 312414
David Carne Tel: 01326 318314
Challenger Marine Tel: 01326 377222
Mylor Chandlery & Rigging
Tel: 01326 375482

Repairs:
Simon Caddy Tel: 01326 372682
Delta Marine Services Tel: 01326 378748
Falmouth Boat Construction
Seafit Marine Services Tel: 01326 313713

Cornwall Maritime Museum
Open to visitors Mon-Sat 10.00-17.00 (April-Oct) and 10.00 -15.00 (Nov-March)
Tel: 01326 240670

Malpas

Bar Creek Yacht Station Tel: 01872 73919
Malpas Marine Tel: 01872 71260

Mylor

Mylor Yacht Harbour
Jonathon Fielding: Manager
Mylor, Falmouth, Cornwall TR11 5UF
Tel: 01326 372121 Fax: 01326 372120
VHF Channel: 37/80
VHF Name: Mylor Yacht Harbour

Mylor Yacht Club
Contact: Secretary Tel: 01326 374391

Penryn

Capt A J Brigdon: Harbourmaster
Tel: 01326 373352

Challenger Marine
Contact: Manager
Freemans Wharf, Falmouth Road, Penryn,
Cornwall TR10 8AS Tel: 01326 377222

St Mawes

St Mawes Harbour
Captain Roy Maddern: Harbourmaster
The Quay, St Mawes, Truro TR2 5DG
Tel: 01326 270553 Fax: 01326 270234

St Mawes Sailing Club
Ronnie Howard: Secretary
No1, The Quay, St Mawes, Truro TR2 5DG
Tel: 01326 270686 Fax: 01326 270040

Moorings:
Malpas Marine Tel: 01872 71260
Pencuil Boatyard Tel: 01872 580564
River Assoc Freshwater Boatyard
Tel: 01326 270443
St Mawes Pier & Harbour Co Tel: 01326 270553

Chandlers:
Percuil Boatyard Tel: 01872 580564
Reg Landon Marine Tel: 01872 272688

Repairs:
Percuil Boatyard Tel: 01872 580564
River Assoc Freshwater Boatyard
Tel: 01326 270443

Truro

Capt A J Brigdon: Harbourmaster Tel: 01872
272130

Royal Cornwall Museum
Open to visitors Mon-Sat (except Bank
Holidays) 10,00-17.00 Tel: 01872 272205

HELFORD RIVER   50.06'.0N 05.06'.0W

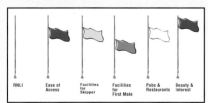

Helford River Moorings
Contact: Moorings Officer
Bridge Farm, Mawgan, Helston TR12 6AE
Tel: 01326 221265
VHF Channel: M
VHF Name: Helford River Moorings Officer

Helford River Sailing Club Tel: 01326 231460
VHF Channel: 80/M
VHF Name: Helford River Sailing Club

Port Navas Yacht Club Tel: 01326 340419
or 01326 340065

Chandler/Moorings/Repairs:
Gweek Quay Boatyard Tel: 01326 221657

The Lizard
No facilities for yachts

The Lizard Lifeboat
Open to visitors weekday mornings through-out the year
Contact: Peter Greenslade Tel: 01326 290974

ST MICHAEL'S MOUNT & MARAZION
                              50.07'.0N 05.28'.5W

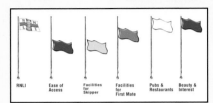

St Michael's Mount Harbour
K Murch: Harbourmaster Tel: 01736 710265

Mounts Bay Sailing Club
Mrs C Martin: Secretary Tel: 01736 710620

Marazion Lifeboat Station
Open to visitors all year, 10.00-18.00 daily
Contact: R Topham Tel: 01736 710125

PENZANCE   50.07'.0N 05.31'.5W

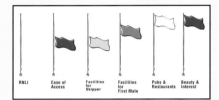

Penzance Harbour
Neil Clark: Harbourmaster
Wharf Road, Penzance, Cornwall
Tel: 01736 366113
VHF Ch: 12   VHF Name: Penzance Harbour

Penzance Yacht Club
Contact: Secretary Tel: 01736 364989

Chandler:
A Mathew Sail Loft Tel: 01736 364004

Repairs:
Penzance Dry Dock & Engineering Co
Tel: 01736 363838

NEWLYN   50.06'.0N 05.32'.5W

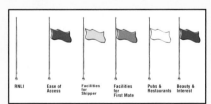

Newlyn Harbour
Andrew Munson: Harbourmaster
Tel: 01736 362523
VHF Ch: 16/12   VHF Name: Newlyn Harbour

Penlee Lifeboat Station
Open to visitors all year round by appointment
Contact: A Munson Tel: 01736 361017

MOUSEHOLE   50.05'.0N 05.32'.0W

Contact: Harbourmaster Tel: 01736 731511

ST MARY'S, SCILLIES   49.55'.0N 06.18'.5W

St Mary's Harbour
Jeff Penhaligon: Harbourmaster

ST MARY'S, SCILLIES cont.

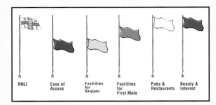

Tel/Fax: 01720 422768
VHF Ch: 14/16
VHF Name: St Mary's Harbour

Scillonian Sailing & Boating Club
Tel: 01720 422208

Chandler:
Isles of Scilly Steamship Co Tel: 01720 423399

Repairs:
Rat Island Sailboat Co Tel: 01720 423399

St Mary's Lifeboat Station
On view to visitors from the boathouse only

SENNEN COVE

No facilities for yachts

Sennen Cove Lifeboat
Open to visitors all year round (but no land-ing facilities) Contact: Dr R Manser
Tel: 01736 871222 (871560 after hours)

ST IVES

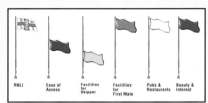

St Ives Harbour
Eric Ward: Harbourmaster Tel: 01736 795018
St Ives Lifeboat Station
Open daily to visitors from Easter through
September, 10.00-16.00 (21.00 in Aug)
Contact: Captain J Moran Tel: 01736 796422

ST AGNES

No facilities for yachts

St Agnes Lifeboat Station
Blue Peter IV lifeboat is at this station
Open to visitors daily April-Oct 10.30-18.30; by
appointment in the winter season
Contact: R Thomas Tel: 01872 552680

NEWQUAY

Newquay Harbour
Contact: M Gater Tel: 01637 872809

Chandlers:
JB Marine Tel: 01637 878185

Newquay Lifeboat Station
The only lifeboat station to incorporate a
church. Open to visitors all year round, early
to late. Contact: R Eglinton
Tel: 01637 873846

PADSTOW   50.32'.5N 04.56'.0W

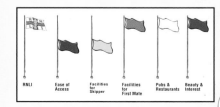

Padstow Harbour
Captain R T Platt: Harbourmaster
Harbour Office, Padstow PL28 8AQ
Tel: 01841 532239 Fax: 01841 533346
VHF Channels: 12/16

Chandlers:
Chapman & Hewitt Tel: 01208 813487
Rigmarine Tel: 01841 532657/532386

Padstow Lifeboat
Positioned 125 steps down, at the bottom of
cliffs over 30 metres high. Open to visitors
Mon-Friday 10.00-16.00 summer,
11.00-14.00 winter. Contact: G Phillips
Tel: 01841 533059

Rock

Rock Sailing & Water Ski Club
P Fuller: Secretary Tel: 01208 862709

Rock Lifeboat
A new station, winner of an architectural
design award. Open to visitors all year
round, by appointment
Contact: Tony Stuart
Tel: 01208 862960

PORT ISAAC

Port Isaac Lifeboat Station
Open daily 09.00-dusk
Contact: E Childs Tel: 01208 880322

BUDE

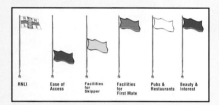

Bude Harbour
Mike Banstone: Harbourmaster
Tel: 01288 353111

Bude Lifeboat Station
Open daily from Easter through October
Contact: P Frost Tel/Fax: 07288 356263

CLOVELLY

No facilities for yachts

Clovelly Lifeboat Station
Open to visitors by appointment
Contact: Boathouse Tel: 01237 431828

RIVERS TAW & TORRIDGE
51.03'.5N 04.12'.0W

Appledore

Limited facilities for yachts

Appledore Lifeboat Station
Open to visitors by appointment
Contact: Boathouse Tel: 01237 473969

ILFRACOMBE   51.12'.5N 04.06'.5W

Ilfracombe Harbour
Contact: Harbourmaster Tel: 01271 862108
VHF Channels: 12/16
VHF Name Ilfracombe Harbour

South West England - Chart Agents

The Foc'sle, Topsham Tel: 01392 874105
Brixham Chandlers, Brixham Tel: 01803 882055
Dart Chandlers, Dartmouth Tel: 01803 833772
Dart Haven, Dartmouth Tel: 01803 752242
Sport Nautique, Dartmouth Tel: 01803 832532
Sport Nautique, Salcombe Tel: 01548 842130
The Sea Chest, Plymouth Tel: 01752 222012
Percuil Boatyard, St Mawes Tel: 01872 580564

ILFRACOMBE cont.

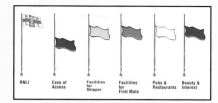

Ilfracombe Yacht Club
Contact: Secretary Tel: 01271 863969

Chandler:
Ilfracombe Marine Tel: 01271 863386

Repairs contact Harbour Manager

Ilfracombe Museum
Placed second out of 18 000 entrants for Blue
Peter Museum of the year. Open daily 10.00-
17.30 April-Oct and Mon-Fri 10.00-12.30 Nov-
March Tel: 01271 863541

Ilfracombe Lifeboat Station
Open daily 10.00-17.00 to visitors from Easter
to late October (also 19.00-21.30 in July and
August) Contact: Mrs B Putt Tel: 01271 863771

PORLOCK WEIR   51.13'.0N 03.37'.5W

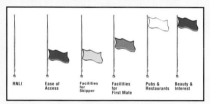

Porlock Weir Harbour (privately owned)
Contact: Harbourmaster Tel: 01643 863187

Porlock Weir Sailing Club
Howard Willicombe: Secretary
Tel: 01752 330774

MINEHEAD   51.13'.0N 03.28'.0W

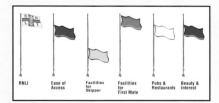

Minehead Harbour
Capt Muller: Harbourmaster Tel: 01643 702566
VHF Ch: 16 VHF
Name Minehead Harbour Radio

Chandlery and repair:
Uphill Boat Centre Tel: 01934 418617

Minehead Lifeboat
Has the latest type fast inshore lifeboat
Open to visitors daily 10.30-18.30 from Easter
to late October, by appointment in winter
months.
Contact: K Escott Tel: 01643 703444

WATCHET   51.11'.0N 03.19'.5W

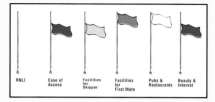

Watchet Harbour
Contact: Harbourmaster Tel: 01984 631264
VHF Channel: 09/12/14/16
VHF Name: Watchet Harbour

Watchet Boatowners Assoc
Bruce Scott: Secretary Tel: 01984 634242

Uphill Boat Centre Tel: 01934 418617

WESTON-SUPER-MARE   51.21'.0N 02.59'.0W

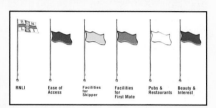

Weston Bay Yacht Club
Contact: Secretary Tel: 01275 620772

Chandler/repairs:
Uphill Boat Centre Tel: 01934 418617

Weston-super-Mare Lifeboat
Open to small parties by appointment
Contact: Pete Holder Tel: 01934 631527

BRISTOL   51.27'.0N 02.37'.5W

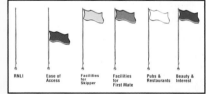

Bristol City Docks
Geoff Lane: Harbourmaster
Harbourmaster's Office, Underfall Yard,
Cumberland Road, Bristol, Avon BS1 6XG
Tel: 0117 9297608 Fax: 0117 9294454 VHF Ch:
16/73 VHF Name: Bristol Floating Harbour

Bristol Marina, Contact: Manager
Hanover Place, Bristol, Avon BS1 6UT
Tel: 0117 9213198 Fax: 0117 9297672
VHF Ch: 80/M VHF Name: Bristol Marina

Cabot Cruising Club Tel: 0117 9268318

Moorings:
Portavon Marina Tel: 0117 9861626

Chandler:
Force 4 Chandlery Tel: 0117 9268396
WF Price Tel: 0117 9292229

Repairs:
Bristol Sails Tel: 0117 9225080

South West England - Chart Agents

Bosun's Locker, Falmouth Tel: 01326 312414
Mylor Rigging, Falmouth Tel: 01326 375482
Rigmarine, Padstow Tel: 01841 532657
Uphill Boat centre, Minehead Tel: 01934 418617

South West England - Pilot Books

West Country Crusing, Mark Fishwick
published by Airlife Publishing ISBN: 1852771070

North Brittany and Channel Islands Cruising, Peter Cumberlidge
published by Yachting Monthly, ISBN: 1852 770 694

Normandy & Channel Islands Pilot, Mark Brackenbury
published by Sheridan House Inc, ISBN: 0713 635 07X

South West England - Pilot Books

The Channel Islands, compiled by Nick Heath, RCC Pilotage
Foundation, published by Imray, Laurie, Norie & Wilson,
Tel: 01480 462114 ISBN: 0852 883 617

Waypoint Directory (English Channel), Peter Cumberlidge 1995
published by Adlard Coles Nautical, Tel: 0207 2420946 ISBN: 0713 641 177

The Shell Channel Pilot, Tom Cunliffe, Revised 1997 Edition
published by Imray, Laurie, Norie & Wilson, Tel: 01480 462114
ISBN: 0852 882 785

Bristol Channel and Severn Pilot, Peter Cumberlidge 1988
published by Adlard Coles Nautical, Tel: 0207 2420946 ISBN: 0540 074 225

Yachtsman's Guide to Scilly, J Norman Gooding
published by Ennor Pubns, ISBN: 0907 205 003

Artist: **Anthony Flemming TINTAGEL** *Courtesy of:* **The Artist**

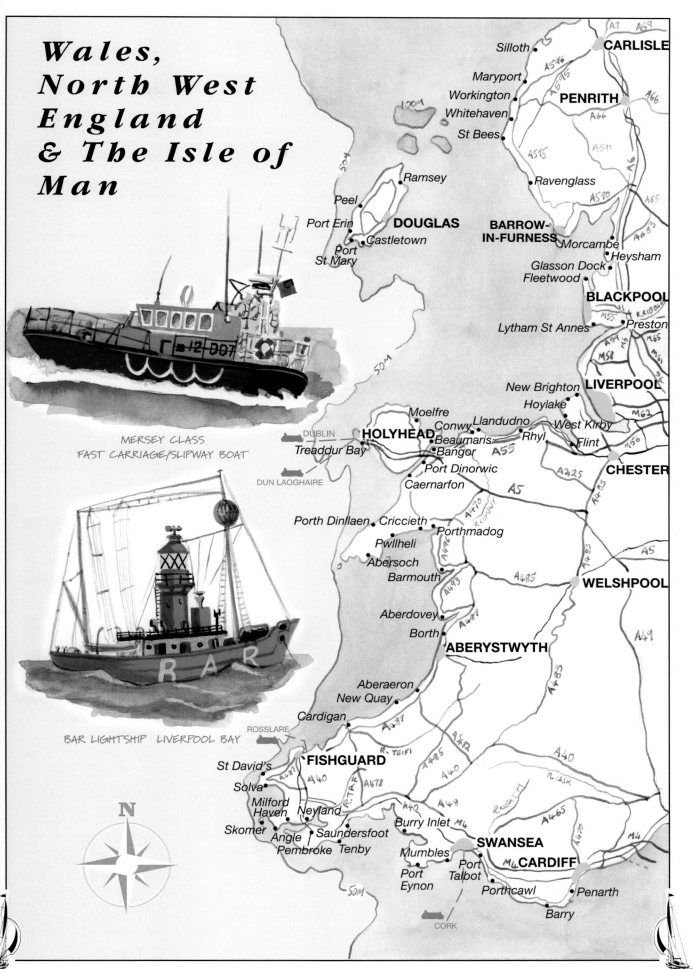

Wales, North West England & The Isle of Man

MERSEY CLASS
FAST CARRIAGE/SLIPWAY BOAT

BAR LIGHTSHIP LIVERPOOL BAY

N

Silloth
CARLISLE
Maryport
PENRITH
Workington
Whitehaven
St Bees
Ravenglass
Ramsey
Peel
Port Erin
DOUGLAS
BARROW-
IN-FURNESS
Castletown
Morcambe
Heysham
Port
St Mary
Glasson Dock
Fleetwood
BLACKPOOL
Lytham St Annes
Preston
New Brighton
LIVERPOOL
Hoylake
Moelfre
Conwy
Llandudno
West Kirby
DUBLIN
HOLYHEAD
Beaumaris
Rhyl
Flint
Treaddur Bay
Bangor
Port Dinorwic
DUN LAOGHAIRE
Caernarfon
CHESTER
Porth Dinllaen
Criccieth
Porthmadog
Pwllheli
Abersoch
Barmouth
WELSHPOOL
Aberdovey
Borth
ABERYSTWYTH
Aberaeron
New Quay
Cardigan
ROSSLARE
St David's
FISHGUARD
Solva
Milford
Haven
Neyland
Burry Inlet
Skomer
Saundersfoot
SWANSEA
Angle
CARDIFF
Pembroke
Tenby
Mumbles
Port
Talbot
Port
Eynon
Porthcawl
Penarth
CORK
Barry

Vale of Glamorgan

While many would perhaps seek to pass by the south coast of Wales as it approaches the Bristol Channel, they would be missing out on a number of places where excellent yachting facilities are available and places of interest are within easy reach. Certainly the tidal conditions in the upper reaches of the Severn Estuary are enough to make those of us who are not used to tidal ranges of over 10 metres quail somewhat, and we may think that the Severn Bore seems more terrifying than tedious. However, we suggest that while you may wish to leave the top of the estuary to the experts, you could tentatively approach Penarth which gives access to the Welsh capital at Cardiff. Further west, Swansea offers good facilities and is readily accessible, and for those who are prepared to spend a night away from the pontoons, The Mumbles is a delightful place to put in.

Cardiff to Swansea

The names of two of Wales's largest cities may strike an uninviting note to some yachtsmen, but it has to be said that the facilities on offer here are excellent, and the marinas in the revamped dock areas of these cities are both worth visiting. **Penarth** is the harbour and dockside face of Cardiff, the Welsh capital city and an attractive centre for both commerce and culture. Cardiff Castle (☎ 029 2082 2083) which overlooks Bute Park is built on the site of an old Roman fort, and much of the existing building dates back to the 12th century. A more modern 20th century building houses the magnificent National Museum of Wales (☎ 029 2039 7951) which is nearby in Cathays Park and contains important collections of paintings and natural history exhibits as well as glass, porcelain and silver. Also well worth a look is the Welsh Industrial and Maritime Museum (☎ 029 2048 1919) which is part of the National Museum. There is a host of other attractions in Cardiff, not least for those who follow Wales's national sport, the headquarters of Welsh rugby football is at Cardiff Arms Park which has recently been completely redeveloped for the World Cup. On the waterfront, Penarth itself has evolved into a seaside resort as the role of its docks for exporting coal has declined, and a busy marina is now in place in the old docks. The new Cardiff Bay Barrage, completed at the end of 1998, now means that 24 hour access to the marina is possible which makes it a much more inviting option than it was before. Once inside, you will find a marina with berths for around 400 boats and the facilities which you would expect in such a large marina are all available within the complex. There's a selection of shops for provisioning locally, and you are only a couple of miles from the centre of Cardiff for a more cosmopolitan selection of shopping opportunities.

As you would expect, there is a wide choice of pubs and restaurants in Cardiff. With this in mind, here are a few suggestions to help you on your way. Just off the High Street, the City Arms (☎ 029 2022 5258) is a popular pub for all ages, as is the Cottage (☎ 029 2023 0600) on St Mary Street, which serves its own home-cooked lunches. The Vulcan (☎ 029 2046 1580) on Adam Street, just outside the city centre is an unpretentious old pub with very good value lunches and a sawdust covered floor, and the Wharf (☎ 029 2045 6101) on Atlantic Wharf, is relaxed with authentic maritime memorabilia. The Cardiff Bay Hotel (☎ 029 2047 5000) also on Atlantic Wharf has a distinctly nautical flavour that stretches to the name of the restaurant, Halyard's. In the city centre, on Charles Street the Metropolis Restaurant (☎ 029 2034 4300) is a modern and up to date conversion of an old factory with à la carte meals and reasonably priced lunches.

In Penarth itself, the Golden Lion (☎ 029 2070 1574) on Glebe Street, is a traditional local, while the Royal Hotel (☎ 029 2070 8048) on Queen's Road overlooks the marina and the River Ely Estuary, yet still seems to be mainly frequented by locals. The Caprice (☎ 029 2070 2424) is an excellent seafood restaurant with splendid views over the Bristol Channel and, finally, the Captain's Wife (☎ 029 2053 0066) is a pub to put on your list of places to try.

Taxi:	Beelines Taxis (☎ 029 2070 9822), K Tax (☎ 029 2070 8525)
Car hire:	Enterprise (☎ 029 2038 9222) or Budget Car Hire (☎ 029 2066 4499)
Cycle hire:	In Cardiff - Taff Trail Cycle Hire (☎ 029 2039 8362)
Bus:	Cardiff bus covers all local areas (☎ 029 2039 6521)
Rail:	Penarth Station, national rail enquiries (☎ 0345 484950)
Airport:	Cardiff International Airport, near Barry (☎ 01446 711111)

for more details, see Directory Section

Artist: **Anthony Fleming BARRY DOCK**
Courtesy of: **The Artist**

Your options along this stretch of coastline are rather limited, and even this far out in the Bristol Channel the tidal streams can be ferocious, so careful attention to your almanac and tidal atlas is essential. Access to Barry Docks is constrained by the tide, and once inside, you will not have to dry out, or if sitting on the bottom holds no terrors for you, there is an attractive but tiny harbour at the seaside resort of Porthcawl. Much of the coastline between Barry and **Porthcawl** is designated as Heritage Coast, but because of the hazards you will probably give most of it a good offing. So as not to miss out, a stroll along at least some of it is to be warmly recommended. Merthyr Mawr is about five miles along the coast path and has splendid castle ruins and delightful thatched cottages and further along the cliffs are magnificent. Porthcawl itself has all the bustle of a seaside resort town, and the long esplanade has a splendid 1930s Grand Pavilion as its centrepiece. The harbour is accessible for about two hours each side of high water, there are visitors' moorings here and a reasonable range of facilities is available at the waterfront. Local shops for provisions are close to hand as is a good selection of places for a drink or a meal. The Atlantic (01656 785011) on West Drive serves a bar dinner on Sundays as well as à la carte meals. The Seabank (01656 782261) is another comfortable hotel, while for pubs that serve good food, look no further than the Rose and Crown (01656 784850) in Nottage, and the Prince of Wales in Kenfig.

Swansea

Swansea Marina is based in the old South Dock which is in an area which has been revamped and developed into the Maritime Quarter. Adjacent is the Maritime and Industrial Museum (☎ 01792 650351) which has a collection of floating exhibits that you can explore as well as exhibitions examining the area's industrial history. For a broader picture, the Swansea Museum (☎ 01792 653763) is just along the road where there are collections of local pottery and porcelain as well as an Egyptian Mummy – there's a bigger collection of Egyptian artefacts at the Egypt Centre (☎ 01792 295960) as well. From your base in the dock, you are well placed for exploring the centre of the town and there are plenty of shops including a supermarket and covered market within a few minutes' walk. One of Wales's most notable men of letters is celebrated at the Dylan Thomas Centre (☎ 01792 463980) which is just beyond the Museum. The Grand Theatre (☎ 01792 475715), a ten screen cinema complex and a tenpin bowling centre are also within easy reach. The Gower Peninsula is an area of outstanding natural beauty so, with your boat safely tucked into the marina, you might consider an excursion to enjoy the countryside. Access to the marina is constrained by the tide, but is straightforward when there's enough water. Facilities are comprehensive and conveniently located. For city centre sailing destinations, they don't get much better than this. There are three pubs on site at the marina which is handy for a drink and a simple meal. The Tug and Turbot (☎ 01792 648785) and The Waterside (☎ 01792 648555) are both reasonable, but the Pumphouse (☎ 01792 651080) is probably ahead by a short nose. There is also Galini's (☎ 01792 456285) which is a respectable restaurant, though you might prefer to take a short taxi ride to Eleos (☎ 01792 648609) in The Kingsway to experience life in the town rather than just at the marina. For excellent French food, the Rendezvous (☎ 01792 467113) in Princess Way is a good choice within about ten minutes walk, or The Slow Boat (☎ 01792 645253) in High Street is a top class Chinese restaurant. The restaurant at the Marriott Hotel (☎ 01792 642020) by the marina is also highly rated.

Taxi:	Diamond (☎ 01792 474747) or Abbacabs (☎ 01792 702333)
Car hire:	Hilton International Car Hire (☎ 01792 310313)
Cycle hire:	Dunvant (☎ 01792 208889)
Bus:	local services and National Express from the Quadrant Centre
Rail:	Swansea Station for Intercity services
Ferry:	Services from Swansea to Cork
Airport:	Cardiff Airport

for more details, see Directory Section

Mumbles

Close to Swansea where everything is convenient and easy, there's a prettier but slightly less straightforward option if the weather is settled. The resort town of Mumbles looks across the bay at Swansea with its backdrop of steep tree-lined hillside. This is good countryside for walking and the clifftops on the peninsula are a popular spot for birdwatching. A central landmark in the town is Oystermouth Castle (☎ 01792 368732) which you can see from the bay. In the bay itself alongside the pier, the lifeboat house, with its built-in slipway, dates back to 1922. Visitors are welcome to look around in the morning on weekdays. Drop your anchor in the bay as close as you can to the shore (watch out for the tidal range) and head for the shore. There's a complete range of local shops in Mumbles village for all your provisioning needs within walking distance. For comprehensive facilities, you need to nip into Swansea, but there are two clubs here which will be happy to see you. The Mumbles Motor Boat and Fishing Club has a bar which serves snacks during normal licensing hours, and the Mumbles Yacht Club also has a bar and offers food as well as showers, but may not be open in the evening at weekends. Alternatively, the food and drink are good at the Pilot Inn (☎ 01792 366643) in Mumbles Road. Verdi's (☎ 01792 369135) on Knab Rock is handy for an inexpensive meal, and a short taxi ride (AA Taxi ☎ 01792 360600) takes you to The High Tide Café (☎ 01792 363462) in Newton Road. Pa's (☎ 01792 367723) is also here for a more extravagant meal, or you might try Patrick's (☎ 01792 360199), which is closer, in Mumbles Road for good food if you are feeling extravagant.

Pembrokeshire

Pembrokeshire boasts some magnificent coastline with imposing cliffs and spectacular islands lying off. That is at the western end of the area, while to the east the land is lower lying and includes extensive sandflats and marshland. This offers a different array of wildlife and a different backdrop to sail past. The sheltered inland cruising area which opens up behind Milford Haven is well worth spending some time in as there is wonderful countryside to be enjoyed in the Pembrokeshire Coast National Park. There are numerous ports of call both large and small as you work your way around the west end of the county, and plentiful opportunities for exploring history and cultural background and of course we have pointed the way to some welcoming hostelries for that important period of recuperation at the end of the day!

Saundersfoot & Tenby

Extensive shallows, tricky tides and frequently shifting sands make access for the visitor to the estuaries which lead to Llanelli and Carmarthen very difficult. Extremely good local knowledge or a pilot are essential for these entrances, so you will probably want to head

for the west end of Carmarthen Bay where there are two small drying harbours. These might well be of interest to those who want to avoid the throng in the marinas at Swansea or Milford Haven. **Saundersfoot** has an attractive little harbour where you might find room alongside or a drying mooring in the middle. There are good sandy beaches and good shopping, pubbing and restauranting to be had as well. The Saundersfoot Sailing Club will be happy to let you make use of their facilities.

Artist: **Anthony Flemming TENBY, PEMBROKESHIRE** Courtesy of: **The Artist**

A few miles to the south, **Tenby** is another small resort town with a little harbour which can be rather crowded. There are suitable places to anchor off in fair weather. Elegant guest houses and hotels peer down to the harbour from their commanding position set back from the waterfront and enjoy an elevated view over the bay. There are 13th century town walls and a castle to explore and a 15th century merchant's house to visit. Tenby Museum and Art Gallery (☎ 01834 842809) on Castle Hill gives you the chance to learn about local history and culture. Caldey Island just offshore to the south of the town has the ruins of a 12th century Benedictine Monastery as well as a more modern version which is still the home of an order of monks. Facilities for yachts are a little limited, but by liaising with the harbour-master and the sailing club, you should be able to find most of the items a cruising yacht might need on arrival, and there's a full range of shops including a supermarket within about half a mile. Within easy range of the harbour, you will be able to quench your thirst at the Hope and Anchor (☎ 01834 842131) in St Julian's Street or the No Name Bar (☎ 01834 845941) in the High Street, both of which serve pub meals as well. The Dennis Café (☎ 01834 842298) on Castle Sands offers inexpensive food, or you might try Candy (☎ 01834 842052) in the High Street for something a bit more elaborate. The top places in town are Mews (☎ 01834 844068) in Upper Frog Street and Pam Pam (☎ 01834 842946) in Tudor Square.

Taxi: (☎ 01834 844603) or (☎ 01834 845843)
Car hire: (☎ 01834 812433)
Cycle hire: (☎ 01834 845955)

Bus: local services and nationwide links
Rail: Tenby Station links to national network
Airport: Cardiff Airport
for more details, see Directory Section

Artist: **Moira Huntly LOW WATER, TENBY** Courtesy of: **The Artist**

Milford Haven

Milford Haven is aptly named and its location makes it a major crossroads for vessels of all sizes navigating their way along the coast of Wales, up from Land's End on passage to points further north or across to Southern Ireland. There are good facilities available, though the entrance can be busy with large commercial traffic and the lower reaches are somewhat blighted with industrial paraphernalia such as tanker terminals and oil refineries. However, the sheltered cruising through the inland area of the Pembrokeshire Coast National Park further upriver is an added treat. Tucked just inside the entrance on the west side, there is a handy little anchorage at **Dale** where there is a yacht club which welcomes visiting yachts to use their facilities. This is a popular sailing centre and most basic requirements can be found here, but shopping in the village is somewhat limited. The Griffin at the top of the slipway is a good spot for a drink and serves bar meals, or head to Bistro Planet Dale (☎ 01646 636642) run by West Wales Windsurfing and Sailing Club. If you are looking for more comprehensive facilities you will need to head further up river, past the Esso Jetty and past the Elf Jetty - you will find the **Milford Marina** just opposite the Texaco Jetty which stretches for over a mile - the other two are not much smaller either! To be fair, Milford Haven is not an unattractive town and the dock area now sees little commercial traffic and has been redeveloped around the marina which was opened in 1991. The history of the docks has been a chequered one. Sir William Hamilton, whose wife is famed for her association with Lord Nelson, obtained the right to build a new town here in 1790 to exploit the superb natural harbour. Most of the detailed work was overseen by his nephew, Charles Francis Greville, who was supported by American Quaker whalers and the Navy Board in developing the town and its docks. However, the naval dockyard was moved to Pembroke in 1814, and during the 19th century the emphasis moved to fishing. From its peak in the 1920s, this industry has now declined, as indeed has the prosperity brought more recently by the oil industry which has a smaller presence now than it did until the early 1980s. More detail about Milford Haven's history can be found at the Heritage and Maritime Museum (☎ 01646 694496) and the Kaleidoscope Discovery Centre (☎ 01646 695374) gives further opportunity for the broadening of younger and not-so-young minds with its range of hands-on scientific and technological exhibits. Also in the redeveloped dock area close to the marina, there's a Go-Kart circuit and adventure playground. The marina offers a full range of facilities and you will find a good choice of shops including supermarkets within walking distance or a short taxi ride away. The Pembrokeshire Yacht Club which is about a mile from the marina overlooking Gellyswick Bay welcomes visiting yachtsmen to use its bar and dining facilities. There are a number of places to eat and drink at the marina. For pub type atmosphere and food, try Martha's Vineyard (☎ 01646 697083) and you can also get inexpensive meals at the Dockside Diner and Ice Cream Parlour (☎ 01646 693040). The Waterfront Bistro (☎ 01646 697058) is a bit smarter and the Windjammer Bistro and Cafe (☎ 01646 693999) is also worth a visit, as is The Water Gardens (☎ 01646 697945) which overlooks the marina. It stays open all day and serves speciality steak dishes on the à la carte menu in the evenings. For other pubs, try Champers Wine Bar (☎ 01646 697135), The Starboard (☎ 01646 692439) and the Priory Inn (☎ 01646 69523) for a selection to keep you busy.

Taxi:	(☎ 01646 697472)
Car hire:	From nearby Pembroke Dock - The Kenning Car, Van & Truck Rental (☎ 01646 684252) or (☎ 0870 1555900)
Bus:	local services by South Wales Transport (☎ 01792 580580)
Rail:	Milford Haven Railway Station a couple of minutes' walk away
Airport:	Swansea Airport

for more details, see Directory Section

Upriver

If you plan to cruise further upriver, you may well wish to take advantage of the marina facilities at **Neyland** which is a few miles up from Milford Haven. This is a large marina with berths for over four hundred boats. It's tucked into a sheltered little creek surrounded with woodland and offers comprehensive facilities. The town of Neyland itself is a little dreary with its uniform terraces of Victorian railway workers houses built when this was the terminus of Brunel's South Wales Railway, but you will find a warm welcome and excellent food at Neyland Yacht Club (☎ 01646 600267). Just across the river from the docks which serve Pembroke, Neyland always struggled to compete for commercial traffic and ultimately failed when the railway was closed in the 1950s. If you want to branch out from the facilities at the marina, for a good range of food and drink head for The Ferry Inn (☎ 01646 600270) which overlooks Hazelbeach at the west end of Neyland. A short taxi ride will take you over to Pembroke, or an alternative option here is to take your boat to **Pembroke Dock** where

the Pembroke Haven Yacht Club is based and visiting yachts are welcomed. The docks which serve Pembroke are a couple of miles from the town itself, but there's a bustling little metropolis here with things to see including The Gun Tower (☎ 01646 622246), which is now a free local museum, and some of the buildings which used to be associated with the now departed naval dockyard are rather fine. A short taxi or train ride will take you into Pembroke itself where there is of course the castle and a delightful mixture of other old buildings. On arrival at the docks, you will find that there are a few berths alongside the quay or on the pontoon and there are often vacant moorings available, though facilities are more limited than at Neyland. The Pembroke Haven Yacht Club's clubhouse is on Hobbs Point and has a bar where bar snacks are available and showers. For provisions shopping, there are several supermarkets and smaller shops within a few hundred yards and there's a selection of places to eat and drink as well. The Rose and Crown (☎ 01646 683067) in Queen Street and the First and Last (☎ 01646 682687) on London Road are good options for a drink, and either a ride in the dinghy or taxi away, The Ferry Inn (☎ 01646 682947) at Pembroke Ferry or The Jolly Sailor (☎ 01646 600378) in Burton serve very good pub food. In Meyrick Street, both Brown's Restaurant (☎ 01646 683645) and Mr Chips (☎ 01646 682699) offer inexpensive meals and The Charcoal Grill (☎ 01646 683645) is a bit more upmarket. The restaurant at the Cheddar Bridge Hotel (☎ 01646 685961) in Essex Road is the best the immediate area has to offer.

At Pembroke Dock:	
Taxi:	Ferry Cabs (☎ 01646 621443) or Fred's Taxis (☎ 01646 682226)
Car hire:	Kennings (☎ 01646 684252) or Central Hire (☎ 01646 683965)
Bus:	local services and national links to Swansea & London
Rail:	Pembroke Dock Station for services to Swansea and London
Ferry:	to Rosslare, Southern Ireland
Airport:	Swansea

for more details, see Directory Section

Pressing on upriver from Neyland and Pembroke, the countryside opens out and you find yourself in an area of mudflats, reedbeds and woodlands. The river is readily navigable for about five miles beyond Neyland as far as Landshipping where the Cleddau River divides, and much further if you take to your tender. A trip to Carew up the creek beyond Lawrenny is worth doing as this is an attractive little village with a fine 13th century castle and restored tidal mill. There are some good moorings and a pontoon as well as facilities at Lawrenny, where there is also a pub, and you will find other watering holes at Landshipping and Carew.

Milford Haven to St David's Head

Leaving the old fortifications and modern industrial outbursts behind, the geological nature of the coastline becomes varied and interesting. Once outside Milford Haven, wildlife is abundant as you head for the point with its off-lying islands. Both Skokholm and Skomer

Islands are bird sanctuaries and there's an anchorage on the south east side of Skomer at South Haven. This is a fair weather spot as the holding is not brilliant, but it's a tremendous place to watch seals and puffins which are regularly here in force in the spring. The Pembrokeshire Coast National Park extends the length of St Bride's Bay and beyond St David's Head almost all the way to Cardigan. This is spectacular and beautiful coastline and though there are a number of fair weather anchorages, there are few places for the yachtsman to take shelter or find facilities. The little harbour at **Solva** offers refuge for small boats if you don't mind drying out. The unspoilt village is well worth visiting, and you have the opportunity to enjoy the coastline and surrounding countryside which provide superb walking and bird-watching. Just along the coast is the tiny cathedral city of St Davids which is barely more than a village. The ruins of the Bishop's Palace (☎ 01437 720517) which date from the 14th century are imposing and there are two oceanaria and several art galleries to browse in. It's also well worth taking a trip to the RNLI's St David's lifeboat station at Porth Stinian. The Station and its slipway are located in a spectacular setting close to the original lifeboat house which dates back to the station's foundation in 1869. At Solva Harbour, there are visitors' moorings and space for a handful of boats to lie alongside the quays - contact the harbour-master on arrival for directions. The Solva Boatowners' Association has a small clubhouse at the waterfront where you can get a shower. There is little else by the harbour and for shops and refreshment, you will need to go just over half a mile to the village. In Lower Solva, The Harbour Hotel, (☎ 01437 720013), The Ship Inn (☎ 01437 721247) and the Cambrian Hotel (☎ 01437 721210) all serve pub meals, as does the Royal George (☎ 01437 720002) in the High Street in Upper Solva. As well as the Window on Wales Coffee Shop (☎ 01437 720659), there are three restaurants in Main Street in Lower Solva. The Anchor Café & Restaurant (☎ 01437 720149) will probably dent your pocket the least, and for slightly more elaborate menus try The Old Pharmacy Restaurant (☎ 01437 720005) or Le Papillon Rouge (☎ 01437 720802).

Fishguard

There's good shelter to be found in Fishguard Harbour unless the wind really pipes up from the north. Off Goodwick and behind the Northern Breakwater, priority is given to commercial vessels - this is where the ferries and day trip boats to southern Ireland leave from. Yachts are not permitted to anchor here unless they can tuck into the shallow area north of the east breakwater. Access is constrained by the tide in the Lower Harbour by Fishguard itself, but this is a more attractive place to moor. It was the scene of a rather half-hearted invasion attempt by the French in 1797 which only lasted a few days before the force of just over 1000 men surrendered to the local militia. With wooded hillsides rising up to the Old Fort on one side and the narrow streets of the town coming down to the waterfront on the other, this little drying harbour is an idyllic spot. This is where the Fishguard Bay Yacht Club is based, and they will direct you to where to moor if there is space, or if there isn't, in settled weather you can anchor just outside. Their clubhouse on The Quay

has a bar and showers and will give you a warm welcome. Shopping is all about a mile away as are most of the places to eat and drink, but there is the Ship Inn (☎ 01348 874033) in the Lower Town where you can quench your thirst. Up in the centre of town, The Royal Oak (☎ 01348 872514) in The Square is famed as the venue for the signing of the French surrender. It still welcomes visitors and is a good choice for a meal. The best food in the area will be found at Three Main Street (☎ 01348 874275) in Main Street (yes, at number three). If you are up at the Goodwich end of the bay, try the Glendower Hotel (☎ 01348 822823) in Glendower Square for a drink, The Rose and Crown (☎ 01348 872305) for pub food or the Ferryboat Inn (☎ 01348 874747) for something a bit more elaborate. You might also like to visit the lifeboat here - who knows, you might have collected milk-bottle tops or silver paper to pay for it as it's "Blue Peter VII".

Taxi:	Bernie's (☎ 01348 874491) or
	Merv's (☎ 01348 875129)
Car hire:	Europcar (☎ 01348 874260)
Cycle hire:	Newport Cycles (☎ 01239 820008)
Bus:	leaves from lower town to Cardigan
	and Haverfordwest
Rail:	Fishguard Harbour Station - services
	to Swansea, Cardiff & London
Ferry:	Fishguard Harbour to Rosslare
Airport:	Cardiff Airport

for more details, see Directory Section

Ceredigion

Challenging pilotage make you feel you have really earned your landfall in several of the harbours along the Ceredigion coastline, and a warm welcome ashore will be well deserved. The coastline is majestic especially as you approach Aberystwyth which is the first major centre of population after Cardigan. Here you will find a marina for a welcome night of convenience or you may choose to base yourself there for longer to explore the surrounding area.

Fishguard to Aberystwyth

This stretch of rocky coastline boasts a wealth of wildlife and much of it is designated as Heritage Coast. It's a good area to see dolphins, porpoises and seals as well as a wide variety of seabirds. There are three small drying harbours along here which may appeal to those with shallow draft and a cool head for pilotage. The entrance to the River Teifi which leads up to **Cardigan** is the most difficult of these, and you'll definitely need a large scale chart. It's also worth getting in touch with someone at the Teifi Boat Club or the harbour-master for advice about the channel. Once you are in, repair to the bar at the Boat Club for a well earned drink, or head up into Cardigan and try the Eagle Inn (☎ 01239 612046) on Castle Hill, or for a very Welsh flavour, The Red Lion (☎ 01239 612482) at Pwllhai which is close to the river. Both serve pub food. You can find an inexpensive meal at Mariners (☎ 01239 614136) on Quay Street and the restaurant at the Grosvenor Hotel (☎ 01239 612046) will offer you something a bit more upmarket. The Teifi Inn (☎ 01239 613284) and the Ferry Inn (☎ 01239 615172), both on the river bank, offer the best food in town. There's a supermarket for provisions and Robin's taxi service will get you about (☎ 01239 612190). Just over ten miles along the coast to the east, you round New Quay Head and are greeted with a long sandy bay with New Quay at one end and Aberaeron at the other. Both are popular destinations for holiday makers but the atmosphere in each is quite different. The harbour at **New Quay** is accessible for a couple of hours each side of high water and there is room for 3 visiting boats alongside the quay. Things to see and do here include the Heritage Centre and Museum (☎ 01545 572142) for local historical flavour, good walking both inland and on the cliffs, sandcastle building and wildlife boat trips for a bit of a busman's holiday. The supermarket and a few other provisions shops are within a quarter of a mile of the harbour and marine diesel is available at the Pier Slipway. The New Quay Yacht Club welcomes the crews of visiting yachts, and you can use the showers at their clubhouse. After just a short walk to build up your thirst, you will find the Dolau Inn (☎ 01545 560 881) in Church Street or the Black Lion (☎ 01545 560209) in Glan Mor Terrace are inviting places for a drink, and The Wellington Inn (☎ 01545 560245) in Wellington Place does good pub food. In South John Street, Mariners (☎ 01545 560467) serves inexpensive meals, and The Old Watch House (☎ 01545 560852) is a bit more elaborate. Top of the range are The Hungry Trout (☎ 01545 560680) in Glanmor Terrace and Cegin Ali (☎ 01545 560265) in Uplands Square.

Just beyond the far end of Little Quay Bay, **Aberaeron** lacks the sandy beach, but makes up for it in other ways. This elegant little town was largely designed by John Nash - the style is more like his London Terraces than the Brighton Pavilion - and in the last century was a bustling port for the export of, among other things, pigs to Spain and France! Around the harbour, you will find a Sea Aquarium (☎ 01545 570142), a honey bee exhibition (The Hive on the Quay, ☎ 01545 570445) and a Toy Museum, which has a model railway and hundreds of toys and models, and there's easy access to the coast for strolling along the shingle beach. Head for the Yacht Club for a shower and water and the Aquarium for marine diesel. There's a full range of shops for provisions within a few hundred yards of the harbour. Close to the harbour on Market Street, the Monachty Arms (☎ 01545 570389) and the Cadwgan (☎ 01545 570149) serve good beer, and The Royal Oak (☎ 01545 570332) on North Street and L'Hirondelle (☎ 01545 570366) in Market Street offer decent pub meals. For an inexpensive meal, try the New Celtic Restaurant (☎ 01545 570369) also on Market Street, or the Prince of Wales (☎ 01545 570366) on Queen Street or the Castle Hotel (☎ 01545 570205) on Bridge Street for something with a more extensive menu. The Harbour Master (☎ 01545 570755) on Quay Parade is the best in town, and a short taxi ride (3 miles) takes you to Plas Morfa (☎ 01974 202515) in Llanon which is worth the journey. Cei Cabs (☎ 01545 560454) will take you there, or if you want to hire a car, contact Forge Garage (☎ 01545 570291). Cycles can be hired from Cyclemart (☎ 01545 470079) for exploring the surrounding countryside.

Aberystwyth

After the series of tricky little harbours, it will come

as a relief to some to find the convenience of a marina - the first since Milford Haven. This is a good base to explore the area, and numerous little harbours are within range to sail to and back in a day. Pwllheli Marina to the north is easily reached in a day's sail as is Abersoch, and to the south New Quay and Fishguard. The tidal access is a bit tight if you draw as much as two metres, but for smaller boats, there's a reasonable window around high water to get in here. Aberystwyth is a bustling tourist resort which caters for the tourist trade all year round. The town offers a cinema, the National Library of Wales (☎ 01970 632800) serving the University of Wales which is based here, theatres and museums including the Ceredigion Museum (☎ 01970 633088) which has a fine and varied collection in the imposing former theatre and cinema, The Coliseum. A ride on the old narrow gauge Vale of Rheidol Railway (☎ 01970 625819) up the valley to the top of Cwm Rheidol with its waterfalls is a must. The town's new promenade passes the Old Castle first built in 1277 by Edward I to subdue the Welsh and ends at the foot of Constitution Hill. At the 430 foot summit of the hill, you will find the Great Aberystwyth Camera Obscura and Victorian Tearooms (☎ 01970 617642) which is in fact a reconstruction rather than genuinely Victorian, but still quite fun all the same. To get to the top of the hill, you might well like to make use of the Aberystwyth Electric Cliff Railway (☎ 01970 617642) which is the longest of its kind in Britain, and really does date from Victorian times. There is plenty for children to do here as well with parks, a leisure centre (☎ 01970 624579) and adventure trails as well as exercise on the beach which is a mixture of sand and shingle. The Ceredigion Heritage and Marine Heritage Coast (☎ 01545 572141) organises guided walks and boat trips in various locations along this stretch of coastline for you to get the most out of it. Facilities at the reassuringly small marina (just over 100 pontoon berths) are comprehensive, and it's about five minutes walk to the centre of town for shopping and thirst and hunger quenching. The Black Lion (☎ 01970 623448) is a good choice for a pub meal, and Elizabeth's (☎ 01970 612583) on North Parade will serve you a good meal which won't burn a hole in your pocket. Gannets (☎ 01970 617164) and Little Italy (☎ 01970 625707) offer slightly more elaborate menus, and the best in the area is probably the restaurant at the Conran Hotel (☎ 01970 617941) at Chancery which is a taxi ride away.

Taxi:	Aber Taxis (☎ 01970 627272)
Car hire:	Budget Rent a Car (☎ 01970 626200)
Bus:	local services leave from Aberystwyth Station
Rail:	Aberystwyth Station links to national rail network
Airport:	Cardiff Airport is about 2 hours away

for more details, see Directory Section

Gwynedd & Anglesey

This northern part of Wales has a profusion of inspiring castles to underline the sense of history and a variety of coastal scenery is set against the backdrop of mountains provided by the Snowdonia National Park. More modern architecture is also on the menu with the

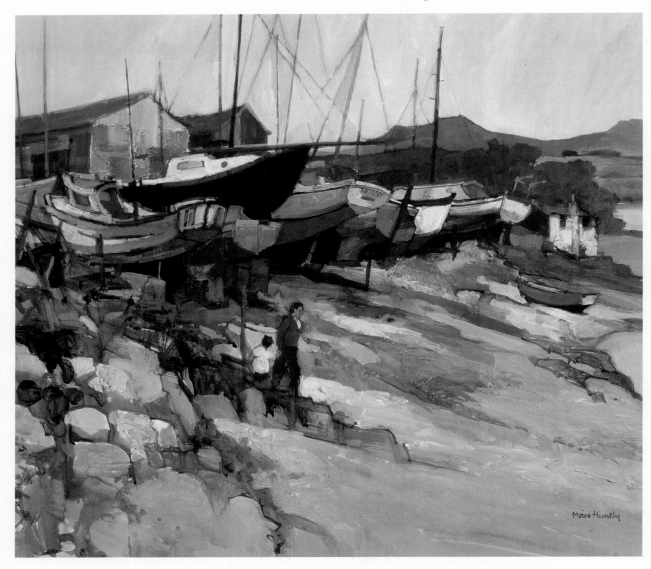

Artist: **Moira Huntly BOATYARD, BEAUMARIS** *Courtesy of:* **The Artist**

flight of fantasy which created Portmeirion and there is a salty "yachtie" feel to be found in Pwllheli and Abersoch. The north coast leads us to Anglesey where there are a number of interesting places to explore including that railway station with the very long platform tickets. There's also the new marina currently being developed at Holyhead which will offer a useful staging post for yachts heading along the coast or across the Irish Sea.

Aberdovey to Pwllheli

As you approach the northern end of Cardigan Bay, there are a series of little harbours which allow you to explore attractive resort towns and villages and to enjoy the wonderful backdrop which the hills of the Snowdonia National Park provide. Though not all accessible or sheltered in all conditions, if the weather is fair, you could hardly ask for a more idyllic cruising ground. Our first Port of Call here is **Aberdovey** or Aberdyfi in local parlance. In settled conditions, the bar at the

entrance to the Dovey should not present too many problems, and once inside this splendid landlocked estuary, there is deep water to moor in or a quay to come alongside, giving space in total for 150 boats including those which live here. Contact the harbourmaster for directions. Aberdovey is set on the edge of Snowdonia National Park and there's a visitor centre here to tell you all about that as well as exploring the local history of the town. There are good sandy beaches, and connections to the local network of scenic railways should you wish to explore the countryside of the National Park from the comfort of a railway carriage rather than on your own pins. The facilities here are good for such a small place, and you will find most shops you might need for provisions, though the minimarket is more of a good general store than a supermarket. The three pubs in the town all serve food and there are several good restaurants and cafés as well. Ten miles or so further north, the entrance to the Mawddach at **Barmouth** is not so tricky, but the depth inside may deter those who don't like to touch or sit on the bottom. This would be their loss as this is a very attractive spot. You can get in for a couple of hours each side of high water, but be warned, at springs the tide can run VERY quickly through the entrance. Call the harbour-master for direction on where to berth. A railway bridge and frequently shifting sandbanks make it tricky to navigate far upriver - maybe this is one to take to the tender for as there are about seven miles of tidal estuary and river running through the valley with fine woodland and mountainscape backdrops. Just half a mile to the north is the first area of land ever donated to the National Trust. The RNLI has a museum at Barmouth (☎ 01341 280940) which is open daily between Easter and the end of September and you won't be able to overlook the lifeboat which lives on a mooring not far from the railway bridge. Facilities are good though it's a bit of a hike to some of the local shops in the centre of the town. The Merioneth Yacht Club at The Quay will supply you with a drink, light snack and shower as required, and there's a good selection of pubs, cafes and restaurants in the town. The Last Inn (☎ 01341 280530) is close to the waterfront and serves good pub food and the Talydon about five minutes walk away is a good spot for a drink. The best food in town is served by Mrs Page at the Inglenook - the harbour-master will tell you how to find it. There's a steam railway along the spit, the Las Vegas Fairground has dodgems and other amusements and, for local history, have a look in the Medieval Tower House (☎ 01341 280467). From Barmouth, it's a short hop up to **Porthmadog** at the head of Cardigan Bay. Here there is another tricky shifting sandbar to be avoided in unsettled conditions. Once inside, if you don't mind taking the ground, you will be well sheltered in the inner harbour. There are a few visitors' mooring buoys, or you might get a space alongside the quay. You are well placed here for a bit of castle visiting with Harlech Castle (☎ 01766 780552) not far to the south and Criccieth Castle (☎ 01766 522227) just to the west. The bizarre architectural fantasyland which is the village of Portmeirion (☎ 01766 770000) is just across the bay and is well worth a visit, even if just to pick up some Portmeirion Pottery seconds at bargain prices. Excellent local railway services will take you to all these places and also up to the remarkable Llechwedd Slate Caverns (☎ 01766 830306) where you will be amazed that mining activity can leave such a beautiful legacy. To get there, take a ride on the famous Ffestiniog narrow gauge steam railway (☎ 01766 512340). In Porthmadog itself, there's a Maritime Museum (☎ 01766 513736) and cinema and lots of souvenir shops to browse or spend money in. There is also a good range of shops for provisions not far from the harbour which is close to the centre of town. Facilities at the Madog Yacht Club are made available for the crews of visiting yachts, so you can shower, drink and eat here. If you want to branch out a bit, The Ship (☎ 01766 512990) on Lombard Street is good for a drink or a meal, and for real extravagance, try the restaurant at the Porthmeirion Hotel (☎ 01766 770228). It's a couple of miles away, so a taxi might be needed so try Port Taxis (☎ 01766 514244), or if you want to hire a car for further exploration, you need Gelli Rentals (☎ 01766 514775).

Pwllheli

Tucked on the inside of the Lleyn Peninsula, Pwllheli is a popular holiday resort and offers good facilities for the itinerant yachtsman. The harbour area has been redeveloped and berths are available at the marina here, or from the harbour-master who manages the commercial end of things - there are about a dozen local fishing boats which still work out of the harbour. This is a less expensive option, but you need to be prepared to dry out alongside, or berth on pile or fore-and-aft moorings. The marina is accessible and has deep water at almost all states of the tide. (At low water springs, the depth on the harbour bar is only about one metre.) The marina is a large one with berths for around 450 boats and the range of facilities reflects this. Pwllheli itself is a jolly little town, and it is a good base for exploring the surrounding area where there is plenty to see and do. In the town, Neuadd Dwyfor (☎ 01758 704088) is both a cinema and theatre and there are bookshops, antique shops and craft shops for you to browse in. For those who fancy action on four wheels, there's Go-Karting and Quad-Biking at Parc Glasfryn (☎ 01766 810202) which is four miles out of town, and at Llanbedrog a few miles to the west, you can try your hand at clay pigeon shooting and archery at the Llanbedrog Shooting School and Archery Centre (☎ 01758 740810). Close to Llanbedrog, there is a splendid Gothic style stately home, Plas Glyn-y-Weddw (☎ 01758 74-763) which has a fine collection of paintings and drawings. This impressive house and its beautiful gardens are open to the public, and exhibitions of notable contemporary artists' work regularly take place here. Two thirds of the Lleyn Peninsula has been designated an area of outstanding natural beauty and so makes for good countryside for walking and birdwatching. A couple of stops along the railway, or a brisk walk away, you will find Butlins Starcoast World (☎ 01758 701441) where there is a spectacular funfair and plenty more besides. If you stay on the train, you can explore the areas around Porthmadog and beyond which were covered in the previous section. David Lloyd George was born in neighbouring Llanystumdwy which is a pretty village worth a visit in its own right, and there is a museum in his honour for you to brush up on your knowledge of this groundbreaking politician and statesman. (The Lloyd George Museum, ☎ 01766 522071.) The crews of visiting yachts are welcomed at the Pwllheli Sailing Club where there is a bar and food is available - get a temporary membership card from the reception at the marina. The range of shops in the centre of town is good and includes a supermarket and, since this is a market town, the market on Wednesdays is worth a visit. There's a bus link to the centre of the town which is about a mile from the marina. Also in the centre of the town, there is a good selection of pubs and restaurants to choose from and there are several places which offer takeaway food. The Boathouse (☎ 01758 612865) is a good choice for a drink and the Victoria (☎ 01758 612834) at South Beach is worth heading to for a pub meal. For a restaurant meal, try the Tex-Mex cuisine at The Village (☎ 01758 613198) at Y Maes or for Italian, Pompei (☎ 01758 614944) on the High Street. The best food in the area is at Plas Bodegroes (☎ 01758 612363) in Nefyn Road which is about three miles from the marina, so you might find a taxi useful but it's well worth the trip.

Taxi:	Rhyd Taxis (☎ 0800 654321)
Car hire:	Abarconwy Car & Van Hire (☎ 01492 874669), from nearby Conwy
Bus:	service form marina to town centre links to local and national network
Rail:	Pwllheli Station on Cambrian Coast Line, links to national network
Airport:	Manchester Airport

for more details, see Directory Section

Pwllheli to Caernarfon

The coastline around the Lleyn Peninsula is attractive and unspoiled – the whole area has seen little modern development and might almost be living in a different era. Designated as Heritage Coast, the views are spectacular and you'll see plenty of wildlife – Bardsey Island lying off the point is a National Nature Reserve, but not somewhere for yachts to explore. The navigator will have an interesting time of it along here as there are tricky currents and off-lying islands to contend with, so some almanac and chartwork before departure is a good idea. It's a long leg to Caernarfon where you need to time your arrival to suit the tides, or further to Holyhead, which is at least accessible in all conditions. If the weather is being kind, there are a few places to put in.

Just along the coast from Pwllheli, the little fishing village of **Abersoch** is now a popular centre for boating of all kinds, and especially dinghy racing which the wide sandy bay is ideal for. The shelter is much as you would expect by looking at the chart and this is not a good place to be in strong easterlies. There are not a huge number of moorings for visitors here, and the gently sloping sands mean that you must moor or anchor a long way offshore if you don't want to sit on the bottom at low water. (See directory for organisations which offer moorings.) Shopping is quite limited as this is a small place, though you will find most essentials and there are several inviting hostelries for a run ashore. On the other side of the peninsula at **Porthdinllaen** there is a sheltered bay which is a popular port of call for yachts. While there are no moorings or general facilities for yachts, it does provide an excellent little anchorage. This is an area of outstanding natural beauty, and the small hamlet of Porthdinllaen is now owned by the National Trust. This is a popular place for holidaymakers, many being drawn to its excellent 27 hole golf course, The Nefyn & District Golf Club (☎ 01758 720966), which overlooks the bay, and the opportunities the area offers for walking. The Porthdinllaen Visitors' Centre (☎ 01758 720308) at the Lifeboat House will be of interest to those who like to find out about lifeboats and other local issues. The Ty Coch Inn (☎ 01758 720498) by the beach is a good spot for a drink and 50 yards up the quiet main road The Cliffs Inn (☎ 01758 720356) serves good pub meals. For provisions, you will need to go half a mile to the village of Morfa Nefyn where there is a general store, post office and garage.

Caernarfon & The Menai Strait

The waterfront at Caernarfon is dominated by the imposing and massive castle (CADW ☎ 01286 677617) which was built by Edward I in the late 13th century. As well as being a military stronghold, it was also intended to be the seat of government and a royal palace, and was where Prince Charles was invested as Prince of Wales in 1969. The old town is surrounded by medieval walls which lead out from the castle walls enclosing a delightful network of narrow streets and is well worth exploring. More recent history can be explored at Caernarfon Air World (☎ 01286 830800) where there is a museum and the opportunity to view the castles of the area and Snowdonia by plane. An alternative view of Snowdon can be had by taking the Snowdon Mountain Railway which climbs to the summit from Llanberis which is just on the edge of the National Park and only a few miles from the centre of town. Set on the banks of the sheltered Menai Strait, Caernarfon is not too difficult to get to as long as you plan your arrival to take account of the swift tides which run through the strait. There are a number of options for berthing and the harbour-master will advise you about where is the most suitable spot for your size and type of boat. A berth alongside under the castle walls is a fine place to come ashore from though you need to be prepared to dry out for this option. Wherever you come ashore, you will find all the facilities and shops you might need within a few minutes walk. There's a good choice of places for a drink or a meal as well.

For a restaurant meal try the Celtic Royal (☎ 01286 674139) on Bangor Street which also serves bar meals at lunchtime. The Seiont Manor Hotel (☎ 01286 673366) in Llanrung, is a little further afield at 3 miles east of Caernarfon, but boasts a three-room restaurant and inventive cooking which is worth the journey.

The scenery as you head on up the Menai Strait from Caernarvon is spectacular, and the navigation is in places quite challenging, especially through the Swellies between the two imposing bridges. The tidal stream can reach eight knots here, so be sure to consult a good pilot book for details of when to make your passage through. The marina at **Port Dinorwick** has space for a few visitors and offers refuge from the swooshing currents. With its wide variety of types of habitat there is a wealth of marine life, both plant and animal, living in the strait and over 1000 different species have been identified. A stroll along the foreshore at low water will enable you to see at least some of them. Once through the Swellies, you approach Bangor and Beaumaris which are covered after our tour around Anglesey.

Taxi:	(☎ 01286 672233)
Car hire:	Rent a Car (☎ 01286 676171)
Cycle hire:	(☎ 01286 676804)
Bus:	Enquiries (☎ 01248 750444)
Rail:	National Rail enquiries (☎ 0345 484950)
Ferry:	Stena Line enquiries (☎ 0990 707070)
Airport:	Liverpool

for more details, see Directory Section

Anglesey

Anglesey is perhaps most widely known for its ferry service to Ireland via Holyhead, and that place with an impossibly long name just by the Menai bridges which can mercifully be abbreviated to Llanfair P.G. – the platform tickets from the station are a popular souvenir and here you will also find the James Pringle Weavers Visitor Centre (☎ 01248 717171). The Stone Science Centre (☎ 01248 450310) in the middle of the island takes you on a quick romp through 650 million years of geology and fossils and panders to children's fascination with dinosaurs. Anglesey Sea Zoo (☎ 01248 430411) which is just opposite Caernarfon over the Menai Strait at Brynsiencyn, gives you an opportunity to look at things which are alive! Not far away, you can see most of Anglesey's landmarks in one place, one twelfth of full size, at the Anglesey Model Village (☎ 01248 440477) at Newborough. Included is Plas Newydd (NT ☎ 01248 714795) which in reality overlooks the strait not far from that place with the platform tickets. It's the traditional home of the Marquess of Anglesey and has fine paintings, an interesting military museum and attractive gardens and woodland. The island offers a wealth of fine countryside with spectacular cliffs especially in the north and around Holy Island, and the contrasting scenery along the narrow Menai Strait which separates the island from the mainland. Good facilities for the yachtsman should by now be in place at the new marina in Holyhead Harbour, and there are smaller, quieter and prettier places to put into as well.

Holyhead

Holyhead Harbour is a fine refuge from foul weather and accessible in pretty much any conditions. Tucked away round the north east side of the spectacular crags and cliffs of Holy Island, this old walled town enjoys good transport links with the rest of the island and so is not a bad place to base yourself for exploration further afield. It's a busy commercial port with ferry traffic heading across to Dublin and Dun Laoghaire in Southern Ireland, so it's no bad thing to contact Port Control on Channel 14 to check on traffic movements. Mooring for yachts is by the Holyhead Sailing Club in the large New Harbour and you should contact the club for directions. Shelter is good, but at the time of writing there's nowhere particularly handy to go alongside. Plans are in hand for the construction of a new 500 berth marina with all the usual facilities, and the first 50-100 berths should be in place by the end of the 1999 season. The Sailing Club welcomes visitors to its facilities which include bar, restaurant and showers. Most basic facilities will be found close by as will shops for essentials. For comprehensive re-provisioning, a trip to the centre of town about a mile away will be needed.

Taxi: (☎ 01407 765000) or (☎ 01407 769090)
Car hire: Hertz (☎ 01407 763818)
Bus: Local and national services
Rail: National Rail enquiries (☎ 0345 484950)
Ferry: Stena Line enquiries (☎ 0990 707070)
Airport: Manchester
for more details, see Directory Section

Moelfre

The bay at Moelfre presents an attractive anchorage on the north east side of the island. Facilities for visiting yachts are limited at this small holiday resort, but there are local shops for provisions, and both The Kimmel Arms (☎ 01248 410231) and The Oak Lodge Hotel (☎ 01248 410494) serve good pub meals - the restaurant in the latter being slightly more elaborate. The Sea Watch Centre (☎ 01248 410277) is intended to spark the imagination of young and old alike and includes a retired lifeboat and displays on marine life, ships and shipwrecks. The latter is certainly of local relevance considering the loss of the Royal Charter and over 300 lives on the point at the north of the bay in 1859 as she returned, heavily laden, from the Australian goldfields, and the wreck of the Hindlea can still be seen. The RNLI have had a station here since 1848 and, as well as the all-weather lifeboat, there has been an inshore lifeboat here since 1965. The current lifeboat house was built in 1909 and welcomes visitors all year. (see directory for more details.) The coastline offers spectacular walking and there's a fine sandy beach just to the north west.

Beaumaris

There's a full range of facilities available if you anchor off at **Bangor** though the tidal stream can make life interesting here. A more attractive spot is across the strait and a little further east at Beaumaris. This historic town has as its centrepiece the partly moated and formidable but unfinished defences of Beaumaris Castle (CADW ☎ 01248 810361), another of Edward I's bastions to subdue the Welsh. More recent history can be explored at the old Gaol & Courthouse (☎ 01286 679098) and the Museum of Childhood (☎ 01248 712498). You might be able to get a mooring from one of the yacht clubs here, and the Royal Anglesey Yacht Club makes visitors welcome in its clubhouse which has a bar and showers. There's a good range of shops all within a few hundred yards and you will not be short of somewhere to take refreshment either. The Sailors Return (☎ 01248 811314) in Church Street is ideal for a drink, and the Liverpool Arms (☎ 01248 810362) in Castle Street serves good pub meals. Also in Castle Street, Bottles Bistro (☎ 01248 810623) won't break the bank for a restaurant meal and The White Lion (☎ 01248 810589) is a bit more elaborate. For the best food in town, head for the Bulls Head (☎ 01248 810329) just along the road.

Taxi: (☎ 01248 490414) or (☎ 01248 490500)
Car hire: Stop Gap (☎ 01248 352772)
Bus: services to Bangor
Rail: Bangor Station for services to Holyhead
             and London
for more details, see Directory Section

Conwy

Regrettably, your options are rather limited along the north coast of Wales. In fair weather, you may like to anchor off outside the harbour at Rhoss-on-Sea, but for the most part, the coast consists of wide sandy beaches which are not greatly hospitable for yachts but paradise for caravans which you will see in profusion. Fortunately, there is one excellent option which is the town of Conwy itself where there is a marina and plenty to see and do.

Conwy

Like so many other towns in the area, Conwy has as its focus a magnificent castle (CADW ☎ 01492 592358) built on the instructions of Edward I. This and the walled town next to it give the town a strong sense of history, and there is plenty to keep the avid historic building explorer busy. Close to the castle, you will find Aberconwy House (NT ☎ 01492 592246), a 14th century merchant's house, and Plas Mawr (CADW ☎ 01492 580167), a well-preserved Elizabethan town-house. The beach resort towns of Llandudno and Colwyn Bay are within easy reach for seaside holiday amusements. To the north west of Llandudno, the towering headland of Great Ormes Head, which you will have seen on your approach to Conwy, is worth a visit for spectacular views, wildlife and a variety of historic attractions including a disused lighthouse and Bronze Age mineworkings. Access to Conwy Harbour is barely constrained by the tide – those drawing more than 1.5 metres may have to wait for a bit around low water springs. You have a choice here and can either get a mooring from the harbour authorities, or head for the well-appointed marina run by Crest Nicholson. The marina is a short walk from the town centre where the range of shops should cater for most provisioning needs. For a drink and a simple meal, the Old White House (☎ 01492 573133) is close to the marina, or you might prefer to head for the splendid old Castle Hotel (☎ 01492 592324) in the High Street for a choice of bar snacks or restaurant meals. The Liverpool Arms (☎ 01492 562161) on The Quay in Conwy, is also a good choice for a drink. Sandwiched between Conwy and Colwyn Bay, Llandudno has the royally named Kings Head (☎ 01492 877993) and Queens Head (☎ 01492 546570), both of which should be easily remembered, and the Cross Keys (☎ 01492 876132) on Madoc Street is ideal for good, reasonably priced food. For an hotel meal, The Esplanade (☎ 01492 860300) and the St Tudno (☎ 01492 874411) are both first rate examples, the latter being particularly noted for its excellent restaurant. On the other side of Llandudno, Colwyn Bay fields a very worthy restaurant by the name of Café Nicoise (☎ 01492 531555) which is definitely worth a visit.

Taxi:	Elwyn's Taxis (☎ 01492 592344)
Car hire:	Aberconwy Car & Van Hire (☎ 01492 874669)
Bus:	(☎ 01492 596969)
Rail:	National Rail enquiries (☎ 0345 484950)
Ferry:	Stena Line enquiries (☎ 0990 707070)
Airport:	Manchester

for more details, see Directory Section

Merseyside

Before you plunge into the River Mersey and the busy docks around Liverpool, you might consider the quieter option offered at **West Kirby** in the wide estuary of the River Dee. Most of the estuary dries at low water, and the tides can be quite fierce, but for those not bothered about drying out in soft mud, a warm welcome awaits you at the West Kirby Sailing Club (☎ 0151 625 5579). Moorings may be available for boats up to 32 foot, or you can drop your anchor clear of the moorings. Shops, pubs and restaurants are all conveniently close to the club, and for more tranquil pursuits, the islands in the mouth are popular with birdwatchers.

Liverpool

The maritime pedigree of Liverpool will not fail to strike you as you cruise past the miles of dockside waterfront. While there are far fewer ships using the Mersey than there were, there is still a considerable amount of traffic and Liverpool continues to be an important part of the transport network for international trade. Considerable re-development around the Canning Docks, not far from the Royal Liver Building (☎ 0151 236 2748 for tours) which is a notable landmark, has given a home to a number of museums and places of interest. You will emerge much better informed by the time you have visited Merseyside Maritime Museum (☎ 0151-478 4499), the HM Customs & Excise National Museum "Anything to declare?" (☎ 0151 478 4499), the Museum of Liverpool Life (☎ 0151 478 4080) and the Northern Branch of the Tate Gallery (☎ 0151 709 0507). If you still want more, within walking distance there's The Beatles Story (☎ 0151 709 1963) – and you can visit The Cavern as well – and in Rumford Street at Western Approaches (☎ 0151 227 2008), you can visit the underground headquarters used for the Battle of the Atlantic. In William Brown Street you'll find The Walker Art Gallery (☎ 0151 478 4199), The Liverpool Museum and Planetarium (☎ 0151 478 4399) and the Central Library (☎ 0151 225 5429). Completed in 1978, Liverpool Cathedral (☎ 0151 709 6271) on St James Mount, is the largest cathedral in Britain and good views can be had from the tower which climbs to 331 feet. The Albert Dock Marina has space for a few visitors and has the considerable advantage of being right in the thick of the area full of museums and dockside attractions. However, if you prefer not to be one of these yourself, you may well choose to head for the Liverpool Marina in Brunswick and Coburg Docks which is about a mile upriver. Here you will find a full range of facilities and you will be made welcome in the Harbourside Club. There is a bar and restaurant (bookings ☎ 0151 709 2683) in the club or if you stroll up to Albert Dock, you will find alternatives there. On the west bank, moorings may also be available from the Wallasea Yacht Club up at the mouth of the river, or the Royal Mersea Yacht Club at Rock Ferry just opposite the marina contact them in advance for availability and pilotage instructions.

Wandering into town, you will not be disappointed with the choice of places to eat and drink. The Albert Dock has a lively bar, Blue (☎ 0151 7097097) which Liverpool Football Club have been known to frequent. The Philharmonic (☎ 0151 7091163) on the corner of Hope Street and Hardman Street, is worth visiting for its extravagant decoration, not least in the gents lavatories! It is only 20 minutes walk from Albert Dock, too. Of course you can't come to Liverpool if you are a Beatles fan, and not visit Matthew Street with the famous Cavern Club (☎ 0151 2361964). The Pump House (☎ 0151 7092367) on Albert Dock, is a conveniently located multi-level conversion of a dock building. On the

Artist: **Anthony Flemming** **LIVERPOOL** *Courtesy of:* **The Artist**

restaurant front, Ziba (☎ 0151 7088870) on Berry Street is a 20 minute walk from Albert Dock and serves good cordon-bleu style food in a modern atmosphere. Cafe Renouf (☎ 0151 7088698) on Rodney Street, is roughly the same distance away from Albert Dock and serves good, simple french cooking and is excellent value for money. Est Est Est (☎ 0151 7086969) on Albert Dock is another good place to eat, as is Don Pepe (☎ 0151 2311909) on Victoria Street, conveniently positioned between the dock and the centre city. To finish off the night, the Mello Mello Bar (☎ 0151 7070898) and Cream (☎ 0151 7091693) which was voted by the Guardian as the Best Club in 1997, are both in the Slater Street/Concert Square area which is famed for clubs and late bars, and is roughly 15 minutes from Albert Dock.

Taxi:	(☎ 0151 427 7909)
Car hire:	Avis (☎ 0151 709 4737)
	Hertz (☎ 0151 709 3580)
Bus:	regular services from marina to town centre
Rail:	local rail services link to national net work
Ferry:	to Belfast, Northern Ireland and Douglas, Isle of Man
Airport:	Liverpool Airport (☎ 0151 486 8877)

for more details, see Directory Section

Lancashire

The sandy beaches and bright lights at Blackpool and Morecambe have made this stretch of coastline popular with holidaymakers for over a century. These are places which mean fun and enjoyment to many, but the yachtsman may be inclined to be disdainful. The beautiful sand dunes which line the shore warn of shifting sandbars off the shore, and much of the coastline here has very shallow water stretching well out to sea. With prevailing winds often making this a lee shore, this is definitely not a place to be pottering about close to the beach if the weather turns nasty. Having said that, with a little thought and a wary eye on the weather forecast, one can plan a cruise along here which will take in the sights and keep you out of trouble.

The River Ribble

The Ribble Estuary is definitely not for the faint hearted. The navigation is tricky and your options are very limited if the weather turns against you. There is no longer any shipping using the river, though there are some navigation marks left over from the old days. Be warned - the channel may well have shifted since. The remains of the training walls are another hazard. Add to that tidal access for only a few hours around high water, and most prudent strangers will tend to steer well clear. It was here that the RNLI suffered its worst ever night on the 9th December, 1886 when, in the course of rescuing a crew of 12 from the *Mexico* of Hamburg, both Southport and St Anne's lifeboats were lost. After several near swampings Lytham Lifeboat successfully brought off the crew of the Mexico, but the cost was high and twenty-seven lifeboatmen lost their lives that night. The Lytham Lifeboat Museum on East Beach pays tribute to this and other services by local lifeboats. If you are determined, you can anchor near **Lytham St Annes** and the Ribble Cruising Club will welcome you ashore, but do plan carefully - local knowledge is advised and the tides are huge. A couple of other options are open to you. The Douglas Boatyard at **Hesketh Bank** up the Douglas River which runs off to the south of the Ribble has a few spaces for visitors on pontoons or quayside moorings and there are reasonable facilities ashore. Ten minutes walk takes you to the Becconsall Hotel where you can get a drink, and in Tarleton which is a couple of miles away, The Cork & Bottle serves pub food and the presence of the Tarleton Bistro provides an alternative choice. This is definitely a place for those who want to be away from it all as it is very much a backwater. The Ribble Marshes between the River Douglas and the sea are a national nature reserve which is especially busy in the migration seasons. For a more cosmopolitan experience, once you have navigated the entrance, following the river up to **Preston** should hold no terrors. There's a marina in the old Preston Dock which has locked access for about four hours around high water. The dock area has been redeveloped as a leisure area, so you will find shops and restaurants in pleasant surroundings, and the centre of town with museums to explain the town's important past role in the textiles industry is a short bus or taxi ride away.

Fleetwood

Fleetwood offers good shelter and a reasonably straightforward entrance from the sea, though you will need to watch out for ferry and other commercial traffic which the harbour still serves and access to the marina is only for a couple of hours each side of high water. Away from the docks which are tucked on the back of the peninsula, Fleetwood is a seaside holiday town and merges with its much bigger and better known brother Blackpool to the south. If you have never been to the top of Blackpool Tower or tried any of the fairground rides on the Pleasure Beach, you really ought at least to go and have a look. The popularity of Blackpool continues to be phenomenal in spite of the ascendancy of the foreign holiday, and from the safe distance of the marina at Fleetwood, you have the option of taking a look and then running back to your boat if you really can't stand it! In Fleetwood itself, there's an interesting local museum (☎ 01253 876621) and the lifeboat station is worth a look - it includes a water-jetting system in the harbour bottom to prevent silting by the lifeboat's berth. The marina is at Fleetwood Harbour Village and has berths for over 300 boats and a good range of facilities. In Dock Street, head for the Fleetwood Arms (☎ 01253 872787) for a drink and Lynn's Diner (☎ 01253 878913) for an inexpensive meal. The Trafalgar (☎ 01253 872266) on North Albert Street will offer you something a little more elaborate and look for Euston (☎ 01253 876525) on The Esplanade for the best food in the area.

Taxi:	Fleetwood Taxi (☎ 01253 822000)
Car hire:	Cleveleys, GMC Self Drive Car Hire (☎ 01253 829922)
Bus/tram:	local services and connections to Blackpool
Rail:	Blackpool Station links to national network at Preston
Ferry:	services to Northern Ireland
Airport:	Manchester

for more details, see Directory Section

Morecambe Bay

This is a difficult stretch of coastline for the yachtsman. Prevailing winds often make it a lee shore and the large areas of shallow water, much of which dry to sand and mud at low water, have made it the scene of numerous disastrous strandings. Most yachts on passage will tend to skip past here and probably head for the Isle of Man as a staging post, or even cruise up the east coast of Ireland which does have easier navigation and probably more appealing places to visit. If there are places along here you really want to go to, can we suggest that the M6 is a splendid road and offers considerably fewer navigational challenges. Having said that, there is a fine marina up the River Lune at **Glasson Dock**. It is accessible for a couple of hours each side of high water, but it's about 5 miles from the historic town of Lancaster and a little further still from the jolly beach resort of Morecambe. **Heysham**, which is closer to Morecambe, is denied to you as it's a busy ferry terminal where yachts are discouraged, though in an emergency it's worth knowing about as a refuge. You will probably not be too disappointed about this as the backdrop of nuclear power stations and dockyards is hardly picturesque. If you don't mind drying out, you might manage to pick up a vacant mooring or anchor off by the Morecambe and Heysham Yacht Club which will give you access to the promenade and theme park and much more besides in this appealing resort town. The shallow waters which recede at low water to leave exposed vast areas of sand, shingle or mud, continue around the head of Morecambe Bay and down to the little group of islands off **Barrow-in-Furness**. Piel Island has the ruins of a 14th century castle (EH ☎ 01229 833609) and the south end of the Isle of Walney and Foulney Island both have nature reserves where amongst others, there are colonies of herring gulls and lesser black-backed gulls. If you are here just after the nesting season, families of eider duck may entertain you. On neighbouring Roa Island, one of the RNLI's newest lifeboathouses has replaced its 70 year old predecessor. You can anchor clear of the dredged fairway which takes commercial traffic up to Barrow Docks. Facilities are very limited on the islands, but better at Barrow which is three miles up the channel. Don't miss the Barrow Dock Museum (☎ 01229 870871) which is open between Wednesday and Sunday each week.

Cumbria

Now that we are in Cumbria, our thoughts turn to the Lake District whose hills form the backdrop as we follow the coast north. The coastline continues to look inhospitable to the yachtsman, though there are one or two places which offer sanctuary of sorts. The large drying harbour at **Ravenglass** is one for the intrepid navigator. Local knowledge, or at least a comprehensive pilot book, is needed to get in here. First used as a harbour by the Romans, the fort which they built here in AD78 is one of the best preserved in the country and has the highest standing Roman walls in the north of England. Once inside, a ride on the narrow gauge Ravenglass and Eskdale Railway (☎ 01229 717171), known affectionately as the "Ratty", gives a gentle introduction to the Lake District scenery, there's a fine stately home in splendid grounds at Muncaster Castle (☎ 01229 717614) just outside the village and a railway museum. Shopping facilities are basic, and as this is a small place, don't expect a huge choice of places to eat and drink. The beer is well kept and there's pub food at the Ratty Arms (☎ 01229 717676) and the Holly House Hotel (☎ 01229 717230) also serves meals.

Whitehaven

Blasting on north from Ravenglass, you pass the forboding outline of Sellafield. Soon after, a more natural outlook beckons as you approach the cliffs of St Bees Head, home to the only colony of black guillemot in England. Just round the corner and you fetch up at Whitehaven which is becoming a delightful place to visit. This traditional coalmining area has suffered from the loss of much employment; however, with its Georgian grid street layout and some very attractive buildings, the money being spent on re-developing the town to boost tourism is definitely to the advantage of passing yachtsmen. The dock area has been extensively refurbished, and there is now a small marina in the locked Inner Harbour. Access is possible for about three hours each side of the tide which makes this one of the most accessible spots with good shelter for a long way. Purpose built as a trading port by the local Lowther family, the town prospered in spite of the interruptions posed by the American War of Independence. Ships were commandeered, and in 1778 John Paul Jones, a former inhabitant of the town and then a captain in the American Navy, launched a raid to destroy the harbour and the shipping in it. Not much damage was done as half his men ended up in a local inn, absolutely pickled - this sets a fine example for visitors from the sea just over two hundred years later! You can find out more about this and other aspects of local history both maritime and otherwise at the Whitehaven Beacon Museum (☎ 01946 592302). Another local link with America can be found in the churchyard of St Nicholas' Church in the town centre where George Washington's grandmother, Mildred Gale, is buried. Just to the south of the town near Egremont, The Florence Mine (☎ 01946 820683) may be of interest as it's the last working iron ore mine in Britain. There's a heritage centre and by prior arrangement underground tours are also available. If you are interested in industrial heritage, you probably ought to have a look at the BNFL Visitors' Centre at Sellafield. It is a bit further away, but is informative and does have the advantage of being free. While you are in the area, St Bees is a pretty little village and the lifeboat station

there is worth a look, and turning inland, get some dubbin on your boots as you are well placed to enjoy some of the Lake District's least congested countryside. Once you have built up a thirst, you will find there are plenty of pubs to choose from. The Paul Jones Tavern (☎ 01946 690916) on Duke Street is a good choice for a drink and you can get bar meals there as well.

Taxi:	Abbey Cars (☎ 01946 63000)
Car hire:	For Rent a Car (☎ 01946 820266)
Bus:	Stagecoach enquiries (☎ 01946 63222)
Rail:	National Rail enquiries (☎ 0345 484950)
Airport:	Carlisle Airport

for more details, see Directory Section

Maryport

It seems appropriate that our last Port of Call in England should have been the site of a Roman Fort whose role was to protect against marauders creeping around the western end of Hadrian's Wall at Bowness-on-Solway. In its day, this was one of Cumbria's busiest ports for exporting locally produced goods to the rest of the world. It is now the home of a small fishing fleet which leaves the outer Senhouse Dock available for use as a marina. It is also the home of the Maryport Steamships Museum (☎ 01900 815954) whose exhibits in Elizabeth Dock can be explored and a full history of Maryport's maritime history can be found at the Maryport Maritime Museum (☎ 01900 813738) in Senhouse Street. Also worth a look is the Senhouse Roman Museum (☎ 01900 816168) by the site of the Roman Fort at The Battery, where you will find the oldest collection of Roman sculpture and inscriptions in Britain. Underwater wonders are explored at the Maryport Aquaria (☎ 01900 817760) on the South Quay by the Elizabeth Dock. Fletcher Christian, of Mutiny on the Bounty fame, is also remembered here – he actually came from Cockermouth just inland, but his parents hailed from Maryport. For less intellectual amusement, Maryport also boasts a good indoor Go-karting track (☎ 01900 816472) on Curzon Street.

With space for over 200 boats, the marina is larger than the one just down the coast at Whitehaven. As it's also been established longer it offers more comprehensive facilities. Shelter is excellent and the marina is accessible for around three hours each side of high water. Like many other small ports, as commercial traffic has dwindled, the harbour has been the focus for redevelopment, so the waterfront provides a lively face to the town and there's a good range of local shops within five minutes walk.

After exploring this historic town, there are several excellent pubs and restaurants to sample. Jollies Bistro (☎ 01900 809214) on Crosby Street and the Waverly Hotel (☎ 01900 812115) on Curzon Street are good for food, while the Captain Nelson (☎ 01900 813109) on Irish Street is a good choice for a drink, as is The Old Mill (☎ 01900 813148) at Dearham. A little further along the coast at Allonby, Seychelle's Restaurant (☎ 01900 881502) has fine waterfront views, and you might try the Baywatch Hotel (☎ 01900 881088) if you fancy a good steak.

Taxi:	Keith's Cabs (☎ 01900 818686)
Car hire:	Practical Car & Van Rental (☎ 01900 819280)
Bus:	Stagecoach (☎ 01946 63222)
Rail:	National Rail Enquiries (☎ 0345 484950)
Airport:	Carlisle Airport

for more details, see Directory Section

Isle of Man

The Isle of Man is ideally located as a place to break voyages up and down the Irish Sea, and also for those crossing between mainland Britain and Ireland. The island's main harbour at Douglas probably offers the best facilities at present (and certainly will once the tidal basin in the inner harbour is fully equipped with pontoons) and there are several other smaller harbours which are interesting places to visit or convenient stopping off places. If you are able to, it is well worth planning to spend a few days on and around the island rather than just treating it as a motorway service station! The island has a very agreeable pace of life and a rich history which includes the longest continuous parliament in the world, dating back over 1000 years to its foundation by the Vikings in 979. The tranquillity which the island is renowned for is only marginally interrupted by the world famous TT (Tourist Trophy) Motorbike Races which take place over a fortnight in late May and early June, and the Manx Grand Prix in late August and early September.

Douglas

Douglas is a busy centre of commerce as well as a popular tourist resort. While financial deals are being transacted ashore, the harbour is busy as well - this is where the ferries from mainland Britain and Ireland dock - and the harbour is also the centre for other commercial traffic which serves the island. The Tower of Refuge on Conister Rock, the rocky islet in Douglas Bay is a reminder that the harbour here was not always as sheltered a haven as it is now. The tower stands as a memorial to the concern for the welfare of seamen shown by Sir William Hillary who arranged for it to be built in 1832. His catchily titled pamphlet, *An Appeal to the British Nation on the Humanity and Policy of forming a National Institution for the Preservation of Lives and Property from Shipwreck,* was published in 1823 and set the ball rolling for the creation of the National Institution for the Preservation of Life from Shipwreck in 1824. In 1854, the name was changed to the Royal National Lifeboat Institution which it has remained ever since. Hillary was a man of action as well as a writer of pamphlets, and as a very active member of the crew of the Douglas lifeboat, was awarded three gold medals by the institution for acts of considerable bravery while engaged in saving lives at sea. This achievement has only been matched by one other lifeboatman in the history of the Institution, namely Henry Blogg, coxswain of the Cromer Lifeboat. For a thorough overview of all aspects of the island's history, a visit to the excellent Manx Museum (☎ 01624 675522) which also contains the National Art Gallery is highly recommended. A ride on the world's oldest horsedrawn trams along the Douglas Promenade offers an alternative way of soaking up the atmosphere. From Douglas,

you are well placed to explore the rest of the island via the Steam Railway which serves the southern end of the island or via the Victorian Manx Electric Railway which will give you a sedate ride up to Ramsey via Laxey where you can admire the world's largest working waterwheel. Lady Isabella, as the wheel is known, is the centrepiece of an interesting museum of industry (☎ 01624 648000). Laxey is also at the bottom of the Snaefell Mountain Railway which will take you gently to the top of the island's highest mountain – a painless way to reach a fine viewpoint. With bus services linking Douglas to Peel and Tynwald Hill as well as the other centres on the island, you may well decide to take advantage of the facilities in Douglas Harbour and explore the rest of the island from there.

The new flap gate on Douglas's Yacht Basin gives deep water berths for yachts, and pontoons should be in place by the early part of the 2000 sailing season. Douglas Bay Yacht Club is moving to new premises in refurbished dock buildings on The Tongue where visitors will be welcome, and the harbour authorities will be providing washing facilities in the same area as well. A full range of shops and a supermarket are all to be found within half a mile. As the Yacht Basin will continue to be accessible for only 3 hours each side of high water, existing arrangements, which include a small pontoon and visitors' moorings in the outer harbour, will remain in place for very short stays or for those waiting for access to the inner harbour. You need permission from the harbour-master to stop here, and it's not a good place to be in strong north easterlies.

There is a wide choice of places to eat and drink in Douglas, and there are plenty close to the harbour. The Market Inn (☎ 01624 675202) and The Albert (☎ 01624 673632), both in Chapel Row close to the North Quay, are both good options for a drink, and the British Hotel (☎ 01624 675464) on the Quay serves good pub food. The Terminus Tavern (☎ 01624 624312) in Strathallan Crescent is a couple of miles away, but worth considering as an alternative for a pub meal. Inexpensive restaurant meals can be had from Coasters (☎ 01624 616020) on North Quay or The Cul de Sac (☎ 01624 623737) on Market Hill just off the Quay. Scotts Bistro (☎ 01624 623764) on John Street or La Tasca (☎ 01624 613992) on Loch Promenade are both a bit further away, but will serve you with something a little more upmarket. If you want to push the boat out, you'll need to take a taxi to L'Experience (☎ 01624 623103) in Summerhill or Ciapelli's (☎ 01624 677442) on Nobles Park.

Taxi:	Available at harbour
Car hire:	Atholl Car Hire (Europcar), Peel Road, Douglas (☎ 01624 623232)
	Ford Rent-a-car, Airport & Sea terminal, Douglas (☎ 01624 662211)
	Isle of Man Rent a Car (Hertz), Douglas (☎ 01624 621844)
Bus:	bus services link all main centres on the island
Rail:	Douglas to Ramsey: Manx Electric Railway
	Douglas to Port St Mary & Port Erin: Isle of Man Steam Railway
	Isle of Man Railways: (☎ 01642 670077)

Ferry: services to Heysham and Liverpool, summer services to Ireland and Isle of Man Steam Packet Company (☎ 01624 661661)

Airport: Isle of Man (Ronaldsway) Airport (☎ 01624 821600) Manx Airlines Reservations (☎ 01624 824313)

for more details, see Directory Section

Ramsey

Ramsey is an attractive leafy town with a fine backdrop of wooded hills rising up to the peak of Snaefell. The harbour here is accessible for three hours each side of high water and offers an alternative port of call for yachtsmen who want to explore, or berth at, the northern less populated end of the island. There are visitors' mooring buoys outside the harbour if you want to stay afloat, or you can join small coasters and fishing boats alongside the harbour walls to dry out. Plans for a marina here are at a very early stage, so we don't expect to see much for a couple of years. Most basic facilities are available, and the shops are close to the waterfront. You will be welcome to use the showers at the Manx Sailing and Cruising Club which is close to hand. The Grove Rural Life Museum (☎ 01624 648000) is just outside the town. At this Victorian period house, you can capture the flavour of life 100 years ago, and there are well maintained gardens for you to enjoy where you may meet those curious tail-less Manx cats. Handy for a drink you will find the Stanley (☎ 01624 812258) on West Quay, and also on West Quay, The Trafalgar (☎ 01624 814601) does good pub food. Close by, Gophers (☎ 01624 815562) serves inexpensive meals and The Harbour Bistro (☎ 01624 814182) on East Quay is a bit smarter and is open in the evenings. The best in the area is the Grand Island (☎ 01624 812455) on Bride Road which is a couple of miles away, so perhaps an occasion for a taxi if you don't fancy the easy walk.

Taxi: (☎ 01624 812239 or (☎ 01624 814141)
Bus: bus services link all main centres on the island
Rail: Douglas to Ramsey: Manx Electric Railway Isle of Man Railways: (☎ 01642 670077)
Ferry: services from Douglas
Airport: Isle of Man (Ronaldsway) Airport (☎ 01624 821600) Manx Airlines Reservations (☎ 01624 824313)

Peel

Roughly half way down the picturesque west coast of the island, Peel nestles behind its fine sandy bay, and the harbour entrance is spectacularly located by the castle (☎ 01624 648000) and cathedral ruins on St Patrick's Isle. The harbour dries, but you can usually get alongside the breakwater at any state of the tide. Gales from four points each side of north can make the entrance inadvisable, but otherwise this is a straightforward place to get into. There are visitors' moorings in the bay and room for visitors in the harbour which is shared with fishing boats as well as small tanker and cargo boats which "do not cause much trouble" according to the Commodore of the Peel Sailing and Cruising Club. Basic facilities are available on the quays around the harbour, and you are welcome to use the facilities at the yacht club. You will find a full range of shops within a few hundred yards, and there's a good choice of places to eat and drink. The White House Hotel (☎ 01624 842252) on Douglas Street is the best spot for a drink and the Creek Inn (☎ 01624 842216) on The Quay is close to the harbour and serves good pub food. In Athol Place, the Hong Kong Delight (☎ 01624 842944) serves inexpensive meals, and The Marine Hotel (☎ 01624 842337) on Shore Road will offer you something a little more elaborate. Karl's Bistro (☎ 01624 844144) on The Quay is top of the range in Peel.

Port Erin & Port St Mary & Castletown

At the southern end of the island, you are faced with a choice of places to put in. There are three little drying harbours, all of which you can anchor outside, and judicious choice should give shelter from almost any direction. Port Erin and Port St Mary back onto each other across the Cregneash Peninsula and Castletown is only a couple of miles away. Wherever you end up, you will be well placed to enjoy these attractive and historic towns. Port St Mary probably offers the most convenience, though the wide sandy beaches in Castletown Bay may well prove tempting to some. The choice of places to visit is considerable and includes the Nautical Museum and magnificent Castle Rushden (☎ 01624 648000) next to the harbour in Castletown, the Railway Museum at the Steam Railway's southern terminus in Port Erin and the Cregneash Village Folk Museum (☎ 01624 648000) just south of Port St Mary. With its intricate coastline of cliffs and coves, this is wonderful countryside for walking, and the nature reserve on the Calf of Man has a wide variety of birdlife to admire. This is one of the last remaining places in Britain where you can see choughs, and you will hardly be surprised to find Manx shearwaters in profusion. In the waters around Man, especially the south and west coasts, you may be able to see various aquatic mammals including seals, dolphins and basking sharks which are relatively recent visitors to the area. The Scarlett Visitor Centre south of Castletown is the place to go if you would like to learn more about the flora and fauna of the Isle of Man.

Both Port Erin and Port St Mary have conveniently located watering holes for the thirsty sailor to visit. The Falcon's Nest Hotel (☎ 01624 834077) on Station Road in Port Erin is a friendly beachside hotel, while the Albert (☎ 01624 832118) on Athol Street in Port St Mary, is particularly popular with both fishermen and 'yachties' and is located next to the harbour. Castletown has several pubs to choose from, including the Castle Arms (☎ 01624 824673) on the Quayside which is reputed to be one of the oldest pubs on the island. It is decorated with a nautical theme and serves good food. The Sidings (☎ 01624 823282) by the Station is a comfortable pub with a good range of beer, which appeals to both locals and visitors alike. A bit further along on Victoria Road is the Viking Hotel, which is again very popular and serves excellent food including barbecues in the garden. Still in Castletown, Chablis Cellar (☎ 01624 823527) on Bank Street, is a good restaurant for something a bit smarter, and Silverburn Lodge (☎ 01624 822343) and Rosa's Place (☎ 01624 822940) are also well worth considering.

Taxi: (☎ 01642 834949)
Car hire: (☎ 0500 823533)

Bus:	local services to destinations throughout the island
Rail:	Isle of Man Steam Railway links Port Erin, Port St Mary & Castletown to Douglas
Airport:	Ronaldsway Airport 1 mile from Castletown

for more details, see Directory Section

Artist: **Anthony Flemming CAERNARFON CASTLE** Courtesy of: **The Artist**

CARDIFF AND PENARTH 51.21'.0N 03.09'.5W

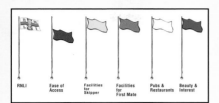

Cardiff Bay Barrage
Contact: Harbourmaster Tel: 02920 471311
VHF Ch: 14 VHF Name: Barrage Control

Penarth Marina
Charles Bush: Manager
Penarth, South Glamorgan CF64 1TQ
Tel: 02920 705021 Fax: 02920 712170
VHF Ch: 80 VHF Name: Penarth Marina

Penarth Motor Boat & Sailing Club
Contact: Secretary Tel: 02920 226575

Penarth Yacht Club
Contact: Secretary Tel: 02920 708196

Chandlers:
Cambrian Marine Tel: 02920 34 549
Marine Scene Tel: 02920 705780
Wigmore Wright Marine Services
Tel: 02920 709983
T J Williams Tel: 02920 487676

Repairs:
Breaksea Sailmakers & Riggers
Tel: 02920 730785
Cambrian Marine Tel: 02920 343549
West Point Marine Tel: 02920 711337
Wigmore Wright Marine Services
Tel: 02920 709983

Penarth Lifeboat Station
Open to visitors by appointment
Contact: A Rabaiotti (Hon Sec)
Tel: 02920 709910

BARRY 51.23'.5N 03.15'.5W

Barry Dock
Contact: Harbourmaster Tel: 01446 700754
VHF Channel: 11 VHF Name: Barry Radio

Barry Yacht Club
Contact: Secretary Tel: 01446 735511

Chandler:
Ray Harris Marine Tel: 01446 740924

Barry Dock Lifeboat
Open to visitors by appointment
Contact: E Powell Tel: 01446 738120

Atlantic College Lifeboat Station
Open to visitors by appointment only
(stands on private grounds)
Contact: Gareth Rees (Hon Sec)
Tel: 01446 796953

PORTHCAWL 51.28'.5N 03.42'.0W

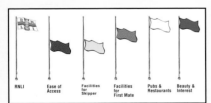

Porthcawl Harbour
Contact: Harbourmaster Tel: 01696 782756

Porthcawl Harbour Boat Club
Contact: Secretary Tel: 01656 782342

Porthcawl Lifeboat Station
Open to visitors most weekends
Contact: P Missen (Hon Sec) Tel: 01656 784113

SWANSEA 51.36'.5N 03.55'.5W

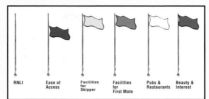

Swansea Harbour
Contact: Harbourmaster Tel: 01792 650855
VHF Ch: 18 VHF Name: Tawe Lock (barrage)

Swansea Marina
Dave Hoskin: Manager
Lockside, Maritime Quarter, Swansea, West
SA1 1WG Tel: 01792 470 310 Fax: 01792 463 948
VHF Ch: 80 VHF Name: Swansea Marina

Swansea Yacht & Sub-Aqua Club
Contact: Secretary Tel: 01792 650855

Chandler:
Cambrian Boat Centre Tel: 01792 467263

Repairs:
Cambrian Boat Centre Tel: 01792 467263
Canard Sails Tel: 01792 367838
Paul Clark Tel: 0831 685202

Swansea Maritime & Industrial Museum
Open daily Tues-Sun and all Bank Holidays
Contact: Mike Lewis Tel: 01792 650351/470371

PORT TALBOT

Port Talbot Lifeboat Station
Open every weekend by appointment
Contact: RV Harris Tel: 01639 884290

MUMBLES 51.34'.0N 03.58'.0W

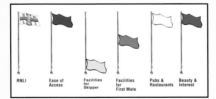

Bristol Channel Yacht Club
Contact: Secretary Tel: 01792 366000

Mumbles Motor Boat & Fishing Club
A E Davies: Secretary
642 Mumbles Road, Mumbles, Swansea
Tel: 01792 369 646

Mumbles Yacht Club
The Clubhouse, Southend, Swansea SA3 4EN
Georgie Thomas: Secretary Tel: 01792 369321

Chandlers:
Cambrian Boat Centre Tel: 01792 467263
The Captain's Cabin Tel: 01792 363448

The Mumbles Lifeboat Station
Open to visitors by appointment weekday
mornings 09.00-13.00 all year
Contact: Paul Leleu (Coxn)
Tel: 01792 361268/366246

HORTON & PORT EYNON

Horton & Port Eynon Lifeboat Station
Open to visitors all year round
Contact: Mr P Muxworthy (Hon Sec)
Tel: 01792 390805

BURRY PORT

(Marina planned here by 2002)

Contact: Superintendant
Burry Port Harbour Office, Burry Port,
Dyfed Tel: 01554 758181/834315

Burry Port Yacht Club
Contact: SecretaryTel: 01554 8336350

Burry Port Lifeboat
Open most weekends by appointment
Contact: G Smith (Hon Sec)
Tel: 01554 832030/833358

SAUNDERSFOOT AND TENBY 51.42'.5N 04.41'.5W

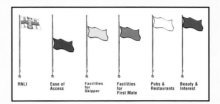

Saundersfoot Harbour
Peter Scourfield: Harbourmaster
Harbour Office, Saundersfoot, Dyfed SA69 9HE
Tel/Fax: 01834 812094
VHF Ch: 16 VHF Name: Saundersfoot Harbour

Tenby Harbour
Contact: Harbourmaster
Tel/Fax: 01834 842717
VHF Ch: 16/80 VHF Name: Tenby Harbour

Tenby Sailing Club
Contact: Secretary Tel: 01834 842762

Chandler:
Jones & Teague Tel: 01834 813429

Tenby Museum & Art Gallery
Open to visitors daily from Easter through
September. Contact: John Beynon
Tel: 01834 842809

Tenby Lifeboat Station
Open to visitors mid May - end Sept, Mon-Fri
11.00-17.00, Suns 14.00-17.00 and during winter
months by appointment
Contact: Arthur Squibbs (Hon Sec)
Tel: 01834 843694

MILFORD HAVEN 51.40'.0N 05.08'.0W

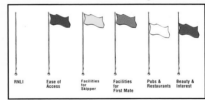

Port of Milford Haven
Contact: Berthing Master
Tel: 01646 692342 Fax: 01646 690179
VHF Channel: 12
VHF Name: Milford Haven Radio

Lawrenny Yacht Station
Contact: Manager Tel: 01646 651367
VHF Channel: M
VHF Name: Lawrenny Yacht Station

Dale Yacht Club
Contact: Secretary Tel: 01646 636 362

Lawrenny Yacht Club
Contact: Secretary Tel: 01646 651212

Milford Marina
Adrian Owens: Manager
Tel: 01646 696312 Fax: 01646 696314
VHF Channel: 37/M
VHF Name: Milford Marina

Chandler:
Brunel Chandlery Tel: 01646 601667
Bosuns Locker Tel: 01646 697834
Cosalt Tel: 01646 692032

Repairs:
Boat & Engine Repairs Wooden Hulls
Tel: 01646 698805
Milford Haven Ship Repairers
Tel: 01646 692691
Neyland Marine Services Tel: 01646 698 968

Angle Lifeboat Station
Open to visitors Mon-Fri 09.00 13.00 (except
Xmas & Boxing Day) by appointment
Contact: John Allen Tel: 01646 641260

Neyland

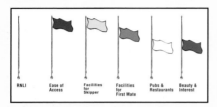

Neyland Yacht Haven
Brunel Quay, Neyland, Milford Haven, Dyfed
SA73 1PY Tel: 01646 601601
VHF Channel 80/M
VHF Name Neyland Yacht Haven

Neyland Yacht Club
The Promenade, Neyland, Milford Haven
Tel: 01646 600267

Pembroke

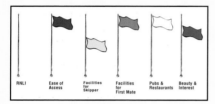

Pembroke Haven Yacht Club
E J Lowe: Secretary Tel: 01646 684403

Pembrokeshire Yacht Club
Tel: 01646 692799

SOLVA   51.52'.0N 05.11'.5W

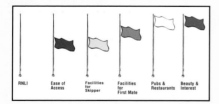

Solva Harbour
Contact: Harbourmaster Tel: 01437 720153

Solva Boatowners Assoc
D Taylor: Secretary
Tan Y Graig, Main Street, Solva
Tel: 01437 721220

Chandler:
Ocean Haze Tel: 01437 720826

Repairs:
Piers Beckett Tel: 01437 720972

LITTLE AND BROAD HAVEN

Little and Broad Haven Lifeboat
Open to visitors by appointment
Contact: C Whitby (Hon Sec)
Tel: 01437 781300

ST DAVIDS

St Davids Lifeboat
Open to visitors all year round
Contact: J Davies Tel: 01437 720716

FISHGUARD   52.00'.0N 04.58'.5W

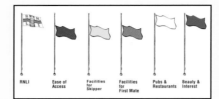

Fishguard Harbour
Contact: Harbourmaster
Harbour Dept, Preseli Pembrokeshire District
Council, Town Hall, Fishguard
Tel: 01348 873231
VHF Ch: 14/16 VHF Name: Fishguard Harbour

Fishguard Bay Yacht Club
David Hughes: Secretary
The Quay, Lower Town, Fishguard, Pembs
SA65 9NB Tel: 01348 872866

Chandlers:
Goodwick Marine Tel: 01348 873955

Repairs:
Contact Goodwick Marine

Fishguard Lifeboat Station
Blue Peter VII lifeboat
Open to visitors all year round
Contact: Coxn F George
Tel: 01348 874616 or 823231 (station)

CARDIGAN   52.07'.0N 04.42'.0W

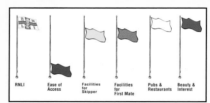

Port Cardigan
Contact: Harbourmaster (New Quay)
Tel: 01545 560 368

Teifi Boating Club
Gareth Jerman: Secretary Tel: 01239 612361

Moorings:
Tywynne Gwbert (DJW Evans)
Tel: 01239 613890
Netpool (Len James) Tel: 01239 612166

Chandler:
Ynys Marine, Station Yard, Cardigan

Repairs:
Cardigan Marine Spares Tel: 01239 711167
Cardigan Outboards Tel: 01239 613966
Ynys Marine, Station Yard, Cardigan

Cardigan Lifeboat
Poppit Beach
Open to visitors by appointment
Contact: F Coates (Hon Sec) Tel: 01239 613896

NEW QUAY & ABERAERON

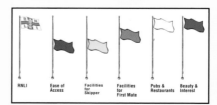

New Quay Harbour   52.13'.0N 04.21'.0W
Captain Chris Corcoran: Harbourmaster
Harbour Office, The Pier, New Quay,
Ceredigion SA45 9NW Tel: 01545 560368

VHF Channels: 16/12/80
VHF Name: New Quay Harbour

New Quay Yacht Club
Contact: Secretary Tel: 01545 560516

New Quay Lifeboat Station
Open to visitors daily 14.00-17.00 from May
through September.
Contact: R G Davies (Hon Sec)
Tel: 01545 561219 or 0468 663666

Aberaeron Harbour   52.14'.5N 04.16'.0W

Captain Chris Corcoran: Harbourmaster
South Beach, Aberaeron, Ceredigion SA 46 0BE
Tel: 01545 571645
VHF Channels: 14/16
VHF Name: Aberaeron Harbour

Aberaeron Yacht Club
Contact: Secretary Tel: 01545 570077

Chandler & Repairs:
Cardigan Outboards Tel: 01239 613966

ABERYSTWYTH   52.24'.5N 04.05'.5W

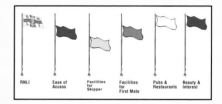

Aberystwyth Harbour
Contact: Harbourmaster Tel: 01970 611433
VHF Channel: 14/16
VHF Name: Aberystwyth Harbour

Y Lanfa Marina
Sion Edwards: Manager
Trefechan, Aberystwyth
Tel: 01970 611422 Fax: 01970 624122
VHF Ch: 80 VHF Name: Aberystwyth Marina

Aberystwyth Boat Club
Contact: Secretary Tel: 01970 611433

Chandler:
Bosuns Chandlers Tel: 01646 697834

Ceredigion Museum
Open daily to visitors Mon-Sat 10.00-17.00;
Sundays in school hols 12.00-17.00
Contact: Gweullion Ashley
Tel: 01970 633086 or 633088 (museum)

Aberystwyth Lifeboat Station
Open to visitors all year round
Contact: D Jenkins (Hon Sec)
Tel: 01970 624469

Borth Lifeboat Station
Open to visitors March through October
Contact: R Davies (Hon Sec) Tel: 01970 871512

ABERDOVEY/ABERDYFI   5232'.5N 04.02'.5W

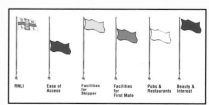

Aberdovey Harbour
Dave Davies: Harbourmaster
Harbour Office, Aberdyfi, Gwynedd LL35 0EB
Tel/Fax: 01654 767626

Dovey Yacht Club
Contact: Secretary Tel: 01827 286514

Moorings:
Aberleri Boatyard, Contact: Manager
Tel: 01970 371152 Fax: 01970 623 311

Chandler:
Dovey Marine Tel: 01654 767581

Repairs:
West Wales Marine Tel: 01654 767478

Aberdovey Lifeboat Station
Open to visitors by appointment most week-ends during summer months
Contact: Nick Dawson Tel: 01654 767225

BARMOUTH 52.43'.0N 04.03'.0W

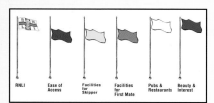

Barmouth Harbour
Captain J Kirkham: Harbourmaster
Harbour Office, Barmouth
Tel/Fax: 01341 280671
VHF Ch: 12 VHF Name: Barmouth Harbour

Merioneth Yacht Club
The Quay, Barmouth, Gwynedd LL42
Julian Greenway: Secretary Tel: 01341 281156

Chandlers:
Glaslyn Marine Tel: 01766 513595
Griffin Marine Tel: 01341 280232
Seafarer Tel: 01341 280978

Repairs:
Cambrian Coastal Cruisers
Griffin Marine Tel: 01341 280232
Tony Sydenham Services Tel: 01341 281212

RNLI Museum
Open to visitors daily, Easter through
September Tel: 01341 280940

Barmouth Lifeboat Station
Open to visitors by appointment only
Contact: boathouse Tel: 01341 280274

PORTHMADOG 52.55'.5N 04.07'.5W

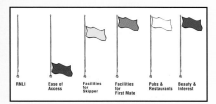

Dafydd Phillips: Harbourmaster
Harbour Offfice, Porthmadog, Gwynedd
LL53 5YT Tel/Fax: 01766 512927
VHF Channels: 14/12/16
VHF Name: Porthmadog Harbour

Madog Yacht Club
Contact: Secretary Tel: 01766 512976

Porthmadog Sailing Club
Contact: Secretary Tel: 01766 513456

Mooring:
Gwynedd Marine Tel: 01766 530684
Madog Boatyard Tel: 01766 514205

Chandlers:
Glaslyn Marine Tel: 01766 513545

Repairs:
Robert Owen Marine Tel: 01766 513435

Criccieth Lifeboat Station
Open to visitors daily May through October
11.00-17.00 and 19.00-21.00 (July & Aug)
Other times by appointment
Contact: Lt Cdr P L Williams (Hon Sec)
Tel: 01766 523183

PWLLHELI 52.53'.0N 04.23'.5W

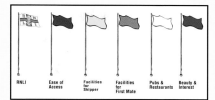

Pwllheli Harbour
Ken Fitzpatrick: Harbourmaster
Outer Harbour, Pwllheli, Gwynedd LL53 5AY
Tel/Fax: 01758 704081
VHF Channel: 12/16
VHF Name: Pwllheli Harbourmaster

Hafan Pwllheli
Wil Williams: Manager
Glan Don, Pwllheli, Gwynedd LL53 5YT
Tel: 01758 701219 Fax: 01758 701443
VHF Channel: 80 VHF Name: Hafan Pwllheli

Marina Boat Club
Contact: Secretary Tel: 01758 612271

Pwllheli Sailing Club
Contact: Secretary Tel: 01758 613343

South Caernavonshire Yacht Club
Contact: Secretary Tel: 01758 712338

Chandlers:
Abersoch Boatyard Tel: 01758 712213

Chandlers/Repairs:
Anson Power & Sail Tel: 01758 701705
Firmhelm (Pwllheli Marine Centre)
Tel: 017658 612251
JKA Sailmakers Tel: 01758 613266
Llyn (Pwllheli Marine Centre)
Tel: 017658 612606
PB Marine Tel: 01758 701254
Rowlands (Pwllheli Marine Centre)
Tel/Fax: 01758 613193
William Partington Marine Tel: 01758 612808

Pwllheli Lifeboat Station
Open all year to visitors
Contact: J Jones
Tel: 01758 613295 or 612200

ABERSOCH 52.49'.5N 04.23'.5W

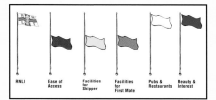

Abersoch Harbour
Contact: Harbourmaster Tel: 01758 712684

Abersoch Power Boat Club
Contact: Secretary Tel: 01758 812027

South Caernarvonshire Yacht Club
Contact: Secretary Tel: 01758 812338

Chandlers/Repairs:
Abersoch Boatyard Tel: 01758 712213
JKA Sailmakers Tel: 01758 613266

Abersoch Lifeboat Station
Open to visitors Thursday evenings from
07.00 throughout the summer
Contact: B McGill Tel: 01758 712213 or 713161

PORTH DINLLAEN 52.56'.5N 04.33'.5W

Contact: Harbourmaster Tel: 01758 720295

Porthdinllaen Lifeboat Station
Open to visitors Easter through September
Contact: R T Morris Tel: 01758 720308

PORTH DINLLAEN cont.

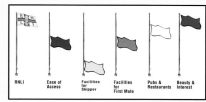

CAERNARFON 53.08'.5N 04.16'.5W

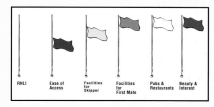

River Harbour
Contact: Harbourmaster
Harbour Office, Slate Quay, Caernarfon,
Gwynedd LL55 2PB
Tel: 01286 672118 Fax: 01286 678279

Port Dinorwic Marina
Contact: Secretary
Port Dinorwic, Gwynedd LL56 4JN
Tel: 01248 671500 Fax: 01248 671252
VHF Ch: 80 VHF Name: Dinorwic Marine

Caernarfon Sailing Club
Contact: Secretary Tel: 01286 672861

Royal Welsh Yacht Club
Contact: Secretary Tel: 01286 672599

BEAUMARIS 53.15'.5N 04.05'.5W

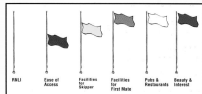

Menai Harbour
Contact: Harbourmaster
Administration, Pier Office, St George's Pier,
Menai Bridge, Anglesey LL77 7TW
Tel: 01248 712312
VHF Channel: 16 VHF Name: Menai Pier

North West Ventures Yacht Club
Contact: Secretary Tel: 01248 810023

Royal Anglesey Yacht Club
J de Leyland-Berry: Secretary
Beaumaris, Anglesey, North Wales
Tel: 01248 810295

Chandler:
ABC Marine Tel: 01248 811413
Dickies Tel: 01248 352 775
Waterfront Marine Tel: 01248 352 313

Beaumaris Lifeboat Station
Home of Blue Peter II
Open to visitors by appointment
Contact: H G Williams Tel: 01248 490268

LLANDUDNO

Yachting facilities and moorings at Conwy

Llandudno Lifeboat
Open to visitors daily except Sundays
Contact: boathouse Tel: 01492 875777

RHYL

No facilities for yachts

Rhyl Lifeboat Station
Open daily to visitors Easter through
September and Sunday mornings all year
Contact: D Archer-Jones (Hon Sec)
Tel: 01745 350068/353607

FLINT

No facilities for yachts

Flint Lifeboat Station
Open to visitors every Sunday morning
Contact: D Moore (Hon Sec) Tel: 01352 732986

HOLYHEAD   53.19'.5N 04'37'.0W

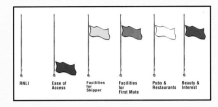

Holyhead Harbour
Contact: Harbourmaster Tel: 01407 762304

Holyhead Marina
Contact: Manager Tel: 01407 764242

Holyhead Sailing Club
Kerry Brown: Secretary
Newry Beach, Holyhead, Gwynedd
Tel/Fax: 01407 762526
VHF Channel: 80
VHF Name: Holyhead Sailing Club

Chandler:
J Watley(Holyhead Chandlery)
Tel: 01407 763632

Repairs:
Trinity Marine Tel: 01407 763855
Mouseloft Tel: 01407 763636

Holyhead Maritime Museum
Open to visitors Easter through September
Contact: John Cave Tel: 01407 764374

Holyhead Lifeboat Station
Open to visitors by appointment only
Contact: J Parry (Hon Sec) Tel: 01407 765608

TREARDDUR BAY

Suitable for small craft only

Trearddur Bay Lifeboat Station
Open to visitors most weekends and public
holidays; other days by appointment
Contact: Jack Abbott (Hon Sec)
Tel: 01407 860794

MOELFRE

Anchorage with limited facilities

Moelfre Lifeboat Station
Open to visitors all year round
Contact: boathouse Tel: 01248 410367

CONWY   53.17'.5N 03.50'.0W

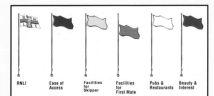

Conwy Harbour
Contact: Harbourmaster Tel: 01492 596253

Conwy Marina:
Contact: Manager Tel: 01492 593000

Bay of Colwyn Sailing Club
Promenade, Rhos-on-Sea, Colwyn Bay
Tel: 01492 544403

Chandler:
North Wales Boat Centre Tel: 01492 580740

Repairs:
ABC Power Marine Tel: 01248 811413
Dickies Tel: 01248 532775
TLC Tel: 01492 580820

Conwy Lifeboat
Open to visitors all year round (situated on
the quay)

WEST KIRBY   53.26'.0N 03.17'.0W

West Kirby Sailing Club
Val Braide: Secretary
Sandy Lane, West Kirby, Wirral L48 3HZ
Tel: 0151 6255579 Fax: 0151 6252800

West Kirby Lifeboat Station
Open to visitors by appointment only
Contact: R H Jones Tel: 0151 6257699

LIVERPOOL   53.24'.0N 03.00'.0W

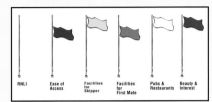

Liverpool Harbour
Contact: Port Operations Tel: 0151 9496134/5
VHF Channel: 12 VHF Name: Mersey Radio

Albert Dock Marina
Contact: Manager
Royal Liver Building, Pier Head, Liverpool,
Merseyside L3 1JH
Tel: 0151 2366090 Fax: 0151 2364986
VHF Channel: M
VHF Name: Canning River Entrance

Liverpool Marina
Jeremy Haughton: Manager
Coburg Wharf, Sefton Street, Liverpool,
Merseyside L3 4BP
Tel: 0151 7085228/7090578 Fax: 0151 709 8731
VHF Ch: M VHF Name: Liverpool Marina

Blundellsands Sailing Club
Contact: Secretary Tel: 0151 9293531
VHF Channel: M
VHF Name: Blundellsands Sailing Club

Hoylake Sailing Club
Contact: Secretary Tel: 0151 6322616

Liverpool Yacht Club
Contact: Secretary Tel: 0151 7220711

Royal Mersey Yacht Club
Contact: Secretary Tel: 0151 6453204

Tranmere Sailing Club
Contact: Secretary Tel: 0151 6453977

Chandlers:
Cosalt Perry's Yacht Centre Tel: 0151 6475751
JP Lamb Tel: 0151 7094861
Steve Roberts Marine Tel: 0151 7078300

Repairs:
Lambs Yachting Tel: 0151 7094861
Mobile Marine Engineering Tel: 01565 733553
Robbins Marine Electronics Tel: 0151 7095431
Steve Roberts Marine Tel: 0151 7078300
Stringer Marine Tel: 0151 5259280

Hoylake Lifeboat Station
Open to visitors by appointment on Sundays
during summer, 14.00-16.00
Contact: Coxsn David Dodd
Tel: 0151 6322103

New Brighton Lifeboat Station
Open occasionally by appointment
Contact: F Brereton (Hon Sec)
Tel: 0151 6395198

RIVER RIBBLE   53.43'.5N 03.00'.0W

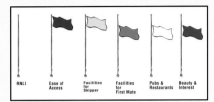

Preston Marina
Contact: Manager
Navigation Way, Riversway, Docklands,
Preston, Lancs PR2 2YP
Tel: 01772 733595 Fax: 01722 731881
VHF Channels: 16/80/37/M
VHF Name: Riversway Control

Douglas Boatyard
Derek M Sheppard: Manager
Becconsall Lane, Hesketh Bank, Preston,
Lancs PR4 6RR Tel/Fax: 01772 812462
VHF Channel: 16
VHF Name: Douglas Boatyard

Moorings:
Freckleton Boatyard Tel: 01722 632439
James Mayor & Co Tel: 01722 812250

Chandlers:
Douglas Boatyard, as above
Preston Marine Services Tel: 01772 733595
Shipsides Marine Tel: 01772 797079

Repairs: see Douglas Boatyard above

LYTHAM ST ANNES

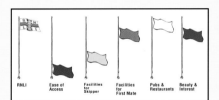

Ribble Cruising Club
Contact: Secretary Tel: 01253 739983

Lytham Lifeboat Museum
Open to visitors end of May through
September on Tues,Thurs and weekends
from 10.30-16.30. Also Weds 13.30-16.30 during
July & Aug
Contact: Frank Kilroy Tel: 01253 730155

Lytham Lifeboat Station
Open to visitors most days by appointment
Contact: Frank Kilroy (Hon Sec)
Tel: 01253 730155

BLACKPOOL

No facilities for yachts

Blackpool Lifeboat Station
Open to visitors all year
Contact: Keith Horrocks Tel: 01253 62042

FLEETWOOD   53.55'.5N 03.00'.0W

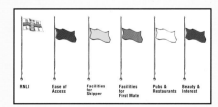

Fleetwood Harbour Control
Contact: Harbourmaster Tel: 01253 872323
VHF Channel: 11
VHF Name: Fleetwood Harbour Control

Fleetwood Harbour Village Marina
Dick Rigby: Manager
Dock Office, Wyre Dock, Fleetwood FY7 6PP
Tel: 01253 872 323 Fax: 01253 777 549
VHF Channels: 16/11/12
VHF Name: Fleetwood Dock

Fleetwood Harbour Yacht Club
Contact: Secretary Tel: 01942 790561

Wardley's Yacht Club
Contact: Secretary Tel: 01253 700429

Mooring:
Skippool Moorings Tel: 01253 891000

Chandler:
Fleetwood Trawler Supply Tel: 01253 873476

Fleetwood Lifeboat Station
Open to visitors daily 10.00-16.00
Contact: P Woodworth (Hon Sec)
Tel: 01253 874 000

GLASSON DOCK   53.60'.0N 02.51'.0W

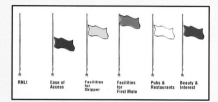

Glasson Dock
Contact: Harbourmaster Tel: 01524 751724

Glasson Basin Yacht Co
Contact: Manager
Glasson Dock, Nr Lancaster, Lancs LA2 0AW
Tel: 01524 751491 Fax: 01524 752626
VHF Channel: 16
VHF Name: Glasson Dock

Glasson Sailing Club
Contact: Secretary
Tel: 01524 751 089

MORECOMBE BAY

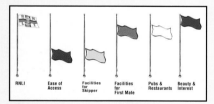

Heysham   54.02'.0N 02.56'.0W

Contact: Harbourmaster Tel: 01524 52373

Morecambe

Morecombe & Heysham Yacht Club
Clive Dugdale: Commodore Tel: 01524 852828

Chandler:
E Nicholson Tel: 01524 417534

Morecombe Lifeboat Station
Open to visitors at all times by appointment
Contact: J Beaty (Hon Sec)
Tel: 01524 415077

BARROW-IN-FURNESS

Contact: Harbourmaster Tel: 01229 822911

Dock Museum
Open to visitors Weds-Sun all year round
Contact: Collections Manager
Tel: 01229 870 871

Barrow Lifeboat Station
Currently closed for rebuilding
Further details contact: Paul Heavyside
Tel: 01229 829867

WHITEHAVEN   54.33'.0N 03.35'.5W

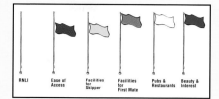

Port of Whitehaven
Captain D Allan: Harbourmaster
Tel: 01946 692435

Whitehaven Marina
Contact: Manager Tel: 01946 692435

ST BEES

No facilities for yachts

St Bees Lifeboat Station
Open Tuesdays on request, 18.00-21.00
Contact: Captain L Goldwater Tel: 01946 830647

WORKINGTON   54.39'.0N 03.34'.5W

Prince of Wales Dock
Contact: Harbourmaster Tel: 01900 602301

Vanguard Sailing Club
Contact: Secretary Tel: 01900 826886

Workington Lifeboat Station
Open to visitors by appointment
Contact: Coxn J Stobbat Tel: 01900 870780

MARYPORT   54.43'.5N 03.30'.5W

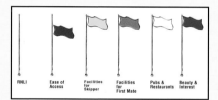

Maryport Harbour
Contact: Harbourmaster Tel: 01900 817440
VHF Channel: 12
VHF Name: Maryport Harbour

Maryport Marina
Keith Williams: Manager
Maryport Harbour, Maryport CA15 8AD
Tel: 01900 814431 Fax: 01900 814583
VHF Ch: 16 VHF Name: Maryport Marina

SILLOTH

Commerical harbour where yachts are not
encouraged.

Silloth Lifebot Station
Open to visitors Sunday mornings 10 am -
12pm. Other times contact Captain C Puxley
(Hon Sec) Tel: 01697 331358

RAMSEY   54.19'.5N 04.22'.5W

Contact: Harbourmaster Tel: 01624 8122445
VHF Channels: 16/12
VHF Name: Ramsey Harbourmaster

Manx Sailing & Cruising Club
Mrs L Wilson: Secretary Tel: 01624 813494
VHF Channel: 12
VHF Name: Ramsey Harbour

Ramsey Lifeboat Station
Open to visitors all year round
Contact: W E Claque (Hon Sec) Tel: 01624
812544

DOUGLAS   54.09'.0N 04.28'.0W

Captain K Horsley: Harbourmaster
Harbours Division, Dept of Transport, Sea
Terminal Building, Douglas, I.O.M. IM1 2RF

DOUGLAS cont.

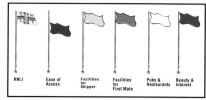

Tel: 01624 686628 Fax: 01624 626403
VHF Ch: 16/12 VHF Name: Douglas Harbour

Douglas Bay Yacht Club
Contact: Secretary Tel: 01624 673965

Chandler:
Manx Marine Tel: 01624 674842

Douglas Lifeboat Station
Open to visitors all year round
Contact: Captain D Cowell (Hon Sec)
Tel: 01624 675629

PORT ST MARY   54.04'.5N 04.43'.5W

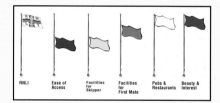

Contact: Harbourmaster Tel: 01624 833205
VHF Channel: 16/12
VHF Name: Port St Mary Harbour

Chandler:
Castle Marine Tel: 01624 835048

Port St Mary Lifeboat Station
Open to very small parties all year round
Contact: Captain A McKaig (Hon Sec)
Tel: 01624 834524

PORT ERIN   54.05'.5N 04.40'.5W

Contact: Harbourmaster Tel: 01624 833206
VHF Channels: 16/12 VHF Name: Port Erin

Port Erin Lifeboat Station
Open to visitors Easter through September
Contact: H Crellin (Hon Sec)
Tel: 01624 835529

CASTLETOWN   54.03'.5N 04.38'.5W

Contact: Harbourmaster Tel: 01624 823549
VHF Ch: 16/12 VHF Name: Castletown Harbour

PEEL   54.13'.5N 04.41'.5W

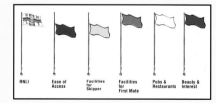

Contact: Harbourmaster Tel: 01624 842338
VHF Ch: 16/12 VHF Name: Peel Harbour

Peel Sailing & Cruising Club
Andrew Sumner: Secretary
Rocket House, Peel Promenade I.O.M.
Tel: 01624 842390

Repairs:
Mike Pollard, Sailmaker Tel: 01624 835831

Peel Lifeboat Station
Open to visitors all year round
Contact: A Corlett (Hon Sec) Tel: 01624 842309

Wales, North West England & The Isle of Man - Chart Agents

Cambrian Boat Centre, Swansea Tel: 01792 467 263

Jones & Teague, Tenby Tel: 01834 813 429

Goodwick Marine, Fishguard Tel: 01348 873 955

Bosun's Locker, Milford Haven Tel: 01646 697 834

Glaslyn Marine, Porthmadog Tel: 01766 513 545

Firmhelm Ltd, Pwllheli Tel: 01758 612 251

Pwllheli Marine Centre, Pwllheli Tel: 01758 612 251

ABC Marine, Beaumaris Tel: 01248 811 413

Conway Marina, Colwyn Bay Tel: 01492 572 777

Douglas Boatyard, Preston Tel: 01772 812 462

Fleetwood Trawler Supplies, Fleetwood Tel: 01253 873 476

E Nicholson, Morecombe Tel: 01524 417 534

Manx Marine, Douglas, I.O.M. Tel: 01624 674 842

Wales, North West England & The Isle of Man - Pilot Books

Lundy and Irish Sea Pilot, David Taylor. 1994. supplement to May 1997
published by Imray, Laurie, Norie & Wilson, Tel: 01480 462114
ISBN: 0852 882 491

A Cruising Guide to Northwest England and Wales, George Griffiths
published by Imray, Laurie, Norie & Wilson, ISBN: 0852 881 908

Yachtsman's Guide to Scilly, J Norman Gooding
published by Ennor Pubns.; ISBN: 0907 205 003

Isles of Scilly, Robin Brandon, John Garey, Fay Garey, New Ed. Feb. 1999
published by Imray, Laurie, Norie & Wilson, ISBN: 0852 884 117

West Country Crusing, Mark Fishwick
published by Airlife Publishing ISBN: 1852 771 070

West Coasts of England & Wales Pilot, 13th Ed. 1996
published by United Kingdom Hydrographic Office, ISBN: 0707 710 375

Artist: **Anthony Flemming MOORINGS AT DUSK** Courtesy of: **The Artist**

Artist: **Anthony Flemming MALDON, ESSEX** *Courtesy of:* **The Artist**

Anthony Flemming was born in London in 1936 into a famous artistic family, and trained at Goldsmiths College of Art where he studied painting, etching, lithography and industrial design. After a period of working as a lithographer he travelled to Spain and Italy where he became interested in the Venetian School of painting.

On returning to England his technical drawings and aerodynamic studies caught the attention of Jack Brabham who commissioned him to design the body and part of the chassis for a new racing car. This led to design work for McLaren, Piper and McKechnie. In 1972 however, his involvement in the automotive design field was broken after his decision to return to painting full time.

A life long interest in boats and water dictated his choice of subject matter. Having sailed since he was very young, the accumulated experience gave him a broad visual and physical knowledge of water, the sky, and places seen from the sea. Since that time he has extended his field to include landscape painting of the highest quality, both in oil and watercolour; at the same time never relinquishing his interest and expertise in etching and engraving.

These intuitive abilities have been reflected in the acclaim and rewards his work now commands. Successful exhibitions have been held in the USA, Japan and London, and in 1975 his work first appeared in calendars for Royle Publications. Subsequently his work has been extensively used by BP, the Woolwich Building Society, Shell, The National Westminster Bank, the Maritime Trust and many others. He exhibits regularly at the RI and RSMA, and has executed numerous private commissions for major British and Overseas Companies.

Artist: **Anthony Flemming WHITE MILL, SANDWICH** *Courtesy of:* **The Artist**

Scotland

Artist: **Anthony Flemming** EILEAN DONNAN CASTLE *Courtesy of:* **The Artist**

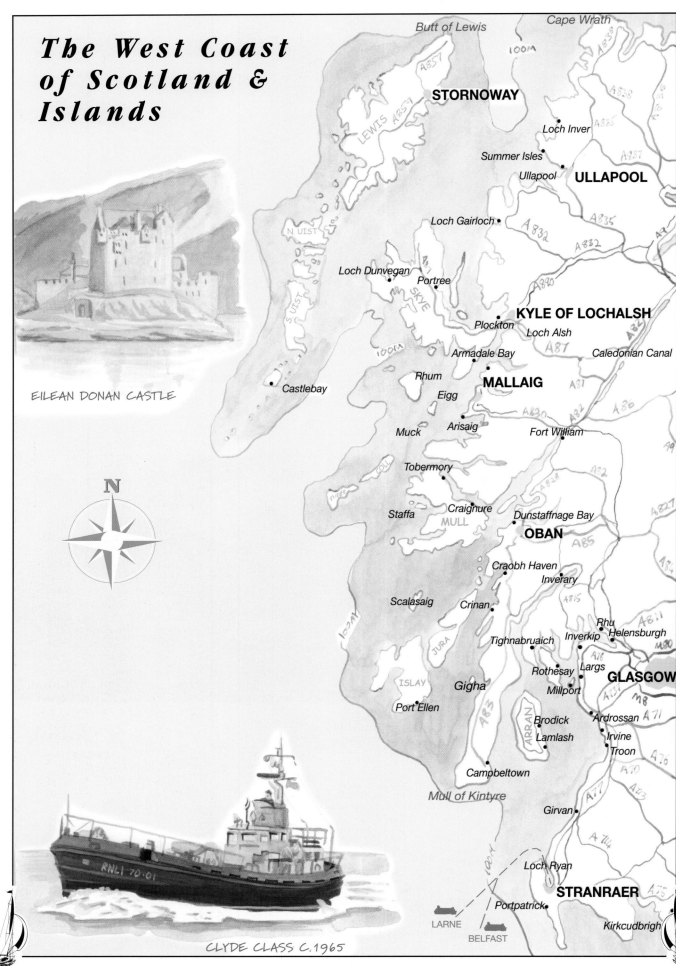

The West Coast of Scotland & Islands

EILEAN DONAN CASTLE

N

Butt of Lewis

Cape Wrath

100M

STORNOWAY

Loch Inver

Summer Isles

Ullapool **ULLAPOOL**

LEWIS

Loch Gairloch

N. UIST

Loch Dunvegan

Portree

SKYE

KYLE OF LOCHALSH

Plockton

Loch Alsh

Armadale Bay

Caledonian Canal

S. UIST

Rhum

MALLAIG

Eigg

Castlebay

Muck

Arisaig

Fort William

Tobermory

COLL

Staffa

Craignure

Dunstaffnage Bay

TIREE

MULL

OBAN

Craobh Haven

Inverary

Scalasaig

Crinan

JURA

Rhu

Helensburgh

Tighnabruaich

Inverkip

Rothesay

Largs

GLASGOW

ISLAY

Gigha

Millport

Port Ellen

ARRAN

Brodick

Ardrossan

Lamlash

Irvine

Troon

Campbeltown

Mull of Kintyre

Girvan

Loch Ryan

STRANRAER

Portpatrick

LARNE

BELFAST

Kirkcudbrigh

RNLI 70·01

CLYDE CLASS C.1965

146

Dumfries & Galloway

In the understandable stampede to get to the scenery further north, many may overlook this southern Scottish cruising area to their loss. As well as the ports examined in some detail below, there are numerous attractive places to anchor for seclusion and enjoyment of the scenery and wildlife which is on offer. Most are also within easy reach of an inn or hotel ashore. Consult your almanac or a good pilot book for more suggestions than we have space to do justice to here. Do also get hold of a copy of "Welcome Ashore" which is an excellent free guide to moorings, harbours and "yachtie friendly" hostelries all around Scotland (available from marina and harbour offices or Sail Scotland, The Promenade, Largs KA30 8BQ ☎ 01475 689899).

Kirkcudbright

Dodging the sandbanks and swift currents which you'll find further up the Solway Firth, our first port of call north of the border is the attractive town of Kirkcudbright. Set at the head of a sheltered bay, with the hills of the Galloway Forest Park rising in the background, Kirkcudbright has lots to offer and is fortunate enough to be several miles off the main road which carries heavy traffic thundering along to the ferry at Stranraer. There is local history to be explored at The Stewartry Museum (☎ 01557 331643), opened in 1892, where you can find out about the social and natural history of The Stewartry, the eastern half of Galloway. MacLellans Castle (☎ 01557 331856) in the town centre is an impressive castellated town house built in 1577 by the Provost Sir Thomas MacLellan. The town is a favourite haunt of artists who have had a colony here since 1880. E.A. Hornel of "The Glasgow Boys" fame lived in Kirkcudbright and at Broughton House & Garden (☎ 01557 330437) which was his home, there is a collection of his work. A wider cross-section of artists is represented at the Tolbooth Art Centre (☎ 01557 331556). Not far out of town, you can visit the Kirkcudbright Wildlife Park (☎ 01557 331645). This is a zoological park and animal conservation centre with animals from all around the world. For something a little different, why not take a guided tour of the dam and generating station at Galloway Hydros Visitors Centre (☎ 01557 330114) which is 2 miles north of Kirkcudbright. There are good beaches here as well. On the western peninsula Brighouse Bay is a popular choice and Doon Beach is another option.

Facilities for yachts are limited, though you will be able to get a shower by the harbour. The harbour-master can direct you to a choice of berthing options including drying berths alongside the quay, pile moorings or a floating pontoon, or you might like to anchor in deeper water towards the mouth of the bay near the Lifeboat Station. There is a tank firing range on this side of the bay and along the coast outside, so check for activity before sailing past or going ashore here especially during the week. (Range Safety Officer ☎ 01557 323236.) Once ashore, Kirkcudbright is a small place so nothing is far from the waterfront. There's a good range of local shops including a supermarket for provisions and a number of craft shops for browsing. There are also plenty of good options for a drink or a meal. Opinion is divided on whether the Masonic Arms (☎ 01557 330517) in Castle Street, the Commercial Hotel in St Cuthbert Street or the Selkirk Arms (☎ 01557 330402) in the High Street is the best spot for a drink. Robbie Burns was a regular visitor to the last of these, and it is claimed that it was here that he wrote the famous Selkirk Grace. The Gordon House (☎ 01557 330670) in the High Street and the Royal Hotel (☎ 01557 331213) in St Cuthbert Street serve pub meals, and for inexpensive restaurant meals, try the Belfry Café (☎ 01557 330861) or Arty's Café in St Cuthbert Street. The best food in town is either at the Auld Alliance (☎ 01557 330569) in Castle Street or in the restaurant at the Selkirk Arms (as above).

Taxi:	Allan's Taxi Service (☎ 01557 331663)
Car hire:	nearest in Dumfries, 30 miles away
Bus:	local services link to Dumfries
Rail:	Dumfries Station for services to Carlisle and the national network
Airport:	Prestwick Airport (60 miles) or Newcastle Airport (150 miles) or some domestic flights from Carlisle (70 miles)

for more details, see Directory Section

The Selkirk Grace

Some hae meat and canna eat,
And some wad eat that want it;
But we hae meat, and we can eat,
And sae the Lord be thanket.

Robert Burns

Portpatrick

To head north from Kirkcudbright, you first need to shape a course with a little south in it to round Burrow Head and then the Mull of Galloway. This rocky peninsula forms the southern end of the Rhins of Galloway, and its bleak isolation makes it a haven for seabirds. You can visit the RSPB Reserve if you find you need to anchor in Tarbet Bay to wait for the tide. From here, it is still quite a long way to Stranraer by sea as you will have to sail round the north of the peninsula. A useful little harbour gives an opportunity to break your journey at Portpatrick. Plans are in hand for pontoons in the dredged inner harbour – consult the harbour-master for direction. For such a small place, facilities are good, though the shopping options are a little limited. If you like, you can pop across to Stranraer which is only a couple of miles away by bus or taxi. There is a selection of places for a run ashore within half a mile of the harbour. For a drink, try the Harbour House Hotel or the Downshire Arms, and for good pub food, The Crown Hotel is handy, or you might like to try the Mount Stewart. The best restaurant in town is at the Fernhill Hotel (☎ 01776 810220).

Loch Ryan and Stranraer

Loch Ryan will give you good shelter although it's probably not the most peaceful spot on earth as Stranraer is a busy commercial port which handles ferry traffic for Ireland. You can find out about local archaeology, farming and folk life at the Stranraer Museum (☎ 01776 705088), and the Castle of St John (☎ 01776

705088) is a late medieval tower house which was latterly used as a Victorian prison. It has displays on the castle, prison life and the Covenanters, a religious group who were persecuted here. For some culture, you will find the work of local artists exhibited at the Waterloo Gallery (☎ 01776 702888). You will be away from the worst of the traffic and the shelter is good if you anchor in The Wig near Kirkholm which is where the Loch Ryan Sailing Club is based. By prior arrangement with the harbour-master, you may be able to go alongside at Stranraer itself or anchor just off as directed. Once ashore, you will find all the shops you need for provisions, and a selection of places to eat and drink as well. The beer is well kept at the Ruddicot Hotel (☎ 01776 702684) in London Road and Bar Pazzerello (☎ 01776 706585) in George Street, serves bar meals till early evening. For a restaurant meal, there's a good Chinese, the Sun Kai Restaurant (☎ 01776 703196) in Queen Street where you can also get takeaway meals, or you might try the Barony Restaurant (☎ 01776 889899) in Hanover Street. For an up-market Italian meal, L'Aperitif (☎ 01776 702991) in London Road is a good choice.

Taxi:	(☎ 01776 705555 or (☎ 01776 704999)
Car hire:	Hertz (☎ 01776 706622) or
	Avis (☎ 01775 706899)
Bus:	Stagecoach enquiries (☎ 01776 704484)
Rail:	Stranraer Station, National Rail Enquiries
	(☎ 0345 484950)
Ferry:	Seacat to Belfast (☎ 0990 523523)
	Stena Line ferries to Belfast (☎ 01776 802165)
Airport:	Prestwick Airport (☎ 01292 479822)

for more details, see Directory Section

Ayrshire, Argyll and Bute

The coastline of Ayrshire offers a fine backdrop to sail along. Sparsely populated hillsides with the first of a series of castles and fortifications lead you up to Girvan. From here, you have several options for a next port of call. The spectacular cruising grounds along the north coast of Ireland are within reach, or if you turn to the north as you round the Mull of Kintyre, the West Coast and Islands of Scotland stretch away, opening up a cruising area that could keep you occupied for a lifetime. Closer to hand, there are good opportunities further north up the Firth of Clyde or over on the east side of the Mull of Kintyre and up into Loch Fyne.

The Ayrshire coastline and the long peninsula which runs down to the Mull of Kintyre enclose a large area of water which has plenty of interest for the yachtsman. This is a superb area to cruise in with fine views across to the hills on the Isle of Arran and the Mull of Kintyre beyond. Your south-west coast Scot clearly likes outdoor activity. The golfer is well catered for with half a dozen courses around Troon, and many more in the surrounding area (see _Following the Fairways_, published by Kensington West Productions). The yachtsman is also favoured with several good marinas and harbours to choose from between Troon and Inverkip towards the northern end of the Firth of Clyde. Heading up the west side of the Mull of Kintyre, the landscape

becomes wilder and the population more sparse and you start to find plentiful opportunities to get away from the crowds and enjoy peace and seclusion in a variety of spectacular settings. Though the area is not always blessed with the most reliable weather, if you have plenty of time you would be unlucky not to find that exhilarating combination of sunny weather and a good sailing breeze. At this point you may well wonder if there is anywhere else in the world which can offer such a wonderful range of places to sail to. The scenery is ever changing and even in the remotest places, you will often find hotels and restaurants which offer excellent menus and a warm welcome.

Girvan

Standing sentinel in the approaches to the Firth of Clyde, and often wearing a woolly hat of cloud, the tiny island of Ailsa Craig towers to over 1000 feet. Just opposite on the mainland, the little harbour at Girvan offers a deep water refuge, though access over the bar is not possible for a couple of hours each side of low water. There's a long pontoon and a wooden jetty for yachts to berth at and most facilities are available - head for the public swimming pool to get a shower. This is a handy place to base yourself for inspecting some fine historic buildings - the well-preserved remains of Crossraguel Abbey (HS ☎ 01655 883113) are just inland from magnificent Culzean Castle (☎ 01655 760274) which looks out over the sea a few miles to the north of Girvan. Neighbouring Turnberry also has a ruined castle as well as its famous golf course and excellent hotel (☎ 01655 331000). In Girvan itself, the McKechnie Institute (☎ 01465 713643) in Dalrymple Street has exhibitions on local arts, fishing and geology and the Town House Aviary and Gardens just opposite the harbour might be of interest. Because this is a small town, the shops are close to hand as is a selection of places for a run ashore. The Harbour Bar (☎ 01465 713174) in Knockcushan Street is a good choice for a drink and just along the road, Swee (☎ 01465 713583) serves pub type meals, as does the Roxy Café Bar (☎ 01465 715261) in Bridge Street. Also in Bridge Street, The Marine Fish Restaurant (☎ 01465 714260) won't break the bank, or in Dalrymple Street, try The Country Club (☎ 01465 713262) or Poppins (☎ 01465 715222) for something a little more upmarket. The best in town is Wildings (☎ 01465 713481) in Montgomerie Street.

Taxi:	(☎ 01465 714444)
Cycle hire:	Carrick Cycles (☎ 01465 714189)
Bus:	services to Ayr, Glasgow and Stranraer
Rail:	Girvan Station (1/4 mile) for services to
	Stranraer, Ayr, Glasgow and Newcastle
Airport:	Prestwick Airport (approx 20 miles)

for more details, see Directory Section

Troon to Inverkip

Troon is our first stop along this stretch and access to the harbour is straightforward. The shelter is good and the marina is accessible at all states of the tide. Part of the Yacht Havens Group, this marina caters for over 300 boats and facilities are comprehensive. There's a chandler and boatyard here, and a full range of shops, including a supermarket, is between five and ten minutes walk from the marina. For a break from on-board catering, the Anchorage (☎ 01292 317448) on Harbour Road and The Lookout (☎ 01292 311523) at the marina are good places to go for a drink and both also serve meals. For a less expensive restaurant meal, try Peckers (☎ 01292 317918) in Ayr Street, and for a meal in dignified surroundings, you could try the Piersland House Hotel (☎ 01292 314747) in Craigend Road by the Royal Troon Golf Club. The top of the range is McCallum's Oyster Bar (☎ 01292 319339) at The Harbour.

Taxi:	C-K Taxis (☎ 01292 312013)
Car hire:	from Prestwick Airport (☎ 01292 479822)
Bus:	coastal & local services and to Ayr and Glasgow
Rail:	Troon Station for services to Ayr & Glasgow
Airport:	Prestwick Airport (5 miles) for services to London, Belfast & Dublin and others

for more details, see Directory Section

For the museum lover, **Irvine** is inviting, even if the prospect of tower blocks which greets you as you approach is not very encouraging. The older parts of the town have a long history and associations with the poet Burns, and there is a long-established Burns Society and Museum here. The Scottish Maritime Museum (☎ 01294 278283) is by the waterfront as is the Magnum Leisure Centre (☎ 01294 278381) for swimming, skating and cinemagoing. A new development on the north bank of the river is dedicated to the life and work of Alfred Nobel and those who have won Nobel Prizes over the years. The exhibition is housed on the site where Nobel established his dynamite works in the 19th century.

Accommodation for visiting yachts is alongside the Visitors' Wharf which is not far beyond the new lifting bridge which allows pedestrian access to the Nobel exhibition site. Access is constrained by the tide, but once inside, the shelter is good. You will find a full range of shops including an extensive mall with two supermarkets less than a mile from the harbourside and there's a small general store much closer. There's also a wide selection of places to eat and drink within easy walking distance. For a drink and pub meals, try The Keys (☎ 01294 279118), The Ship Inn (☎ 01294 279722) or The Marina (☎ 01294 274079) all in Harbour Street. You will also be made welcome in the bar at the Irvine Sailing and Cruising Club which is part of the Irvine Water Sports Club and is based at 66 Harbour Street. Puffers (☎ 01294 278283) on the Maritime Museum Wharf and The Gatehouse (☎ 01294 276596) on Montgomery Street are good choices for an inexpensive meal. Aquarium (☎ 01294 311414) on Harbour Point, and Da Vinci's (☎ 01294 273535) in Glasgow Vennel are good choices for restaurant meals, or you could try the restaurants at Annfield House (☎ 01294 278903) in Castle Street or The Golf Hotel (☎ 01294 278633) in Kilwinning Road which are both a bit further away. A taxi will probably also be needed to head for the Hospitality Inn (☎ 01294 274272) on Annick Road which has a very good restaurant.

Artist: **Anthony Flemming** **SAILING ON THE CLYDE** *Courtesy of:* **The Artist**

Taxi:	Arrow Cabs (☎ 01294 277777) or Tay Cabs (☎ 01294 212111)
Car hire:	Melville's Motors (☎ 01294 277550)
Bus:	services from Irvine Cross to Ayr, Troon, Largs & Glasgow
Rail:	Irvine Station for services to Ayr, Troon, Largs & Glasgow
Airport:	Prestwick Airport (☎ 01292 479822) or Glasgow Airport (☎ 0141 887 1111) – both accessible by rail or road

for more details, see Directory Section

At the north end of Irvine Bay, the rocky outcrop of Horse Island - which is a nature reserve - guards the entrance to **Ardrossan** Harbour. This continues to be a busy ferry port with regular services to the Isle of Arran, and it's well connected by road and rail. There's a new and well-equipped marina in the old Eglinton Dock which is accessible at all states of the tide and offers good shelter. In severe gale conditions (usually only in the winter), the storm gate may be closed to protect those boats already inside. There are some shops locally, but it's a mile to the supermarket. (Taxi: ☎ Clyde Taxis 01294 605400.) The Hip Flask (☎ 01294 465222) is a good choice for a drink or a pub meal, and Laineys (☎ 01294 471860) will serve you an inexpensive restaurant meal. Just up the road near Farland Head, the Seamill Hydro (☎ 01294 822217) offers a more upmarket atmosphere. Sailing on up the coast, as you approach the headland, your view of the two islands of Cumbrae sharpens. South-facing Milport Bay on **Great Cumbrae** is a popular sailing centre and an attractive place to pick up a visitors mooring and go for a stroll ashore. The Cathedral of the Isles is the smallest cathedral in Scotland and is a central feature in this little resort town where you will also find the Museum of the Cumbraes (☎ 01294 464174) for local background. Opposite Cumbrae, the much larger holiday resort of **Largs** spreads along the mainland coast and offers us another well-equipped marina run by the Yacht Havens Group and plenty of interesting places to visit. With its elegant promenades and a fine backdrop of high hillsides in the Clyde Muirshiel Regional Park, Largs has plenty to offer. In 1263, an invasion attempt by the Vikings was successfully beaten off here and the story of the Vikings in Scotland is explored at Vikingar! (☎ 01475 689777) at Barrfields on the Greenock Road. Close to the marina at the family home of the Earls of Glasgow, Kelburn Castle & Country Centre (☎ 01475 568121) offers gardens and woodland to stroll in and a commando assault course, riding and pony trekking for the more energetic. There's a good general store and off-licence at the marina, though for a comprehensive restocking of the lockers, you may want to head for the centre of Largs which is about a mile away. There you will find a supermarket and full range of smaller shops. Similarly, for refreshment ashore, at the marina you can eat at either the Bosun's Table Coffee Shop (☎ 01475 689198) or Nardini at Regattas (☎ 01475 686684) which is a restaurant and bar. To get away from the marina it's worth heading down to Fairlie where the Mudhook (☎ 01475 568432) serves good pub type food, and people travel from far and wide for the seafood at Fins (☎ 01475 568989) on Fencebay. On the Esplanade in Largs, the Brisbane House Hotel (☎ 01475 687200) has a good reputation for both its restaurant and accommodation.

Taxi:	Brisbane Taxis (☎ 01475 689990) or Herbies Taxis (☎ 01475 689689)
Car hire:	Melvilles Car Hire (☎ 0345 525354) or Compass Self Drive (☎ 01294 276777)
Bus:	local services along the coast and to Glasgow
Rail:	from Largs Station services along the coast and to Glasgow
Ferry:	to Isle of Great Cumbrae
Airport:	Prestwick Airport (☎ 01292 479822) or Glasgow Airport (☎ 0141 887 1111) – both accessible by rail or road

for more details, see Directory Section

The marina at **Inverkip** is never hard to find with the high chimneys of the power station just to the south and the lighthouse opposite on Toward Point. This marina offers excellent shelter, and is set in attractive countryside close to the small village of Inverkip. It's an ideal staging post if you are heading further up the Clyde to Gare Loch or Loch Long. Kip Marina, as it is generally shortened to, has a full range of facilities, chandlery and repairs. On site is The Chartroom (☎ 01475 520919) where you can have a drink or a reasonably priced meal. In the village, The Inverkip Hotel (☎ 01475 520478) has good beer and serves pub meals. For an inexpensive restaurant meal, try the Village Inn and if you want to push the boat out, hop in a taxi to Gleddoch House (☎ 01475 540711) in Langbank, or The Scullery (☎ 01475 630033) in Gourock.

Taxi:	Inverclyde Taxis (☎ 01475 734563)
Car hire:	Arnold Clarke (☎ 01475 783535)
Bus:	local services along the coast and to Glasgow
Rail:	from Inverkip Station services along the coast and to Glasgow
Airport:	Prestwick Airport (☎ 01292 479822) or Glasgow Airport (☎ 0141 887 1111)

The Clyde Estuary

The waters of the Clyde Estuary and Loch Fyne provide a splendid cruising ground, and while it is popular (and consequently offers a range of excellent facilities). it's not always crowded either. There are spectacular views of hills and mountains in almost every direction. There is also a wide choice of places to make for, and a series of short hops can take you to a new harbour or anchorage for lunch and dinner for several days. At either end of the season, you can easily find you are the only boat within sight, though even then you should still keep a good lookout. Things can come from underneath here which can be a surprise if you thought you had the place to yourself. Check your almanac for details of "Subfacts" broadcast by Clyde Coastguard which will give you some idea of where and when you might expect to have to keep clear of submarines exercising. We have included a selection of some of the places where you can stop which should give a flavour of the area. For more comprehensive details of places where you will find facilities, get hold of a copy of "Welcome Ashore" which is a useful free guide to moorings, harbours and "yachtie friendly" hostelries all around Scotland (available from marina offices or Sail Scotland, The Promenade, Largs KA30 8BQ ☎ 01475 689899).

Loch Long and Gare Loch

The Clyde becomes quite built up as it approaches Glasgow, and there is a fair amount of commercial traffic to keep you on your toes. Having said that, there are attractive anchorages to be found up Loch Long and its tributaries and in Gareloch as well. For the best yachting facilities in this area, head for **Rhu** Marina in Gareloch. The village of Rhu is set on a wooded hillside close to the mouth of the loch and there are fine views up to the Argyll Forest Park to the North and East. Facilities at the marina are good, though the shopping is a little limited. For major re-provisioning, you will need to take a bus or taxi to the neighbouring town of Helensburgh which is a few miles away and there you will find everything you might need. Helensburgh is an attractive place with some interesting historical connections, not least that this was the birthplace in 1888 of John Logie Baird who we must thank for the small square screen which now dominates so many people's leisure time. The Hill House (NTS ☎ 01436 673900) on Upper Colquhoun Street is well worth a look. Designed by Charles Rennie Mackintosh for the Glasgow publishing family, the Blackies, this fine example of the designer's work is well preserved, appearing as it would have done in 1904 when it was completed. Henry Bell, the builder of the first paddle-steamer, *The Comet*, also hails from the town and you can see a replica of this vessel if you cross to Greenock. This is a good base for exploration further afield. Rail connections make a thorough exploration of Glasgow an easy day trip, and Helensburgh virtually backs onto Loch Lomond which is set in stunning scenery and a good place for strolling or more energetic walking. You can also take boat trips on the Loch from Luss which is about ten miles away. There is a choice of places to find a drink or a meal in Helensburgh. For an inexpensive meal, try the Commodore Hotel (☎ 01436 676924) in West Clyde Street, or close to the marina in Rhu itself, the Rhu Inn (☎ 01436 821048) is a good place for a drink and the Ardencaple Hotel (☎ 01436 820200) serves pub type meals. The Rosslea Hall Hotel (☎ 01436 439955) is also in Rhu and offers a more upmarket atmosphere.

Taxi:	Neptune (☎ 01436 676666)
	Trident (☎ 01436 675555)
	(☎ Rhu 01436 820393)
Car hire:	Arnold Clark (☎ 01436 671409)
Bus:	from outside marina to Helensburgh & Garelochhead
Rail:	from Helensburgh to Glasgow, Oban and Mallaig
Ferry:	from Helensburgh Pier to Gourock
Airport:	Glasgow Airport for domestic and international flights

for more details, see Directory Section

You will probably not wish to get too involved in the naval activity further up the loch at Faslane, and so may choose to nip around into Loch Long which is navigable for much further anyway. Slicing its way up into the Highlands, the scenery is spectacular. There is some Ministry of Defence presence up here as well, so be sure to consult your almanac to check on restrictions to navigation. At the mouth of the Loch, Cove Yacht Club on the east bank has a few visitors' moorings, but is not always attended, and facilities ashore are distinctly limited. There are more visitors' moorings on the opposite bank and in Holy Loch, and further south off Dunoon. Up the loch, there are good views up Glen Finart from Ardentinny and rather contrasting views of the Trident missile base at Coulport on the opposite bank. You may find a visitors' mooring by the Ardentinny Hotel (☎ 01369 810209), or you may prefer to head up to Lochgoilhead where again visitors' moorings may be available and you will find limited facilities ashore.

Isle of Bute & Rothesay

Bute became a popular holiday resort in Victorian times, and the architecture in the capital Rothesay tends to reflect this. With its varied landscape and places of interest to visit, the island is a good place to pause for a while and explore. Rothesay Castle (☎ 01700 502691) just outside the town was a favourite residence of the Stewart Kings, and Robert III made his son the Duke of Rothesay at the end of the fourteenth century, founding a tradition that lasts to this day as Prince Charles holds the title now. The ruins of this castle date back to the 13th century and include a 16th century great hall. A more recent historic house is Mount Stuart House (☎ 01700 503877) which is an awe-inspiring Victorian Gothic mansion with splendid gardens. It's on the coast a few miles south of Rothesay and will make a reasonably unambitious first objective for a tour of the island by bicycle. In Rothesay itself, the Bute Museum (☎ 01700 505067) will give you the background on the island's history, natural history and archaeology.

Pontoon berths are available in the outer harbour which is surrounded by shops, pubs and hotels. Showers and most other facilities needed by yachts are also close to hand. In Rothesay, Ardmory House (☎ 01700 502346) on Ardmory Road is good for a drink and pub grub, and in the evening it serves dinner from an a la carte menu. The Black Bull (☎ 01700 502366) in Albert Place, is a seafront pub, serving good value bar food with a friendly and efficient service.

At Rothesay

Taxi:	(☎ 01700 502275) and (☎ 01700 504000)
Car hire:	From Glasgow, Thrifty Car Rental (☎ 0141 445 444)
Cycle hire:	The Mountain Bike Centre (☎ 01700 502333) 24 East Princess, Rothesay
Ferry:	to Wemyss Bay on mainland
Rail:	from Wemyss Bay on mainland to Glasgow and national network
Airport:	Prestwick Airport (☎ 01292 479822) or Glasgow Airport (☎ 0141 887 1111) – both accessible by rail or road from Wemyss Bay

for more details, see Directory Section

From Rothesay, the sheltered backwaters of the Kyles of Bute offer the shortest route to Loch Fyne and are well worth sailing around even if you plan to head south from here. The northern end of the island is more rugged than the south, and with hillsides running down to the waterside on both sides of the channel this is a beautiful place to potter along, admiring the scenery and the wealth of wildlife

Artist: **Anthony Flemming** **A BREEZY DAY ON THE CLYDE** *Courtesy of:* **The Artist**

which is attracted by this tranquil haven. To name but a few, ringed plover, curlew and eider duck are often to be found around the island's coasts. Opposite the north west corner of the island, the small mainland village of Tignabruaich is set in marvellous scenery and is a fine spot for a run ashore. There's a good general store and opposite some of the visitors' moorings, the Royal Hotel (☎ 01700 811239) offers a warm welcome. For good bar food and a hot shower, try the Kames Hotel (☎ 01700 811489) just along the shore. For a more lavish meal, you'll need to take a taxi up to the Kilfinan Hotel (☎ 01700 821201) on the edge of Loch Fyne about 12 miles away. (Taxi: Gordon MacLellan ☎ 01700 811441.)

Loch Fyne and East Loch Tarbert

Loch Fyne offers wonderful sheltered cruising through highland scenery all the way up to **Inveraray** which is an attractive Georgian town where there are plenty of shops for provisions. The restored jail and courtroom are well presented for historical flavour (☎ 01499 302381) and the Auchindrain Township Open Air Museum (☎ 01499 500235) just down the road gives a good insight into how life was lived in the highlands in centuries gone by. To see how "the other half" managed, a visit to Inveraray Castle (☎ 01499 302203) is a must as it's a splendid pile set in beautiful woodland and gardens. About half way up the loch, there's a useful short-

cut out to the Western Isles at Ardrishaig near Lochgilphead. The Crinan Canal emerges just opposite Jura and saves a passage of over 100 miles around the Mull of Kintyre.

It's worth anchoring in Loch Sween for a run ashore to the Tayvallich Inn (☎ 01546 870282) by Lochgilphead for excellent seafood. Not far from the mouth of Loch Fyne, the little town of **East Loch Tarbert** is a popular sailing destination and the base for The Scottish Series, which is the biggest annual regatta in the area and takes place towards the end of May. Unless you plan to participate, it's worth avoiding the area at that time as several hundred yachts converge on the small harbour which can become a wee bit congested. The good news is that for the rest of the year, there is plenty of space on the pontoons and a good range of facilities for yachtsmen. Local shops for provisions are on the harbourfront, and very fresh fish can often be had as it is landed here. It's a bit of a walk around to the Columba Hotel (☎ 01880 820808) on East Pier Road, but it's worth it as the views are good and so is the beer and whisky. The Victoria Hotel (☎ 01880 820236) on Barmore Road is closer to the visitors' berths and offers bar snacks and restaurant meals. You will need to book early to eat in The Anchorage Restaurant (☎ 01880 820881) in Harbour Street as it has an excellent reputation for its seafood.

The Mull of Kintyre and Arran

Whichever side of Arran you choose to pass, you will enjoy the views and there are good places to drop anchor or pick up a visitors' mooring as well. On the east side, both **Brodick** and **Lamlash** Bays are popular anchorages, with Lamlash offering more shelter, less traffic (the ferries go to Brodick) and fewer facilities. Brodick Castle (☎ 01770 302202) is a fine stately pile built out of red sandstone with impressive collections of silver, porcelain, sporting trophies and paintings, and the woodland gardens are a pleasing place for a stroll. The Heritage Museum (☎ 01770 302636) explores the interesting geology and history of the island. The island offers good opportunities for walking and Goat Fell, just north of Brodick, is the island's highest peak at just under 3000 feet which makes a climb to the top rather more than just a gentle amble! Loch Ranza, at the northern end of the island, is an atmospheric little anchorage close to the ruins of a 13th century castle. Again, visitors' moorings may be available or you can drop your own anchor and there's a hotel and shop ashore in the small village. Shelter is not so easily found on the west side of the island, but opposite on the Mull of Kintyre, Carradale Bay and harbour offer the chance for a run ashore, though facilities are very limited. Not far south of Carradale, Saddell Castle glares out across Kilbrannan Sound at Arran. This solid looking tower house was built in 1508 and is owned by the Landmark Trust, so it's available for rent as a holiday house.

Close to the southern end of the Mull of Kintyre, **Campbeltown** nestles at the head of its sea loch which makes it a superbly sheltered refuge. The Heritage Centre (☎ 01586 551400) at Big Kiln explores the cultural, social, economic and industrial influences which have shaped the town. It is easy to forget how remote from any major centres of population this end of the peninsula is, as it's only an easy day's sail from Largs or Kip which is near Glasgow, but by road – well, just look at the chart! Campbeltown is the biggest place for miles, and does offer a good range of facilities for yachts. Pontoon berths are available and you will find a selection of shops within a couple of hundred yards, though it's half a mile to the supermarket. For a drink ashore, the Ardshel Hotel (☎ 01586 552133) in Kilkerran Road serves real ales, and the White Hart Hotel (☎ 01586 552440) also serves pub food. The Dhorlin Diner on Long Row will serve you an inexpensive meal, and the Palm Bistro in Hall Street is a little more upmarket. For a more lavish meal out, take a taxi to the Putechan Lodge Hotel (☎ 01583 421323) which looks out over the Sound of Jura in Bellochantuy about ten miles up the road.

Taxi:	☎ (01586 552131)
Car hire:	☎ (01586 552030)
Bus:	service to Glasgow (3 times daily)
Ferry:	summer service to Ballycastle, Northern Ireland
Airport:	local service from Macrihanish Airfield to Glasgow (twice daily)

for more details, see Directory Section

The Sound of Jura

Once you round the Mull of Kintyre, you will soon realise that you are approaching some of the finest cruising waters in Europe. One of the great attractions is the scarcity of towns or, in some areas, any centre of population at all. There is a price to pay for the wonderful scenery and space to sail without being surrounded by other boats. Facilities are, at times, pretty limited. However, you don't come sailing here for lots of shops and huge choices of places to eat and drink, though have no fear, we will be pointing the way to a selection of the latter where there are opportunities. If you start with well stocked lockers, you will find places to top up with essentials, and there will be some stunning places to view the world from the tranquillity of your cockpit with a "sundowner" in hand and fine culinary smells wafting up from the galley. In the height of summer, you had better not wait for the sun to go down literally as you could get rather thirsty! The further north you go, the lighter the evenings are, and on clear nights, it barely gets dark at all in June and July.

As you approach the Sound of Jura, your passage is flanked by the islands of Islay to the west and Gigha to the east. Whisky buffs may well wish to take advantage of the moorings offered by the Lagavullin Distillery (☎ 01496 302400) on **Islay** for a run ashore, and there are five more distilleries to inspect on the island. The Museum of Islay Life (☎ 01496 850358) in Port Charlotte, which is an attractive conservation village, is housed in a former Free Church built in 1843. Life on the island is well represented, and the collection includes an illicit whisky still, the tools of the trade for coopers, wheelwrights and crofters as well as distillers and a variety of archaeological artefacts.

Port Charlotte (☎ 01496 850360) is both the name and location of a fine pub which has, as you would expect, a good range of malt whiskies and a restaurant which serves local produce, including seafood. Alternatively, head to Ballygrant, where the Ballygrant Inn (☎ 01496 840277) is another pub that serves good food including a la carte options.

There's better shelter from the south and south west in the lee of the smaller island of **Gigha** in Ardminish Bay on the east side. Visitors' moorings are available, and there's plenty of space to anchor. Facilities ashore include a shop and the Gigha Hotel (☎ 01583 505254) for a drink, meal and shower and even fuel. The landscape is not harsh, and nor apparently is the climate judging by the azaleas and palm trees in the gardens at Achamore House just south of Ardminish! The same cannot be said of the landscape of Jura to the north of Islay. The moorland of the Jura Forest with its impressive high peaks, The Paps of Jura which reach a height of around 2500 feet, makes for an awesome backdrop to sail past. One wonders to what extent George Orwell was influenced by the severity of the scenery while he stayed here as he wrote "1984". Visitors' moorings are available at Craighouse towards the south east of the island which provides a handy spot to stop and wait for a favourable tide up towards Crinan. For those who are in search of remote spots, cut through the Sound of Islay and head for the island of Colonsay a short day's sail to the north. Your route through the Sound of Islay takes you past **Port Askaig** which is where the RNLI has kept its Islay Lifeboat since 1948.

There is space to anchor or go alongside here. As this is where the mainland and Jura ferries berth, it can be a bustling place where you will be able to top up on basic provisions, and the hotel is a hospitable outpost. Pressing on to **Colonsay**, you will find an island of about 16 square miles which has a rocky coastline interspersed with fine sandy bays and an interesting mix of wildlife. Seals abound and otters can be seen if you are patient. Inland, you will find rhododendron woods, moorland, and lily-filled lochs. The Colonsay House Gardens are particularly fine and include surprises like eucalyptus and palm trees which thrive in the mild climate here. A local curiosity is the large number of wild goats which, legend has it, are descended from survivors of wrecks from the Spanish Armada in 1588. 150 different species of birds have been recorded on the island including golden eagles and colonies of fulmars. The main centre of what population there is can be found at Scalasaig where there is space for visiting yachts alongside the pier at all states of the tide. Provisions and fuel are available ashore and the Colonsay Hotel (☎ 01951 200316) is about 400 yards from the pier. It's the only hostelry on the island and serves bar meals, or if you book in advance, there's a table d'hôte menu as well. You can get takeaway meals at The Pantry if you prefer to eat aboard but don't have the urge to cook.

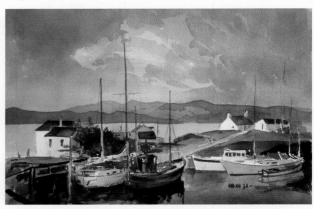

Artist: **Anthony Flemming CRINAN CANAL BASIN**
Courtesy of: **The Artist**

Crinan and the Crinan Canal

Sailing north up the Sound of Jura, Loch Crinan on the west shore is where we meet up with those who took the short cut through the canal from Loch Fyne, and we find a busy crossroads for both commercial and leisure traffic. This used to be the domain of the "Clyde Puffers", as made famous by Para Handy, which were designed to use the canal to ply their trade between Glasgow and the islands, and you may still see one or two in the basin at Crinan. However, the majority of canal users are now yachts and motor cruisers, though fishing boats do take refuge here as well. The canal runs for nine miles from Ardrishaig on Loch Gilp and rises to a height of 64 feet above sea level which results in the sort of view from your cockpit you have probably not seen before! En route, you pass close to Dunadd Fort which was a strong-

hold from the Iron Age onwards. This well-preserved hill fort is where the kings of Dalriada, an ancient kingdom founded around AD 500, were crowned. As well as providing a useful link, the canal basins also offer alongside berthing, and at the Crinan end, there's a boatyard and a very welcome oasis in the shape of the Crinan Hotel (☎ 01546 830261) which has two excellent and very popular restaurants (so be sure to book). The view from the Lock 16 Restaurant is spectacular, and the Westward Restaurant downstairs will make slightly less of a dent in your pocket! The local shop will enable you to stock up on essentials.

Loch Craignish

Just to the north of Crinan, there are some wonderful places to anchor among the islands of Loch Craignish. The Lagoon behind Eilean Dubh and Eilean Mhic Chrion is a particularly beautiful spot. While visitors' moorings are provided in a number of anchorages in this area, you will generally find that anchoring is the norm, so you should have good ground tackle and the confidence to use it, to make the most of cruising as you head further north in this exceptionally beautiful and sparsely populated part of the country. For the anchor-shy, or perhaps just to make a change, the **Ardfern** Yacht Centre at the head of the loch has pontoon berths and mooring buoys for visitors. There's a small general store and a chandlers here and facilities available include showers, launderette and ice. This is a good base for local exploration and as well as the wonderful scenery, there is plenty of historical interest. Kilmartin Glen is about seven miles away, and not only is it beautiful, but there are numerous ancient monuments including a bronze age burial cairn and a stone circle which dates to about 3000 BC. There's an excellent interpretive museum in Kilmartin and a couple of miles north, you find the ruins of the tower house and hall of Carnoustie Castle which dates from the 16th century. Close to the Ardfern Yacht Centre, the Galley of Lorne (☎ 01852 500284) is a good pub for a drink or a meal, and the Crafty Kitchen (☎ 01852 500303) will serve you a reasonably priced restaurant meal. If you want to push the boat out, the Loch Melfort Hotel (☎ 01852 200233) is just over five miles away to the north. Also worth a visit is Arduane Garden (NTS ☎ 01852 200366) which is a 20 acre garden containing rhododendrons, azaleas, woodlands and ponds with water lilies just next to the Loch Melfort Hotel.

From Ardfern	
Taxi:	(☎ 01852 500638)
Cycle hire:	(☎ 01852 500662)
Bus:	from Yacht Centre, services to Oban and Lochgilphead
Rail:	Oban Station is 25 miles away
Airport:	Glasgow Airport is 90 miles away

for more details, see Directory Section

Craobh Haven

The enhanced natural harbour at Craobh (pronounced Croove) is the location of a well-equipped purpose-built yachting centre that more or less backs on to Ardfern which is a mile or so away on the other side of the peninsula. Pontoon berths with the usual services are available for visitors and there's a reasonable general store to top up on provisions. Chandlery and most repairs are also on hand and showers and laundry facilities on site. The "village" is a collection of brightly coloured modern, but sympathetic, houses clustered around the pub, the "Lord of the Isles" (☎ 01852 500658), which still feels rather new, but is mellowing with age. Food and drink is available here, or you could try Creels Restaurant (☎ 01852 500222). Alternatively, refer to the entry for Ardfern for other options in the area.

Taxi:	Oban Taxis (☎ 01631 564666) or (☎ 01631 563784) or freephone (☎ 0800 123444)
Car hire:	via marina office (☎ 01852 500222)
Rail:	Oban Station (☎ 01631 563083) is 25 miles away
Airport:	Glasgow Airport (☎ 0141 8871111) is 90 miles away

for more details, see Directory Section

Careful passage planning is needed to leave the north end of the Sound of Jura. Consult your almanac and pilot book to establish the most suitable route and time to make a break for the Firth of Lorn which will open up the cruising areas around the Isle of Mull and further north. Looking at your chart, you cannot fail to be impressed by the range of the overfalls which emerge from the Gulf of Coryvreckan. This narrow passage between the north end of Jura and the isle of Scarba can be safely negotiated at the right point of the tide, but is to be treated with considerable circumspection at all other times. In stormy conditions, the turbulence extends well over five miles to the west of the passage in what is known as the Great Race. The standing wave over the Cailleach ("The Hag"), a rocky ledge in the middle of the channel which halves the depth to about 30 metres and interrupts the flow of water through this otherwise deep channel, can reach a height of over twenty feet! Once you have successfully navigated your way into the Firth of Lorn, there's a wonderful natural anchorage at Puilladobhrain which is tucked in behind the islands off the northwest side of Seil. From here it's an attractive half mile walk to the nearest pub at Clachan Bridge or, if you are lucky enough to find the anchorage free of other boats, why bother going to the pub? - settle in and enjoy a night at anchor away from civilisation!

Oban

Nestling in a sheltered bay behind the island of Kerrera, which in turn is sheltered by Mull, Oban offers a splendid haven to the yachtsman. It is a major crossroads for traffic both waterborne and otherwise with railway connections to the ferry network operated by Caledonian Macbrayne out of the harbour here. While it can be busy, you may enjoy this after the seclusion you will have found in the surrounding areas, and the shops and supermarkets here offer a welcome chance to stock up the lockers. You can approach Oban from either end of Kerrera and, as the town comes into view, you will be struck by the Coliseum-like folly on the hill behind the town. It was never completed, but stands as a monument to its instiga-

tor, John Stewart McCaig, and certainly kept local stonemasons in work during his lifetime. Once ashore, the Oban Distillery Visitor Centre (☎ 01631 572004) in Stafford Street invites you on a guided tour of the distillery and there's an exhibition on the history of Oban here as well. More local industry is on display at the Caithness Glass Visitor Centre (☎ 01631 563386) on the Waterfront at Railway Pier where you can learn about the art of glassmaking and pick up bargains in the factory shop. Five minutes up the road, Dunstaffnage Castle (HS ☎ 01631 562465) is a fine 13th century castle with the ruins of an exquisite chapel nearby. The marina in Dunstaffnage Bay just west of the Connel Bridge offers an alternative to Oban if you want to avoid the bustle of the town and it's well placed for exploring up Loch Etive. Don't be fooled into thinking that the Oban Sea-life Centre (☎ 01631 720386) is in Oban, it's over the Connel Bridge and a few miles beyond near Barcaldine, but should keep children occupied for an hour or so with over 30 different displays of living marine creatures including rays, octopus, eels and jellyfish to name but a few.

You have several options for berthing at Oban. There are a number of visitors' mooring buoys off The Esplanade north of the harbour, and also by Oban Sailing Club to the south west. For major re-provisioning, you may like to lie alongside the North Pier, though you will have to do battle with commercial vessels here. A good alternative is to head for Oban Yachts and Marine Services in Ardentrive Bay on Kerrera just opposite Oban. Here there are pontoons to lie alongside or moorings, and there's a ferry service to and from the North Pier at Oban Harbour. Showers and most other facilities are available at Ardentrive Bay, though for provisions you will need to get across to Oban.

In Oban, there are plenty of places to go for a drink or a meal. The Oban Inn (☎ 01631 562484) in Stafford Street is a good choice for a drink or a pub meal, and the Boxtree (☎ 01631 563542) in George Street serves good food at modest prices. For something a bit different, you might like to try The Gathering (☎ 01631 565421) on Breadalbane Street which has a splendidly Scottish feel in a Victorian banqueting hall, and there's an Irish Bar just downstairs for alternative Celtic atmosphere and live music. For smart hotel restaurants, the Manor House Hotel (☎ 01631 562087) on Gallanach Road is a good choice and has spectacular views, and the Heatherfield House Hotel (☎ 01631 562681) on Albert Road is probably the best in the area. If you fancy a bit of an excursion, the Knipoch Hotel (☎ 01852 316251) which is about six miles south of Oban also has an excellent reputation.

Taxi:	Alba Taxis (☎ 01631 566676) or West Coast Taxis (☎ 01631 564148)
Car hire:	Hazel Bank Motors (☎ 01631 566476)
Bus:	Enquiries (☎ 01631 563244)
Rail:	Oban station (☎ 01631 563083)
Ferry:	services to Mull and other islands: Caledonian MacBrayne (☎ 0990 650000)

for more details, see Directory Section

Isle of Mull

Just a few miles over the Firth of Lorne from Oban, the Isle of Mull presents its hilly prospect with numerous peaks over 2000 feet. Much of the island is sparsely populated, and there are places where what is marked on a road atlas as a village seems to be little more than an isolated phone box to serve a community scattered around the adjacent hillsides. The main centres of population are on the north east coast of the island so this is where you will need to head for if you are in search of most facilities and the Sound of Mull offers the shortest route to the north beyond the Ardnamurchan Peninsula. Don't ignore the west side though. Tinkers Hole on Erraid at the end of the Ross of Mull is a treasure of an anchorage, and just beyond, the Isle of Iona has a unique atmosphere.

Artist: **Anthony Flemming MULL**
Courtesy of: **The Artist**

Tobermory

The colourful waterfront at Tobermory must be one of the best known harbour views in Scotland and it's always a welcome sight to the itinerant yachtsman. The town is the main centre of population on the island and accordingly the selection of shops is good. It's still an active base for commercial fishing, and ferries and day trip boats are regular users of the harbour, so it can be pretty busy at times. The promise of a good evening ashore will keep you going as you battle to find somewhere to moor. Sadly, there just aren't enough visitors' moorings here and dropping the anchor can be tricky as well. Take the hint and avoid this harbour at weekends in the high season, but do be sure to visit when it's quieter. All the facilities you might need can be found along the harbourfront, and there are some splendid places for a drink or a meal ashore. The Mishnish Hotel (☎ 01688 302009) is always a popular watering hole for yachtsmen, especially as showers are available here as well as good selections of beer, whisky and bar food. The Back Brae Restaurant (☎ 01688 302422) is well-known for its seafood, as is the Lochinvar Restaurant (☎ 01688 302253. The Tobermory Hotel (☎ 01688 302091) on the Main Street is good for local produce such as lamb, steak and seafood. For a less expensive meal, the Waterfront has all manner of establishments from the Captain's Table (☎ 01688 571400) on Stevenson Street and the Gannets (☎ 01688 302203), which both offer good value meals throughout the day to MacGochan's which is more of a bistro/bar with a wide range of good meals. For a smarter meal, the

Western Isles Hotel (☎ 01688 302012) up the hill behind the town is an excellent choice. There are good views over the harbour and a choice of restaurant or bar meals.

Taxi:	(☎ 01688 300441)
Car hire:	MacKays Garage (☎ 01688 302103)
Bus:	to Craignure for ferry to Oban
Ferry:	from Craignure to Oban on Mainland

for more details, see Directory Section

Craignure

As Craignure is where the ferry from Oban docks, this is a convenient spot for crew changes and there are visitors' moorings just north of the ferry pier. There is also a variety of places of interest close to hand. From Old Pier Station at Craignure, Mull Rail (☎ 01680 812494) will take you for a mile and a half's scenic journey along the coast. Views across the Sound of Mull can include Ben Nevis and the Glencoe Hills on a clear day. At the far end of the line, you arrive at Torosay Castle (☎ 01680 812421) which is a fine Victorian family home with an interesting collection of Edwardian contents, and superb gardens which range from formal terraces to attractive woodland. There are good views over the sound of Mull as well and towards Duart Point where Duart Castle (☎ 01680 812309) is perched on a rocky outcrop. This has been the home of the Chief of the Clan Maclean for 700 years and has dungeons to explore and panoramic views from the top of the keep. Though the village is not large, there is a good range of facilities available including a local shop and hotels.

Taxi:	Jimmy Poulson (☎ 01688 302204)
Car hire:	Bay View Garage (☎ 01680 812444) or Mull Car Hire (☎ 01680 812487)
Bus:	to Tobermory
Rail:	from Oban on Mainland
Ferry:	services to Oban via Caledonian MacBrayne

for more details, see Directory Section

Iona

Columba and his followers established themselves here in AD 563 having moved from Ireland to spread the gospel in Scotland and the north of England. The Abbey which was founded in the 13th century is part of an appealing huddle of buildings which includes a museum and gift shop. Managed by the Iona Cathedral Trustees, it is still an active focus for Christian worship and pilgrimage. This small island is now owned by the National Trust for Scotland (01631 570000) and has a population of something just over one hundred people, many of whom still pursue the traditional and simple existence of the crofter on the island's fertile land. You will find the island is at its best after the daytrippers have gone home, so if the weather is settled, consult your pilot book for guidance about where to anchor and prepare for a peaceful night in the strikingly tranquil atmosphere which makes the island so special. Close to the abbey, the village of Iona has a small shop and an hotel though both are pretty basic - let's face it, you have not come here to be impressed by bright lights! An alternative anchorage close by is at **Tinker's Hole** which is in a very picturesque setting next to the isle of Erraid just by the extreme south westernmost point of Mull. The pilotage needed to get in is interesting and nearby you will find another remote community as the cottages ashore are occupied by the Findhorn Community. A short sail away, you will find good shelter in **Loch Lathaich** which is a welcoming natural harbour on the north side of the Ross of Mull. A few miles west of the Sound of Iona, this is a useful anchorage if you plan to explore the west coast of Mull. Quite a good range of facilities for yachts is available from the Bendoran Boatyard and there's a small shop at Bunessan for provisions. The Assapol House Hotel (☎ 01681 700258) in Bunessan is a small country house hotel with well cooked and presented food, or head for Ardfenaig House (☎ 01681 700210) a couple of miles west of Bunessan for a good meal in delightful surroundings. From here, an excellent daytrip is to head north to visit the spectacular island of **Staffa**. This uninhabited island is owned by the National Trust for Scotland (☎ 01631 570000) and is noted for its basaltic formations and distinctive stepped columns. Of several caves, the most famous is Fingal's Cave which inspired part of Mendelssohn's Hebrides overture. There are no facilities ashore and options for anchoring are all a bit precarious making this a fair weather destination if you hope to land. Even if you can't land, the island is magnificent to sail past, and you will certainly get a clear impression of why it has long been considered a remarkable spot.

Highland

Starting with Fort William, well inland and the gateway to the Caledonian Canal, this section includes the coastline all the way to the awe-inspiring headland of Cape Wrath which is impressive even in a flat calm. There are spectacular mountains, sandy beaches and numerous natural harbours some of which even have human habitations and some sort of hostelry. The choice is yours - peace and tranquillity away from it all, or an evening in port with fishing boats and other yachts for company. The West Coast of Scotland would be a yachtsman's dream cruising ground even without the islands, and these add even more to the wealth of opportunities for exploring, and also for finding sheltered places to sail or hole up in the unfortunate event of contrary weather conditions. Skye, with the jagged points of the Cuillin Hills, is an unforgettable sight, and there are impressive peaks forming the backbone of the Outer Hebrides which serve as a splendid breakwater to calm the might of the Atlantic swell. "Welcome Ashore", that handy free guide to moorings, harbours and "yachtie friendly" hostelries all around Scotland has helpful information for this area (it is available from marina offices or Sail Scotland, The Promenade, Largs KA30 8BQ ☎ 01475 689899). Be prepared to be independent as you cruise in this area - supermarkets are a very rare commodity, so you will need well stocked lockers. You will find that chandlers and boatyards are not much more prevalent, so a good range of spares is the right idea. Have no fear that this is a total desert, howev-

er - we have suggested a number of places where really splendid meals are available ashore so you won't be needing to cook aboard every day if you don't want to.

Fort William

Fort William is a focal point in the highlands, and a crossroads for those journeying by various modes of transport. Both rail and road networks pass through. What is of most interest to the yachtsman is that this is where the Caledonian Canal begins its spectacular route through the Great Glen. Twenty two miles of canal cuttings link Loch Lochy, Loch Oich and Loch Ness before reaching Inverness, the Moray Firth and access to the waters of the east coast of Scotland. With mountains of over 3000 feet on each side of the canal, this is a spectacular route to take as well as being a handy shortcut. (For more information about the Caledonian Canal, see Inverness.)

The approach to Fort William is impressive as well for it's a splendid sail up Loch Linnhe and through the Corran Narrows, and if you are lucky, you might even see Ben Nevis at the head of the loch without too much cloud shrouding the top of its huge bulk. As the highest mountain in Scotland, Ben Nevis draws visitors to the area from far and wide, and Fort William is kept busy with visitors coming to walk and climb in the summer and to ski in the winter. It's well worth taking a ride up in the gondola ski-lift which will give you the chance to admire the spectacular panorama of mountain peaks which stretch away in every direction. For some local background, the West Highland Museum (☎ 01397 702169) in Cameron Square has a good collection which will give you a flavour of the history of the area, and has a particularly interesting array of items relating to the Jacobite risings. There is space for visiting yachts to berth alongside the pier close to the centre of the town, and a good range of facilities is available. The alternative is to follow the loch around the corner to Corpach which is the village at the entrance to the Caledonian Canal where you can come alongside or anchor as long as you keep clear of moorings and the approach to the canal. Facilities are more limited here, but there is a shop and you can find somewhere to have a meal and a drink ashore in the village, or hop in a taxi along the road to Fort William to sample the delights of the bright lights.

The Glen Nevis (☎ 01397 705459) is modern and comfortable and serves good value bar food, and there is a restaurant as well. The Grog & Gruel (☎ 01397 705078) on the High Street, is more traditionally decorated and offers pub grub downstairs and a restaurant upstairs. The restaurant at Inverlochy Castle (☎ 01397 702177) is well worth the 3 miles journey out of town, for not only the meals (booking essential) but also for the spectacular views of the loch and mountains from this Victorian castle.

Taxi:	Bluebird (☎ 01397 706070) or Mr Thompson (☎ 01397 705651)
Car hire:	VW Rental (☎ 01397 702432)
Bus:	Highland Country Buses (☎ 01397 702373)
Rail:	Fort William Station, National Rail Enquiries (☎ 0345 484950)
Ferry:	Fort William to Camsnagaul, enquiries (☎ 01397 712102)

Airport: Glasgow Airport (☎ 0141 887 1111)
for more details, see Directory Section

The Small Islands

There is a very satisfactory resonance to the names of the islands which lie between the Ardnamurchan Peninsula and the Isle of Skye. "Eigg, Rhum and Muck" rolls off the tongue splendidly, and one should not forget Canna just to the north. Each is inhabited and their atmospheres are strikingly different, so a thorough explorer will want to visit all four. The largest of the islands, Rhum, is spectacular for its mountainous terrain which reaches over 2,500 feet. It is owned by the Nature Conservancy Council who use the island for research and so access to the island is limited. You will find a range of basic facilities at Loch Scresort which is the only place landing is permitted. This is not a good destination for those who cruise with their dogs as they are not allowed to land at all. Muck and Eigg both have harbours which can be used in fair weather, but do not offer much shelter if conditions deteriorate. For shelter, the harbour on Canna is your best bet, and the bird life and archaeology on this island makes it one of the most interesting islands in the Hebrides. Facilities are very limited indeed - you will need to be prepared to be totally independent while you stay here.

Arisaig Harbour

The village of Arisaig is set in attractive wooded countryside which is perfect for gentle strolling by contrast to the energetic scrambling up highland hillsides which so many places around here invite. There are also superb sandy beaches with clear water for swimming close to the village. The West Highland Line runs from Arisaig to Fort William through spectacular scenery and offers the chance to enjoy a variety of dramatic panoramas quickly and without expending more energy than is needed for the ten minute walk to the station. Steam train excursions are run from Fort William by the West Coast Railway Company (☎ 01524 732100). The harbour is accessible for about two hours each side of high water and it's dredged to give nearly two metres at low tide. There is space for visitors to anchor in the harbour, or you may be able to pick up a visitors' mooring. Fuel and chandlery are available and Arisaig Marine can undertake most basic repair work. The general store has a good range of fresh produce and is only five minutes walk away. For showers and a drink the Arisaig Hotel (☎ 01687 450210) is conveniently close to the pier, and you can get an inexpensive meal or takeaway at the Upstairs-Downstairs Café (☎ 01687 450226) which is also nearby. For more upmarket eating, The Old Library Lodge and Restaurant (☎ 01687 450651) serves good meals and is ten minute's walk from the village centre. If you feel like an excellent feed, it's worth the trip to Arisaig House (☎ 01687 450622) where there's bar food at lunchtime - be warned that dinner here is not cheap but it is superb.

Taxi:	From nearby Mallaig: Dempsters Taxis (☎ 01687 462388)
Car hire:	From nearby Morar, Morar Motors (☎ 01687 462118)

Bus: Shiel Bus Company (☎ 01967 431272)
Rail: Arisaig Station on the West Highland Line for services to Fort William and Glasgow
Airport: Inverness Airport 100 miles, Glasgow Airport 150 miles
for more details, see Directory Section

Artist: **Anthony Flemming MALLAIG**
Courtesy of: **The Artist**

Mallaig

While the views up to the Cuillin Hills on Skye are superb, Mallaig itself is probably not the most attractive town on the coast around here and it's a busy ferry port and also has an active fishing fleet. The Mallaig Heritage Centre (☎ 01687 462085) tells the story of how this traditional crofting area became Europe's busiest herring port, and for a face to face encounter with a range of sealife, Mallaig Marine World (☎ 01687 462292) includes a marine aquarium and fishing exhibition. The RNLI have an Arun lifeboat stationed here which lives on moorings in the harbour, so you will therefore not be surprised to learn that access is not constrained by the tide and is straightforward. No specific facilities for yachts are provided, but the good range of services needed by the fishing fleet are available to yachtsmen as well.

It is hard to get away from the sea in Mallaig, and why try, when there are several pleasing seafood restaurants in the vicinity. The Cabin (☎ 01687 462207) and the Fish Market Restaurant (☎ 01687 462299) are both worth investigation. Hotels for bar and restaurant meals include the West Highland (☎ 01687 462210), the Marine (☎ 01687 462217) and a little further away at 3 miles, is the Morar Hotel (☎ 01687 462346). For a more informal meal, The Café Cornerstone (☎ 01687 462306) and the Fisherman's Mission (☎ 01687 462086) are handy.

Taxi:	Morrison's (☎ 01687 462885)
Car hire:	From nearby Morar, Morar Motors (☎ 01687 462118)
Bus:	Shiel Bus Company, enquiries (☎ 01967 431272)
Rail:	Mallaig Station (☎ 01687 462227)
Ferry:	Service to Skye, Caledonian Macbrayne (☎ 01687 462403)
Airport:	Inverness, enquiries (☎ 01463 232471)

for more details, see Directory Section

Isle of Skye

As you approach Skye from the south, the magnificent pointed peaks of the Cuillin Hills rear up on the western side. There's a dramatic anchorage at the foot of the mountains in Loch Scavaig though this may be an uncomfortable place to be in anything other than the most settled weather as the hills can provoke disconcertingly squally conditions. For a slightly less spectacular setting, but better protected anchorage, Armadale Bay on the south east shore of the island in the Sound of Sleat is a good option. Here you will find the Clan Donald Visitor Centre (☎ 01471 844305) with its ancestral research centre, and there are 40 acres of Armadale Castle Gardens to explore. These include attractive 19th century woodland gardens and the Museum of the Isles is also based here. The Galley (☎ 01471 844252) is a good option for a meal ashore, and it won't cost you an arm and a leg either.

Artist: **Anthony Flemming EILEAN DONAN**
Courtesy of: **The Artist**

Ten miles further along the coast, it's worth dropping anchor at Isleornsay Harbour halfway up the Sound of Sleat for a run ashore to the Hotel Eilean Iarmain (☎ 01471 833332). The hotel is set in magnificent surroundings with views over the sound and has a busy bar with good bar food and offers interesting fish dishes. The Kinloch Lodge Hotel (☎ 01471 833333) a little way down the road is a very good option for a lavish dinner and worth paying a taxi fare for. For those who might like to get better acquainted with the art of whisky distilling, we recommend a day's sailing past the Cuillins to Loch Harport which is towards the top of the south west coast of the island. The Talisker Distillery (☎ 01478 612727) at Carbost will be delighted to show you around and let you sample the product. There are even visitors' moorings close to the distillery to make it easy for you. On the other side of the island, **Portree** is the island's capital, and commands a sheltered harbour tucked behind the island of Raasay. It's also one of the RNLI's more recently established outposts, having had an all-weather lifeboat on the station since only 1991. (See directory for details if you'd like to visit.) The approach from the north gives terrific views of a series of impressive cliffs and geological features such as the Old Man of Storr. Portree is another busy fishing port, and so facilities for boats of one sort or another are available and there are showers and laundry facilities as well. A convenient place for a meal is The Pier which is on the harbourside. It's a

down-to-earth fisherman's bar where, to your advantage, they have much to learn about portion control!

Taxi:	(☎ 01471 844361)
Car Hire:	Macrae's Care Hire (☎ 01478 612554)
Bus:	local services to Kyle of Lochalsh
Rail:	from Kyle of Lochalsh on mainland (over bridge) to Inverness or from Mallaig on mainland to Fort William and Glasgow
Ferry:	from Ardvasar, crosses Sound of Sleat to Mallaig
Airport:	Inverness, (☎ 01463 232471)

for more details, see Directory Section

Kyle of Lochalsh and Inner Sound

Some planning is necessary to get the tides right to negotiate the route around the south eastern side of Skye. The views into Loch Duich past Eilean Donnan Castle (☎ 01599 85202) are spectacular if you have time to dally on your way through, and at the west end of Kyle Akin, controversial though it may be, there is something quite impressive about the Skye Bridge which soars a hundred feet over the channel. There are numerous places to drop anchor or pick up visitors' moorings through here, but be warned that the tidal streams can be strong. There is also pontoon and quayside berthing at **Kyle of Lochalsh** which is where the ferries to Skye traditionally sailed from. A range of shops and facilities is available here, and there are good transport links with trains to Inverness and buses to Glasgow. The Kyle Hotel (☎ 01599 534204) on Main Street will let you have a shower and offers bar and restaurant meals, or for something a little more intimate, try the Seafood Restaurant (☎ 01599 534813) by the piers. To the north of the Skye Bridge, the entrance to Loch Carron opens up, and it's a short sail around to **Plockton** where there is a snug anchorage tucked behind the headland. This is an attractive village set on a sheltered bay fringed with palm trees and wooded hillsides. It has long been a popular holiday destination and the landscape may be familiar to those who saw the T.V. series "Hamish MacBeth", much of which was filmed here. Specific yachting facilities are limited, but with a little ingenuity, you'll find most basic things you might need. There's a good range of local shops for provisions and general browsing, and a selection of places for a meal or a drink. The Plockton Hotel (☎ 01599 544274) is on the seafront where there are good views of the bay and Loch Carron, and The Seafood Restaurant (☎ 01599 534813) up at the station has a varied menu which includes steaks and scotch lamb as well as what its name suggests. The Haven Hotel (☎ 01599 544223) is another good choice for a tasty meal ashore.

Loch Gairloch

The small village of Gairloch is set in stunning scenery on the shore of the loch which looks set to include a marina in the not-too-distant future. Sandy beaches line the shore and the area is popular with sea-anglers and golfers as well as yachtsmen – all drawn by the opportunity to pursue their favourite pastimes in such wonderful surroundings. The village has welcomed visitors since Victorian times when it became a popular holiday destination - hardly surprisingly the popularity has endured. Opposite the village, there's an attractive anchorage behind Horrisdale Island near the Badachro Inn (☎ 01445 741255) on the south side of the loch, or you can come alongside at Gairloch Pier. Once ashore, the Gairloch Heritage Museum (☎ 01445 2287) will give you background about the history and culture of the area and includes material on illicit whisky stills, fishing and the ironworks which was based near here at Loch Maree in the 17th century. The entrance is wide and easy to enter which is great for yachts, but also great for swell in heavy weather, so the shelter is not all one might wish for in boisterous conditions. Basic supplies including fuel can be found locally, and there are several hospitable spots to mention. The Old Inn (☎ 01445 712006) is in an attractive setting and serves good value bar meals. For something a little more elaborate, try the Myrtle Bank Hotel (☎ 01445 712004) which has fine views over to the Isle of Skye. Garden lovers will definitely wish to put into the next inlet to the north. Loch Ewe is also outstanding for its scenery, and at the south end of the loch, a pier gives access to the Inverewe Garden (☎ 01445 86200) where there are spectacular and colourful displays of flowers and shrubs in carefully cultivated gardens which have been maturing for over a hundred years.

Ullapool

Ullapool was purpose built as a fishing town by the British Fisheries Society in the late eighteenth century, and retains an elegant orderliness which its original designers would be delighted by. Rows of neat, white painted houses look out over Loch Broom which is surrounded by magnificent mountainous scenery. The Ullapool Museum & Visitor Centre (☎ 01854 612987) in West Argyll Street is well worth a look to get some of the background about the town and includes innovative displays of "The People of the Loch" and "A Highland Parish Past & Present". Though in the later part of the season the harbour can be busy with fishing boats, this is a well-equipped place to call by boat, and moorings or perhaps berths on the pier are usually available for visitors. A good selection of local shops will enable you to stock up the lockers, and for a run ashore, can we suggest on the outskirts of the town, the Harbour Lights Hotel (☎ 01854 612222) on Garve Road? It is just a short walk from the centre of the town and offers good meals which make use of local produce. Alternatively, the Ferryboat Inn (☎ 01854 612366) on Shore Street is a comfortable waterfront pub bar which serves meals. At the Morefield Motel which is about a mile out of the town on North Road, there's a good bar for a drink or a pub meal, and for something slightly more elaborate, the Mariners Restaurant (☎ 01854 612161) is also part of the same establishment and is well worth the 15 minute walk. If you have time to spend an evening or two ashore, then try the Altnaharrie Inn (☎ 01854 633230). This former drovers' inn is a fantastic experience from the moment you land on the little island. The food is wonderful, but can only be sampled as a resident, and booking is essential.

Taxi:	E & L Taxis (☎ 01854 612966)
Car hire:	Loch Broom Filling Station (☎ 01854 612560)

Artist: **Anthony Flemming** **PLOCKTON** _Courtesy of:_ **The Artist**

The West Coast of Scotland & Islands

Bus: City Link (☎ 0990 505050)
Rail: Nearest station is Garve, National Rail
          Enquiries (☎ 0345 484950)
Ferry: Ullapool to Stornoway
Airport: Inverness (☎ 01463 232471)
for more details, see Directory Section

To the north east of the entrance to Loch Broom, the Summer Isles provide another delightful area to explore. Set against a spectacular mountainous backdrop on the mainland, there are several good anchorages among this group of attractive barely inhabited islands. The largest island, Tanera Mor is noted for its variety of wildlife – boat trips from the mainland bring people across to see the seals and birds here. The "Cabbage Patch" in the bay on the east side is probably the easiest anchorage and is certainly an attractive spot. Limited facilities are available on the mainland at Achiltibuie where there is a local shop and post office. Here you will also find the splendid Summer Isles Hotel (☎ 01854 622282) which serves food all day. For an indulgent meal, the restaurant has a short but excellent menu which varies depending on what fresh ingredients are available.

Lochinver

The coastline here is dominated by a series of impressive mountains which draw walkers and climbers from far and wide. Overshadowed by the towering bulk of Suilven, or "The Sugar Loaf", which rises to nearly 2,400 feet, Loch Inver offers a welcome and secure refuge to both visiting yachts and the lifeboat service whose most northerly West Coast lifeboat station is located here. This is a busy fishing harbour and the fish auction hall is a central focus of activity, and there also are local craftshops to visit in the area including the "Highland Stoneware" Pottery. Visiting yachts may be able to find space alongside the pontoon or harbour quays, or you may prefer to drop anchor in the sheltered water inside the harbour. Be prepared to be directed by the harbour-master. Facilities including fuel, launderette and chandlery are available, and you can get a shower at the Culag Hotel. Wayfairers Bar (☎ 01571 844270) on Culag Pier is handy for a drink, and Caberfeidh (☎ 01571 844321) on Main Street about 15 minutes walk away serves pub-type meals. For something a bit more elaborate, head to the Culag Hotel (☎ 01571 844270) which is on Culag Pier, or the Lochinver Larder (☎ 01571 844356). The top of the range choices are the best part of half an hour's walk - or a taxi ride - away, and are Inver Lodge (☎ 01571 844496) at the far end of Lochinver or Albanach (☎ 01571 844407) at Baddidarach on the peninsula.

Taxi: E. Shairp (☎ 01571 844607)
Bus: services from Lochinver to Inverness
Rail: Laird Station (approx. 45 miles) for
          services to Inverness
Airport: Inverness Airport (approx. 100 miles)
for more details, see Directory Section

Loch Inchard & Kinlochbervie

Unlike the coastline to the south which is backed by picturesque mountains, the prospect as you approach Cape Wrath is stark and inhospitable. You might think that no one would live on a coastline like this, and for the stretch which leads to the grandeur of Cape Wrath, you would be right, but about fifteen miles south, you come to outposts of human existence like Kinlochbervie which has a thriving fishing harbour as its raison d'être. With pontoon accommodation for visiting yachts, this sheltered harbour is a useful place to stop before tackling "the corner" if the conditions look less than promising and, once ashore, you will find basic supplies, plenty of fresh fish and two pleasant hotels - the Kinlochbervie Hotel (☎ 01971 521275) and the Rhiconich Hotel (☎ 01971 521224) where you can get a drink or a meal.

Taxi: Mr Alan Bruce (☎ 01971 521477)
Bus: Inverness Traction (☎ 01463 239292),
          Post Bus Service (☎ 01463 256228)
Airport: Inverness or Wick
for more details, see Directory Section

The Western Isles

The Western Isles, or Outer Hebrides as they are also known, provide a remote and sometimes bleak cruising area which is notable for its solitude and its varied and beautiful landscapes. At the south end of the archipelago which stretches for considerably more than a hundred miles, the island of **Barra** is dominated by the steep slopes of Heaval which rises to a majestic thousand feet above sea level just behind the harbour at Castlebay. The castle on an island in the bay is Kisimul Castle. It's the residence of the local laird, and dates back to the 13th century. Also in the bay, you will find the Barra Lifeboat on its moorings contributing to this spectacular setting. There are visitors' moorings, and basic facilities like fuel, water and some provisions can be found ashore. South Uist which stretches north from here has contrasting coastlines. The west side is low lying and made up of a strip of sandy beaches which are backed by the line of sizeable peaks which march their way up the east shore. Shelter is consequently easier to find on the east side, and there are some stunning places to put in where you will definitely have the place to yourself! Places to find provisions, or even any people at all, are few and far between, but where you do find them, the natives are very friendly and more than happy to pass the time of day with you and tell you about life on the islands. Make sure you have a copy of "Welcome Ashore" which is an excellent free guide to moorings, harbours and "yachtie friendly" hostelries all around Scotland (available from marina offices or Sail Scotland, The Promenade, Largs KA30 8BQ). This guide gives good coverage of where there are moorings and facilities throughout both South and North Uist and, heading north, Harris and Lewis as well. Looking to the north, the RNLI has another outpost at the other end of the archipelago at **Stornoway**. There has been a lifeboat station here since 1887, and 1999 saw a new boat commissioned to cover these often turbulent northern waters - contact the Honorary Secretary if you would like to see the lifeboat facilities. The harbour here is a buzzing hub of activity and the base of an active fishing fleet, though the grandeur of the town's public buildings rightly suggests that in days gone by, the fleet was much bigger and brought much more prosperity to the whole island. This is of course, albeit sadly, to the benefit of the cruising yacht and her crew as there is now good pontoon accommodation in the inner harbour opposite the grandiose mock-Tudor splendour of Lews Castle. A very good range of facilities is available - head for the mission to fishermen on the harbourfront for a shower and a splendid breakfast as well. For a drink and a bar meal, a good option is the Royal Hotel (☎ 01851 702109) on Cromwell Street which also has a restaurant for more formal dining or try the restaurant at The Park Guest House (☎ 01851 702485) on James Street, about 500 yards from the ferry terminal, for fresh modern cooking which makes good use of local produce.

Taxi:	Stornoway Central Cabs (☎ 01851 706900), Barra - Neilie's Cabs (☎ 01871 81002)
Car hire:	Stornoway, Lewis Car Rental (☎ 01851 703760) or Benbecula-Maclennan Bros (☎ 01870 602191)
Cycle hire:	In Stornoway, Alex Dan Cycle Hire (☎ 01851 708025) or Rhan Cycles (☎ 01870 620283)
Bus:	Harris Coaches (☎ 01859 502441) or General Enquiries (☎ 01876 560244)
Ferry:	Caledonian Ferries, Stornoway enquiries (☎ 01851 703673)
Airport:	Stornoway (☎ 01851 703673)

for more details, see Directory Section

Artist: **Anthony Flemming SCOTTISH ANCHORAGE** *Courtesy of:* **The Artist**

KIPPFORD

Limited facilities for yachts

Kippford Lifeboat Station
Open all year round by appointment
Contact: Hon Sec G McQueen Tel: 01556 620201

KIRKCUDBRIGHT   54.50'.5N 04.03'.5W

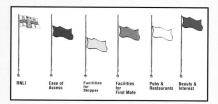

Kirkcudbright Harbour
Gordon Burns: Harbourmaster
Harbour Office, Kirkcudbright DG6 4HY
Tel/Fax: 01557 331135
VHF Channel: 16/12 VHF Name: Kirkcudbright

Kirkcudbright Sailing Club
Terry Hughes, Secretary
Castle Dykes Walk, Kirkcudbright
Tel: 01557 331727

Chandler:
Kirkcudbright Scallop Gear Ltd
Tel: 01557 330399

Kirkcudbright Lifeboat
Open to visitors by appointment only
Contact: Hon Sec R Thomson
Tel: 01557 330835

PORTPATRICK   54.50'.5N 05.07'.0W

Portpatrick Lifeboat Station
Open to visitors weekends by appointment
Easter through Oct (daily during April and
May) Contact: Coxn/Mech Robert Erskine
Tel: 01776 810251/855

Portpatrick Lifeboat Station
Open Easter - September by appointment
Contact: Hon Sec H Harvie (01776 810220) or
Coxn/Mech R Erskine (01776 810542)

LOCH RYAN (STRANRAER)
                        55.01'.0N 05.05'.0W

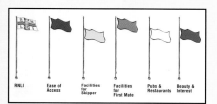

Contact: Harbourmaster Tel: 01776 702460
VHF Channel: 14
VHF Name:

Loch Ryan Sailing Club
P B Hocken: Secretary Tel: 01776 840325

Stranraer Lifeboat
Open to visitors by appointment only
Contact: Hon Sec A Murray
Tel: 01776 702750 (or 703051 office hours)

GIRVAN   55.15'.0N 04.52'.0W

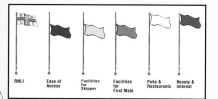

Girvan Harbour
Roderick Leitch: H/master Tel: 01465 713648
VHF Ch: 12 VHF Name: Girvan Harbour

Chandler (nearest):
Troon Yacht Haven

Repairs:
Nobles Boatyar Tel: 01465 71223

Girvan Lifeboat Station
Open daily 10.00-16.00 by appointment
Contact: Hon Sec C M'Kechnie
Tel: 01465 712276/713410

TROON   55.33'.0N 04.05'.0W

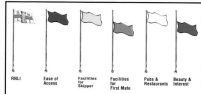

Troon Harbour
Capt N Brown: H/master Tel: 01292 315553

Troon Yacht Haven
Contact: Manager
Troon Marina, Harbour Road, Troon KA10 6DJ
Tel: 01292 315553 Fax: 01292 312836
VHF Ch: 80 VHF Name: Troon Yacht Haven

Troon Cruising Club
Babs Henderson: Secretary Tel: 01292 311908

Troon Yacht Club
Jo Lloyd: Secretary Tel: 01560 322396

Chandler:
Kyle Chandlers Tel: 01292 311880

Repairs:
Boat Electric & Electronics Tel: 01292 315355
Marine Mechanical: Tel: 01292 313400
Troon Marine Services Tel: 01292 316180
West Coast Marine Services Tel: 01292 318121

Troon Lifeboat Station
Open to visitors Saturday mornings only
Contact Hon Sec J Manson
Tel: 01292 313871

IRVINE   55.36'.0N 04.42'.0W

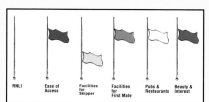

Irvine Harbour
Peter Cartwright: H/master Tel: 01294 278132
VHF Channel: 12 VHF Name: Irvine Harbour

Irvine Sailing & Cruising Club
Keith Gibson: Secretary Tel: 01294 272541

Chandler/Repairs (nearest):
See Troon

ARDROSSAN   55.38'.5N 04.49'.5W

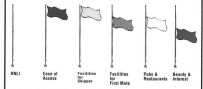

Ardrossan Harbour
VHF Channel: 12/14/16
VHF Name: Ardrossan Harbour

Clyde Marina
David Cook: General Manager
The Harbour, Ardrossan, Ayrshire KA22 8DB
Tel: 01294 607077 Fax: 01294 607076
VHF Channel: 80 VHF Name: Clyde Marina

Chandler:
DDZ Marine Tel: 01475 686 072

Repairs: at marina

LARGS   55.46'.5N 04.52'.0W

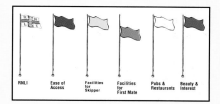

Largs Yacht Haven
Carolyn Elder, Manager
Irvine Road, Largs, Ayrshire KA30 8EZ
Tel: 01475 675333 Fax: 01475 672245
VHF Channel: 80/M37
VHF Name: Largs Yacht Haven

Fairlie Yacht Club
A R Niven: Secretary Tel: 0141 6441004

Largs Sailing Club
Andrew Heron: Secretary Tel: 01475 674782

Chandlers at marina

Repairs:
DDZ Marine Tel: 01475 686072
North Western Automarine Engineers
Tel: 01475 687139
Saturn Sails Tel: 01475 689933

Largs Lifeboat Station
Open to visitors by appointment only
Contact: Hon Sec D Hewitt
Tel: 01475 675 18 (or 894095 office hours)

INVERKIP   55.54'.5N 04.53'.0W

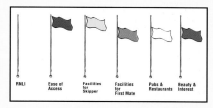

Kip Marina
Duncan Chalmers: Manager
The Yacht Harbour, Inverkip PA16 0AS
Tel: 01475 521485 Fax: 01475 521298
VHF Channel: 37/80 VHF Name: Kip Marina

Clyde Cruising Club
J A Baird: Secretary Tel: 0141 2212774

Royal Gourock Yacht Club
I P C Mackenzie: Secretary Tel: 01475 632983

Royal Scottish Motor Yacht Club
Janice Read: Secretary Tel: 0141 881 1024

Chandler/Repairs at marina

GARELOCH AND LOCH LONG
                        56.00'.5N 04.46'.5W

Cdr Vaughn: Queen's Harbourmaster
Tel: 01436 674321, ext. 6848

Rhu Marina
N Stratton: Manager
Tel: 01436 820 238 Fax: 01436 821 039
VHF Channel: 37/80 VHF Name: Rhu Marina

GARELOCH AND LOCH LONG cont.

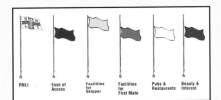

Cove Sailing Club
Ann Bray: Secretary Tel: 01436 842159

Royal Northern & Clyde Yacht Club
Tim Lightoller: Secretary Tel: 01436 820322

Mooring:
McGruer & Co Tel: 01436 831313
Modern Charters Ltd Tel: 01436 831312
Silvers Marine Tel: 01436 831222

Chandler at marina

Repairs:
Jackson Sail Design Tel: 01436 821661
New Century Marine Tel: 01436 831511
New World Yacht Care Tel: 01436 820586
NH Sails Tel: 01436 831356

Helensburgh Lifeboat
Open to visitors Wednesdays 14.00-16.00 in
July and August only. Groups at other times
by appointment: contact Hon Sec J Gorrie
Tel: 01436 672006

ROTHESAY AND ISLE OF BUTE
55.50'.5N 05.03'.0W

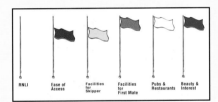

Contact: Harbourmaster Tel: 01700 503842
VHF Channel: 12/16   VHF Name:

Mooring:
Bute Berthing Co Tel: 01700 500630
VHF Ch: 16/12 VHF Name: Bute Berthing Co
St Blane's Hotel Tel: 01700 831244

TIGHNABRUAICH

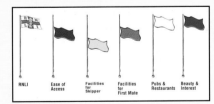

Moorings:
Maramarine Tel: 01436 810971
Melfort Pier & Harbour Tel: 01852 200333
Royal Hotel Tel: 01700 811239

Chandler:
Tighnabruaich Sailing School Shop
Tel: 01700 811580

Tighnabruaich Lifeboat Station
Open all year round by appointment
Contact: Snr Helmsman Ewan Sim
Tel: 01700 811745

TARBERT, LOCH FYNE   55.52'.0N 05.24'0W

Tarbert Harbour
Contact: Harbourmaster
Harbourmaster's Office, Harbour Street,
Tarbert, Argyll PA29 6UD

TARBERT, LOCH FYNE cont.

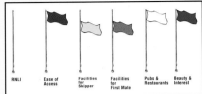

Tel: 01880 820344 Fax: 01880 820719
VHF Ch: 14/16 VHF Name: Tarbert Harbour

Mooring:
Stonefield Castle Hotel (Barmore Island)
Tel: 01880 820836

Repairs:
A McCullum & Co Boatbuilders
Tel: 01880 820 209

ARRAN

Arran Lifeboat Station
Open to visitors weekends during July and
August. Other times by appointment
Contact: Hon Sec G Norris
Tel: 01770 600420 (or 600450 office hours)

CAMPBELTOWN   55.26'.0N 05.32'.5W

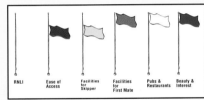

Campbeltown Harbour
Contact: Harbourmaster Tel: 01586 552552
VHF Channels: 12/13/16
VHF Name: Campbeltown Harbour

Campbeltown Lock Berthing Co Ltd
Ian M Silcock: Manager
c/o New Quay Chandlers 1A Longrow,
Campbeltown PA28 6JA Tel/Fax: 01586 554381

Campbeltown Sailing Club
John Mactaggart: Secretary Tel: 01586 552080

Chandler:
New Quay Chandlers Tel: 01586 554381

Repairs:
I A Longrow Tel: 01586 554381

Campbeltown Lifeboat Station
Open all year round by appointment
Contact: Hon Sec Captain D Black
Tel: 01586 552610

PORT ELLEN   55.37'.5N 06.12'.0W

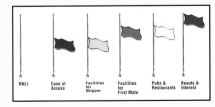

Moorings:
Port Ellen Tel: 01496 810332 (Also Argyll &
Bute Council H/O Tel: 01369 708566)
Lagavulin Distillery Tel: 01496 302400

PORT ASKAIG   55.51'.0N 06.06'.0W

Islay Lifeboat Station
Open to visitors Thursdays 14.00-16.00 from
May through September
Contact: D Boyd Tel: 01496 810464

PORT ASKAIG cont.

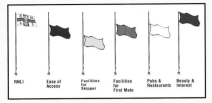

GIGHA ISLAND   55.40'.5N 05.44'.0W

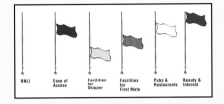

Moorings:
Ardminish Bay Tel/Fax: 01583 506254
(Also Argyll & Bute Council
H/O Tel: 01369 708566)
Gigha Hotel Tel:01583 505254

CRINAN   56.05'.5N 05.33'.5W

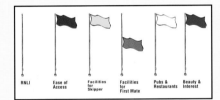

Bellanoch Bay Harbour
Contact: Administration
Tel: 01546 603 210/603797 Fax: 01546 603941
VHF Ch: 16/74 VHF Name: Crinan Canal

Moorings:
Crinan Boats Limited
Contact: Manager
Crinan, Argyll PA31 8SP
Tel: 01546 830232 Fax: 01546 830281
VHF Channel: 16 VHF Name:

Chandler/Repairs at Crinan Boats above

LOCH CRAIGNISH AND ARDFERN
58.08'.0N 05.35'.0W

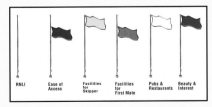

Ardfern Yacht Centre
David Wilkie: Manager
Ardfern, by Lochgilphead, Argyll PA31 8QN
Tel: 01852 500247/500636 Fax: 01852 500624
VHF Ch: 80 VHF Name: Ardfern Yacht Centre

Craignish Boat Club
Jan Brown: Treasurer
c/o Otters, Ardfern, Argyll PA 31 8QN
Tel/Fax: 01852 500689

Chandler/Repairs:
Ardfern Yacht Centre as above

COLONSAY   56.04'.0N 06.11'.0W

Scalasaig Harbour
Contact: Hotel Manager Tel: 01951 20 316

COLONSAY cont.

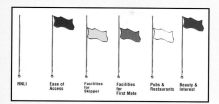

Colonsay Yacht Club
K Byrne: Secretary
Isle of Colonsay, Argyll PA61 7YP
Tel: 01951 200 316

CRAOBH HAVEN   56.13'.0N 05.33'.5W

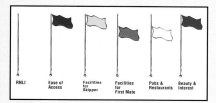

Craobh Marina
Jim Berry: Manager
Tel: 01852 500222 Fax: 01852 500252
VHF Ch: M37/80 VHF Name: Craobh Marina

Chandler/Repairs: at marina

OBAN   56.25'.0N 05.29'.0W

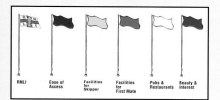

Oban Harbour
Contact: Piermaster Tel: 01631 562892
VHF Channel: 12/16 VHF Name: North Pier

Moorings:
Borro Boats Tel: 01631 563292
Dunstaffnage Marina Tel: 01631 566555
VHF Channel: 80/M37
VHF Name: Dunstaffnage Marina

Horseshoe Bay, Kerrera Tel: 01631 562013
N.A.D.A. Tel: 01631 566955
Oban Marine Centre Tel: 01631 564142
Oban Yachts & Marine Services, Kerresa
Tel: 01631 565333
VHF Channel: 80 VHF Name: Oban Yachts
Puffin Dive Centre Tel: 01631 566088

Chandlers:
Nancy Black Tel: 01631 562550
Oban Yachts & Marine Services
Tel: 01631 565 333

Oban Lifeboat Station
Open mornings daily except Sundays
Contact: Coxn Lorne MacKechnie
Tel: 01631 566377

FORT WILLIAM   58.49'.0N 05.07'.0W

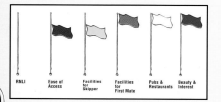

Corpach Basin
Contact: Harbourmaster Tel: 01397 772249
VHF Channel: 74 VHF Name: Corpach Lock

Fort William Pier Tel: 01397 703881

Caledonian Canal
British Waterways Tel: 01463 233140

Lochaber Yacht Club
C B Strong: Secretary Tel: 01397 702370

Moorings:
Underwater Centre Tel: 01397 703786

TOBERMORY   56.37'.5N 06.03'.0W

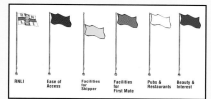

Caledonian MacBrayne Port
Contact: Port Manager Tel: 01688 302017
VHF Channels: 16/12/M
VHF Name: Tobermory Harbour

Western Isles Yacht Club
Mrs M Macgregor: Secretary Tel: 01688 302207

Chandler:
Seafare Tel: 01688 302277 (302386 after hours)
VHF Channels: 16/12/M37 VHF Name Seafare

Moorings:
Argyll & Bute Council Tel (H/O) 01369 708566

Tobermory Lifeboat Station
Open to visitors weekdays 13.45-17.45, also at
weekends by appointment
Contact: John Wilshire Tel: 01688 302250

LOCH LATHAICH   56.19'.5N 06.15'.5W

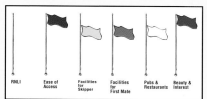

Mooring:
Bendoran Boatyard Tel: 01681 700435

THE SMALL ISLES

Eigg   56.52'.5N 06.07'.5W

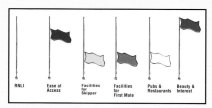

Harbourmaster Tel: 01687 482428
VHF: Channel 8 VHF Name: Eigg Harbour

Canna   57.03'.5N 06.29'.5W

National Trust for Scotland Representative:
Winefride Mackinnon, No 4 Sanday, Isle of
Canna

Local NTS office (Mallaig): 01687 462466

ARISAIG   56.53'.5N 05.54'.5W

Harbourmaster
VHF: Channel: 37(M)/12/16
VHF Name: Arisaig Harbour

ARISAIG

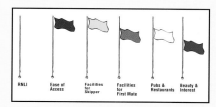

Moorings:
Arisaig Marine
Murdo Grant: Manager
Arisaig Harbour, Highland PH39 4NH
Tel: 01687 450224

Chandlers & all repairs: contact Arisaig
Marine

MALLAIG   57.00'.5N 05.49'.5W

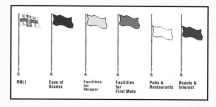

Harbourmaster
Tel: 01687 462154 Fax: 01687 467172
VHF: Channel 9/16
VHF Name: Mallaig Harbour Radio

Chandlers:
Johnson Bros. Tel: 01687 462215

Repairs:
Mallaig Boat Building & Engineering
Tel: 01687 462304

Mallaig Lifeboat
Open by arrangement with M Currie (Cox'n)
Tel: 01687 462125 or 01687 462195 (office)

ARMADALE BAY, SKYE
          57.04'.0N 05.53'.5W

Moorings:
Highland Council Tel: 01478 612727

Sleat Marine Services, Ardvasar, Isle of Skye
Tel: 01471 844216 Fax: 01471 844387

Charter yachts and limited chandlery available from Sleat Marine

KYLE OF LOCHALSH   57.16'.5N 05.43'.0W

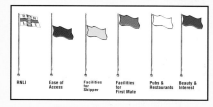

Harbourmaster Tel/Fax: 01599 534167
VHF: Channel: 16/11
VHF Name: Kyle Harbour

Kyle of Lochalsh Lifeboat
Railway Pier, Prospect Road, Kyle of
Lochalsh, Highland
Open by arrangement with A McKerlich
(Hon. Sec.) Hon. Sec.
Tel: 01599 534214 or 01599 534259 (office)

PLOCKTON   57.20'.5N 05.38'.5W

Harbourmaster Tel: 01599 534167

Inner Loch Carron, visitors' moorings:
Lochcarron Pier Trust
Tel: 01520 722215

PLOCKTON cont.

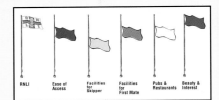

PORTREE   57.24'.5N 06.11'.0W

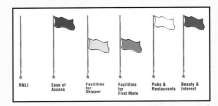

Harbourmaster Tel: 01478 612341
VHF Ch: 16 VHF Name: Portree Harbour

Chandlers:
Skye Fishermen Ltd Tel: 01478 612245

Portree Lifeboat
Open to visitors: by arrangement with David
Beaton, Station Administrator
Station Administrator Tel: 01478 612419

LOCH GAIRLOCH   57.43'.0N 05.45'.0W

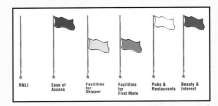

Harbourmaster
Tel: 01445 712140
VHF Ch: 16/14 VHF Name: Gairloch Harbour

Moorings:
Badachro Inn Tel: 01445 741255

ULLAPOOL   57.53'.5N 05.09'.5W

Harbourmaster Tel: 01854 612091
VHF Ch: 14/16/12 VHF Name: Ullapool Harbour

ULLAPOOL cont.

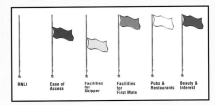

LOCH INVER   58.09'.0N 05.14'.5W

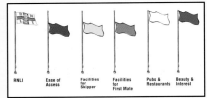

Harbourmaster
Lochinver Harbour, Highland
Tel: 01571 844247
VHF Channel: 9
VHF Name: Lochinver Harbour

Chandlers:
Lochinver Chandlery, Culag Square,
Lochinver, Highland Tel: 01571 844398

Repairs:
G & K Anderson, Culag Square, Lochinver,
Highland Tel: 01571 844221

Lochinver Lifeboat
Lochinver Harbour, Highland IV27 4JP
Open to visitors by appointment with
Neil Gudgeon (Cox'n)
Tel: 01571 844247 or
Graham Anderson (Mechanic)
Tel: 01571 844311

LOCH INCHARD   58.27'.5N 05.04'.0W

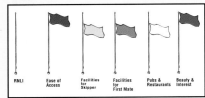

Harbourmaster (Kinlochbervie)
Tel: 01971 521235 Fax: 01971 521718
VHF: Channel: 16/14
VHF Name: Kinlochbervie Harbour

BARRA   56.57'.0N 07.29'.5W

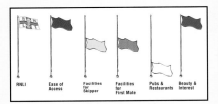

Moorings:
Western Isles Council
Tel: 01870 602425

Barra Lifeboat
Open to vistors: by arrangement with
D MacIssac (Mechanic) Tel: 01871 810767

LEWIS

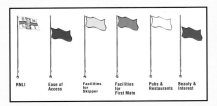

Stornoway Harbour   58.12'.5N 06.23'.0W
Harbourmaster Tel: 01851 702688
VHF Channel: 12/16
VHF Name: Stornoway Harbour

Stornoway Marina, Cromwell St Quay

Chandlers:
Stornoway Fishermen's Co-op
Tel: 0851 702563

Repairs:
J. Fleming Engineering
Tel: 01851 703488

Stornoway Lifeboat
Amity House, Esplanade Quay HS1 2YS
Open to visitors: by arrangement with
Angus MacLeod (Hon. Sec.)
Tel: 01851 702688
Boathouse Tel: 01851 703339

The West Coast of Scotland & Islands - Chart Agents

Kircudbright Scallop Gear, Kirkcudbright Tel: 01557 330399
Maritime Connection, Troon Tel: 01292 315 492
Kelvin Hughes, Glasgow, Langs Chandlers, Largs Tel: 01475 686 026
Kip Chandlery, Inverkip Tel: 01475 521 485
New World Yacht Care, Helensburgh Tel: 01436 820 586
Sailing School Shop, Tighnabruaich Tel: 01700 811 580
New Quay Chandlers, Campbeltown Tel: 01586 554 381
Nancy Black, Oban Tel: 01631 562 550
Lochinvar Chandlery, Lochinvar Tel: 01571 844 398
Stornoway Shipping Services, Stornoway Tel: 01851 704 050

The West Coast of Scotland & Islands - Pilot Books

Clyde Cruising Club Sailing Directions, Firth of Clyde ISBN: 1899 786 155, *Kintyre to Ardnamurchan* ISBN: 1899 786 201,
Ardnamurchan to Cape Wrath, Outerb Hebrides ISBN: 0900 649 690
published by Clyde Cruising Club Sailing Directions, Tel: 0141 221 2774

Yachtsman's Pilot to the West Coast of Scotland, Clyde to Colonsay, ISBN: 0852 881 894
The Yachtsman's Pilot to the Isle of Mull and adjacent coasts, ISBN: 0852 884 044
The Yachtsman's Pilot to the Western Isles, ISBN: 0852 883 395
The Yachtsman's Pilot to Skye and Northwest Scotland, ISBN: 0852 883 644
Martin Lawrence published by Imray, Laurie, Norie & Wilson, Tel: 01480 462114

West Coast of Scotland Pilot. 12th 1995
United Kingdom Hydrographic Office, ISBN: 0707 710 669

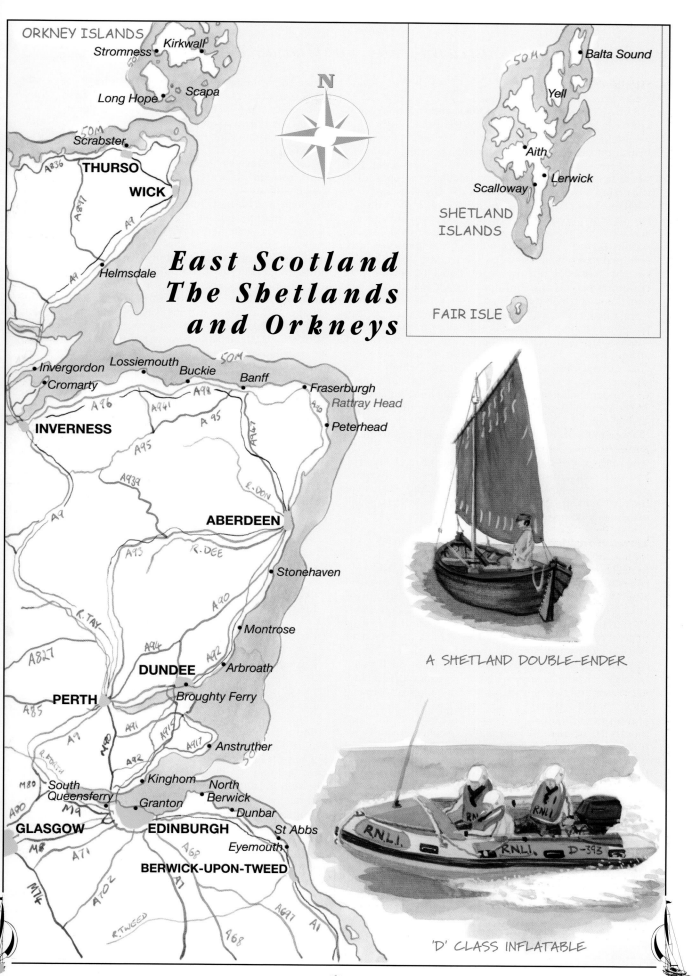

ORKNEY ISLANDS

Kirkwall
Stromness
Long Hope • Scapa

Scrabster
THURSO
WICK

Balta Sound
Yell
Aith
Lerwick
Scalloway
SHETLAND ISLANDS
FAIR ISLE

N

East Scotland The Shetlands and Orkneys

Helmsdale

Invergordon Lossiemouth Buckie Banff Fraserburgh
Cromarty   Rattray Head
INVERNESS   Peterhead

ABERDEEN

Stonehaven

Montrose

DUNDEE Arbroath
PERTH Broughty Ferry

Anstruther
South Queensferry Kinghorn North Berwick
Granton Dunbar
GLASGOW EDINBURGH St Abbs
Eyemouth
BERWICK-UPON-TWEED

A SHETLAND DOUBLE-ENDER

RNLI RNLI D-393

'D' CLASS INFLATABLE

Shetland Islands

Famed for small shaggy ponies and warm woolly knitwear, this northern outpost of the British Isles has a wealth of history and demonstrates a curious mixture of British and Scandinavian influences. Scandinavian rule lasted here until the mid 15th century so Viking and Norse heritage is in many ways much more significant than the more recent links with Britain, and the Shetland identity remains distinctive. The oil industry has recently brought the islands increased prosperity, and while the paraphernalia which necessarily accompanies its operations does not enhance the landscape, it is confined to a few areas and the geography of the area is such that it does not dominate. For a community so comprehensively surrounded by the sea, it will not come as a surprise to find that fishing has traditionally been a major commercial activity here, and many of the harbours around the islands still support this. In high summer, the days are long and it hardly gets dark at all around the longest day. The climate is influenced by the Gulf Stream and is consequently more benign in the summer than might be expected so far north, and there is abundant wildlife. Several important bird sanctuaries are home to a wide variety of seabirds and the low density of human population (less than 25,000) means that of over 100 islands, many are unpopulated and so allow nature to take its course undisturbed. There's nearly 1000 miles of coastline to explore in the group of islands, and different atmospheres and flavours to be experienced as you move from island to island. Historical background can be found in heritage centres and small museums in many of the villages around the islands.

Lerwick and Scalloway

Mainland is the largest of the Shetland Islands, and here you will find, about five miles apart, the two largest towns on the islands. Lerwick is on the east and Scalloway on the west coast of the narrow stretch of land which runs down to Sumburgh Head. Both offer sheltered harbours with good facilities and places of interest to visit ashore. Tucked in behind the island of Bressay, **Lerwick** is now the capital of the islands though historically, this was the role of Scalloway. Lerwick Harbour is busy with commercial traffic including ferries and fishing boats as well as shipping connected to the oil industry. It also claims to welcome more cruise passengers than any other port in Scotland. Once ashore, the Up-Helly-A Exhibition is as close as most visitors are going to get to the traditional Norse fire festival which is held in January every year. A film, photos, costumes and a replica galley give a flavour of the event in the Galley Shed on St Sunniva Street and it's open in the afternoon or evening four days a week. For the full historical perspective, the Shetland Museum (☎ 01595 695057) on the Lower Hillhead is worth a look, as is 17th century Fort Charlotte which was the focus for the development of the town. To the north of the town, the Böd of Gremista (☎ 01595 695057) shows you how 18th century Shetlanders might have lived, and was the birthplace of Arthur Anderson, the co-founder of what is now P & O Ferries, whose life and work are explored in this interesting museum. A daytrip to the anchorage at Nesti Voe off the Isle of Noss will give you the chance

to see the wildlife on this National Nature Reserve (☎ 01595 693345) and to enjoy the spectacular views from the island's 600 foot cliffs. If you prefer to let someone else do the organisation, contact Shetland Wildlife Tours who offer a range of trips around the islands (☎ 01950 460254).

Access to Lerwick Harbour is reasonably straightforward, though do watch out for magnetic anomalies which add to the navigator's headaches in this area. Berthing for visitors is in the docks on each side of the Victoria Pier (consult harbour-master for directions) and facilities are available courtesy of the Lerwick Boating Club whose premises are close by. There's a full range of shops for provisions within a couple of hundred yards, and a supermarket a mile and a half away. Make sure your lockers are full before leaving Lerwick as shopping facilities are very limited elsewhere in the islands. Within walking distance, you will find a good variety of places for a drink or a meal. The Lounge Bar (☎ 01595 692231) in Mountmooly Street is a good choice for a drink, as is Captain Flints (☎ 01595 692249) on Market Cross where you can also get a pub meal. For an inexpensive meal, try the Fisherman's Mission Cafe (☎ 01595 692703) on The Esplanade, or the Isleborough House Café (☎ 01595 692114) in King Harald Street. Monty's Bistro (☎ 01595 696555) on Mountmooly Street, Captain Flints (☎ 01595 692249), and "Oasis" at the Shetland Hotel (☎ 01595 695515) on Holmsgarth Road offer more elaborate fare, and the best in town can be found at either the Kveldsro House Hotel (☎ 01595 692195) in Greenfield Place or the Lerwick Hotel (☎ 01595 692166) on South Road.

Taxi:	Abby's Taxis (☎ 01595 696666) or L.A. Sinclair (☎ 01595 694617) or Sixty Fifty (☎ 01595 696050)
Car hire:	Bolts Car Hire (☎ 01595 693636) or Star Rent-a-Car (☎ 01595 692075)
Cycle hire:	Eric Browns Cycles (☎ 01595 692709)
Bus:	from harbour to locations throughout Mainland
Ferry:	services from Lerwick to Aberdeen (P & O), Stromness and other islands
Airport:	flights to mainland Scotland and thence domestic network from Sumburgh Airport (25 miles)

for more details, see Directory Section

Only five miles from Lerwick by road, but nearer fifty around the coast via Sumburgh Head, **Scalloway** is a busy fishing centre, and the home of the impressive new buildings of the North Atlantic Fisheries College. The ruins of 17th century Scalloway Castle dominate the harbour, as its tyrannical builder Patrick Stewart, Earl of Orkney, dominated the local people when he imposed Scottish feudal law. Scandinavian affiliation is still felt, and perhaps never more so than during the Second World War when the harbour was used as a secret base for Norwegian patriots. A ferry operation known as "The Shetland Bus" carried people and equipment back and forth from Scandinavia. The story is explored in detail at The Scalloway Museum (☎ 01595 880446) which will give you all the historical background of the area.

Artist: **Anthony Fleming SCOTTISH CROFT** *Courtesy of:* **The Artist**

The approach through the outlying islands is particularly scenic and a choice of routes means that it can be reached in any conditions. At a comfortable distance from the main harbour, visiting yachts are welcome on the pontoons by the Scalloway Boat Club which is next to the Fisheries College at Port Arthur. The club has showers, laundry facilities and a cheerful bar, and the place to eat is the Da Haaf Restaurant (☎ 01595 880747) in the college next door which must be one of the smartest and most comfortable college dining rooms in the country. This licensed restaurant does have some choices on the menu other than excellent fresh local fish! The centre of town is a short stroll away, and here you will find more places to eat and drink and a good range of shops for provisions. As the town serves deep sea fishermen whose lives are governed by tides rather than office hours, many of the shops are open until late in the evening.

Taxi:	(☎ 01595 880467) or (☎ 01595 880753)
Bus:	from harbour to locations throughout Mainland
Ferry:	services from Lerwick to Aberdeen (P & O), Stromness and other islands
Airport:	flights to mainland Scotland and thence domestic network from Sumburgh Airport (25 miles)

for more details, see Directory Section

Cruising the Islands

After loading up with supplies at Lerwick or Scalloway, you will be ready for some exploring around the islands, and there are atmospheric anchorages and spectacular scenery in store. We have a few suggestions of places where you will find some evidence of human existence, or if you prefer, a good pilot book will lead you to secluded spots where you can commune with nature in tranquil isolation. A comprehensive pilot book is essential for cruising in this area, and in addition, helpful free guides on harbours and anchorages for yachtsmen are available from Shetland Islands Tourism (☎ 01595 693434) and Sail Scotland (☎ 01475 689899). Starting to the west of Scalloway, the natural harbour of Vaila Sound is an inviting haven and here you will find the village of **Walls**. Pontoon berths are usually available, and the Walls Regatta Club welcomes visitors so you'll be able to have a shower! Nearby, Burrastow House (☎ 01595 809307) has an excellent restaurant with a menu that changes daily. The remote island of Foula, visible on the horizon to the west, has the most isolated community in Britain and can be cut off for weeks in the winter as the harbour is precarious. The population of about 30 people does not support anything like a shop or a pub, but the cliffs to the west, the second highest in the British Isles, are magnificent. There is fine walking though watch out for the great skuas, or "bonxies" as they are known locally, who protect their nests aggressively. Back by the mainland, the sea caves on Papa Stour are impressive, as are the turbulent waters around the island. Heading east, the entrance between uninhabited Vementry Isle with its World War I gun emplacement and Muckle Roe opens up, inviting you to visit the villages at the head of each of three deep inlets. Aith

Voe leads south to the small village of **Aith** which is the RNLI's most northerly outpost. One of only two in the Shetlands, there has been a lifeboat station here since 1932 and Hylton Henry, the coxswain, will be pleased to show you around (☎ 01595 810446). Access to the harbour may be constrained by your draft – at low water, there's only 1.4 metres in the entrance, though once inside, there is over 2 metres. Pontoon berths and most facilities you might hope for are available though the shopping is very limited. You can get a drink and a snack, and meet the locals at the Aith Social Club (☎ 01595 810402). To the north west up the Olna Firth, the village of Voe has a Norwegian appearance and The Pierhead (☎ 01806 588332) is a good pub which also serves food. At the head of Busta Voe, the northern arm, yachtsmen's facilities can be found at the Busta House Hotel (☎ 01806 522506) at **Brae**, and there is even the luxury of a choice of places to eat ashore! Heading back out round Muckle Roe and to the north end of St Magnus Bay, you again get a choice at Hillswick where you will find The Booth (☎ 01806 503348) and St Magnus Bay Hotel (☎ 01806 503372). The stretch of coastline up to the entrance to Yell Sound has sensational cliffs, and the island's highest point, Rønies Hill rises to nearly 1,500 feet in the background. The tidal waters of Yell Sound can be busy with oil tankers and the like heading down to Sullom Voe Oil Terminal. You should contact Sullom Voe Port Control on Channel 14 before entering to explore this fine cruising area where there are good anchorages and plenty of seals to keep you amused. Having come so far, surely you will want to round Muckle Flugga stacks and Out Stack, the northernmost points of the British Isles which are at the top of Unst about twenty miles to the north west. On the west side of Unst, **Balta Sound** is Britain's most northerly yachting centre, and considering its remoteness, a good range of facilities is available in this splendidly sheltered harbour where there is a boatyard, hotel, shop and post office. Here you will also find the Valhalla Brewery (☎ 01957 711348) which is the northernmost brewery in Britain and welcomes visitors. Nearby at Haroldswick, the Unst Boat Haven (☎ 01957 711528) has an interesting collection of traditional small fishing and sailing boats. Heading south, there's a shop, a pub and a boating club at the harbour at **Mid Yell** which is the best base for exploring Yell, the second largest island in the Shetlands. The next spot where reasonably comprehensive facilities are available is Symbister on the island of Whalsey, and to the south of Lerwick, Virkie and Grutness Voe offer a handy refuge right on the southern tip of the islands near the impressive cliffs of Sumburgh Head where 2000 pairs of puffins nest. Here, you are close to Sumburgh Airport for crew changes, and two museums nearby are the Jarlshof Prehistoric Settlement (☎ 01950 460112) and The Shetland Crofthouse Museum (☎ 01595 695057) and Dunrossness for local historical background. Near the airport, the Sumburgh Hotel (☎ 01950 460201) is a fine old building which offers restaurant meals and bar snacks.

Fair Isle

Roughly halfway between the Shetlands and the Orkneys, and an easy day's sailing from either, Fair Isle rears up in isolation from the surrounding emptiness of ocean. The island is a popular destination for birdwatchers and there's a lodge and observatory not far from the harbour in North Haven. Most of us will be familiar with the intricate colourful knitted jumpers which take their name from the island and are still made by the members of the Fair Isle Knitting Co-operative who make up a significant proportion of the island's permanent population of something over 50 people. The island is owned by the National Trust for Scotland who have a number of successful programmes in operation to stem depopulation, and the traditional crofting practices and environmental conservation are interesting to see in action. Facilities for visiting yachts are extremely limited as you would expect. You will probably be able to get a berth alongside the pier in North Haven, but be careful not to block access for the island's ferry which leaves here a couple of times a week. Its slipway will make it quite obvious which side to avoid! Take a stroll ashore to enjoy one of the most isolated spots in the British Isles.

Orkney Islands

The southern islands of the group of around 65 islands which make up the Orkneys surround the huge natural harbour of Scapa Flow which was a major naval base in both World Wars. There is a great deal of earlier history in evidence around the islands, and some of the prehistoric sites here are among the best examples anywhere in Europe and give fascinating insights into how early mankind existed. There is spectacular scenery and imposing coastline to admire – the cliffs along the west side of the island of Hoy are particularly impressive and the 450 foot sandstone stack known as the Old Man of Hoy is a remarkable sight. The area is a popular destination for keen ornithologists and there are numerous RSPB reserves. Of special interest are the breeding populations of arctic terns, curlews, guillemots and hen harriers. Whilst tides can be fierce through some of the narrow channels and around the headlands of the islands, there can be no better way of exploring the area than by boat. There are several useful harbours and numerous sheltered anchorages where you should be able to get away from it all. A comprehensive pilot book is essential for thorough exploration, and will lead you to the secluded anchorages. With a total population of around only 20,000 on the islands, major centres of population are few and far between. The two major towns of Stromness and Kirkwall are both on Mainland, the largest island, and each has facilities for visiting yachts and places of interest to make a run ashore worthwhile.

Stromness

Tucked just inside the western entrance to Scapa Flow, Stromness was traditionally the last stop on the way to the New World for ships trading with Canada. Famous visitors include the notorious William (later Captain) Bligh who was sailing with with Captain Cook in HMS Resolution, and the ill-fated Franklin Expedition on its way to try to find the North West Passage in 1845. For historical background, the Stromness Museum (☎ 01856 850025) is a gem where you can learn about the town's maritime role and there is information about the scuttling of the 74 ships of the German high seas fleet in Scapa Flow at the end of World War I. Within ten miles, there are several interesting historic sites including Skarra Brae (☎ 01856 841815), a stone age village of 10 houses dating from 3,000 BC which is believed to be the best example of a Neolithic Village anywhere in Europe. For culture vultures, the Pier Gallery (☎ 01856 850209) is a must – it includes a collection of abstract art based on work by artists including Ben Nicholson and Barbara Hepworth of St Ives fame. Plans are afoot for a marina in the harbour which will make this a very handy stop-off for visiting yachts cruising in the area, though it has to be said that the facilities which are currently available are pretty comprehensive already. Fuel and water are available and a full range of local shops can be found within a couple of minutes' walk from the harbourfront. The Ferry Inn (☎ 01856 850298) is a short walk away in John Street and here you can get a shower, a drink and a pub meal, or try the Stromness Hotel (☎ 01856 850298) in Victoria Street which has a smarter bar for a drink. There are good views from the Braes Hotel (☎ 01856 850495) which is five minutes' walk up the hill and serves meals which won't burn a hole in your pocket or The Café (☎ 01856 850368) in Victoria Street is a nearer option. The best in the area for more elaborate fayre is Hamnavoe (☎ 01856 850606) in Graham Place.

Taxi:	Brass's (☎ 01856 850750)
Car hire:	Brass's (☎ 01856 850750)
Cycle hire:	Stromness Cycle Hire (☎ 01856 850255)
Bus:	from Pier Head to Kirkwall
Ferry:	from Stromness to Scrabster, Aberdeen and Shetland
Airport:	Kirkwall Airport 15 miles away

for more details, see Directory Section

Kirkwall

The approach to Kirkwall through the sprawl of outlying islands to the north of Mainland gives an idea of the Orkneys' diversity of landscape with its contrasting rocky outcrops and stretches of greenery. Nestling at the foot of Wide Firth, Kirkwall is the capital of the islands and has some interesting and important buildings. You cannot fail to be struck by the plain and severe red stone exterior of St Magnus Cathedral which was built in the middle of the 12th century. The interior is surprisingly spacious and delightfully lit by recently restored stained glass. The Bishop's Palace (HS ☎ 01856 875461) also dates to the mid-12th century but was substantially modified in the 15th and 16th centuries. Adjacent to it is the splendid renaissance-style Earl's Palace (HS ☎ 01856 875461) which was built by the tyrannical Earl of Orkney, Patrick Stewart, between 1600 and 1607. You can get a joint ticket which gives admission to all Historic Scotland's Orkney monuments and buildings in one which is helpful. For a good grounding in Orkney's archaeology and history, you should visit the Tankerness House Museum (☎ 01856 873191) which is based in a fine 16th century townhouse and also has attractive gardens. For culture of a slightly different variety, the Highland Park Distillery (☎ 01856 874619), the most northerly in Scotland, is just outside the town and visitors are welcome to inspect the premises and sample the wares. There's space for visiting yachts to berth inside the inner harbour and most facilities are on hand. Head to the sailing club or one of the harbourside hotels for showers. There's a range of local shops within walking distance, and several places to have a drink or a meal just by the harbour. The Ayre Hotel (☎ 01856 873001) in Ayre Road is a good choice for a smart restaurant meal or, if you fancy getting away from the town, take a taxi to the Scorrabrae Inn (☎ 01856 811262) in Orphir about eight miles away where there are superb views over Scapa Flow. There are several other inviting restaurants near by. The Albert (☎ 01856 876000) on Mounthoolie Lane, in the pedestrian area just off Junction Road, has a pleasant restaurant, while Queens (☎ 01856 872200) on Shore Street, offers a more relaxed atmosphere of carte meals served in the bar. For a change in setting, the Foveran (☎ 01856 876430) in St Ola which is roughly 3 miles southwest of Kirkwall, also has outstanding views of the Scapa Flow.

Taxi:	(☎ 01856 876543) or (☎ 01856 875000)
Car hire:	(☎ 01856 872866)
Bus:	Kirkwall to Stromness
Ferry:	services to other islands in Orkneys. For Shetland and Scottish mainland, services from Stromness
Airport:	Kirkwall Airport for flights to Aberdeen and Inverness

for more details, see Directory Section

Cruising the islands

Scapa Flow has a variety of options for coming alongside or dropping anchor. On the east side, the islands of Burray and South Ronaldsay were linked to Mainland by the Churchill Barriers during World War II to make Scapa Flow easier to protect. The Italian POWs who were set to work constructing these barriers (for improvement of the domestic infrastructure of course, nothing to do with the war effort!) created their own beautifully decorated chapel in two Nissan huts on Lamb Holm. It's definitely worth a look if you are in the area, and just to the south in St Margaret's Hope on South Ronaldsay, The Creel Restaurant (☎ 01856 831311) may help you to make up your mind that this area is not one to miss. On the other side of Scapa Flow, **Longhope** is the base for an RNLI all weather Tyne type lifeboat, and there is space for visitors to berth alongside the pier or anchor here. You can stock up on basic provisions here and fuel and water are available. At neighbouring Lyness, the disused naval base has various quaysides which are available for yachts, and there is a museum here (Lyness Museum ☎ 01856 791300) which explains the role of the naval base in both world wars. Care is needed to make sure that the tide is working for you rather than against, as in places you simply won't be able to make forward progress if you get it wrong. Get it right, and you stand to enjoy the unique atmosphere which Scapa Flow has and the myriad of wildlife which abounds here, including seals, dolphins, porpoises, puffins, gannets and skuas. At the northern end of the Orkneys, the island of Westray makes a good launching off point for Fair Isle and the Shetlands and is well worth a visit. The bird life is spectacular and the RSPB have a reserve at Noup Cliffs and there are two interesting old churches, a castle and good food and drink if you head for Cleaton House (☎ 01857 677508) which is worth the walk from the harbour at Pierowall.

Highland

Thurso Bay to Cromarty

The far north eastern tip of Scotland is low lying and well populated in comparison to the emptiness of the mountainous country to the southwest. At "the end of Scotland", John O'Groats is where you find the Last House in Scotland Museum (☎ 01955 611250) which has an exhibition of photographs of shipwrecks in the Pentland Firth to encourage you to be prudent as you navigate your way around here, as well as material about the island of Stroma which lies just off the coast. It is well worth making the journey to Duncansby Head on the coast to the north east of John O'Groats for good views towards the Orkneys over the spectacular and jagged Duncansby Stacks which tower over 200 feet above sea level. You have several harbours to choose from in this area, and your selection will depend on which direction you are heading in and what the tides are doing. You can opt for Scrabster or Thurso to the west of Duncansby Head or Wick to the south and harbourside berths are available on both sides of Thurso Bay. **Scrabster** is now the ferry terminal for the Orkneys, and is also the base for a fleet of fishing boats. The harbour is accessible at all states of the tide and basic facilities are available on site. For anything other than the most rudimentary provisions, you will need to head to **Thurso**. Here you will find a reasonable range of shops, including a launderette (☎ 01847 893266) on Riverside Place which does service washes. Thurso has its own harbour where the local lifeboat is launched down a slip from a shed built on piles in the harbour. A good range of facilities is available but access is constrained by the tide which probably makes Scrabster a more inviting option as it is only just along the bay.

Artist: **Moira Huntly FISHING BOATS AT WICK**
Courtesy of: **The Artist**

For food and drink, there is a scattering of establishments from which to choose. On the Main Street in Thurso, there is Le Bistro (☎ 01847 893737) and The Redwood Restaurant (☎ 01847 894588) as well as the Pentland (01847 893202). For those of you who are feeling adventurous, Forss House (☎ 01847 861201) on the

Bridge of Forss is just over a 5 mile journey west of Thurso and serves both bar lunches and set dinners.

Taxi:	Harbour Taxis, 2 Miller Place, Scrabster (☎ 01847 892868)
Bus:	services to Inverness
Rail:	services to Inverness
Ferry:	services to Orkney Islands
Airport:	Wick Airport (approx. 20 miles)
	Inverness Airport (approx. 100 miles)

for more details, see Directory Section

Heading south from Duncansby Head, it is a little over ten miles to **Wick** which is tucked into an inlet after you round Noss Head. The town's name is derived from Old Norse, and Old Wick Castle to the south is the ruin of an early Norse tower house which is spectacularly set on a rocky promontory surrounded by the sea. To the north of the town at Auckengill on the way to John O'Groats, the Northlands Viking Centre (☎ 01955 607771) will give you a flavour of the history of the area, and there's another splendid ruined castle perched on the cliffs at Kleiss at the north end of Sinclair Bay. At the south end of the bay in a commanding position on Noss Head, the ruins of Castle Girnigoe and Castle Sinclair which date back to the 15th and 17th centuries are testament to the influence of the Sinclair family over several centuries. In Wick itself, the Heritage Centre (☎ 01955 605393) has a good collection of equipment and photographs relating to matters maritime, especially fishing, with a centrepiece being a restored fisherman's house. Also well worth a visit is the Caithness Glass Visitor Centre (☎ 01955 602286) which is north of Wick, close to the airport. You can watch glass being blown and blow money in the factory shop where bargains may be available. For a drink or a meal ashore, head to Mackays Hotel (☎ 01955 602323) in Union Street where there is an excellent restaurant and Tuesday is Ceilidh night if you fancy some dancing.

Taxi:	(☎ 01955 603192)
Car hire:	(☎ 01955 604125)
Bus:	Highland Country, enquiries (☎ 01847 893123)
Rail:	Wick station
Ferry:	Scrabster to the Orkneys
Airport:	Wick Airport enquiries (☎ 01955 602215)

for more details, see Directory Section

An alternative place to break your journey as you head south along the Highland coast is at **Lybster** where the small harbour offers good shelter, but can be quite tricky to get into. Berth alongside the harbour wall, but do check your almanac to ensure that there is sufficient depth for you, and head ashore where you will find scope for basic re-provisioning and a warm welcome at The Portland Arms Hotel (☎ 01593 721208) where excellent meals are served.

As we approach our next port of call, the backdrop becomes more mountainous, and we reach an area which is noted for scenic valleys with splendid rivers for the fisherman. Helmsdale lies at the mouth of one such river which shares the name, and the harbour offers good refuge to the passing yachtsman. At the best of times the entrance is tricky, and strong easterly winds or a heavy spate in the river will make it wise to pass by, but once inside you will be securely tucked away for some exploring ashore. The countryside is splendid for walking and for those with a yearning to do some personal research on Scotland's premier export, the Clynelish Distillery Visitor Centre (☎ 01408 621444) is about ten miles down the road or railway, in the outskirts of Brora. While it might seem like a long journey to Dunrobin Castle (☎ 01408 633177) which is the other side of Brora, this really is one not to miss. The epitome of a fairytale castle, it has a stunning collection of furniture, paintings and silver. In Brora, there are two pleasant restaurants to eat at, both on Golf Road. For those firmly sticking with the sailing genre, the Royal Marine (☎ 01431 821258) serves good à la carte meals, while its near neighbour the Links (☎ 01408 611225) is great for any closet golfers. It serves dinner, as well as a bar lunch.

Taxi:	A R Macleod (☎ 01431 821338)
Car hire:	Avis (☎ 0990 900500)
Bus:	Scottish City Link (☎ 0990 505050)
Rail:	Helmsdale station, National Rail Enquiries (☎ 0345 484950)
Airport:	Inverness Airport (☎ 01463 232471)

Cromarty Firth

The Cromarty Firth is a large natural harbour which offers good shelter in all conditions. It is renowned for its varied wildlife which includes auks, cormorants and terns, and the waters in this area are home to pilot whales, dolphins and porpoises. Looking over the narrow entrance of the firth from the south, the small town of **Cromarty** is a charming little place and well worth a run ashore. Space in the harbour can be a bit limited, and as the depth is only two metres at low water springs, you may prefer to anchor just to the west. Once ashore, you can enjoy a stroll around the town which is made up of attractive buildings most of which date from 1750 to 1850. You also have the opportunity to visit the Cromarty Courthouse Museum (☎ 01381 600418) in Church Street which is a fine late 18th century building. Hugh Miller's Cottage (NTS 01381 600245) is run by the National Trust for Scotland as a small museum to commemorate the work of this notable local stonemason, geologist and author of folklore. For provisioning, there is only a general store, a bakery and an off-licence so don't plan to do major locker re-stocking here. To save you the trouble, the Royal Hotel (☎ 01381 600217) is right by the harbour and is a good spot for a drink or a meal and a few minutes walk away, the Cromarty Arms (☎ 01381 600230) in Church Street is another option. Also in Church Street, Thistles Restaurant (☎ 01381 600471) will serve you a good meal for a reasonable price. On the north side of the firth, and about four and a half miles to the west, you will find **Invergordon**. This town has developed into a major service and supply centre for the various types of vessel involved in oil exploration and production in the North Sea. Consequently, this is very much a commercial port, though a short stay in the west harbour would give you a good opportunity to stock up on provisions. For a longer stay, the best plan is to anchor by the Invergordon Boating Club as the west harbour can, at times, be rather busy and congested with

working boats and a ferry service to the Orkneys also runs from here. With rail and ferry links, this is a well connected place for crew changes and exploring the local countryside. The town is quite a cosmopolitan outpost which boasts a good selection of shops, pubs, restaurants and hotels. For a drink, the Marine Hotel (☎ 01349 852419) in the High Street is a good option, and Foxes Hotel (☎ 01349 852527) is an Irish pub which serves good bar meals. For a selection of more upmarket places to eat, you will find that Cromarty is where you need to be.

Taxi:	Scobbies Taxis (☎ 01349 852597)
Care hire:	Avis, Inverness (☎ 0990 900500)
Bus:	Inverness Traction (☎ 01463 239292)
Rail:	National Rail enquiries (☎ 0345 484950)
Airport:	Inverness Airport (☎ 01463 232471)

Inverness

Often unofficially regarded as the capital of the Highlands, Inverness is a significant crossroads for both land and water borne traffic. The main rail and road arteries which serve the north pass through here, and Inverness is where the Caledonian Canal meets the sea after linking the long string of lochs which stretch up from Fort William. Either approach by water is spectacular whether it be through the famous and atmospheric deeps of Loch Ness, or from the sea past Fort George, an imposing fortress built by George II to establish control firmly in the area after the Battle of Culloden in 1746. Inverness itself has an impressive castle as its focus, and the views from the esplanade are worth the walk. Nearby, the Inverness Museum (☎ 01463 237114) in Castle Wynd gives a thorough grounding in local history. While you are in the area, you might like to take a trip to the battlefield at Culloden where there is a visitor centre (☎ 01463 790607) run by the National Trust for Scotland which explains the battle and its background. There is a choice of places for visiting yachts to berth. The most comprehensive facilities will be found at Caley Marina and Muirtown Marina which are both within the Caledonian Canal. An alternative, if you don't want to get involved in the canal, is to head for the Longman Yacht Haven which is just up the River Ness and located close to the centre of the town. You should call up in advance to check both whether there is space for you and what commercial traffic may be operating in the river. The town has a population of over 40,000 and so, as you would expect, you will find a wide range of facilities ashore including a cinema, a theatre, art galleries and a plenty of opportunities for shopping. In the town centre, you will find a comprehensive selection of shops for provisions and a good selection of places to eat and drink. The Phoenix Bar (☎ 01463 233685) in Academy Street is a good choice for a drink, and Johnny Foxes (☎ 01463 236577) in Bank Street serves good pub food. For an inexpensive restaurant meal, try the Castle Restaurant (☎ 01463 230925) in Castle Street or for something a little more elaborate, head to Dickens (☎ 01463 713111) in Church Street where the menu includes Chinese and European dishes. The best in town is La Riviera at the Glenmoriston Hotel (☎ 01463 223777) which is at 20 Ness Bank.

Taxi:	(☎ 01463 221111), (☎ 01463 790000), (☎ 01463 719777)

Car hire:	In Inverness, Thrifty Car Rental (☎ 01463 224466) Eurodollar (☎ 01463 238084)
Bus:	links to Aberdeen, Glasgow and London
Rail:	Inverness Station for services to Aberdeen, Edinburgh, Glasgow and London
Airport:	Inverness Airport (☎ 01463 224466) (Dalcross) for flights to most domestic destinations

for more details, see Directory Section

Caledonian Canal

Completed in 1822 after nearly twenty years of work, the Caledonian Canal forms a link through the heart of Scotland's highlands between Fort William and Inverness. Its purpose was as much military as commercial as it allowed British ships to cross between the west and east coasts without running the gauntlet of French warships which often cruised around Scotland's stormy northern waters, though the commercial benefits should not be ignored. Twenty-two miles of canal cuttings link Loch Oich, Loch Lochy and Loch Ness and provide a rich mixture of scenery and waterways to make this more than just a handy shortcut. A passage through the canal and the lochs which it links allows the opportunity to soak up some of Scotland's finest scenery and to see some of Scotland's most famous sights. Your journey through Loch Ness gives you the opportunity to look out for the Loch Ness Monster and, if you are a sceptic, maybe your views will be revised after a look at all the evidence at the Drumnadrochit Loch Ness Monster Exhibition Centre. On the headland which guards Drumnadrochit, the magnificent ruins of Urquhart Castle (HS ☎ 01456 450551) occupy a commanding position with views which take in almost the entire length of the loch. Fort Augustus guards the south end of the loch, and is an attractive village to collect your wits and summon up the strength to contend with a flight of five locks which set you on the route to the smallest of the lochs on the Canal, Loch Oich. With wooded shores and the ruins of Invergarry Castle, this is a really delightful stretch of the journey through the canal. Another stretch of canal cut links Loch Oich to Loch Lochy which takes you to the final and longest canal section which includes Neptune's Staircase where there is a flight of eight locks – a spectacular feat of engineering indeed. This is the Gairlochy to Corpach cut which releases you to the upper reaches of Loch Linnhe next to Fort William, and opens up the cruising grounds of the West Coast, with Oban and Tobermory an easy day's sailing from the canal entrance.

Moray and Aberdeenshire

The Moray coastline is punctuated by a series of small harbours of which we have selected a cross-section to give you a flavour. For comprehensive coverage of all of them a pilot book with good local coverage will be helpful, especially as the tidal constraints of many of them make the navigation and approach tricky. Another useful source of information is the Directory of North-East Council Harbours by Aberdeenshire and Moray Councils which any of the harbours along here will be happy to let you have (see directory for harbour

addresses). The Moray Firth can be a delightful place to sail where you may well be joined by schools of bottle-nosed dolphins which are often to be seen enjoying themselves. Once around Rattray Head, the options for places to put in become much more limited. The marina at Peterhead is a handy place to stop off for a night alongside a pontoon and the harbour at Stonehaven is a real gem.

Artist: **Anthony Flemming BUCKIE**
Courtesy of: **The Artist**

Lossiemouth

The small fishing town of Lossiemouth has a harbour which is busy with fishing boats and a separate basin which is now a marina. It's a good base from which to explore the surrounding area which includes good sandy beaches close to the harbour, the attractive town of Elgin and a number of historic monuments. In Lossiemouth itself, the Fisheries and Community Museum (☎ 01343 813772) will give you a flavour of the town's history and also commemorates Ramsey MacDonald, who was the first Labour prime minister and is the town's most famous son, with a mock-up of his study using his original furnishings. Just inland, the ruined tower of Spynie Palace (HS ☎ 01343 546358) offers spectacular views. Built in the 14th century, this was the residence of the Bishops of Moray until the late 17th century. To the west, the ruins of Dufus Castle are all that remain of a fine motte and bailey castle and, in Elgin itself, what is left of the 13th century cathedral (HS ☎ 01343 547171) gives a good idea of what must have been a stunning building in its prime. Access to the harbour can be tricky so check with the harbour-master before entering. Berthing for visiting yachts is on pontoons or alongside the quay in the dredged yacht basin and most facilities are available, including showers and launderette. A full range of local shops is within a couple of minutes' walk, and there's a supermarket about a mile from the waterfront. For a drink ashore, The Steamboat is handy on Pitgaveny Street or, a little further away, find the Clifton Bar on Clifton Street. For good pub food, head for the Skerry Brae Hotel (☎ 01343 812040) on Scotfield Road about a mile away. Inexpensive meals can be had at the Harbour Tearoom (☎ 01343 814622) on Pitgaveny Quay or at Kandys on Pitgaveny Street. La Caverna (☎ 01343 813027) on Clifton Road is a bit more upmarket, and the best in town is "1629" (☎ 01343 813743) on Clifton Road.

Taxi:	Walker's (☎ 01343 812940) or Andersons (☎ 01343 812149)
Car hire:	D. Smith (☎ 01343 815280)
Bus:	service to Elgin which links to national coach network
Rail:	Elgin Station for trains to Inverness and Aberdeen
Airport:	Inverness Airport for links to UK domestic destinations

for more details, see Directory Section

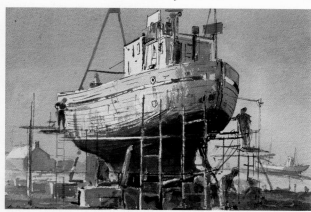

Artist: **Anthony Flemming ON THE SLIP, BANFF**
Courtesy of: **The Artist**

Banff and Macduff

The yachtsman is faced with a choice in Banff Bay as there are two harbours here. **Macduff** Harbour is a busy commercial port where yachts are not enormously welcome, but it does have the advantage of being one of very few harbours along this stretch of coast with enough water to stay afloat at all states of the tide. It is a useful refuge if the weather turns foul, though the entrance is problematic in north easterly gales. A preferable option if you don't mind taking the ground or anchoring just outside is **Banff** Harbour on the west side of the bay. Banff is a former county town and, since Robert the Bruce awarded its charter in 1324, a Royal Burgh. There are a number of fine 17th and 18th century houses, the most spectacular being Duff House (HS ☎ 01261 818181), designed by William Adam and built in about 1740. Set in extensive grounds, it is a masterpiece of its period and, as a bonus, a selection of pictures from the National Galleries of Scotland is displayed here. There are more pictures at the Harbour Gallery and the Banff Museum has a collection of local silverware amongst other exhibits which illustrate the area. Just up the road in Macduff the Marine Aquarium (☎ 01261 833369), with its centre-piece tank, touch pools and audio visual displays, offers alternative mind improvement. Accommodation for visiting yachts at Banff is in the outer harbour, and basic facilities are available. For fuel and chandlery, you need to head for Macduff harbour where there is also a launderette. You can get a shower at Banff Sailing Club and the harbourmaster has a key if it isn't open. There's a full range of shops for provisions including a couple of supermarkets in Banff, and good fresh fish can be found in Macduff. If you are berthed in Macduff, the Macduff Arms on Shore Street is handy for a drink and the

Knowes Hotel in Market Street serves good pub food. Highland Haven (☎ 01261 832408) will serve you an inexpensive restaurant meal, but if you want something a bit smarter, you will need to head along to Banff. The Railway Inn on Castle Street by Banff Harbour is convenient for a drink and the Castle Bar further up the street serves good pub meals. Geo Ellis in the High Street and Scotts in Castle Street are good choices for inexpensive meals and for something a bit more elaborate, try Banff Springs (☎ 01261 812881) on Golden Knowes. The best in town can be found at the County Hotel (☎ 01261 815353) in the High Street or, if you fancy a bit of an excursion, it's worth a trip to the Pennan Inn (☎ 01346 561201) which is about ten miles along the coast to the east and will be familiar to you if you saw the film "Local Hero".

Taxi:	Banff Taxis (☎ 01261 818182) or Victoria Taxis (☎ 01261 833333) in MacDuff
Car hire:	Near Macduff, Deveron Car Hire (☎ 01261 832912)
Bus:	Bluebird Stage Coach enquiries (☎ 01224 212266)
Rail:	20 miles to Huntly or Keith Stations
Airport:	Aberdeen Airport

for more details, see Directory Section

Artist: **Anthony Flemming FISHING BOATS, MACDUFF** *Courtesy of:* **The Artist**

Fraserburgh

Space is not guaranteed for visiting yachts in Fraserburgh Harbour as it is a busy fishing port and commercial craft have priority. However, you might well find it a good staging post as there is plenty of water for access at all states of the tide and it's a useful port of refuge, though the entrance should not be attempted in on-shore gales. A notable local feature is the lighthouse on Kinnaird Head which was incorporated into 16th century Fraserburgh Castle by the Commissioners of the Northern Lighthouses in 1787. Superseded by a modern unmanned lighthouse, this building is now part of Scotland's National Lighthouse Museum (☎ 01346 511022). A guided tour will show you what it was like to be a lighthouse keeper here. The town itself is not desperately attractive, but there's a good range of shops for provisions: a supermarket is close to hand and most other facilities a visiting yacht might need are available. For a run ashore, The Galleon (☎ 01346 515354) on Shore Street is convenient for a pub meal, or you might like to take a taxi to the Watermill Bar (☎ 01346 518219) which is just over a mile away. For a restaurant meal which won't break the bank, try the Saltoun Arms (☎ 01346 518282) in Saltoun Square. Findlay's Bar and Restaurant (☎ 01346 519547) in Smiddyhill Road is worth a try for somethingimg a bit more elaborate.

Taxi:	(☎ 01346 511115)
Car hire:	(☎ 01346 241360) or (☎ 01346 518904)
Cycle hire:	(☎ 01346 512266)
Bus:	services to local towns and Aberdeen
Rail:	Aberdeen Station is on the East Coast Mainline
Airport:	Aberdeen Airport enquiries (☎ 01224 722331)

for more details, see Directory Section

Peterhead

Peterhead Bay boasts a purpose-built yacht marina which is something of a rarity in this part of the country, so to be welcomed. Pontoon berths with all the trimmings make a pleasant change from doing battle with fishing boats and other commercial traffic. Peterhead is still a busy commercial port and the main docks which are adjacent to the town are still the domain of those whose business takes them to sea, so the marina is a little way from the centre of things on the south side of Peterhead Bay. This is good for peace and quiet, but not so good for shopping and exploring the town. However, the Maritime Heritage Centre (☎ 01779 473000) is close to the marina and here you can learn about Peterhead and its people and there's a restaurant for snacks or meals. Round the bay in the centre of town, the Arbuthnot Museum (☎ 01779 477778) in St Peter's Street

focuses on the town's role as a fishing and whaling port. For a practical demonstration of this important element in the local economy, visit the Ugie Fish House (☎ 01779 476209) which is the oldest working fish house in Scotland where traditional methods are still used to smoke salmon and trout. Other than the restaurant at the Maritime Centre, your best bets for bars and restaurants are all a bit of a hike. The Palace Hotel (☎ 01779 474821) in Prince Street and the Bay View (☎ 01779 472523) in St Peter's Street are both the best part of a couple of miles away, so a taxi might be in order if you are heading out for a drink. The Palace Hotel also serves meals, as does the Waterside (☎ 01779 471121) in Fraserburgh Road.

Taxi:	Central (☎ 01779 471000) or Bloo Toon (☎ 01779 471999)
Car hire:	Peterhead Motors (☎ 01779 479787)
Bus:	services to town centre and Aberdeen
Rail:	Aberdeen Station approx. 30 miles
Airport:	Aberdeen Airport (approx. 30 miles) enquiries (☎ 01224 722331)

for more details, see Directory Section

Aberdeen

Yachts are not really encouraged in this busy commercial harbour and as a result there are no specific facilities. This is a pity as it's an interesting city with plenty going on. Still, it's good to know that there's a refuge here for emergencies or just a brief stay (head for Pacific Quay where there is very limited space) and let's hope that in the future a more enlightened attitude towards the yachtsman might emerge.

Artist: **Anthony Flemming** **SLAINS CASTLE** *Courtesy of:* **The Artist**

Stonehaven

The harbour authorities in Stonehaven are much more accommodating, and though this is also a harbour which is busy with commercial traffic and especially fishing boats, yachts are very welcome here. The harbour has good shelter, and is also an attractive place to sit in your cockpit and watch the world go by. To the north, sandy beaches attract the bucket and spade wielding holidaymaker and there's also an amusement park for traditional seaside resort entertainment. The town centre is focussed on the early 19th century Market Buildings which give a distinguished air to the surrounding streets. This air also pervades the harbour area to the south. The Stonehaven Tollbooth Museum (☎ 01779 477778) is at the harbour and will give a good insight into local history and the town's role as a fishing port. A mile or so to the south, the ruins of Dunnottar Castle (☎ 01569 762173) stand out from the coastline on a rocky promontory and make a good objective for a stroll along the cliffs. The harbour approach can be tricky and is not advisable for yachts in strong on-shore winds. Much of the inner harbour dries to a sandy bottom, but you should be able to find enough water to berth alongside in the outer harbour if you want to stay afloat. There's a good range of shops within five minutes walk and a convenient selection of welcoming pubs along the harbour front.

Taxi:	A & I Taxis (☎ 01569 764333) or MacLeod Taxis (☎ 01569 763096)
Car hire:	Arduthie Motors (☎ 01569 762989)
Bus:	Bluebird Bus Company enquiries (☎ 01224 212266)
Rail:	Stonehaven Station enquiries (☎ 01569 762110)
Airport:	Aberdeen Airport (☎ 01224 722331)

for more details, see Directory Section

Angus, Fife & Edinburgh

We are now approaching the more populated areas of Scotland, and both the cities of Dundee and Edinburgh are included in this next section so you will be able to experience the more cosmopolitan face of Eastern Scotland. However, as well as the big cities, there are some charming smaller towns to visit and several fishing harbours with a history that goes back centuries. You will find plenty to see and do once ashore, and furthermore, there are some fine stretches of coastline to admire. The vistas including the bridges over both the Forth and Tay estuaries are impressive, and for a more natural outlook, the coastlines of both Angus and Fife offers pleasing prospects and varied scenery.

Montrose

An expanse of sandy beach fringes Montrose Bay which is the setting for St Cyrus National Nature Reserve (☎ 01674 830736) where there are 227 acres of lava cliffs, sand dunes, saltmarsh and sandflats. Another point of interest is that the visitor centre is housed in the old lifeboat station here. At the south end of the bay, the River South Esk gives access to another nature reserve in the Montrose Basin (Wildlife Centre ☎ 01674 676336) which encloses 750 hectares of estuary as a sanctuary for a wide variety of resident and migrant birds. A bridge across the river prevents yachts from gaining access to the basin. However, there is usually plenty of room for boats to berth in good shelter below the bridge and, while Montrose is a busy port serving the North Sea oil industry, yachts are welcome here. There has been a lifeboat service at Montrose since 1800 which was well before the foundation of the RNLI who took on the management of the station in 1865. Tragedy struck in the winter of 1953 when the lifeboat was caught out in an appalling storm – the entrance here can become impossible for even a lifeboat in severe onshore weather. While waiting to get back in, the lifeboat was capsized and six of the seven crew were lost - a memorial plaque in the lifeboat station pays tribute to those who lost their lives. For more local history, a trip to the Montrose Museum (☎ 01674 673232) which is housed in an elegant Georgian building is warmly recommended and, for more Georgian splendour, the House of Dun (NTS ☎ 01674 810264) which overlooks the Montrose Basin is an excellent example of the work of William Adam who designed and built the house in 1730. The interior is notable for its fine plasterwork and interesting contents and the walled garden on the east side of the house has been restored and is now a good example of a typical late Victorian garden. The approach to the harbour is not immediately obvious, so be sure to consult your almanac or pilot book, and once inside, you may encounter strong currents. Contact the harbourmaster who will be able to direct you to a place to berth alongside one of the quays. From a berth on the north bank, you won't have far to go to find provisions, and a selection of watering holes is available for a spot of refreshment. Montrose is well supplied with a variety of pubs for a drink: The Black Horse Inn (☎ 01674 672179) on Murray Street, Busbys (☎ 01674 674246) on George Street, the Caledonian Bar (☎ 01674 672110) on Ferry Street and the Ferryden Inn (☎ 01674 673266) in Brownlow Place are all good options. For a restaurant meal, try Roos Leap (☎ 01674 672157) on Trail Drive, or for some far eastern flavour, head to Marerosa (☎ 01674 672132) on the High Street, which offers Chinese, or the Indian Cottage Restaurant (☎ 01674 676578) which is just along the street, for a selection of favourites from the sub-continent.

Taxi:	Gutherie Brothers Taxis (☎ 01674 673205) or Dee Jay Taxis (☎ 01674 675166)
Car hire:	Gutherie Brothers Car Hire (☎ 01674 673205)
Bus:	Strathkay Bus Company (☎ 01382 228054) or Scottish City Link (☎ 0990 505050)
Rail:	Montrose Station, National Rail Enquiries (☎ 0345 484950)
Airport:	Aberdeen Airport (☎ 01224 722331)

for more details, see Directory Section,

Arbroath

For many in Scotland and beyond, the name of Arbroath conjures up the image of succulent smoked haddock and the Arbroath 'smokie' continues to be a popular dish. The harbour is still home to a fishing fleet and the town has prospered and become a favoured holiday destination. The Miniature Railway (☎ 01241

879249) is a key attraction, and has been in operation since 1935 and, for more intellectual stimulation, the Signal Tower (☎ 01241 875598) is now an interesting museum. There is plenty of history here – the Abbey (☎ 01241 878756) was founded by William the Lion in 1178 and much of its splendid structure still stands. This was the setting for the signing of the Declaration of Arbroath which re-affirmed Scotland's independence in 1320. The approach to the harbour is reasonably straightforward though a south easterly swell can make the entrance very awkward. The outer harbour dries but the inner harbour has gates which are not closed as a matter of course, but may be on request. You will find a full range of shops for provisions and also plenty of places to refresh and refuel yourself. The Old Brew House (☎ 01241 879945) at Danger Point, is a pub and a restaurant worthy of inspection while the interestingly named Smugglers Tavern (☎ 01241 876927) on Ladybridge Street is handy for a drink. For those of you who feel like venturing out of Arbroath the But 'n' Ben (☎ 01241 877223) is a restaurant in Auchmithie, about 2 miles out of Arbroath which is well worth a visit.

Taxi:	Cooks Taxis (☎ 01241 876266) or Company Cabs (☎ 01241 431333)
Car hire:	Kerr's Self Drive (☎ 01241 877990)
Bus:	Strathtay Scottish (☎ 01382 228345)
Rail:	Arbroath Station, National Rail Enquiries (☎ 0345 484950)
Airport:	Dundee Airport flights to London, for international flights, Aberdeen Airport

for more details, see Directory Section

The River Tay, Broughty Ferry & Dundee

Immortalised in doggerel as the 'silvery Tay' by the poet McGonagle the estuary stretches inland as far as Perth. This was the scene of the terrible collapse of the railway bridge in 1879, barely a year after it was built. With a backdrop of the Sidlaw Hills, Dundee is located on the north bank, and enjoys an enviably picturesque setting which many would say the town fails to match. The oft misapplied sobriquet 'Bonnie Dundee' in fact never referred to the town anyway, but to one of its famous sons, John Graham of Claverhouse. Be that as it may, there is plenty that is interesting about the city that is Scotland's fourth largest and which enjoyed considerable prosperity in Victorian times, prosperity which continues to this day after a shift of emphasis to industries involving modern technology. To start with some old historical background, as you sail up the river Broughty Castle (HS ☎ 01382 76121), which dates back to the 16th century, is a landmark on the starboard bank and is now part of Dundee Museums. A little further up, another 16th century tower house, standing back from the shore, Claypots Castle (HS limited opening – check on ☎ 01786 450000) continues the theme and was at one time the property of 'Bonnie Dundee' himself. There's more history in the centre of town where you will find the oldest British-built ship still afloat at Victoria Dock. HM Frigate Unicorn (☎ 01382 200900) is a 46 gun frigate which was launched in 1824 and, along the front there's another historic ship to visit. The RRS Discovery took Captain Scott to the Antarctic on his

scientific expedition between 1901 and 1904 and the ship forms the focus of an exhibition at Discovery Point (☎ 01382 201245) which is on Discovery Quay. The Barrack Street Museum (☎ 01382 432020) is unsurprisingly on Barrack Street, and has a wide collection of natural history exhibits including the famous and ill-fated Tay Whale which swam up the river in 1883 and the McManus Galleries (☎ 01382 432020) on Albert Square include collections of archeological artefacts, decorative and Scottish Victorian Art, and local historical costume. Industrial history is the theme at the Verdant Works (☎ 01382 225282) in West Henderson's Wynd. Here, the story of the local textile industry is examined with particular emphasis on jute. Not far from Broughty Ferry on the east side of the town, Barry Mill (NTS ☎ 01241 856761) at Carnoustie is a restored 19th century water-mill which was still producing oatmeal until the late 1970s. It's open daily and there are milling demonstrations on Saturdays and Sundays or at other times for pre-booked parties. For those with a sweet tooth, the Shaws Dundee Sweet Factory (☎ 01382 461435) at the Keiller Building on Mains Loan includes a small museum, sweet making demonstrations and, of course, tastings. You have several options for berthing in and around Dundee. The Royal Tay Yacht Club near Broughty Ferry has visitors' moorings or you can anchor off and, whichever you choose, you will be warmly welcomed at the club. For better shelter, head towards the city centre - you can berth in the Victoria Dock, though here you may find the atmosphere rather taken up with commercial shipping. There is space on the south bank at Tayport just opposite the Royal Tay Yacht Club's premises and this harbour, which dries, does not have such a press of commercial traffic, though obviously here you are less well placed for exploring Dundee. No matter where you choose to berth, you will find a plentiful supply of local shops for provisioning and supermarkets are never too far away either. Facilities for yachts are probably most comprehensive at the Royal Tay Yacht Club, although there is no alongside berthing here. For a run ashore in Broughty Ferry, the Broughty Ferry Hotel (☎ 01382 776614) on West Queen Street is where you will find the Bombay Brasserie (☎ 01382 480490) which serves à la carte Indian cuisine in the evenings. The Beach House (☎ 01382 776614) on the Esplanade, is a pleasant, intimate place to enjoy a meal on the seafront, while the Cafe Montmartre (☎ 01382 739313) on Gray Street, is ideal for those of you who have continental hankerings, as it serves French à la carte meals. We can't leave Broughty Ferry without recommending the Fishermans Tavern (☎ 01382 775941) on Fort Street. This nautically decorated town pub, has an impressive range of real ales, wine and malt whiskies; the lunch time bar food is good and the seafront position allows a splendid view of the two Tay bridges.

Dundee is a boat trip or a taxi ride away if you fancy the city centre experience. There are plenty of pubs and restaurants to choose from. For a meal, try the Stakis Dundee (☎ 01382 229271) on Earl Grey Place, which serves a carvery lunch as well as à la carte dinners. Pub-wise, you can't really go wrong with the Hogshead (☎ 01382 205037) on Union Street, or Frew's (☎ 01382

810975) on Strathmartine Road, which is a tastefully decorated Victorian pub.

Firth of Tay to Firth of Forth

For those who are happy to take the ground, there is a series of delightful harbours around the coast of Fife. "Welcome Ashore", Sail Scotland's excellent free guide to moorings, harbours and "yachtie friendly" hostelries all around Scotland has a comprehensive listing of them all and is well worth having aboard for any cruise in Scottish waters (available from marina and harbour offices or Sail Scotland, The Promenade, Largs KA30 8BQ ☎ 01475 689899). We have selected a handful to give you a flavour of what is on offer. The harbour at St Andrews gives you the opportunity to pay homage at the home of the game of golf with its numerous internationally famous courses, and there is plenty more to see besides. This small town has a highly regarded university and, during term time, the streets and pubs in the town are thronged with eager young academics. A visit to the ruins of St Andrews Cathedral and St Rules Tower (HS ☎ 01334 472563) will give you a flavour of the very strong sense of history which the town exudes. Pressing on around Fife Ness, you soon reach **Anstruther** which is a typical Fife fishing harbour and now the home of the Scottish Fisheries Museum (☎ 01333 310628) which is as excellent as it is comprehensive. Also well worth a visit here is the lifeboat station which is based in a splendid boathouse constructed at the turn of the century. The harbour at **Burntisland** offers deep water refuge in the commercial docks in bad weather but, as this is a working facility, yachts are encouraged to use the harbour only in cases of urgency. There are very few facilities which would be useful to a visiting yacht, though by arrangement the Kinghorn Yacht Club which is based at the harbour will be delighted to let you have a shower, and close by, the Auld Hoose (☎ 01592 891074) is a good place for a drink. Kinghorn itself is at the other end of the splendid sandy bay which stretches to the east, and is where the RNLI have an inshore lifeboat station.

Artist: **Anthony Flemming CRAIL HARBOUR**
Courtesy of: **The Artist**

The Firth of Forth

The deep estuary which carves through central Scotland almost as far as Stirling presents a magnificent sailing area which takes in the waterfront of the capital at Edinburgh, spread out around the castle high above the city centre on Castle Rock. With the Pentland and Lammamuir Hills to the south, to the north the high ground in Fife and beyond, there is fine scenery around this splendid stretch of water. The area is popular with yachtsmen as it offers a variety of interesting cruising possibilities and has long been a favoured battleground for racing as well. Furthermore, it is hoped that the 2001 sailing season will see the re-opening of the Forth and Clyde Canal. This will be a tremendous additional connection as it will allow boats to move between the Firth of Forth and the Firth of Clyde on the West Coast without having to go via Inverness or by road. The Forth is spanned by two splendid bridges which carry the railway and the motorway between South Queensferry and North Queensferry. The seaward bridge is the robust Victorian structure which has carried the railway over the estuary since 1890 and, behind it, the more graceful lines of the road bridge make for a pleasing contrast. Nearly three-quarters of a century passed after the completion of the rail bridge before road traffic was able to take a similar shortcut over the Forth in 1964. As you approach the bridges, there's another charming harbour at **Aberdour**, a popular sailing centre which also draws holidaymakers and locals to enjoy excellent golfing and walking opportunities. Aberdour Castle (HS ☎ 01383 860519) looks over the harbour, and dates back to the 13th century. The terraced gardens here are particularly fine. Quayside berths are available in the harbour, which dries, and a limited range of facilities can be found here. For full marina facilities head to **Port Edgar** which is right under the road bridge's southern end. A full selection of yachting facilities is available on site at this council run marina, though for shopping it's a walk of over half a mile to South Queensferry where you will also find a selection of pubs and places to eat. At the marina, the Port Edgar Yacht Club will offer you a warm welcome in their small clubhouse which includes a convivial bar which is always busy on race nights. If you would like to spend a bit of time in **Edinburgh**'s city centre, you should consider taking advantage of the pontoon berths in Granton Harbour. Though still a mile or so from the centre of town, you are a great deal closer than you would be at South Queensferry, and you have the opportunity to take advantage of the hospitality offered by the Royal Forth Yacht Club whose comfortable clubhouse has fine views over the Forth from the harbourside. The list of things to see and do in Edinburgh is almost endless. If you are in the area during August you may well find the Festival and Fringe in full swing when the city has a 24 hours a day buzz of activity. During the rest of the year, life is rather more tranquil, and you will be able to enjoy a stroll up the Royal Mile through the city's Old Town. This takes you from the Palace of Holyroodhouse (☎ 0131 556 1096) which is the Queen's official residence in Edinburgh to the mighty Castle (☎ HS 0131 225 9846) which contains the Scottish Crown Jewels and is the setting for the annual tattoo. The Royal Mile forms the backbone of the Old Town, and to the north, the New Town consists of elegant Georgian ter-races and squares and is where you will find the smartest shops and a wide variety of places to eat and drink. Not far from the Royal Mile, the Royal Museum of Scotland (☎ 0131 247 4422) on Chambers Street has a substantial and varied collection of exhibits and is well worth a visit to admire the contrasting styles of the orig-inal building and the impressive new extension to the west. Close to the museum, Edinburgh University has its central campus, so there are numerous lively pubs and places to eat around here. However, you won't find many students in the excellent Tower Restaurant (☎ 0131 225 3003) which has good views from its location on the top floor of the Royal Museum – the superb food and fine wines on offer here are not cheap. Le Sept (☎ 0131 225 5428) just off the High Street serves splendid crêpes and, for menus which include fresh Scottish pro-duce such as beef, lamb, venison and fish, either The Shore (☎ 0131 553 5080) or Fishers (☎ 0131 5545666) on The Shore in the refurbished docks at Leith are good options. Close to Granton Harbour, the Old Chain Pier (☎ 0131 552 1232) is a lively little bar where you can have inexpensive meals, or just a little further along the front to the east, the Star Bank (☎ 0131 5524141) offers a more elaborate menu and a splendid selection of beers and whiskies.

Taxi:	(☎ 0131 228 1211)
Car hire:	Arnold Clarke Car Hire (☎ 0131 22847747) or Avis (☎ 0131 3376363)
Bus:	L R T enquiries (☎ 0131 5556363)
Rail:	Waverley Station (☎ 0345 484950) is on the East Coast Intercity Mainline
Airport:	Edinburgh Airport (☎ 0131 3331000) about 5 miles form Port Edgar and the city centre

for more details, see Directory Section

Artist: **Anthony Flemming LEITH DOCKS**
Courtesy of: **The Artist**

East Lothian and the Scottish Borders

Several historic fishing towns and villages offer inter-esting and welcoming ports to put into on this stretch of coast. There are spectacular cliffs to admire and a wealth of wildlife as well, especially on those stretches of coastline which escape the fate of having the main road and rail links between Edinburgh and Newcastle right on the foreshore. As you would expect from har-bours which still actively operate fishing fleets, there are good opportunities to sample a variety of locally caught fresh fish. This could take the form of excellent fish & chips or more lavish meals, or why not take advantage of the chance to cook a simple but exquisite meal aboard?

Artist: **Brian Lancaster FIDRA ROCK AND LIGHT**
Courtesy of: **The Artist**

Dunbar

Dunbar is an attractive town which is now a popular resort whose appeal is supported by historical flavours which are amply demonstrated by the town's buildings and atmosphere. Dunbar Castle is now a ruin which was largely demolished to make way for the harbour in the 19th century, and what is left enhances the spectacular approach to the harbour. The magnificent 17th century Town House now houses the Dunbar Town House Museum where a variety of exhibits trace the town's history back to the Iron Age. Another interesting build-ing in the High Street is the birthplace of John Muir (1838-1914) whose family emigrated to the United States in 1849. He grew up to be a leading light in the early development of the conservation movement and the National Parks in America and many other countries around the world owe much to his pioneering determi-nation. John Muir House (☎ 01368 862585) is now a museum dedicated to his memory. Tradition is also upheld here by the presence of one of Scotland's best known independent breweries, the Belhaven Brewery which has been brewing here for over two centuries and whose ales are well worth looking out for. Not far to the north of the town, a striking ruined castle dating back to the 14th century clings to the cliffs at Tantallon (HS ☎ 01620 892727). The views over the Firth of Forth and out to sea from the top of the ramparts are superb. The approach to the harbour includes a number of haz-ards, and the narrow entrance can be tricky. In settled weather, you may prefer to anchor just outside rather than contend with the fishing boats and other commer-cial traffic as well as the shallow water in the harbour. Most facilities you might need can be found near the harbour, and the shops in the High Street, which is about a quarter of a mile away, will allow you to re-stock your lockers comprehensively. The Lothian Hotel (☎ 01368 863205) in the High Street serves bar meals at lunchtime and in the evenings, and a little further up the road, Umberto's Ristorante (☎ 01368 862354) is a good choice for an inexpensive restaurant meal. The Creel Restaurant (☎ 01368 863279) is conveniently placed at the Harbour and draws custom from far and wide as a result of its excellent reputation.

Taxi:	Eve Cars (☎ 01368 863455) or R & I Cabs (☎ 01368 865550)
Car hire:	In nearby East Linton, Torness Motors (☎ 01620 860535)
Bus:	Lowland Scottish Bus Company, enquiries (☎ 0131 6639233)
Rail:	Dunbar Station, call the General Travel Enquiry Line (☎ 0800 232323)
Airport:	Edinburgh (☎ 0131 3331000)

for more details, see Directory Section

St Abbs and Eyemouth

After the towering bulk of the modern landmark which is Torness Power Station, the coastline becomes wilder, and Telegraph Hill serves as a backdrop to the ruins of Fast Castle. The three hundred foot cliffs of St Abbs Head form the next impressive headland, and tucked in around the promontory, we come to the fishing harbour of **St Abbs**. St Abbs Head is a National Nature Reserve (NTS ☎ 018907 71443) managed by the National Trust for Scotland and the Scottish Wildlife Trust. This is an important breeding location for cliff-nesting seabirds and among those which can be seen here are fulmars, kittiwakes, shags and puffins. The adjacent waters have been designated a Voluntary Marine Reserve to broaden the effects of conservation in the area. St Abbs itself is an attractive village where the harbour still bustles with fishing boats and the RNLI have had a station here, now equipped with an Atlantic 21 Lifeboat, since 1911. This is a picturesque small working harbour though facilities for visiting yachts are very limited. If you are not prepared to be independent, you may find it preferable to put into **Eyemouth** about two miles away at the south end of Coldingham Bay. For the historical background of this thriving fishing town, the Eyemouth Museum (☎ 018907 50678) which is in the Old Kirk on Market Place is close to the harbour. A centrepiece here is the 15 foot Eyemouth Tapestry which was embroidered locally to mark the centenary of the loss of 189 fishermen's lives in a storm which is locally known as the Great Fishing Disaster. Links between Eyemouth and neighbouring St Abbs are strong, and in July, the newly elected Herring Queen is escorted by boat from St Abbs to the harbour at Eyemouth is a colourful ceremony which is steeped in tradition.

The harbour offers very good shelter, and though a busy base for fishing boats, yachts are made welcome here. Recent dredging work means that there should be plenty of water inside, but the bar at the entrance can make the approach tricky and if there is any swell, it's a good idea to avoid the entrance for a few hours around low water. A good range of facilities is available close to the waterfront, and all the shops you might need can be found in the centre of the town.

The Tavern on the High Street is a good choice for a drink as it provides good views over the sea and The Ship Hotel (☎ 018907 50224) on Harbour Road is close by and serves bar meals. It's worth taking a taxi two and a half miles inland to the Flemington Inn (☎ 018907 81277) at Ayton where good meals including seafood dishes are available seven days a week.

Taxi:	B & C Taxis (☎ 018907 50821) or Perrymans Taxis (☎ 018907 81533)
Car hire:	Eyemouth Auto Centre (☎ 018907 50554)
Bus:	Cross Country Connections (☎ 01289 308719) or Lowland Bus Company (☎ 01289 307461)
Rail:	Berwick (9 miles), National Rail enquiries (☎ 0345 484950)
Airport:	Edinburgh (☎ 0131 3331000)

for more details, see Directory Section

Artist: **Brian Lancaster SHORELINE, BURNMOUTH** *Courtesy of:* **The Artist**

LERWICK　　　　　　60.09'.5N 01.08'.5W

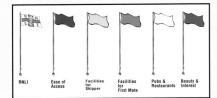

Lerwick Harbour Trust
Captain Archer T L Kemp: Harbourmaster
Albert Building, Lerwick, Shetland ZE1 0LL
Tel: 01595 692991 Fax: 01595 693452
VHF Ch: 16/12 VHF Name: Lerwick Harbour

Lerwick Boating Club
Contact: Secretary Tel: 01595 692407

Chandler:
LHD Marine Supplies Tel: 01595 692882
1 Alexandra Buildings, Lerwick

Repairs:
Malakoff & Wm Moore Ltd Tel: 01595 695544
North Ness, Lerwick

Lerwick Lifeboat Station
Open to visitors all year round
Contact: M Shearer (Hon Sec) (01595 693 768)
or Coxn (01595 693 827)

SCALLOWAY　　　　　60.08'.0N 01.16'.5W

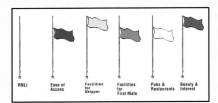

Scalloway Harbour
A Rendall: Harbourmaster
The Harbour Office, Blacksness Pier,
Scalloway Harbour, Shetland ZE1 0TQ
Tel: 01595 880574 Fax: 01595 880566
VHF Ch: 16/12 VHF Name: Scalloway Harbour

Scalloway Marina Tel: 01595 880649

East Voe Marina (under construction)

Scalloway Boat Club
J A Ward: Secretary Tel: 01595 880409

Chandlers:
LHD Marine Supplies
Fishmarket Buildings, Blacksness, Scalloway
Tel: 01595 880220

West Side Fishermen Ltd
Fishmarket Buildings, Blacksness, Scalloway
Tel: 01595 880505

Repairs:
Malakoff & Wm Moore Ltd
West Shore, Scalloway Tel: 01595 880215

AITH

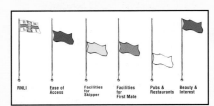

Aith Pier
Victor Grey, Harbourmaster
Tel/Fax: 01595 810378
VHF Channel: 8 VHF Name: Aith Marina

Repairs:
Johnston Garage Tel: 01595 810230

Aith Lifeboat
Open to visitors by appointment
Contact: Coxn Hylton Henry
Tel: 01595 810446

STROMNESS　　　　　　58.58'.0N 03.17'.5W

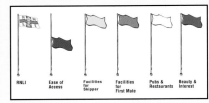

Stromness Harbour
Captain John Banks: Harbourmaster
Stromness, Mainland, Orkney KW16 3AA
Tel: 01856 850744
VHF Ch: 12/16 VHF Name: Stromness Harbour

Orkney Sailing Club
Jimmy Clouston: Secretary Tel: 01856 872331

Stromness Sailing Club
Alan Long: Secretary Tel: 01856 851077

Chandler:
Rope Centre
John Street, Stromness Tel: 01856 850646

Repairs:
Hamnarae Engineering Tel: 01856 850676
Ian Richardson Boatbuilders
Tel: 01856 850321/547

Stromness Lifeboat Station
Open daily except Sundays throughout summer
Contact: Mech R Taylor Tel: 01856 850935

KIRKWALL　　　　　　58.59'.5N 02.57'.5W

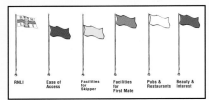

Kirkwall Harbour
Fred Perry: Harbourmaster Tel: 01856 872292
VHF Ch: 12/16 VHF Name: Kirkwall Harbour

Orkney Sailing Club
Contact: Secretary Tel: 01856 872331

Chandler/Repairs:
Ian Richardson Boatbuilders Tel: 01856 850321

Kirkwall Lifeboat
Open to visitors all year round
Contact: Mech D Strutt Tel: 01856 873967

LONGHOPE

Longhope Lifeboat Station
Open to visitors all year round
Contact Dr D Trickett (01856 701460) or
Coxn I McFadyen (01856 701239)

SCRABSTER AND THURSO
　　　　　　　　　　58.36'.5N 03.32'.5W

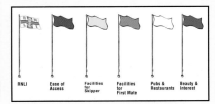

Scrabster Harbour
Pierre Bale: Harbourmaster Tel: 01847 892779
VHF Ch: 12/16 VHF Name: Scrabster Harbour

Pentland Firth Yacht Club
David Lord: Secretary Tel: 01847 896885

Chandler:
Denholm Fishselling Tel: 01847 896968

Thurso Lifeboat
Closed to visitors at present
Contact: G Gibson (Hon Sec) for update
Tel: 01847 893744 (or 01847 892529 office hours)

WICK　　　　　　58.26'.5N 03.04'.5W

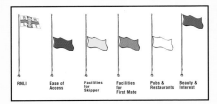

Wick Harbour
Malcolm Bremner: Harbourmaster
Tel: 01955 602030
VHF Channels: 14/16
VHF Name: Wick Harbour

Chandler:
JS Duncan Tel: 01955 602689

Repairs:
J McCaughty Boatbuilders Tel: 01955 602858

Wick Lifeboat
Open to visitors weekdays 10.30-12.30

LYBSTER　　　　　　58.18'.0N 03.17'.5W

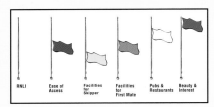

Lybster Harbour
Contact: Harbourmaster Tel: 01593 721325

HELMSDALE　　　　　58.07'.0N 03.39'.0W

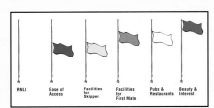

Helmsdale Harbour
Mr Chappey: H/master Tel: 01431 821248

CROMARTY FIRTH　　　57.41'.0N 04.02'.0W

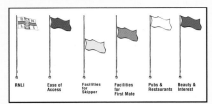

Mr Roehling: H/master Tel: 01381 600479
VHF Channels: 11/16/13
VHF Name: Cromarty Firth Port Control

Cromarty Boat Club
Alex Davidson: Secretary Tel: 01381 600540

Invergordon Boat Club
George O'Hara: Secretary Tel: 01381 877612

Invergordon Lifeboat
Open to visitors by appointment
Contact: Captain I Dunderdale (Hon Sec)
Tel: 01349 852308 (office) or 01862 892211

INVERNESS AND MUIRTOWN
57.30'.0N 04.14'.0W

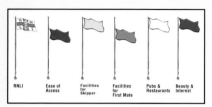

Inverness Harbour
Capt MacLeod: Harbourmaster
Harbour Office, Longman Drive, Inverness,
Inverness-shire IV3 5LS
Tel: 01463 715715 Fax: 01463 715705
VHF Channels: 06/12/16
VHF Name: Inverness Harbour

Longman Yacht Haven
Captain M McLeod: Manager
Longman Drive, Inverness, Inverness-shire
Tel: 01463 715715
VHF Ch: 12 VHF Name: Inverness Harbour

Kessock Lifeboat Station
Open to visitors April through October
Contact: Captain J B Fairgrieve (Hon Sec)
Tel: 01463 715248

Caledonian Canal

British Waterways
Canal Office, Inverness
Tel: 01463 233140 Fax: 01463 710942

Caley Marina
Contact: Manager
Canal Road, Muirtown, Inverness IV3 6NF
Tel: 01463 236539 Fax: 01463 238323

Seaport Marina
Contact: Manager
Muirtown Wharf, Inverness IV3 5LS
Tel: 01463 239475

Chandlers:
Caley Marina as above
Inverness Boat Centre
Main Street, North Kessock
Tel: 01463 731383

Repairs:
Taylor Marine Engineering Ltd
Tel: 01463 711048

BURGHEAD
57.42'.0N 03.30'.0W

Burghead Harbour
John G Mackay: Harbourmaster
Harbour Office, Burghead, Morayshire
Tel/Fax: 01343 835337

Chandler/Repairs (nearest):
See Buckie

LOSSIEMOUTH
57.43'.5N 03.16'.5W

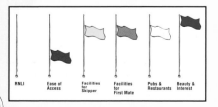

Lossiemouth Harbour
Alex Scott: Harbourmaster
Tel: 01343 813066

Elgin & Lossiemouth Harbour Co
(Lossiemouth Marina)
6 Pitgaveny Quay, Lossiemouth, IV31 6TW
Alex K Scott: Manager Tel: 01343 543355
VHF Ch: 12 VHF Name: Lossiemouth Harbour

Lossiemouth Cruising Club
S Spence: Secretary Tel: 01343 812121

Lossiemouth Sailing Club
I Dorman-Jackson: Secretary
Tel: 01343 812928

Chandler:
Fleetwoods Marine Leisure
4 Pitgaveny Quay, Lossiemouth IN31 6TW
Tel: 01343 813015

Repairs:
P Anderson
50 Yuill Avenue, Buckie Tel: 01542 833988

PORTKNOCKIE
57.42'.5N 02.51'.5W

Herbert D Reid: Harbourmaster
Orcadia, Admiralty Street, Portknockie,
Banffshire Tel: 01542 840833

CULLEN
57.41'.5N 02.49'.0W

Eric Hendry: Harbourmaster
North Arnbath, Portsoy, Banffshire
Tel: 01261 842477

BUCKIE
57.41'.0N 02.57'.5W

Buckie Harbour
Captain William Mackay: Harbourmaster
Tel: 01542 831700
VHF Ch: 16/12 VHF Name: Buckie Harbour

Chandler:
Caley Shop Tel: 01542 832152
Cosalt International Tel: 01542 832978
Fishermen's Fishselling Co Tel: 01542 832584

Repairs:
Forsyths
34 Commercial Road, Buckie Tel: 01542 836400
Buckie Lifeboat
Open to visitors daily 09.00-17.00 from March
through October
Contact: Coxn John Murray Tel: 01542 833245

MACDUFF/BANFF

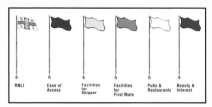

Macduff
57.40'.0N 02.30'.0W

John West:Harbourmaster
32 Shore Street, Macduff
Tel: 01261 832236 Fax: 01261 833612
VHF Ch: 12 VHF Name: Macduff Harbour

Banff

Alasdair M Galloway: Harbourmaster
Harbour Office, Harbour Place, Banff
Tel: 01261 815544
VHF Channel: 14 VHF Name: Banff Harbour

Banff Sailing Club
Mrs J Bowie: Secretary Tel: 01224 868059

Chandlers:
Banffshire Fishselling Co
21 Shore Street, Macduff
Tel: 01261 832891 Fax: 01261 833639

A Paterson
30 Shore Street, Macduff Tel: 01261 832225

Seaway Marine
Station Brae, Macduff
Tel: 01261 832877 Fax: 01261 833377

Repairs:
Macduff Shipyards Tel: 01261 832234
Seaway Marine, details as above

Macduff Lifeboat Station
Open to visitors at any time by appointment
Contact: W J West (Hon Sec) Tel: 01261 832236

FRASERBURGH
57.41'.5N 01.59'.5W

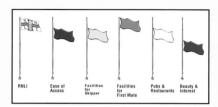

Fraserburgh Port Office
Capt Bob Reid: H/master Tel: 01346 515858
VHF Channel: 12/16 (call on approach)
VHF Name: Fraserburgh Harbour

Fraserburgh Lifeboat Station
Open weekday evenings by appointment
Contact: Jack Provan Tel: 01346 518748

PETERHEAD
57.30'.0N 01.46'.5W

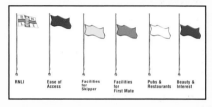

Peterhead Bay Harbour Authority
Capt. Flett: Harbourmaster
Bath House, Bath Street, Peterhead AB42 1DX
Tel: 01779 474020 Fax: 01779 475712
VHF Ch: 14 VHF Name: Peterhead Harbour

Peterhead Bay Marina
Contact: Manager
Tel: 01779 474020 Fax: 01779 475712

Peterhead Sailing Club
Dr B Wilkins: Secretary Tel: 011358 751340

Chandlers:
JNW Services Tel: 01779 477346
Peterhead Watersport Centre Tel: 01779 480888

Peterhead Lifeboat
Open weekdays by appointment Easter
through September
Contact: Coxn A Brown Tel: 01779 471266

ABERDEEN
57.08'.5N 02.03'.5W

Aberdeen Harbour
Capt Colin Parker: Harbourmaster
Tel: 01224 597000
VHF Ch: 12 VHF Name: Aberdeen Harbour

Chandler:
Cosalt International Tel: 01224 588327

Repairs/Chandlery:
Meridian Marine & Technical
Unit 1, Palmerston Road, Aberdeen
Tel: 01224 584182 Fax: 01224 584184

Aberdeen Lifeboat Station
Open to visitors by appointment only
Contact: G Booth (Hon Sec) Tel: 01224 326162

STONEHAVEN
56.57'.5N 02.12'.0W

Stonehaven Harbour
James Brown: Harbourmaster
Harbour Office, Old Pier AB39 2LU
Tel: 01569 762741
VHF Ch: 11 VHF Name: Stonehaven Harbour

STONEHAVEN cont.

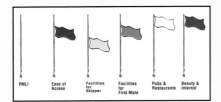

Aberdeen & Stonehaven Yacht Club
Donald Smith: Secretary Tel: 015691 362054

MONTROSE   56.42'.0N 02.26'.5W

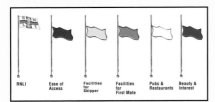

Montrose Harbour
Capt Johansen: H/master Tel: 01674 672302
VHF Ch: 12/16 VHF Name: Montrose Harbour

Montrose Lifeboat Station
Open to visitors by appointment
Contact: N McNab (Hon Sec)
Tel: 01674 675367

ARBROATH   56.33'.0N 02.35'.0W

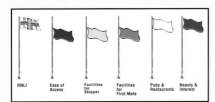

Arbroath Harbour
Douglas Gibson: H/master Tel: 01241 872166
VHF Ch: 11/14 VHF Name: Arbroath Harbour

Arbroath Lifeboat Station
Open daily except Sundays, 10.00-17.00
Contact: Neil McCabe Tel: 01241 875598

RIVER TAY   56.27'.0N 02.53'.0W

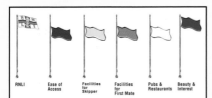

Dundee

Capt Martin Clark: H/master Tel: 01382 224121
VHF Channel: 12
VHF Name: Dundee Harbour Radio

Broughty Ferry Boating Club
Dougal MacIntosh: Vice Commodore
Tel: 01382 452705

Dundee Corinthian Boating Club
Mr Howard: Secretary Tel: 01382 221511

Royal Tay Yacht Club
Stuart Buchanan: Secretary Tel: 01382 477516
VHF Channel: M
HF Name: Royal Tay Yacht Club

Wormit Boating Club
O J Collison: Secretary Tel: 01382 541400

Moorings:
Tayport Harbour Trust Tel: 01382 221331

Chandlers:
Craig Group Catering & Marine Services
Douglas Road, Dundee Tel: 01382 505106

Sea & Shore
Victoria Dock, Camperdown Street, Dundee
Tel: 01382 202666

Simpson W A Marine
1 Logie Avenue, Dundee Tel: 01382 566670

Broughty Ferry Lifeboat Station
Open to visitors daily by appointment
Contact: C Begg (Hon Sec) (01382 778405) or
Coxn J Hughan (01382 350563)

Perth

F G Bissett: Harbourmaster
Tel: 01738 624056

ANSTRUTHER   56.13'.0N 02.41'.5W

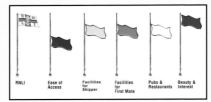

Anstruther Harbour
Bill Smith: Harbourmaster Tel: 01333 310836
VHF Ch: 11 VHF Name: Anstruther Harbour

Anstruther Lifeboat
Open to visitors all year round
Contact: P Murray (01333 310312) or Mech D
Mitchell (01333 310526)

ABERDOUR   56.03'.0N 03.17'.5W

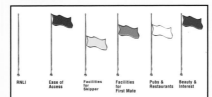

Aberdour Harbour
Contact: Harbourmaster Tel: 01383 860452

Aberdour Boat Club
I McAndie: Secretary Tel: 01592 202827

BURNTISLAND   56.03'.0N 03.14'.0W

Capt Sutherland: H/master Tel: 01333 426725
VHF Ch: 71 VHF Name: Forth Navigation

Kinghorn Sailing Club
R Henderson: Secretary Tel: 01592 872386

KINGHORN

Kinghorn Lifeboat Station
Open to visitors all year round Contact:
C Tulloch Jnr (Hon Sec) Tel: 01592 890105

PORT EDGAR   55.59'.5N 03.24'.5W

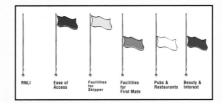

Port Edgar Marina
John F Hainey: Manager

Shore Road, South Queensferry EH30 9SQ
Tel: 0131 3313330 Fax: 0131 3314878
VHF Channel 80/M2 VHF Name: Port Edgar

Port Edgar Yacht Club
Jim Young: Secretary Tel: 0131 3371301

Chandlers:
The Bosun's Locker Tel: 0131 331 3875

GRANTON - EDINBURGH

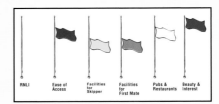

Capt G Vale: Harbourmaster Tel: 0131 555 3866
VHF Ch: 71 VHF Name: Forth Navigation

Forth Corinthian Yacht Club (Edinburgh
Marina joint owner)
Richard Bolton: Secretary
1 Granton Square, Edinburgh EH5 1HE
Tel/Fax: 0131 552 8560

Royal Forth Yacht Club (Edinburgh Marina
joint owner) Richard Bolton: Secretary
Middle Pier, Granton, Edinburgh EH5 1HF
Tel/Fax: 0131 552 8560

Chandler:
Sea Span Tel: 0131 552 2224

Repairs:
Granton Marine Tel: 0131 552 0164

Queensferry Lifeboat
Open to visitors all year round
Contact: T Robertson (Hon Sec)
Tel: 0131 331 1563

NORTH BERWICK   56.03'.5N 02.43'.0W

No facilities for yachts

North Berwick Lifeboat Station
Open to visitors daily from 10.00 Easter
through October.
Contact: J Eldridge (Hon Sec)
Tel: 01620 893418

DUNBAR   56.00'.5N 02.31'.0W

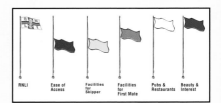

Victoria Harbour
Contact: Harbourmaster Tel: 01368 863206

Dunbar Lifeboat Station
Open to visitors by appointment
Contact: Coxn/Mech N Wright
Tel: 01368 862274

ST ABBS

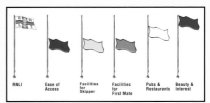

Conact: Harbourmaster Tel: 018907 71323

St Abbs Lifeboat Station
Open during summer months by appointment Contact: A Crowe (Hon Sec)
Tel: 018907 71412

EYEMOUTH

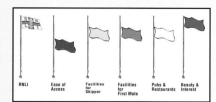

John Johnston: H/master Tel: 018907 50223
Mobile: 0585 742505

Eyemouth Lifeboat Station
Open to visitors all year round
Contact: Captain J Dougal Tel: 018907 50448
or Mech D Collin (Hon Sec) Tel: 018907 50315

East Scotland, The Shetlands & Orkneys - Chart Agents

LHD Lerwick, Aith Tel: 01595 69 2379
Hay & Co, Lerwick Tel: 01595 692 533
Herald Printshop, Stromness Tel: 01856 875 039
Caley Marina, Inverness Tel: 01463 236 539
Thomas Gunn, Aberdeen Tel: 01224 595 045
Fleetwoods, Lossiemouth Tel: 01343 813 015
A Paterson, Macduff Tel: 01261 832 225

East Scotland, The Shetlands & Orkneys - Pilot Books

Clyde Cruising Club Sailing Directions, Shetland Crusing Guide
published by Clyde Cruising Club Sailing Directions, Tel: 0141 221 2774

North Sea (West) Pilot Ed. 1995
published by United Kingdom Hydrographic Office, ISBN: 0707 710 545

North Coast of Scotland Pilot 3rd Ed. 1997
published by United Kingdom Hydrographic Office; ISBN: 0707 710 529

Artist: **Anthony Flemming DUNNOTTAR CASTLE** *Courtesy of:* **The Artist**

Ireland

Artist: **Anthony Flemming** SUNSET Courtesy of: **The Artist**

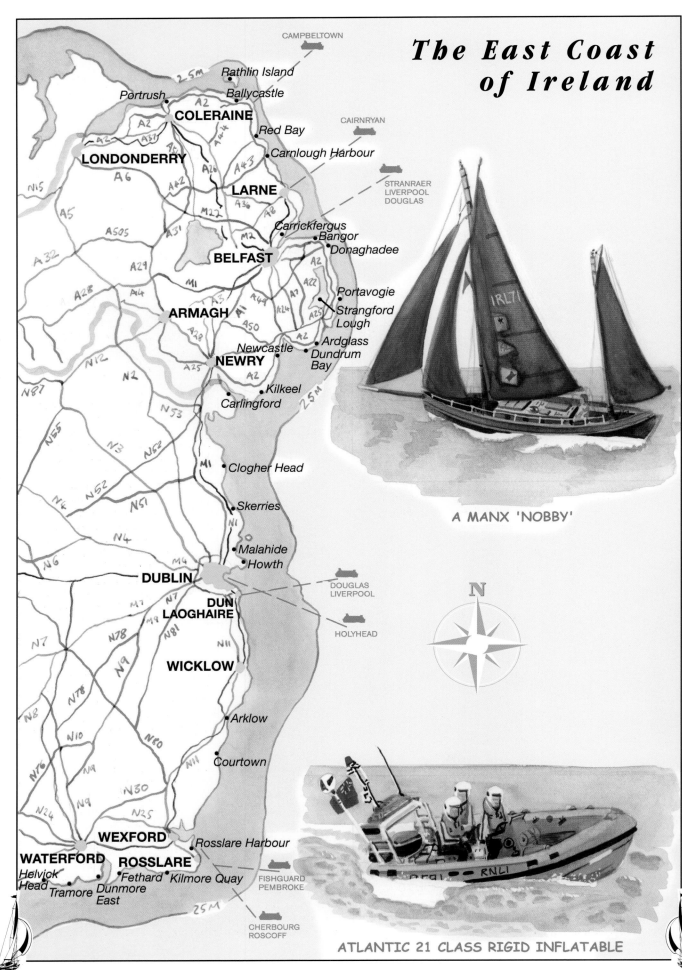

The East Coast of Ireland

CAMPBELTOWN

2.5M

Rathlin Island
Portrush
Ballycastle
COLERAINE
Red Bay
CAIRNRYAN
LONDONDERRY
Carnlough Harbour
STRANRAER
LIVERPOOL
DOUGLAS
LARNE

Carrickfergus
Bangor
BELFAST
Donaghadee

Portavogie
ARMAGH
Strangford
Lough

Newcastle
Ardglass
NEWRY
Dundrum Bay

Kilkeel
Carlingford
25M

Clogher Head

Skerries

Malahide
Howth
DUBLIN
DOUGLAS
LIVERPOOL
DUN LAOGHAIRE
HOLYHEAD

N

WICKLOW

Arklow

Courtown

A MANX 'NOBBY'

WEXFORD
Rosslare Harbour
WATERFORD
ROSSLARE
Helvick Head
Fethard
Kilmore Quay
FISHGUARD
PEMBROKE
Tramore
Dunmore East
25M
CHERBOURG
ROSCOFF

ATLANTIC 21 CLASS RIGID INFLATABLE

Londonderry

Lough Foyle, the wide sea inlet which leads up to Londonderry, is guarded at its entrance by a Martello Tower on east bank which was built to protect this important commercial shipping base during the Napoleonic Wars. The priority here continues to be commercial maritime activity and there are few places where any facilities for yachts are available. Opposite the Martello Tower, the busy fishing harbour at Greencastle is useful to know about as a port of refuge but is otherwise not really a suitable destination for cruising yachts. Berthing is available at Londonderry, though it is not often used by yachts. Yachting facilities are very limited which is a pity as the town is interesting and has plenty of history to explore. If you wish to visit, a pilot book with comprehensive instructions for cruising in this area is essential. However, to be blunt, there are better options around here, so the smart move is to head west to Lough Swilly or east to Coleraine, where there are plentiful facilities, spectacular coastline and welcoming harbours.

Coleraine and the River Bann

With a population of over 20,000, Coleraine is the economic centre of the area and has good shopping and recreational facilities to match this. The Leisure Centre (☎ 01265 56432) has a swimming pool and water slides for indoor exercise and, nearby, the Jet Centre (☎ 01265 58011) has an ice rink, tenpin bowling and 4-screen cinema should you feel in the mood for a little indoor activity. With first class marina accommodation not far from the centre of the town, this is a very good base to explore the surrounding area as transport links to numerous interesting places are good. If the weather is fine, it is well worth taking advantage of the open-top bus which runs north east from Coleraine to Bushmills and stops at Portstewart, Portrush and the Giant's Causeway. (see Portrush entry for more details on Giant's Causeway & Bushmills Distillery). To the north west near Downhill, you will find the Downhill Castle Estate which consists of splendidly landscaped grounds on a rugged stretch of coastline. The brainchild of Frederick Hervey, Earl of Bristol and Bishop of Derry, the estate was laid out in the late 18th century. Now you will find the ruins of the main house which was largely destroyed by fire in 1851, and the remarkable Mussenden Temple (NT ☎ 01265 848728), a stylish folly perched on the cliff top overlooking the sea. In Downhill itself, Hezlett House (NT ☎ 01265 848567) is one of Ireland's oldest surviving buildings. This delightful thatched house dates from the 17th century, though its contents are largely late-Victorian.

Access to the marina is via the River Bann which winds for about four miles from the coast before reaching Coleraine. The river mouth is not easy in all conditions, so consult your almanac or pilot before attempting it. If you don't wish to go all the way to Coleraine, there is an anchorage not far from the mouth, or another marina, Seatons Marina, a mile before Coleraine, though this is not so handy for the facilities the town has to offer. From Coleraine Marina, you have access to a good range of shops and all the city centre attractions are within about half a mile.

Furthermore, Ramparts Wine Bar (☎ 01265 42550) on Park Street, is a good drinking spot and you can also get food there. In addition, there is the Bull's Eye (☎ 01265 43485) on Lime Street for a drink. For a restaurant meal, the Watermargin at the Balthouse (☎ 01265 52992) on Hanover place, serves Chinese food, or on Castle Roe Road, the Salmons Leap Restaurant (☎ 01265 52992) will look after you well, and is owned by the golfer, Darren Clarke.

Taxi:	A1 Taxis (☎ 01265 51705) or Radio Taxis (☎ 01265 53709)
Car hire:	Avis (☎ 01265 43654) Practical Car Rental (☎ 01265 52800)
Bus:	local services by Ulsterbus (☎ 01265 43334)
Rail:	Coleraine Station for services to Belfast & Londonderry (enquiries ☎ 01232 899411)
Airport:	Belfast Airport (☎ 01849 422888) City of Derry Airport (☎ 01504 810784)

for more details, see Directory Section

Antrim

The stretch of coast which runs round from Portstewart to Belfast Lough is the part of Ireland closest to mainland Britain. It is less than twenty miles from Ireland to the Mull of Kintyre which means you have the choice of an easy hop across the Firth of Clyde and Kilbrannan Sound, or further north to Islay and Gigha. Hardly surprisingly, the tides through this narrow gap can be swift, but as long as you plan carefully, this should be something which you can work to your advantage. The Antrim coast itself has some spectacular scenery, and though you will probably find there are one or two others there, you really must grit your teeth to endure the tourists and visit the Giant's Causeway which is remarkable. The seaside resort of Ballycastle is an attractive destination for the yachtsman, especially as it now has a marina, and the small harbours at Cushendall and Carnlough are ideal spots to find a slightly gentler pace of life.

Portrush

Portrush is a jolly seaside resort town with all the trimmings including big dippers and ghost trains and sandy beaches which stretch for miles and behind these links one finds some outstanding holes of golf if you happen to have your clubs aboard! To go with the ice creams and candy floss, the Dunluce Centre (☎ 01265 824444) is an impressive visitor attraction which includes several "virtual reality experiences". A multi-media theatre show brings the mythology of the north coast of Ireland to life using a combination of big screen, sound systems and moving seating which will give you quite a convincing impression that what you are experiencing is real - a bit like being at sea really so maybe not the ideal tonic! The scenarios include Turbo Tours, Earth Quest and Myths & Legends and it's definitely popular with children. To escape the town, there's an open-top bus service that opens up numerous options for exploring (Ulsterbus ☎ 01232 333000) as it runs along the coast between Portrush and The

Giant's Causeway. For a more relaxed encounter with local history, head along the coast to Dunluce Castle (☎ 012657 31938) which is spectacularly set on a craggy outcrop of cliff overlooking the sea with its roofless gable-ends and chimneys reaching for the sky. Neighbouring Dunluce Old Church is also now a ruin and is supposedly connected to the castle by underground passageway. Here we find a reminder of mariners who found this coast distinctly inhospitable - the graves of sailors from the Spanish Armada who were wrecked on the rocks on the coast. Moving to a far merrier situation at Bushmills, the Distillery (☎ 012657 31521) is the world's oldest whiskey distillery and has been operating since 1609. It's an attractive group of buildings with a guided tour, visitor centre and shops. Without question, the most famous attraction along this stretch of coast is the Giant's Causeway. The curious hexagonal stone columns - over 30,000 of them - have drawn visitors from all over the world to marvel. It is an impressive sight and you'll also find a visitor centre (☎ 012657 31855) with audio visual display, shops and cafeteria. To go for a guided walk, telephone to make a booking (☎ 012657 31159). Portrush Harbour is on the west side of the peninsula and it's accessible at all states of the tide and in most conditions, though it can be a bit awkward in north westerly gales especially when the tide is running east. Pontoon or quayside berths and visitors' moorings are available though this is a small harbour and it can be crowded. Facilities are a little limited, but you can get water and diesel, and there are showers at the Portrush Yacht Club where you will also receive a warm welcome in their bar. A range of local shops including a general store and good butcher are to be found within 400 yards of the harbour and, as this is a popular and cosmopolitan resort town, there is a wide choice of places to head to for a drink or a meal. As well as the bar at the yacht club, the Harbour Bar and the Ramore Wine Bar are good choices for a drink and conveniently close to the harbour. For an inexpensive restaurant meal in the harbour area, the Golden Sands is a good option, and for something a bit smarter, the Ramore Restaurant (☎ 01265 824313) serves excellent food. Slightly further afield, Snappers Restaurant (☎ 01265 824945) in Ballyreagh Road is good for a meal, and pub-wise, Donovan's (☎ 01265 822063) on the Main Street, the bar in the Peninsula Hotel (01265 822933) and McLaughlans Bar (☎ 01265 823509) on Ballyreagh Road are all well worth looking into.

Taxi:	Andy Brown (☎ 01265 822223) or Causeway Coast (☎ 01265 823421)
Car hire:	Coastal Self Drive in nearby Coleraine (☎ 01265 52791)
Rail:	Portrush Station for services to Belfast & Londonderry (enquiries ☎ 01232 899411)
Airport:	Belfast Airport (☎ 01849 422888) City of Derry Airport (☎ 01504 810784)

for more details, see Directory Section,

Ballycastle

Ballycastle is a popular holiday resort and it is set in stunning scenery. With Knocklayd Mountain rising up behind and the impressive 600 foot promontory of Fair

Artist: **Anthony Flemming** **DUNLUCE CASTLE** *Courtesy of:* **The Artist**

Head at the end of the bay to the east, the coastline is spectacular, and there are views out to Rathlin Island a couple of miles offshore. This is an attractive little town, and you can learn about local history and folklore at the Ballycastle Museum (☎ 012657 62024) which is in the 18th century court house. For practical historical inspiration, visit the impressive ruins of Bonmargy Friary which used to be home to members of the Franciscan order and it's definitely worth a trip to the Caririck-a-Rede Rope Bridge (☎ 012657 31159) just up the road at Larrybane. This wobbly walkway links the mainland to a beautiful small island which is popular with fisherman – the flimsy bridge is definitely not for the fainthearted or vertigo-prone as it spans a chasm 80 feet above the sea. If you prefer to let someone else do the navigation, there are boat trips across to Rathlin Island which is a popular spot for bird watching. Guillemots and kittiwakes nest on the cliffs and kestrels and buzzards can often be seen here. With excellent walks along the craggy clifftops and the chance to explore the island's caves and rugged scenery, Rathlin is well worth a visit and there's a pub and restaurant to enable you to restore the tissues after an energetic afternoon exploring or just sailing across. The history and folklore of the island is examined at the Rathlin Island Boat House (☎ 012657 62024).

July 1999 saw the opening of a brand new little marina in Ballycastle Harbour. To approach the harbour, you will need to contend with the tides through Rathlin Sound which can be brisk and, as there are also potentially dangerous overfalls in places, you will need to plan your passage carefully. Fully serviced pontoon berths are available for visitors and there are showers and laundry facilities on site. Shopping for provisions is good here as there are a couple of supermarkets which stay open late as well as a range of local shops. There are numerous pubs to choose from in the town. The House of McDonnell (☎ 0126 5762975) has long historic associations and is a good choice for local flavour, and McCarrolls (☎ 012657 62123) on Ann Street, serves good bar meals, or for traditional Irish music, head to the Central Bar (☎ 012657 63877) in the Town Centre. The Marine (☎ 012657 62222) on North Street is situated on the seafront in a scenic position enjoying excellent views of Fair Head and Rathlin Island, and serves bar lunches and à la carte dinners.

Taxi:	Connor's Taxis (☎ 0126 5763611) or Delarby's Taxis (☎ 012657 62822)
Car hire:	Coleraine is nearest car hire
Bus:	Ulster Bus (☎ 012657 62365)
Rail:	Ballymoney Station (approx 15 miles)
Ferry:	Ballycastle to Rathlin (☎ 012657 69299). Ballycastle to Cambeltown (☎ 012657 69229)
Airport:	Belfast Airport (☎ 01849 422888)

for more details, see Directory Section

Rathlin to Belfast Lough

This is an impressive stretch of coastline consisting of dramatic cliffs and white sandy beaches, and there's a fresh vista behind each headland you pass as glens climb their way up into the hills which provide a panoramic backdrop. Several small harbours provide opportunities for a run ashore along here and there are some wonderful places to go for a stroll. Just over ten miles from Rathlin Island, **Red Bay** is the home of a modern "high-tech" lifeboat station and the Cushendall Sailing and Boating Club. There's space for a couple of visiting yachts alongside the quay and the bar at the sailing club will serve you an excellent pint of Guinness. The town itself is about half a mile away and has a good range of shops including a supermarket, as well as a number of inviting hostelries. Joe McCollans in the Main Street is a good choice for a drink and Harry's (☎ 01266 72022) just along the road serves good pub food. For a more elaborate meal, try the Thornlea Hotel (☎ 01266 71223) or just don't stir from the sailing club as they serve food there as well. Just around the headland, there's an attractive small harbour at **Carnlough**. The white limestone harbour is surrounded by bright buildings, and The Londonderry Arms Hotel (☎ 01574 885255) serves good food made from fresh local produce. After soaking up the tranquillity and the hospitality on offer, you may wish to just make another short hop down the coast, and Larne Lough is less than twenty miles to the south. After the isolation and gentle pace of life in the small harbours to the north, the atmosphere here is rather different. **Larne** is a busy ferry port and there's commercial traffic which serves the cement works and power station as well. There's plenty of life, and a good selection of things to see or do ashore if you need a change from just enjoying the scenery and wildlife. The harbour also provides a good refuge from foul weather and offers easy access in any conditions. For local historical background, the Larne Historical Centre (☎ 01574 279482) is a good start, and there's an illuminating model of the Antrim Coast Road at the Larne Interpretive Centre (☎ 01574 260088). For a slightly different local flavour, visit Maud's Ice Cream (☎ 01574 272387) - a tour of the dairy will take you fifteen minutes and then you can get stuck into the delightful task of sampling the wares. In due course, full marina facilities are planned at Larne, but this will not be for a couple of years. In the meantime, visitors' moorings are available from the East Antrim Boat Club (who you should contact in advance) which is based not far from Olderfleet Castle on Curran Point. At present, facilities are rather limited, or a long way away - roll on the marina! Fuel and provisions can all be found, but you may need to go a couple of miles. You will be made welcome in the bar at the Boat Club, or if you want to head into the centre of town which is about 15 minutes walk away, try Dan Campbell's (☎ 01574 277222) in Bridge Street. Mattie Moors (☎ 01574 583252) in Cairncastle about five miles away is a good choice for pub food, and in Main Street in Larne, either Carriages (☎ 01574 275132) or The Wine Bar also known as 'Checkers' (☎ 01574 275305) will serve you a reasonably priced meal. The High Ways Hotel (☎ 01574 272272) in Ballylorn Road offers the best meals in the area.

In Larne

Taxi:	(☎ 01574 260404)
Car hire:	(☎ 01574 278111)
Bus:	local services from Larne Harbour
Rail:	services from Larne Harbour link to Belfast
Ferry:	services to Cairnryan and Stranraer

Airport: Belfast Airport (☎ 01849 422888)
for more details, see Directory Section

Belfast Lough

The wide expanse of Belfast Lough is a popular sailing area, and a particularly favoured area for the racing fraternity. Well-appointed marinas at both Carrickfergus on the north shore and Bangor on the south are the base for large numbers of local boats, and both provide a good range of facilities for the visiting yachtsman as well. The city of Belfast is connected by rail to both if you wish to visit the capital of Ulster, though you may well find that there is plenty to keep you occupied locally, especially if you put into Bangor.

Carrickfergus

The prospect of Carrickfergus is rather splendid, dominated by Carrickfergus Castle (☎ 01960 351273) which was built by John de Courcy in 1180 to guard the entrance to Belfast Lough and confirm Norman control over the area. The sprawling ramparts surround the determined impregnability of the central tower of this well-preserved Norman castle and provide an historic flavour to the waterfront. Once ashore, you can find out about the history of Carrickfergus from as far back as the 6th century by visiting the Knight Ride (☎ 01960 366455) which combines its exhibition with a monorail ride. More recent industrial heritage can be explored at the Carrickfergus Gasworks (☎ 01960 351438) which was one of the last coal gasworks in Ireland and is open Sunday afternoons in July and August. A trans-Atlantic connection is acknowledged by the Andrew Jackson Centre (☎ 01960 366455). The parents of this notable American President (1829-37) emigrated from Carrickfergus in 1765. Should you wish to reverse this trend and stay a while, you will be pleased to hear that fully serviced pontoon berths and all the usual facilities are available at or near the marina. For provisions, you will find a full range of local shops, and the Co-op and Tescos are both close by. You will be made welcome in the bar at the Carrickfergus Sailing Club which is based on Rodgers Quay by the marina, or try the Windrose (☎ 01960 364192) which is also on Rodgers Quay for a drink or a pub meal. Dobbin's Inn (☎ 01960 351905) is in the centre of town on the High Street and is a good choice for a drink, and for an inexpensive meal head for La Casa Pizzeria (☎ 01960 361399) on Woodburn Road. For the best dining in town, you need to visit the Quality Hotel (☎ 01960 364556) on Belfast Road.

Taxi:	Mahoods (☎ 01960 362727)
Car hire:	Avis (☎ 01574 260799)
Bus:	from town centre to Belfast
Rail:	Carrickfergus Station for services to Belfast and Larne
Airport:	Belfast Airport (☎ 01849 422888)

for more details, see Directory Section

Bangor

Bangor is a prosperous town and it presents an elegant façade of attractive terraces which include shops, hotels and restaurants looking down over its sheltered harbour. The town blossomed in Victorian times when it became a popular holiday destination, and has been a favourite spot for the wealthier citizens of Belfast to set up home, away from the city centre, ever since. The harbour is the focus of the town and is now almost exclusively given over to the marina which has over

Artist: **Anthony Flemming** **BELFAST DOCK** *Courtesy of:* **The Artist**

500 berths. Not all the local residents were thrilled when the council decided to re-develop the harbour area as a marina, but as far as the yachtsman is concerned, this was an excellent move. As town centre marinas go, this one is hard to beat as there are good facilities close to hand, plenty of things to do ashore, and an attractive outlook from your cockpit to boot. For historical background, the North Down Heritage Centre (☎ 01247 271200) at Bangor Castle gives a good flavour of the town's development. Five miles west of Bangor, the Ulster Folk and Transport Museum (☎ 01232 428428) has an astonishing collection of preserved buildings, many of which have been reconstructed on site stone by stone, as well as a comprehensive exhibition of Irish Railways material. Just along the road from here, the Crawfordsburn Country Park (☎ 01247 853627) is a good place to go for a stroll through landscaped grounds, and the Park centre has an exhibition on various aspects of the natural history of the park. The restored gun emplacement on Grey Point has good views over the lough - it will take you about an hour to walk there and back. The Pickie Family Fun Park (☎ 01247 274430) is right next to the marina for train rides and swan pedal boats which will delight the children and adults with a penchant for oversized birds! The Museum of Childhood (☎ 01247 471915) in Central Avenue in the middle of town, has a collection of toys, books and clothes which is probably of more interest to "grown-up" children. Access to the marina is very straightforward and all facilities are available on site. The Flagship Shopping Centre is conveniently close to the marina for stocking up on provisions, and there are numerous other local shops and boutiques. There is a considerable choice of places to go for a drink or a meal ashore. Visiting yachtsmen are welcome to use the bar and restaurant at the elegant premises of the Royal Ulster Yacht Club just east of the marina and Donegans Bar (☎ 01247 270362) at 44 High Street is a good choice for a drink and serves meals as well. Just along the road at number 37-9, McElhill's Restaurant (☎ 01247 463928) serves good food in an informal atmosphere or closer to the marina, The Steamer Bar and Restaurant (☎ 01247 467699) serves meals which won't break the bank. The Royal Hotel (☎ 01247 271866) on Quay Street has an excellent restaurant, The Quays Restaurant, for a smart evening ashore and a brace of popular bars for more informal socialising on the waterfront.

Taxi:	(☎ 01247 446466), (☎ 01247 454545), (☎ 01247 451333)
Car hire:	(☎ 01247 271535)
Bus:	local services by Ulsterbus (☎ 01247 271143)
Rail:	Bangor Station for services to Belfast and the rest of Ireland, enquiries (☎ 01232 899411)
Airport:	Belfast Airport (☎ 01849 422888)

for more details, see Directory Section

Down

Stretching south from Belfast Lough, the Ards Peninsula encloses the splendid inland cruising area of Strangford Lough. It's fifty miles from Bangor to Strangford just inside the Lough which is a good day's sailing given a favourable wind and following tide, or you may prefer to break your journey on the way. To the south of Strangford Lough, there is wonderful mountainous scenery and some inviting little harbours to ease you on your way to Carlingford Lough and the border. Another option to consider is a hop across to the Isle of Man as Peel Harbour on the north west coast is only about 50 miles away.

Belfast Lough to Strangford Lough

There's a small marina close to an attractive harbour built of Welsh granite at Donghadee. Access to Copelands Marina is tricky and also constrained by the tide. Furthermore, there's not much space here, so check to see that they can accommodate you in advance. Grace Neill's (☎ 01247 882553) is a popular local hostelry and is thought to be the oldest pub in Ireland. To stock up on fresh fish for a slap-up feast aboard, you should put into Portavogie which is an important fishing harbour. At weekends, there is not much space, if any, for yachts, but during the week there should be room for a short stay.

Strangford Lough

Strangford Lough is a magnificent sheltered cruising area which stretches for about twenty miles inland. It is a Marine Nature Reserve of great beauty and is classed as an area of Special Scientific Interest. With 365 islands, one for every day of the year, eleven yacht clubs which offer a warm welcome to visitors and a host of superb restaurants and inns, there will be plenty to keep you occupied for as long as you have to spend here, and there are numerous places of interest where you can find out about local history and culture. The entrance can be tricky as the currents can run very swiftly, so you will need to consult your almanac or pilot book to get the timing right for your passage through the Strangford Narrows. Not for nothing did the Vikings dub this "Strong Waters". At the head of the Narrows, the villages of Strangford and Portaferry straddle the channel and offer a reasonable range of facilities and scope for an enjoyable run ashore. Behind Strangford, you may notice Castle Ward (NT ☎ 01396 881204) which is a bizarre 18th century mansion which has two very different facades. The east front is classical and the west is Gothic; this was a compromise between the owner and his wife in order to accommodate their contrasting tastes - a splendid example to all about the good old compromise and a handy place to visit if the wife's contemplating a little interior design work back at home. The grounds are magnificent and there are views out over Strangford Lough. While you are in the area, it's worth seeking out the Cuan Restaurant & Bars (☎ 01396 881222). This is a fine shore-side establishment at Strangford village which also provides visitors' moorings. Facilities for visiting yachts are probably most comprehensive in Portaferry on the other side of the channel. The Portaferry Yacht Haven offers fully serviced pontoon berths, and showers are available at the Portaferry Yacht Club's premises close by. Alternatively, you might prefer to pick up one of the visitors' moorings provided by the Portaferry Hotel (☎ 012477 28231).

There's a reasonable supermarket, a range of local shops and a launderette within a couple of hundred yards of the yacht haven, and the Exploris Aquarium (☎ 012477 28062) provides an interesting diversion and claims to be the largest aquarium of its kind in Europe. A good spot for a drink here is Fiddlers Green on Church Street a couple of hundred yards from the pontoons, and The Slip Inn on The Strand is even closer and serves good pub meals. For an inexpensive restaurant meal, try The Narrows (☎ 012477 28148) which is a family run restaurant on Shore Road, or for something a bit more upmarket, the Portaferry Hotel on The Strand serves good food and has a comfortable bar.

From Portaferry
Taxi: S O'Neill (☎ 01247 728771),
            Kieron Donelly (evenings and weekends
            only) (☎ 01247 28771)
            mobile (☎ 0780 3018216)
Car hire: Newtown Aras (☎ 01247 814443)
Bus: local services by Ulsterbus
Rail: Bangor Station
Ferry: between Portaferry and Strangford
            every half an hour
Airport: Belfast Airport (☎ 01849 422888)
for more details, see Directory Section

Artist: **Anthony Flemming EARLY MORNING**
Courtesy of: **The Artist**

Heading up the Lough, you will find the pilotage interesting as you weave your way between the islands and there's a good anchorage just off Kircubbin on the east shore. The Kircubbin Sailing Club can let you have a shower, and their bar is open on Sundays. There's a good range of local shops within easy walking distance in the village, and The Villager is a good pub for a drink. This is a good base to explore some of the surrounding area, and just up the road is Greyabbey (☎ 012477 88585) where there is a ruined abbey and medieval 'physick garden'. Further up towards the head of the lough, Mount Stewart House (NT ☎ 012477 88387) near Newtownards is a good destination to sail to. This fine 18th century house was the childhood home of Lord Castlereagh (1769-1822) who played a major role in Westminster politics and foreign affairs during the period of the Napoleonic Wars. The house is set in very fine formal gardens which enjoy superb vistas and contain plants from all over the world. At the head of the lough, if you climb the tower in the Scrabo

Country Park (☎ 01247 820445) at Newtownards you get fine views over the lough and there's an exhibition about the surrounding countryside.

Opposite Mount Stewart, there are good anchorages around Mahee Island and the ruins of Mahee Castle and Nendrum Monastery make for an historic setting. There's a museum at the Nendrum site where the ruins include the remains of a round tower and walls dating back to the 12th century. Just to the north at the Castle Espie Centre (☎ 01247 874146), you will find a nature reserve which include wetlands for ducks, geese and swans and there are public hides for viewing and a coffee shop. Neighbouring Sketrick Island offers a good range of facilities as it's the home of the Strangford Lough Yacht Club and the Down Cruising Club both of which will greet you hospitably and there's a boatyard here as well. Towards the southern end of the west shore, the village of Killyleagh is well worth making for. The centrepiece is Killyleagh Castle (☎ 01396 828261) which is a picturesque 17th century building and tours are available by appointment. Contact the Killyleagh Yacht Club for moorings here, and a good destination for a run ashore is the Dufferin Arms Coaching Inn (☎ 01396 828229) by the castle where you will find good food, local music and a warm atmosphere. It's ten minutes' walk from the moorings at the yacht club, or the pub staff can collect you and presumably roll you back down if required. Not far down the road, the Delamont Country Park (☎ 01396 828333) is a tranquil spot for a stroll in the gardens and a visit to the heronry, and there's a tea room for refreshments as well. The south west arm of the lough stretches towards Downpatrick up the Quoile River. There is berthing alongside at the Quoile Yacht Club which is a good base for land based excursions to a number of places of interest. The Quoile Countryside Centre (☎ 01396 615520) combines a national nature reserve and a ruined 16th century castle. In Saul nearby the church commemorates St Patrick's arrival in Ireland. The exhibition is open till 6 p.m. and if you are feeling energetic, climb to the top of the hill where there is a huge granite statue of St Patrick and the views are tremendous. While you are in the area, you ought to visit Downpatrick where you will find the Down County Museum (☎ 01396 615218). Located in the former gaol it includes the St Patrick Heritage Centre and, at Downpatrick Cathedral (☎ 01396 614922), a stone marks the spot in the graveyard where St Patrick is thought to have been buried.

From Quoile and Downpatrick
Taxi: Downpatrick Taxis (☎ 01396 612958)
Car hire: C McKeown (☎ 01396 613055)
Bus: local services by Ulsterbus
Rail: Belfast Station (25 miles)
Airport: Belfast Airport (☎ 01849 422888) (25 miles)
for more details, see Directory Section

Ardglass

Pressing on down the coast from the entrance to Strangford Lough it's not far to our next port of call. The fine natural harbour at Ardglass meant that once upon a time this was the busiest fishing port in Ulster. This position has now been usurped by more modern harbours, but it is still a splendidly sheltered haven and is a useful staging post on one's way up or down the coast. For a flavour of local history, Jordan's Castle is a well preserved tower house which is open to the public and, for something a little different, the Sheepland Open Farm (☎ 01396 842268) just up the road is interesting. Its attractions include pet lambs (in season!) and other livestock and an exhibition of farming implements. Access to the harbour is straightforward and there is space for visiting yachts at the Phennick Cove Marina which was opened in 1996. This small yacht haven has space for visitors on fully serviced pontoons and many facilities are available, though bear in mind that this is a small place and the marina is quite new so don't expect a town centre experience.

Dundrum Bay

With the soft green curves of the Mountains of Mourn, which climb to nearly 3,000 feet, to the west providing a scenic setting, there are a couple of options here for small boats and those who can cope with shallow waters or don't mind taking the ground. The entrance to **Dundrum Harbour** is fairly complicated and you will need a good pilot book such as the Irish Cruising Club Sailing Directions to find your way in here. Dundrum Castle, poised on a hill opposite the entrance, was built in 1177 and had a violent existence until it was destroyed by Oliver Cromwell's troops in 1649 - it is open to the public most days. For more tranquil reflection, the magnificent and ancient sand dunes to the south of the entrance to the harbour form the Murlough National Nature Reserve where a wide variety of plant and bird-life thrives. At the south end of

Dundrum Bay, the small resort town of **Newcastle** nestles at the foot of the mountains and is a popular holiday destination. The small harbour which dries is only accessible for three hours each side of high water, and is only really suitable for visiting yachts in settled weather. Having said that, this is an idyllic spot so, if conditions allow, it's well worth popping into. If you have your walking boots aboard, there are excellent opportunities to enjoy the countryside and mountains and you'll find some good hostelries to enjoy once you have built up a thirst and an appetite. Once again there's terrific golf as well so pack those plus fours.

There are a couple of visitors' mooring buoys and space for a few visiting yachts alongside the quay. Facilities are limited – fuel can be ordered and you need to prevail on the good nature of the proprietors of the hotel to get a shower. However, there is a good range of local shops for provisions within a few minutes walk. The Harbour House Inn (☎ 013967 23445) on the South Promenade has a welcoming bar and serves inexpensive pub food. A handy alternative for a meal is The Stone Boat (☎ 013967 24118) which is just next to the harbour or, for the best in the area, it's only a couple of hundred yards to Marios (☎ 013967 23912) further along the South Promenade.

Taxi:	(☎ 013967 71404), (☎ 013967 24100), (☎ 013967 26030)
Car hire:	from Clough, Paul McKibben (☎ 01396 811679)
Bus:	local services by Ulsterbus, enquiries (☎ 013967 22296)
Rail:	from Newry Station (30 miles)

Artist: **Anthony Flemming ESTUARY** *Courtesy of:* **The Artist**

Airport: Belfast Airport (☎ 01849 422888) (30 miles)
for more details, see Directory Section

Carlingford Lough

With the Mountains of Mourn running down to its north shore and Carlingford Mountain to the south, the long inlet of Carlingford Lough provides a variety of sheltered anchorages, and there are several places where you can lie alongside pontoons. The lough forms part of the border between Northern Ireland and its southern neighbour, and while this should not cause undue difficulties for the visitor, customs formalities do need to be observed. Also be prepared for the possibility that the authorities just might wish to know who you are and what you are up to. The entrance is guarded by the ruins of an Anglo-Norman fortress on the north bank at Greencastle Point (☎ 01232 235000) and, further up the lough, you reach the atmospheric little town of Carlingford itself. Here there are plenty of historic buildings, though there is not much sign of some of the thirty-two fortifications which the town apparently once boasted. The ruins of King John's Castle, so named after his visit in 1210, dominate the waterfront to the north of the harbour and 15th century Taafe's Castle stands sentinel over the harbour itself. This is another popular holiday destination and the attractions of the area include its scenery for walking and wildlife and the profusion of historic sites. At Warrenpoint at the head of the lough, a little local cultural flavour can be found at the Burren Heritage Centre (☎ 016937 73378), and a couple of miles up the river, you come to Narrow Water Castle (☎ 01232 23500) in its scenic setting overlooking the narrows at the mouth of the river. It's best to ring first to check when it will be open if you would like a look around.

In strong southerlies, the lough can be affected by uncomfortable squalls and, in onshore winds, the entrance may be impassable. Furthermore, the currents in the entrance can be brisk and it's worth bearing in mind that if you miss the tide or conditions are unsuitable there is shelter for small boats at the busy fishing harbour of Kilkeel a few miles to the north east. At Kilkeel, consult the harbour-master on arrival for instructions on where you can berth. You will find a good selection of boating facilities, though for provisions and refreshment it's a bit of a hike to the town which is nearly a mile away. Once through the entrance to Carlingford Lough, navigation should present few difficulties, though be warned that there is quite a lot of commercial traffic using the dredged channel up the centre to reach Warrenpoint at the head of the lough. Pontoon berthing for visitors is available at Carlingford Marina where there are reasonable facilities and the centre of the town for shopping is only ten minutes walk away. There are also pontoons as well as visitors' moorings at Warrenpoint where you will also find that the shopping is more convenient and comprehensive. If you anchor off and take your tender ashore, you will be given a warm welcome at the Carlingford Lough Yacht Club which is on the north shore near Killowan Point and, just to the west, Rostrevor is an attractive little town where you will find a reasonable range of shops for provisions. Again, you will need to anchor off. . . and don't try to

get ashore at low water – you will find it much easier if you wait for a bit. If it is a restaurant meal you are after, Kilboney Restaurant (☎ 016937 38134) will serve you a decent meal. As for liquid refreshment, O'Neils Bar, is a good spot to rest a while, it should not be too hard to find as it is in The Square. A bit more in the way of choice awaits you in Warrenpoint, where Diamonds Restaurant (☎ 016937 52053) is good for a meal as is the more relaxed Duke Bar and Restaurant (☎ 016937 52084) . Other places to try include, The Marine Bar and Night Club (☎ 016937 53227) Shenanigans Bar, (☎ 016937 53743) Jack Ryan's Bar and Restaurant and for a taste of Italy, you need look no further than Vecchi Roma (☎ 016937 52082)

From Warrenpoint
Taxi: Ace Taxis (☎ 016937 52666),
               AV Taxis (☎ 016937 73966)
Car hire: From nearby Newry - Autotex
               Rent a Car (☎ 01693 838173)
Bus: Ulster Bus Company (☎ 013967 22296)
Rail: From nearby Newry Station, Irish Rail
               enquiries (☎ 0183 6622)
Airport: Belfast Airport (☎ 01849 422888)
for more details, see Directory Section

Dublin

The area around Dublin is a popular one for yachting and there are several places to put in where you will find comprehensive facilities and a warm welcome. After the shortage of havens between here and Carlingford Lough, a run ashore and a shower will probably be most welcome, and there are places of interest to visit and, if you feel the need to regain your land legs, fine countryside for a gentle stroll or invigorating walk.

Malahide

In sight of the Howth Peninsula to the south and with the picturesque Isle of Lambay just to the north, Malahide is set on a long estuary with sandy beaches just to the north of Dublin. This was where the Scandinavian kings who once held control of this area had their summer palace and the town continues to attract people for summer recreation. A slightly more recent historic house is Malahide Castle (☎ 01 846 2516) which was the home of the Talbot family for nearly 800 years until 1976 when it was sold to Dublin County Council. With a 14th century tower, 15th century Great Hall and reception rooms dating from the 18th century, there is a spectacular mix of styles to admire and the portrait collection of the National Gallery of Ireland is also housed here. The grounds, which extend to 270 acres, include the Talbot Botanical Gardens which contain over 5000 different varieties of plants and, in the castle courtyard, the Fry Model Railway Exhibition (☎ 01 846 3779) is one of the most extensive in Europe. For the historic house fan, this area is a bit of a paradise as, just one stop up the railway, you can visit Newbridge House (☎ 01 843 6534) as well. Set in attractive woodlands, this is a fine Georgian house with many original furnishings and interesting collections of paintings, silver and porcelain. For the big city experience, Dublin is just 25 minutes away by train and there is an endless amount to see and do there. (In Dublin, The Guinness in the Shelbourne is a rare treat and if you can book a table at the Unicorn ☎ 01 676 2182 - it's sensational.) Accommodation for visiting yachts is at the ever-expanding Malahide Marina which offers fully serviced pontoon berths and all facilities ashore including a bar and restaurant. The dredged channel which allows access to the marina is subject to change and so it is worth checking with the marina for the latest details about the approach. Once you are safely moored up, the centre of town is a short walk away for a comprehensive range of local shops including a supermarket and plenty of restaurants for a meal ashore. For a drink, you will be made welcome at the Malahide Yacht Club which is open every evening except Monday and from mid-afternoon at the weekend. For local atmosphere, head for Gibneys Traditional Irish pub (☎ 01 845 0606) on New Street where you can get good bar food as well, and, for an excellent restaurant meal, try Les Visages Restaurant (☎ 01 845 1233) in Marine Court.

Taxi:	Malahide Cabs (☎ 01 845 5555)
Car hire:	Malahide Cars (☎ 01 845 2554)
Bus:	services to Dublin city centre and airport
Rail:	services to Dublin and Belfast
Airport:	Dublin Airport (☎ 01 844 4900)

for more details, see Directory Section

Howth

Set on its peninsula which in ancient times was an island, just about wherever you are in Howth you will find a sea view. Still very much commercially involved in the sea with an active fishing fleet, the harbour also offers separate marina accommodation exclusively for the use of yachts. There are undemanding walks along the clifftops to the south and a visit to the National Transport Museum (☎ 01 848 0831) next to Howth Castle on the hill is an alternative way to while away a relaxed afternoon. For more excitement, a short train ride on the Dart takes you into Dublin where there are numerous places of interest and plenty of lively places for a meal or a drink. There is a good range of facilities provided at the Howth Yacht Club Marina and the staff are friendly and helpful. A useful general store and selection of local shops can be found within a couple of hundred yards and there's a supermarket just over half a mile away. The bar in the Yacht Club is open daily, and meals are available in the dining room for lunch or dinner on most days. For café meals, Dee Gee's (☎ 01 839 2641) opposite the railway station is handy and, for an inexpensive restaurant meal, try Casa Pasta (☎ 01 839 3823) opposite the Yacht Club on Harbour Road. For something a little more upmarket, Adrian's (☎ 01 839 1696) on Abbey Street is a good bet, or for excellent seafood, head for the King Sitric (☎ 01 832 5235) on the East Pier. If you are looking for a smart hotel dinner ashore or lunch, The Carvery Restaurant at the Saint Lawrence Hotel (☎ 01 832 2643) is a good option and there are several bars and a nightclub here as well for those in the mood for a bit of a boogie!

Taxi:	S. McConkey (☎ 01 832 2104 or 2836) or Village Cabs (☎ 01 832 1222)
Car hire:	Kennings (☎ 01 677 2723)
Bus:	services to Dublin city centre
Rail:	local services to Dublin city centre. enquiries Irish Rail (☎ 01 836 6222)
Ferry:	from Dublin to Isle of Man & Liverpool, Stena (☎ 01 204 7777), Irish Ferries (☎ 01 661 0511)
Airport:	Dublin Airport (☎ 01 844 4900)

for more details, see Directory Section

Dublin Bay and Dun Laoghaire

As the main docks in Dublin are busy with commercial traffic, yachts are not encouraged unless they are too big for Dun Laoghaire (pronounced Leary) Harbour which is a couple of miles to the south east. Dun Laoghaire is also a busy ferry port, but with four yacht clubs based here as well, this is a major yachting centre and visiting yachts will be made to feel very welcome. Transport links to Dublin are good, so you needn't feel deprived of the opportunity to visit Ireland's capital. Once just a small fishing village, the town became a significant route for trade in the 18th century and its seafaring role makes it an apt location for the National Maritime Museum of Ireland (☎ 01280 0969). It is located in the Mariners Church which is close to the southern corner of the harbour. There is material relating to the RNLI here as well as paintings, photographs and ship models including one of a Guinness barge. A French longboat captured after an invasion attempt in Bantry Bay in 1796 and a cannon from the Spanish Armada are among the centrepieces of the collection. Just to the south of the town, a Martello Tower on the coast is the home of the James Joyce Museum (☎ 01280 9265) which celebrates the life and work of one of Ireland's most eminent men of letters with a collection of the great man's personal effects and papers. The view from here makes it worth the trip even if literature is not your thing! The countryside around the town is attractive and ideal for a bracing walk, and if you fancy a slightly more urban flavour, then Dublin's city centre is only a twenty minute train journey away on the Dart.

Facilities for visiting yachts are good, and may well be about to get better as plans are afoot to build a 500 berth marina at the harbour though this will not be in place until 2002 at the earliest. Meanwhile, visiting yachts are most welcome to berth on the pontoons which belong to the Royal St George Yacht Club and the National Yacht Club, both of which are located in the southern corner of the harbour. It's worth letting them know in advance if you plan to put in here, or you can call them on the VHF (Ch. 37) as you approach. The National Yacht Club is slightly nearer to the Maritime Museum, and the Dun Laoghaire Shopping Centre and the Dart Station are only a couple of hundred yards away. Facilities available at both of these clubs include fuel and water, showers, bars and restaurants. To try out the town itself, a trip to the top floor of Dun Laoghaire shopping centre will bring you by the way of the Barrels pub (☎ 01 2846595) or, in the curiously named, Dun Laoghaire Olds, the Purty Kitchen (☎ 01 2843576) is a good place for a drink. You might also like to try Dunphy's (☎ 01 2801668). There are several good places to eat at in the town; Morels Bistro (☎ 01 2300210) on Glasthule Road; the Brasserie Na Mara (☎ 01 2806767) on Harbour Road; the Powerscourt Restaurant (☎ 01 2801911) and the Cafe au Lait (☎ 01 2804855) will all serve you a meal to satisfy the hunger built up by a day at sea.

Taxi:	Afe Taxis (☎ 01 284 4444)
	Cab Charge (☎ 01 454 4070)
Car hire:	County Car Rentals (☎ 01 235 2030)
Bus:	Dublin Bus (☎ 01 873 4222)
Rail:	Irish Rail enquiries (☎ 01 873 6622)
Ferry:	Stena Line (☎ 0990 707070)
Airport:	Dublin Airport (☎ 01 844 4900)

for more details, see Directory Section

Wicklow

Fine mountainous scenery gives good views as you cruise along this stretch of coastline and the harbours at Wicklow and Arklow are both inviting prospects for some shore leave.

Wicklow

Set in front of the fine backdrop given by the Wicklow Mountains and located at the mouth of the Leitrim River, Wicklow has been a maritime centre since the Danish Vikings established a port here in the 9th century. This is a busy shopping town, and there are also several places of historical interest to explore. The ruins of Black Castle, which was built in the 12th century, stand guard over the harbour to the south and provide a good spot to admire the views over the town and surrounding countryside. The harbour front offers a pleasing tree lined prospect and this is an attractive and bustling town to put into.

For berthing, there are a number of options. Probably the most convenient option is to moor alongside the East Pier and you will find you don't have to go far for most facilities you might need; or contact the Wicklow Sailing Club who may be able to let you have a mooring. Shops for provisions are within easy reach and there is a good choice of places for a meal or a drink ashore. Starting on the Main Street, Phil Healy's Pub (☎ 0404 67380) will set you up with good Irish atmosphere, or The Old Forge (☎ 0404 67032) in the same street, is both a pub and a restaurant. In the Market Square, The Old Court Inn (☎ 0404 67680) is a decent pub and near by The Opera House (☎ 0404 66422) will satisfy your appetite. Two more suggestions include The Bakery (☎ 0404 66770) on Church Street, and the pub The Bridge Tavern (☎ 0404 67718) on Bridge Street. Not far away for great craic in a very popular pub, Quinns Bar (☎ 0508 81266) on the Main Street in Baltinglass, is decorated with old horse racing memorabilia and serves excellent food, providing an excellent place to enjoy a drink.

Taxi:	Reid's Taxis (☎ 040 67671),
	Coffey's Taxis (☎ 0404 68341)
Car hire:	(☎ 0404 67212)
Bus:	Bus Eireann (☎ 01836 6111)
Rail:	Wicklow Station (☎ 0404 67329)
Airport:	Dublin Airport (☎ 01 844 4900)

for more details, see Directory Section

Arklow

The coastline between Wicklow and Arklow 15 miles to the south is unspoiled and offers a delightful scenic backdrop to a gentle day's sailing along the coast. Established in 1824, Arklow can lay claim to having one of the oldest lifeboat stations in the British Isles. There is a new lifeboat house, and the crew is always happy to show visitors around and let you see the Trent class lifeboat. The town combines its roles of being an important fishing port and a popular seaside resort and is steeped in history as well. This was the scene of a famous battle during the Rising of 1798, and a statue and monument stand in the town centre to commemorate the event. The town's Maritime Museum (☎ 0402 32868) has an interesting collection of exhibits which relate to both local and national maritime history. Perhaps the most famous boat to be built here was Gypsy Moth III which took Francis Chichester around the world in 1967. This is a good base for exploring some of the most attractive scenery in Ireland and Gleddalough with its lakes and round tower is within easy reach. The Wicklow Way offers the chance of some exercise and excellent views, and the Vale of Avoca, which may be familiar to those who have seen the TV series Ballykissangel, is only six miles away. Access to the harbour is straightforward except when the wind is strong from the south and south east, and there are quayside berths for visitors which the harbour-master can direct you to. A good range of facilities is available at the quayside, and you can get a shower at the lifeboat house. Alternatively, you may like to head up river a bit to the Arklow Yacht Club on the east bank where there is limited space for visitors on moorings or alongside their jetty. The club is only open a couple of evenings a week, but when it is, you will be welcome to use their bar and showers. For provisions, a full range of shops, including supermarkets which are open 7 days a week, can be found within 10 minutes' walk and within the same distance, you will find plenty of places for a drink or a meal. The Westwood Lounge (☎ 0402 39565) on Main Street is a good choice for a drink, and the 19 Arches (☎ 0402 31076) on Lower Main Street serves good pub meals. The Riverwalk Restaurant (☎ 0402 31657) on Riverbank will serve you an inexpensive meal, though for something a little more upmarket, you might want to try An Ostan Beag (☎ 0402 33044) on Main Street. The best in town is Kitty's Restaurant (☎ 0402 31669) which is just before you get to An Ostan Beag.

Taxi:	(☎ 0402 33600) or (☎ 0402 32560)
Cycle hire:	Blacks Cycles (☎ 0402 31898) or
	John Caulfield (☎ 0402 32284)
Bus:	services to Dublin and Rosslare
Rail:	Arklow Station for services to Dublin and Rosslare
Ferry:	to Wales and France from Rosslare
Airport:	Dublin Airport (☎ 01 844 4900)

for more details, see Directory Section

Wexford

Your options for convenient ports of call between Arklow and Waterford round the corner on the south coast are a little limited. The entrance at **Wexford** is dis-

couragingly tricky, and facilities once inside are limited, but it is an attractive spot if you have a good pilot book to guide you in. **Rosslare Harbour** just to the south is a handy refuge if the weather becomes unkind, but it's a busy commercial and ferry port and does not offer particularly helpful facilities for yachts. As you round the headland at Carnsore Point, the scenery starts to change and you are in for some spectacular coastline. There's a handy but small marina at **Kilmore Quay** where limited facilities are available. This is a charming little fishing village with old world atmosphere and a retired lightship moored in the harbour serves as a Maritime Museum (☎ 053 29655) whose collection includes a splendid five foot model of HMS Africa, sister ship to Nelson's HMS Victory. Make tracks to the Wooden House (☎ 053 99804) for a drink in historic surroundings.

Waterford

It's well worth spending a few days exploring around here, even if you are anxious to get to the renowned cruising waters around Cork Harbour and beyond. There is some lovely countryside, and the network of rivers which wind their way inland from Watermouth Harbour offers the opportunity for sheltered cruising to get a change from open horizons.

Waterford Harbour

The estuary of the Rivers Barrow and Suir opens up a sheltered cruising area which takes you through the Wexford and Waterford countryside and offers a number of places to anchor or moor. On the west shore at the entrance, the fishing village of **Dunmore East** has a Breton quality to its architecture and includes a number of thatched cottages. The harbour is very much geared towards its commercial users, and is not overly welcoming to yachts. If you contact the Waterford Harbour Sailing Club, you may be able to pick up a vacant mooring or space might be available in the harbour itself on the West Quay. Contact the sailing club if you would like a shower, and the shops are close to the harbourfront for you to top up with provisions. Sailing on up the estuary, the shoreline is punctuated with castles from Slade Castle on the promontory at the entrance to 16th century Duncannon Fort (☎ 051 389454) and Ballyhack Castle (☎ 051 389468) built by the Knights Templar in the mid 15th century. The River Suir is navigable all the way to the town of **Waterford** which is of course famed for its crystal glassware. Factory tours are available (☎ 051 73311). With a population of 40,000, this is one of the biggest towns in the area, and boasts a suitable range of places of entertainment and several museums which explore the history of the town and the significant role of Viking settlers in the area. On the waterfront at the end of Custom House Parade, Reginald's Tower was built by the Vikings in 1003 and is now the City Museum (☎ 051 71227). Close by in Greyfriar's Street, the Heritage Centre (☎ 051 71227) has a collection of Viking and medieval relics which have been discovered locally. A pontoon is available for berthing in the town centre by Reginald's Tower which places you conveniently close to the city's shopping centre.

The City Arms (☎ 051 872220) in Arundel Square, is a wonderfully warm, charming Victorian pub with a wide variety of really good food which ranges from bar snacks to an à la carte menu, thus catering for all price ranges. Other really good pubs include Egans (☎ 051 875619) on Barronstrand Street, which draws customers of all ages with good food and music. (The pub becomes a nightclub on Fridays and Saturdays.) The Olde Stand (☎ 051 879488) on Michael Street is right in the heart of the city and provides a choice of three bars, and there's an excellent seafood and steak restaurant upstairs. This is definitely one to visit. Restaurants and Bistros are easily as numerous as the bars and pubs in Waterford. On The Quay, The New Ship Restaurant at Dooley's Hotel (☎ 051 873531) is a pleasant family affair which caters for all tastes. The Barden's Restaurant at Jury's Hotel (☎ 051 832111) at Ferrybank, enjoys splendid views of Waterford and has great cuisine on offer, while at the Waterfront Restaurant and Bar at The Marina (☎ 051 856600) on Canada Street, you can enjoy bar lunches or smarter à la carte dining in the evening in a fantastic waterside setting. For something a little more cosmopolitan, Cafe Luna (☎ 051 843539) on John's Street, is a twilight continental cafe for lots of coffee and hot and cold sandwiches. Another cafe option, Sui Sios (☎ 051 841063) on the High Street, also has a wide choice of tea, coffee and light meals.

There's a good anchorage just above the ferry ramp at Ballyhack where waterfront houses huddle around the castle, and from here, a good excursion is to head across to the spectacular ruins of Tintern Abbey (☎ 051 397124), a daughter house of Tintern in Monmouthshire. Quench your thirst on your return at Byrne's Bar (☎ 051 389107) before rejoining your boat or heading to the well-respected Neptune Restaurant (☎ 051 389284) by the castle. If you are feeling intrepid, the River Barrow is narrow but navigable to **New Ross** - the railway bridge across the mouth will be opened on request. The Mariners Inn (☎ 051 421325) on The Quay serves bar meals all day and more formal meals can be had at the Galley Cruising Restaurant (☎ 051 421723) and John V's Gourmet Restaurant (☎ 051 425188) which are also on The Quay.

Dungarvan Bay

With the Drum Hills to the south and Monavullagh and Comeragh Mountains to the north, Dungarvan Bay enjoys a scenic setting. There are two harbours here which may be of interest to the visiting yachtsman, but you will need large-scale charts or instructions from a comprehensive pilot book. **Helvick Harbour** is a busy commercial fishing harbour and there is not much room for yachts, though it might provide a good overnight break while on passage if you don't mind lying alongside fishing vessels. As ever, it's worth checking to find out if they plan to go to sea during the night and being prepared to move accordingly. Alternatively, in settled weather, you can anchor west of Helvick Pier but watch out for rocks and drying patches. There's a good pub half a mile from the pier, and fuel and a supermarket are about a mile and a half away. Along the bay, **Dungarvon** is a bustling town with a cinema and museum (☎ 058 41231) which specialises in maritime material with a particular focus on shipwrecks. King John's Castle was built around the turn of the 13th century and is a good place to admire the views. Dungarvan Town Quay is accessible to those who don't mind taking the ground, and note that the channel, which dries almost completely at low water, shifted considerably in 1996. Berthing is alongside the Dungarvon Harbour Sailing Club pontoon at the quayside where you will dry out in deep mud. Visitors are very welcome and may use the clubhouse's facilities – there's a bar and showers. A full range of shops is close to the quayside, and there are restaurants to suit all sizes of wallets.

Before moving into the town itself, the Davitt's Quay offers amongst others, pubs like The Anchor Bar (☎ 058 41249) which overlooks the harbour and serves lunch from Monday to Friday, or the Interlude Bistro (☎ 058 45898) which has a cafe, wine bar and bistro all in one, and serves lunch all day and opens for evening meals on Thursdays, Fridays and Saturdays. Moving on up to Dungarvon itself, Bridie Dee's (☎ 058 44688) on Mary Street in the town centre, is reputed to be one of the

town's oldest pubs, while on the Main Street, Downey's Bar (☎ 058 42993) is good if you are after a lively atmosphere. Merry's (☎ 058 41974) also on Main Street, is a pleasant old style restaurant and pub with plenty of music and traditional Irish food - fresh seafood is a speciality. If you are still left wanting, try O'Connell Street and Gratton Square for more good pubs and restaurants.

Taxi:	Fahey's (☎ 0584 4688),
	Noel Murray (☎ 0584 3495)
Car hire:	In nearby Clonmel, Donal Ryan Car Hire
	(☎ 0522 9777)
Bus:	Bus Eireann (☎ 021 508188)
Rail:	Waterford Station
Airport:	Cork Airport (☎ 021 327 1555)

for more details, see Directory Section

Artist: **Steven Dews** ***TWO YACHTS RACING*** *Courtesy of:* **Rosenstiel's**

COLERAINE
55.10'5N 06.46'.5W

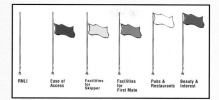

Lionel Duddy: Harbourmaster
Tel: 028 7034 2012 Fax: 028 7035 2000
VHF Channel: 12
VHF Name: Coleraine Harbour Radio

Coleraine Marina Tel: 028 7034 4768

Seaton Marina Tel: 028 7083 2086

Coleraine Yacht Club
The Marina, Portstewart Road, Coleraine
BT52 1RN Tel: 028 7034 4503

Chandlers:
Seaton Sail And Power Co. Tel: 028 7083 2086

PORTRUSH
55.12'.5N 06.39'.5W

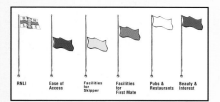

Mr McKay: Harbourmaster
Tel: 028 7082 2307
VHF Ch: 12/16 VHF Name: Portrush Harbour

Portrush Yacht Club
Andy Bradley: Secretary
7 Harbour Road, Portrush Tel: 028 7082 3932

Portrush Lifeboat
The Boathouse, Kerr Street, Portrush
Open to visitors most times by arrangement
Contact: Hon Sec J Scott Tel: 028 7082 3216

Portrush Lifeboat Museum in Boathouse
Open 7 days per week during summer
If closed contact Fay Scott Tel: 028 7082 3216

BALLYCASTLE
55.12'5N 06.14'.5W

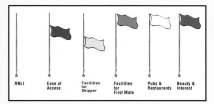

Ballycastle Marina
Contact: Harbour and Marina Supervisor
14 Bay View Road, Ballycastle, Co. Antrim
Tel: 028 2076 8525

RED BAY
55.04'.0N 06.03'.0W

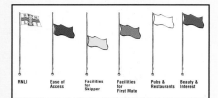

Cushendall Sailing and Boating Club
Jim Farrel: Secretary

Coast Road, Cushendall BT44 0SU
Tel: 028 2567 7167

Chandlers:
Red Bay Boats, Coast Road, Cushendall
Tel: 028 2577 1331

Repairs:
Red Bay Boats
Boat and Engine Repairs.

Red Bay Lifeboat Station
Coast Road, Cushendall, BT44 0QW
A modern high tech building housing
Atlantic 75. Open to visitors by appointment
only on Monday evenings
Contact Hon Sec J. Ferris
Boathouse: 012667 71483
Hon Sec: 012667 71417

LARNE
54.51'.0N 05.47'.5W

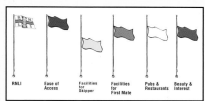

Capt A Gardiner: Harbourmaster
Tel: 01574 872100
VHF Channel: 14/16
VHF Name: Larne Harbour

East Antrim Boat Club
Contact Secretary for advice on moorings
Curran Point, Larne, Co. Antrim, BT40 1AU
Tel: 01574 277204

Larne Lifeboat Station
Coastguard Road, Larne
Open to visitors by arrangement - contact
Hon. Sec. N. Fekkes Tel: 01574 273352
Boathouse Tel: 01574 274490

CARRICKFERGUS
54.42'.0N 05.48'.5W

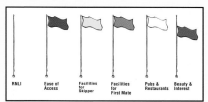

Carrickfergus Marina Tel: 01960 366666
VHF Ch: 37 VHF Name: Carrickfergus Marina

Carrickfergus Sailing Club
Robert J. Logan: Secretary
Rodgers Quay, Carrickfergus BT 389 SP
Tel: 01960 359302 Fax: 01960 359302

Chandlers:
Caters, Irish Quarter West, Carrickfergus
Tel: 01960 351919

Repairs:
The Boatyard, 108 Larne Road, Carrickfergus
Boat Repairs. Engine Repairs. Sail Repairs.
Tel: 01960 366655

BANGOR
54.40'.0N 05.40'.0W

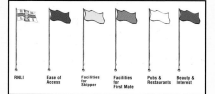

Bangor Marina
Andrew Jaggers: Harbour Manager
Bangor, Co. Down, BT20 5ED
Tel: 01247 453297 Fax: 01247 453450
VHF Channel: 80 VHF Name: Bangor Marina

Royal Ulster Yacht Club
101 Clifton Road, Bangor BT20 5HY
Tel: 01247 270568

Chandlery and Repairs:
B. J. Marine Ltd, Bangor Marina.
Tel: 01247 271434/271395 Fax: 01247 271529

PORTAFERRY

Portaferry Lifeboat
Open to visitors: Contact J Murray (Hon Sec)
Tel: 01247 728414

DONAGHADEE

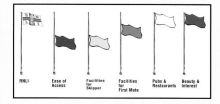

Andrew Firzell: Harbourmaster
Tel: 01247 882377

Copelands Marina
Contact: Manager Tel: 01247 882184

Donaghadee Lifeboat
Arun Harbour, Donaghadee
Open to visitors: All year
Contact: J McAuley (Hon Sec)
(Hon Sec) Tel: 01247 883253
(Office) Tel: 01232 351321

STRANGFORD LOUGH
54.19'.5N 0531'.0W

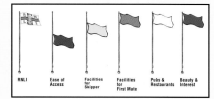

D Pedlow: Harbourmaster
Tel: 01396 881637

Portaferry Yacht Haven
11 The Strand, Portaferry, BT22 1PF
Tel: 012477 29598
VHF Channel: 37
VHF Name: Portaferry Yacht Haven

Strangford Lough Yacht Club
2 Whiterock Bay, Killinchy, BT23 6QA
Tel: 01238 541202

Down Cruising Club
52 Ballydorn Road, Killinchy BT23 6QB
Tel: 01238 541727

East Down Yacht Club Tel: 01396 828375

Killyleagh Yacht Club
Cuan Beach, Killyleagh, Co. Down, BT30 9QU
Tel: 01396 828250

Quoile Yacht Club
21 Castle Island Rd, Downpatrick BT30 7LD
Tel: 01396 612266

Kircubbin Sailing Club   54.29'.5N 532'.5W
Ralph McCutcheon: Secretary
106 Lough Road, Kircubbin, Co. Down
Tel: 012477 38422 Fax: 012477 58069

Chandler:
Sketrick Marine, Sketrick Island, Killinchy

ARDGLASS 54.15'.5N 05.36'.0W

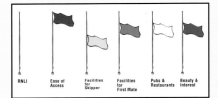

John Smith: Harbourmaster Tel: 01396 841291
VHF Channel: 12/14/16
VHF Name: Ardglass Harbour

Ardglass Marina Tel: 01396 842332
VHF Ch: 80 VHF Name: Ardglass Marina

NEWCASTLE 54.12'.0N 05.49'.5W

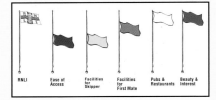

Limited facilities for yachts

Newcastle Lifeboat Station
Lifeboat Station, South Promenade,
Newcastle. The oldest lifeboat station in
Northern Ireland. Open to visitors 09.00 to
17.00 or later by arrangement.
Contact Boathouse Attendant: Hugh Paul
Boathouse Tel: 013967 25138
Boathouse Attendant Tel: 013967 22809

KILKEEL 54.03'.5N 05.59'.5W

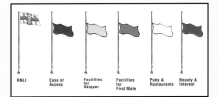

Contact: Harbourmaster Tel: 016937 62287

Chandler:
Kilkeel Trawler Supplies, Kilkeel Harbour
Tel: 016937 62655

Kilkeel Lifeboat Station
Open to visitors by appointment
Contact: The Hon. Sec. M Hanna
Tel: 016937 62497

CARLINGFORD LOUGH 54.01'.5N 06.04'.5W

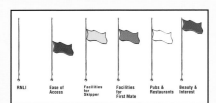

Terry Stevenson: Harbourmaster Warrenpoint
Tel: 016937 73381 Fax: 016937 73962

Carlingford Marina Tel: 042 73492
Carlingford Lough Yacht Club
Tel: 016937 38604

CLOUGHER HEAD

No facilities for yachts

Clougher Head Lifeboat
Open to visitors Easter to September;
at other times or for parties contact Hon Sec
Contact: P Hodgins (Hon Sec) Tel: 041 22225

SKERRIES

No facilities for yachts

Skerries Lifeboat
Open to visitors all year round
Contact: S Shiels (Hon Sec)
Tel: 01 8490579/8322735 (office)

MALAHIDE 53.27'.0N 06.09'.0W

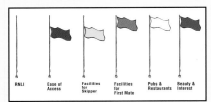

Malahide Marina
Damien Offer: Marina Manager
Malahide, Co. Dublin
Tel: 01 845 4129 Fax: 01 845 4255
VHF Channel: 80 VHF Name: Yacht Base

Malahide Yacht Club
St. James's Terrace, Malahide, Co. Dublin
Tel: 01 8453372 Fax: 01 8454125

HOWTH 53.23'.5N 06.04'.0W

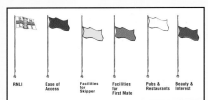

Capt John Burrows: Harbourmaster
Tel: 01 832 2252
VHF Ch: 16 08 VHF Name: Howth Harbour

Howth Yacht Club Marina
Liam Lalor: Marina Manager
Tel: 01 8392777 Fax: 01 8392430
VHF Channel: 80 VHF Name: Howth Marina

Howth Yacht Club
Rupert Jeffares: Secretary
Harbour Road. Howth, Co. Dublin
Tel: 01 8322141 Fax: 01 8392430

Chandler:
Dinghy Supplies, Dublin Road, Sutton, Dublin
Tel: 01 8322312

Repairs:
M.G. Marine
64 The Walled Gardens, Celbridge
Boat Repairs. Engine Repairs. Sail Repairs.
Tel: 087 2770291

Howth Lifeboat Station
Open to visitors: contact Hon. Sec. R Jeffares
Tel: 01 8390130 or Tel Hon Sec: 01 8323524

DUN LAOGHAIRE 53.18'.0N 06.07'.5W

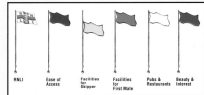

Jim Carter: Harbourmaster Tel: 01 2801130
VHF Ch: 14 VHF Name: Dun Laoghaire Harbour

National Yacht Club
Tel: 01 2805725 Fax: 01 2807837

Royal St George Yacht Club
Tel: 01 2801811 Fax: 01 2843002

Dun Laoghaire Lifeboat Station
Open to Visitors: all year
Contact: Hon. Sec. S. Wynne
Tel: 01 2802879

WICKLOW 52.59'.0N 06.02'.5W

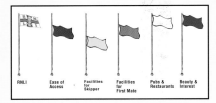

Contact: Harbourmaster Tel: 0404 67455
VHF Channel: 12/14/16
VHF Name: Wicklow Harbour.

Wicklow Sailing Club Tel: 0404 67526

Wicklow Lifeboat Station
Open to visitors: All year round
Contact: J. Potts - Mechanic
Tel: 0404 69411

ARKLOW 52.47'.5N 06.08'.0W

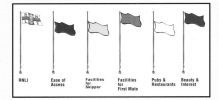

Contact: Harbourmaster Tel: 0402 32426
VHF Channel: 16
VHF Name: Arklow Harbour

Arklow Sailing Club
North Quay, Arklow Tel: 0402 33100

Chandler:
Kevin Kearon, South Quay, Arklow

Repairs:
Bill Brickley, Arklow Slipway, Arklow
Harbour, Boat and Engine Repairs.
Tel: 0402 33233

Arklow Lifeboat Station
The Boathouse, South Quay, Arkloe, Co.
Wicklow. Arklow is the oldest station in the
RNLI established 1826. Open to visitors: Mon-
Fri 9am -5pm, Sat 9am-12pm, Sun 9am-3pm
Tel: 0402 32850

WATERFORD HARBOUR 52.15'.5N 07.06'.0W

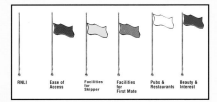

Capt P Cowman: Harbourmaster Tel: 051
874499
VHF Channel: 12/14/16
VHF Name: Waterford Harbour

Waterford Harbour Sailing Club
Tel: 051 83389

COURTOWN

Not suitable for yachts

Courtown Lifeboat Station
Open to visitors: All year, parites by
arrangement Contct: J Kennedy (Hon Sec)
Tel: 055 25648

ROSSLARE

Limited facilities for yachts

Rosslare Harbour Lifeboat Station
Open to visitors: by arrangement
Contact: B Miller (Hon Sec) Tel: 053 58836

KILMORE QUAY   52.10'.5N 06.35'.0W

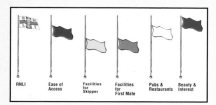

Eddie Barrett: Harbourmaster Tel: 053 29955

Killmore Quay Marina Tel/Fax: 053 29955

Kilmore Lifeboat Station
Open to visitors: All year, parties by

arrangment Contact S Radford (Hon Sec)
Tel 053 29707 or 053 29690 (Boathouse durng
office hours)

FETHARD

Not suitable for yachts

Fethard Lifeboat Station
Open to visitors: contact Mr J Doyle
(Hon Sec) Tel: 051 397184

DUNMORE EAST

Patrick Kavanagh: Harbourmaster
Tel: 051 383166
VHF Channel: 14/16
VHF Name: Dunmore East Harbour

Dunmore East Lifeboat Station
Open to visitors: By arrangement
Contact: The Hon. Sec. Lt. Cdr. P Kavanagh
Tel: 051 383808 or 051 383166

TRAMORE

No facilities for yachts

Tramore Lifeboat Station
Open to visitors: By arrangement
Contact: Boathouse
Boathouse Tel: 051 381622

DUNGARVAN BAY   52.05'.0N 07.36'.5W

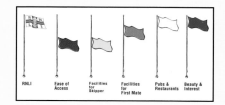

Dungarven Harbour Sailing Club
Dungarvan Town Quay, Waterford

HELVICK HEAD

No facilities for yachts

Helvick Head Lifeboat
Open to visitors: All year
Contact: I Walsh (Hon Sec) Tel: 058 46363

YOUGHAL

Harbourmaster Tel: 024 92820
Youghal Lifeboat
Open to visitors: All year
Contact T Kelleher (Hon Sec)
Hon Sec Tel: 024 93119 or 024 93315 (Office)

The East Coast of Ireland - Pilot Books

Irish Coast Pilot
United Kingdom Hydrographic Office, ISBN: 0707 710 405

East and North Coasts of Ireland Sailing Directions, Irish Cruising Club
published by Imray, Laurie, Norie & Wilson, Tel: 01480 462114 ISBN: 0950 171 76X

South and West Coasts of Ireland Sailing Directions, Irish Cruising Club.
published by Imray, Laurie, Norie & Wilson, Tel: 01480 462114 ISBN: 0950 171 778

Lundy and Irish Sea Pilot, David Taylor
published by Imray, Laurie, Norie & Wilson, Tel: 01480 462114 ISBN: 0852 882 491

New codes for Northern Ireland

After September 2000, you must use the new dialling codes in Northern Ireland.

01238 xxxxxx	becomes	028 97xx xxxx
01247 xxxxxx	becomes	028 91xx xxxx
01265 xxxxx	becomes	028 703x xxxx
01265 xxxxxx	becomes	028 70xx xxxx
01266 xxxxx	becomes	028 256x xxxx
01266 xxxxxx	becomes	028 25xx xxxx
01396 xxxxxx	becomes	028 44xx xxxx
01504 xxxxxx	becomes	028 71xx xxxx
01574 xxxxxx	becomes	028 28xx xxxx
01693 xxxxx	becomes	028 302x xxxx
01693 xxxxxx	becomes	028 30xx xxxx
01849 xxxxxx	becomes	028 94xx xxxx
01960 xxxxxx	becomes	028 93xx xxxx

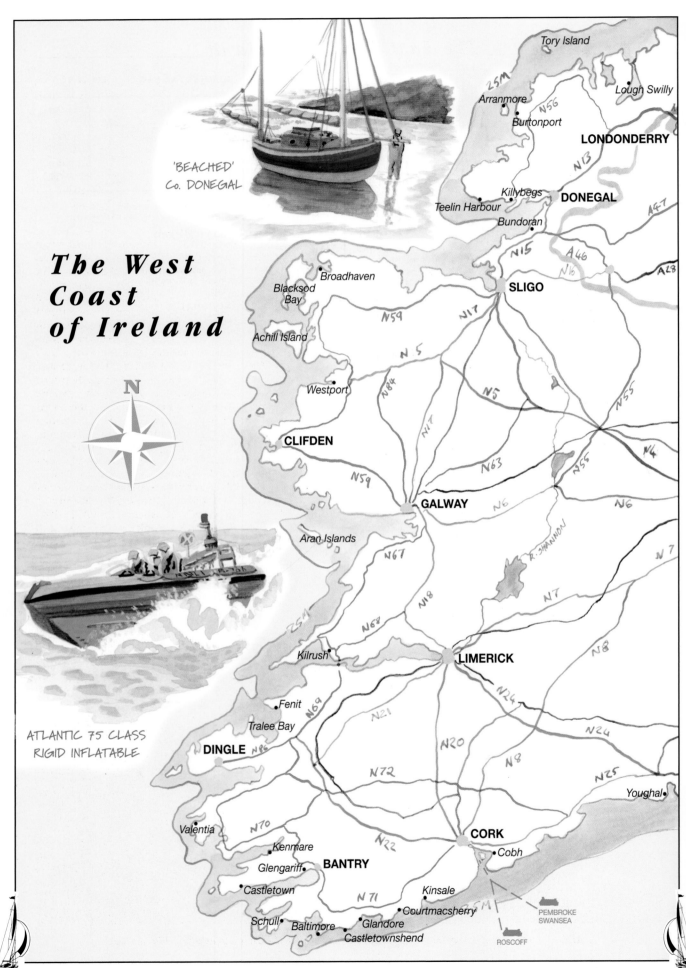

The West Coast of Ireland

N

'BEACHED'
Co. DONEGAL

ATLANTIC 75 CLASS
RIGID INFLATABLE

Tory Island
Lough Swilly
Arranmore
Burtonport
LONDONDERRY
Killybegs
Teelin Harbour
DONEGAL
Bundoran

Broadhaven
Blacksod Bay
Achill Island
Westport
SLIGO

CLIFDEN

GALWAY
Aran Islands

Kilrush
Fenit
Tralee Bay
DINGLE
LIMERICK

Valentia
Kenmare
Glengariff
Castletown
Schull
Baltimore
Glandore
Castletownshend
BANTRY
Kinsale
Courtmacsherry
CORK
Cobh
Youghal

PEMBROKE
SWANSEA
ROSCOFF

Cork

The coastline of Cork provides a variety of excellent sailing options and must be one of the most appealing places in Europe to spend some time cruising. The big sailing centre is Cork Harbour which is a splendid enclosed natural harbour and the venue for much enthusiastic racing as well as providing an excellent range of facilities which will be useful to the cruising sailor. You have the opportunity to take in some big city life in Cork itself, or there are quieter backwaters and anchorages for a more tranquil approach. The coastline is attractive and the adjoining countryside lush and you will find numerous delightful small harbour villages where you can enjoy a quiet run ashore. For those in search of the finest restaurants, Kinsale is just a short hop from Cork Harbour and is widely acclaimed as Ireland's gourmet capital with an impressive selection of highly regarded restaurants. They are all within easy reach of a pontoon berth so you needn't get indigestion trying to start the outboard to get back to the boat! If you are unlucky enough to encounter weather which is a little on the damp side, the warmth and friendliness of the local people will more than make up for it and, if the weather is fine, you will be in for a simply wonderful cruise.

Cork Harbour

The extensive natural harbour and network of rivers and creeks which make up Cork Harbour is a real treat as there are numerous places of interest to visit and some really delightful anchorages. Furthermore, the pilotage through the well-marked and sheltered channels is straightforward. Boating for recreation has long been popular here and, in 1720, the Water Club of the Harbour of Cork was the first yacht club to be formed anywhere in the world. Ford Cork Week which takes place every two years is now challenging Cowes to be the biggest regatta in the British Isles, and for racing yachtsmen and cruisers alike, there can be little doubt that this is one of the key places to sail. The tidal streams through the entrance are not unduly fierce and this is a spectacular place to arrive at as you pass between Fort Meagher and Fort Davis which guard the entrance. Turning to port around Fort Meagher, you approach the Owenboy River which leads to **Crosshaven**, the principal yachting centre in Cork Harbour. This village may lack some of the historical appeal of some of the other towns and villages around the harbour, but as the headquarters of the Royal Cork Yacht Club, and with three marinas, it is a buzzing centre of "yachtie" activity. For most, its convenient location near the entrance to the harbour and the abundance of facilities will make it the obvious first port of call in Cork Harbour. Fully serviced pontoon berths are available at almost all states of the tide from the Royal Cork Yacht Club Marina, Crosshaven Boatyard Marina and Salve Marine which also has visitors' moorings. Between them, they have all the facilities you could possibly need, and though there is no supermarket in the town, there is a reasonable range of local shops for provisions. What the village may lack in terms of shopping is more than made up for by the range of excellent places to eat and drink. Visitors are most welcome at the Royal Cork's clubhouse where there is a convivial bar and the food is excellent, but do strike out and investigate the hostelries in town as well. The Admiral Drake (☎ 021 831687), Cronins (☎ 021 831207) and The Anchor (☎ 021 831799) are all splendid places to have a drink or a bar meal, and are all within a few hundred yards of the Royal Cork.

Artist: **Anthony Flemming GENTLE BREEZE AND HAZE** *Courtesy of:* **The Artist**

Reasonably priced meals can be had at the Schooner Restaurant (☎ 021 832328), or for something a bit smarter, hop in a taxi or bus to Carrigaline about 4 miles away where you will find Gregorys (☎ 021 371512). The best food in the area is probably at Lovetis (☎ 021 294909) in Douglas which is about 8 miles away. Having sailed into Cork Harbour, it would be a crime to just stay in Crosshaven when there is so much more to see. Not far up the River Owenboy, there's a beautiful anchorage at Drake's Pool which is where Sir Francis is said to have taken advantage of the winding river to hide from marauding Spanish pursuers. Back out in the main harbour, on the south side of Great Island and facing the entrance to the harbour, the brightly coloured houses along the waterfront at **Cobh** (pronounced Cove) smile out over the water. The elegant terraces are dwarfed by the impressive neo-Gothic splendour and spire of St Colman's Cathedral which is perched on the hillside behind. This little town was a popular health resort and, as a port of call for the transatlantic liners, it was the last place the Titanic touched land. You can find out all about the town's maritime history and role as a port at the Cobh Heritage Centre (☎ 021 813 591), and there's more maritime history at the Cobh Museum (☎ 021 814 240). To explore local history in a slightly different way, Clippers Bar and Restaurant is in the former clubhouse of the Water Club of the Harbour of Cork which is a rather splendid building on the waterfront. To the north of Cobh on adjoining Fota (or Foaty) Island, the Fota Wildlife Park (☎ 021 812 678) has an array of animals which will delight children and adults alike and is famous for breeding cheetahs which are unsurprisingly kept separate from the antelopes, giraffes and zebras. The neighbouring Arboretum (☎ 021 270244) contains trees from all over the world and is extensive and stunning. For more local flavour, a trip to the Jameson Heritage Centre (☎ 021 613 594) at Middleton is to be warmly recommended. A tour of the distillery buildings will familiarise you with the theory, and of course you won't be leaving without a taste of the local drop! There is space to berth alongside at Cobh or you can drop anchor close to the town, but probably a better option is to head to the marina at **East Ferry** which is in a quiet backwater and there is a pub and a restaurant here as well. Access to the marina, which is in East Passage on the east side of Great Island, is possible at all states of the tide, and there is fuel and water here too. It would be a shame to miss the opportunity to sail up to **Cork City** which is about eight miles beyond Cobh. Here you will find cinemas, theatres, historic buildings, museums - the list could be endless. With a population of a quarter of a million people, this is Ireland's largest city other than Dublin, and it's a major commercial and administrative centre. It also has a pleasantly continental feel as the climate is so much more benign than in most of mainland Britain, the café-society atmosphere is not therefore forced as it can be in many other cities in the British Isles. The university building by Fitzgerald Park is of historical interest and is worth a visit, as is the English Market which is a Victorian-style food market where fresh local produce is available and the selection of fish is outstanding. The Crawford Art Gallery (☎ 021 273 377) in the Old Custom House on Emmet Place has a comprehensive collection of paintings by notable Irish

artists of recent centuries. For the historical perspective, the Cork Public Museum (☎ 021 270 679) in Fitzgerald Park on the Western Road gives a thorough and interesting overview of Cork through the ages and, from Cork, it's not far to Blarney Castle (☎ 021 385 252) - one of Ireland's oldest castles where you will no doubt receive the "gift of the gab" if you manage to kiss the Blarney Stone. There is space for visiting yachts to berth in the very centre of the town – you should consult the Port Operations Office in Cobh for permission to berth before heading up river, they will be able to tell you how to find all the facilities you might need.

If the number and variety of places to eat and drink around Cork harbour have not exhausted your zest for discovery, then the city of Cork itself awaits. Several of the hotels have excellent bars and restaurants, such as Morrisons Island (☎ 021 275858) on Morrisons Quay which serves à la carte dinners, as does Jurys (☎ 021 276622) on Western Road whose two restaurants, Glandore and Fastnet, both offer plenty of choice. Jacques (☎ 021 277387) on Phoenix Street, near the centre of Cork, is another good option for a meal. The Old Oak Bar (☎ 021 276165) on Oliver Plunkett Street, is a friendly pub in the centre of Cork City, drawing a younger crowd. It serves bar food and features some good live bands. On the outskirts of Cork, the Crow's Nest (☎ 021 543330) at Victoria Cross, is great for a meal or bar snack with your drink, and there's loads of choice and a lively atmosphere.

Taxi:	Crosshaven: (☎ 021 832138)
Car hire:	From Cork City Airport, Budget Rent A Car (☎ 021 314000)
Bus:	Local services link Crosshaven and Cork. National network from Cork
Rail:	services from Cork to Dublin, timetable enquiries (☎ 021 508188)
Ferry:	from Cork, Irish Ferries (☎ 021 504333)
Airport:	Cork Airport, Aer Lingus (☎ 021 3271555)

for more details, see Directory Section

Kinsale & Oysterhaven

If you are in search of good food, then Kinsale is a must on your itinerary along Ireland's south coast. Widely fêted as Ireland's Gourmet Capital, there is a tremendous selection of places to eat well in this attractive and historic town. Tucked around the corner near the mouth of the River Barndon, the sheltered harbour's entrance is spectacularly flanked by Charles Fort and James Fort, both dating back to the 17th century and underlining the town's significant strategic importance in days gone by. The Kinsale Regional Museum (☎ 021 772 044) in the town hall gives a good flavour of the history of the area, and there are further exhibitions at Charles Fort (☎ 021 772 263) and Desmond Castle (☎ 021 774 855) where you will also find the International Museum of Wine. There are several options for berthing here. Kinsale Yacht Club Marina is the closest to the centre of town and in high season there is a ferry which will bring you across from Castlepark Marina which is on the peninsula by James Fort. The trade-off is that the facilities are slightly better at Castlepark, though from here you still need to cross to the town to get at the good range of shops for provisions. There is a bar and restaurant (☎ 021 774959) at the mari-

Artist: **Steven Dews** **TACKING DUEL** *Courtesy of:* **Rosenstiel's**

na, but perhaps you will want to try one of the town's excellent restaurants. . . For a drink ashore, the Spaniard and the Greyhound are good options or, if you have the time to stroll to Sandy Cove, the Bulman is well worth a visit. It is difficult to categorise the wide choice of restaurants here – Chez Jean Marc (☎ 021 774625) is as good a choice as any for a reasonably priced meal, and The Vintage (☎ 021 772502) is probably the most expensive. The Cottage Loft (☎ 021 772803), The Man Friday (☎ 021 772260), and The Blue Haven (☎ 021 772209) all have good reputations as well and there are many more, so perhaps you had better plan to spend a few days here! Another option worth mentioning is to moor in **Oysterhaven** which is in a little bay just to the east of Kinsale Harbour. By this quiet anchorage, there is a small village and good meals can be had at The Oystercatcher Restaurant (☎ 021 770822).

From Kinsale

Taxi:	(☎ 021 773000) or (021 772642)
Car hire:	Avis (☎ 021 965045)
Cycle hire:	C & B Cycles (☎ 021 774884)
Bus:	local services to Cork which links to national network
Rail:	services from Cork to Dublin
Ferry:	services from Dublin and Ringaskiddy
Airport:	Cork Airport, Aer Lingus (☎ 021 3271555)

for more details, see Directory Section,

Kinsale to Roaring Water Bay

Sailing west from Kinsale, the broken coastline is punctuated by numerous small natural harbours many of which offer secluded anchorages. There are also several villages which offer some facilities for visiting yachts, and almost invariably at least one place to head ashore to soak up the local hospitality. To make the most of this area, comprehensive instructions from a pilot book with good local coverage will enable you to explore some of the remoter spots to find secluded anchorages not listed in most almanacs. The Irish Cruising Club's *South and West Coast Sailing Directions* is very helpful. Pontoon berths are available in **Courtmacsherry** which is a quiet little seaside village and is now the home of an RNLI all-weather Trent lifeboat. Courtmacsherry Lifeboat was the second of 13 lifeboats launched to assist those in difficulties during the notorious 1979 Fastnet race. Hopefully, you will not experience anything like the storm to hurricane force winds which struck the racing fleet when it was in this area. In settled weather, the entrance should not present undue difficulties here, and once ashore, a stroll through the woods to Wood Point is a good way to stretch your legs. This is a tiny place, so don't expect to find many facilities here. With a fair wind, it's a short day's sail on to **Glandore** which is an attractive village surrounded with wooded hillsides and there are visitors' moorings available in the sheltered natural harbour. Here you will find a couple of excellent restaurants and pubs for a run ashore, and local shops in Glandore and Unionhall opposite will give you the chance to do limited provision stocking. On the west side of the peninsula you will find Castle Haven, a quiet anchorage close to another very small village, **Castletownshend**. This is a tempting place to stop since Mary Anne's (☎ 028 36146) is a wonderful pub which serves fabulous food.

Artist: **Steven Dews SAILING TO WINDWARD** *Courtesy of:* **Rosenstiel's**

Baltimore and Roaring Water Bay

As you round the next headland, Cape Clear Island, the first of numerous islands and rocky outcrops comes into view, and you will be pleased to know that you are approaching **Baltimore** and the wonderful cruising waters of Roaring Water Bay. Baltimore Harbour is tucked between the mainland and Sherkin Island and is a wonderful sheltered harbour, and for a small place, there is a good range of facilities for visiting yachts. This very attractive area is a popular sailing centre, and is also one of the locations used by the Glenans Sailing School. Baltimore is an unspoiled traditional fishing village, and there is plenty to make the visitor feel welcome. The small marina can let you have a berth alongside or visitors' mooring and there are several suitable places to anchor in the immediate area. Once ashore, The Baltimore Harbour Hotel has a leisure centre and The Baltimore Yacht Club will be happy to let you have a shower. Caseys Cabin (☎ 028 20197) is a good choice for a drink or a meal, and The Customs House (☎ 028 20200) and the Mews (☎ 028 20390) all serve excellent food. And for a real treat, the best seafood platter in town is at Chez Yuan (☎ 028 20136). Alongside berthing is also available opposite on **Sherkin Island** close to the ruins of the castle and Franciscan Friary. Here there is good shelter from south westerlies, and there is a

good anchorage as well. Stroll ashore to enjoy the unspoiled beauty of rural Ireland and enjoy a pint in the Jolly Roger (☎ 028 20379) to quench your thirst. Another island in the area which is well worth a visit is Heir Island where you can anchor off to spend the night in perfect solitude with the loom of the Fastnet Light in your cabin. For a run ashore on the island, you will get a good dinner at The Island Cottage (☎ 028 38102). A trip to Cape Clear is a must – this island is a magnet for birdwatchers keen to see the huge seabird colonies, and you will also find Paddy Burkes (☎ 091 796226), Ireland's most southerly pub here. You will need to check in your pilot book for details of the approach and where to anchor at North Harbour on the island. Having got so close, it would be almost rude not to sail around Fastnet Rock about five miles from Clear Island! This rocky outcrop is topped by the impressive tower of the lighthouse which was built at the turn of the century and is now automatic like all lighthouses around the coasts of the British Isles. Heading back to the coast, we find **Schull** tucked in behind Long Island and Castle Island in the centre of Roaring Water Bay. This is a popular holiday area as the scenery is wonderful and the pace of life is relaxed. The harbour of this little market town offers good shelter and is used by a still active fishing fleet and there's a modern fish processing plant here as well. However there is also plenty of room for yachts and there is an active sailing club on the waterfront. The entrance is not difficult, there is always plenty of water and shelter is good in most conditions. Visitors' moorings are available or you may be able to berth alongside the pier, though here you will probably have to contend with fishing boats. There are plenty of shops for provisions and more general browsing – this is a great place to visit as it has lots of atmosphere, and the pubs and restaurants are excellent. For a drink try An Tigin (☎ 028 28830) or the Bunratty Inn (☎ 028 28341) on Main Street which serves bar meals all day. There's bar food and local music at the Galley Inn (☎ 028 28733) also on Main Street. For something a bit smarter, try the Restaurant in Blue (☎ 028 28305) in Gubbeen or for French flavour, La Coquille (☎ 028 28642) in Main Street. For a hotel restaurant meal and fine views, head to The Colla House Hotel (☎ 028 28105) a few miles along Colla Road or the East End Hotel (☎ 028 28101) on Main Street.

Taxi: Schull Hackney Cabs (☎ 028 28320) or Betty Johnson's (☎ 028 28410)

Bus: Eireann Bus Company, enquiries (☎ 021 508188)

Rail: (☎ 021 506766) for nearest service

Ferry: From Cork, Irish Ferries (☎ 021 504333)

Airport: Cork Airport (☎ 021 3271555)

for more details, see Directory Section

At the west end of Roaring Water Bay, **Crookhaven** offers a handy little anchorage though facilities here are limited and, backing onto it, Goleen is an even smaller village on a little inlet which is a good place to anchor in fair weather. Village stores are on hand in both places to top up on essentials, and there is a choice of pubs and restaurants for a run ashore. In Goleen, Heron's Cove (☎ 028 35225) serves food all day, and in Crookhaven, head to O'Sullivan's Bar (☎ 028 35319) for bar food and local music. Ty Ar Mor (☎ 028 35319) on The Pier serves excellent fresh local seafood, and the smartest in town is Journey's Inn (☎ 028 35183) where you are asked to book in advance. Just along on the headland, the Mizen Head Radio Signal Station was where Marconi sent the first Transatlantic radio signal, and his old house in Crookhaven contains an exhibition about his pioneering work with radio communication. Tempting though it is to pause indefinitely in this remote and peaceful spot, there are good reasons to press on as there are some real treats in store around the corner. The next inlet just around Mizen Head is **Dunmanus Bay** which is a breathtaking cruising area. This is a wonderfully out of the way spot, so don't expect to find anything other than the most basic facilities here – centres of population are few and far between and small as well. Consequently, the top class Japanese Restaurant at Ahakista is a bit of a surprise. It's called Shiro (☎ 027 67030) and its specialities include Sashimi, Tempura and Sushi. There's also good food at Blair's Cove (☎ 027 611127) in Durrus.

Bantry Bay

Surrounded by mountains and moorland, the extensive waters of Bantry Bay offer numerous anchorages, especially on the north shore where you can find good shelter. A good pilot book will give a comprehensive selection for you to choose somewhere suitable for the prevailing weather conditions. This area has been the scene of many historical dramas – uprisings, famines and even an unsuccessful invasion attempt by the French in 1796. The weather drove them off, but it has to be said that the middle of winter was probably not a hugely bright time of year for visitors, hostile or otherwise, to be trying to navigate their way in here. To mention just a few of the places you could visit in the bay, Castletown, Glengarriff and Bantry offer the most comprehensive facilities in the area for stocking up on provisions and entertainment ashore. **Castletownbere** is closest to the entrance, so may well prove a useful first or last port of call here. Tucked behind Bear Island which gives good shelter once inside, the entrance is narrow and there are hazards to watch out for, so be sure to have a large scale chart or comprehensive pilotage instructions. This is the home of one of the RNLI's newest stations - a new all-weather Arun lifeboat was stationed here in April 1998. It is also a busy fishing port, and as a consequence, there is a fair range of facilities that are also useful to the yachtsman including showers, fuel and a reasonable range of shops for provisions. For a meal, O'Donoghues (☎ 027 70007) in the Square, is a nice mixture of old and new and bar lunches are available. Its seafood reputedly attracts diners from far and wide, and the atmosphere, needless to say, is typically Irish.

For more charm, you should sail on up the bay to **Glengarriff** which was a popular destination for intrepid Victorian tourists, and played host to the Queen herself who stayed at the Eccles Hotel (☎ 027 63003) which is still a good hostelry to head for. Close to Glengarriff, Garinish Island is one of the most beautiful islands in the bay and has a spectacular sub-tropical garden (☎ 027 63040) which is crammed with unusual plants and flowers and is well worth a visit. The largest town on the bay is **Bantry** itself which boasts a population of nearly 3,000 and consequently has a good range of shops and places of entertainment. The key place to visit here is Bantry House (☎ 027 50047) which was built in the early eighteenth century. Set in elegant grounds and with fine views over Bantry Bay, the house is richly furnished and has interesting contents. At Bantry House you will also find the 1796 French Armada Exhibition which is a comprehensive survey of the ill-fated invasion attempt and its historical background. Bantry Harbour is tucked behind Whiddy Island which has several old gun emplacements, and was the site of an oil refinery until 1979 when the oil tanker Betelgeuse exploded causing considerable public alarm. The harbour is littered with islands and rocky outcrops, and care is needed to keep clear of these as well as numerous mussel rafts which can be an irritation until you get ashore to enjoy the result!

There are numerous options for anchoring in the harbour, so consult your pilot book to see which is most suitable for you. The town is full of good shops for stocking up the boat as well as craft shops and boutiques, and there is a good selection of pubs and restaurants. Right in the centre of town you will find the Bantry Bay Hotel (☎ 027 50289) which has a warm and friendly atmosphere. Alternatively, for a more peaceful drink with views of the Caha Mountains, try the bar at The Westlodge Hotel (☎ 027 50360) which is only a short drive out of Bantry. The Anchor Tavern (☎ 027 50012) on New Street, is one to visit with its lively atmosphere as is Barry Murphy's (☎ 027 50900) on The Quay. This is by no means an exhaustive list and you will be spoilt for choice particularly in the High Street, the Main Street and around The Quay.

Taxi:	From nearby Bandon, Bandon Cabs (☎ 023 41258)
Car hire:	From Cork Airport, Avis (☎ 021 281111)
Bus:	Eireann National Bus Company (☎ 021 508188)
Rail:	Cork Station, enquiries (☎ 021 506766)
Ferry:	Cork/Swansea Ferries (☎ 021 378036)
Airport:	Cork Airport (56 miles) Aer Lingus (☎ 021 327100)

for more details, see Directory Section

Kerry and Clare

The Kerry coastline encloses some of the highest ground and tallest mountains in Ireland and offers the most spectacular vistas you are likely to see this side of the Scottish Border. With rugged shorelines and isolated islands which are often home only to huge colonies of birds, this really is somewhere to get away from it all, and most of the harbours you will find are small and the towns and villages in the area are quiet but welcoming. Beyond the Dingle Peninsula, the landscape changes somewhat and the River Shannon invites you to take advantage of the sheltered inland cruising it offers. This may prove a welcome break from the rugged coastline and the Atlantic Ocean which even in playful mood can be gruelling, and if more than playful then distinctly intimidating. Since rounding Mizen Head near Schull, you will have been aware that there is nothing between you and the United States apart from miles and miles of the Atlantic. Comfortable cruising in these waters starts to be very dependent on fair weather and there may be occasions when sudden changes in the weather or, more disconcertingly, visibility may require you to stand off until conditions improve. The Atlantic swell can cause quite challenging conditions, so to cruise here safely, the prudent will be equipped with a seaworthy boat which is provisioned to stay at sea for several days at a time. We hope, however, that the weather will be kind and that you get to see this coastline at its best, bathed in sunshine.

Kenmare River

The estuary of the Kenmare River stretches inland almost as far as Galway Bay and offers a particularly beautiful cruising ground for those who are in search of out-of-the-way places. The countryside to the north on the Inveragh Peninsula includes some of the highest mountains in Ireland and makes for splendid panoramic views and, with mountains to the south as well, this estuary is surrounded with spectacular scenery indeed. Be sure to have your lockers well stocked before heading in here as shopping options are quite limited. You will find some charming little harbours and picturesque anchorages and very little to disturb the peace and tran-

Artist: **Cloé Cloberty RING OF KERRY FROM THE BEARA PENINSULA**
Courtesy of: **Osborne Studio Gallery**

quillity that makes the pace of life so refreshing. A particularly attractive spot is Sneem Harbour on the north shore, though swell can be a problem in here. While energetic members of the crew may fancy a stroll to the village a couple of miles away where there is a museum and limited shopping, the likely need for an anchor watch is a handy refuge if enthusiasm is lacking! Once again, large scale charts and a good pilot book will ease the tension when approaching some of the secluded refuges in this estuary and will help you to select the most suitable destinations for the weather conditions prevailing during your visit.

There are a some excellent options for a meal in Kenmare. The Park (☎ 064 41200) is perfectly situated to enjoy fabulous views of Kenmare Bay and Hills while serving sumptuous à la carte dinners. The restaurant d'Arcys (☎ 064 415 89) on the Main Street is also an inviting option. The Lime Tree (☎ 064 41225) on Shelbourne Street is a splendid choice for good value meals as is An Leath Phingin (☎ 064 41559) on the Main Street, which serves Italian food. Alternatively, you might like to try Cafe Indigo (☎ 064 42356) in the Square, or for a more relaxed pub atmosphere, The Square Pint (☎ 064 42357) serves a good lunch. Moerans Pub (☎ 064 42254) is an excellent place to enjoy the atmosphere of old Ireland; it serves very good, traditional Irish food including seafood and, of course, Irish Stew.

Dingle

Set on the south of the Dingle Peninsula, which is noted for its spectacular scenery and impressive views, Dingle is a busy fishing port which benefits from a splendid natural harbour. This is one of the larger towns in the area and has an astonishing 52 pubs! This town is an attractive place to visit, and its increasing popularity as a tourist destination means that visitors are welcome and well provided for, and there are plenty of places to eat as well as drink. There is also a good selection of shops for both provisions and browsing. The area has numerous religious sites dating back over the centuries and organised mini-bus tours, with an archaeologist as a guide, take about two hours and serve as an excellent introduction to the uninitiated visitor (contact the Tourist Office: 066 51188). Even if you don't visit any other sites, you should try to get to the Gallarus Oratory about 5 miles north of the town. Perfectly intact after a thousand years, this remarkable building looks a bit like an upside-down boat and is set in glorious countryside. For an informative exhibition about local history, head to the Dingle Library (☎ 066 51499) which contains a worthwhile collection. Off the end of the peninsula, the Blasket Islands are a good destination for a day trip either in your own boat, or on an organised tour if you prefer to let someone else worry about the navigation. Attractive scenery, sea views and exploration of ruined buildings combine to make for an interesting day, and in the summer, the islanders run a simple tea shop for refreshments. The approach to Dingle Harbour is straightforward unless the conditions are poor, and the marina offers fully serviced pontoon accommodation for visiting yachts and a comprehensive range of facilities. For a run ashore you really are spoiled for choice. Krugers Guesthouse & Bar (☎ 066 56127) is Europe's most westerly pub and offers bar meals and traditional

Artist: **Clive Madgwick DINGLE HARBOUR** *Courtesy of:* **Rosenstiel's**

music, and for a simple café type meal, try Tig Lise (☎ 066 51001). Danno's Restaurant & Bar (☎ 066 51855) serves good food made from fresh local produce and there are many, many more places to try so you should have no difficulty in finding something to suit your tastes and budget.

Taxi:	Sheehy (☎ 066 51301), Brown (☎ 066 51259) or Begley (☎ 066 51440)
Car hire:	from Tralee - Duggan (☎ 066 21124), Sheehy (☎ 066 21080), O'Connor (☎ 066 24782)
Cycle hire:	4 outlets close to marina
Bus:	local bus service to Tralee links to main bus routes
Rail:	mainline rail services from Tralee Station (30 miles away)
Airport:	Kerry Airport (35 miles away)

for more details, see Directory Section

Fenit and Tralee Bay

A recently built marina makes Fenit a convenient staging post, and the village is set in an attractive area which is worth spending some time in. The nearest large town is Tralee which is eight miles away and a major tourist destination. Places of interest here include the National Folk Theatre (☎ 066 23055) and the Kerry County Museum (☎ 066 27777) which is set in the town park near the ruins of Geraldine Castle. The museum includes an impressive multimedia recreation of the medieval town called "Kerry - The Kingdom", and the area also has a narrow gauge steam railway, the Tralee-Blennerville Light Railway (☎ 066 28888). A train ride will take you a couple of miles to Blennerville where there is a restored windmill (☎ 066 21064) which is fully operational, and in a neighbouring building, you can visit an interesting exhibition about emigration to America in the 19th century. Fenit itself is a small village, so does not offer quite the same range of tourist attractions which does mean that it is less crowded than Tralee. Fenit Sea World (☎ 066 36544) on the pier is the village's main tourist lure and gives an interesting insight into local sealife, and includes the retrieved timbers of a wrecked ship. You will also be welcome if you visit the lifeboat station which was founded in 1879 and then re-opened in 1994 after a gap of twenty-five years. Fenit Harbour and the marina are straightforward to enter in almost all conditions and are accessible at all states of the tide. Most facilities are available on site, though you will need to go to Tralee to find chandlery or petrol. The shop in the village will tide you over for basic supplies and will also deliver to the marina, or for a comprehensive range of shops including a supermarket, you can head along to Tralee. Fortunately, you don't need to commute to find a drink or a meal. The West End Bar (☎ 066 36246) is a good choice for a drink or a pub meal. Godfrey's Hotel (☎ 066 36108) and the slightly smarter Lighthouse Hotel (☎ 066 36444) both serve reasonably priced restaurant meals. For a treat, two famous seafood restaurants are located nearby: it's a couple of miles to the Tankard Restaurant (☎ 066 36349) in Kilfenora and less than 5 miles to the Oyster Tavern (☎ 066 36102) in Spa and both merit the modest taxi fare it will cost you to get to them.

Taxi:	Bertie Carmody (☎ 066 36191), Mike O'Sullivan (☎ 088 610453),
Minibus:	Mike O'Donnell (☎ 066 36212)
Cycle hire:	Tralee Gas Supplies
Bus:	from Tralee (8 miles) to Dublin, Cork & Limerick
Rail:	from Tralee (8 miles) to Dublin & Cork
Airport:	Kerry Airport for flights to Dublin, London & Frankfurt

for more details, see Directory Section

The River Shannon

The marina at **Kilrush** is about fifteen miles up river from Loop Head on the end of the peninsula. This is a bit of a bore if you are on passage, and you may choose to stop over at one of the anchorages nearer the entrance if the conditions allow. In fair weather, there are a couple of places where you can anchor below Kilrush, and if the weather is looking unsettled, The Shannon offers miles of inland cruising and plenty of places to anchor or go alongside. Half way to Kilrush, and overlooked by a 16th century towerhouse, Carrigaholt Bay offers reasonable shelter from winds from the south, west and north and you can get basic supplies from Carrigaholt which is ten minutes' walk from the quay on the waterfront. Kilrush itself is one of the main centres of population in the area, though this does not make it very big! It is a popular holiday destination as there are five beaches close by and the town offers a good range of facilities to the passing yachtsman. To find out about the area's history, the Kilrush Heritage Centre (☎ 065 51577) is the place to head for and the Kilrush Forest Park just outside the town is an attractive place for a stroll. The grounds include the ruins of a once fine house which was destroyed by fire at about the turn of the century. A good spot to drop anchor for a few hours to do some exploring ashore is just off Scattery Island which is opposite the entrance to Kilrush Creek. Here you will find the remains of five medieval churches and a 6th century monastery, and there's a Visitor Centre (☎ 065 52139) near the Merchant's Quay in Kilrush on the mainland where you can find out about the island's history.

Access to the marina is via a lock which operates at all tides and the approach is well marked and not difficult. Fully serviced pontoons are available for visitors and a good range of facilities including launderette, showers and fuel will be found on site. The marina is five minutes walk from the town centre where there is a good range of shops and a choice of places for a drink or a meal as well. The Central Restaurant (☎ 065 9052477) is ideal for quick and basic meals, with full Irish breakfasts being served all day, lunch, and hot and cold snacks until 6pm. Crotty's Pub (☎ 065 9052470) is a traditional, relaxed place to enjoy a drink and eat some home-cooked lunch while you can pass the summer nights listening to traditional music. For a pub with really good food, the Haven Arms (☎ 065 9051267) is both a local and tourist pub which has won numerous Bar Food awards. Seafood here is a speciality. For a slightly smarter pub meal, the award winning Kelly's Bar and Restaurant (☎ 065 905 1811) serves food all day and there's an à la carte menu in the evening in the restaurant where local seafood is a particular speciality.

From Kilrush
Taxi: (☎ 065 51825)
Cycle hire: (☎ 065 51127)
Bus: from town centre to Limerick (approx. 45 miles)
Rail: Limerick Station
Ferry: Shannon Ferry (☎ 065 53124) from Kilmar (4 miles) to Tarbert on south shore
Airport: Shannon Airport
for more details, see Directory Section

Upriver

The Shannon is the longest navigable river in the British Isles, and it is quite straightforward to take a yacht as far as Limerick which is 50 miles inland from Loop Head. As you head up towards Limerick, pontoon berths and a warm welcome will be found at the Foynes Yacht Club about fifteen miles above Kilrush, and there is a good range of facilities for yachts here. Pontoon berths are also available at Kildysart a couple of miles further up and there are visitors' moorings at Labasheda up the Fergus River beyond Shannon Airport. You can also moor alongside in Limerick which is Ireland's fourth largest city. The Limerick Museum (☎ 061 417826) on John's Square is a good source of historical background and has interesting collections of photographs, local silverware and lace as well as historical and archeological relics. For more historical flavour, King John's Castle (☎ 061 414624) is a splendid, sprawling Norman castle dating from the early 13th century. It has some interesting exhibits and you get good views from the ramparts which overlook the river from King's Island. The cultural arts are well represented here and there are varied collections at The City Gallery of Art (☎ 061 310633) and the Hunt Museum (☎ 061 360788). The city also boasts some fine religious buildings. The centrepiece is St Mary's Cathedral (☎ 061 416238) on King's Island and there are a number of lesser churches and buildings which are interesting for their variety of styles and decoration. A good selection of places for shopping and places to eat and drink completes the picture of an excellent city to visit by boat, and a city which offers what may well be a welcome change from the small and sometimes sleepy places that are accessible to the yachtsman in the surrounding area.

To quench a well-earned thirst, Limerick offers a wide choice. In the heart of the city on O'Connell Street, An Sibin (☎ 061 414566) will undoubtedly get you in the mood with its nightly music sessions, and the Brazen Head Sports Bar (☎ 061 417412) is another popular bar. On Denmark Street, in the centre of town the Nancy Blake (☎ 061 416443) is a lively, all ages pub which serves bar snacks and has a sizeable beer garden. Dolan's (☎ 061 314483) on Dock Road is a traditional musical pub with a superb restaurant attached which serves breakfast, lunch and dinner and has fresh seafood available. The Old Quarter (☎ 061 401190) on Little Ellen Street, combines open air drinking with a strong French influence. For a real piece of history and excellent seafood, The Locke Bar (☎ 061 413733) on George's Quay, dates back to 1724 making it one of Limerick's oldest pubs. Quenelle's on the Waterfront (☎ 061 411111) at Steamboat Quay, Dock Road, is a pleasant setting for dinner while for something special, try the Copper Room at Jurys (☎ 061 327777) on Ennis Road.

Galway and Mayo

The exposed Aran Islands in Galway Bay contrast with the sheltered islands with their fringes of sandy beach in Clew Bay. Add to these the dramatic hills of Connemara which lie between them and you have a magnificent range of scenery which makes an inspiring backdrop to sail past. At the head of Galway Bay, the town of Galway is a welcome centre of energetic life just in case you feel in need of a trip to the cinema or the stimulus of a buzzing city. This can be offset by a visit to Belmullet between Broad Haven and Blacksod Bay which is probably the most remote village in Ireland. If you have come from outside Ireland, you may feel a real sense of satisfaction at reaching one of the most remote, and often challenging, cruising areas in the British Isles. With nothing but the Atlantic stretching away for thousands of miles to the west, this area can be very exposed if the weather turns against you, so a seaworthy boat and prudent attention to weather forecasts with a view to a quick dash for refuge are essential. In places, it can be a long way between harbours, so your planning needs to be thorough and flexible to ensure that you know what your options are and where you can find shelter if needed. If the conditions are favourable, this is a breathtaking area to cruise in, and all the time you can afford to spend here will almost certainly not be enough.

Aran Islands

The exposed Aran Islands are harsh but beautiful and lie some miles from the coast in Galway Bay. If you are in search of out-of-the-way places, these islands with their population of barely 2000 people will be an essential stop-off on your itinerary, though the shelter here is limited and the best anchorage, Killeany Bay on Inishmore, can be crowded with fishing boats. Once ashore, you will find that the Aran Heritage Centre in Kilronan (☎ 099 61355) offers a good introduction to matters historical and cultural and a trip to Dun Aenghus, about 5 miles along the island, is a must as this is one of the best examples of a prehistoric fort in Europe. Like many other buildings on the islands, and the walls which protect the intricate network of small fields, the fort's construction is of dry stone walls whose longevity and resilience is remarkable. There are more prehistoric sites on the smaller islands of Inishmaan and Inisheer which can easily be reached by ferry or light aircraft. The early Christian Church's habit of locating outposts in the most inaccessible places means that these islands have several very ancient church and monastic sites which are interesting, and more recent culture is for sale at several craft shops where you will find locally made curios and souvenirs. There has been a lifeboat station at Kilronan since 1927, and the crew will be pleased to meet you to talk about their role in search and rescue. The harbour is accessible in all states of the tide, and you can get alongside the pier for a few hours around high water. A couple of visitors' moorings may be available in the bay, or alternatively, you can drop your anchor off Kilronan Pier. There is quite a good range of shops within a few hundred yards walk, and fuel is available here as well. You will find a good selection of bars in Kilronan. Ti Joe Mac's (☎ 099 61248) and the American Bar (☎ 099 61130) are both conveniently close for a drink, and you will get a good pub meal at Tigh Joe Watty (☎ 099 61155). A mile away round the bay at Killeany, Tigh Fitz (☎ 099 61213) also serves bar food, and for a restaurant meal, the place to go is the Aran Fisherman (☎ 099 61104) in Kilronan.

Taxi:	(☎ 099 61241) or (☎ 099 61109)
Cycle hire:	(☎ 099 61402) or (☎ 099 61132)
Ferry:	from Kilronan Pier to other islands & mainland Aran Ferries (☎ 091 568903) and Island Ferries (☎ 091 561767)
Airport:	Kilronan Airstrip - Aer Arann (☎ 091 593034) for flights to other islands and mainland

for more details, see Directory Section

Galway Harbour

Galway is the largest town on the west coast of Ireland, and is a bustling and attractive university city with many places of interest to visit. With a central area of narrow streets which date back to medieval times, this is an atmospheric place and, as it has good transport links, it is a good base to explore the surrounding area. Built into the remains of the city walls by the Spanish Arch, the Galway City Museum (☎ 091 567641) has an assorted collection of local material which will give a feel for the history of the area and, being close to the docks, it's a good place to start your explorations of the city. The entrance to the harbour is well marked, and in good conditions, not difficult. The dock gates are only open for a couple of hours before high water and you should contact the harbour-master for instructions about berthing. Alternatively, the Galway Yacht Club will often be able to supply a visitors' mooring – their bar is open on Wednesday evenings and at weekends. Though the docks are busy with commercial traffic, yachts are very welcome, and with rail and air services available from here, this is an ideal place for crew changes or even to leave the boat for a while. As you would expect in a city with over 50,000 inhabitants, there is plenty of scope for shopping both for provisions and more general purchases, and there are plenty of places to find a meal or a convivial drink. Close by, Brennans Bar (☎ 091 564828) in the New Docks is a good choice for a drink and you'll get a good pub meal at O'Flahertys (☎ 091 564041) on Eyre Square. McSwiggins (☎ 091 568917) on Wood Quay will serve you a meal that won't burn a hole in your pocket or try De Burgo's (☎ 091 562188) on St Augustine Street for something a little more elaborate. The best in the area is probably Kirwans Lane (☎ 091 568266) on Kirwans Lane, and for a takeaway meal, McDonachs on Quay Street does good fish and chips and McDonalds offers exactly the same as it does the world over. If you happen to enjoy horse racing then try to visit the Galway Festival in late July-early August - it will knock your socks off!

Taxi:	Omni Cabs (☎ 091 565900)
Car hire:	Windsor Car Hire (☎ 091 770707)
Bus:	nationwide services available from here
Rail:	Galway Station for services to Dublin and Limerick
Ferry:	services to the Aran Islands
Airport:	flights from Dublin and Limerick

for more details, see Directory Section,

Artist: **Clive Madgwick ROUNDSTONE HARBOUR**
Courtesy of: **Rosenstiel's**

Galway Harbour to Sligo Bay

In settled weather, there are some lovely places to put into as you work your way around the Connemara peninsula and beyond. However, some of the entrances can be difficult, and the pilotage through the islands and off the headlands of this wild stretch of coastline should not be undertaken lightly. For the intrepid, there will be a warm welcome at the Clifden Yacht Club at the head of Clifden Bay. This is a spectacular little inlet with a choice of places to berth. If you don't mind taking the ground, then you can dry out alongside the quay, or further down the creek you will be able to find a quiet place to anchor if you consult your pilot book, and you can then take your dinghy up to the town. The selection of shops here is good, and there are some excellent places to have a well-earned drink or meal. For a drink, head for E.J. Kings (☎ 095 21058) on The Square or Guy's (☎ 024 91564) in Main Street where the food is good as well. You are assured of a warm welcome in the bar at the Yacht Club which also serves simple meals, or try Derryclare (☎ 095 21440) in The Square for an inexpensive meal. Mitchells (☎ 095 21867) in Market Street is a bit more upmarket and for a treat, go to O'Gradys Seafood Restaurant (☎ 095 21450) just along the street.

Taxi:	(☎ 095 21268)
Cycle hire:	(☎ 095 21160)
Bus:	services to Galway
Rail:	services from Galway Station

for more details, see Directory Section

Following the coast on round from Clifden, the scenery is spectacular and there are numerous inlets where visitors' moorings are often provided by the Local Authority or County Council. A useful list with a location map of where you can find such moorings all around Ireland called "Visitor Moorings in Ireland" is available from tourist boards, harbour-masters, marinas and some yacht clubs and is well worth having in your library. The off lying islands here can also be spectacu-

Artist: **Clive Madgwick FISHING BOATS ON LAKE CONNEMARA** *Courtesy of:* **Rosenstiel's**

lar, and one such is Inishbofin Island which has a very snug anchorage, and fabulous scenery with deserted sandy bays and the ruins of historic buildings clinging to its rocky shoreline. For island lovers, **Clew Bay** just to the north is a stunning spot with its myriad grassy islands flanked by sandy beaches. Clare Island, where there are visitors' moorings, is set at the mouth of the bay, and is a hilly outpost with the ruins of a friary and a castle to add atmosphere. The enclosed bay is a popular sailing area for both dinghy sailors and those with cruising yachts as well. The scenery is wonderful and there is a good choice of secluded spots to drop anchor. An indication of the appeal of Clew Bay is that the Glenans Sailing School has chosen it as their dinghy sailing training base in Ireland to take advantage of the attractive surroundings and plentiful open water. They are based on Collan More Island, but have no fears that the area will be overrun with enthusiastic novices - there are several hundred more islands and you will find plenty of room to get away from any crowds. For provisions and a run ashore, you can go alongside at **Westport**, though the approach to the quay is only navigable for about two hours around high water. You need to be prepared to sit on the bottom here if you plan to stay for more than a quick trip ashore. The town was planned and built in the late 18th century, and includes an elegant tree-lined waterfront and a number of interesting places to visit. On Westport Quay, the Clew Bay Heritage Centre will bring you up to speed on historical and cultural background, and it's well worth a trip to Westport House (☎ 098 25141) which is a fine Georgian stately home set in wonderful landscaped formal gardens. There are shops for provisions here and on The Quay, the Asgard Tavern and

Restaurant (☎ 098 25319) commands impressive views of Clew Bay and Clare Island and is decorated with a nautical theme. It will come as no surprise, therefore, that its restaurant is famous for seafood. The Restaurant at Knockranny House (☎ 098 28600) at Knockranny, which is about 1/2 mile east of Westport, is a good place for either a bar lunch or an à la carte dinner. Roughly the same distance in the other direction from Westport is the Westport Woods (☎ 098 25811) on Louisburgh Road, which is also a good choice for a slightly more upmarket meal.

To the north of Clew Bay, **Achill Island** has impressive cliffs and a spectacular promontory at Achill Head. With hills rising to over two thousand feet and sandy bays on the coastline, this is a beautiful backdrop to sail past. Tucked in behind the island in Achill Sound, you will find one of the RNLI's newest stations (opened in 1996), and an Arun class lifeboat swinging on its picturesque mooring by 15th century Castle Kildavnet. There are overhead cables and a swing bridge to contend with in the sound, and the tide can sluice through making anchoring awkward, so consult your pilot book before making any irrevocable decisions. It is, however, a wonderfully secluded spot to drop the hook - the attendant caveat is that facilities are extremely limited. For contrasting scenery, **Blacksod Bay** is a magnificent natural harbour on the mainland just north of Achill Island. There are numerous inner bays to choose from to find shelter, and some council managed visitors' moorings are available. Bear in mind that this is an extremely isolated spot, and the nearest place to buy even the most basic provisions is a few miles away at Belmullet which is one of the most remote villages in Ireland. Approaching from the north via Broad Haven Bay you reach Ballyglass, where an all-weather Severn class lifeboat is on station, and there are several sheltered places to choose from to anchor. There's a small shop on the mainland near the anchorage off Inver Point and you can reach Belmullet in your tender.

Sligo and Donegal

With backdrops of high hills and mountains behind craggy coastlines punctuated with fortifications from the Napoleonic period, this is an impressive stretch of coastline to cruise along. As well as wonderful scenery, there are numerous harbours and anchorages which give access to delightful small villages and fishing communities offering scope for convivial refreshment ashore and wonderful fresh seafood. Given reasonable weather conditions, you can drop anchor and head ashore to explore many of the islands you will pass along these shores. You will find varying landscapes, some islands with large populations such as Aran, some with much smaller communities like Tory Island and some, for real solitude, with no one at all.

Sligo

If you are in search of bright lights and a more bustling pace of life after the isolation and tranquillity which many of the ports of call in this area offer, then a visit to Sligo may be just what you are after. The town is in a picturesque setting with a backdrop of mountains behind a coastline of sandy beaches and, as a busy market town, there is plenty going on ashore. The Niland Gallery and Museum (☎ 071 43728) in Stephen Street houses various examples of modern Irish art and the Yeats Memorial Collection of letters, manuscripts and photographs. Sligo Abbey is just across the river - it dates back to the early 15th century and is well worth a look. A few miles north of Sligo,

Benbulben is a spectacular and massive mountain which rises to over 1700 feet, and its neighbour Truskmore is even higher at over 2000 feet. The energetic may wish to admire the view from the top, but for many it may well be enough to admire the hills from a distance! Sligo Bay is the site of the RNLI's most recently established lifeboat station which was opened in March 1999 - an Atlantic 21 inshore lifeboat is now stationed here.

The approach to the harbour at Sligo is pretty tricky and should not be attempted without good pilotage instructions. There's an anchorage opposite the north end of Coney Island near the Sligo Yacht Club who will make you very welcome at their clubhouse on the mainland near Deadman's Point (basic provisions can also be found here). If the shelter is insufficient, or you want to get into the thick of things, follow the channel up to the centre of Sligo (about four miles) where there is space to berth alongside. Here, you are well placed for a good range of shops, and places to eat and drink including The Blue Lagoon (☎ 071 42530) on the riverside, which is an easy 5 minute stroll from Sligo Town Centre and holds a weekly traditional Irish Night with plenty of music. The Tower (☎ 071 44000) on Quay Street serves bar lunches and à la carte dinners for something a bit smarter. The Yeats Tavern Restaurant and Davis's Pub (☎ 071 63117) in Drumcliff Bridge is 5 miles from Sligo town and walking distance from Yeat's grave. It offers very good food at reasonable prices and is worth making the trip for if you have time on your hands.

Taxi:	(☎ 071 43000)
Car hire:	Hertz (☎ 071 44068)
Bus:	Sligo bus station, enquiries (☎ 071 60066)
Rail:	(☎ 071 69888)
Airport:	Strandhill Airport in Sligo (☎ 071 68280)

for more details, see Directory Section

Artist: **David James A SUMMER MORNING** *Courtesy of:* **Rosenstiel's**

Donegal Bay to Loch Swilly

On the north side of Donegal Bay, there are several places where you can comfortably put in for the night as the broken rocky coastline has numerous deep inlets which create wonderful natural harbours. The scenery is spectacular and the countryside is sparsely populated, so you can cruise in real peace and quiet as long as the weather is kind to you. **Killybegs** is an excellent natural harbour where you will find a good range of facilities. This is also a useful port of refuge if the weather turns against you as the entrance is straightforward in most weather conditions and at all states of the tide. The shore rises steeply from the seashore here, and the town clusters its way up the hillside. There is superb countryside for stretching your legs and burning off some energy. The peace and quiet is periodically shattered as fishing boats return to unload their catches as this is a thriving outpost of the fishing industry. As well as being famous for its fish, the town has a long standing reputation for the hand-made carpets which have been made here for over a hundred years.

When berthing, you may well have to contend with fishing boats and you should contact the harbour-master in advance of coming alongside to avoid getting in the way. Shops for provisions are close to hand and there are some good places for a drink or a meal. The Bay View (☎ 073 31950) on the Main Street serves bar lunches and à la carte dinners and at Cope House (☎ 073 31836) the nautically themed Galleon Bar is known for its excellent food and music - it also has a Chinese Restaurant. Wandering up to the Main Street, you will find two more pubs to choose from - these are The Pier Bar and Guest House (☎ 073 31386) and the Sail Inn (☎ 073 31130), both of which will offer a warm welcome.

Taxi:	(☎ 073 31056)
Car hire:	Donegal Car Hire (☎ 075 48232)
Bus:	local services to Londonderry and Sligo
Rail:	Londonderry Station (50 miles approx)
	Sligo Station (45 miles approx)
Airport:	Donegal Airport enquiries (☎ 075 48284)

for more details, see Directory Section

A few of miles to the west, the harbour at **Teelin** is an outstandingly beautiful place to put in for a quiet evening or lunch stop. The tiny harbour is set in superb scenery and is a delightful place to spend some time sitting in the cockpit watching the world drift by. Facilities are extremely limited and, though some supplies can be had at Carrick a few miles inland, you would be well advised to sail to Killybegs if you need anything, so only come in here if you are fully prepared to be independent. Pressing on from Teelin, there is some magnificent coastline to sail past and the steep shore which rises up towards the peak of Slieve League to the west of Teelin is precipitous and spectacular. We are soon heading north after rounding Rossan Point, and the coastline breaks here into numerous inlets and islets all the way to Bloody Foreland. The Aran Roads around the island of **Aran** (or Aranmore) present an attractive cruising area which you could easily spend some time in. A central landmark, which you can see for miles around the coast here, is the imposing peak of Errigal which reaches over 2000 feet away in the distance on the mainland. The island of Aran has had an RNLI station since 1883, though its current location on the north-east side of the island has only been in use for about the last ten years. The island's coast includes some spectacular cliffs and this is a good place for walking and bird watching. Visitors' moorings are available by the island and, as this is a popular holiday area there are reasonably good opportunities for finding fuel and provisions. For refreshments, Earlys Bar is a good place for a drink at the harbour and the Ferry Boat Restaurant (☎ 075 20532) is excellent. There's also pub food in Neily's Bar (☎ 075 20509) which is about a mile from the harbour. A couple of miles away on the mainland, **Burtonport** is the mainland base for the ferry which serves Arranmore and has a snug if rather crowded harbour. Fuel and provisions are available and there's a good restaurant right by the pier which serves splendid local seafood. Gola, a smaller island to the north east of Aran, is a really beautiful spot to anchor for a stroll ashore, and with just a handful of holiday houses the chances are you will have the place almost to yourself. Surrounded by lovely white sandy beaches, the tranquillity here is really wonderful. Beyond Bloody Foreland, the most north-westerly point on this stretch of coast, Tory Island is also well worth a visit. Nearly ten miles from the mainland, this isolated island offers a very insular existence to a population of a couple of hundred who have a distinctly different outlook to their neighbours on the mainland. The spectacular coastline of broken cliffs and jagged outcrops to the south east is topped by flat ground which can be a little bleak where the covering of peat has been cut for fuel. A walk ashore will reveal spectacular views from the cliffs and a pace of life which is both relaxed and hardy – just imagine what this place must be like in winter storms! The island has two little harbours, but shelter for yachts is very limited, so this is really only a suitable destination in settled weather.

For better shelter, you might consider putting into **Mulroy Bay** which is an extensive inlet to the west of Lough Swilly. The entrance is one to approach cautiously at the right state of the tide, and onshore winds or swell may result in it being unsafe for yachts, but if the conditions are good, you are in for a treat. The scenery is spectacular and there are several attractive anchorages. A run ashore to the Rosapenna Hotel (☎ 074 55301) is warmly recommended as the bill of fare on offer amply rewards you for the ten minute walk from Fanny's Bay on the west shore.

Lough Swilly

For wonderful scenery and delightful places to put into, Lough Swilly is certainly one that you should consider. Roughly ten miles to the south west of the imposing promontory of Malin Head, the lough stretches inland for nearly twenty miles as it winds its way in towards Donegal's mountainous countryside. There are several places where you can either berth alongside or anchor to enjoy the tranquil atmosphere and idyllic settings. About five miles from the entrance, there is a handy anchorage off **Pincher** where you will find limited provisions and a bar for a drink. To earn it, perhaps you might like to stretch your legs and your lungs as there are terrific views from the Knockalla Mountain which climbs to around 2000 feet not far to the south. On the east shore at the mouth of Fahan Creek, you will come to the Lough Swilly Yacht Club where you will be most welcome, though from here it is a bit of a hike to find much in the way of supplies. Opposite at **Rathmullan**, there is pontoon berthing available for visitors and a good range of services is available. There is a strong sense of history here with the ruins of a 15th century Carmelite Priory close to the waterfront and "The Flight of the Earls Exhibition" (☎ 074 58229) in the Martello Tower near the pier gives an interesting account of one significant episode. The local shop will enable you to stock up on essential provisions and there are several hotels within reach for a drink or a meal ashore. The Rathmullan House (☎ 074 58188) is an attractive 19th century country house, and serves splendid meals and The Fort Royal (☎ 074 58100) is not far away and is equally good for a leisurely bar lunch or dinner, if you prefer. The White Hart Bar (☎ 074 58154)

is handy for a drink. Other options in area include the St John's Country House (☎ 077 60289) in Fahan which enjoys a spectacular loughside setting in which to enjoy either lunch or a delicious à la carte dinner. In Milford, The Milford Inn (☎ 074 53313) and the Traveller's Inn (☎ 074 53293) on the Main Street, are both ready to serve you a well-earned drink. In Ramelton, The Pin Tavern (☎ 074 26000) is a good place to head for to quench your thirst.

From Rathmullan:
Taxi: (☎ 074 24309)
Car hire: From Londonderry, Avis (☎ 01504 811708)
Bus: Letterkenny Bus Station to Londonderry
             and Belfast
Rail: Londonderry Station, Irish Rail
             (☎ 0181 686 0994)
Airport: Belfast Airport (☎ 01849 422888)
for more details, see Directory Section

Artist: **Cloé Cloberty TOWARDS THE ATLANTIC** _Courtesy of:_ **Osborne Studio Gallery**

BALLYCOTTON

Limited facilities for yachts

Ballycotton Lifeboat
Open to visitors by arrangement with Mech
M Walsh Tel: 021 646721

CORK HARBOUR   51.47'.5N 08.15'.5W

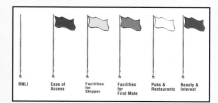

Captain Pat Farnan: Harbourmaster
Port Operations Office, Cork Harbour, Cork
Tel: 021 273125 Fax: 021 276484
Port Operation and Information (24 hr)
Tel: 021 811380
VHF Channel: 12/14/16
VHF Name: Cork Harbour Radio

Crosshaven

Royal Cork Yacht Club Marina
Kim Wood: Manager
Tel: 021 831023 Fax: 021 831586
VHF Channel: 37
VHF Name: Royal Cork Marina

Crosshaven Boat Yard Marina
Matt Foley: Manager
Crosshaven Boat Yard Co. Ltd, Crosshaven,
Tel: 021 831161 Fax: 021 831603
VHF Channel: 37
VHF Name: Crosshaven Marina

Salve Marine
Crosshaven, Co. Cork
Tel: 021 831145 Fax: 021 831747

Chandlers and Repairs:
Contact Crosshaven Boat Yard or Salve
Marine, as above or
Union Chandlery, Anderson Quay, Cork
Tel: 021 271643
McWilliam Sailmakers Tel: 021 831505

East Ferry

East Ferry Marina
Contact: Manager
Tel: 021 811342

KINSALE   51.41'.0N 08.30'.0W

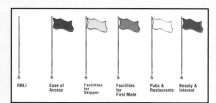

Capt Phil Tait: Harbourmaster
Tel: 021 772503
VHF Channel: 16 VHF Name: Kinsale
Harbour

Kinsale Yacht Club Marina
Tel: 021 772196 Fax: 021 774455

Castlepark Marina
Eddie McCarthy: Manager
Kinsale, Co. Cork, Ireland
Tel: 021 774959 Fax: 021 774958
VHF Channel: 6/16/37
VHF Name: Castlepark Marina

Repairs:
Contact the Castlepark Marina Manager
Boat repairs. Engine repairs. Sail repairs.

COURTMACSHERRY   51.38'.0N 08.41'.0W

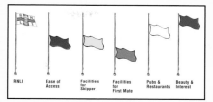

Harbourmaster Tel: 023 46311

Courtmacsherry Harbour Lifeboat.
Open to visitors: By arrangement
Contact: Hon. Sec. J Crowley or Mech. M
Hurley Tel: 023 40394 (Hon. Sec.) or 023 46218
(Mech.)

GLANDORE   51.33'.5N 09.07'.0N

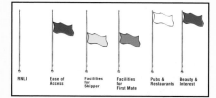

CASTLETOWNSHEND   51.31'.0N 09.10'.5W

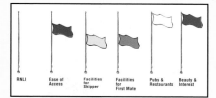

BALTIMORE   51.28'.5N 09.23'.5W

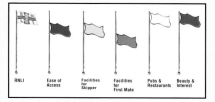

Harbourmaster Tel: 028 20132
VHF Ch: 09/16 VHF Name: Baltimore Harbour

Baltimore Marina
Tel: 021 774959 Fax: 021 774959

Baltimore Sailing Club Tel/Fax: 021 20426

Baltimore Lifeboat
Open to visitors most days.
Contact: B O'Driscoll (Hon. Sec.)
Tel: 028 20101 or 028 20143

SCHULL   51.31'.0N 09.32'.0W

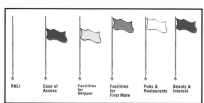

Harbourmaster Tel: 028 28136

Schull Sailing Club Tel: 028 37532

Chandler:
Schull Watersports Centre, The Pier, Schull
Tel: 028 28554

Repairs:
Rossbrin Boatyard, Schull, Co. Cork
Tel: 028 37352 Fax: 028 37104

BANTRY BAY   51.34'.0N 09.57'.0W

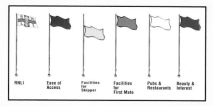

Harbourmaster - Bantry Tel: 0270 50525
VHF Channel: 14/11/16
VHF Name: Bantry Harbour

Harbourmaster - Castletown Tel: 027 70220
VHF Channel: 08/16
VHF Name: Castletown Harbour

Castletownbere Lifeboat
Open to visitors by arrangement with
D. O'Driscoll (Hon. Sec.)
Tel: 027 70055 Mobile: 087 2246369

VALENTIA   51.56'.0N 10.19'.5W

Des Lavelle: Harbourmaster Tel: 066 76124

Valentia Lifeboat Station
Open to visitors by arrangement with
P. Gallagher (Hon. Sec.) Tel: 066 76126

DINGLE   52.07'.0N 10.15'.5W

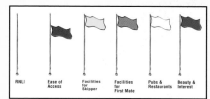

Harbourmaster Tel: 066 51629
VHF Channel: 14 VHF Name: Dingle Harbour

Dingle Marina
LT CDR Brian Farrell: Manager
Harbour Office, Dingle, Co. Kerry, Ireland
Tel: 066 51629 Fax: 066 52629
VHF Channel: M814
VHF Name: Dingle Marina

Chandler:
O' Sullivan Marine, Monavalley, Tralee
Tel: 066 24524

Repairs:
Michael O'Connor, Dingle Tel: 087 625176

FENIT   52.16'.0N 09.51'.5W

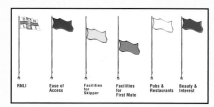

Billy Revington: Harbourmaster
Tel/Fax: 066 36231   Mobile: 087 460516

Fenit Harbour Marina
David Buttimer: Manager
Fenit, Co. Kerry, Ireland
Tel: 066 36231 Fax: 066 36473
VHF Channel: 37 VHF Name: Fenit Harbour

Chandler:
O'Sullivan Marine, Monavalley, Tralee
Tel: 066 24524

Repairs:
Jimmy Brown, Fenit Tel: 066 36199
Boat and Engine repairs.
Bob Bolt, Fenit Tel: 066 36114
Engine repairs.

Fenit Lifeboat
Open to visitors 7 days a week when
mechanic present. Contact: Bob Bolt or
G O Donnchadha (Hon. Sec.)
Tel: 066 36376 or 066 36114

RIVER SHANNON

Kilrush   52.38'.0N 09.29'.5W

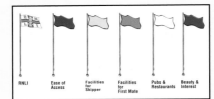

Gerald Griffin: Harbourmaster Tel: 065 51327

Kilrush Marina
John Hehir: Manager
Tel: 065 52072 Fax: 065 51692
VHF Channel: 80   VHF Name: Kilrush Marina

Chandler:
Glynn Marine Tel: 065 51040

Repairs:
Kilrush Marine Tel: 065 52566
Boat repairs. Engine repairs. Sail repairs.

Kilrush Lifeboat
The Boathouse, Kilrush.
Open to visitors: By arrangement with
A O'Connel (Hon. Sec.)
Tel: 065 52566   Mobile: 087 2208567

Foynes Yacht Club Tel: 069 65261
Limerick Harbour Commission
Tel: 061 315377

GALWAY HARBOUR   53.12'.0N 09.08'.0W

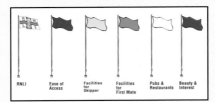

Capt Frank Sheridan: Harbourmaster
Tel: 091 561874 Fax: 091 563738
VHF Channel: 12/16
VHF Name: Harbourmaster Galway

Galway Sailing Club Tel: 091 794527

Chandler:
Galway Maritime, Merchants Road, Galway
Tel: 091 566568

Repairs:
Rynn Engineering, New Docks
Tel: 081 567804
Boat repairs. Engine repairs

The West Coast of Ireland - Pilot Books

East and North Coasts of Ireland Sailing Directions, Irish Cruising Club
published by Imray, Laurie, Norie & Wilson, Tel: 01480 462114 ISBN: 0950 171 76X

South and West Coasts of Ireland Sailing Directions, Irish Cruising Club.
published by Imray, Laurie, Norie & Wilson, Tel: 01480 462114 ISBN: 0950 171 778

Galway Lifeboat
New Docks, Galway
Open to visitors by appointment only with
Pat Lavelle (Hon. Sec.)
Tel: 091 567707 Mobile: 087 2418970

CLIFDEN BAY   53.29'.5N 10.06'.0W

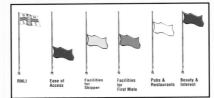

Clifden Yacht Club
John Le Dorvan: Commodore
Tel: 095 21711

Clifden Lifeboat
Open to visitors all year round
Contact: Jack O'Grady (Hon. Sec.)
Tel: 095 21437 or 095 21450

CLEW BAY   53.48'.0N 09.35'.5W

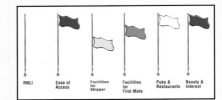

Mayo Sailing Club Tel: 098 26160

Glenans Irish Sailing Club Tel: 098 26046

ACHILL ISLAND

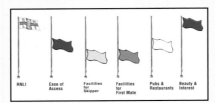

Achill Island Lifeboat
Kildavnet, Achill Island.
Open to visitors: By arrangement with
Bob Kingston (Hon. Sec.) Tel: 098 43496

BALLYGLASS

Ballyglass Lifeboat
Open to visitors all year round
Contact: P Leech (Hon. Sec.)
Hon. Sec. Tel: 097 82227

SLIGO   54.18'.0N 08.34'.5W

Harbourmaster Tel: 071 61197
VHF Channel: 12/16
VHF Name: Sligo Harbour

Sligo Yacht Club Tel: 071 77168

SLIGO cont.

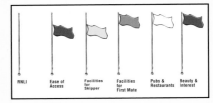

BUNDORAN

Bundoran Lifeboat
Open for visitors: May to September
Contact: Captain H McGowan (Hon. Sec.)
Tel: 072 41552 or 072 41455 Mobile: 087 2246373

KILLYBEGS   54.37'.0N 08.27'.0W

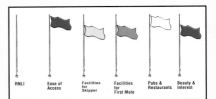

Harbourmaster Tel: 073 31032
VHF Ch: 16/14 VHF Name: Killybegs Harbour

ARRANMORE   55.01'.0N 08.33'.5W

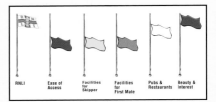

Arranmore Harbour
Visitors moorings available
VHF Channel: 10 VHF Name: Ferry Office

Arranmore Lifeboat Station
Arranmore, Co. Donegal
Open to visitors Easter through September
Contact: Hon. Sec. A Gallagher
Tel: 075 20928 or 075 20533

LOUGH SWILLY   55.17'.0N 07.34'.0W

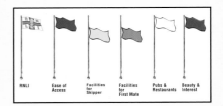

Lough Swilly Yacht Club Tel: 074 60189

Lough Swilly Lifeboat
Open to visitors all year round
Contact: L Magee (Hon. Sec.)
Tel: 077 61700/61209 or 077 61710

Acknowledgements

An enormous number of people – RNLI personnel, harbour-masters, yacht club officers and secretaries, marina managers and others – have contributed to this book and we are really grateful to them all. This book could not have been put together without their involvement. The editors would particularly like to thank Sally O'Leary, Peter Cumberlidge, John Myatt, Rodney Wright and Barry Cox for their kind support and advice. We would also like to thank all of the following who have given up their time to this project:

Colin Price • Kenderick Horne • Jonathan Milton • Alison Bird • Andrew Sackett • John Bartholomew • Nick Willmer •
Ron Whitehead • Jenny Hesse • Ian Gardner • Captain J H Jenkinson • Captain PMH Blanch • G S Howlett • David Allan Clarke •
Mrs Linda Sweaney • Ian Reay • Richard J Martin • Mr JC Scott • P Q Mitchell • J W K Smith • Martin Kenny • Alison Marsh •
Mr P Murphy • Ian Gilbraith • Paul Lane • D Porritt • Richard Willis • Captain J A H Gray • Keith Stuart • Peter Thomson •
Samantha Fielding • Mrs S Scholes • Mrs M M Wilkins • Captain C Hoskison • J H Evans • Barrie Brigham • Brian Bevan •
A G Credland • Captain David King • Howard Anguish • John Clegg • R Broughton • Peter Root • David Harrison • A D Cross •
Peter Beck • Allen Frary • Lorraine Marshall • Mr A Watson • P M Jackson • Frank H Muirhead • C Cox • Thomas Carr •
Andrew Donovan • Captain J N Wooley • John Cooper • P Parker • E M Caines • D S G Reid • I Firman • Peter Wilson •
Chris Garnett • Richard Sampson • A Rutter • David Conner • Diana Pickard • Gary Edwards • Anthea Wade •
David Lewin • M Hemmingway • R J L Stace • John Langrick • Marjory Hall • David G Brown • G R Baker • T Plane •
Rod Jenkins • Adam Cars • Valerie Green • R A Rush • Don Cockrill • Peter Barker • Captain Ken Gray • A G Hawkins •
Carol Partridge • C E Sharrod • Captain I M Shearer • Dan Hughes • N J Tubb • John Knapp • Mr A Lay • David Skinner •
Helen Poole • John Mitchell • Keith Stevens • Martin Rudwick • Ian Clarke • Nigel Roper • William Bowman •
Stephen Duncan-Brown • Steven Gordon • Caroline Millar • Hugh Knight • Mrs Jane Moody • Peter Bedwell • Alan Tribbeach •
Cuan Marsh • Ken Campling • R Kemp • Alan Young • Don Hickman • Dave Brown • Captain G R Hall • G R Hall •
Lt Col M J Samuelson RM • Mrs S Tribe • Chris Brown • J Horton • John Edward • Brian May • Michael Webb • C Rossiter •
Mr P T Reakes • D Grierson • David Henson • Captain D T Stabler • Lt DRG Mannard RNR • Roger Clarke • Mike Hill •
E S Tucker • Peter Harris • Neal Rickets • Neil Slater • John Tarr • Mrs M Smallwood • Tony Tucker • Ian Quick • Alan Mayne •
A P Hodges • Mr M A Gaunt • Peter Hodges • Steve Tooke • Andrew Matthews • Julian Stapley • A Barber • J B Heaton •
Mr A G Smith • Robin Page • M J K Stuart • Captain Roy Maddern • Ronnie Howard • Captain D G Banks • David Edwards •
J Seagrove • John Young • Mr Andrew de Labat • Mr D J Prior • Mr Windebank • Jonathon Fielding • Caroline Dudley •
Mrs C Martin • Keith Murch • Terry George • Captain J J Moran • Mr J S Crossland • R C Thomas • Captain Malcolm Gator •
Ron Eglinton • Captain R T Platt • George C Phillips • B Rush • D P Parr • Paddy Frost • Mark R Myers • Andrew Putt •
Colin Knill • J Slocombe • Howard Willicombe • Mark Blathwayte • K G Escott • Bruce Scott • Charles Bush • John Barr •
R V Harris • Dave Hoskin • Mike Lewis • Georgie Thomas • Paul Leleu • Tim Clement • P R Muxworth • Arthur Squibbs •
John Beynon • F J Penfold • Jeremy Rees • Adrian Owens • D H Grainger • Anthony Evans • Chris Williams • David Hughes •
D J Evans • F Coates • Captain Chrtis Corcoran • Mike Jones • Roger Davies • Captain Chris Corcoran • Gwenllion Ashley •
Sion Edwards • Dave Davies • Captain J Kirkham • J G C Greenway • Dafydd Philips • Peter Williams • Ken Fitzpatrick •
Wil Williams • B D McGill • R T Morris • Jack Abbott • Kerry Brown • Anthony Barclay • Sarah Anderson • David Jones •
Huw Glynn Williams • R H Williamson • Stan Zalot • Philip Schofield • Steve Lovell • R H Jones • David Dodd • F Brereton •
N Brereton • Jeremy Haughton • M.K. Stannis • Derek M Sheppard • Frank Kilroy • Dick Rigby • P Woodworth •
S J Hayhow • J F Hodgson • Captain L Goldwater • Captain D Allan • Captain K Horsley • Harry Owens • Neil Boyes •
D F Devereaux • Mr G Burns • Terry Hughes • Robert Erskine • Roderick Leitch • Jilly Sharp • J M Leldesley • Keith Gibson •
David Cook • Carolyn Elder • Duncan Chalmers • J G Gorrie • Ann Bray • N Stratton • Robin Stephens • Ewan Sim • Ian M Silcook •
Bob Hunter • David Willice • Mrs Jan Brown • K Byrne • Jim Berry • Lorne MacKechnie • R Kincaid • Willie Melville •
John Wilshire • Mr Brian Swingbanks • Murdo Grant • A Ross McKerlich • John Mannall • Neil Gudgeon • Angus M MacLeod •
A Rendall • Hylton Henry • Kevin Henry • Victor Gray • Captain Archer T L Kemp • Alan Long • Captain John Banks •
Captain R Moore • Alex Davidson • Captain J B Fairgrieve • Captain M Macleod • John Mackay • Alex K Scott •
Herbert D Reid • John Murray • Eric Hendry • Alasdair Galloway • Andrew Findlay • W J West • Jack Provan • James Watt •
J J Ferguson • John Edwards • Margaret H King • J K Lindsay • R Henderson • John F Hainey • Richard Bolton •
Mr D Horsburgh • Alistair Crowe • Alan Wilson • Robert Cardwell • Joseph Ferris • Jim Farrell • Frank Healy •
Robert J Logan • Andrew Jaggers • John Murray • Ralph McCutcheon • F Morgan • Damien Offer • Rupert Jeffares •
Ned Dillon • John Doyle • Donal Walsh • Matt Foley • Eddie McCarthy • Lt Cdr Brian Farrell • Bob Bolt • David Buttmer •
John Heffir • Padraic Dillane • Pat Lavelle • Jack O'Grady • Francis Bonner • John Taylor • Graham Trebert •
P M Sarl • Geoff Mead • R Daley • Bruce Ferguson • Barry Macneaney

We must also thank the many staff of tourist boards and other organisations who have been kind enough to send information from all around the British Isles and Ireland and whose modesty has been such that we do not know their names to thank them personally – nevertheless, we are enormously grateful to them all.

Index & Abbreviations

CADW — Welsh Historic Monuments, Crown Building, Cathays Park, Cardiff CF1 3NQ Tel: 029 205 00200
EH — English Heritage, PO Box 9019, London W1A 0JA Tel: 020 7973 3434
EN — English Nature, Northminster House, Northminster PE1 1UA Tel: 01733 340345
HS — Historic Scotland, Longmore House, Salisbury Place, Edinburgh EH9 1SH Tel: 0131 668 8800
NT — National Trust, PO Box 39, Bromley, Kent BR1 3XL Tel: 020 8315 1111
NTS — National Trust for Scotland, 5 Charlotte Square, Edinburgh EH2 4DU Tel: 0131 226 5922
NTG — National Trust for Guernsey, 26 Cornet Street, St Peter Port, Guernsey Tel: 01481 728451
RSPB — Royal Society for the Protection of Birds, The Lodge, Sandy, SG19 2DL Tel: 01767 680551

Aberaeron . . . 125, 138
Aberdeen . . . 176, 183
Aberdeenshire . . . 174
Aberdour . . . 179, 183
Aberdovey . . . 126, 138
Aberdyfi . . . 126, 138
Abersoch . . . 128, 139

*Artist: **Clive Madgwick STAITHES***
*Courtesy of: **Rosenstiel's***

Aberystwyth . . . 125, 138
Achill Island . . . 215, 220
Aith . . . 170, 182
Aldeburgh . . . 37, 51
Alderney . . . 83, 88
Amble . . . 19, 27
Anglesey . . . 128, 139
Angus . . . 177
Anstruther . . . 179, 183
Antrim . . . 189
Appledore . . . 117
Aran . . . 217
Aran Islands . . . 213
Aranmore . . . 217, 220
Arbroath . . . 178, 183
Ardfern . . . 154, 164
Ardglass . . . 194, 202
Ardrossan . . . 150, 163
Argyll and Bute . . . 148
Arisaig Harbour . . . 158, 165
Arklow . . . 198, 202
Armadale Bay . . . 159, 165
Arran . . . 153, 164
Avon . . . 110
Ayrshire . . . 148
Ballycastle . . . 190, 201
Ballycotton . . . 219
Ballyglass . . . 220
Balta Sound . . . 170
Baltimore . . . 208, 219
Bamburgh . . . 18
Banff . . . 175, 183
Bangor, N.Ireland . . . 192, 201
Bangor, N.Wales . . . 129
Bantry . . . 209
Bantry Bay . . . 209, 219
Barmouth . . . 127, 139
Barra . . . 161, 166
Barrow-in-Furness . . . 132, 141
Barry . . . 120, 137
Bawdsey . . . 38, 51
Beadnell . . . 19, 27
Beaucette . . . 85, 88
Beaulieu River . . . 67, 78
Beaumaris . . . 129, 139
Belfast Lough . . . 192
Bembridge . . . 70, 78
Benfleet . . . 44, 53
Berwick-on-Tweed . . . 17, 27
Birdham Pool . . . 61
Blackpool . . . 140
Blacksod Bay . . . 215
Blakeney . . . 33, 50
Blyth . . . 20, 27
Bosham . . . 62, 77
Bradwell-on-Sea . . . 42, 52
Brancaster Staithe . . . 50
Braye Bay . . . 83
Breydon Water . . . 34
Bridlington . . . 24, 28
Bridport . . . 74, 78
Brightlingsea . . . 41, 52
Brighton . . . 60, 76
Bristol . . . 112, 117
Brixham . . . 93, 114
Brodick . . . 153
Brough Haven . . . 25
Broughty Ferry . . . 178
Buckie . . . 183
Buckler's Hard . . . 67, 78
Bude . . . 110, 117
Bundoran . . . 220
Burgh Castle . . . 34, 50
Burghead . . . 183
Burlesden . . . 65, 78
Burnham Overy Staithe . . . 32, 50
Burnham-on-Crouch . . . 42, 52
Burntisland . . . 179, 183
Burry Port . . . 137
Burtonport . . . 217
Caernarfon . . . 128, 139
Caledonian Canal . . . 174, 183
Campbeltown . . . 153, 164
Canna . . . 158, 165
Canvey Island . . . 44, 53
Cardiff . . . 120, 137
Cardigan . . . 124, 138
Carrickfergus . . . 192, 201
Carlingford Lough . . . 196, 202
Carnlough . . . 191
Castlebay . . . 161
Castletown . . . 135, 141
Castletownbere . . . 209
Castletownshend . . . 207
Ceredigion . . . 124
Channel Islands . . . 83
Charlestown . . . 102
Chatham . . . 46
Chelsea Harbour . . . 45
Chichester . . . 61
Chichester Harbour . . . 61, 77
Christchurch . . . 72, 78
Clacton-on-Sea . . . 52
Clare, County . . . 210
Cleethorpes . . . 29
Clew Bay . . . 215, 220
Clifden . . . 214, 220
Clougher Head . . . 202
Clovelly . . . 117
Clyde Estuary . . . 150
Cobh . . . 206
Coleraine . . . 189, 201

*Artist: **Clive Madgwick BRIXHAM***
*Courtesy of: **Rosenstiel's***

Colonsay . . . 154, 164
Conwy . . . 129, 140
Conyer Creek . . . 47, 54
Cork City . . . 206, 219
Cork Harbour . . . 205
Cork, County . . . 205
Cornwall, North Coast . . . 108
Cornwall, South Coast . . . 100
Coryvreckan, Gulf of . . . 155
Courtmacsherry . . . 207, 219
Courtown . . . 202
Cowes . . . 69, 78
Craignure . . . 156
Craobh Haven . . . 154, 165
Craster . . . 19, 27
Crinan . . . 154, 164
Crinan Canal . . . 154
Cromarty . . . 173
Cromarty Firth . . . 173, 182
Cromer . . . 33, 50
Crookhaven . . . 209
Crosshaven . . . 205, 219
Cullen . . . 183
Cullercoats . . . 27
Cumbria . . . 132
Dale . . . 122
Dartmouth . . . 94, 114
Devon South . . . 92
Devon, North . . . 110
Dingle . . . 211, 219
Donegal . . . 216
Donghadee . . . 193, 201

*Artist: **Clive Madgwick CROMER***
*Courtesy of: **Rosenstiel's***

Dorset . . . 71
Douglas . . . 134, 141
Dover . . . 48, 55
Down . . . 193
Dublin . . . 196
Dublin Bay . . . 197
Dumfries & Galloway . . . 147
Dun Laoghaire . . . 197, 202
Dunbar . . . 180, 183
Dundee . . . 178, 183
Dundrum . . . 195
Dungarvon . . . 199, 203
Dungeness . . . 49
Dunmanus Bay . . . 209
Dunmore East . . . 199, 203
East Ferry . . . 206, 219
East Loch Tarbert . . . 152, 164
East Lothian . . . 180
East Riding of Yorkshire . . . 24
East Sussex . . . 58
Eastbourne . . . 59, 76
Edinburgh . . . 179
Eigg . . . 158, 165
Emsworth . . . 63, 77
Essex . . . 40
Exeter . . . 92, 114
Exmouth . . . 92, 114
Eyemouth . . . 181, 183
Fair Isle . . . 170
Falmouth . . . 103, 115
Fareham . . . 65, 77
Farne Islands . . . 18
Faversham Creek . . . 47, 54
Felixstowe Ferry . . . 38, 51
Fenit . . . 212, 219
Fethard . . . 203
Fife . . . 177
Filey . . . 28
Firth of Forth, The . . . 179
Fishguard . . . 124, 138
Flamborough . . . 28
Fleetwood . . . 132, 140
Flint . . . 140
Fort William . . . 157, 165
Fowey . . . 101, 115
Fraserburgh . . . 175, 183
Gallions Point . . . 45
Galway . . . 214
Galway Harbour . . . 214, 220
Galway, County . . . 213
Gareloch . . . 151, 164
Gigha . . . 153, 164
Gillan Creek . . . 105
Gillingham . . . 46, 54
Girvan . . . 148, 163
Glamorgan, Vale of . . . 120
Glandore . . . 207, 219
Glasson Dock . . . 132, 141
Glengarriff . . . 209
Gorey . . . 85, 88
Gosport . . . 64, 77
Granton . . . 179, 183
Gravesend . . . 44, 53
Great Cumbrae . . . 150
Great Yarmouth . . . 33, 50
Greenwich . . . 45
Grimsby . . . 25, 29
Guernsey . . . 83, 88
Gulf of Coryvreckan . . . 155
Gwynedd . . . 125
Hamble . . . 65, 78
Hampshire . . . 63
Happisburgh . . . 50
Hartlepool . . . 22, 28
Harwich . . . 40, 51
Hastings . . . 58
Hayle Estuary . . . 109
Hayling Island . . . 63
Helensburgh . . . 151
Helford River . . . 105, 116
Helmsdale . . . 172, 182
Helvick Harbour . . . 199
Helvick Head . . . 203
Herm . . . 85
Hesketh Bank . . . 132
Heybridge Basin . . . 42, 52
Heysham . . . 132, 141
Highland . . . 157, 172
Holy Island . . . 17, 27
Holyhead . . . 129, 140
Hoo . . . 46, 54
Horton & Port Eynon . . . 137
Howth . . . 197, 202
Hugh Town . . . 107, 116
Hull . . . 25, 28
Hunstanton . . . 50
Ilfracombe . . . 110, 117
Inveraray . . . 152
Invergordon . . . 173, 183
Inverkip . . . 150, 163
Inverness . . . 173, 183
Iona . . . 156
Ipswich . . . 39, 51
Irvine . . . 149, 163
Islay . . . 153
Isle of Bute . . . 151, 164
Isle of Man . . . 134
Isle of Mull . . . 156
Isle of Skye . . . 159, 165
Isle of Wight . . . 68
Isles of Scilly . . . 107, 116
Itchenor . . . 61
Jersey . . . 85, 88
Kenmare River . . . 210
Kent . . . 46
Kerry, County . . . 210

*Artist: **Clive Madgwick FOWEY***
*Courtesy of: **Rosenstiel's***

Kilkeel . . . 196, 202
Killybegs . . . 217, 220
Kilmore Quay . . . 199, 203
Kilrush . . . 212, 220
Kinghorn . . . 183
Kingsbridge Estuary . . . 95

Artist: *Clive Madgwick*
CHARLESTOWN
Courtesy of: **Rosenstiel's**

Kingston-upon-Hull 25, 28
Kingswear 94
Kinlochbervie 161
Kinsale 206, 219
Kippford 163
Kircubbin 194
Kirkcudbright 147, 163
Kirkwall 171, 182
Kyle of Lochalsh 159, 165
Lamlash 153
Lancashire 131
Langstone Harbour 63, 77
Largs 150, 163
Larne 191, 201
Lerwick 168, 182
Levington 39, 51
Lewis 161, 166
Limehouse Basin 45
Limerick 213
Lincolnshire 26
Lindisfarne 17
Littlehampton 61, 76
Liverpool 130, 140
Llandudno 129, 139
Loch Craignish 154, 164
Loch Fyne 152
Loch Gairloch 159, 166
Loch Inchard 161, 166
Loch Lathaich 157, 165
Loch Long 151, 164
Loch Ryan 147, 163
Lochalsh 159
Lochinver 161, 166
London 44
Londonderry 189
Longhope 171, 182
Looe 101, 115
Lossiemouth 174, 183
Lough Foyle 189
Lough Swilly 217, 220
Lowestoft 36, 50
Lulworth Cove 74
Lybster 172, 182
Lyme Regis 74, 78
Lymington 67, 78
Lytham St Annes 132, 140
Mablethorpe 29
Macduff 175, 183
Malahide 196, 202
Maldon 42, 52
Mallaig 158, 165
Malpas 104, 116
Marazion 105, 116
Margate 47, 54
Marylandsea 52
Maryport 133, 141
Mayo 213
Medway, The 46, 54
Menai Strait, The 128
Mersea Island 41, 52
Merseyside 130
Mevagissey 102
Mid Yell 170
Milford Haven 122, 138
Milport 150
Minehead 111, 117
Moelfre 129, 140
Montrose 177, 183
Moray 174
Morecambe Bay 132, 141
Mousehole 107, 116
Muck 158
Mudeford 78
Mull of Kintyre 153
Mull, Isle of 156
Mulroy Bay 217
Mumbles 121, 137
Mylor Creek 104, 116
Newbiggin 20, 27

Newcastle, N. Ireland 195, 202
Newcastle-upon-Tyne 21, 27
Newhaven 59, 76
Newlyn 107, 116
Newport 70, 78
Newquay, Cornwall 109, 116
New Quay, Ceredigion 125, 138
Newtown River 69, 78
Neyland 123, 138
Norfolk 32
North Berwick 183
North Fambridge 43, 54
North Shields 27
North Sunderland 19, 27
North Yorkshire 22
Northumberland 17
Oban 155, 165
Orford 37, 51
Orkney Islands, The 170, 182
Outer Hebrides, The 161
Oysterhaven 206
Padstow 109, 116
Peel 135, 141
Pembroke 123, 138
Pembrokeshire 121
Penarth 120, 137
Penzance 106, 116
Perth 183
Peterhead 176, 183
Pin Mill 39, 51
Pincher 217
Plockton 159, 165
Plymouth 98, 115
Polperro 101
Poole Harbour 73, 78
Porlock Weir 111, 117
Port Askaig 154, 164
Port Dinorwick 128
Port Edgar 179, 183
Port Ellen 164
Port Erin 135, 141
Port Isaac 117
Port St Mary 135, 141
Port Talbot 137
Portaferry 201
Portavogie 193
Portchester 65, 77
Porthcawl 120, 137
Porthdinllaen 128, 139
Porthleven 105
Porthmadog 127, 139
Portknockie 183
Portland Harbour 74, 78

Artist: *Clive Madgwick* **MALDON**
Courtesy of: **Rosenstiel's**

Portpatrick 147, 163
Portree 159, 166
Portrush 189, 201
Portsmouth 63, 77
Preston 132, 140
Pwllheli 127, 139
Queenborough 46, 54
Ramsey 135, 141
Ramsgate 47, 54
Ramsholt 38, 51
Rathlin Island 191
Ravenglass 133
Red Bay 191, 201
Redcar 28
Restonguet Creek 104
Rhu 151, 164
Rhum 158
Rhyl 157
River Alde 37, 51
River Bann 189
River Blackwater 41, 52
River Colne 41, 52
River Coquet 19
River Crouch 42, 52
River Dart 94, 114
River Deben 38

River Exe 92, 114
River Fal 104, 115
River Hamble 65, 78
River Humber 24
River Medina 69, 78
River Ore 37
River Orwell 39, 51
River Ribble 131, 140
River Roach 43, 53
River Shannon 212, 220
River Stour 40, 51
River Tamar 100, 114
River Tay 178, 183
River Thames 44, 53
River Tyne 21
River Yealm 95, 114
Rochester 47, 54
Rock 117
Rosslare 199, 203
Rothesay 151, 164
Runswick Bay 22, 28

Artist: *Clive Madgwick* **CLOVELLY**
Courtesy of: **Rosenstiel's**

Ryde 70, 78
Rye 58, 76
Salcombe 95, 114
Sark 85
Saundersfoot 121
Scalloway 168, 182
Scapa Flow 171
Scarborough 23, 28
Schull 208, 219
Scilly Isles 107, 116
Scottish Borders, The 180
Scrabster 172, 182
Seahouses 19
Selsey 77
Sennen Cove 116
Sheerness 54
Sheringham 50
Sherkin Island 208
Shetland Islands 168, 182
Shoreham 60, 76
Shotley Point 40, 52
Silloth 141
Skegness 26, 29
Skerries 202
Skye, Isle of 159
Sligo 216, 220
Sligo, County 216
Small Islands, The 158, 165
Snape 38
Solva 124, 138
Somerset 110
Sound of Jura 153
South Ferriby 25, 29
South Queensferry 179
Southampton 65, 78
Southend-on-Sea 43, 53
Southwold 36, 50
Spurn Head 28
St Abbs 181, 183
St Agnes 116
St Anne 83
St Bees 141
St Helier 86, 88
St Ives 108, 116
St Katherine Haven 45
St Mary's 107, 116
St Mawes 103, 116
St Michael's Mount 105, 116
St Peter Port 85, 88
Staffa 157
Starcross 92, 114
Stonehaven 177, 183
Stornoway 161, 166
Strangford Lough 193, 201
Stranraer 147, 163
Stromness 170, 182
Studland Bay 74
Suffolk 34

Summer Isles 161
Sunderland 21, 27
Sussex, East and West 58
Swanage Bay 74, 78
Swansea 121, 137
Swanwick 65, 78
Symbister 170
Tarbert, Loch Fyne 152, 164
Teelin 217
Teesmouth 28
Tenby 121
The Broads 33, 50
The Swale 47
Thorney Island 62, 77
Thurso 172, 182
Tignabruaich 152, 164
Tinker's Hole 157
Tobermory 156, 165
Tollesbury 42, 52
Topsham 92, 114
Tor Bay 93, 114
Torquay 93, 114
Tralee Bay 212
Tramore 203
Trearddur Bay 140
Troon 148, 163
Truro 104, 116
Tyne & Wear 20
Tynemouth 27
Ullapool 160, 166
Vale of Glamorgan 120
Valentia 219
Virkie 170
Waldringfield 38, 51
Wallasea Island 43, 53
Walls 169
Walton-on-the-Naze 41, 52
Wareham 73
Warsash 65, 78
Watchet 111, 117
Waterford 199, 202
Waterford, County 199
Wells-next-the-Sea 32, 50
West Kirby 130, 140
West Mersea 52
West Sussex 58
Western Isles, The 161
Weston-super-Mare 112, 117
Westport 215
Wexford 198
Wexford, County 198
Weymouth 74, 78
Whitby 22, 28
Whitehaven 133, 141
Whitstable 47, 54
Wick 172, 182
Wicklow 198, 202
Wicklow, County 198
Winteringham Haven 25
Withernsea 28
Wivenhoe 41, 52
Woodbridge 38
Woolverstone 39, 51

Artist: *Clive Madgwick* **WIVENHOE**
Courtesy of: **Rosenstiel's**

Wooton Creek 70
Workington 141
Yarmouth 68, 78
Yorkshire, East Riding 24
Yorkshire, North 22
Youghal 203

Artist: **Cloé Cloherty** **ATLANTIC SEAS** *Courtesy of:* **The Artist**